WHO'S WHO IN BRITISH OPERA

WHO'S WHO IN BRITISH OPERA

=

EDITED BY

NICKY ADAM

.

FOREWORD BY

THE EARL OF HAREWOOD

Scolar Press

© Nicky Adam, 1993

Published by
SCOLAR PRESS
Gower House
Croft Road
Aldershot
Hants GU11 3HR
England

Ashgate Publishing Company
Old Post Road
Brookfield
Vermont 05036
USA

British Library Cataloguing-in-Publication data.
Adam, Nicky
Who's Who in British Opera
I. Title
782.1092

Library of Congress Cataloging-in-Publication Data
Adam, Nicky
Who's Who in British Opera / Nicky Adam; foreword by the Earl of Harewood.
p.   cm.
ISBN 0–85967–894–6
1. Opera—Great Britain—Biography—Dictionaries. I. Title.
ML102.O6A3   1993
782.1′092′245—dc20
[B]   93–12314
CIP
MN

ISBN 0 85967 894 6 hardback
1 85928 044 7 paperback

Typeset in Bodoni and Helvetica by
Poole Typesetting (Wessex) Ltd., Bournemouth
and printed in Great Britain by Hartnolls Ltd, Bodmin

CONTENTS

FOREWORD
==
by the Earl of Harewood

WHO HAS NOT SIGHED WITH IRRITATION at finding no potted biographies of singer, conductor, director, even composer when attending an operatic performance? We have all wanted at some time or another to know something more about the previous experience, even the present status, of a performer; we have all looked for information about someone's teacher and been frustrated.

Here is the perfect antidote to such a sting, with most of the information as accurate as only the person concerned can make it; there is even mention of an appropriate address.

All opera enthusiasts thrive on the information to be found in old or new yearbooks of major or minor opera companies – I still remember my delight at finding the great Wilhelm Furtwängler had conducted *The Merry Widow* in (was it?) Zurich in his early days – and we search for listings, analyses of one kind or another. Anyone wanting more or less complete information on the heroes and heroines of the British operatic scene will find it here.

I hope this book finds its way into many a personal as well as every public reference library; that it will be part of the equipment of all critics; and that the labour which has gone into compiling it will be felt to have been richly rewarded.

PREFACE

=

*Opera lovers will be aware
of several excellent reference books
already in print.*
Who's Who in British Opera,
*however, is the first to concentrate
on people who are currently
active in opera in the UK.*

IT MUST BE ADMITTED THAT THIS is not as simple a definition as it may seem. Clearly it includes artists who are British or who frequently work in Britain (though not those who are retired or, of course, deceased). However, artists tend nowadays to be globetrotters, so to some extent entries or omissions may appear arbitrary. For instance, a number of internationally well known names do not feature in the book, whereas some artists will be found who have not appeared in a work of reference before, often in spite of a well-established career. Readers will find that some artists are included who are neither British nor even resident in Britain, and some British artists who are presently working abroad, but whose contribution to British opera is nevertheless significant. I can only say that I have tried to temper strict logic with common sense.

The entries comprise singers, conductors, composers, directors, designers, administrators, editors, librettists, teachers, translators, critics and writers; almost five hundred in all. They range from relative newcomers to those whose careers span decades. Each entry encapsulates an artist's career and includes recordings, videos and publications where relevant.

The data were obtained from questionnaires, supplemented by research where necessary. In all cases a proof of the intended entry was submitted to the artist for correction and approval.

It is in the nature of a reference book of this kind to be out of date by the time it is published. In order to alleviate this problem, the artists have been asked to include their engagements up to the end of the 1992/1993 season, but obviously future plans may be subject to change. In any case, it would be surprising if no errors or omissions were to find their way into the entries, so the editor would be grateful for any corrections and updated information for use in future editions.

ACKNOWLEDGEMENTS: It would have been impossible to compile this book without reference to a number of publications. Of especial value were: *The New Grove Dictionary of Music and Musicians* edited by Stanley Sadie, *Kobbé's Complete Opera Book* edited and revised by the Earl of Harewood, *The Penguin Dictionary of Musical Performers* compiled by Arthur Jacobs, *The Metropolitan Opera Encyclopedia* edited by David Hamilton, and the monthly journal *Opera*. Artists' agents, the press officers of all the main opera companies and festivals and the staff of the Westminster Central Music Library have been more than generous with their time and patience. I am extremely grateful to them. Among the many individuals who have given help and encouragement, I should particularly like to thank James Bevan, Mel Cooper, Flora Fraser, the Earl of Harewood, Thomas Heinitz, Arthur Jacobs, Ashley Leiman, Rodney Milnes, Lady Sieff, Deidre Tilley and Lord Weidenfeld. Above all I am deeply indebted to the artists themselves, without whose co-operation it would have been impossible to produce the book.

The following people were instrumental in the actual preparation of the book: Katherine Fry, Assistant Editor; Karen Cull, initial research; Peter Birrel, literary research, Henry Levy, database and computer management; Ellen Keeling, Senior Editor, Scolar Press.

The joy of opera lies in the music, the voices and the dramatic spectacle. Any experience, however, can be enhanced by additional knowledge. If this book can add something to the reader's pleasure, it will have performed a useful function.

NICKY ADAM
July 1993

Katherine Fry – Assistant Editor and Chief Researcher

I am greatly indebted to Katherine Fry for her endeavour and commitment to this book. Often almost on her own she kept the project on an even keel. She has been a valuable colleague and I look forward to future co-operation with her.

N.A.

A GUIDE TO THE USE OF THE BOOK

===

IN GENERAL THE STRUCTURE OF THE book should be self-evident. Further details are given below

ABBREVIATIONS: See Page xvii.

CROSS REFERENCES: Appendix 1 indexes all those included in the biographical section under 27 different headings.

OPERAS AND THEIR COMPOSERS: Composers are mentioned in the biographical section only in the case of world premières or world stage premières or where two operas have the same title. A complete list of the works mentioned in the book, together with their composers, can be found in Appendix 2.

TITLES: There can be no hard and fast rules regarding the language of opera titles. For example, some titles are traditionally given in the original regardless of the language of performance, such as, *Così fan tutte*. In other cases the title is translated; for instance, *Le Nozze di Figaro/The Marriage of Figaro* or *Figaro's Wedding; Les Vêpres Siciliennes/I Vespri Siciliani*.

The capitalization of titles is, with very few exceptions, in the English manner.

ROLES: Titles such as King, Count, Steersman, are translated into English but, in general, proper names are given in the original language. There are some exceptions: for example, where a character's name appears in a translated title, as in *Samson and Delilah*; or when a mythical or historical character might not be clearly recognized in the original language, for example, *Caronte (Charon)* or *Giunone (Juno)*.

PRODUCER: The person who supervises the stage action of an operatic performance was formerly, and in some cases is still known as, the producer. Current usage, however, prefers the term Director, and this usage has been followed. In this book the word Producer refers only to radio, recordings, television and theatre – to the person who is in overall charge of the production.

CONTRALTO: This designation would nowadays appear to be out of favour, and any female voice which is not termed soprano is therefore called Mezzo-Soprano.

PERSONAL DETAILS: As far as possible, where they are shown, these details are as returned on a questionnaire. A spouse's occupation is mentioned only if it is a related profession.

EDUCATION/TRAINING: In general, secondary education is omitted unless it relates specifically to music.

London Royal Schools' Vocal Faculty was formed in 1992 by combining the opera departments and vocal faculties of the Royal Academy of Music and the Royal College of Music.

The National Opera Studio has had four names: from 1950 to 1957 it was The Opera School, from 1957 to 1963 it was the National School of Opera, from 1963 to 1977 it was the London Opera Centre.

The Royal Northern College of Music was formed in 1971 by an amalgamation of the Royal Manchester College of Music and the Northern School of Music, Manchester.

PERFORMANCES: The book is concerned for the most part with staged performances. However, in some circumstances, concert, radio and television performances have been included.

DATES AND PRODUCTIONS: In the case of directors and designers, a given date refers to the first performance of a new production. In the case of singers and conductors the date refers to their first appearance in the production.

MAJOR DEBUTS: A major debut is determined either by role or venue or sometimes both.

RECORD LABELS: These are listed in Appendix 3 with their abbreviations.

VIDEOS: Most videos are identified by the name of the opera company rather than by the video label.

AWARDS AND HONOURS: These relate to the UK unless otherwise stated.

The recipient of an award is usually a single individual, but some awards are made to a production as a whole. Where the latter is the case that fact is indicated in the entry by the addition of the word 'production' after the name of the company. For instance, *English National Opera production of Xerxes*, as opposed to *Xerxes (English National Opera)*, which is an award made to an individual.

Awards as distinct from honours are normally included only when they are specifically for work in opera.

OPERA COMPANIES: What follows does not purport to be an exhaustive survey of British opera companies and festivals, but is concerned only with elucidating possible obscurities and confusions.

The Almeida Festival, at the Almeida Theatre in London, ceased in 1990. Almeida Opera's first season was in 1992.

Batignano Festival features the company Musica nel Chiostro. The company's name is used only when it performs elsewhere.

City of Birmingham Touring Opera was formed in 1987 as an amalgamation of Birmingham Music Theatre and English Touring Opera. (Not to be confused with the company of the same name below.)

Chelsea Opera Group gives only concert performances.

Earls Court refers to arena productions originally staged at Earls Court by Classical Productions (UK) Ltd.

English Opera Group was expanded and re-formed as English Music Theatre in 1975 but has not functioned since 1979.

English Touring Opera was known as Opera for All until 1980 and as Opera 80 until 1992. This company should not be confused with the company of the same name referred to under City of Birmingham Touring Opera. If an entry spans the changeover year, Opera 80/ English Touring Opera is used.

Glyndebourne Education presents projects in colleges, schools and special schools and projects for adults, including community opera.

Glyndebourne Touring Opera was formed as an offshoot of Glyndebourne Festival Opera in 1968. Where an artist has appeared with both companies reference is simply made to Glyndebourne Festival and Touring Opera.

Kent Opera existed between 1969 and 1989.

London Chamber Opera took over the productions of the Intimate Opera Company in 1983.

London Opera Festival was London International Opera Festival until 1992, but is always referred to by its current name.

London Opera Players was Opera Players until 1986.

New Opera Company is affiliated to English National Opera (formerly to Sadler's Wells Opera).

Opera Factory was known as Opera Factory London Sinfonietta from 1984 to 1990, but is always referred to as Opera Factory.

Opera North was known as English National Opera North from 1978 to 1981, but is always referred to as Opera North.

Opera Northern Ireland was formed in 1985 as an amalgamation of the Northern Ireland Opera Trust and the Studio Opera Group, but is always referred to as Opera Northern Ireland even prior to 1985.

Opera Restor'd grew out of the Holme Pierrepont Opera Trust in 1985.

The Royal Opera, Covent Garden is normally referred to simply as Covent Garden even when the company is performing elsewhere.

Sadler's Wells Opera moved to the London Coliseum in 1968, and became English National Opera in 1974. If an entry spans the changeover year, Sadler's Wells Opera/English National Opera is used. New Sadler's Wells Opera was a completely independent company formed at Sadler's Wells Theatre after the departure of Sadler's Wells Opera to the London Coliseum.

Scottish Opera for All existed from 1966–1974 as Scottish Opera's small-scale touring operation.

Scottish Opera Go Round is the small-scale touring arm of Scottish Opera and was founded in 1978.

Welsh National Opera for All was founded in 1963 as Welsh National Opera's small-scale touring operation, but the name is no longer in use.

LIST OF ABBREVIATIONS

b.   =   born
m.   =   married
m. diss.   =   marriage dissolved
d.   =   died
BBC   =   British Broadcasting Corporation
HTV   =   Harlech Television
LWT   =   London Weekend Television
Op.   =   Opus
UK   =   United Kingdom
USA   =   United States of America

For Record Labels see Appendix 3

ABULAFIA JOHN   Director

POSITION: Director of Productions, Mecklenburgh Opera.

PERSONAL DETAILS: b. 22 March 1951, London.

EDUCATION/TRAINING: University of Sussex.

PROFESSIONAL DEBUT: 1974, Open Space Theatre, *Edgar Allan's Late Night Horror* by Robert Nye/*Down Red Lane* by B. S. Johnson.

OPERATIC DEBUT: 1986, Mecklenburgh Opera, *The Marriage of Figaro*.

CAREER: 1973-1975, Artistic Director, Pool Theatre, Edinburgh; since 1976, freelance theatre and opera director; since 1986, founder and Director of Productions, Mecklenburgh Opera; since 1988, staff director, English National Opera.

OPERATIC WORLD PREMIÈRES INCLUDE: 1990, English National Opera Contemporary Opera Studio, *Snatched by the Gods* by Param Vir.

OPERA PRODUCTIONS IN THE UK INCLUDE: Since 1986: Mecklenburgh Opera: *The Emperor of Atlantis*, *Die Weisse Rose* (1989, British première), *Mannekins* (1990, British première), *The Soldier's Tale*; *Petrified* (1992, British première); Queen Elizabeth Hall, *Zaide*; Royal College of Music, *Sister Aimee* (1987, British première).

RELATED PROFESSIONAL ACTIVITIES: Author, stage and television writer; translator with Brian Bannatyne-Scott, *Mannekins*.

AWARDS INCLUDE: 1991, Prudential Award for Opera to Mecklenburgh Opera.

ADDRESS: 98a Petherton Road, Highbury, London N5 2RG or c/o English National Opera, London Coliseum, St Martin's Lane, London WC2N 4ES.

ADAMS DONALD   Bass

PERSONAL DETAILS: b. 20 December 1928, Bristol; m. 1952, Muriel Harding (soprano), one child.

EDUCATION/TRAINING: Bristol Cathedral School; studied acting with Hedley Goodall.

PROFESSIONAL DEBUT: As actor: 1944, member, BBC Repertory Company, Bristol; as singer: 1951, member, D'Oyly Carte Opera.

EARLY CAREER INCLUDED: 1953–1969, Principal Bass, D'Oyly Carte Opera, singing all leading Gilbert and Sullivan bass roles in the UK and abroad; 1963, co-founder and member, Gilbert and Sullivan for All; until 1983, career primarily in operetta.

MAJOR DEBUTS INCLUDE: 1983: Covent Garden, Frontier Guard, *Boris Godunov*; Lyric Opera, Chicago, title role, *The Mikado*; 1984, Welsh National Opera, Baron Zeta, *The Merry Widow*; 1986: English National Opera, Dikoy, *Katya Kabanova*; Canadian Opera Company, Toronto, title role, *The Mikado*; 1988, Glyndebourne Festival Opera, Dikoy, *Katya Kabanova*; 1991, Aix-en-Provence Festival, Quince, *A Midsummer Night's Dream*.

CAREER IN THE UK INCLUDES: Since 1983: Covent Garden: Quince, *A Midsummer Night's Dream*; Frank, *Die Fledermaus*; Sacristan, *Tosca*; Badger/Priest, *The Cunning Little Vixen*; English National Opera: Benoit/Alcindoro, *La Bohème*; Bartolo, *The Marriage of Figaro*; Woodcutter, *Königskinder*; Glyndebourne Festival and Touring Opera: Antonio and Bartolo, *Le Nozze di Figaro*; Swallow, *Peter Grimes*; Opera North: Monterone, *Rigoletto*; Bartolo, *The Marriage of Figaro*; Scottish Opera, Bartolo, *Il Barbiere di Siviglia*; Welsh National Opera: Monterone, *Rigoletto*; Bartolo, *The Barber of Seville*; Frank, *Die Fledermaus*; Baron Ochs, *Der Rosenkavalier*.

RELATED PROFESSIONAL ACTIVITIES: Numerous concerts and recitals in the UK and abroad.

RECORDINGS INCLUDE: Sullivan: *HMS Pinafore, Iolanthe, Patience, The Pirates of Penzance, Ruddigore, The Sorcerer,*

1

The Yeomen of the Guard (all DECC), *The Mikado* (DECC/TELA).
VIDEOS INCLUDE: Sullivan: *Patience, Ruddigore, The Sorcerer* (all Walker); Janáček, *Katya Kabanova* (Glyndebourne Festival Opera).
ADDRESS: c/o Harrison/Parrott Ltd, 12 Penzance Place, London W11 4PA.

AINSLEY JOHN MARK
Tenor

PERSONAL DETAILS: b. 9 July 1963, Cheshire.
EDUCATION/TRAINING: 1982–1983, Magdalen College, Oxford, studied music; 1983-1985, lay clerk, Christ Church, Oxford; currently with Anthony Rolfe Johnson and Diane Forlano.
PROFESSIONAL DEBUT: 1984, Royal Festival Hall, (Stravinsky) *Mass*.
MAJOR DEBUTS INCLUDE: 1988, Innsbruck Festival, Eurillo, *Gli Equivoci nel Sembiante* (operatic debut); 1989, English National Opera, Eurimaco, *The Return of Ulysses*; 1990, Opera Northern Ireland, Tamino, *The Magic Flute*; 1991: Scottish Opera, Fenton, *Falstaff*; Welsh National Opera, Idamante, *Idomeneo*; Lyons Opera, Don Ottavio, *Don Giovanni*; 1992, Glyndebourne Festival Opera, Ferrando, *Così fan tutte*; 1993, Aix-en-Provence Festival, Don Ottavio, *Don Giovanni*.
RELATED PROFESSIONAL ACTIVITIES: Concerts and recitals in the UK and abroad; leading exponent of baroque music.
RECORDINGS INCLUDE: Beethoven, *Fidelio* (PHIL); Handel: *Acis and Galatea* (HYPE/L'OI), *Nisi Dominus* (DG), *Saul* (PHIL); Monteverdi, *Orfeo* (DECC); Mozart, *Requiem* (EMI); Purcell, *Hail Bright Cecilia* (HYPE); Great Baroque Arias (PICK).
ADDRESS: c/o Lies Askonas Ltd, 186 Drury Lane, London WC2B 5RY.

ALBERY TIM   Director

OPERATIC DEBUT: 1983, Batignano Festival, *The Turn of the Screw*.
CAREER: Freelance opera and theatre director in the UK and abroad.
MAJOR OPERATIC DEBUTS: 1985, Opera North, *The Midsummer Marriage*; 1986–1990, Opera North/Scottish Opera/Welsh National Opera co-production, *The Trojans* (also 1990, at Covent Garden); 1988, English National Opera, *Billy Budd*; 1990, Bregenz Festival, *La Wally*; 1991, Netherlands Opera, *Benvenuto Cellini*; 1992, Australian Opera, Sydney, *Le Nozze di Figaro*.
OPERA PRODUCTIONS IN THE UK INCLUDE: Since 1985: English National Opera: *Beatrice and Benedict, Peter Grimes, Lohengrin*; Opera North: *La Finta Giardiniera, Don Giovanni, Don Carlos*; Scottish Opera, *The Midsummer Marriage*.
VIDEOS INCLUDE: Britten, *Billy Budd* (English National Opera).
ADDRESS: c/o Harriet Cruickshank, 97 Old South Lambeth Road, London SW8 1XU.

ALDEN DAVID   Director

PERSONAL DETAILS: b. New York City, USA.
EDUCATION/TRAINING: University of Pennsylvania.
CAREER: Freelance opera director in the USA and abroad; currently affiliated to Opera at the Academy, New York and New Israeli Opera, Tel Aviv.
MAJOR OPERATIC DEBUTS INCLUDE: 1978: New Orleans Opera, *La Bohème*; Washington Opera, *The Seraglio*; 1979: Scottish Opera, *Rigoletto* (British debut); Houston Grand Opera, *Werther*; 1980, Metropolitan Opera, New York, *Fidelio*; 1981, Canadian Opera Company, Toronto, *Die Entführung aus dem Serail*; 1982, Netherlands Opera, *The Rake's Progress*; 1983: Opera North, *Beatrice and Benedict*; Santa Fe Opera, *The Turn of the Screw*; 1984: English National Opera, *Mazeppa*; Long Beach Opera, California,

Don Carlos; 1985, Lyric Opera, Chicago, *La Traviata*; 1988, Los Angeles Music Center Opera, *Wozzeck*; 1989/1990, English National Opera/Netherlands Opera co-production, *A Masked Ball*; 1992/1993, Welsh National Opera/State Opera of South Australia, Adelaide co-production, *Elektra*.

OPERATIC WORLD PREMIERES INCLUDE: 1976, Michigan Opera, *Washington Square* by Thomas Pasatieri; 1978, Wolf Trap Opera, Virginia, *The Duchess of Malfi* by Stephen Douglas Burton; 1990, American Music Theater Festival, Philadelphia, *Casino Paradise* by William Bolcom.

OPERA PRODUCTIONS IN THE UK INCLUDE: Since 1980: English National Opera: *Simon Boccanegra*, *Oedipus Rex*, *Duke Bluebeard's Castle*, *The Duel of Tancredi and Clorinda*; Scottish Opera: *Wozzeck*, *The Rise and Fall of the City of Mahagonny*; English National Opera/Welsh National Opera co-production, *Ariodante*.

ADDRESS: c/o Harrison/Parrott Ltd, 12 Penzance Place, London W11 4PA.

ALLEN THOMAS   Baritone

PERSONAL DETAILS: b. 10 September 1944, County Durham; m. 1968, Margaret Holley, one child; m. 1988, Jeannie Lascelles.

EDUCATION/TRAINING: 1964–1968, Royal College of Music, studied the organ and singing with Hervey Alan.

PROFESSIONAL DEBUT: 1969, Welsh National Opera, d'Obigny, *La Traviata*.

EARLY CAREER INCLUDED: 1969, chorus member, Glyndebourne Festival Opera; 1969–1972, Principal Baritone, Welsh National Opera: Morales, *Carmen*; Guglielmo, *Così fan tutte*; Schaunard, *La Bohème*; Falke, *Die Fledermaus*; Paolo, *Simon Boccanegra*; Papageno, *The Magic Flute*; title roles: *Billy Budd*, *The Barber of Seville*, *The Marriage of Figaro*.

MAJOR DEBUTS INCLUDE: 1971, Covent Garden, Donald, *Billy Budd*; 1973, Glyndebourne Festival Opera, Papageno, *Die Zauberflöte*; 1976, Covent Garden at La Scala, Milan, Marcello, *La Bohème*; 1978, Scottish Opera, Pelléas, *Pelléas et Mélisande*; 1979: Paris Opera, Marcello, *La Bohème*; Teatro Comunale, Florence, Count, *Le Nozze di Figaro*; 1980, Teatro Colón, Buenos Aires, Pelléas, *Pelléas et Mélisande*; 1981: Grand Théâtre, Geneva, Sharpless, *Madama Butterfly*; Metropolitan Opera, New York, Papageno, *Die Zauberflöte*; 1982, English National Opera, Andrei, *War and Peace*; 1983: Houston Grand Opera, title role, *Il Barbiere di Siviglia*; Vienna State Opera, Marcello, *La Bohème*; 1985, Salzburg Festival, title role, *Il Ritorno d'Ulisse in Patria* (new version by Henze); 1987, La Scala, Milan, title role, *Don Giovanni*.

OPERATIC WORLD PREMIERES INCLUDE: 1974, English Opera Group at the Aldeburgh Festival, Count, *The Voice of Ariadne* by Thea Musgrave.

CAREER IN THE UK INCLUDES: Since 1972: Covent Garden (1972-1978, member): Valentin, *Faust*; Ned Keene, *Peter Grimes*; Silvio, *Pagliacci*; Morales, *Carmen*; Belcore, *L'Elisir d'Amore*; Guglielmo, *Così fan tutte*; Marcello, *La Bohème*; Harlequin, *Ariadne auf Naxos*; Demetrius, *A Midsummer Night's Dream*; High Priest, *Idomeneo*; Count, *Le Nozze di Figaro* (also 1992, Japan tour); *Pelléas*, *Pelléas et Mélisande*; Papageno, *Die Zauberflöte*; Dapertutto, *Les Contes d'Hoffmann*; Wolfram, *Tannhäuser*; Sharpless, *Madama Butterfly*; Eisenstein, *Die Fledermaus*; Malatesta, *Don Pasquale*; Forester, *The Cunning Little Vixen*; Count, *Capriccio*; title roles: *Billy Budd*, *Eugene Onegin*, *Don Giovanni* (also 1992, Japan tour); English National Opera, title roles: *Doctor Faust* (1986, British stage première), *Billy Budd*; Glyndebourne Festival Opera: Guglielmo, *Così fan tutte*; Forester, *The Cunning Little Vixen*; Perrucchetto, *La Fedeltà Premiata*; title roles: *Le Nozze di Figaro*, *Don Giovanni*; Welsh National Opera:

Count Danilo, *The Merry Widow*; Germont, *La Traviata*; title role, *Eugene Onegin*.

RELATED PROFESSIONAL ACTIVITIES: Regular concerts, recitals, broadcasts and television appearances in the UK and abroad.

RECORDINGS INCLUDE: Berlioz, *Béatrice et Bénédict* (PHIL); Bizet, *Carmen* (DECC); Gluck, *Iphigénie en Tauride* (TELA); Gounod, *Faust*; Janáček, *The Cunning Little Vixen*; Léoncavallo, *Pagliacci* (all EMI); Mozart: *Così fan tutte* (PHIL), *Don Giovanni* (EMI/PHIL), *Le Nozze di Figaro* (DECC/EMI/PHIL), *Die Zauberflöte* (PHIL); Orff, *Carmina Burana* (EMI); Rossini, *Il Barbiere di Siviglia* (PHIL); Tchaikovsky, *Eugene Onegin* (DG); Tippett, *King Priam* (DECC); Wolf, lieder; Love Songs and Lullabies (both VIRG).

VIDEOS INCLUDE: Britten, *Billy Budd* (English National Opera); Mozart: *Così fan tutte* (Glyndebourne Festival Opera), *Don Giovanni* (La Scala, Milan); Puccini, *La Bohème* (Covent Garden).

HONOURS INCLUDE: 1984, Honorary Master of Arts, University of Newcastle upon Tyne; 1986, Olivier Award, English National Opera production of *Doctor Faust* (specially recommended with Graham Clark); 1988: Honorary Doctorate of Music, University of Durham; Fellow, Royal College of Music; Honorary Member, Royal Academy of Music; 1989, Commander, Order of the British Empire (CBE).

ADDRESS: c/o Lies Askonas Ltd, 186 Drury Lane, London WC2B 5RY.

ANGAS RICHARD   Bass

POSITION: Principal Bass, English National Opera.

PERSONAL DETAILS: b. 18 April 1942, Surrey; m. Rosanne Creffield (mezzo-soprano), one child.

EDUCATION/TRAINING: 1960–1964, Royal Academy of Music, with Olive Groves and George Baker; 1965–1966, Vienna State Academy, with Ilse Rapf and Erik Werba; currently with Josephine Veasey.

PROFESSIONAL DEBUT: 1966, Scottish Opera, Lodovico, *Otello*.

EARLY CAREER INCLUDED: 1967–1979, appearances with New Opera Company, Scottish Opera, Welsh National Opera, Krefeld/Mönchengladbach Opera; roles included: Fafner, *Das Rheingold*; King Marke, *Tristan und Isolde*; Heinrich, *Lohengrin*; Baron Ochs, *Der Rosenkavalier*; Archbishop of Palermo, *King Roger* (1975, New Opera Company, British stage première); Don Alfonso, *Così fan tutte*; Osmin, *Die Entführung aus dem Serail*; Rocco, *Fidelio*.

MAJOR DEBUTS INCLUDE: 1969, English Opera Group (Aldeburgh Festival and Australia tour), Abbot, *Curlew River*; 1972, Teatro São Carlos, Lisbon, Sleep/Corydon/Winter/Hymen, *The Fairy Queen*; 1975: Covent Garden, First Apprentice, *Wozzeck*; Welsh National Opera, General Boum, *The Grand Duchess of Gérolstein*; 1976, Koblenz, Méphistophélès, *Faust*; Police Commissar, *Der Rosenkavalier*; 1977, La Monnaie, Brussels; 1978, Gran Teatre del Liceu, Barcelona; 1980, English National Opera, Ramfis, Aida; 1981, Angers, Commendatore, *Don Giovanni*; 1984, Metropolitan Opera, New York, Balaga/Bennigsen/Davout, *War and Peace*; 1988, Opera North, Cook, *The Love for Three Oranges*; 1989, Netherlands Opera, Johor, *The Making of the Representative for Planet 8*.

OPERATIC WORLD PREMIERES INCLUDE: 1974, Scottish Opera, Cato, *The Catiline Conspiracy* by Iain Hamilton; 1976, Covent Garden, Attendant 1, *We Come to the River* by Hans Werner Henze; 1986, English National Opera, Troupe of Ceremony/Judge, *The Mask of Orpheus* by Harrison Birtwistle; 1989, Paris Opera, Pontius Pilate, *Der Meister und Margarita* by York Höller.

CAREER IN THE UK INCLUDES: Since 1980, Principal Bass, English National Opera: Seneca, *The Coronation of Poppea*; Don Basilio, *The Barber of Seville*; Pluto and

Charon, *Orfeo*; Osmin, *The Seraglio*; Angelotti, *Tosca*; Balaga/Bennigsen/Davout, *War and Peace*; Pimen, *Boris Godunov*; Jupiter, *Orpheus in the Underworld*; Daland, *The Flying Dutchman*; Pistol, *Falstaff*; Reciter, *Pacific Overtures*; Johor, *The Making of the Representative of Planet 8* (1988, British première); Time/Antinöo, *The Return of Ulysses*; Cook, *The Love for Three Oranges*; Doctor, *Wozzeck*; Spinelloccio, *Gianni Schicchi*; Gloucester, *Lear*; Arkel, *Pelléas and Mélisande*; Magistrate, *Werther*; Bartolo, *The Marriage of Figaro*; Innkeeper, *Königskinder*; Zuniga, *Carmen*; title role, *The Mikado*.

RELATED PROFESSIONAL ACTIVITIES: Numerous concerts, recitals, broadcasts and television appearances in the UK and abroad.

RECORDINGS INCLUDE: Offenbach: *Orpheus in the Underworld*, *The Tales of Hoffmann* (both TER); Schoenberg, *Moses und Aron* (CBS); Sondheim, *Pacific Overtures*; Sullivan, *The Mikado* (both TER).

VIDEOS INCLUDE: Sullivan, *The Mikado* (English National Opera).

AWARDS AND HONOURS INCLUDE: 1964, Kathleen Ferrier Memorial Scholarship; 1965, Richard Tauber Memorial Prize; 1966, Deutsche Gramophon Prize (Vienna); 1990, Honorary Associate, Royal Academy of Music.

ADDRESS: c/o English National Opera, London Coliseum, St Martin's Lane, London WC2N 4ES.

ANGEL MARIE   Soprano

PERSONAL DETAILS: b. Australia; m. 1985, David Freeman (director), one child.

EDUCATION/TRAINING: Adelaide Conservatorium, with Donald Munro; 1977–1978, with Erich Vietheer, Geoffrey Parsons and Peter Gellhorn in London; privately with Audrey Langford.

EARLY CAREER INCLUDED: 1977–1982, appearances with English Bach Festival, Morley Opera, Opera Factory Zurich;

roles included: High Priestess, *Hippolyte et Aricie*; Vitellia, *La Clemenza di Tito*; Galatea, *Acis and Galatea*; Fiordiligi, *Così fan tutte*; Lilian, *Happy End*.

MAJOR DEBUTS INCLUDE: 1982, Opera Factory, Pretty Polly, *Punch and Judy*; 1983, English National Opera, Euridice/Hope, *Orfeo*; 1984, Queen Tye, *Akhnaten*: Houston Grand Opera, New York City Opera; 1986: Welsh National Opera, Queen of the Night, *The Magic Flute*; Adelaide Festival, title role, *Iphigenias*; 1988, Opera North, Musetta, *La Bohème*; 1990: Glyndebourne Touring Opera, Jo Ann, *New Year*; Victoria State Opera, Melbourne, Donna Anna, *Don Giovanni*.

OPERATIC WORLD PREMIERES INCLUDE: 1986: English National Opera, Oracle of the Dead/Hecate, *The Mask of Orpheus* by Harrison Birtwistle; Opera Factory, several roles, *Hell's Angels* by Nigel Osborne; 1991, Covent Garden (debut), Morgan le Fay, *Gawain* by Harrison Birtwistle.

CAREER IN THE UK INCLUDES: Since 1982: English National Opera, Queen Tye, *Akhnaten* (1985, British première); Opera Factory: Lucy, *The Beggar's Opera*; Denise, *The Knot Garden*; Juno and title role, *La Calisto*; Donna Anna, *Don Giovanni*; Countess, *The Marriage of Figaro*; Hannah, *Yan Tan Tethera*; title roles: *Iphigenias*, *The Coronation of Poppea*.

RELATED PROFESSIONAL ACTIVITIES: Concerts, recitals and television appearances in the UK including several Opera Factory productions for Channel Four.

ADDRESS: c/o Allied Artists, 42 Montpelier Square, London SW7 1JZ.

ANGUS DAVID
Conductor and Chorus Master

POSITIONS: Chorus Master, Glyndebourne Festival Opera; Chorus Director, Scottish Chamber Orchestra.

PERSONAL DETAILS: b. 2 February 1955, Reading; m. 1990, Johanna Mayr (German language coach and translator).
PREVIOUS OCCUPATION: 1978–1985, secondary school music teacher.
EDUCATION/TRAINING: 1973–1976, University of Surrey, studied music performance and piano with Martin Hughes; 1985–1988, Conducting Fellowship, Royal Northern College of Music, with Timothy Reynish.
PROFESSIONAL DEBUT: 1988, Bradford Chamber Orchestra.
OPERATIC DEBUT: 1989, New Sussex Opera at the Brighton Festival, *Faust*.
CAREER: 1988–1989, répétiteur and Deputy Chorus Master, Opera North; since 1989, Chorus Master and staff conductor, Glyndebourne Festival Opera; since 1991, Chorus Director, Scottish Chamber Orchestra.
OPERA PERFORMANCES INCLUDE: Since 1989: Glyndebourne Festival and Touring Opera: *New Year*, *The Magic Flute*, *Così fan tutte*, *Katya Kabanova*; Icelandic Opera, *Pagliacci*.
RELATED PROFESSIONAL ACTIVITIES: Conductor for numerous British choral groups.
AWARDS INCLUDE: 1986, 1987 and 1988, Ricordi Conducting Prize.
ADDRESS: c/o Glyndebourne Festival Opera, Lewes, East Sussex BN8 5UU.

ARCHER NEILL   Tenor

PERSONAL DETAILS: b. 31 August 1961, Northampton; m. 1986, Marilyn Dale (soprano), one child.
EDUCATION/TRAINING: 1979–1982, University of East Anglia, studied music; 1981 and 1982, Brevard Music Center, North Carolina; privately with Eduardo Asquez.
PROFESSIONAL DEBUT: 1987, Kent Opera, Tamino, *The Magic Flute*.
MAJOR DEBUTS INCLUDE: 1988: Scottish Opera, Ferrando, *Così fan tutte*; Welsh National Opera, Don Ottavio, *Don Giovanni*; 1989: Teatro Regio, Parma,

Andrès, *Wozzeck*; Opera North, Count, *The Barber of Seville*; 1990: Covent Garden, Jacquino, *Fidelio*; English National Opera, Tamino, *The Magic Flute*; 1991, Basle, Pylade, *Iphigénie en Tauride*.
OPERATIC WORLD PREMIERES INCLUDE: 1992, Almeida Opera, Servant/Captain, *Terrible Mouth* by Nigel Osborne.
CAREER IN THE UK INCLUDES: Since 1987: Buxton Festival: Ubaldo, *Armida*; title role, *Don Quixote in Sierra Morena*; Covent Garden, Steersman, *Der Fliegende Holländer*; Ferrando, *Così fan tutte*; Glyndebourne Touring Opera, Opera Factory; Opera North, Achilles, *King Priam*; Welsh National Opera: Cassio, *Otello*; Pelléas, *Pelléas et Mélisande*; Count, *The Barber of Seville*.
RELATED PROFESSIONAL ACTIVITIES: Concerts, broadcasts and television appearances in the UK and abroad.
VIDEOS INCLUDE: Beethoven, *Fidelio* (Covent Garden); Debussy, *Pelléas et Mélisande* (Welsh National Opera).
ADDRESS: c/o Harrison/Parrott Ltd, 12 Penzance Place, London W11 4PA.

ARMSTRONG RICHARD
Conductor

POSITIONS: Music Director, Scottish Opera; Chief Conductor, National Orchestra of Scotland.
PERSONAL DETAILS: b. Leicester.
EDUCATION/TRAINING: 1961–1964, Corpus Christi College, Cambridge.
PROFESSIONAL AND OPERATIC DEBUT: 1969, Welsh National Opera, *The Marriage of Figaro*.
CAREER: 1966–1968, member, music staff, Covent Garden; Welsh National Opera: 1968–1973, Head of Music Staff; 1973–1986, Music Director; 1987–1993, Principal Guest Conductor; 1988–1990, Principal Guest Conductor, Frankfürt Opera; since 1993/1994 season: Music Director, Scottish Opera; Chief Conductor, National Orchestra of Scotland.
MAJOR OPERATIC DEBUTS INCLUDE: 1977, Scottish Opera, *Jenůfa*; 1980: English National Opera, *Aida*; Frankfürt Opera,

Der Fliegende Holländer; Komische Oper, East Berlin, *Peter Grimes*; Netherlands Opera, *Elektra*; 1982, Covent Garden, *Billy Budd*; 1988, Grand Théâtre, Geneva, *Don Carlos*; 1991, Paris Opera, *Falstaff*; 1992, Edinburgh International Festival, *Moses and Aaron* (concert performance).

OPERATIC WORLD PREMIERES INCLUDE: Welsh National Opera: 1974, *The Beach of Falesá* by Alun Hoddinott; 1990, *Tornrak* by John Metcalf.

OPERA PERFORMANCES IN THE UK INCLUDE: Since 1973: Covent Garden: *Andrea Chénier, Un Ballo in Maschera, Don Carlos*; English National Opera: *Salome, Wozzeck*; Scottish Opera: *Katya Kabanova, The Cunning Little Vixen, The Makropoulos Case, From the House of the Dead, Billy Budd, Il Trovatore*; Welsh National Opera: *The Flying Dutchman, Manon Lescaut, Jenůfa, Il Trovatore, The Midsummer Marriage, I Masnadieri, La Bohème, Elektra, Peter Grimes, The Makropoulos Case, Ernani, The Cunning Little Vixen, Die Frau ohne Schatten, Fidelio, La Forza del Destino, Katya Kabanova, Un Ballo in Maschera, From the House of the Dead, Rigoletto, Otello, The Ring of the Nibelung* (also 1986, at Covent Garden), *Falstaff, Ernani.*

RECORDINGS INCLUDE: Beethoven: *Fidelio*, Symphony No. 6 (both ACAD); Verdi, operatic extracts (CFP).

HONOURS INCLUDE: 1978, Janáček Medal (Czechoslovakia); 1993, Commander, Order of the British Empire (CBE).

ADDRESS: c/o Scottish Opera, 39 Elmbank Crescent, Glasgow G2 4PT.

ASHE ROSEMARY   Soprano

PERSONAL DETAILS: b. 28 March 1953, Lowestoft.

EDUCATION/TRAINING: 1970–1974, Royal Academy of Music; 1975–1977, London Opera Centre, with Richard Alda, Peter Harrison and Joy Mammen.

PROFESSIONAL DEBUT: 1978, Opera North, Venus, *Orpheus in the Underworld.*

CAREER INCLUDES: Since 1979: Earls Court, Frasquita, *Carmen* (also 1990, Japan tour); English National Opera: Fiakermilli, *Arabella*; Esmeralda, *The Bartered Bride*; Ankhesenpaaten, *Akhnaten* (1985, British première); Papagena, *The Magic Flute*; Venus, *Orpheus in the Underworld*; New Sadler's Wells Opera: *Manon* and Sari, *Bitter Sweet*; Josephine, *HMS Pinafore*; title role, *La Belle Hélène*; Opera North: Alice, *Count Ory*; Queen of the Night, *The Magic Flute*; Julie Le Verne, *Show Boat*; Opera Northern Ireland, Musetta, *La Bohème*; Wexford Festival, Marionette, *La Vedova Scaltra.*

OPERATIC WORLD PREMIERES INCLUDE: 1979, Covent Garden, Marie Regnault, *Thérèse* by John Tavener.

RELATED PROFESSIONAL ACTIVITIES: Regular broadcasts for BBC Radio; television and West End appearances include: Lucy, *The Beggar's Opera*; Despina, *Così fan tutte*; Carlotta, *The Phantom of the Opera*; Cunegonde, *Candide.*

RECORDINGS INCLUDE: Coward, *Bitter Sweet*; Romberg, *The Student Prince*; Wilson, *The Boyfriend* (all TER); Wright and Forrest, *Kismet*; Lloyd Webber, *The Phantom of the Opera* (POLY).

ADDRESS: c/o Portfolio Management, 58 Alexandra Road, London NW4 2RY.

ASHMAN MIKE
Director, Translator and Writer

POSITION: Associate Director, Opera Department, London Royal Schools' Vocal Faculty.

PERSONAL DETAILS: b. 16 April 1950, Hertford.

PREVIOUS OCCUPATIONS: Fringe theatre director, road manager and sub editor/journalist for various music publications.

EDUCATION/TRAINING: 1968–1972, Magdalene College, Cambridge.

OPERATIC DEBUT: 1982, Malvern Festival, *Noye's Fludde.*

7

CAREER: Staff director: 1979–1984, Welsh National Opera; 1984–1986, Covent Garden; since 1986, freelance director in the UK and abroad; Associate Director: 1988–1992, Opera School, Royal College of Music; since 1992, Opera Department, London Royal Schools' Vocal Faculty.
MAJOR OPERATIC DEBUTS INCLUDE: 1983, Welsh National Opera, *Parsifal*; 1986, Covent Garden, *Der Fliegende Holländer*, Dublin Grand Opera: 1987, *La Bohème*; 1990, *Tosca*; 1991, Teatro La Zarzuela, Madrid, *Peter Grimes*; Norwegian Opera, Oslo: 1989, *Der Fliegende Holländer*; 1993-1996, *Der Ring des Nibelungen*.
OPERATIC WORLD PREMIERES INCLUDE: 1990, Welsh National Opera, *Tornrak* by John Metcalf.
OPERA PRODUCTIONS IN THE UK INCLUDE: Since 1986: Covent Garden, *Médée*; Opera Northern Ireland, *The Bartered Bride*; Royal College of Music: *Paul Bunyan*, *Eugene Onegin*, *Le Comte Ory*, *The Rake's Progress*; Scottish Opera Go Round, *Cavalleria Rusticana/Pagliacci*; University College Opera: *Lakmé*, *Le Roi d'Ys*.
RELATED PROFESSIONAL ACTIVITIES: Translations: *The Bartered Bride* (Welsh National Opera and Opera Northern Ireland), *The Yes-Sayer* (Banff Centre, Alberta).
PUBLICATIONS INCLUDE: Contributor: *Wagner in Performance* (Yale University Press); Opera Guides: *Parsifal*, *Tannhäuser*, *Stage Works of Belá Bartók* (all Calder); frequent contributor to programmes for Covent Garden and Welsh National Opera.
AWARDS INCLUDE: 1990, Canadian National Opera Association Production Competition, *Tornrak*.
ADDRESS: c/o Gillian Clench, International Artists' Management, 1 Mount Pleasant Cottages, Rhiwbina Hill, Cardiff CF4 6UP.

ATHERTON DAVID
Conductor

POSITIONS: Music Director: Hong Kong Philharmonic Orchestra; Mainly Mozart Festival, San Diego.
PERSONAL DETAILS: b. 3 January 1944, Lancashire; m. Ann Drake, three children.
EDUCATION/TRAINING: 1962–1966, Fitzwilliam College, Cambridge.
PROFESSIONAL DEBUT: 1968, London Sinfonietta at the Queen Elizabeth Hall.
OPERATIC DEBUT: 1968, Covent Garden, *Il Trovatore*.
CAREER: Covent Garden: 1967–1968, répétiteur; 1968–1980, Resident Conductor; 1968–1973 and 1989–1991, founder and Music Director, London Sinfonietta; Royal Liverpool Philharmonic: 1980–1983, Principal Conductor; 1983–1986, Principal Guest Conductor; 1980–1987, Music Director, San Diego Symphony Orchestra; 1985–1989, Principal Guest Conductor, BBC Symphony Orchestra; since 1989, Music Director: Hong Kong Philharmonic Orchestra; Mainly Mozart Festival, San Diego.
MAJOR OPERATIC DEBUTS INCLUDE: 1976, Covent Garden at La Scala, Milan, *Peter Grimes*; *Billy Budd*: 1978, San Francisco Opera; 1984, Metropolitan Opera, New York; 1988, English National Opera.
OPERATIC WORLD PREMIERES INCLUDE: English Opera Group at the Aldeburgh Festival: 1968, *Punch and Judy* by Harrison Birtwistle; 1969, *The Grace of Todd* by Gordon Crosse; 1969: Music Theatre Ensemble at the Edinburgh International Festival, *Pharsalia* by Iain Hamilton; Music Theatre Ensemble at the Brighton Festival, *Down by the Greenwood Side* by Harrison Birtwistle; 1976, Covent Garden, *We Come to the River* by Hans Werner Henze; 1977, BBC Radio 3, *Tamburlaine* by Iain Hamilton.
OPERA PERFORMANCES IN THE UK INCLUDE: Since 1980: Covent Garden: *L'Africaine*, *The Rake's Progress*, *The Nightingale/L'Enfant et les Sortilèges*, *Les Huguenots*, *Jenůfa*; English National

Opera: *The Love for Three Oranges*,
Peter Grimes.
RELATED PROFESSIONAL ACTIVITIES:
Concerts, broadcasts and television
performances with leading orchestras
worldwide; 1973: editor, instrumental and
chamber music of Arnold Schoenberg
and Roberto Gerhard; ballet
arrangements, *Pandora* and *Don Quixote*
(both by Gerhard); Artistic Director: 1979–
1982, London Stravinsky Festival; 1983–
1984, Ravel/Varèse Festival
(performances included *L'Heure
Espagnole/L'Enfant et les Sortilèges*).
RECORDINGS INCLUDE: Birtwistle, *Punch
and Judy* (ETCE); Janáček, operatic and
chamber works; Ligeti: *Melodien* for
chamber orchestra, Chamber Concerto
(all DECC): Tippett: *The Ice Break* (VIRG),
King Priam (DECC); Weill: Concerto for
violin and wind orchestra, *Kleine
Dreigroschenmusik* – orchestral suite,
Mahagonny-Gesänge (all DG).
VIDEOS INCLUDE: Britten, *Billy Budd*
(English National Opera).
PUBLICATIONS INCLUDE: Contributor: 1977,
The Musical Companion (Gollancz); 1980,
*The New Grove Dictionary of Music and
Musicians* (Macmillan).
AWARDS INCLUDE: 1971, Conductor of the
Year, Composers' Guild of Great Britain;
1973, Edison Award (USA); 1977, Grand
Prix du Disque (France); 1981,
Koussevitzky Prize (USA); 1982:
International Critics' Award, *King Priam*;
Prix Caecilia (Belgium).
ADDRESS: c/o Harold Holt Ltd, 31 Sinclair
Road, London W14 0NS.

ATKINSON LYNTON   Tenor

POSITION: Member, The Royal Opera,
Covent Garden.
PERSONAL DETAILS: b. 11 October 1962,
London; m. Joy Robinson (mezzo-
soprano).
EDUCATION/TRAINING: 1980–1983, St John's
College, Cambridge, studied music with
George Guest; further studies with Gita
Denise and David Mason in London.

PROFESSIONAL DEBUT: 1985, Brighton
Festival Chorus, Soloist, *Mass in B Minor*
(Bach).
EARLY CAREER INCLUDED: 1985–1988,
primarily a concert performer.
CAREER IN THE UK INCLUDES: Since 1988:
Midsummer Opera, Acis, *Acis and
Galatea* (1988, operatic debut); Covent
Garden (since 1991, member): First
Prisoner, *Fidelio* (1990, debut); Servant,
Capriccio; Borsa, *Rigoletto*; Pang,
Turandot; Nathanael, *Les Contes
d'Hoffmann*; Strolling Player, *Death in
Venice*; Fourth Jew, *Salome*; Zefirino, *Il
Viaggio a Reims*; Jacquino, *Fidelio*;
Federico, *Stiffelio*; also: Buxton Festival,
Emilio, *Il Sogno di Scipione*; Spitalfields
Festival, Damon, *Acis and Galatea*;
Travelling Opera, Ernesto, *Don Pasquale*.
OPERATIC WORLD PREMIERES INCLUDE:
1991, Covent Garden, Ywain, *Gawain* by
Harrison Birtwistle.
RELATED PROFESSIONAL ACTIVITIES:
Regular concerts and recitals with
leading conductors and orchestras in the
UK and abroad.
RECORDINGS INCLUDE: Haydn and
Schubert masses (MERI).
VIDEOS INCLUDE: Beethoven, *Fidelio*
(Covent Garden).
AWARDS INCLUDE: 1988, Richard Tauber
Memorial Prize; 1990, Alfredo Kraus
International Singing Competition (Las
Palmas).
ADDRESS: c/o Magenta Music International
Ltd, 64 Highgate High Street, London N6
5HX.

AYRTON NORMAN
Director and Teacher

PERSONAL DETAILS: b. 25 September 1924,
London.
EDUCATION/TRAINING: 1947–1948, acting
course, Old Vic Theatre School, London.
PROFESSIONAL DEBUT: As actor: 1949, Old
Vic Theatre Company.
OPERATIC DEBUT: 1962, Handel Opera
Society, *Artaxerxes*.

9

CAREER: Since 1963, opera and theatre director with leading companies in the UK, Australia, Canada and USA; 1949–1951, appearances at the Old Vic and several repertory theatres; 1949–1952, staff member, Old Vic Theatre School; 1952, opened teaching studio; 1953, dramatic coach, Covent Garden; London Academy of Music and Dramatic Art: 1954–1966, Assistant Principal; 1966–1972, Principal; director and teacher: 1974–1978, Loeb Drama Center, Harvard; 1974–1985, Juilliard School of Music and Mannes College of Music, New York; 1980–1981, National Opera Studio; 1981–1985, Resident Stage Director, American Opera Center, New York; 1986-1990, Director of Opera, Royal Academy of Music; since 1986, Dean, British American Drama Academy, London.

MAJOR OPERATIC DEBUTS INCLUDE: 1963, Covent Garden, *La Traviata*; 1965, Sutherland-Williamson Opera Company, Australia tour: *Lucia di Lammermoor, La Traviata, Semiramide, Faust*; 1976, Australian Opera, Sydney, *Lakmé*.

OPERA PRODUCTIONS IN THE UK INCLUDE: Since 1963: Covent Garden, *Manon*; Handel Opera: *Giulio Cesare, Theodora*; Royal Academy of Music: *The Carmelites, Giulio Cesare, The Rape of Lucretia*.

HONOURS INCLUDE: 1989, Honorary Member, Royal Academy of Music.

ADDRESS: 40A Birchington Road, London NW6 4LJ.

* * * *

BAILEY NORMAN
Baritone and Teacher

PERSONAL DETAILS: b. 23 March 1933, Birmingham; m. 1957, Doreen Simpson, three children; m. 1985, Kristine Ciesinski (soprano).

PREVIOUS OCCUPATIONS: 1950–1951, accountant; 1956–1958, school teacher.

EDUCATION/TRAINING: 1951–1956, Rhodes University, South Africa, studied music; 1958–1960, Vienna State Academy.

PROFESSIONAL DEBUT: 1959, Vienna Chamber Opera, Tobias Mill, La Cambiale di Matrimonio.

EARLY CAREER INCLUDED: Principal Baritone: 1960–1963, Linz; 1963–1964, Wuppertal; 1964–1967, Deutsche Oper am Rhein, Düsseldorf; roles included: Tonio, *Pagliacci*; Alfio, *Cavalleria Rusticana*; Escamillo, *Carmen*; Herald, *Lohengrin*; Speaker, *Die Zauberflöte*; Music Master, *Ariadne auf Naxos*; Golaud, *Pelléas et Mélisande*; 1967–1971, Principal Baritone, Sadler's Wells Opera, roles included: Count and title role, *The Marriage of Figaro*; Count di Luna, *Il Trovatore*; Wotan, *The Ring of the Nibelung*; Don Pizarro, *Fidelio*; title role, *The Flying Dutchman*.

MAJOR DEBUTS INCLUDE: 1967, La Scala, Milan, Priest, *Job*; Hans Sachs, *Die Meistersinger von Nürnberg*: 1968, Sadler's Wells Opera; 1969: Covent Garden, Bayreuth Festival; 1975, New York City Opera; 1976, Metropolitan Opera, New York; 1978, Australian Opera, Sydney; 1973: Scottish Opera, Kurwenal, *Tristan und Isolde*; Paris Opera, Amfortas, *Parsifal*; 1974, Welsh National Opera, title role, *The Flying Dutchman*; 1976: Scottish Opera at the Edinburgh International Festival, title role, *Macbeth*; Vienna State Opera, Wanderer, *Siegfried*; 1978, Lyric Opera, Chicago, Jokanaan, *Salome*; 1981, Opera North, Lindorf/Coppelius/Dapertutto/Dr Miracle, *The Tales of Hoffmann*; 1988, Nancy Opera, title role, *King Priam*.

OPERATIC WORLD PREMIERES INCLUDE: 1985, Deutsche Oper am Rhein, Duisburg, Jan Mathys, *Die Wiedertäufer (Behold The Sun)* by Alexander Goehr.

CAREER IN THE UK INCLUDES: Since 1971: Covent Garden: Amfortas and Klingsor, *Parsifal*; Balstrode, *Peter Grimes*; Kurwenal, *Tristan und Isolde*; Wolfram, *Tannhäuser*; Jokanaan, *Salome*; Ford, *Falstaff*; Wotan, *Der Ring des Nibelungen*; Orest, *Elektra*; Germont, *La Traviata*; Music Master, *Ariadne auf Naxos*; Sadler's Wells Opera/English National Opera: Kutuzov, *War and Peace* (1972, British stage première); Germont, *La Traviata*; Scarpia, *Tosca*; Kurwenal, *Tristan and Isolde*; Leporello, *Don Giovanni*; Music Master, *Ariadne auf Naxos*; Ballad Singer, *Gloriana*; Sharpless, *Madam Butterfly*; Father, *Hänsel and Gretel*; Forester, *The Cunning Little Vixen*; Prince Gremin, *Eugene Onegin*; Water Sprite, *Rusalka*; Ariodate, *Xerxes*; title role, *The Flying Dutchman*; Opera North: King René, *Yolande*; title role, *Nabucco*; Scottish Opera: Sharpless, *Madama Butterfly*; Welsh National Opera: Barak, *Die Frau ohne Schatten*; Scarpia, *Tosca*.

RELATED PROFESSIONAL ACTIVITIES: Numerous concerts, recitals, broadcasts and television appearances in the UK and abroad; Professor of Singing, Royal College of Music.

RECORDINGS INCLUDE: Mozart, *Die Zauberflöte*; Tippett, *King Priam*; Wagner: *Der Fliegende Holländer*, *Die Meistersinger von Nürnberg* (all DECC), *The Rhinegold*, *The Valkyrie*, *Siegfried* (all EMI).

VIDEOS INCLUDE: Britten: *Gloriana* (English National Opera), *Peter Grimes* (Covent Garden).

AWARDS AND HONOURS INCLUDE: 1977: Sir Charles Santley Memorial Award; Commander, Order of the British Empire (CBE); 1981, Honorary Member, Royal Academy of Music; 1986, Honorary Doctorate of Music, Rhodes University.

ADDRESS: c/o Music International, 13 Ardilaun Road, London N5 2QR.

BAINBRIDGE ELIZABETH
Mezzo-soprano

PERSONAL DETAILS: b. 28 March 1930, Lancashire; m. P. Morris (d. 1988), one child.

EDUCATION/TRAINING: Guildhall School of Music and Drama, with Norman Walker.

PROFESSIONAL DEBUT: 1957, chorus member, Glyndebourne Festival Opera.

EARLY CAREER INCLUDED: 1958–1964, appearances with Glyndebourne Festival Opera, Welsh National Opera, Wexford Festival; roles included: Pallas Athene, *L'Incoronazione di Poppea*; Third Lady, *Die Zauberflöte*; Azucena, *Il Trovatore*.

MAJOR DEBUTS INCLUDE: Auntie, *Peter Grimes*: 1976, Covent Garden at La Scala, Milan; 1977, Lyric Opera, Chicago; 1979: Covent Garden Far East tour; Teatro Colón, Buenos Aires; 1988, Maggio Musicale, Florence.

OPERATIC WORLD PREMIERES INCLUDE: 1976, Covent Garden, May/Madwoman 4, *We Come to the River* by Hans Werner Henze.

CAREER IN THE UK INCLUDES: Since 1965: Covent Garden (1965–1990, member): Suzuki, *Madama Butterfly*; Mamma Lucia, *Cavalleria Rusticana*; Frugola, *Il Tabarro*; Emilia, *Otello*; Maddalena, *Rigoletto*; Mistress Quickly, *Falstaff*; Alisa, *Lucia di Lammermoor*; Evadne, *Troilus and Cressida*; She-Ancient, *The Midsummer Marriage*; Auntie, *Peter Grimes*; Madame Arvidson, *Un Ballo in Maschera*; Amneris, *Aida*; Erda, *Der Ring des Nibelungen*; Clotilde, *Norma*; Marcellina, *Le Nozze di Figaro*; Filipyevna, *Eugene Onegin*; Grandmother, *Jenůfa*; First Norn, *Götterdämmerung*; Innkeeper's Wife, *The Cunning Little Vixen*; Hostess, *Boris Godunov*; Hostess, *The Fiery Angel*; English Opera Group, Bianca, *The Rape of Lucretia*; Handel Opera Society, Irene, *Theodora*; Scottish Opera: Hostess, *Boris Godunov*; Mistress Quickly, *Falstaff*; Auntie, *Peter Grimes*.

RELATED PROFESSIONAL ACTIVITIES: Concerts in the UK and abroad.

11

RECORDINGS INCLUDE: Bellini, *Norma* (RCA); Britten: *Peter Grimes, The Rape of Lucretia* (both PHIL); Janáček, *The Cunning Little Vixen* (EMI); Massenet, *Cendrillon* (CBS); Tippett, *The Midsummer Marriage* (PHIL); Vaughan Williams, *Sir John in Love* (EMI); Verdi, *Il Trovatore* (RCA); Walton, *Troilus and Cressida* (EMI).

VIDEOS INCLUDE: Britten, *Peter Grimes* (Covent Garden); Sullivan, *The Yeomen of the Guard* (Walker).

ADDRESS: c/o Music International, 13 Ardilaun Road, London N5 2QR.

BALCOMBE RICHARD
Conductor and Répétiteur

PERSONAL DETAILS: b. 8 September 1955, Eastbourne; m. 1983, two children.

EDUCATION/TRAINING: 1973–1978, Guildhall School of Music and Drama: piano with Cimbro Martin, David Wilde and Mary Peppin; violin with Walter Gerhardt and Suzanne Rosza.

OPERATIC DEBUT: 1989, Travelling Opera, *La Bohème*.

CAREER: Since 1979, chorus master, orchestrator, répétiteur, pianist and accompanist in the UK and abroad; since 1989, Conductor, Travelling Opera.

OPERA PERFORMANCES IN THE UK INCLUDE: Since 1989, Travelling Opera: *Cosi fan tutte, Don Giovanni, The Marriage of Figaro, Rigoletto, The Barber of Seville, Orpheus in the Underworld, Don Pasquale, The Messiah, Carmen.*

AWARDS INCLUDE: 1976, Countess of Munster Award.

ADDRESS: c/o Travelling Opera, 125 St Mary's Road, Market Harborough, Leicestershire LE16 7DT.

BANKS BARRY   Tenor

PERSONAL DETAILS: b. Stoke-on-Trent.

EDUCATION/TRAINING: Royal Northern College of Music, with Joseph Ward; National Opera Studio; masterclasses with Geraint Evans and Elisabeth Schwarzkopf; currently with Iris dell'Acqua.

PROFESSIONAL DEBUT: 1982, Buxton Festival, Napoleon, *Háry János.*

EARLY CAREER INCLUDED: 1983-1985, chorus member, Glyndebourne Festival Opera.

MAJOR DEBUTS INCLUDE: 1985, Glyndebourne Touring Opera, Flute, *A Midsummer Night's Dream*; 1986, Théâtre du Châtelet, Paris, Florville, *Il Signor Bruschino*; 1987: English National Opera, Count, *The Barber of Seville*; Opera North, Don Basilio, *The Marriage of Figaro*; Welsh National Opera, Count, *The Barber of Seville*; 1988, Netherlands Opera, Pedrillo, *Die Entführung aus dem Serail*; 1989: Covent Garden, Beppe, *Pagliacci*; Kent Opera, Reverend Adams, *Peter Grimes*; 1990, Batignano Festival, Mercury, *King Priam*; Tamino, *Die Zauberflöte*; 1990, Leipzig Opera; 1991, La Monnaie, Brussels and Landestheater, Salzburg; 1993: Salzburg Festival, Shepherd/Spirit, *Orfeo*; Salzburg Mozart Week, Aufidio, *Lucia Silla.*

OPERATIC WORLD PREMIERES INCLUDE: 1991, Opera North, Pedrolino, *The Jewel Box* by Mozart/Paul Griffiths; 1993, English National Opera, Josh, *Inquest of Love* by Jonathan Harvey.

CAREER IN THE UK INCLUDES: Since 1986: Buxton Festival, Grimbald, *King Arthur*; English National Opera: Novice, *Billy Budd*; Fenton, *Falstaff*; Nanki-Poo, *The Mikado*; Brighella, *Ariadne auf Naxos*; Glyndebourne Touring Opera: Tamino, *Die Zauberflöte*; title role, *The Rake's Progress*; Opera North: Iopas, *The Trojans*; Arturo, *Lucia di Lammermoor*; Giannetto, *The Thieving Magpie.*

RELATED PROFESSIONAL ACTIVITIES: Regular concerts and recitals in the UK and abroad.

VIDEOS INCLUDE: Mozart at Buckingham Palace (EMI).

AWARDS INCLUDE: 1983, Peter Moores Foundation Scholarship.

ADDRESS: c/o Robert Gilder & Company, Enterprise House, 59–65 Upper Ground, London SE1 9PQ.

BANNATYNE-SCOTT BRIAN
Bass and Translator

PERSONAL DETAILS: b. 4 November 1955, Edinburgh; m. 1979.
EDUCATION/TRAINING: 1973–1977, University of St Andrews, studied French and medieval history; 1978-1981, Guildhall School of Music and Drama, with Laura Sarti; further studies with Peter Pears, Hans Hotter and Gerhard Husch; currently with Norman Bailey.
PROFESSIONAL DEBUT: 1981, Teatro La Fenice, Venice, First Magician, *Oberon* by Niccolò Castiglioni (world première).
EARLY CAREER INCLUDED: 1982–1985, Principal Bass, Scottish Opera: Sergeant, *Manon Lescaut*; Nourabad, *The Pearl Fishers*; Colline, *La Bohème*; Speaker, *The Magic Flute*; Night, *L'Egisto*; Voice of Neptune, *Idomeneo*; Don Fernando, *Fidelio*; Micha, *The Bartered Bride*; Monterone, *Rigoletto*; Theseus, *A Midsummer Night's Dream*; La Roche, *Capriccio*.
MAJOR DEBUTS INCLUDE: 1982, Rome Opera, First Magician, *Oberon*; 1987, English National Opera, Monterone, *Rigoletto*; 1988, Opera London, Mercury, *L'Incoronazione di Poppea*; 1989, Wexford Festival, Father Augustine, *The Duenna* (Prokofiev); 1991, Polythemus, *Acis and Galatea*: Salzburg Festival and National Arts Centre, Ottawa.
CAREER IN THE UK INCLUDES: Since 1986: City of Birmingham Touring Opera, Fafner and Hagen, *The Ring Saga*; English National Opera: Schwarz and Pogner, *The Mastersingers of Nuremberg*; Tall Englishman, *The Gambler*; Flemish Deputy, *Don Carlos*; Monterone, *Rigoletto*; Commendatore, *Don Giovanni*; Banquo, *Macbeth*; Mecklenburgh Opera: Death, *The Emperor of Atlantis*; Jakob, *Mannekins* (1990, British première); Opera North, Varlaam, *Boris Godunov*; Grand Inquisitor, *Don Carlos*.
RELATED PROFESSIONAL ACTIVITIES: Numerous concerts in the UK and abroad; translator with John Abulafia, *Mannekins*.

RECORDINGS INCLUDE: Monteverdi, *L'Incoronazione di Poppea (VIRG)*; Purcell, *King Arthur* (ARCH).
AWARDS INCLUDE: 1981, Decca-Kathleen Ferrier Prize; 1990, Wagner Society Bayreuth Bursary.
ADDRESS: c/o Magenta Music International Ltd, 64 Highgate High Street, London N6 5HX.

BARCLAY YVONNE   Soprano

POSITION: Member, The Royal Opera, Covent Garden.
PERSONAL DETAILS: b. 30 January 1960, Ayrshire.
EDUCATION/TRAINING: Royal Scottish Academy of Music and Drama, with Neilson Taylor; 1984–1985, National Opera Studio; currently with Iris dell'Acqua.
PROFESSIONAL DEBUT: 1983, Scottish Opera, First Boy, *The Magic Flute*.
EARLY CAREER INCLUDED: 1983–1988, appearances with Opera East, Opera West, Scottish Opera; roles included: Despina, *Così fan tutte*; Frasquita, *Carmen*; Musetta, *La Bohème*; Sandman, *Hansel and Gretel*; Strawberry Seller/Lace Seller/Strolling Player, *Death in Venice*; Dawn/Winter, *L'Egisto*.
MAJOR DEBUTS INCLUDE: 1988: Glyndebourne Festival Opera, Shepherdess, *L'Enfant et les Sortilèges*; Glyndebourne Touring Opera, Blonde, *Die Entführung aus dem Serail*; 1989: Opera 80, Susanna, *The Marriage of Figaro*; Opera North, First Niece, *Peter Grimes*; 1990, Leipzig Opera: Gretel, *Hänsel und Gretel*; Blonde, *Die Entführung aus dem Serail*; 1992, English National Opera, Echo, *Ariadne auf Naxos*.
OPERATIC WORLD PREMIERES INCLUDE: 1991, Royal Opera Garden Venture: Woman, *The Panic* by David Sawer; Aphrodite, *The Judgement of Paris* by John Woolrich.
CAREER IN THE UK INCLUDES: Since 1989: English National Opera, Dew Fairy, *Hansel and Gretel*; Glyndebourne

Festival Opera, Emmie, *Albert Herring*;
Opera North, Eurydice, *Orpheus in the
Underworld*; Opera Northern Ireland,
Esmeralda, *The Bartered Bride*; Scottish
Opera, Barbarina, *The Marriage of
Figaro*.
ADDRESS: c/o Royal Opera House, Covent
Garden, London WC2E 9DD.

BARDON PATRICIA
Mezzo-soprano

PERSONAL DETAILS: b. 1965, Dublin.
EDUCATION/TRAINING: Dublin College of
Music, with Veronica Dunne.
PROFESSIONAL DEBUT: 1985, Welsh
National Opera, Flosshilde,
Götterdämmerung.
MAJOR DEBUTS INCLUDE: 1985, Dublin
Grand Opera, Olga, *Eugene Onegin*;
1987: Opera North, Anna, *The Trojans*;
Basle, Suzy, *La Rondine*; 1990: Scottish
Opera, Anna, *The Trojans*; Dublin Grand
Opera, title role, *The Rape of Lucretia*;
Teatro Filarmonico, Verona, Third Lady,
Die Zauberflöte; 1991, Covent Garden,
Wowkle, *La Fanciulla del West*; 1992:
English National Opera, Maddalena,
Rigoletto; Flanders Opera, Antwerp,
Helen, *King Priam*; Teatro La Fenice,
Venice, Arsace, *Semiramide*.
OPERATIC WORLD PREMIERES INCLUDE:
1990, Munich Biennale, Mrs Grainger, *63:
Dream Palace* by Hans-Jürgen von Bose.
CAREER IN THE UK INCLUDES: Since 1986:
Covent Garden: Maddalena, *Rigoletto*;
Hedwige, *Guillaume Tell*; Opera North:
Helen, *King Priam*; Suzuki, *Madama
Butterfly*; Maddalena, *Rigoletto*; Welsh
National Opera: Olga, *Eugene Onegin*.
RELATED PROFESSIONAL ACTIVITIES:
Regular concerts and recitals in the UK
and abroad.
AWARDS INCLUDE: 1983, prize winner,
Cardiff Singer of the World Competition.
ADDRESS: c/o Ingpen & Williams Ltd, 14
Kensington Court, London W8 5DN.

BARHAM EDMUND   Tenor

PERSONAL DETAILS: b. 22 March 1954,
London.
EDUCATION/TRAINING: 1973–1975, Trinity
College of Music; 1975-1977, London
Opera Centre.
PROFESSIONAL DEBUT: 1977, Opera for All,
Count, *The Barber of Seville*.
EARLY CAREER INCLUDED: 1977–1979,
several roles with Opera for All and New
Opera Company; 1980–1985, appearances
with opera houses in Cologne, Darmstadt,
Dortmund and Heidelberg; Principal
Tenor: 1980–1984, Wuppertal Opera;
1984–1985, Gärtnerplatz, Munich; roles
included: Rodolfo, *La Bohème*; Manrico,
Il Trovatore; Don Alvaro, *La Forza del
Destino*; Alfredo, *La Traviata*; Belmonte,
Die Entführung aus dem Serail; Konrad,
Hans Heiling; title roles: *La Clemenza di
Tito, Don Carlos*.
MAJOR DEBUTS INCLUDE: 1978, La
Monnaie, Brussels, Mayor, *Albert
Herring*; 1980, Wuppertal Opera,
Nemorino, *L'Elisir d'Amore*; 1985, English
National Opera, Jeník, *The Bartered
Bride*; 1987, Opera North, Boris, *Katya
Kabanova*; 1988, Lucerne, Jimmy,
Aufstieg und Fall der Stadt Mahagonny;
1990, English National Opera Soviet
Union tour (Bolshoi and Kirov), Macduff,
Macbeth; 1991: Bregenz Festival, Don
José, *Carmen*; Lucerne, title role, *Otello*;
1992, Welsh National Opera, Pinkerton,
Madam Butterfly.
CAREER IN THE UK INCLUDES: Since 1985:
English National Opera (1988-1990,
Principal Tenor): Turiddu, *Cavalleria
Rusticana*; Gabriele, *Simon Boccanegra*;
Narraboth, *Salome*; Pinkerton, *Madam
Butterfly*; Vakula, *Christmas Eve* (1988,
British stage première); Cavaradossi,
Tosca; Macduff, *Macbeth*; Gustavus, *A
Masked Ball*; Don Alvaro, *The Force of
Destiny*; title roles: *Don Carlos,
Lohengrin*; Opera North: *Don José,
Carmen*; Foresto, *Attila*; Enzo, *La
Gioconda*.

RELATED PROFESSIONAL ACTIVITIES:
Numerous concerts and recitals in the UK
and abroad.

RECORDINGS INCLUDE: Mozart, *Die
Zauberflöte* (PHIL); Rossini, *Petite Messe
Solennelle* (CHAN); Vivaldi, *Gloria* (ERAT);
Opera Spectacular (IMP).

AWARDS INCLUDE: 1975, Ricordi Opera
Prize.

ADDRESS: c/o Stafford Law Associates, 26
Mayfield Road, Weybridge, Surrey KT13
8XB.

BARKER CHERYL   Soprano

PERSONAL DETAILS: b. 22 April 1960,
Sydney, Australia; m. Peter Coleman-
Wright (baritone).

EDUCATION/TRAINING: 1977–1984, with
Joan Hammond in Sydney.

PROFESSIONAL DEBUT: 1984, State Opera
of South Australia, Adelaide, Blonde, *Die
Entführung aus dem Serail*.

CAREER INCLUDES: Since 1984: English
National Opera: (1989 debut), Governess,
The Turn of the Screw; Foreign Princess,
Rusalka; Oksana, *Christmas Eve*; Mimi,
La Bohème; Glyndebourne Touring
Opera: (1989, debut), Cherubino, *Le
Nozze di Figaro*; Marzelline, *Fidelio*;
Opera 80, Micaëla, *Carmen*; Scottish
Opera: (1991, debut), Annio, *La Clemenza
di Tito*; Tatyana, *Eugene Onegin*;
Australian Opera, Sydney: Mimi, *La
Bohème*; Marzelline, *Fidelio*; Victoria
State Opera, Melbourne: First Lady, *Die
Zauberflöte*; Mimi, *La Bohème*; Violetta,
La Traviata; Antonia, *Les Contes
d'Hoffmann*.

RELATED PROFESSIONAL ACTIVITIES:
Concerts and recitals in the UK and
abroad.

AWARDS INCLUDE: 1989, Royal Over-Seas
League Music Competition.

ADDRESS: c/o Stafford Law Associates, 26
Mayfield Road, Weybridge, Surrey KT13
8XB.

BARKER JOHN
Conductor, Chorus Master,
Répétiteur and Translator

POSITION: Head of Music Department, The
Royal Opera, Covent Garden.

PERSONAL DETAILS: b. 23 September 1931,
Middlesex.

EDUCATION/TRAINING: Royal College of
Music, studied piano, viola and
conducting; Mozarteum, Salzburg, with
Lovro Von Matacic.

PROFESSIONAL AND OPERATIC DEBUT:
1958, Touring Opera, *Pagliacci*.

CAREER: 1958: member, music staff,
Glyndebourne Festival Opera; Chorus
Master and Conductor, Touring Opera;
1959–1974, conductor, Chorus Master and
subsequently Head of Music Staff,
Sadler's Wells Opera; since 1975,
conductor, Chorus Master, Head of Music
Staff and currently Head of Music
Department, Covent Garden.

MAJOR OPERATIC DEBUTS INCLUDE: 1959,
Sadler's Wells Opera, *The Merry Widow*;
1976, Covent Garden, *Le Nozze di Figaro*.

OPERATIC WORLD PREMIERES INCLUDE:
1969, Sadler's Wells Opera, *Lucky Peter's
Journey* by Malcolm Williamson.

OPERA PERFORMANCES IN THE UK
INCLUDE: 1959–1974, Sadler's Wells Opera,
more than 800 performances including:
*Cinderella, Count Ory, Hansel and Gretel,
Oedipus Rex, Orpheus and Eurydice, The
Rake's Progress, The Ring of the
Nibelung, The Thieving Magpie, The
Violins of St Jacques*; since 1975, Covent
Garden: *Don Giovanni, Troilus and
Cressida, Madama Butterfly, Tosca, Lucia
di Lammermoor, Il Trovatore, Carmen, La
Bohème, Peter Grimes, Turandot, La
Cenerentola*.

RELATED PROFESSIONAL ACTIVITIES:
Numerous concerts and broadcasts in the
UK and abroad.

RECORDINGS INCLUDE: Covent Garden
Gala Concert (EMI).

PUBLICATIONS INCLUDE: Translation,
Boccaccio (Weinberger).

ADDRESS: c/o Royal Opera House, Covent
Garden, London WC2E 9DD.

BARKER PAUL
Composer, Conductor and Répétiteur

POSITIONS: Artistic Director, Modern Music Theatre Troupe; Composer in Residence, West Sussex.

PERSONAL DETAILS: b. 1 July 1956, Cambridge.

EDUCATION/TRAINING: 1974–1978, Guildhall School of Music and Drama, composition with Patric Standford and piano with Edith Vogel; 1983–1985, University of Durham, composition with John Casken.

FIRST PROFESSIONAL PERFORMANCE OF A COMPOSITION: 1979, Nottingham Festival, Dialogue for flute and piano.

CAREER: Compositions include five operas, 10 contemporary dance scores, numerous orchestral, vocal and choral works; 1978–1984, Music Director, Dancers Anonymous; 1983: Conductor, North Tyne and Wear Choral Society; répétiteur, European Opera Centre, Belgium; since 1985, founder and Artistic Director, Modern Music Theatre Troupe.

OPERATIC WORLD PREMIERES: 1985, Opera Viva, *The Marriages Between Zones 3, 4 & 5*, after the novel by Doris Lessing, conductor Chris Willis, director Christopher Newell; Modern Music Theatre Troupe: 1986, *Phantastes*, after the Victorian novel by George McDonald, conductor Chris Willis, director Christopher Newell; 1988, *The Pillow Song*, after 10th-century Japanese writer Sei Shonagan, conductor the composer, director Akemi Horie; 1989, *La Malinche*, conductor the composer, director Akemi Horie (all librettos by the composer); 1990, *Albergo Empedocle*, libretto by Nicholas Till, conductor the composer, director Nicholas Till.

RELATED PROFESSIONAL ACTIVITIES: 1978–1983, Visiting Lecturer, City University, London; 1984–1990, Associate Lecturer, Kingsway College, London; 1988–1990, vocal coach; 1990, opera education workshops, Opera North.

RECORDINGS INCLUDE: *The Pied Piper of Hamelin*, *Fanfare for Barbican* (both UNIC).

ADDRESS: c/o British Music Information Centre, 10 Stratford Place, London W1N 9AE.

BARLOW STEPHEN
Conductor

PERSONAL DETAILS: b. 30 June 1954, London; m. 1986, Joanna Lumley (actress and writer).

EDUCATION/TRAINING: 1972–1975, Organ Scholar, Trinity College, Cambridge; 1975-1976, Guildhall School of Music and Drama, with Vilem Tausky.

PROFESSIONAL AND OPERATIC DEBUT: 1978, Glyndebourne Touring Opera, *The Rake's Progress*.

CAREER: Freelance conductor in the UK and abroad; 1977–1985, member, music staff and Associate Conductor, Glyndebourne Festival Opera; 1982–1985, staff conductor, English National Opera; Opera 80: 1980–1988, Associate Conductor; 1988-1990, Music Director.

MAJOR OPERATIC DEBUTS INCLUDE: 1979, Glyndebourne Festival Opera, *Die Schweigsame Frau*; 1980, English National Opera, *The Damnation of Faust*; Opera 80, *The Barber of Seville*; 1989: Covent Garden, *Turandot*; Netherlands Opera, *Il Barbiere di Siviglia*; Vancouver Opera, *The Rake's Progress*; 1990, San Francisco Opera, *Capriccio*; 1991, Victoria State Opera, Melbourne, *Die Zauberflöte*.

OPERATIC WORLD PREMIERES INCLUDE: 1986, Royal Society of Arts, *Exposition of a Picture* by Stephen Oliver.

OPERA PERFORMANCES IN THE UK INCLUDE: Since 1979: Covent Garden, *Die Zauberflöte*; Glyndebourne Festival and Touring Opera: *Der Rosenkavalier, La Cenerentola, Arabella, Così fan tutte, Orfeo ed Euridice, The Love for Three Oranges, Higglety Pigglety Pop!/Where the Wild Things Are*; Opera 80/English Touring Opera: *The Seraglio, Eugene Onegin, A Masked Ball, The Rake's Progress, Falstaff*; Opera North: *Intermezzo, Le Nozze di Figaro*; Opera

Northern Ireland; *Faust*; Scottish Opera:
The Bartered Bride, *Intermezzo*.
RELATED PROFESSIONAL ACTIVITIES:
Numerous appearances with leading
British orchestras.
RECORDINGS INCLUDE: Gay, *The Beggar's
Opera* (HYPE).
AWARDS AND HONOURS INCLUDE: 1979,
Leverhulme Award, Glyndebourne; 1984,
Fellow, Guildhall School of Music and
Drama.
ADDRESS: Not available.

BARSTOW JOSEPHINE
Soprano

PERSONAL DETAILS: b. 27 September 1940,
Sheffield; m. 1964, Terry Hands (theatre
director); m. 1969, Ande Anderson
(formerly General Manager, The Royal
Opera, Covent Garden).
PREVIOUS OCCUPATION: English teacher.
EDUCATION/TRAINING: University of
Birmingham, studied English; 1965–1966,
London Opera Centre.
PROFESSIONAL DEBUT: 1964, Opera for All,
Mimi, *La Bohème*.
EARLY CAREER INCLUDED: Principal
Soprano: 1967–1968, Sadler's Wells
Opera; 1968–1970, Welsh National Opera;
roles included: Cherubino, *The Marriage
of Figaro*; Violetta, *La Traviata*; Fiordiligi,
Così fan tutte; Mimi, *La Bohème*; Amelia,
Simon Boccanegra; also 1968, Camden
Festival, title role, *Yolande* (British
première).
MAJOR DEBUTS INCLUDE: 1969, Covent
Garden, Niece, *Peter Grimes*; 1971, Aix-
en-Provence Festival, Alice, *Falstaff*;
1972, Glyndebourne Festival Opera, Lady
Macbeth, *Macbeth*; 1977: Scottish Opera,
Leonore, *Fidelio*; Metropolitan Opera,
New York, Musetta, *La Bohème*; 1979,
Deutsche Staatsoper, East Berlin, title
role, *Salome*; 1981, Lyric Opera, Chicago,
Lady Macbeth, *Macbeth*; 1983, Bayreuth
Festival, Gutrune, *Götterdämmerung*;
1986: Soviet Union (Bolshoi, Riga, Tiblisi):
Lady Macbeth, *Macbeth*; title role, *Tosca*;
Vienna State Opera, Benigna, *Die

Schwarze Maske*; 1988, Opera Company
of Boston, title role, *Médée*.
OPERATIC WORLD PREMIERES INCLUDE:
Covent Garden: 1970, Denise, *The Knot
Garden* by Michael Tippett; 1976, Young
Woman, *We Come to the River* by Hans
Werner Henze; 1977, Gayle, *The Ice
Break* by Michael Tippett; 1974, Sadler's
Wells Opera, Marguérite, *The Story of
Vasco* by Gordon Crosse; 1986, Salzburg
Festival, Benigna, *Die Schwarze Maske*
by Krzysztof Penderecki.
CAREER IN THE UK INCLUDES: Since 1971:
Covent Garden: Alice, *Falstaff*; Santuzza,
Cavalleria Rusticana; Ellen Orford, *Peter
Grimes*; Odabella, *Attila*; Leonore,
Fidelio; title role, *Salome*; Glyndebourne
Festival Opera: Elettra, *Idomeneo*;
Leonore, *Fidelio*; Sadler's Wells Opera/
English National Opera: Emilia Marty, *The
Makropoulos Case*; Olympia/Giulietta/
Antonia, *The Tales of Hoffmann*; Natasha,
War and Peace (1972, British stage
première); Jeanne, *The Devils of Loudun*
(1973, British première); Autonoë, *The
Bassarids* (1974, British stage première);
Violetta, *La Traviata*; Marschallin, *Der
Rosenkavalier*; Leonora, *The Force of
Destiny*; Senta, *The Flying Dutchman*;
Mimi, *La Bohème*; Sieglinde, *The
Valkyrie*; Katerina, *Lady Macbeth of
Mtsensk* (1987, British stage première);
Ellen Orford, *Peter Grimes*; title roles:
Salome, Tosca, Aida, Arabella; Welsh
National Opera: Elisabeth de Valois, *Don
Carlos*; Ellen Orford, *Peter Grimes*;
Tatyana, *Eugene Onegin*; Amelia, *Un
Ballo in Maschera*; title roles: *Jenůfa,
Tosca*.
RELATED PROFESSIONAL ACTIVITIES:
Numerous concerts, recitals, broadcasts
and television appearances in the UK and
abroad.
RECORDINGS INCLUDE: Porter, *Kiss Me
Kate* (EMI); Tippett, *The Knot Garden*
(PHIL); Verdi: *Un Ballo in Maschera* (DG),
Verdi, arias (TER); Weill, *Street Scene*;
Opera Finales (both DECC).
VIDEOS INCLUDE: Mozart, *Idomeneo*; Verdi,
Macbeth (both Glyndebourne Festival
Opera).

AWARDS AND HONOURS INCLUDE: 1985: Commander, Order of the British Empire (CBE); Honorary Doctorate of Music, University of Birmingham; Fidelio Medal, Association of International Opera Directors.

ADDRESS: c/o John Coast, 31 Sinclair Road, London W14 ONS.

BAYLEY CLIVE   Bass

PERSONAL DETAILS: b. 15 November 1960, Manchester; m. 1989, Paula Bradley.

EDUCATION/TRAINING: 1979–1985, Royal Northern College of Music, with Nicholas Powell; 1985–1986, National Opera Studio.

PROFESSIONAL DEBUT: 1985, Opera North, Schwarz, *The Mastersingers of Nuremberg*.

EARLY CAREER INCLUDED: 1986–1987, Opera North: King, *Aida*; Don Basilio, *The Barber of Seville*; Colline, *La Bohème*; Banquo, *Macbeth*; Bartolo, *The Marriage of Figaro*; Ghost of Hector, *The Trojans*.

MAJOR DEBUTS INCLUDE: 1987: Covent Garden, Second Prisoner, *Fidelio*; English National Opera, Pietro, *Simon Boccanegra*; 1988, Netherlands Opera, Truffaldino, *Ariadne auf Naxos*.

OPERATIC WORLD PRÉMIERES INCLUDE: 1991, Covent Garden, Agravain, *Gawain* by Harrison Birtwistle; 1992, Almeida Opera, Surgeon, *Terrible Mouth* by Nigel Osborne.

CAREER IN THE UK INCLUDES: Since 1988: Covent Garden: Colline, *La Bohème*; Porter, *The Fiery Angel*; English National Opera: Monk, *The Stone Guest*; Mr Ratcliffe and Claggart, *Billy Budd*; Count Horn, *A Masked Ball*; Neptune, *The Return of Ulysses*; Wagner/Gravis/Master of Ceremonies/Law Student, *Doctor Faust*; Masetto, *Don Giovanni*; Opera Factory, Leporello, *Don Giovanni*; Opera North: Raimondo, *Lucia di Lammermoor*; Angelotti, *Tosca*; Papal Legate, *Jérusalem* (1990, British stage première); Simone, *Gianni Schicchi*; Jeronimus, *Masquerade* (1990, British première);

Sparafucile, *Rigoletto*; Ibn-Hakia, *Yolande*; Monk, *Don Carlos*.

RECORDINGS INCLUDE: Bernstein, *Candide* (DG).

VIDEOS INCLUDE: Britten, *Billy Budd* (English National Opera).

ADDRESS: c/o Harrison/Parrott Ltd, 12 Penzance Place, London W11 4PA.

BECHTLER HILDEGARD
Designer

PERSONAL DETAILS: b. 14 November 1951, Stuttgart, Germany; m., two children.

EDUCATION/TRAINING: Camberwell School of Art, Central School of Art and Design.

PROFESSIONAL DEBUT: 1981, ICA Theatre, London, *Ella* by Herbert Achternbusch.

OPERATIC DEBUT: 1987, Almeida Festival, *Jakob Lenz* (British première).

CAREER: Since 1981, freelance opera, theatre, film and television designer in the UK and Europe including Almeida Theatre, Royal National Theatre, Royal Shakespeare Company and Abbey Theatre, Dublin.

MAJOR OPERATIC DEBUTS INCLUDE: 1989, Bregenz Festival, *La Wally*; 1991, *Peter Grimes*: English National Opera and Bavarian State Opera, Munich; 1993: English National Opera, *Lohengrin*; Opera North: *Don Carlos*, *Wozzeck*; Netherlands Opera, *La Wally*.

OPERATIC WORLD PREMIERES INCLUDE: 1992, English National Opera, *Bakxai* by John Buller; costume designs: 1988, Théâtre de la Bastille, Paris (co-production with the Almeida Festival), *The Undivine Comedy* by Michael Finnissy; 1989, Almeida Festival, *Golem* by John Casken.

ADDRESS: c/o London Management, 235/241 Regent Street, London W1R 7AG.

BEDFORD STEUART
Conductor

POSITIONS: Co-Artistic Director, Aldeburgh Festival; Artistic Director, English Sinfonia.

PERSONAL DETAILS: b. 31 July 1939, London; m. 1969, Norma Burrowes (soprano); m. 1980, Celia Harding, two children.

EDUCATION/TRAINING: 1957–1961, Royal Academy of Music; 1961–1964, Organ Scholar, Worcester College, Oxford.

PROFESSIONAL DEBUT: 1964, Oxford Chamber Orchestra.

OPERATIC DEBUT: 1967, English Opera Group at Sadler's Wells Theatre, *The Beggar's Opera*.

CAREER: 1965–1967, member, music staff, Glyndebourne Festival Opera; 1967–1975, member, music staff and conductor, English Opera Group; 1965–1972, professor, Royal Academy of Music (1972, conducted first modern performance of *Belisario*); Artistic Director: 1975–1979, English Music Theatre; since 1973, Aldeburgh Festival; since 1981, English Sinfonia.

MAJOR OPERATIC DEBUTS INCLUDE: 1973, Covent Garden, *Owen Wingrave* (world stage première by Benjamin Britten); 1974: Welsh National Opera, *Idomeneo*; Metropolitan Opera, New York, *Owen Wingrave*; 1975, Royal Opera, Copenhagen, *A Midsummer Night's Dream*; 1978: La Monnaie, Brussels, *Peter Grimes*; Santa Fe Opera, *The Duchess of Malfi*; Teatro Colón, Buenos Aires: *Dido and Aeneas, Arlecchino*.

OPERATIC WORLD PREMIERES INCLUDE: English Opera Group at the Aldeburgh Festival: 1972, *The Visitors* by John Gardner; 1973, *Death in Venice* by Benjamin Britten; 1976, English Music Theatre at the Aldeburgh Festival, *Tom Jones* by Stephen Oliver; 1979, English Music Theatre at the Old Vic Theatre, *An Actor's Revenge* by Minoru Miki.

OPERA PERFORMANCES IN THE UK INCLUDE: Since 1967: Covent Garden: *Così fan tutte, Death in Venice*; English Opera Group/English Music Theatre and/or Aldeburgh Festival: *The Rape of Lucretia, A Midsummer Night's Dream, Idomeneo, Iolanta/Trial by Jury, Sāvitri/The Wandering Scholar, Sandrina's Secret, Cinderella, Paul Bunyan* by Benjamin Britten (1976, world stage première), *The Fairy Queen, The Magic Flute, Curlew River, La Cubana* (1978, British première), *The Prodigal Son, Owen Wingrave, Rodelinda, Albert Herring*; English National Opera: *Madam Butterfly, The Rape of Lucretia*.

RELATED PROFESSIONAL ACTIVITIES: Numerous concerts, broadcasts and television performances with leading orchestras in the UK and abroad; 1976, conducted première of Britten's cantata, *Phaedra*.

RECORDINGS INCLUDE: Britten: *Death in Venice, Phaedra* (both DECC), orchestral works; Britten and Saxton, works for solo instruments and orchestra (both COLL); Grainger, Salute to Percy Grainger (DECC); Holst: *The Wandering Scholar*, orchestral and choral works (both EMI); Shostakovich, orchestral works (COLL).

HONOURS INCLUDE: Fellow: Royal Academy of Music, Royal College of Organists.

ADDRESS: c/o Harrison/Parrott Ltd, 12 Penzance Place, London W11 4PA.

BEGLEY KIM   Tenor

PERSONAL DETAILS: b. 1955, Cheshire.

PREVIOUS OCCUPATION: Actor, appearing with numerous repertory companies, Royal Shakespeare Company and in the West End.

EDUCATION/TRAINING: 1980–1982, Guildhall School of Music and Drama, with Rudolf Piernay; 1982–1983, National Opera Studio.

PROFESSIONAL DEBUT: 1983, Covent Garden, Archangel Gabriel, *Taverner*.

MAJOR DEBUTS INCLUDE: 1984, Covent Garden at the Olympic Arts Festival, Los Angeles: Reverend Adams, *Peter Grimes*; Pang, *Turandot*; 1985, Covent Garden at the Athens Festival, Achilles,

King Priam; 1986, Glyndebourne Touring Opera, Don Ottavio, *Don Giovanni*; 1988: Glyndebourne Festival Opera, Gaston, *La Traviata*; Opera North, Prince Shuisky, *Boris Godunov*; Scottish Opera, Nadir, *The Pearl Fishers*; 1989: English National Opera, Jove, *The Return of Ulysses*; Dortmund Opera, Prince Shuisky, *Boris Godunov*; 1990, Frankfurt Opera, Dancing Master, *Ariadne auf Naxos*; 1991, Théâtre des Champs Elysées, Paris, Don Basilio, *Le Nozze di Figaro*; 1992, Frankfurt Opera, title role, *Lohengrin*; 1993: Grand Théâtre, Geneva, Grigory, *Boris Godunov*; Salzburg Festival, Dr Caius, *Falstaff*.

CAREER IN THE UK INCLUDES: Since 1983: Covent Garden (1983–1988, member): First Japanese Envoy, *The Nightingale and Frog*, *L'Enfant et les Sortilèges*; Herald, *Esclarmonde*; Andrès, *Wozzeck*; Reverend Adams, *Peter Grimes*; Pang, *Turandot*; Heinrich and Walther, *Tannhäuser*; Major-Domo, *Der Rosenkavalier*; Philistine Man, *Samson*; Achilles, *King Priam*; Scaramuccio, *Ariadne auf Naxos*; Guido Bardi, *A Florentine Tragedy* (1985, British première); Don Basilio, *Le Nozze di Figaro*; Lysander, *A Midsummer Night's Dream*; Cassio, *Otello*; Guide, *The King Goes Forth to France* (1987, British première); Hervey, *Anna Bolena*; Froh, *Das Rheingold*; Prince Shuisky, *Boris Godunov*; Young Servant, *Elektra*; Monostatos, *Die Zauberflöte*; English National Opera: Dancing Master, *Ariadne auf Naxos*; Don Ottavio, *Don Giovanni*; Male Chorus, *The Rape of Lucretia*; Glyndebourne Festival Opera: Elemer, *Arabella*; Boris, *Katya Kabanova*; Pelegrin, *New Year*; High Priest, *Idomeneo*; Laca, *Jenůfa*; Handel Opera Society, Tiridate, *Radamisto*; Opera North: Fritz, *Der Ferne Klang* (1992, British première); Vaudemont, *Yolande*; Opera Northern Ireland, Don Ottavio, *Don Giovanni*.

RELATED PROFESSIONAL ACTIVITIES: Regular concerts, recitals, broadcasts and television appearances in the UK and abroad; 1992, founder, Broomhill International Opera Course, Tunbridge Wells.

RECORDINGS INCLUDE: Bellini, *Norma* (DECC).

VIDEOS INCLUDE: R. Strauss, *Der Rosenkavalier* (Covent Garden).

ADDRESS: c/o Lies Askonas Ltd, 186 Drury Lane, London WC2B 5RY.

BENNETT RICHARD RODNEY
Composer

PERSONAL DETAILS: b. 29 March 1936, Kent.

EDUCATION/TRAINING: 1953–1956, Royal Academy of Music, with Lennox Berkeley and Howard Ferguson; 1957-1959, with Pierre Boulez in Paris.

FIRST PROFESSIONAL PERFORMANCE OF A COMPOSITION: 1954, London, Sonata for piano.

CAREER: Since 1954, compositions in all genres including five operas, one ballet, numerous orchestral, chamber, instrumental, vocal and choral works and incidental music for film, theatre and television; 1963–1965, Professor of Composition, Royal Academy of Music; 1970–1971, Composer in Residence, Peabody Institute, Johns Hopkins University, Baltimore.

OPERATIC WORLD PREMIERES: Sadler's Wells Opera: 1961, *The Ledge*, opera in one act, libretto by Adrian Mitchell, conductor Alexander Gibson, director John Blatchley, designer Timothy O'Brien; 1965, *The Mines of Sulphur*, opera in three acts, libretto by Beverley Cross, conductor Colin Davis, director Colin Graham, designer Alix Stone; 1967, *A Penny for a Song*, opera in two acts, libretto by Colin Graham after the play by John Whiting, conductor Bryan Balkwill, director Colin Graham, designer Alix Stone; 1969, Coventry, *All the King's Men*, opera for children in one scene, libretto by Beverley Cross; 1970, Covent Garden, *Victory*, opera in three acts, libretto by Beverley Cross after Joseph Conrad, conductor Edward Downes, director Colin Graham, designer Alix Stone.

RELATED PROFESSIONAL ACTIVITIES: Regular performances as jazz musician and pianist; Vice-president, London College of Music; since 1975, member, General Council, Performing Right Society.

RECORDINGS INCLUDE: *What Sweeter Music* (TELA), *After Syrinx* for oboe and piano (DENO), Four Piece Suite for two pianos (EMI), Sonata for soprano, saxophone and piano, Four etudes for piano (both HYPE).

AWARDS AND HONOURS INCLUDE: 1964, Arnold Bax Prize; 1965, Ralph Vaughan Williams Award; 1975, Society of Film and Television Award, *Murder on the Orient Express*; 1977, Commander, Order of the British Empire (CBE); Honorary Fellow, London College of Music.

ADDRESS: c/o Lemon, Unna & Durbridge Ltd, 24 Pottery Lane, London W11 4LZ.

BERNAS RICHARD
Conductor

POSITION: Artistic Director, Music Projects, London.

PERSONAL DETAILS: b. 21 April 1950, New York City, USA; m. 1974, Deirdre Busenburg; m. 1981, Beatrice Harper, two children.

EDUCATION/TRAINING: 1968–1970, University of York; 1973-1974, with Witold Rowicki in Warsaw; 1979, with Franco Ferrara in Siena.

OPERATIC DEBUT: 1984, Lyons Opera, *Medea* by Gavin Bryars (world première).

CAREER: 1979–1982, Conductor in Residence, University of Sussex; since 1979, Artistic Director, Music Projects, London; since 1987, Guest Conductor, The Royal Ballet, Covent Garden.

MAJOR OPERATIC DEBUTS INCLUDE: 1984, Théâtre des Champs Elysées, Paris, *Medea*; 1987, Almeida Festival, *Jakob Lenz* (British première); 1988, Scottish Opera, *Death in Venice*; 1990: Aldeburgh Festival, *Triptych*; English National

Opera, *Greek*; 1991, Netherlands Opera, *Die Glückliche Hand*.

OPERATIC WORLD PREMIERES INCLUDE: 1989, Almeida Festival, *Golem* by John Casken.

RELATED PROFESSIONAL ACTIVITIES: Regular concerts with leading British orchestras; television performances include 1990, *Greek* (BBC); since 1990, member, Music Advisory Panel, Arts Council of Great Britain.

RECORDINGS INCLUDE: Casken, *Golem* (VIRG); Satie, *Socrate* (FACT)

PUBLICATIONS INCLUDE: Contributor, Opera Guides: *The Force of Destiny*, *Moses* (both Calder).

AWARDS INCLUDE: 1990, Royal Philharmonic Society/Charles Heidsieck Award, BBC Television production of *Greek*; 1991, *Gramophone* Contemporary Award, *Golem*.

ADDRESS: c/o Robert Gilder & Company, Enterprise House, 59–65 Upper Ground, London SE1 9PQ.

BESCH ANTHONY   Director

PERSONAL DETAILS: b. 5 February 1924, London.

EDUCATION/TRAINING: Worcester College, Oxford.

PROFESSIONAL DEBUT: 1949, Theatre Royal, Windsor, *Northanger Abbey*.

OPERATIC DEBUT: 1957, Glyndebourne Festival Opera, *Der Schauspieldirektor*.

CAREER: Since 1950, freelance opera and theatre director for leading British companies, and many worldwide including those in Argentina, Australia, Belgium, Canada, France, Germany, Holland, USA.

OPERATIC WORLD PREMIERES INCLUDE: 1962, Morley College, *The Abbot of Drimock* by Thea Musgrave; 1968, English Opera Company at the Aldeburgh Festival, *Punch and Judy* by Harrison Birtwistle; 1972, New Opera Company at Sadler's Wells Theatre, *Time Off? Not a Ghost of a Chance*! by Elisabeth Lutyens;

1974, Scottish Opera, *The Catiline Conspiracy* by Iain Hamilton.

OPERA PRODUCTIONS IN THE UK INCLUDE: Since 1957: Covent Garden, *La Clemenza di Tito*; Handel Opera Society: *Alcina, Theodora, Rodelinda, Jephtha*; New Opera Company: *The Nose* (1973, British stage première), *King Roger* (1975, British stage première), *Bomarzo* (1976, British première), *Julietta* (1978, British première); Opera North: *The Tales of Hoffmann, Johnny Strikes Up* (1984, British première); Sadler's Wells Opera/ English National Opera: *Count Ory, Tannhäuser, Andrea Chénier, Ariadne auf Naxos, The Thieving Magpie, Don Giovanni, The Magic Flute*; Scottish Opera: *Otello, L'Heure Espagnole, Faust, Albert Herring, Così fan tutte, The Marriage of Figaro, The Turn of the Screw, Der Rosenkavalier, The Coronation of Poppea, The Merry Widow, Alceste, Ariadne auf Naxos, The Rape of Lucretia, Tosca*.

RELATED PROFESSIONAL ACTIVITIES: 1986-1989, Head of Opera Studies, Guildhall School of Music and Drama.

ADDRESS: 19 Church Lane, Aston Rowant, Oxfordshire OX9 5SS.

BEST JONATHAN   Bass

PERSONAL DETAILS: b. Kent.

EDUCATION/TRAINING: St John's College, Cambridge, studied English; 1981-1983, Guildhall School of Music and Drama.

PROFESSIONAL DEBUT: 1983, Welsh National Opera, Sarastro, *The Magic Flute*.

EARLY CAREER INCLUDED: 1983, Batignano Festival, Erasto, *La Dori*; 1984–1986, Principal Bass, Welsh National Opera: Jago, *Ernani*; Masetto, *Don Giovanni*; Montano, *Otello*; Walton, *I Puritani*.

MAJOR DEBUTS INCLUDE: 1984, Maggio Musicale, Florence, Pluto, *Orfeo*; 1985, Scottish Opera, Masetto, *Don Giovanni*; 1987: Kent Opera, Sarastro, *The Magic Flute*; La Monnaie, Brussels: Montano, *Otello*; Luther, *Les Contes d'Hoffmann*;

1989, Covent Garden, Flemish Deputy, *Don Carlos*; 1990: Opera North, Bluebeard, *Ariane and Bluebeard*; Dublin Grand Opera, Sarastro, *The Magic Flute*; 1991: English National Opera, Johann, *Werther*; Opera 80, Sarastro, *The Magic Flute*; 1992: Edinburgh International Festival, Ephraimite, *Moses and Aaron* (concert performance); English Bach Festival, Polyphemus, *Acis and Galatea*.

OPERATIC WORLD PREMIERES INCLUDE: 1987, Kent Opera, Mongolian Soldier, *A Night at the Chinese Opera* by Judith Weir; 1991, Opera North, Bishop Henry of Norwich, *Caritas* by Robert Saxton.

CAREER IN THE UK INCLUDES: Since 1986: Covent Garden, Schwarz, *Die Meistersinger von Nürnberg*; English Touring Opera (City of Birmingham Touring Opera), Colline, *La Bohème*; Kent Opera, Hobson, *Peter Grimes*; Opera North: Zuniga, *Carmen*; Sparafucile, *Rigoletto*; Mr Ratcliffe, *Billy Budd*; Scottish Opera: Zuniga, Carmen; Private Willis, *Iolanthe*; Speaker, *The Magic Flute*; Colline, *La Bohème*; title role, *The Marriage of Figaro*.

RELATED PROFESSIONAL ACTIVITIES: Regular concerts, recitals and broadcasts in the UK and abroad.

RECORDINGS INCLUDE: Saxton, *Caritas* (COLL); British choral works (HYPE); A Hundred Years of Italian Opera (OPRA).

ADDRESS: c/o Music International, 13 Ardilaun Road, London N5 2QR.

BEST MATTHEW
Bass-baritone, Conductor and Composer

PERSONAL DETAILS: b. 6 February 1957, Kent; m. 1983, Rosalind Mayes, two children.

EDUCATION/TRAINING: 1976–1979, Choral Scholar, King's College, Cambridge, studied music; 1979–1980, National Opera Studio; further studies with John Carol Case, Otakar Kraus, Robert Lloyd, Patrick McGuigan and Janine Reiss.

PROFESSIONAL DEBUT: 1980, Aldeburgh Festival, Snug, *A Midsummer Night's Dream*.

MAJOR DEBUTS INCLUDE: 1980, Covent Garden, Herald, *Otello*; 1982, Welsh National Opera, Count Ribbing, *Un Ballo in Maschera*; 1983, Glyndebourne Touring Opera, Don Fernando, *Fidelio*; 1986, Alte Oper, Frankfurt, Judge, *The English Cat*; 1987, Opera North, Narbal, *The Trojans*; 1990, Netherlands Opera, First Nazarene, *Salome*.

CAREER IN THE UK INCLUDES: Since 1980: Covent Garden (1980–1986, member): Montano, *Otello*; Police Commissioner, *Lulu* (1981, British première, three act version); Second Philistine and Old Hebrew, *Samson et Dalila*; Coryphée, *Alceste*; Foltz, *Die Meistersinger von Nürnberg*; Second Commissary, *The Carmelites*; Timur, *Turandot*; Masetto, *Don Giovanni*; Fiorello, *Il Barbiere di Siviglia*; Monk, *Don Carlos*; Colline, *La Bohème*; Hobson, *Peter Grimes*; Lorenzo, *I Capuleti e i Montecchi*; Lamoral, *Arabella*; Zaretsky, *Eugene Onegin*; Second Prisoner, *Fidelio*; Singer, *Un Re in Ascolto* (1989, British première); Opera North: Polyphemus, *Acis and Galatea*; Raimondo, *Lucia di Lammermoor*; Count des Grieux, *Manon*; Shchelkalov and Pimen, *Boris Godunov*; Fernando, *The Thieving Magpie*; Welsh National Opera: Colline, *La Bohème*; Sparafucile, *Rigoletto*; First Nazarene, *Salome* (also 1990, Tokyo).

RELATED PROFESSIONAL ACTIVITIES: Regular concerts with leading orchestras in the UK and Europe; Guest Conductor: BBC Singers, City of London Sinfonia, English Chamber Orchestra, London Mozart Players; founder and Director: since 1973, Corydon Singers; since 1991, Corydon Orchestra; several compositions including 1979, Aldeburgh Festival, *Alice* (chamber opera).

RECORDINGS INCLUDE: Berlioz, *L'Enfance du Christ* (EMI); Borodin, *Polovtsian Dances* (DECC); Falla, *El Retablo de Maese Pedro* (ASV); Rossini, *Il Barbiere di Siviglia* (PHIL); Stravinsky, *The Rake's Progress* (DECC); Tippett, *The Midsummer Marriage* (NIMB); as conductor: choral works by Britten, Bruckner, Howells and Vaughan Williams (all HYPE).

VIDEOS INCLUDE: Saint-Saëns, *Samson et Dalila*; Verdi, *Don Carlos* (both Covent Garden).

AWARDS INCLUDE: 1982, Decca-Kathleen Ferrier Prize.

ADDRESS: Not available.

BICKET HARRY
Conductor, Chorus Master, Harpsichordist and Organist

POSITION: Chorus Master, English National Opera.

PERSONAL DETAILS: b. 15 May 1961, Liverpool.

EDUCATION/TRAINING: 1978–1980: Royal College of Music, piano with Yonty Solomon; Duke of Edinburgh's Organ Scholar, St George's Chapel, Windsor Castle; 1980–1983, Christ Church, Oxford, organ with Simon Preston.

OPERATIC DEBUT: 1992, English National Opera, *Orfeo*.

CAREER: Since 1983, freelance harpsichordist with numerous British orchestras; Westminster Abbey: 1984–1987, Sub-organist; 1987–1988, Acting Organist and Master of the Choristers; English National Opera: 1988–1990, Assistant Chorus Master; since 1990, Chorus Master.

OPERA PERFORMANCES IN THE UK INCLUDE: Since 1992, English National Opera, *The Duel of Tancredi and Clorinda*.

ADDRESS: c/o English National Opera, London Coliseum, St Martin's Lane, London WC2N 4ES.

23

BICKLEY SUSAN
Mezzo-soprano

PERSONAL DETAILS: b. 27 May 1955,
Liverpool; m., two children.

PREVIOUS OCCUPATIONS: Child portrait
photographer and shop assistant.

EDUCATION/TRAINING: 1977–1980, City
University, London, studied music; 1980-
1981, Guildhall School of Music and
Drama, with Noelle Barker.

PROFESSIONAL DEBUT: 1984, Early Opera
Project at Maggio Musicale, Florence,
Proserpina, *Orfeo*.

MAJOR DEBUTS INCLUDE: 1987,
Glyndebourne Touring Opera, Florence
Pike, *Albert Herring*; 1989, Glyndebourne
Festival Opera, Hippolyta, *A Midsummer
Night's Dream*; 1990: Innsbruck Festival,
Dido, *Dido and Aeneas*; Opéra Bastille,
Paris, Kabanicha, *Katya Kabanova*; 1991,
Covent Garden, Fyodor, *Boris Godunov*;
1992, English National Opera, Second
Lady, *The Magic Flute*.

CAREER IN THE UK INCLUDES: Since 1984:
Aldeburgh Festival, Jezebel, *Naboth's
Vineyard*; Glyndebourne Festival and
Touring Opera: Anna, *The Electrification
of the Soviet Union*; Mrs Sedley, *Peter
Grimes*; Kostelnička, *Jenůfa*; Kabanicha,
Katya Kabanova; Marcellina, *Le Nozze di
Figaro*; Opera 80: Madame Arvidson, *A
Masked Ball*; Baba the Turk, *The Rake's
Progress*.

RECORDINGS INCLUDE: Purcell, *Dido and
Aeneas* (COLL); Satie, *Socrate* (FACT); A
Hundred Years of Italian Opera (OPRA).

ADDRESS: c/o Allied Artists, 42 Montpelier
Square, London SW7 1JZ.

BIRTWISTLE, SIR HARRISON
Composer

PERSONAL DETAILS: b. 15 July 1934,
Lancashire; m., three children.

EDUCATION/TRAINING: Royal Manchester
College of Music, studied clarinet with
Frederick Thurston and composition with
Richard Hall; Royal Academy of Music,
studied clarinet with Reginald Kell.

FIRST WORK TO ACHIEVE PROMINENCE:
1959, Cheltenham Festival, *Refrains and
Choruses* for wind quintet.

CAREER: Numerous compositions in all
genres including five operas and several
music theatre works; 1962–1965, Director
of Music, Cranborne Chase School,
Dorset; 1966–1968, Visiting Harkness
Fellow, Princeton University; co-founder:
1967, Pierrot Players; 1971, Matrix;
Visiting Professor of Music: 1973,
Swarthmore College, Pennsylvania; 1974–
1975, State University of New York at
Buffalo; Royal National Theatre: 1975–
1982, Music Director (1977, music theatre,
Bow Down; 1981, incidental music, *The
Oresteia*); currently Associate Director;
1991, Composer in Residence, Aldeburgh
Festival; currently Visiting Tutor in
Composition, Royal Northern College of
Music.

OPERATIC WORLD PREMIERES: 1968,
English Opera Group at the Aldeburgh
Festival, *Punch and Judy*, a tragical
comedy or comical tragedy in one act,
libretto by Stephen Pruslin, conductor
David Atherton, director Anthony Besch,
designer Peter Rice; 1969, Music Theatre
Ensemble at the Brighton Festival, *Down
by the Greenwood Side*, a dramatic
pastoral in one act, text by Michael
Nyman based on the traditional English
mummers' play and the ballad of the
Cruel Mother, conductor David Atherton,
director John Cox, designer Anthony
Denning; 1986: English National Opera,
The Mask of Orpheus, opera in three acts,
text by Peter Zinovieff, conductor Elgar
Howarth, director David Freeman,
designer Jocelyn Herbert; Opera Factory,
Yan Tan Tethera, a mechanical pastoral,
text by Tony Harrison based on traditional
folk tales, conductor Elgar Howarth,
director David Freeman, designer David
Roger; 1991, Covent Garden, *Gawain*,
opera in two acts, libretto by David
Harsent after *Gawain and the Green
Knight*, conductor Elgar Howarth, director
Di Trevis, designer Alison Chitty.

RECORDINGS INCLUDE: *Punch and Judy, Refrains and Choruses, Secret Theatre, Silbury Air, Carmen Arcadiae Mechanicae Perpetuum and For O, for O, The Hobby-Horse is Forgot* (all ETCE), *Verses for Ensembles, Monody for Corpus Christie, Nenia-the Death of Orpheus* (all DECC), *Earth Dances* (COLL), *Endless Parade* (PHIL), *Tragoedia* (EMI).

AWARDS AND HONOURS INCLUDE: 1986, Evening Standard Award, *The Mask of Orpheus* (English National Opera); 1987, Grawemeyer Award, University of Louisville (Kentucky); 1988: Knighthood, Chevalier de l'Ordre des Arts et des Lettres (France); 1991, *Evening Standard Award* and Royal Philharmonic Society Award, *Gawain* (Covent Garden); Fellow, Royal Manchester College of Music and Royal Northern College of Music.

ADDRESS: c/o Universal Edition (London) Ltd, 2/3 Fareham Street, London W1V 4DU.

BJØRNSON MARIA   Designer

PERSONAL DETAILS: b. Paris, France.

EDUCATION/TRAINING: Central School of Art and Design.

PROFESSIONAL DEBUT: 1971, Citizens Theatre, Glasgow, *The Life of Galileo* by Bertolt Brecht.

OPERATIC DEBUT: 1972, Wexford Festival, *Katya Kabanova* (co-design with Sue Blane).

CAREER: Freelance opera and theatre designer in the UK and abroad; designs for Almeida Theatre, Chichester Festival Theatre, Nottingham Playhouse, Royal Shakespeare Company, West End and Broadway include *Follies, The Phantom of the Opera* and *Aspects of Love*.

MAJOR OPERATIC DEBUTS INCLUDE: 1975: Welsh National Opera, *Jenůfa*; Cassel, *The Queen of Spades*; Netherlands Opera, *The Gambler*; 1976, Scottish Opera, *Die Meistersinger von Nürnberg*; 1978: Australian Opera, Sydney, *Die Meistersinger von Nürnberg*; Houston Grand Opera, *Jenůfa*; 1979, Opera North, *Rigoletto*; 1982/1983, Netherlands Opera/ English National Opera co-production, *The Queen of Spades*; 1985, Covent Garden, *Donnerstag aus Licht* (British première); 1989, Grand Théâtre, Geneva, *Le Nozze di Figaro*; 1990, Maggio Musicale, Florence, *Aufstieg und Fall der Stadt Mahagonny*; 1991, Glyndebourne Festival Opera, *Così fan tutte*.

OPERATIC WORLD PREMIERES INCLUDE: 1977, English National Opera, *Toussaint* by David Blake.

OPERA DESIGNS IN THE UK INCLUDE: Since 1973: English National Opera: *The Gambler, The Valkyrie, Carmen, The Cunning Little Vixen, The Makropoulos Case*; English Opera Group, *La Rondine*; Opera North, *Werther*; Welsh National Opera: *Ernani, From the House of the Dead*; co-productions: Scottish Opera/ Opera North, *Don Giovanni*; Scottish Opera/Welsh National Opera: *Jenůfa, The Makropoulos Case, Katya Kabanova, The Cunning Little Vixen*; costume designs include: Covent Garden: *Les Contes d'Hoffmann, Der Rosenkavalier*; Scottish Opera: *The Magic Flute, The Golden Cockerel, The Bartered Bride, The Seraglio, Hansel and Gretel*; Welsh National Opera, *Il Trovatore*.

VIDEOS INCLUDE: Offenbach, *Les Contes d'Hoffmann*; R. Strauss, *Der Rosenkavalier* (both Covent Garden).

AWARDS INCLUDE: British entry, Gold Medal, International Exhibition of Stage Design, Prague Biennale for Janáček Cycle (Scottish Opera/Welsh National Opera).

ADDRESS: c/o Lies Askonas Ltd, 186 Drury Lane, London WC2B 5RY.

BLACK JEFFREY   Baritone

PERSONAL DETAILS: b. 6 September 1962, Brisbane, Australia; m. 1986, Jan St John (soprano).

EDUCATION/TRAINING: 1980–1984, Queensland Conservatorium of Music, Brisbane; privately with Janet Delpratt in

Australia and Audrey Langford in London; currently with Janice Chapman.

PROFESSIONAL DEBUT: 1985, Australian Opera, Sydney, Mercutio, *Roméo et Juliette*.

MAJOR DEBUTS INCLUDE: 1986: Monte Carlo Opera, Harlequin, *Ariadne auf Naxos* (European debut); Glyndebourne Festival Opera, Sid, *Albert Herring* (British debut); 1987: Covent Garden, Harlequin, *Ariadne auf Naxos*; Lyric Opera of Queensland, Malatesta, *Don Pasquale*; 1988, Los Angeles Music Center Opera, Guglielmo, *Così fan tutte*; 1989: Australian Opera, Sydney, title role, *Il Barbiere di Siviglia*; Netherlands Opera, Harlequin, *Ariadne auf Naxos*; 1990, Victoria State Opera, Melbourne, Zurga, *Les Pêcheurs de Perles*; 1991: Australian Opera, Sydney, title role, *Don Giovanni*; Opéra Bastille, Paris, Lescaut, *Manon Lescaut*; 1992: San Francisco Opera, title role, *Il Barbiere di Siviglia*; Victorian State Opera, Melbourne, Rodrigo, *Don Carlos*; 1993, Lyric Opera, Chicago, Guglielmo, *Così fan tutte*; San Diego Opera, title role, *Il Barbiere di Siviglia*.

CAREER INCLUDES: Since 1985: Covent Garden: Sid, *Albert Herring*; Dandini, *La Cenerentola*; Count de Nevers, *Les Huguenots*; title role, *Il Barbiere di Siviglia*; Glyndebourne Festival Opera: Demetrius, *A Midsummer Night's Dream*; Count, *Capriccio*; Count, *Le Nozze di Figaro*; Australian Opera, Sydney (1985–1990, Principal Baritone): Schaunard, *La Bohème*; Papageno, *The Magic Flute*; Falke, *Die Fledermaus*; Dandini, *La Cenerentola*; Ottone, *L'Incoronazione di Poppea*; Guglielmo, *Così fan tutte*.

RELATED PROFESSIONAL ACTIVITIES: Numerous concerts and recitals in the UK and abroad including London Philharmonic Orchestra: 1989, *Carmina Burana*; 1992, *St Matthew Passion*.

RECORDINGS INCLUDE: Orff, *Carmina Burana* (EMI).

AWARDS INCLUDE: 1980, Margaret Nickson Lieder Prize; 1983, Marianne Mathy Competition; 1985, Queensland Youth of the Year Award (all Australia).

ADDRESS: c/o Lies Askonas Ltd, 186 Drury Lane, London WC2B 5RY.

BLAKE DAVID
Composer and Conductor

POSITION: Professor of Music, University of York.

PERSONAL DETAILS: b. 2 September 1936, London; m. 1960, Rita Muir, three children.

EDUCATION/TRAINING: 1957–1960, Gonville and Caius College, Cambridge; 1960-1961, Akademie der Künste, East Berlin.

FIRST PROFESSIONAL PERFORMANCE OF A COMPOSITION: 1960, Cheltenham Festival, Divertimento for flute and piano.

CAREER: Since 1960, numerous compositions in all genres; University of York: 1963–1964, Granada Arts Fellow; 1964–1976, Lecturer in Music; since 1976, Professor of Music.

OPERATIC WORLD PREMIERES: English National Opera: 1977, *Toussaint*, opera in three acts, libretto by Anthony Ward, conductor Mark Elder, director David Pountney, designer Maria Bjørnson; 1989, *The Plumber's Gift*, opera in two acts, libretto by John Birtwhistle, conductor Lionel Friend, director Richard Jones, designer Nigel Lowery.

RECORDINGS INCLUDE: Concerto for violin, *In Praise of Krishna* (both ARGO), Variations for piano (EMI).

PUBLICATIONS INCLUDE: 1977, vocal score, *Toussaint* (Novello).

ADDRESS: Mill Gill, Askrigg, Nr Leyburn, North Yorkshire.

BLANE SUE   Designer

EDUCATION/TRAINING: Wolverhampton College of Art, Central School of Art and Design.

PROFESSIONAL DEBUT: 1971, Citizens Theatre, Glasgow.

OPERATIC DEBUT: 1972, Wexford Festival, *Katya Kabanova* (co-design with Maria Bjørnson).

CAREER: Freelance set and costume designer for opera, theatre and film in the UK and abroad including Citizens Theatre, Royal National Theatre, Royal Shakespeare Company, West End and Broadway; films include costumes for *The Rocky Horror Picture Show*, *The Draughtsman's Contract* and *Absolute Beginners*.

OPERA DESIGNS INCLUDE: Since 1973: English National Opera: *Christmas Eve*, *Königskinder*; Opera North: *The Thieving Magpie*, *The Duenna* (1992, British stage première); Scottish Opera: *The Golden Cockerel*, *The Bartered Bride*, *Hansel and Gretel*, *The Two Widows*, *Il Barbiere di Siviglia*; Welsh National Opera, *Le Nozze di Figaro*; Batignano Festival, *Zaide*; costume designs include: Covent Garden, *Porgy and Bess*; English National Opera: *The Gambler*, *The Mikado*; Glyndebourne Festival Opera, *Porgy and Bess*; Opera North, *Die Fledermaus*; Opera North/ English National Opera co-production, *The Love for Three Oranges*; La Scala, Milan, *La Fanciulla del West*; Maggio Musicale, Florence: *Così fan tutte*, *Le Nozze di Figaro*.

VIDEOS INCLUDE: Sullivan, *The Mikado* (English National Opera).

ADDRESS: c/o Susan Angel Associates Ltd, 12 D'Arblay Street, London W1V 3FP.

BLYTH ALAN
Critic, Broadcaster and Writer

PERSONAL DETAILS: b. 27 July 1929, London; m. 1961.

EDUCATION/TRAINING: Pembroke College, Oxford.

CAREER: As critic: 1963–1976, *The Times* and *Financial Times*; 1965-1967, *The Listener*; since 1966, *Gramophone*; since 1977, *Daily Telegraph*; since 1965, regular contributor, BBC Radio 3; *Opera*:

1966-1983, Assistant Editor; currently, member, Editorial Board.

PUBLICATIONS INCLUDE: 1969, *The Enjoyment of Opera* (Oxford University Press); 1981: *Introduction to Wagner's Ring*; *Remembering Britten*; Editor, *Opera on Record*, Vols 1–3 (all Hutchinson); contributor: 1980, *The New Grove Dictionary of Music and Musicians*; 1992, *The New Grove Dictionary of Opera* (both Macmillan).

ADDRESS: 22 Shilling Street, Lavenham, Suffolk.

BOLTON ANDREA   Soprano

PERSONAL DETAILS: b. 27 June 1959, Manchester; m. 1981, one child.

EDUCATION/TRAINING: Royal Northern College of Music; 1984–1985, National Opera Studio.

PROFESSIONAL DEBUT: 1985, Welsh National Opera, Despina, *Così fan tutte*.

MAJOR DEBUTS INCLUDE: 1986, Batignano Festival, Lisetta, *Il Re Teodoro in Venezia*; 1987, Opera North, Valencienne, *The Merry Widow*; 1988: Scottish Opera, Cunegonde, *Candide*; Wexford Festival, Donna Elvira, *Don Giovanni*.

CAREER IN THE UK INCLUDES: Since 1986: Scottish Opera, Ascagne, *The Trojans* (also 1990, at Covent Garden); Welsh National Opera: Oscar, *Un Ballo in Maschera*; Adele, *Die Fledermaus*; Susanna, *Le Nozze di Figaro*; Echo, *Ariadne auf Naxos*; Blonde, *Die Entführung aus dem Serail*.

RELATED PROFESSIONAL ACTIVITIES: Concerts and recitals in the UK and Ireland.

ADDRESS: c/o Korman International Management, Crunnells Green Cottage, Preston, Hertfordshire SG4 7UQ.

BOLTON IVOR
Conductor and Harpsichordist

POSITIONS: Music Director: Glyndebourne Touring Opera, St James's Baroque Players.

PERSONAL DETAILS: b. 17 May 1958, Lancashire; m., one child.

EDUCATION/TRAINING: 1976–1980, Clare College, Cambridge; 1980–1981, Conducting Scholar, Royal College of Music; 1981–1982, National Opera Studio.

OPERATIC DEBUT: 1986, Opera 80, *The Rake's Progress*.

CAREER: Glyndebourne Festival Opera: 1982–1984, Assistant Chorus Master and staff conductor; 1985–1989, Chorus Master; Opera 80: 1990–1991, Associate Music Director; 1991–1992, Music Director; since 1984, founder and Music Director, St James's Baroque Players; since 1992, Music Director, Glyndebourne Touring Opera.

MAJOR OPERATIC DEBUTS INCLUDE: 1989, Glyndebourne Festival Opera, *Orfeo ed Euridice*; 1990, Batignano Festival, *King Priam*; 1991, Leipzig Opera, *Die Zauberflöte*; 1992: English National Opera, *Xerxes*; Opera North, *The Thieving Magpie*; 1993: Teatro Comunale, Bologna, *L'Incoronazione di Poppea*; Opera Zuid, Holland, *Ariadne auf Naxos*.

OPERA PERFORMANCES IN THE UK INCLUDE: Since 1986: Britten-Pears School for Advanced Musical Studies, *Così fan tutte*; Glyndebourne Touring Opera: *Die Entführung aus dem Serail, Il Barbiere di Siviglia, Die Zauberflöte, La Bohème, The Rake's Progress*; Guildhall School of Music and Drama, *L'Ormindo*; Opera 80/English Touring Opera: *Cinderella, Carmen, The Marriage of Figaro, Lucia di Lammermoor, La Bohème, The Magic Flute, Don Giovanni, Così fan tutte*.

RELATED PROFESSIONAL ACTIVITIES: Regular concerts in the UK and abroad; particularly associated with the Lufthansa Festival of Baroque Music at St James's Church, Piccadilly.

RECORDINGS INCLUDE: Brahms and Mendelssohn violin concertos with Xue Wei (both ASV); Lesley Garrett, Prima Donna (SILV); as harpsichordist/conductor: Bach, harpsichord concertos (PICK).

AWARDS INCLUDE: 1985, Jani Strasser Award, Glyndebourne.

ADDRESS: c/o Ingpen & Williams Ltd, 14 Kensington Court, London W8 5DN.

BOOTH-JONES CHRISTOPHER   Baritone

POSITION: Principal Baritone, English National Opera.

PERSONAL DETAILS: b. 4 October 1943, Somerset; m. Jillian Summerfield (soprano), two children.

PREVIOUS OCCUPATION: School teacher.

EDUCATION/TRAINING: 1965–1970, Royal Academy of Music, with Joy Mammen.

PROFESSIONAL DEBUT: 1971, Welsh National Opera for All, title role, *The Marriage of Figaro*.

EARLY CAREER INCLUDED: 1971–1978, appearances with English Music Theatre, Glyndebourne Touring Opera, Opera for All, Park Lane Opera, Phoenix Opera, Unicorn Opera, Camden and City of London Festivals; roles included: Niels, *Fennimore and Gerda*; Clodomiro, *Lotario*; Antonio, *Le Nozze di Figaro*.

MAJOR DEBUTS INCLUDE: 1978, Welsh National Opera, Schaunard, *La Bohème*; 1980, Kent Opera, Monostatos, *The Magic Flute*; 1981, Opera North, Ottokar, *Der Freischütz*; 1983, English National Opera, Gregory, *Romeo and Juliet*; 1991, Covent Garden, Morales, *Carmen*.

OPERATIC WORLD PREMIERES INCLUDE: 1976, English Music Theatre at the Aldeburgh Festival, Northerton, *Tom Jones* by Stephen Oliver; 1992, English National Opera, Soldier/Herdsman, *Bakxai* by John Buller.

CAREER IN THE UK INCLUDES: Since 1978: English National Opera (since 1983, Principal Baritone): Grosvenor, *Patience*; Denisov, *War and Peace*; Poet/Dreamy Cloud/Vašek, *The Adventures of Mr*

Brouček; Lhotsky/Verva, *Osud* (1984, British stage première); Herman and Yeletsky, *The Queen of Spades*; Falke, *Die Fledermaus*; Papageno, *The Magic Flute*; Schaunard, *La Bohème*; Silvio, *Pagliacci*; Horemhab, *Akhnaten* (1985, British première); Manjiro, *Pacific Overtures*; Sacristan, *Tosca*; Novice's Friend, *Billy Budd*; Pantaloon, *The Love for Three Oranges*; Guglielmo, *Così fan tutte*; Elviro, *Xerxes*; Duke of Albany, *Lear* (1989, British première); Claudio, *Beatrice and Benedict*; Christian, *A Masked Ball*; Music Master, *Ariadne auf Naxos*; Marullo, *Rigoletto*; Opera North, Demetrius, *A Midsummer Night's Dream*; Welsh National Opera, title role, *The Marriage of Figaro*.
RELATED PROFESSIONAL ACTIVITIES: Numerous concerts, recitals, broadcasts and festival appearances in the UK and abroad.
RECORDINGS INCLUDE: Handel, *Julius Caesar* (EMI); Sondheim, *Pacific Overtures* (TER).
VIDEOS INCLUDE: Bizet, *Carmen* (Covent Garden); Britten, *Billy Budd*; Handel, *Xerxes* (both English National Opera); Sullivan: *The Gondoliers*, *Princess Ida* (both Walker).
HONOURS INCLUDE: Associate, Royal Academy of Music.
ADDRESS: c/o Music International, 13 Ardilaun Road, London N5 2QR.

BOTES CHRISTINE
Mezzo-soprano

PERSONAL DETAILS: b. Kingston-upon-Thames; m. 1982, John Lees.
EDUCATION/TRAINING: 1972–1975, University of Durham, studied modern history; 1975–1979, Royal Northern College of Music, with Frederic Cox; 1979–1980, National Opera Studio; since 1980, privately with Rupert Bruce-Lockhart.
PROFESSIONAL DEBUT: 1981, Glyndebourne Touring Opera, Meg Page, *Falstaff*.

EARLY CAREER INCLUDED: 1982-1983, Cambridge University Opera: Dorotea, *Stiffelio*; Fenena, *Nabucco*.
MAJOR DEBUTS INCLUDE: 1984, Opera Factory: Diana, *La Calisto*; Thea, *The Knot Garden*; 1985, Kent Opera, Sorceress, *Dido and Aeneas*; 1986, Scottish Opera, title role, *Iolanthe*; 1989, English National Opera, Hansel, *Hansel and Gretel*.
OPERATIC WORLD PREMIERES INCLUDE: 1984, Batignano Festival, Sister, *La Bella e la Bestia* by Stephen Oliver; 1986, Opera Factory, several roles, *Hell's Angels*, by Nigel Osborne.
CAREER IN THE UK INCLUDES: Since 1984: Cambridge Opera Trust, Idamante, *Idomeneo*; English National Opera: Fox, *The Cunning Little Vixen*; Pitti-Sing, *The Mikado*; Cherubino, *The Marriage of Figaro*; Proserpina, *Orfeo*; Minerva/Amor, *The Return of Ulysses*; Music Theatre Wales, Venus, *Euridice*; Musica nel Chiostro, Sister, *Beauty and the Beast* (1985, British première); Opera Factory: Dorabella, *Così fan tutte*; Nurse, *Eight Songs for a Mad King* and Mezzo-soprano, *Aventures et Nouvelles Aventures*; Dark Lady/Mummy, *The Ghost Sonata* (1989, British première); Scottish Opera, Second Lady, *The Magic Flute*; Travelling Opera: Cherubino, *The Marriage of Figaro*; Rosina, *The Barber of Seville*.
AWARDS INCLUDE: 1981, South East Arts Young Musicians Platform; 1982, Miriam Licette Scholarship.
ADDRESS: c/o Robert Gilder & Company, Enterprise House, 59–65 Upper Ground, London SE1 9PQ.

BOTTONE BONAVENTURA
Tenor

PERSONAL DETAILS: b. 19 September 1950, London; m. 1973, Jennifer Dakin (soprano), four children.
EDUCATION/TRAINING: Royal Academy of Music, with Bruce Boyce.

PROFESSIONAL DEBUT: 1973, Welsh National Opera for All, Count, *The Barber of Seville*.

EARLY CAREER INCLUDED: 1973–1982: Glyndebourne Touring Opera, Bardolph, *Falstaff*; Opera Northern Ireland, Arturo, *Lucia di Lammermoor*; Opera Rara: Georges, *L'Etoile du Nord*; Appio, *Virginia*; Phoenix Opera, Pyramus, *Pyramus and Thisbe*; Wexford Festival: Second Croupier, *The Gambler*; Count, *La Serva e l'Ussero*; Count, *Crispino e la Comare*.

MAJOR DEBUTS INCLUDE: 1982: English National Opera, Cassio, *Otello*; Nice Opera, Ruedi, *Guillaume Tell*; 1987: Covent Garden, Italian Tenor, *Der Rosenkavalier*; Houston Grand Opera, Pedrillo, *The Seraglio*; 1988, Scottish Opera, Governor General, *Candide*; 1990: Glyndebourne Festival Opera, Italian Tenor, *Capriccio*; Opera North, Alfredo, *La Traviata*; 1991: Welsh National Opera, title role, *Count Ory*; Bavarian State Opera, Munich, Alfred, *Die Fledermaus*.

OPERATIC WORLD PREMIERES INCLUDE: 1974, University College Opera, Sailor, *Clytemnestra* by Peter Wishart.

CAREER IN THE UK INCLUDES: Since 1983: Covent Garden: Alfred, *Die Fledermaus*; Italian Tenor, *Capriccio*; Raoul, *Les Huguenots*; Arnold, *Guillaume Tell*; Count Libenskof, *Il Viaggio a Reims*; English National Opera: Major Domo/ Bonnet, *War and Peace*; Duke, *Rigoletto*; Mercury, *Orpheus in the Underworld*; David, *The Mastersingers of Nuremberg*; Nanki-Poo, *The Mikado*; Beppe, *Pagliacci*; Gregor, *The Makropoulos Case*; Sam Kaplan, *Street Scene*; Truffaldino, *The Love for Three Oranges*; Zinovy, *Lady Macbeth of Mtsensk*; Fenton, *Falstaff*; Mazal/Starry-Eyes/ Petřík, *The Adventures of Mr Brouček*; Scottish Opera: Jack, *The Midsummer Marriage*; Loge, *Das Rheingold*; Narraboth, *Salome*; Welsh National Opera, Fernando, *La Favorita* (also 1993, at Covent Garden).

RELATED PROFESSIONAL ACTIVITIES: Numerous concerts, recitals, broadcasts and television appearances in the UK and abroad.

RECORDINGS INCLUDE: Bernstein, *Candide* (TER); Donizetti, *Lucia di Lammermoor* (EMI); Offenbach, *Orpheus in the Underworld*; Romberg, *The Student Prince*; Sondheim, *A Little Night Music*; Sullivan, *The Mikado* (all TER); Tippett, *The Ice Break* (VIRG); Verdi, *Otello* (EMI); Weill, *Street Scene* (TER).

VIDEOS INCLUDE: J. Strauss, *Die Fledermaus* (Covent Garden); Sullivan, *The Mikado* (English National Opera).

HONOURS INCLUDE: Honorary Member, Royal Academy of Music.

ADDRESS: c/o Stafford Law Associates, 26 Mayfield Road, Weybridge, Surrey KT13 8XB.

BOVINO MARIA   Soprano

PERSONAL DETAILS: b. West Yorkshire; m. 1983, Christopher Newell (director), one child.

EDUCATION/TRAINING: University of Sheffield, studied music; Guildhall School of Music and Drama, with Johanna Peters.

PROFESSIONAL DEBUT: 1982, Opera 80, Adele, *Die Fledermaus*.

EARLY CAREER INCLUDED: 1983–1986: English Bach Festival, Amour, *Orphée et Eurydice*; English National Opera: First Boy, *The Magic Flute*; Peep-Bo, *The Mikado*; London Savoyards: Mabel, *The Pirates of Penzance*; Josephine, *HMS Pinafore*; Gianetta, *The Gondoliers*; Opera 80: Despina, *Cosi fan tutte*; Elvira, *The Italian Girl in Algiers*.

MAJOR DEBUTS INCLUDE: 1985, Glyndebourne Festival Opera, Emmie, *Albert Herring*; 1987, Scottish Opera, Blonde, *The Seraglio*; 1988: English National Opera, Queen of the Night, *The Magic Flute*; Glyndebourne Touring Opera, Tytania, *A Midsummer Night's Dream*; 1989, Covent Garden, Emmie, *Albert Herring*.

CAREER IN THE UK INCLUDES: Since 1987: Covent Garden, Strolling Player, *Death in Venice*; Mid Wales Opera, Adele, *Die Fledermaus*; Scottish Opera, Papagena and Queen of the Night, *The Magic Flute*; Travelling Opera: Mimi, *La Bohème*; Gilda, *Rigoletto*.

RELATED PROFESSIONAL ACTIVITIES: Concerts and recitals in the UK.

VIDEOS INCLUDE: Britten, *Albert Herring* (Glyndebourne Festival Opera).

ADDRESS: c/o Musicmakers, Little Easthall Farmhouse, St Paul's Walden, Nr Hitchin, Hertfordshire SG4 8DH.

BOWDEN PAMELA
Teacher (formerly Contralto)

POSITIONS: Head of Singing, London College of Music; Visiting Professor, Royal Scottish Academy of Music and Drama.

PERSONAL DETAILS: b. 17 April 1925, Rochdale; m. D.J.P. Edwards, two children.

EDUCATION/TRAINING: 1941–1944 and 1947–1948, Royal Manchester College of Music, with Norman Allin and Leslie Langford; privately with Roy Henderson.

CAREER INCLUDES: 1950–1978, appearances with Covent Garden, Glyndebourne Festival and Touring Opera and leading international opera companies; roles included: Madame Larina, *Eugene Onegin*; Sorceress, *Dido and Aeneas*; Gertrude, *Roméo et Juliette*; Venus, *Il Ballo delle Ingrate*; Orfeo, *Orfeo ed Euridice*; numerous concerts, oratorios and recitals with leading conductors and orchestras in the UK and abroad; repertoire included *Carmen*, several Handel roles, *The Dream of Gerontius*, *Alto Rhapsody*, *The Enchantress* and Five William Blake Songs by Malcolm Arnold dedicated to her; 1978, retired from performing; currently teacher, international adjudicator and examiner; since 1984, Head of Singing, London College of Music.

RELATED PROFESSIONAL ACTIVITIES: 1987–1988, Chairman, Association of Teachers of Singing; 1988–1989, President, Incorporated Society of Musicians.

RECORDINGS INCLUDE: Sullivan, *Ruddigore* (EMI); Tippett, *A Child of Our Time* (DECC); (Herrmann, *Wuthering Heights* – created role of Isabella Linton, currently unavailable).

HONOURS INCLUDE: Fellow: 1965, Royal Manchester College of Music; 1988, London College of Music.

ADDRESS: c/o London College of Music, Polytechnic of West London, St Mary's Road, London W5 5RF.

BOWMAN JAMES
Counter-tenor

PERSONAL DETAILS: b. 6 November 1941, Oxford.

PREVIOUS OCCUPATIONS: 1965–1967, school teacher; 1969, lay vicar, Westminster Abbey.

EDUCATION/TRAINING: Ely Cathedral Choir School; 1960–1963, New College, Oxford, studied history.

PROFESSIONAL DEBUT: 1967, English Opera Group, Oberon, *A Midsummer Night's Dream*.

EARLY CAREER INCLUDED: 1967–1976: numerous concerts and appearances with Early Music Consort, English Opera Group, Glyndebourne Touring Opera, Handel Opera Society, Sadler's Wells Opera; roles included: Endymion, *La Calisto*; Polinesso, *Ariodante*; Ruggiero, *Alcina*; Lichas, *Hercules*; title role, *Ottone*.

MAJOR DEBUTS INCLUDE: 1970: Glyndebourne Festival Opera, Endymion, *La Calisto*; Sadler's Wells Opera, Anthamas, *Semele*; 1971, Netherlands Opera, Ottone, *L'Incoronazione di Poppea*; 1974, Santa Fe Opera, Lidio, *L'Egisto*; 1978: Verona Arena, Ruggiero, *Orlando Furioso*; Oberon, *A Midsummer Night's Dream*: Welsh National Opera and Australian Opera, Sydney; 1980, Dallas

Civic Opera, Ruggiero, *Orlando Furioso*; 1982: Scottish Opera, Lidio, *L'Egisto*; San Francisco Opera, Tolomeo, *Julius Caesar*; 1985, Goffredo, *Rinaldo*: Teatro Municipale, Reggio Emilia and Théâtre du Châtelet, Paris; 1986, Polinesso, *Ariodante*: Buxton Festival and Grand Théâtre, Geneva; 1988, La Scala, Milan, Epafo, *Fetonte*; 1992, Teatro La Fenice, Venice, Anthamas, *Semele*.

OPERATIC WORLD PREMIERES INCLUDE: 1972, Covent Garden (debut), Priest Confessor/God the Father, *Taverner* by Peter Maxwell Davies; 1973, English Opera Group at the Aldeburgh Festival, Voice of Apollo, *Death in Venice* by Benjamin Britten; 1977, Covent Garden, Astron, *The Ice Break* by Michael Tippett.

CAREER IN THE UK INCLUDES: Since 1976: Barber Institute, Birmingham, title role, *Julius Caesar*; Covent Garden, Oberon, *A Midsummer Night's Dream*; English National Opera: Tolomeo, *Julius Caesar*; Anfinomo, *The Return of Ulysses*; Glyndebourne Festival Opera, Oberon, *A Midsummer Night's Dream*; Handel Opera Society, title roles: *Serse*, *Scipione*, *Giustino*; Phoenix Opera at the Camden Festival, Theramene, *Eritrea* (1982, British première); Scottish Opera, title role, *Orlando*.

RELATED PROFESSIONAL ACTIVITIES: Regular concerts, recitals, broadcasts and television appearances in the UK and abroad; 1983–1986, voice teacher, Guildhall School of Music and Drama.

RECORDINGS INCLUDE: Bach: *St Matthew Passion* (TELD), solo cantatas (HYPE); Britten, *Death in Venice* (DECC); Handel: *Giulio Cesare*, *Messiah* (both EMI), *Israel in Egypt* (DECC), *Joshua* (HYPE), *Orlando* (L'OI); Monteverdi, *L'Incoronazione di Poppea* (VIRG); Orff, *Carmina Burana* (DECC); Telemann, cantatas; James Bowman recital (both MERI).

VIDEOS INCLUDE: Britten, *A Midsummer Night's Dream* (Glyndebourne Festival Opera); Handel, *Julius Caesar* (English National Opera).

ADDRESS: 4 Brownlow Road, Redhill, Surrey RH1 6AW.

BREDIN HENRIETTA
Administrator, Dramaturg, Editor and Writer

POSITION: Artistic Administrator, English National Opera Contemporary Opera Studio.

PERSONAL DETAILS: b. 10 April 1959, London.

EDUCATION/TRAINING: St Mary's Convent, Ascot.

CAREER: English National Opera: 1983–1989, assistant editor and subsequently editor, various English National Opera publications (1985–1989, member, Dramaturgy Department); since 1989, co-founder and Artistic Administrator, English National Opera Contemporary Opera Studio focusing on collaborations between composers and writers; commissions include: 1992: *Soundbites*, a triple bill: *Pig* by Jonathan Dove and *April de Angelis*/*The Rebuilding of Waterloo Bridge* by Giles Chaundy and Caroline Gawn/*Nevis* by Kenneth Dempster and Gavin Pagan; *Mary of Egypt* by John Tavener and Mother Thekla (co-commission with Aldeburgh Foundation); *Terrible Mouth* by Nigel Osborne and Howard Barker (co-commission with Almeida Theatre); 1993, *The Man at the Heels of the Wind* by Kevin Volans and Roger Clarke (co-commission with Dancelines Productions).

PUBLICATIONS INCLUDE: 1992, children's books: *Christmas Eve*, *The Prince and the Goosegirl* (both Child's Play International).

ADDRESS: c/o Contemporary Opera Studio, English National Opera, London Coliseum, St Martin's Lane, London WC2N 4ES.

BRONDER PETER   Tenor

PERSONAL DETAILS: b. 22 October 1953, Hertfordshire (of German/Austrian parentage).

PREVIOUS OCCUPATION: Electronics engineer.

EDUCATION/TRAINING: 1979–1984, Royal Academy of Music, with Joy Mammen; 1984-1985, National Opera Studio.

PROFESSIONAL DEBUT: 1985, Glyndebourne Touring Opera, Remendado, *Carmen*.

MAJOR DEBUTS INCLUDE: 1986: Covent Garden, Arturo, *Lucia di Lammermoor*; Welsh National Opera, Arturo, *I Puritani*; 1989: English National Opera, Vanya, *Katya Kabanova*; Netherlands Opera, Ernesto, *Don Pasquale*; 1989–1990, Welsh National Opera in Milan, New York and Tokyo, Dr Caius, *Falstaff*; 1990, Glyndebourne Festival Opera, Mr Upfold, *Albert Herring*; 1991, Théâtre des Champs Elysées, Paris, Dr Caius, *Falstaff*; 1992, Scottish Opera, Rodolfo, *La Bohème*.

CAREER IN THE UK INCLUDES: Since 1986: Covent Garden: First Prisoner, *Fidelio*; Major-Domo, *Der Rosenkavalier*; Apparition of a Youth, *Die Frau ohne Schatten*; English National Opera: Andrès, *Wozzeck*; Shepherd, *Oedipus Rex*; Count, *The Barber of Seville*; Welsh National Opera (1986–1990, Principal Tenor): Count, *The Barber of Seville*; Tamino, *The Magic Flute*; Cassio, *Otello*; Rodolfo, *La Bohème*; Iopas, *The Trojans*; Narraboth, *Salome*; Lensky, *Eugene Onegin*; Edgardo, *Lucia di Lammermoor*; Elvino, *La Sonnambula*; Ferrando, *Così fan tutte*; Alfredo, *La Traviata*, Alfred, *Die Fledermaus*; Pylade, *Iphigénie en Tauride*.

RELATED PROFESSIONAL ACTIVITIES: Private voice teacher.

RECORDINGS INCLUDE: Cilea, *Adriana Lecouvreur* (DECC); Janáček, *Osud* (EMI); Rossini, *Il Turco in Italia* (PHIL).

HONOURS INCLUDE: 1989, Associate, Royal Academy of Music.

ADDRESS: c/o Allied Artists, 42 Montpelier Square, London SW7 1JZ.

BROTHERSTON LEZ
Designer

PERSONAL DETAILS: b. 6 October 1961, Liverpool.

EDUCATION/TRAINING: 1981–1984, Central School of Art and Design.

PROFESSIONAL DEBUT: 1984, *Letter to Brezhnev* (film).

OPERATIC DEBUT: 1985, Royal Northern College of Music, *Teseo*.

CAREER: Freelance designer for numerous British opera, theatre and ballet companies.

MAJOR OPERATIC DEBUTS INCLUDE: 1988, Scottish Opera, *The Pearl Fishers*; 1989, Opera North, *The Flying Dutchman*; 1990/1991, Welsh National Opera/Opera Northern Ireland co-production, *Hansel and Gretel*; 1991: Hong Kong Arts Festival, *The Marriage of Figaro*; Opera Zuid, Holland, *Werther*.

OPERA DESIGNS IN THE UK INCLUDE: Since 1985: Abbey Opera at the Camden Festival: *The Protagonist* (1986, British stage première), *The Silverlake* (1987, British stage première); Buxton Festival: *David and Goliath*, *Il Sogno di Scipione*, *The Impresario*; Guildhall School of Music and Drama: *Julietta*, *L'Ormindo*; Opera 80, *Don Giovanni*; Opera North, *Masquerade* (1990, British première); Opera Northern Ireland, *Rigoletto*; Phoenix Opera, *La Traviata*; Royal Academy of Music: *The Cunning Little Vixen*, *Les Boréades* (1985, British stage première); Surrey Opera, *Don Giovanni*.

RELATED PROFESSIONAL ACTIVITIES: Visiting Lecturer, Central School of Art of Design.

ADDRESS: c/o Mayer Management Ltd, Suite 44, 2–3 Golden Square, London W1R 3AD.

BROWN PAUL   Designer

PERSONAL DETAILS: b. 13 May 1960, South Glamorgan.
EDUCATION/TRAINING: 1979–1983, University of St Andrews, studied English; 1983–1984, Riverside Studios design course, with Margaret Harris.
PROFESSIONAL DEBUT: 1985, Royal Court Theatre, *Ourselves Alone* by Anne Devlin.
OPERATIC DEBUT: 1987, City of Birmingham Touring Opera, *Falstaff.*
CAREER: Since 1985, freelance theatre and opera designer including Royal Court Theatre: *A Lie of the Mind* by Sam Shepard, *Road* by Jim Cartwright (also Lincoln Center, New York).
OPERA DESIGNS INCLUDE: Since 1988: City of Birmingham Touring Opera: *Ghanashyam, Zaide*; Covent Garden, *Mitridate, Rè di Ponto*; Deutsche Oper, Berlin, *Otello*; Teatro Comunale, Bologna, *L'Incoronazione di Poppea.*
ADDRESS: c/o Kate Lewthwaite Associates, 6 Windmill Sreet, London W1P 1HF.

BRYDON RODERICK
Conductor, Pianist and Accompanist

PERSONAL DETAILS: b. 8 January 1939, Edinburgh; two children.
EDUCATION/TRAINING: University of Edinburgh, studied composition with Kenneth Leighton; Accademia Chigiana, Siena, with Sergiu Celibidache; Vienna State Academy.
PROFESSIONAL AND OPERATIC DEBUT: 1964, Sadler's Wells Opera, *Attila.*
CAREER: Freelance conductor in the UK and abroad; 1963–1969, staff conductor, Sadler's Wells Opera; 1965–1967, Associate Conductor, Scottish National Orchestra; 1966–1970, staff conductor, Scottish Opera; 1974–1983, Artistic Director and Chief Conductor, Scottish Chamber Orchestra; Music Director: 1979–1984, Opera School, Royal Scottish Academy of Music and Drama; 1984–1987, Lucerne City Theatre; 1987–1990, Berne City Theatre.

MAJOR OPERATIC DEBUTS INCLUDE: 1970, Netherlands Opera, *La Bohème*; 1983: Grand Théâtre, Geneva, *Death in Venice*; Munich Festival, *The Turn of the Screw*; 1984: Covent Garden, *A Midsummer Night's Dream*; Lucerne, *Le Mystère de la Nativité*; Teatro La Fenice, Venice, *Mitridate, Rè di Ponto*; 1990: Los Angeles Music Center Opera, *Idomeneo*; Victoria State Opera, Melbourne, *Madam Butterfly*; 1993, Australian Opera, Sydney, *A Midsummer Night's Dream.*
OPERATIC WORLD PREMIERES INCLUDE: Royal Scottish Academy of Music and Drama: 1981, *Columba* by Kenneth Leighton; 1988, *On the Razzle* by Robin Orr.
OPERA PERFORMANCES IN THE UK INCLUDE: Since 1964: Opera North: *La Traviata, The Rake's Progress*; Phoenix Opera at the Camden Festival, *Zemir and Azor*; Scottish Opera: *La Bohème, Il Ballo delle Ingrate, The Turn of the Screw, A Midsummer Night's Dream, Lucia di Lammermoor, The Rape of Lucretia, The Marriage of Figaro, The Bartered Bride, L'Egisto, Werther, Death in Venice, Jenůfa, Fidelio.*
RELATED PROFESSIONAL ACTIVITIES: Numerous appearances as piano accompanist at lieder recitals and conductor with leading orchestras in the UK and abroad.
HONOURS INCLUDE: Fellow, Royal Scottish Academy of Music and Drama.
ADDRESS: c/o Lies Askonas Ltd, 186 Drury Lane, London WC2B 5RY.

BRYSON ROGER
Bass-baritone

PERSONAL DETAILS: b. 11 February 1944, London; m. 1980, Catherine McCord (soprano).
EDUCATION/TRAINING: 1967–1972, Guildhall School of Music and Drama, with Walther Gruner; 1972–1974, London Opera Centre, with Otakar Kraus.
PROFESSIONAL DEBUT: 1975, Kent Opera, Ceprano, *Rigoletto.*

EARLY CAREER INCLUDED: 1975–1978, appearances with Chelsea Opera Group, English Opera Group, Glyndebourne Touring Opera, Kent Opera.

MAJOR DEBUTS INCLUDE: 1979, Glyndebourne Festival Opera, Neptune, *Il Ritorno d'Ulisse in Patria*; 1982: English National Opera, Black Minister, *Le Grand Macabre* (British première); Opera Factory, Doctor, *Punch and Judy*; 1984, Welsh National Opera, Peachum, *The Threepenny Opera*; 1987, Scottish Opera, Schigolch, *Lulu*; 1988, Nancy Opera, Old Man, *King Priam*.

OPERATIC WORLD PREMIERES INCLUDE: 1991, Opera North, William, *Caritas* by Robert Saxton.

CAREER IN THE UK INCLUDES: Since 1979: Buxton Festival, Sancho Panza, *Don Quixote in Sierra Morena*; English National Opera, Bosun, *Billy Budd*; Glyndebourne Festival and Touring Opera: Second Priest/Second Armed Man, *Die Zauberflöte*; Lictor, *L'Incoronazione di Poppea*; Bottom and Quince, *A Midsummer Night's Dream*; Antonio and Bartolo, *Le Nozze di Figaro*; Lawyer, *Intermezzo*; Notary, *Der Rosenkavalier*; Cook/Herald, *L'Amour des Trois Oranges*; Rocco, *Fidelio*; Osmin, *Die Entführung aus dem Serail*; Don Alfonso, *Così fan tutte*; Leporello, *Don Giovanni*; Dikoy, *Katya Kabanova*; Opera North: Schmidt, *Werther*; Masetto, *Don Giovanni*; Schigolch, *Lulu*; Tchelio, *The Love for Three Oranges*; Swallow, *Peter Grimes*; Mr Flint, *Billy Budd*; title role, *Don Pasquale*; Scottish Opera, Bartolo, *Le Nozze di Figaro*; University College Opera, Méphistophélès, *Faust* (Spohr).

RELATED PROFESSIONAL ACTIVITIES: Numerous concerts and recitals in the UK.

RECORDINGS INCLUDE: Boughton, *The Immortal Hour*; Gay, *The Beggar's Opera* (both HYPE); Monteverdi, *Il Ritorno d'Ulisse in Patria* (CBS); Saxton, *Caritas* (COLL).

VIDEOS INCLUDE: Monteverdi, *L'Incoronazione di Poppea* (Glyndebourne Festival Opera); Sullivan, *Trial by Jury* (Walker).

ADDRESS: c/o Music International, 13 Ardilaun Road, London N5 2QR.

BUCHAN CYNTHIA
Mezzo-soprano

PERSONAL DETAILS: b. Edinburgh.

EDUCATION/TRAINING: 1968–1972, Royal Scottish Academy of Music and Drama, with Marjorie Blakeston; further studies with Ilse Rape in Vienna and Hans Hotter in Munich.

PROFESSIONAL DEBUT: 1968, Scottish Opera at the Edinburgh International Festival, *Solo Ingrate, Il Ballo delle Ingrate*.

MAJOR DEBUTS INCLUDE: 1972, Wexford Festival, Varvara, *Katya Kabanova*; 1974, Glyndebourne Festival Opera, Nature, *La Calisto*; 1975, Angers, Rosina, *Il Barbiere di Siviglia*; 1977, English National Opera, Dorabella, *Così fan tutte*; 1978, Cherubino, *Le Nozze di Figaro*: Frankfurt Opera and La Monnaie, Brussels; 1979, State Opera of South Australia, Adelaide, Charlotte, *Werther*; 1980: Covent Garden, Flower Maiden, *Parsifal*; Welsh National Opera, Olga, *Eugene Onegin*; 1982: Kent Opera, Nero, *Agrippina*; Berlioz Festival, Lyons, Ascanio, *Benvenuto Cellini*; 1983, Opera North, Dorabella, *Così fan tutte*; 1984, Hamburg State Opera, Harmony/Mirinda, *L'Ormindo*; 1986, Glyndebourne Festival Opera at the Hong Kong Arts Festival, Hermia, *A Midsummer Night's Dream*; 1988, Netherlands Opera, Varvara, *Katya Kabanova*; 1990, Los Angeles Music Center Opera, Jennie, *Higglety Pigglety Pop!*; 1991, Angers, Adalgisa, *Norma*.

OPERATIC WORLD PREMIERES INCLUDE: 1984, Glyndebourne Touring Opera, Jennie, *Higglety Pigglety Pop!* preliminary version by Oliver Knussen; 1992, Womens Playhouse Trust, Mother-in-Law/Wedding Guest, *Blood Wedding* by Nicola LeFanu.

CAREER IN THE UK INCLUDES: Since 1969: Buxton Festival: Orsze, *Háry János*; title role, *Griselda* (1983, first modern performance); Covent Garden: Bersi, *Andrea Chénier*; Annina, *Der Rosenkavalier*; English National Opera: Pippo, *The Thieving Magpie*; Preziosilla, *The Force of Destiny*; Isolier, *Count Ory*; Rosina, *The Barber of Seville*; Varvara, *Katya Kabanova*; Glyndebourne Festival and Touring Opera: Olga, *Eugene Onegin*; Cherubino, *Le Nozze di Figaro*; Dorabella, *Così fan tutte*; Hermia, *A Midsummer Night's Dream*; Jennie, *Higglety Pigglety Pop!* (1985, provisional complete version); title role, *L'Enfant et les Sortilèges*; Opera North: Azucena, *Il Trovatore*; Charlotte, *Werther*; title role, *Carmen*; Scottish Opera: Cherubino, *The Marriage of Figaro*; Hansel, *Hansel and Gretel*; Hermia, *A Midsummer Night's Dream*; Prince Orlofsky, *Die Fledermaus*; Annina, *Der Rosenkavalier*; Varvara, *Katya Kabanova*; Olga, *Eugene Onegin*; Charlotte, *Werther*; Welsh National Opera: Varvara, *Katya Kabanova*; Suzuki, *Madam Butterfly*; Rosina, *The Barber of Seville*; Mistress Quickly, *Falstaff*; title role, *Carmen*.

RELATED PROFESSIONAL ACTIVITIES: Numerous concerts, recitals and broadcasts in the UK and Europe.

RECORDINGS INCLUDE: Verdi, *La Traviata* (EMI).

VIDEOS INCLUDE: Britten, *A Midsummer Night's Dream* (Glyndebourne Festival Opera); Giordano, *Andrea Chénier* (Covent Garden); Knussen, *Higglety Pigglety Pop!* (Glyndebourne Festival Opera); R. Strauss, *Der Rosenkavalier* (Covent Garden).

AWARDS INCLUDE: 1972, Richard Tauber Memorial Prize.

ADDRESS: c/o Robert Gilder & Company, Enterprise House, 59–65 Upper Ground, London SE1 9PQ.

BULLER JOHN   Composer

PERSONAL DETAILS: b. 7 February 1927, London; m., four children.

PREVIOUS OCCUPATION: Architectural surveyor.

EDUCATION/TRAINING: 1959–1964, University of London, with Anthony Milner.

FIRST WORK TO ACHIEVE PROMINENCE: 1970, *The Cave* for ensemble.

CAREER: Since 1970, compositions include orchestral, instrumental, vocal and choral works; Composer in Residence: 1975–1976, University of Edinburgh; 1985–1986, Queens University, Belfast.

OPERATIC WORLD PREMIERES: 1992, English National Opera, *Bakxai*, opera in seventeen scenes, libretto by the composer after Euripides, conductor Martin André, director Julia Hollander, designer Hildegard Bechtler.

RELATED PROFESSIONAL ACTIVITIES: 1965–1976, member (1971–1972, Chairman), MacNaghten Concerts Committee.

RECORDINGS INCLUDE: *The Theatre of Memory* for orchestra; *Proença* for mezzo-soprano, electric guitar and orchestra (both UNIC).

AWARDS INCLUDE: 1978, Arts Council bursary; International Rostrum of Composers (Paris): 1978, *Proença*; 1982, *The Theatre of Memory*.

ADDRESS: c/o Oxford University Press, 7–8 Hatherley Street, London SW1P 2QT.

BULLOCK SUSAN   Soprano

PERSONAL DETAILS: b. 9 December 1958, Cheshire; m. 1983, Lawrence Wallington (bass-baritone).

EDUCATION/TRAINING: 1977–1980, Royal Holloway College, London; 1980–1983, Royal Academy of Music, with Marjorie Thomas; 1984–1985, National Opera Studio; currently with Audrey Langford.

PROFESSIONAL DEBUT: 1986, English National Opera, Pamina, *The Magic Flute*.

CAREER INCLUDES: Since 1986: Batignano Festival, Andromache, *King Priam*; English National Opera (1986–1989, Principal Soprano): Micaëla, *Carmen*; Marzelline, *Fidelio*; Gilda, *Rigoletto*; Marguérite, *Faust*; Peep-Bo and Yum-Yum, *The Mikado*; First Lady, *The Magic Flute*; Sandman, *Hansel and Gretel*; Greta Fiorentino, *Street Scene*; Tatyana, *Eugene Onegin*; Ellen Orford, *Peter Grimes*; Alice Ford, *Falstaff*; title role, *Madam Butterfly*; Glyndebourne Touring Opera, title roles: *Jenůfa*, *Katya Kabanova*; Opera Northern Ireland, Rosalinde, *Die Fledermaus*.

RELATED PROFESSIONAL ACTIVITIES: Concerts and television appearances in the UK.

RECORDINGS INCLUDE: Sullivan, *The Mikado*; Weill, *Street Scene* (both TER).

VIDEOS INCLUDE: Sullivan, *The Mikado* (English National Opera).

AWARDS AND HONOURS INCLUDE: 1983, Royal Over-Seas League Music Competition; 1984: Decca-Kathleen Ferrier Prize; Royal Society of Arts Award for study with Elisabeth Schwarzkopf; 1986: Shell-Scottish Opera Award; Associate, Royal Academy of Music.

ADDRESS: c/o Stafford Law Associates, 26 Mayfield Road, Weybridge, Surrey KT13 8XB.

BUNNING CHRISTINE
Soprano

PERSONAL DETAILS: b. 24 February 1958, Luton.

EDUCATION/TRAINING: 1979–1983, Guildhall School of Music and Drama; 1983-1984, with Irmgaard Seefried in Vienna; privately with David Mason and Audrey Langford in London.

PROFESSIONAL DEBUT: 1985, chorus member and small roles, Buxton Festival.

EARLY CAREER INCLUDED: 1985–1988, chorus member and small roles: Buxton Festival, English Bach Festival, Glyndebourne Festival Opera, New Sadler's Wells Opera, Wexford Festival.

MAJOR DEBUTS INCLUDE: 1988: Glyndebourne Festival Opera, Sashka, *The Electrification of the Soviet Union*; Opera North, title role, *Katya Kabanova*; 1989, Welsh National Opera, Mimi, *La Bohème*; 1990: English National Opera, Miss Jessel, *The Turn of the Screw*; Opera Factory, Donna Elvira, *Don Giovanni*.

CAREER IN THE UK INCLUDES: Since 1989: Central Festival Opera, Northampton, Violetta, *La Traviata*; English National Opera: Greta Fiorentino, *Street Scene*; Tebaldo, *Don Carlos*; Harrogate International Festival, Miss Jessel, *The Turn of the Screw*; Kentish Opera, Lady Macbeth, *Macbeth*; Welsh National Opera: Mařenka, *The Bartered Bride*; title role, *Tosca*.

RELATED PROFESSIONAL ACTIVITIES: Numerous concerts and recitals in the UK including 1987, Wigmore Hall, first performance of *Seven Sin Songs* by Alan Belk.

RECORDINGS INCLUDE: Pergolesi, *La Serva Padrona*; Rossini, *Petite Messe Solennelle* (both MERI).

AWARDS INCLUDE: 1986, Richard Tauber Memorial Prize; 1987, National Federation of Music Societies Award for Female Singers.

ADDRESS: c/o Music International, 13 Ardilaun Road, London N5 2QR.

BURGESS SALLY
Mezzo-soprano

POSITION: Principal Mezzo-soprano, English National Opera.

PERSONAL DETAILS: b. 9 October 1953, Durban, South Africa; m. 1988, Neal Thornton (jazz musician), one child.

EDUCATION/TRAINING: Royal College of Music, with Hervey Alan; privately with Marion Studholm, Esther Salaman and Josephine Veasey.

PROFESSIONAL DEBUT: As soprano: 1976, Bach Choir at the Royal Festival Hall, *Requiem* (Brahms).

37

EARLY CAREER INCLUDED: 1977–1983: Principal Soprano, English National Opera: Bertha, *Euryanthe*; Diana, *Orpheus in the Underworld*; Zerlina, *Don Giovanni*; Foreign Woman, *The Consul*; Phyllis, *Iolanthe*; Micaëla, *Carmen*; Cherubino, *The Marriage of Figaro*; Pamina, *The Magic Flute*; Marzelline, *Fidelio*; Mimi, *La Bohème*; Composer, *Ariadne auf Naxos*; Charlotte, *Werther*; Stephano, *Romeo and Juliet*; Pauline, *The Gambler*; also: New Opera Company, title role, *Julietta* (1978, British première); Opera North, Jenny, *The Mines of Sulphur*; Phoenix Opera at the Camden Festival, title role, *Eritrea* (1982, British première); Spitalfields Festival, Phénice, *Armide*; since 1983, mezzo-soprano.

MAJOR DEBUTS INCLUDE: 1983: Covent Garden, Siebel, *Faust*; Glyndebourne Festival Opera, Smeraldina, *L'Amour des Trois Oranges*; 1986, English National Opera, title role, *Carmen*; Amneris, *Aida*: 1988, Opéra du Rhin, Strasbourg; 1990: Lausanne Opera, Nancy Opera; 1991: Scottish Opera, Fricka, *Die Walküre*; Bregenz Festival, title role, *Carmen*.

OPERATIC WORLD PREMIÈRES INCLUDE: 1989, English National Opera, Sylvia Galway, *The Plumber's Gift* by David Blake.

CAREER IN THE UK INCLUDES: Since 1983: Principal Mezzo-soprano, English National Opera: Octavian, *Der Rosenkavalier*; Nicklausse, *The Tales of Hoffmann*; Lady Angela, *Patience*; Nefertiti, *Akhnaten* (1985, British première); Public Opinion, *Orpheus in the Underworld*; Sesto, *Julius Caesar*; Prince Orlofsky, *Die Fledermaus*; Laura, *The Stone Guest*; Sonyetka, *Lady Macbeth of Mtsensk* (both 1987, British stage premières); Meg Page, *Falstaff*; Minerva/Amor, *The Return of Ulysses*; Fennimore, *Fennimore and Gerda*; Judith, *Duke Bluebeard's Castle*; Witch, *Königskinder*; Messenger, *Orfeo*; also: Covent Garden, Maddalena, *Rigoletto*; Opera North: Andronico, *Tamburlaine* (Handel); Amneris, *Aida*; Dido, *The Trojans*; Julie Le Verne, *Show Boat* (also London

Palladium); Orpheus, *Orpheus and Eurydice*; Laura, *La Gioconda*; title role, *Carmen*; Scottish Opera, Amneris, *Aida*.

RELATED PROFESSIONAL ACTIVITIES: Numerous concerts, recitals, broadcasts and television appearances in both opera and jazz.

RECORDINGS INCLUDE: Gluck, *Armide*; Handel, *Saul* (both EMI); McCartney, *Liverpool Oratorio* (EMI); Offenbach, *Orpheus in the Underworld* (TER); Ravel, *Five Greek Folk Songs* (CALA); Rossini, *Il Barbiere di Siviglia*; Vivaldi, Sacred Choral Music (both PHIL); Sally Burgess Sings Jazz (TER).

VIDEOS INCLUDE: McCartney, *Liverpool Oratorio* (EMI).

HONOURS INCLUDE: Associate, Royal College of Music.

ADDRESS: c/o Harrison/Parrott Ltd, 12 Penzance Place, London W11 4PA.

BURROWS STUART   Tenor

PERSONAL DETAILS: b. 7 February 1933, South Wales; m. 1957, Enid Lewis, two children.

PREVIOUS OCCUPATION: School teacher.

EDUCATION/TRAINING: Trinity College, University of Wales.

PROFESSIONAL DEBUT: 1963, Welsh National Opera, Ismaele, *Nabucco*.

EARLY CAREER INCLUDED: 1963–1968, Welsh National Opera: Malcolm and Macduff, *Macbeth*; Rodolfo, *La Bohème*; Eleazor, *Moses*; Jeník, *The Bartered Bride*; Don Ottavio, *Don Giovanni*; Ernesto, *Don Pasquale*; Duke, *Rigoletto*.

MAJOR DEBUTS INCLUDE: 1965, National Opera of Greece, Athens, title role, *Oedipus Rex*; 1967, Covent Garden, First Prisoner, *Fidelio*; Tamino, *Die Zauberflöte*: 1967, San Francisco Opera; 1970, Vienna State Opera; Don Ottavio, *Don Giovanni*: 1970, Salzburg Festival; 1971, Metropolitan Opera, New York; 1975, Paris Opera; 1978, Grand Théâtre, Geneva, title role, *La Damnation de Faust*; 1982, La Monnaie, Brussels, title role, *La Clemenza di Tito*.

CAREER IN THE UK INCLUDES: Since 1967,
Covent Garden: Beppe, *Pagliacci*; Erik,
Der Fliegende Holländer; Tamino, *Die
Zauberflöte* (also 1979, Far East tour);
Des Grieux, *Manon Lescaut*; Elvino, *La
Sonnambula*; Don Ottavio, *Don Giovanni*;
Lensky, *Eugene Onegin*; Fenton, *Falstaff*;
Leicester, *Maria Stuarda*; Ernesto, *Don
Pasquale*; Ferrando, *Così fan tutte*;
Pinkerton, *Madama Butterfly*; Alfredo, *La
Traviata*; title roles: *Faust, Idomeneo, La
Clemenza di Tito*.
RELATED PROFESSIONAL ACTIVITIES:
Numerous concerts, recitals, broadcasts
and television appearances in the UK and
abroad including since 1978, annual
series, *Stuart Burrows Sings* (BBC).
RECORDINGS INCLUDE: Berlioz: *La
Damnation de Faust* (DG), *Requiem* (CBS);
Donizetti, *Maria Stuarda* (DECC); Mozart:
La Clemenza di Tito (PHIL), *Don Giovanni*
(PHIL/DECC), *Die Entführung aus dem Serail*
(PHIL), *Die Zauberflöte, Famous Mozart
Arias*; Tchaikovsky, *Eugene Onegin* (all
DECC).
AWARDS AND HONOURS INCLUDE: 1959,
Blue Riband, National Eisteddfod of
Wales; University of Wales: 1981,
Honorary Doctorate of Music; 1990,
Fellowship.
ADDRESS: c/o John Coast, 31 Sinclair Road,
London W14 ONS.

BURY JOHN   Designer

PERSONAL DETAILS: b. 27 January 1925,
Aberystwyth; m. 1947, Margaret
Greenwood, one child; m. 1966, Elizabeth
Duffield, three children.
EDUCATION/TRAINING: Cathedral School,
Hereford; University College, London.
PROFESSIONAL DEBUT: 1946, member, Joan
Littlewood's Theatre Workshop at Theatre
Royal, Stratford East.
OPERATIC DEBUT: 1965, Covent Garden,
Moses and Aaron (British première).
CAREER: 1946–1962, actor, stage manager,
lighting and set designer, Theatre
Workshop (1955–1962, Principal
Designer); Royal Shakespeare Theatre:

1962–1973, Associate Designer; 1964–
1968, first Head of Design; 1973–1985,
Head of Design, Royal National Theatre;
since 1985, freelance designer working
mainly in opera.
MAJOR OPERATIC DEBUTS INCLUDE: 1970,
Glyndebourne Festival Opera, *La Calisto*;
1982, Metropolitan Opera, New York,
Macbeth; 1987, Lyric Opera, Chicago, *Le
Nozze di Figaro*; 1991, Bavarian State
Opera, Munich, *Peter Grimes*; Los
Angeles Music Center Opera: 1986,
Salome; 1989, *Così fan tutte*; 1991,
Elektra.
OPERA DESIGNS IN THE UK INCLUDE: Since
1966: Covent Garden: *Die Zauberflöte,
Tristan und Isolde, Salome*;
Glyndebourne Festival Opera: *Il Ritorno
d'Ulisse in Patria, Le Nozze di Figaro,
Don Giovanni, Così fan tutte, Fidelio, A
Midsummer Night's Dream, Orfeo ed
Euridice, L'Incoronazione di Poppea,
Carmen*.
RELATED PROFESSIONAL ACTIVITIES:
1962–1978, member, Designers' Working
Group, Arts Council of Great Britain;
1975-1985, Chairman, Society of British
Theatre Designers; wide experience as
consultant to theatre architects.
VIDEOS INCLUDE: Beethoven, *Fidelio*; Bizet,
Carmen; Britten, *A Midsummer Night's
Dream*; Gluck, *Orfeo ed Euridice*;
Monteverdi: *Il Ritorno d'Ulisse in Patria,
L'Incoronazione di Poppea*; Mozart: *Così
fan tutte, Don Giovanni, Le Nozze di
Figaro* (all Glyndebourne Festival Opera).
HONOURS INCLUDE: 1969, Fellow, Royal
Society of Arts; 1979, Officer, Order of the
British Empire (OBE); 1990, Honorary
Fellow, Royal College of Art.
ADDRESS: Burleigh House, Burleigh,
Stroud, Gloucestershire GL5 2PQ

BUTLIN ROGER   Designer

PERSONAL DETAILS: b. Stafford.
EDUCATION/TRAINING: West of England
College of Art, Bristol; University of
Southampton.

39

PREVIOUS OCCUPATION: Art teacher and lecturer.

PROFESSIONAL DEBUT: 1969, Greenwich Theatre, *Forget-Me-Not Lane* by Peter Nichols.

OPERATIC DEBUT: 1972, Welsh National Opera, *Billy Budd*.

CAREER: 1969–1972, Head of Design, Greenwich Theatre; since 1972, freelance opera and theatre designer in the UK and abroad.

MAJOR OPERATIC DEBUTS INCLUDE: 1973, Australian Opera, Sydney (opening season of Sydney Opera House), *Il Barbiere di Siviglia*; 1974, Glyndebourne Festival Opera, *Idomeneo*; 1977, Kent Opera, *Iphigenia in Tauris*; 1978, La Monnaie, Brussels, *Peter Grimes*; 1979: Buxton Festival, *Lucia di Lammermoor*; English National Opera, *Cinderella*; Scottish Opera, *Eugene Onegin*; Cologne Opera, *La Périchole*; *Alceste*: 1981, Covent Garden; 1982, Kentucky Opera; 1983, Opera North, *Eugene Onegin*; 1992, Dallas Civic Opera, *L'Elisir d'Amore*.

OPERA DESIGNS IN THE UK INCLUDE: Since 1980: Buxton Festival: *Don Quixote in Sierra Morena*, *Torquato Tasso*, *L'Italiana in Londra*, *Il Pittor Parigino*; English National Opera, *Così fan tutte*; Kent Opera: *Agrippina*, *The Seraglio*, *The Barber of Seville*, *The Coronation of Poppea*, *Pygmalion*, *Dido and Aeneas*, *The Magic Flute*, *The Return of Ulysses*; Scottish Opera, *Idomeneo*.

VIDEOS INCLUDE: Mozart, *Idomeneo* (Glyndebourne Festival Opera).

ADDRESS: c/o Curtis Brown Group Ltd, 162-168 Regent Street, London W1R 5TB.

BYLES EDWARD   Tenor

POSITION: Principal Tenor, English National Opera.

PERSONAL DETAILS: b. Ebbw Vale; m., two children.

EDUCATION/TRAINING: Royal College of Music, with H. Arnold Smith and Clive Carey.

EARLY CAREER INCLUDED: 1957–1973, appearances with English Opera Group, Glyndebourne Festival Opera, Handel Opera Society, Opera for All, Welsh National Opera (1960–1972, Principal Tenor) and Elizabethan Opera, Sydney; roles included: Brighella, *Ariadne auf Naxos*; Pinkerton, *Madam Butterfly*; Rodolfo, *La Bohème*; Arnold, *William Tell*; Amenophis, *Moses*; Alfred, *Die Fledermaus*; Ernesto, *Don Pasquale*; Count, *The Barber of Seville*; Don Basilio, *The Marriage of Figaro*; Monostatos, *The Magic Flute*; Pang, *Turandot*; title roles: *Albert Herring* (also 1964, English Opera Group Soviet Union tour), *Faust*.

OPERATIC WORLD PREMIERES INCLUDE: 1960, English Opera Group at the Aldeburgh Festival, Snout, *A Midsummer Night's Dream* by Benjamin Britten; 1974, Welsh National Opera, Father Galuchet, *The Beach of Falesá* by Alun Hoddinott; English National Opera: 1977: Vasca, *The Royal Hunt of the Sun* by Iain Hamilton; Saint Leger/Abbé Maury/Spanish General/French Officer, *Toussaint* by David Blake; 1991, Philotus, *Timon of Athens* by Stephen Oliver.

CAREER IN THE UK INCLUDES: Since 1974: Principal Tenor, English National Opera: Guillot, *Manon*; Monostatos, *The Magic Flute*; Menelaus, *La Belle Hélène*; Hauk Šendorf and Vítek, *The Makropoulos Case*; Trabuco, *The Force of Destiny*; Isaac, *The Thieving Magpie*; Don Curzio, *The Marriage of Figaro*; Mime, *The Ring of the Nibelung*; Blind, *Die Fledermaus*; Missail, *Boris Godunov*; Karataev, *War and Peace* (also 1984, USA tour); Gamekeeper, *Rusalka*; Prince Nilsky/Hunchbacked Gambler, *The Gambler*; Moser, *The Mastersingers of Nuremberg*; Manfredo, *The Sicilian Vespers*; Shepherd, *Tristan and Isolde*; John Styx, *Orpheus in the Underworld*; Shogun's Wife/British Sailor, *Pacific Overtures*; Red Whiskers, *Billy Budd*; Bardolph, *Falstaff*; Priest, *Christmas Eve*; Monsieur Triquet, *Eugene Onegin*; Eumete, *The Return of Ulysses*; Idiot, *Wozzeck*; Reverend Adams, *Peter Grimes*;

Broomstick-maker, *Königskinder*; Composer/Harper/Miroslav, *The Adventures of Mr Brouček*; also: Covent Garden, Idiot, *Wozzeck*; New Opera Company, Official, *Julietta* (1978, British première); Welsh National Opera: Vítek, *The Makropoulos Case*; Benda, *The Jacobin* (1980, British stage première).

RELATED PROFESSIONAL ACTIVITIES: Numerous concerts, recitals, oratorios and broadcasts in the UK.

RECORDINGS INCLUDE: Offenbach, *The Tales of Hoffmann*; Sondheim, *Pacific Overtures* (both TER); Verdi, *La Traviata* (EMI).

VIDEOS INCLUDE: Britten, *Billy Budd*; Dvořák, *Rusalka* (both English National Opera).

HONOURS INCLUDE: Associate, Royal College of Music.

ADDRESS: c/o English National Opera, London Coliseum, St Martin's Lane, London WC2N 4ES.

BYRNE ELIZABETH   Soprano

PERSONAL DETAILS: b. 3 June 1953, Lancashire; m. 1989, James Asher.

EDUCATION/TRAINING: 1972–1975, Birmingham School of Music, with Linda Vaughan; 1975–1978, Royal Northern College of Music, with Frederic Cox; 1978–1979, National Opera Studio; 1980–1981, International Opera Studio, Zurich; currently with Gita Denise.

PROFESSIONAL DEBUT: 1981, Glyndebourne Touring Opera, Alice Ford, *Falstaff*.

MAJOR DEBUTS INCLUDE: 1982, Zurich Opera: Flower Maiden, *Parsifal*; Gingerbread Woman, *A Village Romeo and Juliet*; 1984, Welsh National Opera, title role, *The Drama of Aida*; 1985, Lucerne, Amelia, *Un Ballo in Maschera*; 1986, Batignano Festival, Minerva, *Il Ritorno d'Ulisse in Patria*; 1987, Scottish Opera, High Priestess, *Aida*; 1988, English National Opera, title role, *Madam Butterfly*; 1990, Lyric Opera Center for American Artists, Chicago, Stepdaughter, *Six Characters in Search of an Author*; 1991, Lyric Opera, Chicago, Pale Lady, *The Gambler*.

CAREER IN THE UK INCLUDES: Since 1981: Abbey Opera at the Camden Festival: Asteria, *Nerone*; Sister, *The Protagonist* (1986, British stage première); English National Opera: First Lady, *The Magic Flute*; Oksana, *Christmas Eve*; Miss Jessel, *The Turn of the Screw*; Amelia, *A Masked Ball*; Glyndebourne Touring Opera: Donna Elvira, *Don Giovanni*; Fata Morgana, *The Love for Three Oranges*; Welsh National Opera: Gerhilde, *The Valkyrie*; Third Norn, *Götterdämmerung*.

RELATED PROFESSIONAL ACTIVITIES: Numerous concerts, recitals and broadcasts in the UK and USA.

ADDRESS: c/o Chicago Concert Artists, Suite 906, 431 South Dearborn Street, Chicago, IL 60605, USA.

*   *   *   *

CADDY IAN   Bass-baritone

PERSONAL DETAILS: b. 1 March 1947, Southampton; m. Kathryn Ash, three children.

EDUCATION/TRAINING: 1965–1970, Royal Academy of Music: piano with Madeleine Windsor, vocal studies with Henry Cummings; privately with Otakar Kraus and Iris dell'Acqua.

PROFESSIONAL DEBUT: 1970, Opera for All, Guglielmo, *Così fan tutte*.

EARLY CAREER INCLUDED: 1970–1973: chorus member and small roles, Glyndebourne Festival Opera; New Opera Company, Harold, *Time Off? Not a Ghost of a Chance!*; Opera for All: Geronio, *Il Turco in Italia*; Schlemil, *The Tales of Hoffmann*.

MAJOR DEBUTS INCLUDE: 1973, Glyndebourne Touring Opera, Schaunard, *La Bohème*; 1975, Wexford Festival: Boreas/Nicondia, *Eritrea* (first modern performance); Pacuvio, *La Pietra del Paragone*; 1976: English National Opera on tour, Ajax II, *La Belle Hélène*; Kent Opera, Adonis, *Venus and Adonis*; 1978, Opera North, Aeneas, *Dido and Aeneas*; 1981, Scottish Opera, Macheath, *The Beggar's Opera*; 1982: Covent Garden, Varsonofiev, *Khovanshchina*; Welsh National Opera, Don Pizarro, *Fidelio*; 1989, Houston Grand Opera, Pooh-Bah, *The Mikado*.

OPERATIC WORLD PREMIERES INCLUDE: 1977, English National Opera, Boucannier, *Toussaint* by David Blake.

CAREER IN THE UK INCLUDES: Since 1974: Covent Garden: Happy, *La Fanciulla del West*; Yamadori, *Madama Butterfly*; English Bach Festival: Don Quixote, *El Retablo de Maese Pedro*; Pollux, *Castor et Pollux*; Jupiter/Telenus, *Naïs*; Aeneas, *Dido and Aeneas*; English National Opera: Mountarrarat, *Iolanthe*; Falke, *Die Fledermaus*; Bobinet, *La Vie Parisienne*; Pooh-Bah, *The Mikado*; Glyndebourne Festival and Touring Opera: Commercial Councillor, *Intermezzo*; Count, *Capriccio*; Opera North: Theatre Director, *Les Mamelles de Tirésias*; Falke, *Die Fledermaus*; Oxford University Opera, title role, *Orfeo*; Phoenix Opera: Bobinet, *La Vie Parisienne*; Macheath, *The Beggar's Opera*; Scottish Opera: Falke, *Die Fledermaus*; Guglielmo, *Così fan tutte*; Count, *Capriccio*.

RELATED PROFESSIONAL ACTIVITIES: Numerous concerts, recitals and broadcasts in the UK and abroad; editor: songs, cantatas and orchestral works by Mayr and Donizetti.

RECORDINGS INCLUDE: Donizetti, songs (MERI); Gabrieli, choral and instrumental works (ARGO).

VIDEOS INCLUDE: Puccini, *La Fanciulla del West* (Covent Garden); R. Strauss, *Intermezzo* (Glyndebourne Festival Opera).

AWARDS AND HONOURS INCLUDE: 1967, Ricordi Opera Prize; 1970, Countess of Munster Award; 1984, Associate, Royal Academy of Music.

ADDRESS: c/o Music International, 13 Ardilaun Road, London N5 2QR.

CAHILL TERESA   Soprano

PERSONAL DETAILS: b. 30 July 1944, Maidenhead; m. 1971, John Kiernander (m. diss.).

EDUCATION/TRAINING: 1962–1967, Guildhall School of Music and Drama, with Joyce Newton; 1967–1969, London Opera Centre; privately with Andrew Field, Audrey Langford, Vera Rozsa and John Caunce; Licentiate, Royal Academy of Music.

PROFESSIONAL DEBUT: 1967, Phoenix Opera, Rosina, *The Barber of Seville*.

MAJOR DEBUTS INCLUDE: 1970: Covent Garden, Barbarina, *Le Nozze di Figaro*; Welsh National Opera, Micaëla, *Carmen*; 1971, Glyndebourne Festival Opera, First Lady, *Die Zauberflöte*; 1973: English Opera Group, title role, *Iolanta*; Santa Fe Opera, Donna Elvira, *Don Giovanni*; 1974, Scottish Opera, Sophie, *Der Rosenkavalier*; 1976, Covent Garden at La Scala, Milan: Servilia, *La Clemenza di Tito*; First Niece, *Peter Grimes*; 1977, English National Opera, Antonia, *The Tales of Hoffmann*; 1979, Opera North, Countess, *The Marriage of Figaro*; 1981: Kent Opera, Tatyana, *Eugene Onegin*; Opera Company of Philadelphia, Alice Ford, *Falstaff*.

OPERATIC WORLD PREMIERES INCLUDE: 1976, Covent Garden, Madwoman 1/Lady, *We Come to the River* by Hans Werner Henze; 1977, English National Opera, Pauline Leclerc, *Toussaint* by David Blake.

CAREER IN THE UK INCLUDES: Since 1970: Covent Garden: Donna Elvira and Zerlina, *Don Giovanni*; Fiordiligi, *Così fan tutte*; Servilia, *La Clemenza di Tito*; Woodbird, *Siegfried*; Flower Maiden, *Parsifal*; Woglinde, *Das Rheingold*; Xenia, *Boris*

Godunov; Lisa, *La Sonnambula*; Sophie, *Der Rosenkavalier*; First Niece, *Peter Grimes*; Glyndebourne Festival and Touring Opera: Pamina, *Die Zauberflöte*; Naiad, *Ariadne auf Naxos*; Destiny, *La Calisto*; Alice Ford, *Falstaff*; Donna Elvira, *Don Giovanni*; Fiordiligi, *Così fan tutte*; Handel Opera Society, title role, *Semele*; Kent Opera, Leonore, *Fidelio*; London Sinfonietta at the Queen Elizabeth Hall, Elisabeth, *Elegy for Young Lovers*; New Opera Company, Columbine, *Commedia* (1982, British première).

RELATED PROFESSIONAL ACTIVITIES: Regular concerts, recitals, broadcasts and television appearances in the UK and abroad; masterclasses: Dartington Hall Summer School of Music, Elgar Society; guest lecturer, Trinity College of Music; teacher, Guildhall School of Music and Drama; adjudicator for several UK competitions.

RECORDINGS INCLUDE: Britten, *Peter Grimes* (PHIL); Cavalli, *La Calisto* (ARGO); Massenet, *Cendrillon* (CBS); Mozart, *Le Nozze di Figaro*; R. Strauss, *Der Rosenkavalier* (both EMI).

VIDEOS INCLUDE: Mozart, *Die Zauberflöte* (Glyndebourne Festival Opera).

AWARDS AND HONOURS INCLUDE: 1970, John Christie Award; Associate, Guildhall School of Music and Drama.

ADDRESS: 65 Leyland Road, London SE12 8DW.

CAIRNS JANICE   Soprano

POSITION: Principal Soprano, English National Opera.
PERSONAL DETAILS: b. Northumberland; m. Michael Collins, two children.
EDUCATION/TRAINING: 1970–1974: Royal Scottish Academy of Music and Drama; privately with John Hauxvell; 1974–1977, with Arthur Hammond in London and with Tito Gobbi in Rome.
PROFESSIONAL DEBUT: 1974, chorus member, Scottish Opera.

EARLY CAREER INCLUDED: 1978–1981: Craig-y-nos: Dido, *Dido and Aeneas*; title role, *Tosca*; Kent Opera, Alice Ford, *Falstaff*; University College Opera, Odabella, *Attila*.
MAJOR DEBUTS INCLUDE: 1978, Thessaloniki Festival, Desdemona, *Otello*; 1982, English National Opera, Musetta, *La Bohème*; Reiza, *Oberon*: 1985, Scottish Opera; 1987, Teatro La Fenice, Venice; 1988, Opera North, Leonore, *Fidelio*.
CAREER IN THE UK INCLUDES: Since 1982: Principal Soprano, English National Opera: Eva, *The Mastersingers of Nuremberg*; Maria, *Mazeppa*; Rosalinde, *Die Fledermaus*; Lisa, *The Queen of Spades*; Amelia, *Simon Boccanegra*; Alice Ford, *Falstaff*; Amelia, *A Masked Ball*; Anna Maurrant, *Street Scene*; title roles: *Ariadne auf Naxos*, *Madam Butterfly*, *Aida*, *Tosca*; also: Kent Opera, Donna Anna, *Don Giovanni*; New Sussex Opera, Madeleine, *Andrea Chénier*; Opera North: Hélène, *Jérusalem* (1990, British stage première); title role, *Aida*; Scottish Opera: Leonora, *Il Trovatore*; title roles: *Aida*, *Madama Butterfly*.
RELATED PROFESSIONAL ACTIVITIES: Numerous concerts, recitals, broadcasts and television appearances in the UK and abroad.
ADDRESS: c/o John Coast, 31 Sinclair Road, London W14 ONS.

CAIRNS TOM
Director and Designer

PERSONAL DETAILS: b. 1 November 1952, County Down, Northern Ireland.
PREVIOUS OCCUPATION: 1976–1980, school teacher.
EDUCATION/TRAINING: Belfast College of Art and Design; Goldsmith's College; Riverside Studios design course, with Margaret Harris.
PROFESSIONAL DEBUT: As designer: 1983, Crucible Theatre, Sheffield, *Hamlet*.

OPERATIC DEBUT: As designer: 1984, Opera Northern Ireland, *Don Giovanni*; as director and designer: 1991, Opera North, *King Priam*.

CAREER: 1985–1987, Associate Artist, Crucible Theatre, Sheffield; since 1988, freelance director and designer for numerous opera and theatre companies including Citizens Theatre, Glasgow; Royal Exchange, Manchester; Royal National Theatre; Royal Shakespeare Company.

OPERA PRODUCTIONS INCLUDE: Since 1985: as designer: Bregenz Festival, *Samson et Dalila*; Opera 80, *Don Giovanni*; Opera North: *La Finta Giardiniera*, *L'Heure Espagnole/Gianni Schicchi*; co-designs with Antony McDonald: English National Opera: *Billy Budd*, *Beatrice and Benedict*; Opera North, *The Midsummer Marriage*; Opera North/Scottish Opera/Welsh National Opera co-production, *The Trojans* (also 1990, at Covent Garden); Netherlands Opera, *Benvenuto Cellini*; as director and designer: Scottish Opera, *Don Giovanni*; Stuttgart State Opera, *La Bohème*.

VIDEOS INCLUDE: Britten, *Billy Budd* (English National Opera)

ADDRESS: c/o Harriet Cruickshank, 97 Old South Lambeth Road, London SW8 1XU.

CALEY IAN   Tenor

PERSONAL DETAILS: b. 22 February 1948, Preston; m. 1972, Susan Ashworth, three children.

EDUCATION/TRAINING: Royal Manchester College of Music: 1966–1967, studied piano; 1967–1971, vocal studies with Gwilym Jones and Joseph Ward; privately with Frederic Cox, Denis Dowling and Erich Vietheer.

PROFESSIONAL DEBUT: 1972, Glyndebourne Festival Opera, Telemaco, *Il Ritorno d'Ulisse in Patria*.

EARLY CAREER INCLUDED: 1972–1977: English Bach Festival, Hippolyte, *Hippolyte et Aricie*; English Opera Group/ English Music Theatre: Ruggero, *La Rondine*; Ramiro, *Cinderella*; title role, *Albert Herring*; Glyndebourne Festival and Touring Opera: Malcolm, *Macbeth*; Loby, *The Visit of the Old Lady* (1973, British première); Pedrillo, *Die Entführung aus dem Serail*; title role, *The Rake's Progress*; Sadler's Wells Opera/ English National Opera: Camille, *The Merry Widow*; Idamante, *Idomeneo*; Paris, *La Belle Hélène*.

MAJOR DEBUTS INCLUDE: 1977, Opéra Comique, Paris, title role, *The Rake's Progress*; 1978, Covent Garden, Roderigo, *Otello*; 1981: Berlioz Festival, Lyons, Bénédict, *Béatrice et Bénédict*; Grand Théâtre, Geneva, title role, *Albert Herring*; 1983, Teatro Massimo, Palermo, title role, *Idomeneo*; 1988, Paris Opera, Vanya, *Katya Kabanova*; Berne, title roles: 1988, *Peter Grimes*; 1989, *Parsifal*.

OPERATIC WORLD PREMIERES INCLUDE: 1981, Venice Biennale at La Fenice, Silenus, *Oberon* and Entheus, *The Lords' Masque*, double-bill by Niccolò Castiglioni; 1986, Frankfurt Opera, Simeon, *Stephen Climax* by Hans Zender; Paris Opera: 1988, Sosie, *La Celestine* by Maurice Ohana; 1989, Byezdomny, *Der Meister und Margarita* by York Höller.

CAREER IN THE UK INCLUDES: Since 1978: Almeida Festival, Kaufman, *Jakob Lenz* (1987, British première); Covent Garden: Rodolphe, *Guillaume Tell*; Agrippa, *The Fiery Angel*; English National Opera: Ramiro, *Cinderella*; Drum Major, *Wozzeck*; Glyndebourne Festival and Touring Opera: Jacquino, *Fidelio*; Fileno, *La Fedeltà Premiata*; Baron Lummer, *Intermezzo*; Opera North, Narraboth, *Salome*; Scottish Opera: Nadir, *Les Pêcheurs de Perles*; Idamante, *Idomeneo*; Flamand, *Capriccio*; Baron Lummer, *Intermezzo*; Florestan, *Fidelio*; title roles: L'Egisto, *Orion*.

RELATED PROFESSIONAL ACTIVITIES: Concert career with regular broadcasts and recital work in the UK and abroad.

RECORDINGS INCLUDE: Rameau: *Hippolyte et Aricie* (CBS), *Naïs*; Stravinsky, *Le Rossignol* (both ERAT); Weill, *The Seven Deadly Sins* (EMI).

VIDEOS INCLUDE: Beethoven, *Fidelio*; Monteverdi, *Il Ritorno d'Ulisse in Patria*; R. Strauss, *Intermezzo*; Verdi, *Macbeth* (all Glyndebourne Festival Opera).

AWARDS INCLUDE: 1972, John Christie Award.

ADDRESS: c/o Ingpen & Williams Ltd, 14 Kensington Court, London W8 5DN.

CANNAN PHYLLIS   Soprano

PERSONAL DETAILS: b. 22 August 1947, Paisley; m., two children.

EDUCATION/TRAINING: Royal Scottish Academy of Music, London Opera Centre.

PROFESSIONAL DEBUT: 1974, Opera For All, appeared in *Rigoletto*.

EARLY CAREER INCLUDED: 1974–1983, as mezzo-soprano: Camden Festival, Fatme, *Zemire and Azor*; Covent Garden (1980–1983, member): Spirit of Antonia's Mother, *Les Contes d'Hoffmann*; Lady in Waiting, *Macbeth*; Frederica, *Luisa Miller*; Fortune Teller, *Arabella*; Teresa, *La Sonnambula*; Mrs Cratchit, *A Christmas Carol* (1981, British première at Sadler's Wells Theatre); Magdalene, *Die Meistersinger von Nürnberg*; Susanna, *Khovanshchina*; Lola, *Cavalleria Rusticana*; Mercédès, *Carmen*; Glyndebourne Touring Opera: Clairon, *Capriccio*; Forester's Wife, *The Cunning Little Vixen*; University College Opera, title role, *Hérodiade*; since 1983, soprano.

MAJOR DEBUTS INCLUDE: 1977, Glyndebourne Festival Opera, Innkeeper's Wife, *The Cunning Little Vixen*; 1979: English National Opera, Mercédès, *Carmen*; Opera North, Flora, *La Traviata*; Welsh National Opera, Suzuki, *Madam Butterfly*; 1980, Covent Garden, Wellgunde, *Der Ring des Nibelungen*; 1983 (debut as soprano), Buxton Festival, Ottone, *Griselda* (first modern performance); 1985, Covent Garden at the Athens Festival, Hecuba, *King Priam*; 1986, Scottish Opera, Miss Jessel, *The Turn of the Screw*; 1987: Grand Théâtre, Geneva, Mother/Witch, *Hänsel und Gretel*; Hong Kong Arts Festival, Senta, *Der Fliegende Holländer*; 1990, Cologne Opera, Miss Jessel, *The Turn of the Screw*; 1992, Teatro La Fenice, Venice, Mrs Grose, *The Turn of the Screw*.

CAREER IN THE UK INCLUDES: Since 1984: Covent Garden: Margret, *Wozzeck*; Marianne, *Der Rosenkavalier*; Hecuba, *King Priam*; Gerhilde and Second Norn, *Der Ring des Nibelungen*; English National Opera: Foreign Princess, *Rusalka*; Goneril, *Lear* (1989, British première); Anna Maurrant, *Street Scene*; Fata Morgana, *The Love for Three Oranges*; Mother/Witch, *Hansel and Gretel*; title role, *Tosca*; Glyndebourne Touring Opera, Lady Billows, *Albert Herring*; Opera North, Santuzza, *Cavalleria Rusticana*; Welsh National Opera: Kostelnička, *Jenůfa*; Katerina, *The Greek Passion*.

RELATED PROFESSIONAL ACTIVITIES: Numerous concerts and recitals in the UK and abroad.

RECORDINGS INCLUDE: Verdi, *Il Trovatore* (PHIL).

VIDEOS INCLUDE: Dvořák, *Rusalka* (English National Opera); Offenbach, *Les Contes d'Hoffmann*; R. Strauss, *Der Rosenkavalier* (both Covent Garden).

ADDRESS: c/o Lies Askonas Ltd, 186 Drury Lane, London WC2B 5RY.

CAPRONI BRUNO   Baritone

POSITION: Principal Baritone, Darmstadt State Theatre.

PERSONAL DETAILS: b. Bangor, Northern Ireland.

EDUCATION/TRAINING: 1983–1988, Royal Northern College of Music, with Frederic Cox; 1988–1989, National Opera Studio; currently with Dennis Wicks.

PROFESSIONAL DEBUT: 1988, chorus member, Glyndebourne Festival Opera.

CAREER INCLUDES: Since 1989: Covent Garden (1989–1992, member): Yamadori, *Madama Butterfly* (debut); Marullo, *Rigoletto*; Herald, *Otello*; Nachtigall, *Die Meistersinger von Nürnberg*; Fiorello, *Il*

Barbiere di Siviglia; Kilian, *Der Freischütz*; Dancaïro, *Carmen*; Ping, *Turandot*; Second Philistine, *Samson et Dalila*; Schlemil, *Les Contes d'Hoffmann*; Méru and Count de Nevers, *Les Huguenots*; English Clerk, *Death in Venice*; Mathias, *The Fiery Angel*; Schaunard, *La Bohème*; Riccardo, *I Puritani*; Antonio, *Il Viaggio a Reims*; Masetto, *Don Giovanni*; since 1992, Principal Baritone, Darmstadt State Theatre: Anckarström, *Un Ballo in Maschera*; Rodrigo, *Don Carlos*; Marcello, *La Bohème*.

RELATED PROFESSIONAL ACTIVITIES: Concerts in the UK.

AWARDS INCLUDE: 1987, Frederic Cox Award, Royal Northern College of Music; 1988, Ricordi Opera Prize.

ADDRESS: c/o Harrison/Parrott Ltd, 12 Penzance Place, London W11 4PA.

CARNEGY PATRICK
Dramaturg

POSITION: Dramaturg, Royal Opera House, Covent Garden.

PERSONAL DETAILS: b. 23 September 1940, Leeds.

EDUCATION/TRAINING: 1960–1963, Trinity Hall, Cambridge.

CAREER: *The Times Educational Supplement*: 1964–1969, member, editorial staff; 1966–1988, Opera Critic; 1969–1978, Special Writer/Assistant Editor, *The Times Literary Supplement*; 1978–1988: Music Books Editor, Faber and Faber Ltd; Director, Faber Music Ltd; since 1988, Dramaturg, Royal Opera House, Covent Garden (new post).

OTHER PROFESSIONAL ACTIVITIES INCLUDE: Course Director: since 1968, Bayreuth International Youth Festival; since 1980, Britten-Pears School for Advanced Musical Studies; BBC: 1986–1989, member, Music Advisory Committee; since 1990, member, General Advisory Council; regular broadcasts for BBC Radios 3 and 4.

PUBLICATIONS INCLUDE: 1973, *Faust as Musician: A Study of Thomas Mann's Doctor Faustus* (Chatto & Windus); contributor: 1987, *The novella transformed: Thomas Mann as opera, in Benjamin Britten: Death in Venice*, editor Donald Mitchell (Cambridge University Press); 1992: *Designing Wagner: Deeds of Music Made Visible?, Wagner in Performance*, editors Barry Millington and Stewart Spencer (Yale University Press); *Allegory in opera since 1800, The New Grove Dictionary of Opera*, editor Stanley Sadie (Macmillan); articles and reviews for numerous journals.

ADDRESS: c/o Royal Opera House, Covent Garden, London WC2E 9DD.

CASKEN JOHN
Composer and Teacher

POSITION: Professor of Music, University of Manchester.

PERSONAL DETAILS: b. 15 July 1949, Barnsley.

EDUCATION/TRAINING: University of Birmingham, with John Joubert and Peter Dickinson; 1971–1972, with Andrzej Dobrowolski and Witold Lutoslawski in Warsaw.

FIRST WORK TO ACHIEVE PROMINENCE: 1972, Music for cello and piano.

CAREER: Numerous compositions in all genres including orchestral, instrumental, ensemble, vocal and choral works; 1973–1979, lecturer, University of Birmingham; 1980–1981, Fellow in Composition, Huddersfield Polytechnic; 1981–1992, lecturer, University of Durham; since 1991, first Composer in Association, Northern Sinfonia; since 1992, Professor of Music, University of Manchester; Featured Composer: 1980, Bath Festival; 1984, Musica Nova Festival, Glasgow; 1990, Music Today, Tokyo; 1986 and 1991, Huddersfield Contemporary Music Festival.

OPERATIC WORLD PREMIERES: 1989, Almeida Festival, *Golem*, chamber opera, libretto by the composer in collaboration

with Pierre Audi, conductor Richard
Bernas, director Pierre Audi, designer
Kyoji Takubo (1990, US première, Opera
Omaha, Nebraska).
RECORDINGS INCLUDE: *Golem* (VIRG),
Firewhirl, *String Quartet*, *la Orana*,
Gauguin (all WERG), *Clarion Sea* (MERL).
AWARDS INCLUDE: 1990, first Britten Award
for Composition.
ADDRESS: c/o Schott & Co. Ltd, 48 Great
Marlborough Street, London W1V 2BN.

CAULTON JEREMY
Administrator

POSITION: Director of Opera Planning,
English National Opera.
PERSONAL DETAILS: b. 24 November 1944,
Bombay, India; m. 1966, Celia Toynbee
(radio journalist), one child.
EDUCATION/TRAINING: 1964–1967, Christ
Church, Oxford, studied modern history.
CAREER: 1967–1968, violinist, The Royal
Ballet, Covent Garden; 1969–1972,
Assistant Director, Contemporary Music
Department, Schott & Co. Ltd; English
National Opera: 1972–1976, Personal
Assistant to Managing Director; 1976–
1979, Controller of Opera Planning; since
1979, Director of Opera Planning.
OTHER PROFESSIONAL ACTIVITIES INCLUDE:
1972–1984, General Manager, New Opera
Company.
ADDRESS: c/o English National Opera,
London Coliseum, St Martin's Lane,
London WC2N 4ES.

CHANCE MICHAEL
Counter-tenor

PERSONAL DETAILS: b. 7 March 1955,
Buckinghamshire; m. 1991.
PREVIOUS OCCUPATION: 1977–1980, Stock
Exchange dealer.
EDUCATION/TRAINING: 1974–1977, Choral
Scholar, King's College, Cambridge,
studied English; 1980–1990, privately with
Rupert Bruce-Lockhart.

PROFESSIONAL DEBUT: 1984, Buxton
Festival, Apollo, *Jason*.
MAJOR DEBUTS INCLUDE: 1985, Lyons
Opera, Andronico, *Tamerlano*; 1988,
Paris Opera, Tolomeo, *Giulio Cesare*;
1989: Glyndebourne Festival Opera,
Oberon, *A Midsummer Night's Dream*;
Glyndebourne Touring Opera, Voice of
Apollo, *Death in Venice*; 1990,
Netherlands Opera, Anfinomo/Human
Frailty, *Il Ritorno d'Ulisse in Patria*; 1991,
Teatro São Carlos, Lisbon, Goffredo,
Rinaldo; 1992: Covent Garden, Voice of
Apollo, *Death in Venice*; English National
Opera, Anfinomo, *The Return of Ulysses*;
Scottish Opera, title role, *Julius Caesar*.
OPERATIC WORLD PREMIERES INCLUDE:
1987, Kent Opera, Military Governor, *A
Night at the Chinese Opera* by Judith
Weir.
CAREER IN THE UK INCLUDES: Since 1985:
Cambridge University Opera, Orfeo,
Orfeo ed Euridice; English Bach Festival,
title role, *Teseo*; Glyndebourne Festival
Opera, Voice of Apollo, *Death in Venice*;
Kent Opera: Ottone, *Agrippina*; Ottone,
The Coronation of Poppea.
RELATED PROFESSIONAL ACTIVITIES:
Numerous concerts and recitals in the UK
and abroad.
RECORDINGS INCLUDE: Cavalli, *Giasone*
(HARM); Gluck, *Orfeo ed Euridice* (SONY);
Handel: *Agrippina* (PHIL), *Semele* (DG),
Tamerlano (ERAT); Monteverdi, *Orfeo* (DG);
Mozart, *Ascanio in Alba* (ADDA); Orff,
Carmina Burana (EMI); Purcell, *The Fairy
Queen* (COLL).
VIDEOS INCLUDE: Britten, *Death in Venice*
(Glyndebourne Tourng Opera).
ADDRESS: c/o Lies Askonas Ltd, 186 Drury
Lane, London WC2B 5RY.

CHITTY ALISON   Designer

PERSONAL DETAILS: b. 16 October 1948,
London.
EDUCATION/TRAINING: 1966–1967, St
Martin's School of Art; 1967–1970, Central
School of Art and Design.

47

PROFESSIONAL DEBUT: 1970, Victoria Theatre, Stoke-on-Trent, *Pinocchio*.

OPERATIC DEBUT: 1987, Royal National Theatre Studio with the Aquarius Ensemble, *Bow Down/Down by the Greenwood Side*.

CAREER: 1970–1979, Victoria Theatre, Stoke-on-Trent (1975–1979, Head of Design); since 1979, freelance opera, theatre and film designer including Royal National Theatre, Royal Shakespeare Company and West End; films include 1990, *Life is Sweet*.

MAJOR OPERATIC DEBUTS INCLUDE: 1987, Opera North, *The Marriage of Figaro*; 1990, Glyndebourne Festival Opera, *New Year*; 1992, Opera Theatre of St Louis, *The Vanishing Bridegroom*.

OPERATIC WORLD PREMIERES INCLUDE: 1989, Houston Grand Opera, *New Year* by Michael Tippett; 1991, Covent Garden, *Gawain* by Harrison Birtwistle.

RELATED PROFESSIONAL ACTIVITIES: Teacher: Central School of Art and Design, Slade School of Art, Wimbledon College of Art.

ADDRESS: c/o Curtis Brown Group Ltd, 162–168 Regent Street, London W1R 5TB.

CHRISTIE, SIR GEORGE
Administrator

POSITION: Chairman, Glyndebourne Productions Ltd.

PERSONAL DETAILS: b. 31 December 1934; m. 1958, Patricia Nicholson, four children.

EDUCATION/TRAINING: Eton College, Windsor.

CAREER: 1957–1962, assistant to Secretary of Gulbenkian Foundation; since 1959, Chairman, Glyndebourne Productions Ltd.

OTHER PROFESSIONAL ACTIVITIES INCLUDE: 1968–1988, founding Chairman, The London Sinfonietta; since 1988, Chairman, Music Advisory Panel, Arts Council of Great Britain.

HONOURS INCLUDE: 1984, Knighthood; 1986: Fellow, Royal College of Music; Honorary Member, Royal Northern College of Music; 1990, Honorary Doctorate, University of Sussex; 1991, Honorary Member, Guildhall School of Music and Drama.

ADDRESS: Glyndebourne, Lewes, East Sussex BN8 5UU

CHRISTIE NAN   Soprano

PERSONAL DETAILS: b. Irvine, Scotland; m. 1972, Andrew Hendrie (trumpeter), one child.

EDUCATION/TRAINING: Royal Scottish Academy of Music, with Winifred Busfield; London Opera Centre, with Vera Rozsa; currently with Charles Craig.

PROFESSIONAL DEBUT: 1969, Scottish Opera, Fiametta, *The Gondoliers*.

EARLY CAREER INCLUDED: 1969–1976: Principal Soprano, Scottish Opera: First Niece, *Peter Grimes*; Flora, *The Turn of the Screw*; Xenia, *Boris Godunov*; Papagena, *The Magic Flute*; Tytania, *A Midsummer Night's Dream*; Queen of Shemakha, *The Golden Cockerel*; Susanna, *The Marriage of Figaro*; Amor, *The Coronation of Poppea*; Lucia, *The Rape of Lucretia*; Blonde, *The Seraglio*; also: English Music Theatre: Pamina, *The Magic Flute*; title role, *Sandrina's Secret*; Opera Northern Ireland, Blonde, *The Seraglio*; Opera Rara, Orazia, *Gli Orazi ed i Curiazi*.

MAJOR DEBUTS INCLUDE: 1971, Covent Garden, Esquire, *Parsifal*; 1972, La Monnaie, Brussels, Lauretta, *Gianni Schicchi*; 1977, Glyndebourne Festival Opera, Isotta, *Die Schweigsame Frau*; 1978, Netherlands Opera, Despina, *Così fan tutte*; 1981, Frankfurt Opera (1981–1983, Principal Soprano), Marie, *Die Soldaten*; 1982: Opera North, Tytania, *A Midsummer Night's Dream*; Zurich Opera, Giunia, *Lucio Silla*; 1984, English National Opera, Queen of the Night, *The Magic Flute*; 1990, Earls Court Japan tour, Frasquita, *Carmen*; 1991, Teatro La Fenice, Venice, Arbate, *Mitridate, Rè di Ponto*.

OPERATIC WORLD PREMIERES INCLUDE: Scottish Opera: 1969, Juliette, *The Undertaker* by John Purser; 1974, Galla, *The Catiline Conspiracy* by Iain Hamilton; 1976, English Music Theatre at the Aldeburgh Festival, Sophie, *Tom Jones* by Stephen Oliver; 1993, English National Opera, Psychopomp, *Inquest of Love* by Jonathan Harvey.

CAREER IN THE UK INCLUDES: Since 1977: Buxton Festival, Sandrina, *La Buona Figliuola*; English National Opera: Zdenka, *Arabella*; Eurydice, *Orpheus in the Underworld*; Adele, *Die Fledermaus*; Countess Adele, *Count Ory*; Glyndebourne Festival Opera: Despina, *Così fan tutte*; Nightingale/Fire, *L'Enfant et les Sortilèges*; Scottish Opera: Nannetta, *Falstaff*; Zerbinetta, *Ariadne auf Naxos*; Queen of the Night, *The Magic Flute*; Despina, *Così fan tutte*; Birdie, *Regina* (1991, British première).

RELATED PROFESSIONAL ACTIVITIES: Numerous concerts, recitals, broadcasts and television appearances with leading conductors and orchestras in the UK and abroad.

RECORDINGS INCLUDE: Cimarosa, *Gli Orazi ed i Curiazi* (OPRA); Maw, *La Vita Nuova* (CHAN); A Hundred Years of Italian Opera (OPRA).

VIDEOS INCLUDE: Sullivan: *The Gondoliers*, *Princess Ida*, *The Sorcerer* (all Walker).

ADDRESS: c/o Lies Askonas Ltd, 186 Drury Lane, London WC2B 5RY.

CIESINSKI KRISTINE
Soprano

PERSONAL DETAILS: b. 5 July 1952, Delaware, USA; m. C. William Henry (violinist, d. 1984); m. 1985, Norman Bailey (baritone).

EDUCATION/TRAINING: Bachelor of Fine Arts, Boston University.

PROFESSIONAL DEBUT: 1976, Central City Opera, Denver, Countess, *Capriccio*.

EARLY CAREER INCLUDED: 1976–1985: Chesapeake Opera: Countess, *The Marriage of Figaro*; title role, *Madam Butterfly*; Cincinatti Opera, Eva, *Die Meistersinger von Nürnberg*; Cleveland Opera, title role, *Aida*; Kentucky Opera, Fiordiligi, *Così fan tutte*; Landestheater, Salzburg: Rosalinde, *Die Fledermaus*; Marguérite, *Faust*; title role, *Iphigénie en Tauride*; Milwaukee Opera, title role, *Salome*; Northern Virginia Opera, Pamina, *The Magic Flute*; Opera Delaware, title role, *Tosca*; Washington Opera, Second Lady, *The Magic Flute*.

MAJOR DEBUTS INCLUDE: 1985: Scottish Opera, Donna Anna, *Don Giovanni* (British debut); Bremen Opera, title role, *La Wally*; title role, *Salome*: 1986, Canadian Opera Company, Toronto; 1987, Mexico City; 1988, Zagreb National Theatre; 1989, Bavarian State Opera, Munich; 1990, Baltimore Opera; 1987, Freiburg, title role, *Médée*; 1989: English National Opera, Anna Maurrant, *Street Scene*; Teatro Massimo Bellini, Catania, title role, *Médée*; 1990, English National Opera Soviet Union tour (Bolshoi and Kirov), Lady Macbeth, *Macbeth*; 1992, title role, *Lady Macbeth of Mtsensk*: Opéra Bastille, Paris and La Scala, Milan.

CAREER IN THE UK INCLUDES: Since 1986: English National Opera: Marie, *Wozzeck*; Lady Macbeth, *Macbeth*; Foreign Princess, *Rusalka*; title role, *Salome*; Opera North: Cassandra, *The Trojans*; Senta, *The Flying Dutchman*; Scottish Opera, Anna Maurrant, *Street Scene*; Welsh National Opera: Cassandra, *The Trojans*; title role, *Tosca*.

RELATED PROFESSIONAL ACTIVITIES: Numerous concerts and recitals in the UK and abroad, frequently with her sister, Katherine Ciesinski (mezzo-soprano).

RECORDINGS INCLUDE: Weill, *Street Scene* (TER).

AWARDS INCLUDE: 1977: Geneva International Competition, Salzburg Annual Opera Competition; 1978, Metropolitan Opera Competition (New York).

ADDRESS: c/o Trawick Artists Management Inc., 129 West 72nd Street, New York, NY 10023, USA.

CLARK GRAHAM   Tenor

PERSONAL DETAILS: b. 10 November 1941, Lancashire; m. Joan Lawrence (soprano).

PREVIOUS OCCUPATIONS: 1964–1969, physical education teacher; 1971–1975, Senior Regional Officer, The Sports Council.

EDUCATION/TRAINING: 1961–1964, Loughborough College of Education; 1969–1970, University of Loughborough; privately with Bruce Boyce.

PROFESSIONAL DEBUT: 1975, Scottish Opera, Cassio, *Otello*.

EARLY CAREER INCLUDED: 1975–1978: Principal Tenor, Scottish Opera: Brighella, *Ariadne auf Naxos*; Malcolm, *Macbeth*; David, *Die Meistersinger von Nürnberg*; Jacquino, *Fidelio*; Ernesto, *Don Pasquale*; Pedrillo, *The Seraglio*; Italian Tenor, *Der Rosenkavalier*.

MAJOR DEBUTS INCLUDE: 1976: New Opera Company, title role, *Bomarzo* (British première); Vancouver Opera, Camille, *The Merry Widow*; 1978, English National Opera, Rinuccio, *Gianni Schicchi*; 1981, Bayreuth Festival, David, *Die Meistersinger von Nürnberg*; 1982, Welsh National Opera, Skuratov, *From the House of the Dead*; 1985, Metropolitan Opera, New York, Števa, *Jenůfa*; David, *Die Meistersinger von Nürnberg*: Munich Festival, Vienna State Opera, Zurich Opera; 1986: Welsh National Opera at Covent Garden, Loge, *The Ring of the Nibelung*; Netherlands Opera, David, *Die Meistersinger von Nürnberg*; 1988, Loge and Mine, *Der Ring des Nibelungen*: Bayreuth Festival and Théâtre des Champs Elysées, Paris; 1989, Canadian Opera Company, Toronto, Gregor, *The Makropoulos Case*; Metropolitan Opera, New York: 1989, Herod, *Salome*; 1990, Captain, *Wozzeck*; 1981: Opéra Bastille, Paris, Director, *Un Re in Ascolto*; Théâtre du Châtelet, Paris, Painter/Negro, *Lulu*; 1992: Lyric Opera, Chicago, Vašek, *The Bartered Bride*; Metropolitan Opera, New York, Captain Vere, *Billy Budd*.

OPERATIC WORLD PREMIERES INCLUDE: 1991, Metropolitan Opera, New York, Bégearss, *The Ghost of Versailles* by John Corigliano.

CAREER IN THE UK INCLUDES: Since 1978: English National Opera: Ramiro, *Cinderella*; Quint, *The Turn of the Screw*; Caramello, *A Night in Venice*; Camille, *The Merry Widow*; Count, *The Barber of Seville*; Matteo, *Arabella*; Italian Tenor, *Der Rosenkavalier*; Rodolfo, *La Bohème*; Grigory, *Boris Godunov*; Herman, *The Queen of Spades*; Alexei, *The Gambler*; David, *The Mastersingers of Nuremberg*; Gregor, *The Makropoulos Case*; Vašek, *The Bartered Bride*; Mephistopheles, *Doctor Faust* (1986, British stage première); Don Juan, *The Stone Guest* (1987, British stage première); title roles: *The Tales of Hoffman*, *Count Ory*, *The Adventures of Mr Brouček*; Scottish Opera: Skuratov, *From the House of the Dead*; Števa, *Jenůfa*.

RELATED PROFESSIONAL ACTIVITIES: Since 1987, masterclasses: Abbey Opera, National Opera School, Royal College of Music.

RECORDINGS INCLUDE: Mozart, *Le Nozze di Figaro* (ERAT); R. Strauss, *Der Rosenkavalier* (EMI); Wagner, *Der Fliegende Holländer* (PHIL).

VIDEOS INCLUDE: Wagner: *Der Fliegende Holländer*, *Die Meistersinger von Nürnberg*, *Der Ring des Nibelungen* (all Bayreuth Festival).

AWARDS INCLUDE: 1986, Olivier Award, English National Opera production of *Doctor Faust* (specially recommended with Thomas Allen).

ADDRESS: c/o Ingpen & Williams Ltd, 14 Kensington Court, London W8 5DN.

CLARKE ADRIAN   Baritone

PERSONAL DETAILS: b. Northampton.

EDUCATION/TRAINING: 1972–1976, Royal College of Music; 1976–1978, London Opera Centre.

PROFESSIONAL DEBUT: 1978, Opera North.

CAREER IN THE UK INCLUDES: Since 1978: Buxton Festival: Don Quixote, *Master Peter's Puppet Show*; title role, *Robin Hood*; New Sussex Opera, Nick Shadow, *The Rake's Progress*; Northern Stage, Maharal, *Golem*; Opera 80: Taddeo, *The Italian Girl in Algiers*; Escamillo, *Carmen*; Opera Factory, several roles, *The Martyrdom of St Magnus*; Opera North: Morales and Escamillo, *Carmen*; Theatre Director, *Les Mamelles de Tirésias*; Falke, *Die Fledermaus*; Spalanzani, *The Tales of Hoffmann*; Matt, *The Threepenny Opera*; Sid, *La Fanciulla del West*; Afron, *The Golden Cockerel*; Pish-Tush, *The Mikado*; Don Ferdinand, *The Duenna* (1992, British stage première); Scottish Opera, title role, *The Barber of Seville*; Scottish Opera Go Round: Rodrigo, *Don Carlos*; Silvio, *Pagliacci* and Alfio, *Cavalleria Rusticana*.

OPERATIC WORLD PREMIERES INCLUDE: 1989, Almeida Festival, Maharal, *Golem* by John Casken.

RELATED PROFESSIONAL ACTIVITIES: Regular concerts and recitals in the UK and Europe.

RECORDINGS INCLUDE: Casken, *Golem* (VIRG).

ADDRESS: c/o M & M Lyric Artists, 6 Princess Road, London NW1 7JJ.

CLEOBURY NICHOLAS
Conductor

POSITIONS: Artistic Director: Aquarius, Cambridge Festival, Cambridge Symphony Orchestra.

PERSONAL DETAILS: b. 23 June 1950, Kent; m. Heather Kay, two children.

EDUCATION/TRAINING: 1968–1971, Worcester College, Oxford.

PROFESSIONAL DEBUT: 1978, BBC Scottish Orchestra.

OPERATIC DEBUT: 1979, Glyndebourne Touring Opera, *Fidelio*.

CAREER: Assistant Organist: 1971–1972, Chichester Cathedral; 1972–1976, Christ Church, Oxford; 1977–1979, Chorus Master, Glyndebourne Festival Opera;

1977–1980, Assistant Director, BBC Singers; 1981–1987, Principal Conductor, Royal Academy of Music; 1989–1991, Principal Guest Conductor, Gavle Symphony Orchestra, Sweden; Artistic Director: since 1983, Aquarius; since 1990, Cambridge Symphony Orchestra; since 1992, Cambridge Festival.

MAJOR OPERATIC DEBUTS INCLUDE: 1979, English National Opera, *The Marriage of Figaro*; 1980, Wexford Festival, *Zaide*; 1981, Welsh National Opera, *The Marriage of Figaro*; 1983, Flanders Opera, Antwerp, *Les Contes d'Hoffmann*; 1985, Opera North, *A Village Romeo and Juliet*; 1990, Royal Opera, Stockholm, *Le Nozze di Figaro*.

OPERA PERFORMANCES IN THE UK INCLUDE: Since 1979: Aldeburgh Festival, *Punch and Judy*; Cambridge Festival, *Thérèse*; Park Lane Opera: *La Finta Semplice, La Finta Giardiniera*; Royal Academy of Music: *The Magic Flute, La Rondine, Albert Herring, Street Scene, Eugene Onegin, L'Incoronazione di Poppea, Orpheus in the Underworld, The Knot Garden, The Cunning Little Vixen, Le Nozze di Figaro, Dialogues des Carmélites, Triptych*; Welsh National Opera, *La Traviata*.

RELATED PROFESSIONAL ACTIVITIES: Numerous concerts, broadcasts and recordings with leading orchestras in the UK and abroad.

RECORDINGS INCLUDE: Maxwell Davies, film score suites: *The Boyfriend/The Devils* (COLL).

HONOURS INCLUDE: 1985, Honorary Member, Royal Academy of Music

ADDRESS: c/o Allied Artists, 42 Montpelier Square, London SW7 1JZ.

COE DENIS   Administrator

POSITION: Executive Chairman, British Youth Opera.

PERSONAL DETAILS: b. 5 June 1929, Northumberland; m. 1953, four children; m. 1979.

51

EDUCATION: 1950–1952, teacher training, Bede College, Durham; 1955–1960, London School of Economics.

CAREER: 1952–1959, music and history teacher; 1959–1961, deputy headmaster; 1961–1966, Senior Lecturer in Public Administration, Politics and Political Science, Manchester College of Commerce; 1966–1970, Labour Member of Parliament for Middleton and Prestwich (including: 1968–1970, member, Council of Europe and Western European Union; Parliamentary Private Secretary to Minister of Health); 1970–1974, Dean of Students, North East London Polytechnic; 1974–1982, Assistant Director, Middlesex Polytechnic; 1983–1989, Performing Arts Officer and subsequently Director, Cleveland Arts; since 1987, co-founder and Executive Chairman, British Youth Opera.

OTHER RELATED ACTIVITIES INCLUDE: 1969–1972, member, Archbishops' Commission on Church and State; 1972–1982, founder and Chairman, National Bureau for Handicapped Students; 1975–1979, member, Warnock Committee for Special Needs; National Youth Theatre: 1968–1992, Council member; since 1992, Vice-president.

HONOURS INCLUDE: 1992, Fellow, Royal Society of Arts.

ADDRESS: c/o British Youth Opera, South Bank University, 58 Clapham Common North Side, London SW4 9RZ.

COLEMAN-WRIGHT PETER
Baritone

PERSONAL DETAILS: b. 13 October 1958, Victoria, Australia; m. Cheryl Barker (soprano).

EDUCATION/TRAINING: Victorian College of Arts, Melbourne, with Joan Hammond.

PROFESSIONAL DEBUT: 1982, Opera 80, Guglielmo, *Così fan tutte*.

EARLY CAREER INCLUDED: 1983–1986, appearances with Dublin Grand Opera, Glyndebourne Touring Opera, Klagenfurt Opera, Opera Northern Ireland and Victoria State Opera, Melbourne; roles included: Zurga, *The Pearl Fishers*; Guglielmo, *Così fan tutte*; Demetrius, *A Midsummer Night's Dream*; Sid, *Albert Herring*; Wolfram, *Tannhäuser*; Eisenstein, *Die Fledermaus*; Masetto, *Don Giovanni*; Papageno, *Die Zauberflöte*.

MAJOR DEBUTS INCLUDE: 1987, Netherlands Opera, Soldier/Brother, *Doktor Faust*; 1988, English National Opera, title role, *The Barber of Seville*; 1990, Covent Garden, Dandini, *La Cenerentola*; 1991: Aix-en-Provence Festival, Theseus, *A Midsummer Night's Dream*; Grand Théâtre, Geneva, Ned Keene, *Peter Grimes*; Count, *Le Nozze di Figaro*: 1991, Teatro La Fenice, Venice; 1992, Australian Opera, Sydney.

OPERATIC WORLD PREMIERES INCLUDE: English National Opera: 1989, Colin Lovell, *The Plumber's Gift* by David Blake; 1993, John, *Inquest of Love* by Jonathan Harvey.

CAREER IN THE UK INCLUDES: Since 1987: Covent Garden: Don Alvaro, *Il Viaggio a Reims*; Papageno, *Die Zauberflöte*; English National Opera: Niels Lyhne, *Fennimore and Gerda*; title roles: *Billy Budd*, *Don Giovanni*; Glyndebourne Festival and Touring Opera, Morales, *Carmen*.

RELATED PROFESSIONAL ACTIVITIES: Numerous lieder recitals in the UK and abroad.

RECORDINGS INCLUDE: Stravinsky, *Oedipus Rex* (EMI).

AWARDS INCLUDE: 1984, Esso/ Glyndebourne Touring Opera Award; 1986, Shell Opera Aria Competition (Australia).

ADDRESS: c/o Lies Askonas Ltd, 186 Drury Lane, London WC2B 5RY.

COLLINS ANNE
Mezzo-soprano

PERSONAL DETAILS: b. 29 August 1943, Durham.
EDUCATION/TRAINING: Royal College of Music, with Oda Slobodskaya and Meriel St Clair.
PROFESSIONAL DEBUT: 1970, Sadler's Wells Opera, Governess, *The Queen of Spades*.
EARLY CAREER INCLUDED: 1970–1975, Principal Mezzo-soprano, Sadler's Wells Opera/English National Opera: Ragonde, *Count Ory*; Madame Akhrosimova, *War and Peace* (1972, British stage première); Suzuki, *Madam Butterfly*; Arnalta, *The Coronation of Poppea*; Mamma Lucia, *Cavalleria Rusticana*; Beroë, *The Bassarids* (1974, British stage première); Madame Arvidson, *A Masked Ball*; Erda, Rossweisse and Waltraute, *The Ring of the Nibelung*.
MAJOR DEBUTS INCLUDE: 1974, English Opera Group, Mrs Herring, *Albert Herring*; 1975, Covent Garden, Grimgerde, *Die Walküre*; 1976: Grand Théâtre, Bordeaux, Erda, *Siegfried*; Wexford Festival, Mrs Page, *The Merry Wives of Windsor*; 1977: Welsh National Opera, Sosostris, *The Midsummer Marriage*; Grand Théâtre, Geneva, First Norn, *Götterdämmerung*; 1986, Glyndebourne Festival Opera, Florence Pike, *Albert Herring*.
CAREER IN THE UK INCLUDES: Since 1976: Covent Garden: Anna, *The Trojans at Carthage*; Mother, *L'Enfant et les Sortilèges*; Mother Superior, *The Fiery Angel*; English National Opera: Zita, *Gianni Schicchi*; Lady Jane, *Patience* (also 1984, USA tour); Adelaide, *Arabella*; Mistress Quickly, *Falstaff*; Princess Clarissa, *The Love for Three Oranges*; Marcellina, *The Marriage of Figaro*; Mrs Sedley, *Peter Grimes*; Katisha, *The Mikado*; Lady Blanche, *Princess Ida*; Glyndebourne Festival Opera, Fortune, *L'Incoronazione di Poppea*; Handel Opera Society: Onoria, *Ezio*; Dejanira, *Hercules*; Opera North: Auntie, *Peter Grimes*; Nurse, *Ariane and Bluebeard*; Scottish Opera, Madame Larina, *Eugene Onegin*; Welsh National Opera: Erda, *The Ring of the Nibelung*; Madame Arvidson, *Un Ballo in Maschera*; Filipevna, *Eugene Onegin*.
RECORDINGS INCLUDE: Mozart, *Die Zauberflöte* (PHIL); Puccini, *Suor Angelica* (DECC); Wagner, *The Rhinegold, The Valkyrie, Siegfried, Twilight of the Gods* (all EMI).
VIDEOS INCLUDE: Sullivan: *The Gondoliers, Iolanthe, The Mikado, Patience, Princess Ida* (all Walker).
ADDRESS: c/o Lies Askonas Ltd, 186 Drury Lane, London WC2B 5RY.

COMBOY IAN Bass

PERSONAL DETAILS: b. 19 February 1941, Cheshire; m. 1968, Dianne Chidgey (violin teacher), three children.
PREVIOUS OCCUPATION: 1957–1962, research chemist.
EDUCATION/TRAINING: 1962–1966, Royal Northern College of Music, with Albert Haskayne and Ellis Keeler; 1966–1968, Vienna State Academy, with Wolfgang Steinbruck and Erik Werba; privately with Otakar Kraus.
PROFESSIONAL DEBUT: 1968, Glyndebourne Touring Opera, Second Priest, *Die Zauberflöte*.
EARLY CAREER INCLUDED: 1968–1970, Principal Bass, Sadler's Wells Opera: Nightwatchman, *The Mastersingers of Nuremberg*; Leporello, *Don Giovanni*; Speaker, *The Magic Flute*; Colline, *La Bohème*; Truffaldino, *Ariadne auf Naxos*.
MAJOR DEBUTS INCLUDE: 1969, Glyndebourne Festival Opera, Osmano, *L'Ormindo*; 1972: Covent Garden, Captain, *Taverner*; Scottish Opera, Theseus, *A Midsummer Night's Dream*; 1976, Wexford Festival, Mr Page, *The Merry Wives of Windsor*; 1978, Opera North, Bartolo, *The Marriage of Figaro*; 1981, Kent Opera, Prince Gremin, *Eugene Onegin*; 1982, Welsh National Opera, Doctor, *Wozzeck*; 1986, Rennes,

Sparafucile, *Rigoletto*; 1987, Lille Opera, Osmin, *Die Entführung aus dem Serail*.

OPERATIC WORLD PREMIERES INCLUDE: 1977: St Magnus Festival, Håkon, *The Martyrdom of St Magnus* by Peter Maxwell Davies; Scottish Opera at the Edinburgh Festival, Morton, *Mary, Queen of Scots* by Thea Musgrave; 1988, Berlin Kammeroper, Zeus, *Europa und der Stier* by Helge Jörns; 1990, Welsh National Opera, Captain, *Tornrak* by John Metcalf.

CAREER IN THE UK INCLUDES: Since 1971: Covent Garden, Flemish Deputy, *Don Carlos*; English National Opera: Nikitich, *Boris Godunov*; Russian Admiral, *Pacific Overtures*; title role, *The Mikado*; Handel Opera Society: Varo, *Ezio*; Ernando, *Scipione*; Polidarte, *Giustino*; New Opera Company, Black Will, *Arden Must Die* (1974, British première); University College Opera, Rarach, *The Devil's Wall* (1987, British première); Welsh National Opera: Cuno, *Der Freischütz*; Truffaldino, *Ariadne auf Naxos*; Governor, *From the House of the Dead*.

RECORDINGS INCLUDE: Sondheim, *Pacific Overtures* (TER); Handel, *Scipione* (French label).

VIDEOS INCLUDE: Verdi, *Don Carlos* (Covent Garden).

ADDRESS: c/o Music International, 13 Ardilaun Road, London N5 2QR.

CONNELL ELIZABETH
Soprano

PERSONAL DETAILS: b. 22 October 1946, Port Elizabeth, South Africa.

EDUCATION/TRAINING: University of Witwatersrand, Johannesburg; London Opera Centre, with Otakar Kraus.

PROFESSIONAL DEBUT: As mezzo-soprano: 1972, Wexford Festival, Varvara, *Katya Kabanova*.

EARLY CAREER INCLUDED: Principal Mezzo-soprano: 1973–1975, Australian Opera, Sydney: Venus, *Tannhäuser*; Maria, *War and Peace*; Rosina, *Il Barbiere di Siviglia*; Amneris, *Aida*; Kostelnička, *Jenůfa*; 1975–1980: English

National Opera: Eboli, *Don Carlos*; Maria, *War and Peace*; Herodias, *Salome*; Azucena, *Il Trovatore*; Kabanicha, *Katya Kabanova*; Eglantine, *Euryanthe*; Judith, *Duke Bluebeard's Castle*; Marina, *Boris Godunov*; title role, *The Italian Girl in Algiers*; also, Covent Garden: Frederica, *Luisa Miller*; Eboli, *Don Carlos*; 1980, began soprano repertoire, roles included: Covent Garden, Vitellia, *La Clemenza di Tito*; English National Opera: Sieglinde, *The Valkyrie*; Donna Elvira, *Don Giovanni*; Santuzza, *Cavalleria Rusticana*; since 1983, soprano.

MAJOR DEBUTS INCLUDE: 1976: Covent Garden, Viclinda, *I Lombardi*; Welsh National Opera, Kostelnička, *Jenůfa*; 1977: Australian Opera, Sydney, Lady Macbeth, *Macbeth*; Netherlands Opera, Eboli, *Don Carlos*; 1979, Teatro Regio, Turin, Geneviève, *Pelléas et Mélisande*; 1980: Opera Company of Boston, Amneris, *Aida*; Bayreuth Festival, Ortrud, *Lohengrin*; 1981: Holland Festival, Kundry, *Parsifal*; La Scala, Milan, Ortrud, *Lohengrin*; 1982: Bonn Opera, Marie, *Wozzeck*; Hamburg State Opera, Ortrud, *Lohengrin*; 1983: La Scala, Milan: Corine, *Anacréon*; Fiordiligi, *Così fan tutte*; Salzburg Festival, Elettra, *Idomeneo*; 1984: Grand Théâtre, Geneva, title role, *Norma*; Teatro San Carlo, Naples, Lady Macbeth, *Macbeth*; 1985: Glyndebourne Festival Opera, Elettra, *Idomeneo*; Bavarian State Opera, Munich, Lady Macbeth, *Macbeth*; Metropolitan Opera, New York, Vitellia, *La Clemenza di Tito*; 1986: Edinburgh International Festival, Reiza, *Oberon*; La Scala, Milan, Giselda, *I Lombardi*; 1987: Australian Opera, Sydney, title role, *Médée*; Opera Company of Philadelphia, Donna Anna, *Don Giovanni*; Paris Opera, Senta, *Der Fliegende Holländer*; Rome Opera, Lady Macbeth, *Macbeth*; 1988, San Francisco Opera, Leonore, *Fidelio*; 1990, Teatro Regio, Turin, Elisabeth de Valois, *Don Carlos*; 1991, San Francisco Opera, Odabella, *Attila*.

CAREER IN THE UK INCLUDES: Since 1983, Covent Garden: Fiordiligi, *Così fan tutte*; Leonora, *Il Trovatore*; Leonore, *Fidelio*; Lady Macbeth, *Macbeth*; Elettra, *Idomeneo*; Odabella, *Attila*.

RELATED PROFESSIONAL ACTIVITIES: Regular concerts, recitals, broadcasts and masterclasses in the UK and abroad.

RECORDINGS INCLUDE: Donizetti, *Poliuto* (NUOV); Rossini, *Guillaume Tell* (DECC); Schoenberg, *Gurrelieder* (DENO); Schubert, Complete Lieder, Vol. 5 (HYPE); Verdi, *I Due Foscari* (PHIL); Wagner, *Lohengrin* (SONY), *The Valkyrie* (EMI).

VIDEOS INCLUDE: Wagner, *Lohengrin* (Bayreuth Festival).

AWARDS INCLUDE: 1972, Maggie Teyte Prize.

ADDRESS: c/o Columbia Artists Management Inc., 165 West 57th Street, New York, NY 10019, USA.

CONNELL JOHN   Bass

PERSONAL DETAILS: b. 11 April 1956, Glasgow.

EDUCATION/TRAINING: Royal Northern College of Music, with Patrick McGuigan; National Opera Studio.

PROFESSIONAL DEBUT: 1984, Opera North, First Soldier, *Salome*.

EARLY CAREER INCLUDED: 1985–1988, Principal Bass, English National Opera: Monk, *Don Carlos*; Commendatore, *Don Giovanni*; Colline, *La Bohème*; Wagner/Gravis/Master of Ceremonies/Law Student, *Doctor Faust* (1986, British stage première); Ferrando, *Il Trovatore*; Angelotti, *Tosca*; Leporello, *The Stone Guest*; Old Convict, *Lady Macbeth of Mtsensk* (both 1987, British stage premières); First Nazarene, *Salome*; Don Basilio, *The Barber of Seville*; Dansker, *Billy Budd*; Chub, *Christmas Eve* (1988, British stage première); Sarastro, *The Magic Flute*; Pogner, *The Mastersingers of Nuremberg*.

MAJOR DEBUTS INCLUDE: 1985, English National Opera, Ramfis, *Aida*; 1988, Covent Garden, Titurel, *Parsifal*; 1990,

English National Opera Soviet Union tour (Bolshoi and Kirov), Banquo, *Macbeth*; 1992, Welsh National Opera, Sarastro, *The Magic Flute*.

CAREER IN THE UK INCLUDES: Since 1989: Covent Garden: Monk, *Don Carlos*; Sparafucile, *Rigoletto*; English National Opera: Banquo, *Macbeth*; Arkel, *Pelléas and Mélisande*; Swallow, *Peter Grimes*; Padre Guardiano, *The Force of Destiny*; Opera North: Don Basilio, *The Barber of Seville*; Colline, *La Bohème*; Welsh National Opera, Da Silva, *Ernani*.

RELATED PROFESSIONAL ACTIVITIES: Concerts and broadcasts in the UK and Spain.

RECORDINGS INCLUDE: Mendelssohn, *Elijah* (PHIL); Vaughan Williams, *Serenade to Music* (HYPE).

VIDEOS INCLUDE: Britten, *Billy Budd* (English National Opera).

ADDRESS: c/o John Coast, 31 Sinclair Road, London W14 0NS.

COPLEY JOHN   Director

PERSONAL DETAILS: b. 12 June 1933, Birmingham.

EDUCATION/TRAINING: Sadler's Wells Ballet School; Central School of Arts and Crafts, studied theatre design.

PROFESSIONAL DEBUT: As actor: 1950, Covent Garden, Apprentice, *Peter Grimes*.

OPERATIC DEBUT: 1965, Covent Garden, *Suor Angelica*.

CAREER: 1953–1959, stage manager, Sadler's Wells Theatre and West End; Covent Garden: 1960–1963, Deputy Stage Manager; 1963–1966, Assistant Resident Director; 1966–1972, Associate Resident Director; 1972–1975, Resident Director; 1975–1988, Principal Resident Director; since 1988, freelance.

MAJOR OPERATIC DEBUTS INCLUDE: 1967, Welsh National Opera, *La Bohème*; 1968, Wexford Festival, *La Clemenza di Tito*; 1970: Sadler's Wells Opera, *Carmen*; Australian Opera, Sydney, *Fidelio*; *Lucia di Lammermoor*. 1970, Netherlands

Opera; 1972, Dallas Civic Opera; 1974, Scottish Opera; 1975, Lyric Opera, Chicago; 1976, National Opera of Greece, Athens, *Madama Butterfly*; 1977, New York City Opera, *Le Nozze di Figaro*; 1978, Opera North, *Les Mamelles de Tirésias*; 1982, San Francisco Opera, *Giulio Cesare*; 1984: Bavarian State Opera, Munich, *Adriana Lecouvreur*; Victoria State Opera, Melbourne, *Don Carlos*; 1985, San Diego Opera, *Eugene Onegin*; 1987, Santa Fe Opera, *Ariodante*; 1988: Deutsche Oper, Berlin, *L'Elisir d'Amore*; Metropolitan Opera, New York, *Giulio Cesare*; 1989, Los Angeles Music Center Opera, *Tancredi*.

OPERA PRODUCTIONS IN THE UK INCLUDE: Since 1966: Covent Garden: *Così fan tutte*, *Orfeo ed Euridice*, *Le Nozze di Figaro*, *Don Giovanni*, *La Bohème*, *Faust*, *L'Elisir d'Amore*, *Benvenuto Cellini*, *Ariadne auf Naxos*, *Maria Stuarda*, *Werther*, *La Traviata*, *Lucrezia Borgia*, *Alceste*, *Semele*, *Norma*, *Alcina*; Opera North, *Madama Butterfly*; Sadler's Wells Opera/ English National Opera: *Carmen*, *The Seraglio*, *Il Trovatore*, *La Traviata*, *Mary Stuart*, *Der Rosenkavalier*, *La Belle Hélène*, *Werther*, *Manon*, *Aida*, *Julius Caesar*; Scottish Opera: *Un Ballo in Maschera*, *Dido and Aeneas*; Welsh National Opera: *La Traviata*, *Falstaff*, *Peter Grimes*, *Tosca*.

VIDEOS INCLUDE: Donizetti, *Mary Stuart* (English National Opera); Puccini, *La Bohème* (Covent Garden).

ADDRESS: c/o Harrison/Parrott Ltd, 12 Penzance Place, London W11 4PA.

COX JOHN   Director

POSITION: Production Director, The Royal Opera, Covent Garden.

PERSONAL DETAILS: b. 12 March 1935, Bristol.

EDUCATION/TRAINING: St Edmund Hall, Oxford, studied English.

PROFESSIONAL DEBUT: 1961, Theatre Royal, York, *Roots* by Arnold Wesker.

OPERATIC DEBUT: 1965, Sadler's Wells Opera, *L'Enfant et les Sortilèges*.

CAREER: Since 1961, opera and theatre director in the UK and abroad; Glyndebourne Festival Opera: 1959–1961, Assistant Director; 1962–1969, Guest Associate Director; 1971–1981, Director of Productions; 1963–1965, director, BBC Television; Scottish Opera: 1981–1985, General Administrator; 1985–1986, Artistic Director; since 1988, Production Director, Covent Garden.

MAJOR OPERATIC DEBUTS INCLUDE: 1970, Glyndebourne Festival Opera, *Il Turco in Italia*; 1979, San Francisco Opera, *Arabella*; 1980, La Scala, Milan, *The Rake's Progress*; 1982, Metropolitan Opera, New York, *Il Barbiere di Siviglia*; 1986, Bavarian State Opera, Munich, *Daphne*; 1989: Landestheater, Salzburg, *Il Rè Pastore*; Maggio Musicale, Florence, *Idomeneo*; 1990, Covent Garden, *Guillaume Tell*; 1990/1991, San Francisco Opera/Covent Garden co-production, *Capriccio*; 1992/1993, Covent Garden/Los Angeles Music Center Opera co-production, *Die Frau ohne Schatten*.

OPERATIC WORLD PREMIERES INCLUDE: 1969: Music Theatre Ensemble at the Brighton Festival, *Down by the Greenwood Side* by Harrison Birtwistle; Music Theatre Ensemble at the Edinburgh International Festival, *Pharsalia* by Iain Hamilton; Sadler's Wells Opera, *Lucky Peter's Journey* by Malcolm Williamson; 1971, Music Theatre Ensemble at the Brighton Festival, *Triptych* by Alexander Goehr.

OPERA PRODUCTIONS IN THE UK INCLUDE: Since 1971: Covent Garden, *Il Viaggio a Reims*; English National Opera: *Così fan tutte*, *Patience*; Glyndebourne Festival and Touring Opera: *Ariadne auf Naxos*, *Die Entführung aus dem Serail*, *The Visit of the Old Lady* (1973, British première), *Capriccio*, *Idomeneo*, *Intermezzo*, *The Rake's Progress*, *Der Freischütz*, *Die Schweigsame Frau*, *Die Zauberflöte*, *La Bohème*, *La Fedeltà Premiata*, *Der Rosenkavalier*, *Il Barbiere di Siviglia*, *La Cenerentola*; Scottish Opera: *L'Egisto*,

Manon Lescaut, The Marriage of Figaro, Lulu.
VIDEOS INCLUDE: Mozart: *Idomeneo, Die Zauberflöte*; Rossini: *Il Barbiere di Siviglia, La Cenerentola*; R. Strauss: *Arabella, Intermezzo*; Stravinsky, *The Rake's Progress* (all Glyndebourne Festival Opera).
AWARDS AND HONOURS INCLUDE: 1974, *Evening Standard* Award, Glyndebourne Festival Opera production of *Intermezzo*; 1980, Society of West End Theatre Award, English National Opera production of *Così fan tutte*; 1991, Honorary Fellow, St Edmund Hall, Oxford.
ADDRESS: c/o Royal Opera House, Covent Garden, London WC2E 9DD.

CRAIG RUSSELL   Designer

PERSONAL DETAILS: b. 23 March 1948, Whangerei, New Zealand.
EDUCATION/TRAINING: University of Auckland, studied fine arts.
PROFESSIONAL DEBUT: 1969, Mercury Theatre, Auckland, *The Narrow Road to the Deep North* by Edward Bond.
OPERATIC DEBUT: 1975, University College Opera, *The Snow Maiden.*
CAREER: Freelance opera and theatre designer in the UK and abroad.
MAJOR OPERATIC DEBUTS INCLUDE: 1978, Scottish Opera, *The Elixir of Love*; 1981, Wexford Festival, *I Gioielli della Madonna*; 1983: English National Opera, *The Rape of Lucretia*; Opera North, *Così fan tutte*; 1985: Bonn Opera, *Don Pasquale*; Gelsenkirchen, *Die Entführung aus dem Serail*; 1986, Vancouver Opera/Welsh National Opera/Opera North co-production, *The Barber of Seville*; 1987: Grand Théâtre, Geneva, *Hänsel und Gretel*; Minnesota Opera, *Ariadne auf Naxos*; Teatro La Fenice, Venice, *Oberon*; 1988, Hesse State Opera, Wiesbaden, *Lohengrin*; 1989: La Monnaie, Brussels, *L'Elisir d'Amore*; Netherlands Opera, *Ariadne auf Naxos.*

OPERATIC WORLD PREMIERES INCLUDE: 1978, Scottish Opera Go Round, *Peace* by Carl Davis; 1984, Batignano Festival, *La Bella e la Bestia* by Stephen Oliver; 1985, Scottish Opera, *Hedda Gabler* by Edward Harper.
OPERA DESIGNS IN THE UK INCLUDE: Since 1976: City of Birmingham Touring Opera, *Peace*; D'Oyly Carte Opera: *Trial by Jury, HMS Pinafore*; English National Opera, *Ariadne auf Naxos*; Glyndebourne Touring Opera, *La Bohème*; Opera North: *Così fan tutte, The Magic Flute, A Village Romeo and Juliet, The Barber of Seville, Acis and Galatea, Boris Godunov*; Scottish Opera: *Sāvitri/Fanny Robin, The Silken Ladder/The Marriage Contract, Oberon*; Welsh National Opera: *The Seraglio, Ariadne auf Naxos, Count Ory*; Opera North/Royal Shakespeare Company co-production, *Show Boat.*
RELATED PROFESSIONAL ACTIVITIES: Teacher, Trent Polytechnic.
VIDEOS INCLUDE: Britten, *The Rape of Lucretia* (English National Opera).
ADDRESS: c/o Performing Arts, 6 Windmill Street, London W1P 1HF.

CROOK PAUL   Tenor

PERSONAL DETAILS: b. 17 April 1936, Blackburn; m. Maria Cleva (Italian language coach), three children.
PREVIOUS OCCUPATION: 1951–1961, coal miner.
EDUCATION/TRAINING: 1964–1968, privately with E. Herbert Caesari; 1969–1972, Centre Lyrique, Geneva, with Herbert Graf and Lotfi Mansouri.
PROFESSIONAL DEBUT AS A PRINCIPAL: 1969, Grand Théâtre, Geneva, Spoletta, *Tosca.*
EARLY CAREER INCLUDED: 1961–1969, chorus member, Sadler's Wells Opera.
MAJOR DEBUTS INCLUDE: 1971, Teatro San Carlo, Naples, Mime, *Das Rheingold*; 1972: Sadler's Wells Opera, Spalanzani, *The Tales of Hoffmann*; La Monnaie, Brussels, Simpleton, *Boris Godunov*; Teatro Massimo, Palermo, Valzacchi, *Der*

Rosenkavalier; 1975, Covent Garden,
Hunchback Brother, *Die Frau ohne
Schatten*; 1976, San Francisco Opera,
Bob Boles, *Peter Grimes*; Mime, *Der Ring
des Nibelungen*: 1974, Seattle Opera;
1976, Covent Garden; 1986, Deutsche
Oper, Berlin; 1987, Metropolitan Opera,
New York; 1989, Teatr Wielki, Warsaw;
Herod, *Salome*: 1977, Covent Garden;
1988, New Orleans Opera; 1990, Santiago.
CAREER IN THE UK INCLUDES: Since 1972:
Sadler's Wells Opera/English National
Opera (1972–1975, Principal Tenor):
Alfred, *Die Fledermaus*; Vanya, *Katya
Kabanova*; Narraboth, *Salome*; Pedrillo;
The Seraglio; Covent Garden (1975–1990,
member): Spoletta, *Tosca*; Don Basilio,
Le Nozze di Figaro; Shepherd, *Tristan
und Isolde*; Bardolph, *Falstaff*; Harry, *La
Fanciulla del West*; Eisslinger, *Die
Meistersinger von Nürnberg*; Scribe,
Khovanshchina; Notary, *Don Pasquale*;
Normanno, *Lucia di Lammermoor*;
Altoum, *Turandot*; Monostatos, *Die
Zauberflöte*; Andrès/Cochenille, *Les
Contes d'Hoffmann*; Bois-Rosé, *Les
Huguenots*; Hotel Porter, *Death in Venice*.
RECORDINGS INCLUDE: Bellini, *Norma*;
Cilea, *Adriana Lecouvreur*; Massenet:
Cendrillon (all CBS), *Werther* (PHIL);
Offenbach, *Les Contes d'Hoffmann* (DG);
Puccini: *La Bohème* (CBS), *La Fanciulla
del West* (DG); Verdi, *Otello* (RCA).
VIDEOS INCLUDE: Offenbach, *Les Contes
d'Hoffmann*; Puccini, *La Fanciulla del
West*; R. Strauss, *Der Rosenkavalier* (all
Covent Garden).
ADDRESS: Not available.

CROWLEY BOB   Designer

POSITION: Associate Designer, Royal
National Theatre and Royal Shakespeare
Company.
PERSONAL DETAILS: b. 10 February 1952,
Cork.
EDUCATION/TRAINING: Presentation
Brothers, Cork.
OPERATIC DEBUT: 1982, Kent Opera, *Don
Giovanni*.

CAREER: Since 1977, freelance opera and
theatre designer with leading companies
in the UK and abroad including Bristol
Old Vic, Royal Court Theatre and Royal
Exchange, Manchester; Associate
Designer: since 1981, Royal Shakespeare
Company; since 1983, Royal National
Theatre.
MAJOR OPERATIC DEBUTS INCLUDE: 1986,
Los Angeles Music Center Opera, *Alcina*;
1987, Covent Garden, *The King Goes
Forth to France* (British première); 1988,
English National Opera/Netherlands
Opera co-production, *The Magic Flute*;
1993: Welsh National Opera/Opera North/
Lyric Opera of Queensland co-production,
Eugene Onegin; Bavarian State Opera,
Munich, *Don Giovanni*.
OPERA DESIGNS IN THE UK INCLUDE: Since
1985: Covent Garden, *The Knot Garden*;
Spitalfields Festival, *Alcina*.
ADDRESS: c/o Simpson Fox Associates Ltd,
52 Shaftesbury Avenue, London W1V 7DE.

CULLIS RITA   Soprano

PERSONAL DETAILS: b. 25 September 1949,
Cheshire.
EDUCATION/TRAINING: Royal Manchester
College of Music.
PROFESSIONAL DEBUT: 1973, chorus
member, Welsh National Opera.
EARLY CAREER INCLUDED: 1973–1976,
Welsh National Opera: Second Boy, *The
Magic Flute*; Voice from Heaven, *Don
Carlos*; Musician, *Manon Lescaut*;
Barena, *Jenůfa*; Miss Wordsworth, *Albert
Herring*; Inez, *Il Trovatore*; Xenia, *Boris
Godunov*.
MAJOR DEBUTS INCLUDE: 1977, Welsh
National Opera, Leïla, *The Pearl Fishers*;
1979, Scottish Opera, Tytania, *A
Midsummer Night's Dream*; 1981, Buxton
Festival, Elisetta, *Il Matrimonio Segreto*;
1984, Glyndebourne Touring Opera,
Countess, *Le Nozze di Figaro*; 1985,
Opera North, Jenifer, *The Midsummer*

Marriage; 1986, New Israeli Opera, Tel Aviv, Countess, *Le Nozze di Figaro*; 1987, English National Opera, Donna Anna, *Don Giovanni*; 1989, Netherlands Opera, title role, *Ariadne auf Naxos*; 1991: Canadian Opera Company, Toronto, Countess, *Le Nozze di Figaro*; Vitoria, Sieglinde, *Die Walküre*; 1992, San Diego Opera, Countess, *Le Nozze di Figaro*; 1993, Covent Garden, Fox, *The Cunning Little Vixen*.

CAREER IN THE UK INCLUDES: Since 1976: Buxton Festival, La Marchesa, *La Buona Figliuola*; English National Opera: Fox, *The Cunning Little Vixen*; Composer, *Ariadne auf Naxos*; Fiordiligi, *Così fan tutte*; Musetta, *La Bohème*; Glyndebourne Touring Opera, title role, *Katya Kabonova*; Opera North, Christine, *Intermezzo*; Opera Northern Ireland, title role, *Ariadne auf Naxos*; Scottish Opera: Leïla, *The Pearl Fishers*; Fox, *The Cunning Little Vixen*; Welsh National Opera (1976–1984, Principal Soprano): Tytania, *A Midsummer Night's Dream*; Musetta, *La Bohème*; Governess, *The Turn of the Screw*; Liù, *Turandot*; Virtue, *The Coronation of Poppea*; Tatyana, *Eugene Onegin*; Countess, *The Marriage of Figaro*; Lenio, *The Greek Passion* (1981, British première); Gilda, *Rigoletto*; Marzelline, *Fidelio*; Pamina, *The Magic Flute*; Donna Anna, *Don Giovanni*; Ellen Orford, *Peter Grimes*; Fox, *The Cunning Little Vixen*; Agathe, *Der Freischütz*; Marschallin, *Der Rosenkavalier*.

RELATED PROFESSIONAL ACTIVITIES: Numerous concerts and recitals in the UK.

RECORDINGS INCLUDE: Martinů, *The Greek Passion* (SUPR); Tippett, *The Midsummer Marriage* (NIMB); Wagner, *Parsifal* (EMI).

ADDRESS: c/o Kaye Artists Management Ltd, Barratt House, 7 Chertsey Road, Woking, Surrey GU21 5AB.

CURTIS MARK   Tenor

PERSONAL DETAILS: b. Hertfordshire.

EDUCATION/TRAINING: 1976–1980, Royal Northern College of Music, with Frederic Cox; 1980–1981, National Opera Studio.

PROFESSIONAL DEBUT: 1980, Glyndebourne Festival Opera, First Armed Man, *Die Zauberflöte*.

MAJOR DEBUTS INCLUDE: 1981, Covent Garden, Coryphée, *Alceste*; 1982, Opera North, Steersman, *Der Fliegende Holländer*; 1983, Scottish Opera, First Armed Man, *The Magic Flute*; 1988, Singapore Festival of Arts, Don Ottavio, *Don Giovanni*; 1989, Buxton Festival, Broccardo, *Il Pittor Parigino*.

OPERATIC WORLD PREMIERES INCLUDE: 1986, English National Opera (debut), Priest, *The Mask of Orpheus* by Harrison Birtwistle; 1991, Opera North, Dottore, *The Jewel Box* by Mozart/Paul Griffiths.

CAREER IN THE UK INCLUDES: Since 1981: Covent Garden: Lamplighter, *Manon Lescaut*; Gaston, *La Traviata*; English National Opera: First Armed Man, *The Magic Flute*; Don Ottavio, *Don Giovanni*; Hilarion, *Princess Ida*; Glyndebourne Touring Opera: Fenton, *Falstaff*; Jacquino, *Fidelio*; Kent Opera: Jacquino, *Fidelio*; Don Ottavio, *Don Giovanni*; Young Guard, *King Priam*; Monostatos, *The Magic Flute*; Opera North: Vašek, *The Bartered Bride*; Stroh, *Intermezzo*; Don Basilio, *The Marriage of Figaro*; Simpleton, *Boris Godunov*; Reverend Adams, *Peter Grimes*; Arv, *Masquerade* (1990, British première); Hermes, *King Priam*; Don Ottavio, *Don Giovanni*; Tapioca, *L'Etoile*; Goro, *Madama Butterfly*; Nexus Opera, Madwoman, *Curlew River*; Scottish Opera: Hylas, *The Trojans* (also 1990, at Covent Garden); Nadir, *The Pearl Fishers*.

RELATED PROFESSIONAL ACTIVITIES: Concerts and broadcasts in the UK and abroad.

RECORDINGS INCLUDE: Puccini, *Madama Butterfly* (DG); Tippett, *The Midsummer Marriage* (NIMB); Verdi, *La Forza del Destino* (DG).

VIDEOS INCLUDE: Puccini, *Manon Lescaut* (Covent Garden); Tippett, *King Priam* (Kent Opera).

AWARDS INCLUDE: 1981, Leverhulme Award, Glyndebourne.

ADDRESS: c/o Music International, 13 Ardilaun Road, London N5 2QR.

* * * *

DALE LAURENCE   Tenor

PERSONAL DETAILS: b. 10 September 1957, Sussex.

EDUCATION/TRAINING: 1976–1980, Guildhall School of Music and Drama, with Rudolf Piernay; 1980, Salzburg Mozarteum, with Richard Miller; further studies with Peter Pears, Ernst Hufliger and Seth Riggs.

PROFESSIONAL DEBUT: 1981, English National Opera, Camille, *The Merry Widow*.

MAJOR DEBUTS INCLUDE: 1981, Bouffes du Nord, Paris, Don José, *La Tragédie de Carmen*; 1983: English National Opera, title role, *Orfeo*; Glyndebourne Festival Opera, Don Ramiro, *La Cenerentola*; Basle, Roméo, *Roméo et Juliette*; 1984: Covent Garden, Pong, *Turandot* (also at the Olympic Arts Festival, Los Angeles); Opera North, Jeník, *The Bartered Bride*; Welsh National Opera, Don Ottavio, *Don Giovanni*; Netherlands Opera, Ferrando, *Così fan tutte*; 1987: La Monnaie, Brussels, Fenton, *Falstaff*; Paris Opera, Pluto, *Orphée aux Enfers*; 1990, Zurich Opera, Roméo, *Roméo et Juliette*; 1991, Stuttgart State Opera, Pylade, *Iphigénie en Tauride*; Tamino, *Die Zauberflöte*; 1989, Canadian Opera Company, Toronto; 1990, Vienna State Opera; 1991, Salzburg Mozart Week.

CAREER IN THE UK INCLUDES: Since 1981: Covent Garden: Nobleman, *Lohengrin*; Young Sailor, *Tristan und Isolde*; Jacquino, *Fidelio*; Steersman, *Der Fliegende Holländer*; English National Opera: Shepherd, *Orfeo*; Telemaco, *The Return of Ulysses*; Opera North: Tamino,

The Magic Flute; Belmonte, *The Seraglio*; Welsh National Opera: Ferrando, *Così fan tutte*; Eisenstein, *Die Fledermaus*; Lensky, *Eugene Onegin*; Alfredo, *La Traviata*; Fenton, *Falstaff*.

RELATED PROFESSIONAL ACTIVITIES: Concerts, recitals and television appearances in the UK and abroad; research and revival of early 19th century French operatic repertoire including first modern performances of *Gustave III* and *Joseph*.

RECORDINGS INCLUDE: Gounod, *St Cecilia Mass* (EMI); Rossini, *Maometto II* (PHIL); Méhul, *Joseph*; French Operatic Recital (both CHNT).

VIDEOS INCLUDE: Rossini, *La Cenerentola* (Glyndebourne Festival Opera); Sullivan, *Princess Ida* (Walker).

AWARDS AND HONOURS INCLUDE: 1980, Salzburg Mozarteum Prize; 1982, Medal of the City of Paris.

ADDRESS: c/o Musicaglotz, 11 Rue le Verrier, 75006 Paris, France.

DANIEL PAUL   Conductor

POSITION: Music Director, Opera North.

PERSONAL DETAILS: b. 5 July 1958, Birmingham; m. 1988, Joan Rodgers (soprano), one child.

EDUCATION/TRAINING: 1976–1979, King's College, Cambridge; 1979–1980, Guildhall School of Music and Drama.

PROFESSIONAL AND OPERATIC DEBUT: 1982, Opera Factory, *The Beggar's Opera*.

CAREER: English National Opera: 1980–1985, member, music staff; 1985–1987, staff conductor; Opera Factory: 1982–1987, Associate Conductor; 1987–1990, Music Director; since 1990, Music Director, Opera North.

MAJOR OPERATIC DEBUTS INCLUDE: 1985, English National Opera, *Fidelio*; 1988, Nancy Opera, *King Priam*; 1990, Opera North, *Jérusalem* (British stage première).

OPERA PERFORMANCES IN THE UK INCLUDE: Since 1980: English National Opera: *Akhnaten* (1985, British première), *Don Giovanni*, *La Bohème*, *The Mask of Orpheus*, *Carmen*, *Rigoletto*, *Orpheus in the Underworld*, *Tosca*, *The Stone Guest* (1987, British stage première), *Lear* (1989, British première), *The Return of Ulysses*, *The Marriage of Figaro*; Opera Factory: *Punch and Judy*, *La Calisto*, *Così fan tutte*, *Eight Songs for a Mad King*, *Aventures et Nouvelles Aventures*, *The Ghost Sonata* (1989, British première), *Don Giovanni*; Opera North: *Ariane and Bluebeard*, *Attila*, *King Priam*, *Don Giovanni*, *Der Ferne Klang* (1992, British première), *Boris Godunov*, *Rigoletto*, *Don Carlos*, *Wozzeck*.

RELATED PROFESSIONAL ACTIVITIES: Regular concerts with leading orchestras in the UK and abroad; Opera Factory productions conducted for Channel Four Television include: *Così fan tutte*, *Don Giovanni*; translations: with Joan Rodgers, *The Stone Guest* (English National Opera); *Der Ferne Klang* (Opera North).

ADDRESS: c/o Harrison/Parrott Ltd, 12 Penzance Place, London W11 4PA.

DAVIES ARTHUR   Tenor

PERSONAL DETAILS: b. Wrexham; m., two children.

EDUCATION/TRAINING: Royal Northern College of Music.

PROFESSIONAL DEBUT: 1972, Welsh National Opera, Squeak, *Billy Budd*.

EARLY CAREER INCLUDED: 1973–1985, Principal Tenor, Welsh National Opera: Arbace, *Idomeneo*; Nemorino, *L'Elisir d'Amore*; Count, *The Barber of Seville*; Ferrando, *Così fan tutte*; Nadir, *The Pearl Fishers*; Jack, *The Midsummer Marriage*; Števa, *Jenůfa*; Lysander, *A Midsummer Night's Dream*; Janek, *The Makropoulos Case*; Peter Quint and Prologue, *The Turn of the Screw*; Nero, *The Coronation of Poppea*; Lensky, *Eugene Onegin*; Fox, *The Cunning Little Vixen*; Yannakos, *The Greek Passion* (1981, British première); Bob Boles, *Peter Grimes*; Jeník, *The Bartered Bride*; Rodolfo, *La Bohème*; Don José, *Carmen*; Pinkerton, *Madam Butterfly*; title roles: *Albert Herring*, *Orpheus in the Underworld*.

MAJOR DEBUTS INCLUDE: 1980, Scottish Opera, Fox, *The Cunning Little Vixen*; 1981: English National Opera, Pedrillo, *The Seraglio*; Opera North, Jeník, *The Bartered Bride*; 1982: English National Opera, Duke, *Rigoletto*; Ludwigsburg, title role, *La Clemenza di Tito*; 1984, English National Opera USA tour (including Metropolitan Opera, New York): Anatol, *War and Peace*; Duke, *Rigoletto*; 1985, Cincinnati Opera, Don José, *Carmen*; 1986, Santiago Opera, Duke, *Rigoletto*.

OPERATIC WORLD PREMIÈRES INCLUDE: 1976, Covent Garden (debut), Gentleman 1/Victim 8, *We Come to the River* by Hans Werner Henze.

CAREER IN THE UK INCLUDES: Since 1985: Covent Garden: Arturo, *Lucia di Lammermoor*; Alfredo, *La Traviata*; Italian Tenor, *Der Rosenkavalier*; Števa, *Jenůfa*; Pinkerton, *Madama Butterfly*; Foresto, *Attila*; English National Opera: Alfredo, *La Traviata*; Don Ottavio, *Don Giovanni*; Rodolfo, *La Bohème*; Megaros/Lieutenant/Duke of Parma/Student, *Doctor Faust* (1986, British stage première); Leicester, *Mary Stuart*; Gabriele, *Simon Boccanegra*; Don José, *Carmen*; Turiddu, *Cavalleria Rusticana*; Nadir, *The Pearl Fishers*; Lensky, *Eugene Onegin*; Gustavus, *A Masked Ball*; Pinkerton, *Madam Butterfly*; title roles:

Faust, *The Diary of One Who Disappeared* (1986, British stage première), *Werther*; Opera North: Nadir, *The Pearl Fishers*; Gaston, *Jérusalem* (1990, British première); Scottish Opera: Pinkerton, *Madama Butterfly*; Cavaradossi, *Tosca*; Rodolfo, *La Bohème*; Don José, *Carmen*.
RELATED PROFESSIONAL ACTIVITIES: Concerts and recitals in the UK and abroad.
RECORDINGS INCLUDE: Elgar, *The Dream of Gerontius* (CHAN); Martinů, *The Greek Passion* (SUPR); Mendelssohn, *Elijah* (CHAN); Verdi, *Rigoletto* (EMI).
VIDEOS INCLUDE: Donizetti, *Mary Stuart*; Verdi, *Rigoletto* (both English National Opera).
ADDRESS: c/o Stafford Law Associates, 26 Mayfield Road, Weybridge, Surrey KT13 8XB.

DAVIES EIRIAN   Soprano

PERSONAL DETAILS: b. Llangollen, Wales; m. 1989, Timothy Wilson (counter-tenor), one child.
PREVIOUS OCCUPATIONS: Information consultant and librarian.
EDUCATION/TRAINING: University College of Wales; Royal Academy of Music, with Peter Harrison.
PROFESSIONAL DEBUT: 1983, Buxton Festival, Sylvie, *La Colombe*.
EARLY CAREER INCLUDED: 1984–1985, Welsh National Opera: Olga, *The Merry Widow*; Barena, *Jenůfa*; Flora, *La Traviata*; Woglinde, *Götterdämmerung*.
MAJOR DEBUTS INCLUDE: 1986, Opera North, Mimi, *La Bohème*; 1991, Semur, Constanze, *Die Entführung aus dem Serail*; 1992, Zurich Opera, Venus/Chief of the Secret Police, *Le Grand Macabre*.
OPERATIC WORLD PREMIERES INCLUDE: 1987, Glyndebourne Touring Opera, Mrs Frestln, *The Electrification of the Soviet Union* by Nigel Osborne; 1991, Opera North, Christine, *Caritas* by Robert Saxton.

CAREER IN THE UK INCLUDES: Since 1986: Buxton Festival, Lucinda, *Don Quixote in Sierra Morena*; City of Birmingham Touring Opera, First Lady, *The Magic Flute*; English National Opera: Venus, *Orpheus in the Underworld*; Frasquita, *Carmen*; Pamina, *The Magic Flute*; Welsh National Opera: Woglinde and Ortlinde, *The Ring of the Nibelung*; Lisa, *La Sonnambula*; Ännchen, *Der Freischütz*.
RELATED PROFESSIONAL ACTIVITIES: Regular concerts, broadcasts and television appearances in the UK and abroad.
RECORDINGS INCLUDE: Ligeti, *Le Grand Macabre* (WERG); Saxton, *Caritas* (COLL).
AWARDS INCLUDE: 1984, Francisco Vinas International Singing Competition (Barcelona).
ADDRESS: c/o John Coast, 31 Sinclair Road, London W14 ONS.

DAVIES LYNNE   Soprano

PERSONAL DETAILS: b. Wales.
EDUCATION/TRAINING: 1980–1985, Royal Academy of Music; 1987–1988, National Opera Studio, with Patricia Clark.
PROFESSIONAL DEBUT: 1985, Opera 80, Anne Trulove, *The Rake's Progress*.
MAJOR DEBUTS INCLUDE: 1987, Glyndebourne Festival Opera: Frasquita, *Carmen*; Louis XV Chair/Bat, *L'Enfant et les Sortilèges*; 1989, City of Birmingham Touring Opera, Pamina, *The Magic Flute*; 1990: Music Theatre Wales, Dafne, *Euridice*; Dublin Grand Opera, First Lady, *The Magic Flute*; 1991, Opera North, Zerlina, *Don Giovanni*.
OPERATIC WORLD PREMIERES INCLUDE: Batignano Festival: 1988, Signora Angiolieri, *Mario ed il Mago* by Stephen Oliver; 1991, Auretta, *L'Oca del Cairo* by Mozart/Stephen Oliver; 1992, Womens Playhouse Trust, Girl/Bridesmaid, *Blood Wedding* by Nicola LeFanu.
CAREER INCLUDES: Since 1985: Almeida Opera, Signora Angiolieri, *Mario and the Magician* (1992, British première); City of Birmingham Touring Opera, Papagena,

The Magic Flute; Downshire Players, Eurilla, *Orlando Paladino*; Glyndebourne Festival and Touring Opera: Jano, *Jenůfa*; Mother/Cat, *L'Enfant et les Sortilèges*; Matrix Ensemble at the Queen Elizabth Hall, Eurydice, *Les Malheurs d'Orphée*; Opera 80: Donna Elvira, *Don Giovanni*; Gilda, *Rigoletto*; Batignano Festival: Fe-an-nich-ton, *Ba-ta-clan*; title role, *Rodelinda*.

RELATED PROFESSIONAL ACTIVITIES: Numerous concerts with leading conductors and orchestras in the UK; recital tour of Oman.

RECORDINGS INCLUDE: A Hundred Years of Italian Opera (OPRA).

VIDEOS INCLUDE: Janáček, *Jenůfa* (Glyndebourne Festival Opera).

ADDRESS: Not available.

DAVIES MALDWYN   Tenor

PERSONAL DETAILS: b. 24 October 1950, Merthyr Tydfil; m. Christine Powell, two children.

EDUCATION/TRAINING: 1970–1973, Welsh College of Music and Drama; 1973–1976, University College, Cardiff, studied music; 1980, further studies with Erik Werba in Salzburg and with Anton Dermota in Vienna; privately with Rupert Bruce-Lockhart.

PROFESSIONAL DEBUT AS A PRINCIPAL: 1979, University College, Cardiff, Satyavan, *Sāvitri*.

EARLY CAREER INCLUDED: 1976, Sherman Theatre, Cardiff, Angelo, *The Magician* by Alun Hoddinott (world stage première); 1976–1979, chorister, St George's Chapel, Windsor; 1980–1982, member, Covent Garden: Judge, *Un Ballo in Maschera*; Second Jew, *Salome*; Novice, *Billy Budd*; Zorn, *Die Meistersinger von Nürnberg*; Nobleman, *Lohengrin*; Evandre, *Alceste*.

MAJOR DEBUTS INCLUDE: 1982: Lyric Opera of Queensland, Ferrando, *Così fan tutte*; Wexford Festival, Gernando, *L'Isola Disabitata*; 1983, Bayreuth Festival, Froh, *Der Ring des Nibelungen*; 1984: Kent Opera, Belmonte, *The Seraglio*; Grand Théâtre, Geneva, Evandre, *Alceste*; 1985, English National Opera, Jack, *The Midsummer Marriage*; 1987, Scottish Opera, Belmonte, *The Seraglio*; 1988, Opera North, Acis, *Acis and Galatea*.

OPERATIC WORLD PREMIERES INCLUDE: 1977, Fishguard Festival, Second Traveller, *What the Old Man Does is Always Right* by Alun Hoddinott.

CAREER IN THE UK INCLUDES: Since 1982: English National Opera: Ferrando, *Così fan tutte*; Don Ottavio, *Don Giovanni*; Tamino, *The Magic Flute*; Scottish Opera: Ferrando, *Così fan tutte*; Tamino, *The Magic Flute*; Spitalfields Festival, Oronte, *Alcina*.

RELATED PROFESSIONAL ACTIVITIES: Regular concerts, recitals and broadcasts with leading conductors and orchestras in the UK and abroad.

RECORDINGS INCLUDE: Boughton, *The Immortal Hour* (HYPE); Bridge, *Christmas Rose* (PEAR); Handel: *Alcina* (EMI), *Messiah* (HYPE); Haydn, *Nelson Mass* (DG).

ADDRESS: c/o Lies Askonas Ltd, 186 Drury Lane, London WC2B 5RY.

DAVIES MENAI
Mezzo-soprano

PERSONAL DETAILS: b. 17 November 1935, Wales; m. G. Wyn Davies, two children.

PREVIOUS OCCUPATION: 1957–1973, school teacher.

EDUCATION/TRAINING: Normal College, Bangor; University College, Cardiff; Welsh College of Music and Drama, with Valletta Jacopi.

PROFESSIONAL DEBUT: 1974, chorus member, Welsh National Opera.

EARLY CAREER INCLUDED: 1975–1986, Principal Mezzo-soprano, Welsh National Opera, more than 20 roles including: Marcellina, *The Barber of Seville*; Mrs Herring, *Albert Herring*; Grandmother, *Jenůfa*; Marcellina, *The Marriage of Figaro*; Governess, *The Queen of Spades*; Auntie, *Peter Grimes*; Mrs Grose, *The Turn of the Screw*; Arnalta, *The Coronation of Poppea*; Filipyevna,

Eugene Onegin; Innkeeper's Wife/Hen, *The Cunning Little Vixen*; Háta, *The Bartered Bride*; Countess, *Andrea Chénier*; Mrs Peachum, *The Threepenny Opera*.

MAJOR DEBUTS INCLUDE: 1987, Glyndebourne Touring Opera, Louis XV Chair/Bat, *L'Enfant et les Sortilèges*; 1988, Scottish Opera, Filipyevna, *Eugene Onegin*; 1989, Glyndebourne Festival Opera, Grandmother, *Jenůfa*; Mrs Grose, *The Turn of the Screw*. 1989, English National Opera; 1990: English National Opera Soviet Union tour (Bolshoi, Kirov and Kiev), Cologne Opera, Schwetzingen Festival; 1991, Montpellier Festival.

OPERATIC WORLD PREMIERES INCLUDE: 1981, Welsh National Opera, Gwen, *The Journey* by John Metcalf; 1992, Théâtre du Châtelet, Paris, Governess, *Le Chevalier Imaginaire* by Philippe Fénelon.

CAREER IN THE UK INCLUDES: Since 1987: English National Opera, Human Frailty/ Ericlea, *The Return of Ulysses*; Glyndebourne Festival Opera: Auntie, *Peter Grimes*; Glyndebourne Touring Opera, Mrs Herring, *Albert Herring* (also 1989, Teatro Olimpico, Rome and Teatro Valli, Reggio Emilia); Filipyevna, *Eugene Onegin*.

VIDEOS INCLUDE: Janáček, *Jenůfa* (Glyndebourne Festival Opera).

ADDRESS: c/o Harlequin Agency Ltd, 1 University Place, Cardiff CF2 2JU.

DAVIES NOEL
Conductor, Editor, Harpsichordist and Répétiteur

POSITION: Staff Conductor, English National Opera.

PERSONAL DETAILS: b. 1 January 1945, London.

EDUCATION/TRAINING: 1955–1963, Hereford Cathedral School; 1963–1967, Royal College of Music, with Sir Adrian Boult, James Lockhart, Richard Austin and Hubert Dawkes.

PROFESSIONAL AND OPERATIC DEBUT: 1967, Kentish Opera, *Il Signor Bruschino/ Cavalleria Rusticana*.

CAREER: 1967–1974, répétiteur and conductor, Sadler's Wells Opera; 1974– 1984, Conductor, London Welsh Festival Chorus; since 1974, staff conductor, English National Opera.

MAJOR OPERATIC DEBUTS INCLUDE: 1984, English National Opera USA tour (including Metropolitan Opera, New York), *Gloriana*; 1989, Houston Grand Opera, *Giulio Cesare*; 1991, Icelandic Opera, *Rigoletto*.

OPERA PERFORMANCES IN THE UK INCLUDE: Since 1974: English National Opera: *The Magic Flute*, *Mary Stuart*, *Carmen*, *La Traviata*, *The Seraglio*, *La Belle Hélène*, *The Coronation of Poppea*, *Don Giovanni*, *The Barber of Seville*, *Il Trovatore*, *Count Ory*, *Rigoletto*, *Faust*, *Die Fledermaus*, *The Pearl Fishers*, *The Makropoulos Case*, *Madam Butterfly*, *Gianni Schicchi*, *The Love for Three Oranges*, *Rusalka*, *Peter Grimes*, *Xerxes*, *The Adventures of Mr Brouček*.

RECORDINGS INCLUDE: As harpsichordist: Handel, *Julius Caesar* (EMI).

VIDEOS INCLUDE: As assistant conductor and harpsichordist: Handel: *Julius Caesar*, *Xerxes* (both English National Opera).

PUBLICATIONS INCLUDE: Editor, full and vocal scores: 1979, *Julius Caesar* (English National Opera); 1985, *Xerxes* (Chester Music).

ADDRESS: c/o English National Opera, London Coliseum, St Martin's Lane, London WC2N 4ES.

DAVIES WYN
Conductor and Coach

POSITION: Staff Conductor, Welsh National Opera.

PERSONAL DETAILS: b. 8 May 1952, South Wales; m. 1975, Jane Baxendale.

EDUCATION/TRAINING: Christ Church, Oxford.

PROFESSIONAL AND OPERATIC DEBUT:
1974, Welsh National Opera, *L'Elisir
d'Amore*.

CAREER: Since 1974: staff conductor, Welsh
National Opera; guest conductor: Buxton
Festival, English National Opera, New
Sadler's Wells Opera, Opera North,
Opera Northern Ireland, Scottish Opera,
BBC Welsh and Scottish Orchestras, City
of Birmingham Symphony and English
Chamber Orchestras; Assistant
Conductor: Metropolitan Opera, New York
and Banff Centre, Alberta; founder:
London Opera Ensemble, Welsh Chamber
Ensemble.

OPERA PERFORMANCES IN THE UK
INCLUDE: Since 1974: English National
Opera, *The Barber of Seville*; New
Sadler's Wells Opera, *The Gondoliers*;
Opera North: *The Cunning Little Vixen*,
Showboat, *Orpheus in the Underworld*;
Opera Northern Ireland, *The Daughter of
the Regiment*; Scottish Opera, *Iolanthe*;
Welsh National Opera: *Così fan tutte*, *The
Grand Duchess of Gérolstein*, *The
Seraglio*, *La Bohème*, *The Barber of
Seville*, *The Marriage of Figaro*, *Don
Carlos*, *The Magic Flute*, *The Coronation
of Poppea*, *Eugene Onegin*.

RELATED PROFESSIONAL ACTIVITIES:
Coach: Guildhall School of Music and
Drama, National Opera Studio, Royal
Academy of Music.

ADDRESS: c/o Performing Arts, 6 Windmill
Street, London W1P 1HF.

DAVIS ANDREW
Conductor, Harpsichordist and Organist

POSITIONS: Music Director, Glyndebourne
Festival Opera; Chief Conductor, BBC
Symphony Orchestra; Conductor
Laureate, Toronto Symphony Orchestra.

PERSONAL DETAILS: b. 2 February 1944,
Hertfordshire; m. Felicity Vincent (cellist);
m. Nancicarole Monohan (double-
bassist); m. Gianna Rolandi (soprano),
one child.

EDUCATION/TRAINING: 1961–1963, Royal
Academy of Music, organ studies with
Peter Hurford and Piet Kee; 1963–1967,
Organ Scholar, King's College,
Cambridge; 1967–1968, Accademia di
Santa Cecilia, Rome, conducting with
Franco Ferrara.

PROFESSIONAL DEBUT: 1969, Royal
Liverpool Philharmonic Orchestra.

OPERATIC DEBUT: 1973, Glyndebourne
Festival Opera, *Capriccio*.

CAREER: 1968–1970, freelance organist and
continuo player; 1970–1972, Assistant
Conductor, BBC Scottish Symphony
Orchestra; 1973–1977, Associate
Conductor, New Philharmonia Orchestra;
1974–1977, Principal Guest Conductor,
Royal Liverpool Philharmonic Orchestra;
Toronto Symphony Orchestra: 1975–1988,
Artistic Director and Chief Conductor;
since 1988, Conductor Laureate; since
1988, Music Director, Glyndebourne
Festival Opera; since 1989, Chief
Conductor, BBC Symphony Orchestra.

MAJOR OPERATIC DEBUTS INCLUDE: 1981:
Metropolitan Opera, New York, *Salome*;
Théâtre des Champs Elysées, Paris, *Der
Rosenkavalier*; 1983, Covent Garden, *Der
Rosenkavalier*; 1987, Lyric Opera,
Chicago, *Le Nozze di Figaro*; 1991,
Bavarian State Opera, Munich, *Peter
Grimes*.

OPERA PERFORMANCES IN THE UK
INCLUDE: Since 1973, Glyndebourne
Festival Opera: *Eugene Onegin*, *Die
Schweigsame Frau*, *Die Zauberflöte*,
Falstaff, *Arabella*, *Don Giovanni*, *Katya
Kabanova*, *Jenůfa*, *New Year* (1990,
British première), *Le Nozze di Figaro*, *La
Clemenza di Tito*, *The Magic Flute*, *Peter
Grimes*, *The Queen of Spades*.

RELATED PROFESSIONAL ACTIVITIES:
Guest appearances with leading
orchestras worldwide; regular Proms
conductor including since 1988, Last Night
of the Proms.

RECORDINGS INCLUDE: Borodin, orchestral
works (CBS); Britten: Four Sea Interludes
and Passacaglia from *Peter Grimes*,
Variations on a Theme of Frank Bridge,
*The Young Person's Guide to the

Orchestra (all TELD); Duruflé, *Requiem*;
Elgar: *Enigma Variations* (both CBS),
Pomp and Circumstance, Symphonies
Nos 1 & 2 (all TELD); R. Strauss: *Die Liebe
der Danae, Salome* (both CBS); Tippett:
The Mask of Time (EMI), *New Year* (VIRG);
Vaughan Williams, Symphony No. 6
(TELD); complete symphonies of Dvořák
and Mendelssohn (all CBS); as
harpsichordist: Bach, harpsicord and
keyboard concertos; Pergolesi and
Vivaldi, choral music (all PHIL); as
organist: Tallis motets (ARGO).
VIDEOS INCLUDE: Janáček: *Jenůfa, Katya
Kabanova* (both Glyndebourne Festival
Opera).
AWARDS AND HONOURS INCLUDE: 1984,
Honorary Doctorates of Literature,
Universities of York and Toronto; 1990,
Royal Philharmonic Society/Charles
Heidsieck Award; 1992, Commander,
Order of the British Empire (CBE); *The
Mask of Time*: 1987, *Gramophone* Record
of the Year; 1988, Grand Prix du Disque
(France).
ADDRESS: c/o Harold Holt Ltd, 31 Sinclair
Road, London W14 ONS.

DAVIS, SIR COLIN   Conductor

POSITIONS: Principal Guest Conductor,
London Symphony Orchestra; Honorary
Conductor, Dresden Staatskapelle.
PERSONAL DETAILS: b. 25 September 1927,
Weybridge; m. 1949, April Cantelo
(soprano), two children; m. 1964, Ashraf
Naini, five children.
EDUCATION/TRAINING: Royal College of
Music, clarinet with Frederick Thurston.
PROFESSIONAL DEBUT: Kalmar Orchestra,
London: 1948, as clarinettist; 1949, as
conductor.
CAREER: 1950, founder and Principal
Conductor, Chelsea Opera Group; 1950–
1957, freelance conductor with several
orchestras, opera and ballet companies;
1957–1959, Assistant Conductor, BBC
Scottish Orchestra; 1959–1965, Music
Director, Sadler's Wells Opera; 1967–
1975, Principal Conductor, then Principal

Guest Conductor, BBC Symphony
Orchestra; 1971–1986, Music Director, The
Royal Opera, Covent Garden
(performances included *Les Troyens, Der
Ring des Nibelungen*, and 1981, British
première, three act version of *Lulu*);
1972–1984, Principal Guest Conductor,
Boston Symphony Orchestra; 1983–1992,
Principal Conductor, Bavarian Radio
Symphony Orchestra; since 1975,
Principal Guest Conductor, London
Symphony Orchestra; since 1990,
Honorary Conductor, Dresden
Staatskapelle.
MAJOR OPERATIC DEBUTS INCLUDE: 1958,
Sadler's Wells Opera, *The Seraglio*; 1960,
Glyndebourne Festival Opera, *Die
Zauberflöte*; 1965, Covent Garden, *Le
Nozze di Figaro*; 1967, Metropolitan
Opera, New York, *Peter Grimes*; 1977,
Bayreuth, *Tannhäuser* (first appearance
by a British conductor); Covent Garden on
tour: 1976 (La Scala, Milan): *Benvenuto
Cellini, Peter Grimes*; 1979 (Far East):
Peter Grimes, Tosca, Die Zauberflöte;
1984 (Olympic Arts Festival, Los
Angeles): *Peter Grimes, Turandot, Die
Zauberflöte*; 1986, Vienna State Opera,
Werther; 1991, Salzburg Festival, *La
Clemenza di Tito*.
OPERATIC WORLD PREMIERES INCLUDE:
1965, Sadler's Wells Opera, *The Mines of
Sulphur* by Richard Rodney Bennett;
Covent Garden: 1970, *The Knot Garden*;
1977, *The Ice Break* (both by Michael
Tippett).
OPERA PERFORMANCES IN THE UK
INCLUDE: Since 1986, Covent Garden:
*Ariadne auf Naxos, Fidelio, Don Giovanni,
La Clemenza di Tito, Die Zauberflöte, Der
Freischütz, Turandot, La Damnation de
Faust.*
RELATED PROFESSIONAL ACTIVITIES:
Numerous concerts and broadcasts
worldwide; 1969, Artistic Director, Bath
Festival; since 1989, International Chair of
Conducting and Orchestral Studies, Royal
Academy of Music.
RECORDINGS INCLUDE: Berlioz: *Béatrice et
Bénédict, Benvenuto Cellini, La
Damnation de Faust, Les Troyens*;

Gounod, *Faust*; Massenet, *Werther*; Mozart: *La Clemenza di Tito, Così fan tutte, Don Giovanni, Die Entführung aus dem Serail, Idomeneo, Le Nozze di Figaro*; Puccini: *La Bohème, Tosca*; Purcell, *Dido and Aeneas* (all PHIL).

VIDEOS INCLUDE: Britten, *Peter Grimes*; Saint-Saëns, *Samson et Dalila* (both Covent Garden); Wagner, *Tannhäuser* (Bayreuth Festival); Mozart at Buckingham Palace (EMI).

AWARDS AND HONOURS INCLUDE: 1965, Commander, Order of the British Empire (CBE); 1976: *Evening Standard* Award, *Der Ring des Nibelungen* (Covent Garden); Commendatore of the Republic of Italy; 1977, Sibelius Medal (Finland), complete cycle of Sibelius symphonies; 1978, Grosse Schallplattenpreis (Federal Republic of Germany), complete works of Berlioz; 1980, Knighthood; 1982, Chevalier, Legion d'Honneur (France); 1983, *Gramophone* Record of the Year, Triple Concerto by Tippett; 1984, Shakespeare Prize (Hamburg); 1987, Commander's Cross of the Order of Merit (Federal Republic of Germany); 1990, Commandeur de l'Ordre des Arts et des Lettres (France); 1992: Commander First Class, Order of the Lion of Finland; Bayerischen Verdienstorden (Germany); Grammy Awards (USA): *Peter Grimes*, *Così fan tutte*.

ADDRESS: c/o Jill Segal, 39 Cathcart Road, London SW10 9JG.

DAWSON ANNE   Soprano

PERSONAL DETAILS: b. Cheshire; m. Robin Martin-Oliver (counter-tenor).

EDUCATION/TRAINING: 1976–1982, Royal Northern College of Music, with Caroline Crawshaw.

PROFESSIONAL DEBUT: 1982, English National Opera in Manchester, Xenia, *Boris Godunov*.

MAJOR DEBUTS INCLUDE: 1982, Glyndebourne Touring Opera, Euridice, *Orfeo ed Euridice*; 1983, English National Opera, Naiad, *Ariadne auf Naxos*; 1984,

Glyndebourne Festival Opera, Barbarina, *Le Nozze di Figaro*; 1985: Welsh National Opera, Gilda, *Rigoletto*; Netherlands Opera, Angelica, *Orlando*; 1988: Opera North, Galatea, *Acis and Galatea*; Vancouver Opera, title role, *The Cunning Little Vixen*; 1989: Covent Garden, Tebaldo, *Don Carlos*; Frankfurt Opera, Gilda, *Rigoletto*; 1991, Scottish Opera, title role, *The Cunning Little Vixen*.

CAREER IN THE UK INCLUDES: Since 1982: English National Opera: Sophie, *Der Rosenkavalier*; Marguérite, *Faust*; Gilda, *Rigoletto*; Hero, *Béatrice and Bénédict*; title role, *The Cunning Little Vixen*; Glyndebourne Festival and Touring Opera: Chloë, *The Queen of Spades*; Susanna, *Le Nozze di Figaro*; Micaëla, *Carmen*; Mimi, *La Bohème*; Anne Trulove, *The Rake's Progress*; Opera North: Leïla, *The Pearl Fishers*; Sandrina, *La Finta Giardiniera*; Marguérite, *Faust*; Ninetta, *The Thieving Magpie*; Welsh National Opera: Pamina, *The Magic Flute*; Susanna, *Le Nozze di Figaro*; title role, *The Cunning Little Vixen*.

RELATED PROFESSIONAL ACTIVITIES: Regular concerts and recitals with leading conductors and orchestras in the UK and Europe.

RECORDINGS INCLUDE: Boughton, *Immortal Hour*; Gay, *The Beggar's Opera* (both HYPE); Mendelssohn: *Elijah* (PHIL), choral music (HYPE); Mozart, *Le Nozze di Figaro* (EMI); Vaughan Williams, vocal works (HYPE).

AWARDS INCLUDE: 1979, John Ireland Centenary Competition; 1981: Gerald Finzi Song Award; International Vocal Competition, s'Hertogenbosch (Netherlands); 1982: Esso/Glyndebourne Award; Kathleen Ferrier Memorial Scholarship.

ADDRESS: c/o Harrison/Parrott Ltd, 12 Penzance Place, London W11 4PA.

DAWSON LYNNE   Soprano

PERSONAL DETAILS: b. 3 June 1953, York.
PREVIOUS OCCUPATION: 1973–1978, French interpreter and translator.
EDUCATION/TRAINING: 1978–1981, Guildhall School of Music and Drama, with Ellis Keeler; 1981–1990, privately with Rae Woodland.
PROFESSIONAL DEBUT: 1984, Kent Opera, Countess, *The Marriage of Figaro.*
MAJOR DEBUTS INCLUDE: 1987, Maggio Musicale, Florence, Music, *Orfeo*; 1988: Opera North, Mimi, *La Bohème*; Scottish Opera, Pamina, *The Magic Flute*; Théâtre du Châtelet, Paris, Zdenka, *Arabella*; 1989: Ludwigshafen Opera at Sadler's Wells Theatre, Constanze, *Die Entführung aus dem Serail*; Aix-en-Provence Festival, Night/Mystery, *The Fairy Queen*; Lausanne Opera, Sandrina, *La Finta Giardiniera*; 1990, La Monnaie, Brussels, Constanze, *Die Entführung aus dem Serail*; 1991: Naples, Fiordiligi, *Così fan tutte*; Netherlands Opera, Teresa, *Benvenuto Cellini*; Opéra du Rhin, Strasbourg, Countess, *Le Nozze di Figaro*; Théâtre du Châtelet, Paris, Sifare, *Mitridate, Rè di Ponto.*
CAREER IN THE UK INCLUDES: Since 1984: Opera 80, Violetta, *La Traviata*; Opera North, Sandrina, *La Finta Giardiniera.*
RELATED PROFESSIONAL ACTIVITIES: Extensive concert repertoire with regular performances and broadcasts in the UK and abroad.
RECORDINGS INCLUDE: Blow, *Venus and Adonis* (HARM); Gluck: *Iphigénie en Aulide, Les Pèlerins de la Mecque* (both ERAT); Handel: *Acis and Galatea* (L'OI), *Saul* (PHIL); Monteverdi, *Orfeo* (ARCH); Mozart: *Don Giovanni* (EMI), *Die Entführung aus dem Serail* (DECC), *Requiem* (SONY); Purcell: *Dido and Aeneas* (ARCH), *The Fairy Queen* (HARM).
ADDRESS: c/o Lies Askonas Ltd, 186 Drury Lane, London WC2B 5RY.

DEAN ROBERT
Conductor (formerly Baritone)

POSITION: Head of Music, Scottish Opera.
PERSONAL DETAILS: b. 4 September 1954, Surrey.
EDUCATION/TRAINING: 1973–1976, University of Durham; 1976–1978, Royal Northern College of Music, with John Cameron; 1978–1980, National Opera Studio, as répétiteur and subsequently as baritone.
PROFESSIONAL DEBUT: As baritone: 1979, Musica nel Chiostro, Alidoro, *Orontea*; as conductor: 1987, Batignano Festival, *Leonore.*
EARLY CAREER INCLUDED: 1979–1986, appearances with Covent Garden, English National Opera, Glyndebourne Festival and Touring Opera, Musica nel Chiostro, Scottish Opera, University College Opera, Batignano Festival; roles included: Fiorello, *Il Barbiere di Siviglia*; Count, *Le Nozze di Figaro*; Orfeo, *Euridice*; Osmin, *Zaide*; Junius, *The Rape of Lucretia*; Patroclus, *King Priam* (also 1985, Covent Garden at the Athens Festival); Raoul, *La Vie Parisienne*; Albert, *Werther*; Schlemil, *Les Contes d'Hoffmann*; title roles: *Don Giovanni, Faust* (Spohr).
MAJOR DEBUTS INCLUDE: 1981, English National Opera, Pelléas, *Pelléas and Mélisande*; 1982, Opera North, Guglielmo, *Così fan tutte*; 1984, Covent Garden, Second Apprentice, *Wozzeck*; 1985, Scottish Opera, title role, *Il Barbiere di Siviglia*; 1986, Downshire Players of London, Doctor, *La Chute de la Maison Usher* (1986, British première); as conductor: 1987, Scottish Opera, *Così fan tutte.*
OPERATIC WORLD PREMIERES INCLUDE: 1984, Batignano Festival, Beast, *La Bella e la Bestia* by Stephen Oliver; 1985, Scottish Opera, Tesman, *Hedda Gabler* by Edward Harper; 1986, Royal Academy of Arts, Marcello, *Exposition of a Picture* by Stephen Oliver.

OPERA PERFORMANCES IN THE UK
INCLUDE: Since 1987, Scottish Opera:
Tosca, The Barber of Seville, Don Giovanni, Jenůfa, Eugene Onegin (since 1990, Head of Music).
RELATED PROFESSIONAL ACTIVITIES: 1979–1980, accompanist and Assistant Conductor, London Choral Society; 1979–1981, Conductor, Chamber Choir Polyphony; 1988, Music Director, Travelling Opera; 1990, masterclasses, Salt Lake City, Utah.
RECORDINGS INCLUDE: As baritone: Handel, *Coronation Anthems* (PHIL).
VIDEOS INCLUDE: Rossini, *Il Barbiere di Siviglia* (Glyndebourne Fesival Opera).
ADDRESS: c/o Scottish Opera, 39 Elmbank Crescent, Glasgow G2 4PT.

DEAN STAFFORD
Bass-baritone

PERSONAL DETAILS: b. 20 June 1937, Surrey; m. Carolyn Lambourne (soprano and pianist), four children; m. 1981, Anne Howells (mezzo-soprano), two children.
EDUCATION/TRAINING: Royal College of Music, with Gordon Clinton; privately with Howell Glynne and Otakar Kraus.
PROFESSIONAL DEBUT: 1964, Sadler's Wells Opera, Zuniga, *Carmen*.
EARLY CAREER INCLUDED: 1964–1970: Principal Bass-baritone, Sadler's Wells Opera: Daland, *The Flying Dutchman*; Sarastro, *The Magic Flute*; Padre Guardiano, *The Force of Destiny*; Sparafucile, *Rigoletto*; Colline, *La Bohème*; Pluto, *Orfeo*; also: English Opera Group, Abednego, *The Burning Fiery Furnace*; Glyndebourne Festival Opera: Lictor, *L'Incoronazione di Poppea*; Major Domo, *Capriccio*; Magistrate, *Werther*; Rochefort, *Anna Bolena*; Scottish Opera: Leporello, *Don Giovanni*; Sarastro, *The Magic Flute*.
MAJOR DEBUTS INCLUDE: 1969, Covent Garden, Masetto, *Don Giovanni*; Leporello, *Don Giovanni*. 1969, Sadler's Wells Opera (opening production at the London Coliseum); 1971, Hamburg State

Opera; 1974, San Francisco Opera; title role, *Le Nozze di Figaro*: 1973, Bavarian State Opera, Munich; 1975: Cologne Opera and Lyric Opera, Chicago; 1976, Metropolitan Opera, New York.
OPERATIC WORLD PREMIERES INCLUDE: 1967, Sadler's Wells Opera, Samuel Breze, *A Penny for a Song* by Richard Rodney Bennett; 1977, Scottish Opera at the Edinburgh International Festival, Riccio/Cardinal Beaton, *Mary, Queen of Scots* by Thea Musgrave.
CAREER IN THE UK INCLUDES: Since 1971: Covent Garden: Alfonso, *Lucrezia Borgia*; Lindorf, *Les Contes d'Hoffman*; Leporello, *Don Giovanni*; Ferrando, *Il Trovatore*; Publio, *La Clemenza di Tito*; Magistrate, *Werther*; Bottom, *A Midsummer Night's Dream*; Rangoni, *Boris Godunov*; Don Estoban, *The Birthday of the Infanta* (1985, British première); Prime Minister, *The King Goes Forth to France* (1987, British première); Don Alfonso, *Così fan tutte* (also 1992, Japan tour); Gessler, *Guillaume Tell*; Melisso, *Alcina*; title role, *Le Nozze di Figaro*; English National Opera: Kecal, *The Bartered Bride*; Don Pedro, *Béatrice and Bénédict*; Glyndebourne Festival Opera: Leporello, *Don Giovanni*; Don Alfonso, *Così fan tutte*; Scottish Opera: Seneca, *The Coronation of Poppea*; Osmin, *The Seraglio*; La Roche, *Capriccio*; title role, *The Marriage of Figaro*; Welsh National Opera: Sparafucile, *Rigoletto*; Philip II, *Don Carlos*; Seneca, *The Coronation of Poppea*; Kecal, *The Bartered Bride*; Sarastro, *The Magic Flute*; Rocco, *Fidelio*.
RELATED PROFESSIONAL ACTIVITIES: Numerous concerts, oratorios and television appearances in the UK and abroad.
RECORDINGS INCLUDE: Britten, *The Burning Fiery Furnace* (DECC); Delius, *A Village Romeo and Juliet* (ARGO); Monteverdi, *Il Ballo delle Ingrate* (PHIL); Stravinsky: *Oedipus Rex, The Rake's Progress* (both DECC); Verdi, *I Lombardi* (PHIL).

VIDEOS INCLUDE: Mozart: *Così fan tutte*, *Don Giovanni* (both Glyndebourne Festival Opera); Sullivan, *The Mikado* (Walker).

ADDRESS: c/o Harrison/Parrott Ltd, 12 Penzance Place, London W11 4PA.

DEAN TIMOTHY
Conductor, Chorus Master and Repetiteur

POSITION: Music Director, British Youth Opera.

PERSONAL DETAILS: b. 23 April 1956, Buckinghamshire; m. 1981, two children.

EDUCATION/TRAINING: 1973–1974, Guildhall School of Music and Drama, piano with Edith Vogel; 1974–1977, University of Reading, piano with John Barstow; 1977–1979, Royal College of Music: piano with Roger Vignoles and Peter Wallfisch, conducting with Michael Lankester and Norman Del Mar.

PROFESSIONAL AND OPERATIC DEBUT: 1981, Kent Opera, *The Magic Flute*.

CAREER: Répétiteur: Batignano Festival, Buxton Festival, Covent Garden, Kent Opera, Opera North; Kent Opera: 1983–1989, Chorus Master and Assistant Conductor; 1987–1989, Head of Music; Music Director: 1983–1987, London Music Theatre Group; 1988–1989, London Bach Society; 1990–1992, Assistant Music Director, D'Oyly Carte Opera; since 1987, British Youth Opera.

MAJOR OPERATIC DEBUTS INCLUDE: 1991: English National Opera, *Duke Bluebeard's Castle*; Scottish Opera, *The Barber of Seville*.

OPERA PERFORMANCES IN THE UK INCLUDE: Since 1982: British Youth Opera: *Don Giovanni*, *The Marriage of Figaro*, *Così fan tutte*, *Eugene Onegin*, *Carmen*; Kent Opera: *La Traviata*, *Carmen*, *Don Giovanni*, *Count Ory*, *Peter Grimes*, *Fidelio*, *The Burning Fiery Furnace*; London Music Theatre Group, *Juditha Triumphans* (1984, British première).

ADDRESS: 40 Elm Park Road, London N3 1EB.

DICKIE BRIAN   Administrator

POSITION: General Director, Canadian Opera Company, Toronto.

PERSONAL DETAILS: b. 23 July 1941, Nottinghamshire; m. 1968, Victoria Sheldon, three children; m. 1989, Nancy Gustafson (soprano).

EDUCATION/TRAINING: Trinity College, Dublin.

CAREER: Glyndebourne Festival Opera: 1962–1966, Assistant Administrator; 1967–1981, Administrator, Glyndebourne Touring Opera; 1970–1981, Opera Manager; 1981–1989, General Administrator; since 1989, General Director, Canadian Opera Company, Toronto.

OTHER PROFESSIONAL ACTIVITIES INCLUDE: 1967–1973, Artistic Director, Wexford Festival; 1978–1985, Chairman, London Choral Society; 1981–1987, Artistic Adviser, Théâtre Musical de Paris; since 1991, member, Board of Directors, Opera America.

ADDRESS: c/o Canadian Opera Company, 227 Front Street E, Toronto, Ontario M5A 1E8, Canada.

DICKINSON MERIEL
Mezzo-soprano

PERSONAL DETAILS: b. 8 April 1940, Lancashire; m. 1991, Robert Gardner.

EDUCATION/TRAINING: 1958–1963, Royal Manchester College of Music; 1964–1966, Vienna State Academy, with Hans Karg.

PROFESSIONAL DEBUT: 1964, concert with Park Lane Opera.

CAREER INCLUDES: Since 1970: Abbey Opera at the Camden Festival, Frau von Luber, *The Silverlake* (1987, British stage première); Barber Institute, Birmingham: Erenice, *Sosarme*; Cornelia, *Julius Caesar*; English National Opera, Mrs Jones, *Street Scene*; Handel Opera Society: Micah, *Samson*; Hamor, *Jephtha*; Opera North, Magdelone, *Masquerade* (1990, British première); Scottish Opera, Mrs Jones, *Street Scene*;

Welsh National Opera, Madame Larina, *Eugene Onegin*.

RELATED PROFESSIONAL ACTIVITIES: Regular concerts, recitals and broadcasts in the UK and abroad; numerous appearances as an actress/singer.

RECORDINGS INCLUDE: Weill, *Street Scene* (DECC/TER).

AWARDS INCLUDE: 1964, Countess of Munster Award.

ADDRESS: c/o Music International, 13 Ardilaun Road, London N5 2QR.

DOBSON JOHN Tenor

POSITIONS: Member, The Royal Opera, Covent Garden; Director, The Royal Opera Young Singers Programme.

PERSONAL DETAILS: b. 1930, Derby.

EDUCATION/TRAINING: Guildhall School of Music and Drama, with Norman Walker; further studies with Giovanni Inghilleri in Italy.

PROFESSIONAL DEBUT: As baritone: 1950, chorus member, Glydebourne Festival Opera; as tenor: 1956, Bergamo Opera, Pinkerton, *Madama Butterfly*.

EARLY CAREER INCLUDED: Appearances with Bergamo Opera, Glyndebourne Festival Opera, New Opera Company, Scottish Opera, Wexford Festival.

MAJOR DEBUTS INCLUDE: 1959, Covent Garden, Faninal, *Der Rosenkavalier*; 1963, Welsh National Opera, Alfredo, *La Traviata*; 1976: Covent Garden at La Scala, Milan, Bob Boles, *Peter Grimes*; Deutsche Oper am Rhein, Düsseldorf, Loge, *Das Rheingold*; 1977, English National Opera, Mime, *The Ring of the Nibelung*; 1979, Covent Garden Far East tour: Bob Boles, *Peter Grimes*; First Priest, *Die Zauberflöte*; Spoletta, *Tosca*; 1982, Maggio Musicale, Florence, Sellem, *The Rake's Progress*; 1985, Covent Garden at the Athens Festival, Young Guard, *King Priam*; 1986, Covent Garden Far East tour, Altoum, *Turandot*; 1987, Deutsche Oper, Berlin Japan tour, Mime, *Der Ring des Nibelungen*; 1992, Covent Garden Japan tour, Don Curzio, *Le Nozze di Figaro*.

OPERATIC WORLD PREMIERES INCLUDE: Covent Garden: 1962, Paris, *King Priam* (at the Coventry Festival); 1977, Luke, *The Ice Break* (both by Michael Tippett).

CAREER IN THE UK INCLUDES: Since 1959, member, Covent Garden, more than 95 roles including: Jacquino, *Fidelio*; David and Moser, *Die Meistersinger von Nürnberg*; Loge, *Das Rheingold*; Bob Boles, *Peter Grimes*; Prince Shuisky, *Boris Godunov*; Melot, *Tristan und Isolde*; Dr Caius, *Falstaff*; Lysander and Snout, *A Midsummer Night's Dream*; Normanno, *Lucia di Lammermoor*; Pang and Altoum, *Turandot*; Messenger, *Samson et Dalila*; Roderigo and Cassio, *Otello*; Third Jew, *Salome*; Sellem, *The Rake's Progress*; Trin, *La Fanciulla del West*; Mime, *Der Ring des Nibelungen*; Spalanzani, *Les Contes d'Hoffmann*; Father Confessor, *The Carmelites*; Incredibile, *Andrea Chénier*; Monsieur Triquet, *Eugene Onegin*; Count Lerma, *Don Carlos*; Doctor, *Un Re in Ascolto* (1989, British première); Innkeeper, *The Cunning Little Vixen*; Monsieur Taupe, *Capriccio*; Missail, *Boris Godunov*; Jakob Glock, *The Fiery Angel*; Spoletta, *Tosca*; also, Welsh National Opera: Luigi, *Il Tabarro*; Prince Shuisky, *Boris Godunov*; Eisenstein, *Die Fledermaus*.

RELATED PROFESSIONAL ACTIVITIES: Numerous concerts, recitals and broadcasts in the UK; since 1989, Director, Covent Garden Young Singers Programme; Council member, British Youth Opera.

RECORDINGS INCLUDE: Janáček, *The Cunning Little Vixen* (EMI); Menotti, *Amahl and the Night Visitors* (TER); Puccini, *La Fanciulla del West* (DG); Stravinsky, *The Rake's Progress* (DECC); Verdi, *Otello* (NUOV).

VIDEOS INCLUDE: Britten, *Peter Grimes*; Giordano, *Andrea Chénier*; Puccini, *La Fanciulla del West*; Saint-Saëns, *Samson et Dalila*; J. Strauss, *Die Fledermaus*; R. Strauss, *Der Rosenkavalier*; Verdi: *Don Carlos*, *Falstaff* (all Covent Garden).

HONOURS INCLUDE: 1985, Officer, Order of
the British Empire (OBE); 1991, Honorary
Fellow, Guildhall School of Music and
Drama.
ADDRESS: c/o Royal Opera House, Covent
Garden, London WC2E 9DD.

DOGHAN PHILIP   Tenor

PERSONAL DETAILS: b. 1949, London; one
child.
EDUCATION/TRAINING: 1967–1970,
University of Durham, studied music.
PROFESSIONAL DEBUT: As boy soprano:
1962, Covent Garden at the Coventry
Festival, Boy Paris, *King Priam* by
Michael Tippett (world première); as
principal tenor: 1976, English Music
Theatre at the Aldeburgh Festival,
Square, *Tom Jones* by Stephen Oliver
(world première).
EARLY CAREER INCLUDED: 1972–1973,
appearances with the Royal Shakespeare
Company; 1974–1977, chorus member:
English Opera Group/English Music
Theatre, Glyndebourne Festival Opera;
1977–1981: University College Opera:
Jonathan, *Saul and David* (1977, British
stage première); Antonio, *The Duenna*
(Prokofiev); John the Baptist, *Hérodiade*;
Batignano Festival: Aeneas, *Dido and
Aeneas*; Sempronio, *Lo Speziale*.
MAJOR DEBUTS INCLUDE: 1982: Opera 80,
Eisenstein, *Die Fledermaus*; Théâtre des
Champs Elysées, Paris, Alessandro, *Il Rè
Pastore*; 1983: English National Opera,
Shepherd, *Orfeo*; Cologne Opera, title
role, *The Rake's Progress*; Rennes,
Paolino, *Il Matrimonio Segreto*; 1984:
Opera Factory, Mangus, *The Knot
Garden*; Grand Théâtre, Tours, Ferrando,
Così fan tutte; 1986: Teatro Massimo,
Palermo, Fritz, *La Grand-Duchesse de
Gérolstein*; Wexford Festival, Laerte,
Mignon; 1987, Berlin Kammeroper, Don
Juan, *The Stone Guest*; 1989, Lausanne
Opera, Fritz, *La Grande-Duchesse de
Gérolstein*; 1990, Dublin Grand Opera,
Goro, *Madama Butterfly*.

OPERATIC WORLD PREMIERES INCLUDE:
1981, Teatro La Fenice, Venice, Orfeo,
The Lords' Masque by Niccolò
Castiglioni; 1986, Opera Factory, Bad'Un/
Piper, *Yan Tan Tethera* by Harrison
Birtwistle; 1989, English National Opera,
James Singleton, *The Plumber's Gift* by
David Blake; 1992, Théâtre du Châtelet,
Paris, Curate, *Le Chevalier Imaginaire* by
Philippe Fénelon.
CAREER IN THE UK INCLUDES: Since 1983:
Almeida Festival, Comrade, *Die
Massnahme* (1987, British première);
English National Opera: Pisandro, *The
Return of Ulysses*; Beelzebub/Lieutenant/
Duke of Parma/Student, *Doctor Faust*;
Northern Stage, Schoolmaster, *Comedy
on the Bridge*; Opera Factory: Linfea, *La
Calisto*; Johansson, *The Ghost Sonata*
(1989, British première).
RELATED PROFESSIONAL ACTIVITIES:
Regular concerts, broadcasts and
television appearances chiefly in France.
RECORDINGS INCLUDE: A Hundred Years of
Italian Opera (OPRA).
AWARDS INCLUDE: 1980, Toulouse
International Singing Competition; 1991,
John McCormack Medal (Dublin).
ADDRESS: c/o Musilyre, 6 Rue Saulnier,
75009 Paris, France.

DOLTON GEOFFREY
Baritone

PERSONAL DETAILS: b. 30 December 1958,
Shrewsbury; m. Susan Bradley, one child.
EDUCATION/TRAINING: 1977–1982, Royal
Academy of Music; 1982–1983, National
Opera Studio.
PROFESSIONAL DEBUT: 1983, Opera North,
Guglielmo, *Così fan tutte*.
EARLY CAREER INCLUDED: 1983–1986:
Opera 80, Guglielmo, *Così fan tutte*;
Opera North, Silvio, *Pagliacci*; Opera
Northern Ireland: Malatesta, *Don
Pasquale*; Harlequin, *Ariadne auf Naxos*;
Scottish Opera, Sherasmin, *Oberon*;
Batignano Festival, Plistene, *La Grotta di
Trofonio*.

MAJOR DEBUTS INCLUDE: 1986: Opera
Factory, Guglielmo, *Così fan tutte*; Welsh
National Opera, Papageno, *The Magic
Flute*; 1990, English National Opera,
Guglielmo, *Così fan tutte*.
CAREER IN THE UK INCLUDES: Since 1987:
Buxton Festival, title role, *Le Huron*;
English National Opera, Florian, *Princess
Ida*; Opera Factory: Oreste, *Iphigenias*;
Count, *The Marriage of Figaro*; Ottone,
The Coronation of Poppea; Alan, *Yan Tan
Tethera*; Opera North: Lescaut, *Manon*;
Count, *The Marriage of Figaro*; Henrik,
Masquerade (1990, British première);
Hector, *King Priam*; Valentin, *Faust*;
Opera Northern Ireland, Papageno, *The
Magic Flute*; Scottish Opera, Schaunard,
La Bohème.
RECORDINGS INCLUDE: Donizetti, *Emilia di
Liverpool*; A Hundred Years of Italian
Opera (both OPRA).
AWARDS INCLUDE: 1981, Royal Over-Seas
League Music Competition.
ADDRESS: c/o Allied Artists, 42 Montpelier
Square, London SW7 1JZ.

DON ROBIN   Designer

PERSONAL DETAILS: b. 1941, Fife.
PREVIOUS OCCUPATION: Sculptor.
EDUCATION/TRAINING: University of
Edinburgh, studied engineering; Dundee
College of Art.
PROFESSIONAL DEBUT: 1971, Open Space
Theatre, London, *Four Little Girls* by
Pablo Picasso.
OPERATIC DEBUT: 1977, Scottish Opera,
Mary, Queen of Scots by Thea Musgrave
(world première).
CAREER: Since 1971, freelance opera, ballet
and theatre designer in the UK and
abroad.
MAJOR OPERATIC DEBUTS INCLUDE: 1978,
Opera North, *Les Mamelles de Tirésias*;
1979, Aldeburgh Festival, *Eugene
Onegin*; 1983: Welsh National Opera,
Peter Grimes; San Francisco Opera, *The
Midsummer Marriage*; 1985: Lyons
Opera, *Tamerlano*; San Diego Opera,
Eugene Onegin; 1986: Covent Garden, *A

Midsummer Night's Dream*; Australian
Opera, Sydney, *Peter Grimes*; New York
City Opera, *Don Quichotte*; 1987:
Canadian Opera Company, Toronto, *La
Forza del Destino*; Houston Grand Opera,
Norma; 1991: Icelandic Opera, *Die
Zauberflöte*; Teatro La Zarzuela, Madrid,
Peter Grimes.
OPERATIC WORLD PREMIERES INCLUDE:
1981, Royal Northern College of Music,
The Trumpet Major by Alun Hoddinott.
OPERA DESIGNS IN THE UK INCLUDE: Since
1978: Aldeburgh Festival: *A Midsummer
Night's Dream*, *The Prodigal Son*; Buxton
Festival, *Jason*; Covent Garden, *Norma*;
Opera North: *The Flying Dutchman*,
Tosca, *The Marriage of Figaro*, *Madama
Butterfly*; Opera Northern Ireland: *Così
fan tutte*, *L'Elisir d'Amore*.
AWARDS INCLUDE: 1980, Gold Troika,
International Exhibition of Stage Design,
Prague Quadriennale.
ADDRESS: c/o MLR Ltd, 200 Fulham Road,
London SW10 9PN.

DONNELLY MALCOLM
Baritone

PERSONAL DETAILS: b. 8 February 1943,
Sydney, Australia; m. 1967, Dolores
Ryles.
PREVIOUS OCCUPATION: 1959–1963 and
1967–1970, signwriter/display artist.
EDUCATION/TRAINING: 1963–1966, Sydney
Conservatorium of Music, with Marianne
Mathy; 1970–1971, London Opera Centre,
with Vida Harford.
PROFESSIONAL DEBUT: 1967, Elizabethan
Opera, Sydney, Ceprano, *Rigoletto*.
EARLY CAREER INCLUDED: 1971–1981:
Glyndebourne Touring Opera, Don
Pizarro, *Fidelio*; Scottish Opera:
Leporello, *Don Giovanni*; Count, *The
Marriage of Figaro*; Malatesta, *Don
Pasquale*; Scarpia, *Tosca*; title roles: *The
Barber of Seville*, *Macbeth*, *Rigoletto*,
Simon Boccanegra; Wexford Festival,
Herod, *Hérodiade*.

73

MAJOR DEBUTS INCLUDE: 1981, Don
Pizarro, *Fidelio*: English National Opera,
Glyndebourne Festival Opera; 1982,
Opera North, title role, *Der Fliegende
Holländer*; 1984, Victoria State Opera,
Melbourne, Rodrigo, *Don Carlos*; 1985,
Australian Opera, Sydney, Count di Luna,
Il Trovatore; 1987, Netherlands Opera,
Sharpless, *Madama Butterfly*; 1988,
Welsh National Opera, Scarpia, *Tosca*;
1990: English National Opera Soviet
Union tour (Bolshoi and Kirov), title role,
Macbeth; Adelaide Festival, Kurwenal,
Tristan und Isolde; 1992, Covent Garden,
Sharpless, *Madama Butterfly*.

OPERATIC WORLD PREMIERES INCLUDE:
1974, Scottish Opera, Lentulus, *The
Catiline Conspiracy* by Iain Hamilton.

CAREER IN THE UK INCLUDES: Since 1982:
Earls Court, Scarpia, *Tosca*; English
National Opera: Marcello, *La Bohème*;
Napoleon, *War and Peace*; Count di Luna,
Il Trovatore; Huntsman's Voice, *Rusalka*;
Paolo Orsini, *Rienzi*; Ourrias, *Mireille*;
Cuffe, *Gloriana*; Sharpless, *Madam
Butterfly*; Tonio, *Pagliacci*; Scarpia,
Tosca; Ford, *Falstaff*; Creon, *Oedipus
Rex*; Anckarström, *A Masked Ball*;
Eisenstein, *Die Fledermaus*; title roles:
Rigoletto, Mazeppa, Macbeth; Opera
North: Jack Rance, *La Fanciulla del West*;
Balstrode, *Peter Grimes*; title role, *Prince
Igor*; Welsh National Opera: Shishkov,
From the House of the Dead; Don Carlo,
Ernani.

RELATED PROFESSIONAL ACTIVITIES:
Numerous concerts, recitals and
broadcasts in the UK and abroad.

RECORDINGS INCLUDE: Mozart, *Le Nozze di
Figaro* (EMI).

VIDEOS INCLUDE: Britten, *Gloriana* (English
National Opera); Donizetti, *Lucia di
Lammermoor* (Australian Opera, Sydney).

AWARDS INCLUDE: 1969, *Sun* Aria
Competition (Sydney).

ADDRESS: c/o Ingpen & Williams Ltd, 14
Kensington Court, London W8 5DN.

DONNELLY PATRICK
Bass-baritone

PERSONAL DETAILS: b. 15 March 1955,
Sydney, Australia; m. Gaynor Morgan
(soprano).

PREVIOUS OCCUPATION 1978–1980, school
teacher.

EDUCATION/TRAINING: 1974–1977,
Macquarie University, Sydney; 1975–1978,
New South Wales State Conservatorium
of Music, with William Blankenship; 1982–
1983, Guildhall School of Music and
Drama.

PROFESSIONAL DEBUT: 1985, Glyndebourne
Touring Opera, Theseus, *A Midsummer
Night's Dream*.

MAJOR DEBUTS INCLUDE: 1986,
Glyndebourne Festival Opera at the Hong
Kong Arts Festival, Theseus, *A
Midsummer Night's Dream*; 1987,
Wexford Festival, First Minister,
Cendrillon; 1990: Australian Opera,
Sydney, Herald, *Lohengrin*; Grand
Théâtre, Tours, Polyphemus, *Acis and
Galatea*; Victoria State Opera,
Melbourne: 1990, Zurga, *Les Pêcheurs de
Perles*; 1991, title role, *The Marriage of
Figaro*; 1992, English National Opera,
Count Lerma, *Don Carlos*.

OPERATIC WORLD PREMIERES INCLUDE:
1990, Munich Biennale, Hayden, *63:
Dream Palace* by Hans-Jürgen Von Bose.

CAREER IN THE UK INCLUDES: Since 1985:
Glyndebourne Touring Opera: Voice of
Neptune, *Idomeneo*; Masetto, *Don
Giovanni*; Grenville, *La Traviata*; Bartolo,
Le Nozze di Figaro; Opera 80/English
Touring Opera: Ford, *Falstaff*; title role,
The Marriage of Figaro; Opera Factory:
Caleb Raven, *Yan Tan Tethera*; title role,
The Marriage of Figaro.

RELATED PROFESSIONAL ACTIVITIES:
Concerts and broadcasts in the UK and
Australia.

RECORDINGS INCLUDE: Milhaud, *Les
Malheurs d'Orphée* (ASV); Pergolesi, *La
Serva Padrona* (MERI); Stravinsky, *Renard*
(ASV).

AWARDS INCLUDE: 1985, Esso/
Glyndebourne Touring Opera Award.

ADDRESS: c/o Ron Gonsalves Personal Artists & Concert Management, 10 Dagnan Road, London SW12 9LQ.

DOUGLAS NIGEL
Tenor, Broadcaster, Director, Translator and Writer

PERSONAL DETAILS: b. 9 May 1929, Kent; m. 1973, Alexandra Roper, three children.
PREVIOUS OCCUPATION 1951–1953, Lloyd's insurance broker.
EDUCATION/TRAINING: 1949–1951, Magdalen College, Oxford; 1956–1959, Vienna Music Academy; further vocal studies: 1955–1958, with Alfred Piccaver; 1958–1959, with Lilly Kundegraber; since 1959, with Rupert Bruce-Lockhart.
PROFESSIONAL DEBUT: 1959, Vienna Chamber Opera, Rodolfo, *La Bohème*.
CAREER INCLUDES: Principal Tenor: 1959–1960, Biel/Solothurn; 1960–1961, Koblenz; roles included: Pinkerton, *Madama Butterfly*; Alfredo, *La Traviata*; Don Ottavio, *Don Giovanni*; Count, *Il Barbiere di Siviglia*; Camille, *Die Lustige Witwe*; Duke, *Rigoletto*; Lyonel, *Martha*; Alfred, *Die Fledermaus*; Sou-Chong, *Das Land des Lächelns*; Guest Artist: 1962–1970, Basle; 1964–1973, Zurich Opera; 1980–1987, Deutsche Oper am Rhein, Düsseldorf; roles included: Count Danilo, *Die Lustige Witwe*; Drum Major, *Wozzeck*; Flamand, *Capriccio*; Edwin, *Die Csárdásfürstin*; Robespierre, *Dantons Tod*; Count Zedlau, *Wiener Blut*; Eisenstein, *Die Fledermaus*; Antonio, *Der Sturm*; Lord Cockburn, *Fra Diavolo*; title roles: *Peter Grimes*, *Albert Herring*, *Boccaccio*, *Ein Engel kommt nach Babylon*.
MAJOR DEBUTS INCLUDE: 1964: Sadler's Wells Opera, Barinkay, *The Gipsy Baron*; Vienna Volksoper, Count Danilo, *Die Lustige Witwe*; 1968, Edinburgh International Festival, title role, *Peter Grimes*; 1971, Welsh National Opera, Alwa, *Lulu*; 1973, Covent Garden, Lechmere, *Owen Wingrave* by Benjamin Britten (world stage première).

OPERATIC WORLD PREMIERES INCLUDE: 1964, Basle, Jack Worthing, *Bunbury* by Paul Burkhard; 1967, Zurich Opera, L'Heureux, *Madame Bovary* by Heinrich Sutermeister; 1969, New Opera Company at the Camden Festival, Kyril, *Under Western Eyes* by John Joubert; 1971, BBC Television, Lechmere, *Owen Wingrave* by Benjamin Britten; 1975, Scottish Opera, Frank Innes, *Hermiston* by Robin Orr.
CAREER IN THE UK INCLUDES: Since 1973: Covent Garden, Aschenbach, *Death in Venice*; English National Opera: Count Danilo, *The Merry Widow*; Devil, *Christmas Eve* (1988, British stage première); Hauk-Šendorf, *The Makropoulos Case*; Kent, *Lear* (1989, British première); Opera North: Herod, *Salome*; Pluto, *Orpheus in the Underworld*; Scottish Opera: Shapkin, *From the House of the Dead*; Eisenstein, *Die Fledermaus*; Welsh National Opera: Captain Vere, *Billy Budd*; Loge, *The Rhinegold*; Captain, *Wozzeck*; Herod, *Salome*.
RELATED PROFESSIONAL ACTIVITIES: Since 1970, writer and presenter of over 300 programmes for BBC Radio including series *Singer's Choice* and *Operetta Nights with Nigel Douglas*; since 1982, as director: four Viennese operettas for New Sadler's Wells Opera (also translations) and operettas for Australian Opera and Flanders Opera; 1987–1989, member, Music Advisory Committee, BBC; since 1987, member, Music Advisory Committee, British Council.
RECORDINGS INCLUDE: Britten, *Owen Wingrave* (DECC); J. Strauss, *The Gipsy Baron* (HMV); R. Strauss, *Salome* (DECC); Operetta Recital (PHIL).
PUBLICATIONS INCLUDE: Translations: *The Count of Luxembourg*, *Countess Maritza*, *The Gypsy Princess*, *The Merry Widow* (all Weinberger); 1992, *Legendary Voices* (André Deutsch).
ADDRESS: Eythorne House, Eythorne, Dover, Kent CT15 4BE.

75

DOVE JONATHAN
Composer, Pianist and Accompanist,
Répétiteur,

PERSONAL DETAILS: b. 18 July 1959,
London.
EDUCATION/TRAINING: 1977–1980, Trinity
College, Cambridge, with Robin
Holloway; 1982–1983, University of
London.
FIRST PROFESSIONAL PERFORMANCE OF A
COMPOSITION: 1983, Koenig Ensemble,
Consequences (instrumental).
CAREER: Since 1983, compositions in
several genres including theatre and film
scores; 1983–1987, freelance répétiteur,
pianist and accompanist; 1987–1988,
Assistant Chorus Master, Glyndebourne
Festival Opera; 1989, Composer in
Residence, Salisbury Festival; since 1985,
Adaptor/Orchestrator, English Touring
Opera/City of Birmingham Touring Opera;
operas include: *Cinderella*, *La Bohème*,
Falstaff, *The Magic Flute*, *The Ring Saga*.
OPERATIC WORLD PREMIERES: 1990,
Glyndebourne Education on Hastings
Pier, *Hastings Spring*, community opera,
libretto by Nick Ridout, conductor the
composer, director Tim Hopkins, designer
Nigel Lowery; 1992, English National
Opera Contemporary Opera Studio, *Pig*,
libretto by April de Angelis, conductor
David Parry, director Tim Hopkins,
designer Nigel Lowery.
RECORDINGS INCLUDE: *Figures in the
Garden* for wind ensemble, based on *Le
Nozze di Figaro* (EMI).
ADDRESS: 6 Caithness Road, London W14
0JB.

DOWNES, SIR EDWARD
Conductor, Editor and Translator

POSITION: Associate Music Director and
Principal Conductor, The Royal Opera,
Covent Garden.
PERSONAL DETAILS: b. 17 June 1924,
Birmingham; m., two children.

EDUCATION/TRAINING: University of
Birmingham, studied English and music;
Royal College of Music, studied
composition and french horn; 1948–1950,
Carnegie Scholarship, studied and
worked with Hermann Scherchen.
OPERATIC DEBUT: 1948, University of
Aberdeen, *The Marriage of Figaro*.
CAREER: 1945–1948, freelance orchestral
player; 1948, lecturer, University of
Aberdeen; 1950–1952, member, music
staff, Carl Rosa Opera Company; Covent
Garden: 1952–1966, staff conductor; 1966–
1969, Assistant Music Director; 1972–
1976, Music Director, Australian Opera,
Sydney; 1980–1983, Chief Conductor,
Netherlands Radio Orchestra; 1980–1991,
Artistic Director and Principal Conductor,
BBC Philharmonic Orchestra; since 1991,
Associate Music Director and Principal
Conductor, The Royal Opera, Covent
Garden.
OPERATIC WORLD PREMIERES INCLUDE:
Covent Garden: 1970, *Victory* by Richard
Rodney Bennett; 1972, *Taverner* by Peter
Maxwell Davies; 1979, *Thérèse* by John
Tavener; 1979, BBC Radio 3, *Maddalena*
by Sergei Prokofiev.
OPERA PERFORMANCES INCLUDE: Since
1953: Covent Garden, more than 750
performances of over 30 operas
including: *La Bohème*, *Carmen*, *Der
Freischütz*, *Madama Butterfly*, *Les Contes
d'Hoffmann*, *Un Ballo in Maschera*,
Jenůfa, *Rigoletto*, *Il Trovatore*, *Otello*,
Aida, *Peter Grimes*, *Macbeth* (also 1985,
Athens Festival), *Il Barbiere di Siviglia*,
Der Rosenkavalier, *Tosca*, *Gianni
Schicchi*, *Don Carlos*, *Falstaff*, *La Forza
del Destino*, *Katerina Ismailova* (1963,
first staged production in the West),
Khovanshchina, *Arabella*, *Boris Godunov*,
Elektra, *Simon Boccanegra*, *Der Ring des
Nibelungen* (1967, first English conductor
to perform the complete Ring Cycle at
Covent Garden since Thomas Beecham
in 1939), *Hamlet* (Searle, 1969, British
première), *Tannhäuser*, *Billy Budd*,
Eugene Onegin, *Lohengrin*, *Attila*,
Turandot, *The Fiery Angel*, *Salome*,
Stiffelio; also: Welsh National Opera, *The*

Flying Dutchman; Australian Opera, Sydney: *Der Rosenkavalier, War and Peace* (1973, opening of Sydney Opera House); Graz, *Maddalena* by Sergei Prokofiev (1985, world stage première); Teatro Colón, Buenos Aires, *Salome.*

RELATED PROFESSIONAL ACTIVITIES: Regular appearances with leading orchestras in the UK and abroad; translations include: *The Birthday of the Infanta, The Fiery Angel, A Florentine Tragedy, Gianni Schicchi, Jenůfa* (with Otakar Kraus), *Katerina Ismailova, Khovanshchina, Lady Macbeth of Mtsensk, Maddalena, The Nose, The Stone Guest, War and Peace*; performing editions include: *Die Feen, Das Liebesverbot, Maddalena, Rienzi.*

RECORDINGS INCLUDE: Maxwell Davies, Symphony No. 3 (BBC); Puccini, Greatest Hits (RCA); Famous Opera Choruses (DECC), Italian Operatic Favourites (EMI), Opera's Greatest Hits (RCA).

PUBLICATIONS INCLUDE: 1976, *Everyman's Guide to Orchestral Music* (Dent); 1978, *The New York Philharmonic Guide to the Symphony* (Walker); contributor, music journals.

AWARDS AND HONOURS INCLUDE: 1986, Commander, Order of the British Empire (CBE); 1990, *Evening Standard* Award, *Attila* (Covent Garden); 1991, Knighthood; 1992, Honorary Doctorate of Music, University of Manchester; 1993, Olivier Award: *The Fiery Angel, Stiffelio* (both Covent Garden).

ADDRESS: c/o Ingpen & Williams Ltd, 14 Kensington Court, London W8 5DN.

DRUIETT MICHAEL Bass

POSITION: Member, The Royal Opera, Covent Garden.

PERSONAL DETAILS: b. 23 January 1967, London; m. 1988.

EDUCATION/TRAINING: 1983–1985, West London Institute of Higher Education, with Sonja Nerdrum and Eduardo Asquez; 1987: European Opera Centre, Belgium; Scuola Superiore, Acquasparta, Italy (both with Elio Battaglia); 1989–1990,

National Opera Studio, with Norman Bailey.

PROFESSIONAL DEBUT: 1989, Kent Opera, Second Prisoner, *Fidelio.*

CAREER IN THE UK INCLUDES: 1989: Kent Opera, chorus member and small roles; Nonsuch Opera, Ramfis, *Aida*; 1990–1993, Principal Bass, English National Opera: Herald/King of Clubs, *The Love for Three Oranges* (debut); First Workman, *Wozzeck*; Betto, *Gianni Schicchi*; First Nazarene, *Salome*; Badger, *The Cunning Little Vixen*; Banquo, *Macbeth*; Boris, *Lady Macbeth of Mtsensk*; Colline, *La Bohème*; Count Ribbing, *A Masked Ball*; Charon, *Orfeo*; Monk, *Don Carlos*; Sparafucile, *Rigoletto*; Arac, *Princess Ida*; King of Scotland, *Ariodante.*

ADDRESS: c/o John Coast, 31 Sinclair Road, London W14 ONS.

DUDLEY WILLIAM Designer

POSITION: Associate Designer, Royal National Theatre.

PERSONAL DETAILS: b. 4 March 1947.

EDUCATION/TRAINING: St Martin's School of Art, Slade School of Art and University College, London.

PROFESSIONAL DEBUT: 1970, Nottingham Playhouse, *Hamlet.*

OPERATIC DEBUT: 1972, Hamburg State Opera, *Billy Budd.*

CAREER: Freelance opera and theatre designer in the UK and abroad including Royal Court Theatre and Royal Shakepeare Company; since 1981, Associate Designer, Royal National Theatre.

MAJOR OPERATIC DEBUTS INCLUDE: 1974, Welsh National Opera, *Der Fliegende Holländer*; 1978, Metropolitan Opera, New York, *Billy Budd*; 1980: Covent Garden, *Les Contes d'Hoffmann*; Glyndebourne Festival Opera, *Die Entführung aus dem Serail*; 1983, Bayreuth Festival, *Der Ring des Nibelungen*; 1989, Salzburg Festival, *Un Ballo in Maschera*; 1990, Lyric Opera, Chicago, *Lucia di Lammermoor.*

OPERA DESIGNS IN THE UK INCLUDE: Since 1974: Covent Garden: *Don Giovanni*, *Der Rosenkavalier*, *The Cunning Little Vixen*; Glyndebourne Festival Opera, *Il Barbiere di Siviglia*; Welsh National Opera: *The Barber of Seville*, *Idomeneo*.

VIDEOS INCLUDE: Offenbach, *Les Contes d'Hoffmann*; R. Strauss, *Der Rosenkavalier* (both Covent Garden).

ADDRESS: c/o Curtis Brown Group Ltd, 162–168 Regent Street, London W1R 5TB.

*   *   *   *

EAGLEN JANE   Soprano

PERSONAL DETAILS: b. 4 April 1960, Lincoln.

EDUCATION/TRAINING: 1978–1983, Royal Northern College of Music; masterclasses with Elisabeth Schwarzkopf and Tito Gobbi; currently with Joseph Ward.

PROFESSIONAL DEBUT: 1984, English National Opera, Lady Ella, *Patience*.

MAJOR DEBUTS INCLUDE: 1987, Lyric Opera of Queensland, title role, *Madama Butterfly*; 1988: Scottish Opera, Mimi, *La Bohème*; Western Australian Opera, title role, *Tosca*; 1989, Covent Garden, First Lady, *Die Zauberflöte*; 1990–1991, Teatro Comunale, Bologna: Donna Anna, *Don Giovanni*; Amelia, *Un Ballo in Maschera*; 1991, Grand Théâtre, Geneva, Mathilde, *Guillaume Tell*; 1991–1992, Vienna State Opera: Donna Anna, *Don Giovanni*; Senta, *Der Fliegende Holländer*; Elettra, *Idomeneo*; 1992: La Monnaie, Brussels, Elena, *La Donna del Lago*; Bavarian State Opera, Munich, Donna Anna, *Don Giovanni*.

CAREER IN THE UK INCLUDES: Since 1984: Covent Garden: Berta, *Il Barbiere di Siviglia*; Mathilde, *Guillaume Tell*; English National Opera (1984–1991, Principal Soprano): Leonora, *Il Trovatore*; Queen Elizabeth, *Mary Stuart*; Santuzza, *Cavalleria Rusticana*; High Priestess, *Aida*; Sinaida, *Moses*; Micaëla, *Carmen*; Donna Elvira and Donna Anna, *Don Giovanni*; Fata Morgana, *The Love for Three Oranges*; Eva, *The Mastersingers of Nuremberg*; title role, *Tosca*; Scottish Opera: Donna Anna, *Don Giovanni*; Fiordiligi, *Così fan tutte*; Brünnhilde, *Die Walküre*; title role, *Norma*.

RELATED PROFESSIONAL ACTIVITIES: Numerous concerts, recitals, broadcasts and television appearances in the UK and abroad.

RECORDINGS INCLUDE: Mahler, Symphony No. 8 (EMI).

AWARDS INCLUDE: Countess of Munster Award, The Friends of Covent Garden Dame Eva Turner Award, Peter Moores Foundation Scholarship.

ADDRESS: c/o Harrison/Parrott Ltd, 12 Penzance Place, London W11 4PA.

EARLE RODERICK
Bass-baritone

POSITION: Member, The Royal Opera, Covent Garden.

PERSONAL DETAILS: b. 29 January 1952, Winchester; m. Angela Bostock (soprano), two children.

EDUCATION/TRAINING: 1971–1974, St John's College, Cambridge; 1974–1976, Royal College of Music; privately with Otakar Kraus.

PROFESSIONAL DEBUT: 1978, English National Opera, Spinelloccio, *Gianni Schicchi*.

EARLY CAREER INCLUDED: 1978–1980, English National Opera: Zuniga, *Carmen*; Grenville, *La Traviata*; King, *Aida*; Calatrava, *The Force of Destiny*; Angelotti, *Tosca*; Brander, *The Damnation of Faust*.

MAJOR DEBUTS INCLUDE: 1980, Covent Garden, Antonio, *Le Nozze di Figaro*; 1983: Opera North, Leporello, *Don Giovanni*; Welsh National Opera, Fafner, *The Rhinegold*; 1984, Buxton Festival, Oreste, *Jason*; 1986, Scottish Opera, title role, *Le Nozze di Figaro*.

CAREER IN THE UK INCLUDES: Since 1980, member, Covent Garden, more than 30 roles including: Montano, *Otello*; Angelotti, *Tosca*; Monterone, *Rigoletto*; Abimelech, *Samson et Dalila*; Bonze, *Madama Butterfly*; Schaunard, *La Bohème*; Masetto, *Don Giovanni*; Mandarin, *Turandot*; Nightwatchman, *Die Meistersinger von Nürnberg*; Theseus, *A Midsummer Night's Dream*; Hobson, *Peter Grimes*; Orest, *Elektra*; Alberich, *Der Ring des Nibelungen*; Zuniga, *Carmen*; Leuthold, *Guillaume Tell*; Faust, *The Fiery Angel*; One-armed Brother, *Die Frau ohne Schatten*; Brander, *La Damnation de Faust*; Foreman, *Jenůfa*; Harašta, *The Cunning Little Vixen*; Zaretsky, *Eugene Onegin*; also: Opera North: Giorgio, *I Puritani*; He-Ancient, *The Midsummer Marriage*; Welsh National Opera, Hunding, *The Valkyrie*.

RECORDINGS INCLUDE: Donizetti, *Maria Padilla*; Meyerbeer, *Dinorah* (both OPRA); Rossini, *Stabat Mater* (CHAN); Verdi: *La Traviata* (EMI), *Il Trovatore* (PHIL).

VIDEOS INCLUDE: Bizet, *Carmen*; Giordano, *Andrea Chénier*; Puccini: *La Fanciulla del West*; *Manon Lescaut*; R. Strauss, *Der Rosenkavalier* (all Covent Garden).

ADDRESS: c/o John Coast, 31 Sinclair Road, London W14 ONS.

EATHORNE WENDY
Soprano and Teacher

POSITION: Head of Vocal Department, Trinity College of Music.

PERSONAL DETAILS: b. 25 September 1939, Cornwall; one child.

EDUCATION/TRAINING: 1959–1965, Royal Academy of Music (Licentiate), with May Blyth and Flora Nielson.

CAREER INCLUDES: Since 1968, appearances with Covent Garden, Glyndebourne Festival Opera, Sadler's Wells Opera/English National Opera; roles include: Marguérite, *Faust*; Sophie, *Werther*; Julia, *La Vestale*; Echo, *Ariadne auf Naxos*; tours abroad with Glyndebourne Festival Opera and Handel Opera Society; numerous concerts, recitals and broadcasts with leading British orchestras and conductors (repertoire ranges from Bach to contemporary composers); international adjudicator and examiner.

OPERATIC WORLD PREMIERES INCLUDE: 1970, Glyndebourne Festival Opera, Atalanta, *The Rising of the Moon* by Nicholas Maw.

RECORDINGS INCLUDE: Bridge, *The Christmas Rose* (PAVI); Delius, *A Village Romeo and Juliet;* Vaughan Williams: *The Pilgrim's Progress*, *Sir John in Love* (all EMI).

HONOURS INCLUDE: Associate: Royal Academy of Music, Royal College of Music.

ADDRESS: 23 King Edward's Road, Ruislip, Middlesex HA4 7AQ.

EBRAHIM OMAR   Baritone

EDUCATION/TRAINING: Guildhall School of Music and Drama.

PROFESSIONAL DEBUT: 1980, Glyndebourne Touring Opera, Schaunard, *La Bohème*.

MAJOR DEBUTS INCLUDE: 1981, Glyndebourne Festival Opera, Wig Maker, *Ariadne auf Naxos*; 1982, Opera Factory, Punch, *Punch and Judy*; 1984, Kent Opera, Hector, *King Priam*; 1986, Scottish Opera, Billy, *The Rise and Fall of the City of Mahagonny*; 1987, Paris, title role, *Eight Songs for a Mad King*; 1989, Covent Garden, Singer, *Un Re in Ascolto* (British première).

OPERATIC WORLD PREMIERES INCLUDE: 1986, Opera Factory: several roles, *Hell's Angels* by Nigel Osborne; Alan, *Yan Tan Tethera* by Harrison Birtwistle; 1987, Glyndebourne Touring Opera, Serezha,

The Electrification of the Soviet Union by Nigel Osborne; 1988, Batignano Festival, Cipolla, *Mario ed il Mago* by Stephen Oliver; 1990, Munich Biennale, Parkhearst, *63: Dream Palace* by Hans-Jürgen von Bose; 1991, Covent Garden, Fool, *Gawain* by Harrison Birtwistle; 1992, Almeida Opera, Voice of Goya, *Terrible Mouth* by Nigel Osborne.

CAREER IN THE UK INCLUDES: Since 1982: City of Birmingham Touring Opera, Beast, *Beauty and the Beast*; Glyndebourne Festival and Touring Opera: Serezha, *The Electrification of the Soviet Union*; Fiorello, *Il Barbiere di Siviglia*; Donny, *New Year* (1990, British première); Opera Factory: Filch, *The Beggar's Opera*; Mel, *The Knot Garden*; Mercury, *La Calisto*; Baritone, *Aventures et Nouvelles Aventures* and Billy, *Mahagonny Songspiel*; title role, *Don Giovanni*; Scottish Opera: Strephon, *Iolanthe*; Prince Orlofsky, *Die Fledermaus*; Scottish Opera Go Round, title role, *Macbeth*.

RELATED PROFESSIONAL ACTIVITIES: Numerous concerts and television appearances in the UK and abroad; as actor: roles with Royal Shakespeare Company and Leeds Playhouse.

ADDRESS: c/o Allied Artists, 42 Montpelier Square, London SW7 1JZ.

EDWARDS JACK
Director, Designer, Teacher and Writer

POSITION: Artistic Director, Opera Restor'd.

PERSONAL DETAILS: b. 28 May 1937, Cornwall.

EDUCATION/TRAINING: 1946–1953, Truro School, Cornwall.

OPERATIC DEBUT: 1979, Holme Pierrepont Opera Trust, *Cupid and Death*.

CAREER: Regular appearances as an actor; director and designer for theatre and opera; Artistic Director: 1979–1985, Holme Pierrepont Opera Trust; since 1985, Opera Restor'd.

OPERA PRODUCTIONS INCLUDE: Since 1980: Holme Pierrepont Opera Trust: *Venus and Adonis*, *The Death of Dido* (1981, first modern performance), *Thomas and Sally*, *Dido and Aeneas*, *Phoebe* (1984, first modern performance), *Pyramus and Thisbe*; Opera Restor'd: *The Ephesian Matron*, *The Brickdust Man*, *The Grenadier*, *Peleus and Thetis*, *The Portrait* (1990, first modern performance), *Lo Speziale*, *La Serva Padrona*; Utrecht: *The Ephesian Matron*, *Pyramus and Thisbe*.

RELATED PROFESSIONAL ACTIVITIES: 1979–1980, Lecturer in Drama, Dance and Design, Universidad Catolica, Santiago; 1990–1991, Director, residential opera workshops, Little Benslow Music School, Hertfordshire.

ADDRESS: c/o Opera Restor'd, 54 Astonville Street, London SW18 5AJ.

EDWARDS SIAN   Conductor

POSITION: Music Director, English National Opera.

PERSONAL DETAILS: b. 27 August 1959, West Sussex; one child.

EDUCATION/TRAINING: Royal Northern College of Music: 1977–1981, french horn with Ifor James; 1981–1983, with Charles Groves and Timothy Reynish; further studies with Norman Del Mar as an external student at the Royal College of Music; 1983–1985, Leningrad State Conservatoire, with Ilya Alexandrovitch Musin.

PROFESSIONAL DEBUT: 1985, Scottish National Orchestra.

OPERATIC DEBUT: 1986, Scottish Opera, *The Rise and Fall of the City of Mahagonny*.

CAREER: 1985–1993, freelance conductor in the UK and abroad; since 1993/1994 season, Music Director, English National Opera.

MAJOR OPERATIC DEBUTS INCLUDE: 1987, Glyndebourne Festival Opera, *La Traviata*; 1988: Covent Garden, *The Knot Garden*; Opera 80, *Carmen*; 1990, English National Opera, *The Gambler*.

OPERATIC WORLD PREMIERES INCLUDE:
1988, Munich Biennale, *Greek* by Mark-
Anthony Turnage.

OPERA PERFORMANCES IN THE UK
INCLUDE: Since 1986: Covent Garden:
Rigoletto, *Il Trovatore*, *Carmen*, *Madama
Butterfly*; Edinburgh International
Festival, *Greek* (1988, British première);
English National Opera: *The Queen of
Spades*, *Lohengrin*; Glyndebourne
Festival and Touring Opera: *L'Heure
Espagnole/L'Enfant et les Sortilèges*,
Katya Kabanova, *New Year*; Scottish
Opera, *Carmen*.

RELATED PROFESSIONAL ACTIVITIES:
Numerous concerts and broadcasts with
leading orchestras in the UK and abroad.

AWARDS INCLUDE: 1984, first recipient,
Leeds Conductors Competition.

ADDRESS: c/o English National Opera,
London Coliseum, St Martin's Lane,
London WC2N 4ES.

EDWARDS TERRY
Chorus Master

POSITIONS: Chorus Director, The Royal
Opera, Covent Garden; Artistic Director:
Electric Phoenix, London Sinfonietta
Voices and Chorus; Director, London
Voices.

PERSONAL DETAILS: b. 1939; two children.

EDUCATION/TRAINING: Trinity College of
Music (Licentiate, Royal Academy of
Music).

PROFESSIONAL DEBUT: As bass: 1966,
Albert Hall, chorus member, Promenade
concert.

CAREER: 1968–1974, bass, Covent Garden
Extra Chorus; 1970–1986, bass then
manager, John Alldis Choir and Schütz
Choir; 1973–1978, sound designer and
record producer, The Swingle Singers;
since 1973, founder and Director, London
Voices (incorporating London Opera
Chorus), providing chorus for recording
sessions; since 1978, founder and Artistic
Director, Electric Phoenix (avant-garde
vocal group); since 1980, Artistic Director,
London Sinfonietta Voices and Chorus;

1987–1989, Guest Chorus Master, Chicago
Symphony Chorus; since 1992, Chorus
Director, The Royal Opera, Covent
Garden.

RELATED PROFESSIONAL ACTIVITIES:
Regular concerts, particularly of newly
commissioned works (close association
with Luciano Berio and György Ligeti);
workshops with school children and
music students; chorus master on many
recordings and film sound tracks; 1991,
member, Panel of Judges, BBC/Sainsbury
Choir of the Year Competition.

RECORDINGS INCLUDE: As chorus master:
Verdi, *Otello* (DECC); as conductor: Britten,
choral works; Messiaen, *Trois Petites
Liturgies* (both VIRG).

ADDRESS: c/o Royal Opera House, Covent
Garden, London WC2E 9DD.

EGERTON FRANCIS   Tenor

POSITION: Member, The Royal Opera,
Covent Garden.

PERSONAL DETAILS: b. 14 July 1930,
Limerick; three children.

PREVIOUS OCCUPATION: Engineer.

PROFESSIONAL DEBUT AS A PRINCIPAL:
1965, Scottish Opera, Missail, *Boris
Godunov*.

EARLY CAREER INCLUDED: 1961–1963,
chorus member, Glyndebourne Festival
Opera; 1966–1972: Principal Tenor,
Sadler's Wells Opera: Andrès/Cochenille/
Pittichinaccio/Frantz, *The Tales of
Hoffmann*; Count, *The Barber of Seville*;
title role, *Count Ory*; also: appearances
with English Opera Group/English Music
Theatre, Scottish Opera, Wexford
Festival; roles included: Mime, *Das
Rheingold*; Captain, *Wozzeck*; Dema,
L'Egisto; Judge, *Trial by Jury*; Podestà,
La Finta Giardiniera; Nicias, *Thaïs*.

MAJOR DEBUTS INCLUDE: 1972, Covent
Garden, Iopas, *Les Troyens*; 1978, San
Francisco Opera, Red Whiskers, *Billy
Budd*; 1980, Glyndebourne Festival
Opera, Monostatos, *Die Zauberflote*;
1982, Los Angeles Music Center Opera,
Bardolph, *Falstaff*; 1983, Royal Court

Theatre, Drottningholm, Romolo, *Il Fanatico Burlato*; 1984, Netherlands Opera, Nick, *La Fanciulla del West*; 1988, Teatro Regio, Parma, Andrès/Cochenille/Pittichinaccio/Frantz, *Les Contes d'Hoffmann*.

OPERATIC WORLD PREMIERES INCLUDE: Covent Garden: 1972, First Monk, *Taverner* by Peter Maxwell Davies; 1976, Soldier 1, *We Come to the River* by Hans Werner Henze.

CAREER IN THE UK INCLUDES: Since 1972, member, Covent Garden: Captain, *Wozzeck*; Nick, *La Fanciulla del West*; Andrès/Cochenille/Pittichinaccio/Frantz, *Les Contes d'Hoffmann*; Flute, *A Midsummer Night's Dream*; Pong, *Turandot*; Don Basilio, *Le Nozze di Figaro*; Goro, *Madama Butterfly*; Monostatos, *Die Zauberflöte*; Vogelgesang, *Die Meistersinger von Nürnberg*; Bardolph, *Falstaff*; Remendado, *Carmen*; Missail, *Boris Godunov*; Brighella, *Ariadne auf Naxos*; Eroshka, *Prince Igor*; Doctor, *The Fiery Angel*; First Philistine, *Samson et Dalila*; Hunchback Brother, *Die Frau ohne Schatten*; Monsieur Triquet, *Eugene Onegin*.

RECORDINGS INCLUDE: Mozart, *Le Nozze di Figaro* (DECC); Puccini: *La Fanciulla del West* (DG), *Tosca* (RCA); Verdi, *Falstaff* (DG).

VIDEOS INCLUDE: Bizet, *Carmen*; Offenbach, *Les Contes d'Hoffmann*; Puccini, *La Fanciulla del West*; Verdi, *Falstaff* (all Covent Garden); Sullivan, *The Gondoliers* (Walker).

ADDRESS: c/o Athole Still International Management Ltd, Greystoke House, 80–86 Westow Street, London SE19 3AF.

ELDER MARK   Conductor

POSITIONS: Music Director, Rochester Philharmonic Orchestra, New York; Principal Guest Conductor, City of Birmingham Symphony Orchestra.

PERSONAL DETAILS: b. 2 June 1947, Northumberland; m. 1980, Amanda Stein (Planning Administrator, English National Opera), one child.

EDUCATION/TRAINING: 1964–1965, National Youth Orchestra, played bassoon; 1966–1969, Choral and Music Scholar, Corpus Christi College, Cambridge.

PROFESSIONAL AND OPERATIC DEBUT: 1972, Australian Opera, Melbourne, *Rigoletto*.

CAREER: 1970–1971, Chorus Master and member, music staff, Glyndebourne Festival Opera; 1970–1972, member, music staff, Covent Garden; 1972–1974, staff conductor, Australian Opera, Melbourne; English National Opera: 1974–1979, staff conductor; 1979–1993, Music Director; Principal Guest Conductor: 1979, London Mozart Players; 1982, BBC Symphony Orchestra; since 1989, Music Director, Rochester Philharmonic Orchestra, New York; since 1992, Principal Guest Conductor, City of Birmingham Symphony Orchestra.

MAJOR OPERATIC DEBUTS INCLUDE: 1974, English National Opera, *The Bassarids*; 1975, Covent Garden, *La Bohème*; 1978, Komische Oper, East Berlin, *Madama Butterfly*; 1981, Bayreuth Festival, *Die Meistersinger von Nürnberg*; 1988, Metropolitan Opera, New York, *Le Nozze di Figaro*; English National Opera: 1984, USA tour (including Metropolitan Opera, New York): *Gloriana*, *Rigoletto*, *War and Peace*; 1990, Soviet Union tour (Bolshoi and Kirov), *Macbeth*.

OPERATIC WORLD PREMIERES INCLUDE: 1977, Bath Festival, *A Gentle Spirit* by John Tavener; English National Opera: 1977, *Toussaint* by David Blake; 1993, *Inquest of Love* by Jonathan Harvey.

OPERA PERFORMANCES IN THE UK INCLUDE: Since 1979, English National Opera: *Fidelio*, *Arabella*, *Otello*, *War and Peace*, *Pelléas and Mélisande*, *The Flying Dutchman*, *The Makropoulos Case*, *Rigoletto*, *The Queen of Spades*, *Rusalka*, *Rienzi*, *The Valkyrie*, *The Mastersingers of Nuremberg*, *The Sicilian Vespers*, *Gloriana*, *Osud* (1984, British stage première), *Mazeppa*, *The Midsummer Marriage*, *Orpheus in the Underworld*, *Don Giovanni*, *Doctor Faust* (1986, British stage première), *Carmen*, *Simon Boccanegra*, *Lady Macbeth of Mtsensk* (1987, British stage première), *Werther*, *The Barber of Seville*, *Hansel and Gretel*, *The Cunning Little Vixen*, *La Traviata*, *Falstaff*, *Eugene Onegin*, *A Masked Ball*, *Beatrice and Benedict*, *Macbeth*, *Wozzeck*, *Oedipus Rex*/*Duke Bluebeard's Castle*, *Königskinder*, *Don Carlos*, *The Force of Destiny*.

RELATED PROFESSIONAL ACTIVITIES: Concerts, broadcasts and television performances with leading orchestras in the UK and abroad.

RECORDINGS INCLUDE: Offenbach: *The Tales of Hoffmann*, *Orpheus in the Underworld* (both TER); Verdi: *Otello*, *Rigoletto* (both EMI); Josephine Barstow sings Verdi Arias (TER).

VIDEOS INCLUDE: Britten, *Gloriana*; Dvořák, *Rusalka*; Verdi, *Rigoletto* (all English National Opera).

RELEVANT PUBLICATIONS INCLUDE: 1992, *Power House: The English National Opera Experience* (Lime Tree).

AWARDS AND HONOURS INCLUDE: 1989, Commander, Order of the British Empire (CBE); 1991, Olivier Award: *Duke Bluebeard's Castle*, *Macbeth*, *Pelléas and Mélisande*, *Wozzeck* (all English National Opera).

ADDRESS: c/o Ingpen & Williams Ltd, 14 Kensington Court, London W8 5DN.

ELLIOTT ALASDAIR   Tenor

PERSONAL DETAILS: b. 18 July 1954, Hamilton, Scotland; m. 1978, one child.

EDUCATION/TRAINING: 1972–1977, Royal Scottish Academy of Music and Drama, with Lilian Liddell; 1977–1978, Guildhall School of Music and Drama, with Laura Sarti (since 1978, privately); Britten-Pears School for Advanced Musical Studies; 1984–1985, National Opera Studio.

PROFESSIONAL DEBUT: 1981, Kent Opera, Don Curzio, *The Marriage of Figaro*.

EARLY CAREER INCLUDED: 1981–1986, appearances with Kent Opera, Opera Northern Ireland, Aldeburgh and Batignano Festivals; roles included: Filch, *The Beggar's Opera*; Brighella, *Ariadne auf Naxos*; Pisandro, *Il Ritorno d'Ulisse in Patria*.

MAJOR DEBUTS INCLUDE: 1987: English National Opera, Second Jew, *Salome*; Scottish Opera, Squeak, *Billy Budd*; 1988: Buxton Festival, Roberto, *Torquato Tasso*; Glyndebourne Touring Opera, Belmonte, *Die Entführung aus dem Serail*; 1990, Covent Garden, Ruedi, *Guillaume Tell*; 1991: Amadeus Festival, Switzerland, Aceste, *Ascanio in Alba*; Netherlands Opera, Innkeeper, *Benvenuto Cellini*.

OPERATIC WORLD PREMIERES INCLUDE: 1992, English National Opera, Servant, *Bakxai* by John Buller.

CAREER IN THE UK INCLUDES: Since 1986: Buxton Festival, Crotignac, *Il Pittor Parigino*; Covent Garden, Gelsomino, *Il Viaggio a Reims*; English National Opera: Priest, *Christmas Eve*; Andrès, *Wozzeck*; Neath Opera Group, title role, *Count Ory*; Opera 80: Ramiro, *Cinderella*; Belmonte, *The Seraglio*; Opera Northern Ireland: Pedrillo, *The Seraglio*; Leicester, *Mary Stuart*; Scottish Opera: Don Basilio, *Le Nozze di Figaro*; Iopas, *The Trojans* (also 1990, at Covent Garden).

RELATED PROFESSIONAL ACTIVITIES: Concerts and recitals in the UK and Netherlands.

AWARDS INCLUDE: BP Peter Pears Award, Britten-Pears Award for Concert Singers.

ADDRESS: c/o Athole Still International Management Ltd, Greystoke House, 80–86 Westow Street, London SE19 3AF.

EPSTEIN MATTHEW
Administrator

POSITION: General Director, Welsh National Opera.

PERSONAL DETAILS: b. 23 December 1947, New York City, USA.

EDUCATION/TRAINING: University of Pennsylvania, studied modern history.
CAREER: Since 1969: concert and opera agent (Vice-president and Special Consultant, Columbia Artists Management Inc.); consultant on production concepts and casting for opera companies (Netherlands Opera, San Francisco Opera, Santa Fe Opera), recording companies (BMG Classics/RCA Records), symphony orchestras in the USA and Europe; 1982–1986, Artistic Consultant, Carnegie Hall; 1987–1990, Artistic Director, Opera Programme, Brooklyn Academy of Music (1989, responsible for first visit of Welsh National Opera to USA); since 1991, General Director, Welsh National Opera.
OTHER PROFESSIONAL ACTIVITIES INCLUDE: 1989 and 1991, member, Jury Panel, Cardiff Singer of the World Competition.
ADDRESS: c/o Welsh National Opera, John Street, Cardiff CF1 4SP.

ESSWOOD PAUL
Counter-tenor and Teacher

POSITION: Professor in Baroque Vocal Interpretation, Royal Academy of Music.
PERSONAL DETAILS: b. 6 June 1942, Nottingham; m. 1966, Mary Lillian Cantrill, two children; m. 1990, Aimée Desirée Blattmann (soprano).
PREVIOUS OCCUPATION: 1964–1971, lay vicar, Westminster Abbey.
EDUCATION/TRAINING: 1961–1964, Royal College of Music, with Gordon Clinton.
PROFESSIONAL DEBUT: 1965, BBC Radio 3, *Messiah*.
MAJOR DEBUTS INCLUDE: 1968, University of California, Berkeley, Orimeno, *L'Erismena* (operatic debut); 1969, Basle, title role, *Il Tigrane*; 1970, Netherlands Opera, Orimeno, *L'Erismena*; Zurich Opera: 1976, Ottone, *L'Incoronazione di Poppea*; 1977, Anfinomo, *Il Ritorno d'Ulisse in Patria*; 1981, David, *Saul*; 1978, Scottish Opera at the Aix-en-Provence Festival, Spirit, *Dido and Aeneas*; 1980, La Scala, Milan, Death, *Paradise Lost*; 1981, Lyons Opera, David, *David et Jonathas*; Salzburg Festival: 1983, Hamor, *Jephtha*; 1984, David, *Saul*; 1987, Cologne Opera, Oberon, *A Midsummer Night's Dream*; 1990, Karlsruhe, title role, *Admeto*.
OPERATIC WORLD PREMIERES INCLUDE: 1979, Lyric Opera, Chicago, Death, *Paradise Lost* by Krzysztof Penderecki; 1984, Stuttgart State Opera, title role, *Akhnaten* by Philip Glass.
CAREER IN THE UK INCLUDES: Since 1969: English Bach Festival at Covent Garden, title role, *Riccardo Primo*; Handel Opera Society: Ahasuerus, *Esther*; Arsace, *Partenope*; Kent Opera, Ottone, *Agrippina*; Phoenix Opera, Spirit, *Dido and Aeneas*.
RELATED PROFESSIONAL ACTIVITIES: Numerous concerts, recitals, broadcasts, television appearances and masterclasses in the UK and abroad; 1967, co-founder, Pro Cantione Antiqua; 1977–1980, Professor of Singing, Royal College of Music; since 1985, Professor in Baroque Vocal Interpretation, Royal Academy of Music.
RECORDINGS INCLUDE: J.S. Bach, complete cantatas (TELD); Charpentier, *David et Jonathas* (ERAT); Glass, *Akhnaten* (CBS); Handel: *Giulio Cesare* (TELD), *Israel in Egypt* (ARCH), *Jephtha* (TELD), *Il Pastor Fido* (HUNG), *Rinaldo* (CBS), *Saul* (TELD), *Serse* (CBS); Monteverdi: *L'Incoronazione di Poppea*, *Il Ritorno d'Ulisse in Patria* (both TELD); Telemann, *Der Geduldige Socrates* (HUNG).
VIDEOS INCLUDE: Monteverdi, *L'Incoronazione di Poppea* (Zurich Opera).
AWARDS AND HONOURS INCLUDE: 1964: Associate, Royal College of Music; Henry Blower Prize for Singing; 1990, Honorary Member, Royal Academy of Music; 1992, Handel Prize (Germany).
ADDRESS: c/o Transart (UK) Ltd, 18b Pindock Mews, London W9 2PY.

EVANS ANNE   Soprano

PERSONAL DETAILS: b. 20 August 1941, London; m. 1962, Melvyn Jones; m. 1981, John Lucas.

EDUCATION/TRAINING: 1962–1966, Royal College of Music, with Ruth Packer; 1966–1968, Centre Lyrique, Geneva, with Maria Carpi; further studies with Vida Harford.

PROFESSIONAL DEBUT: 1967, Grand Théâtre, Geneva, Annina, *La Traviata*.

EARLY CAREER INCLUDED: 1968–1977, Principal Soprano, Sadler's Wells Opera/English National Opera: Mimi, *La Bohème* (British debut); Countess, *The Marriage of Figaro*; Fiordiligi, *Così fan tutte*; Pamina, *The Magic Flute*; Ilia, *Idomeneo*; Violetta, *La Traviata*; Musetta, *La Bohème*; Elsa, *Lohengrin*; Marschallin, *Der Rosenkavalier*; Penelope, *Gloriana*; Milada, *Dalibor*; Giulietta/Antonia/Stella, *The Tales of Hoffmann*; Sieglinde and Third Norn, *The Ring of the Nibelung*; title role, *Tosca*.

MAJOR DEBUTS INCLUDE: 1974, Welsh National Opera, Senta, *The Flying Dutchman*; 1978: Covent Garden, Rosalinde, *Die Fledermaus*; San Francisco Opera, Elsa, *Lohengrin*; 1980, Rome Opera, Chrysothemis, *Elektra*; 1985, Marseilles Opera, Elsa, *Lohengrin*; 1988, Zurich Opera, Brünnhilde, *Die Walküre*; 1988–1989, Brünnhilde, *Der Ring des Nibelungen*: Paris Opera, Bayreuth Festival, Washington Opera and Deutsche Oper, Berlin; 1991, Teatro Colón, Buenos Aires, Elsa, *Lohengrin*; 1992, Metropolitan Opera, New York, Elisabeth, *Tannhäuser*.

CAREER IN THE UK INCLUDES: Since 1978: Covent Garden: First Lady, *Die Zauberflöte*; Freia, *Der Ring des Nibelungen*; English National Opera: Kundry, *Parsifal*; title role, *Ariadne auf Naxos*; Opera North, Senta, *Der Fliegende Holländer*; Welsh National Opera: Chrysothemis, *Elektra*; Empress and Barak's Wife, *Die Frau ohne Schatten*; Leonore, *Fidelio*; Brünnhilde, *The Ring of the Nibelung*; Donna Anna, *Don Giovanni*; Cassandra, *The Trojans*; Isolde, *Tristan und Isolde* (also 1993, at Covent Garden).

RELATED PROFESSIONAL ACTIVITIES: Numerous concerts and recitals in the UK and abroad.

RECORDINGS INCLUDE: Wagner, *Götterdämmerung* (ASV), *The Valkyrie*, *Twilight of the Gods* (both EMI).

VIDEOS INCLUDE: Wagner, *Der Ring des Nibelungen* (Bayreuth Festival).

ADDRESS: c/o Ingpen & Williams Ltd, 14 Kensington Court, London W8 5DN.

EWING MARIA   Soprano

PERSONAL DETAILS: b. 27 March 1950, Detroit, USA; m. 1982, Peter Hall (director, m. diss.), one child.

EDUCATION/TRAINING: Cleveland Institute of Music; further studies with Marjorie Gordon, Eleanor Steber, Jennie Tourel and Otto Guth.

PROFESSIONAL DEBUT: 1973, Ravinia Festival, Chicago, concert with Chicago Symphony Orchestra.

MAJOR DEBUTS INCLUDE: (1973–1986, mezzo-soprano; since 1987, soprano); 1976: Cherubino, *Le Nozze di Figaro*: Metropolitan Opera, New York and Salzburg Festival; La Scala, Milan, Mélisande, *Pelléas et Mélisande*; 1977: Lyric Opera, Chicago, Idamante, *Idomeneo*; Metropolitan Opera, New York, Blanche, *Dialogues des Carmélites*; 1978: Glyndebourne Festival Opera, Dorabella, *Così fan tutte* (British debut); San Francisco Opera, Charlotte, *Werther*; 1980, La Monnaie, Brussels, Cherubino, *Le Nozze di Figaro*; Grand Théâtre, Geneva: 1980, Zerlina, *Don Giovanni*; 1981, title role, *La Cenerentola*; 1982, title role, *La Périchole*; 1983, Susanna, *Le Nozze di Figaro*; 1981: Houston Grand Opera, Rosina, *Il Barbiere di Siviglia*; Paris Opera, Zerlina, *Don Giovanni*; Metropolitan Opera, New York: 1982, Dorabella, *Così fan tutte*; 1985, Composer, *Ariadne auf Naxos*; 1986, title role, *Carmen*; 1986: Los Angeles Music Center Opera, title role, *Salome*; Lyric

Opera, Chicago, title role, *The Merry Widow*; 1988, Covent Garden, title role, *Salome*; Los Angeles Music Center Opera: 1989, title role, *Tosca*; 1991, title role, *Madama Butterfly*; 1991, Vienna State Opera, Mélisande, *Pelléas et Mélisande*.

CAREER IN THE UK INCLUDES: Since 1981: Covent Garden, title roles: *Carmen*, *Tosca*; Earls Court, title role, *Carmen*; Glyndebourne Festival Opera: Rosina, *Il Barbiere di Siviglia*; Composer, *Ariadne auf Naxos*; title roles: *L'Incoronazione di Poppea*, *Carmen*.

RELATED PROFESSIONAL ACTIVITIES: Regular concerts, recitals, broadcasts and television appearances worldwide.

RECORDINGS INCLUDE: Debussy, *Pelléas et Mélisande* (DG); Giordano, *Andrea Chénier* (RCA); Mozart, *Don Giovanni* (EMI); Verdi, *I Vespri Siciliani* (RCA).

VIDEOS INCLUDE: Bizet, *Carmen* (Covent Garden, Earls Court, Glyndebourne Festival Opera); Monteverdi, *L'Incoronazione di Poppea*; Rossini, *Il Barbiere di Siviglia* (both Glyndebourne Festival Opera).

ADDRESS: c/o Harold Holt Ltd, 31 Sinclair Road, London W14 0NS.

*　*　*　*

FARNCOMBE CHARLES
Conductor

POSITIONS: Music Director: London Chamber Opera, Malcolm Sargent Festival Choir; Chief Conductor, Handel Festival, Karlsruhe.

PERSONAL DETAILS: b. 29 July 1919, London; m. 1963, Sally Mae Felps (music teacher), one child.

PREVIOUS OCCUPATIONS: 1940–1941, civil engineer; 1941–1947, Captain, Royal Electrical and Mechanical Engineers.

EDUCATION/TRAINING: 1936–1940, University of London, studied engineering; 1948–1951, Royal Academy of Music, studied french horn with Aubrey Brain.

PROFESSIONAL AND OPERATIC DEBUT: 1955, Handel Opera Society, *Deidamia* (first modern performance).

CAREER: 1955–1985, founder and Music Director, Handel Opera Society; 1970–1979, Principal Conductor, Royal Court Theatre, Drottningholm; since 1979, Chief Conductor, Handel Festival, Karlsruhe; Music Director: since 1985, Malcolm Sargent Festival Choir; since 1986, London Chamber Opera.

MAJOR OPERATIC DEBUTS INCLUDE: 1957, Handel Opera Society, *Alcina* (with Joan Sutherland); 1969, Royal Court Theatre, Drottningholm, *Il Pastor Fido*; 1974, Royal Opera, Stockholm, *Don Carlos*; 1981, English Bach Festival at Covent Garden, *Castor et Pollux*.

OPERA PERFORMANCES IN THE UK INCLUDE: 1955–1985, Handel Opera Society: *Hercules*, *Theodora*, *Semele*, *Rodelinda*, *Radamisto*, *Rinaldo*, *Jephtha*, *Giulio Cesare*, *Riccardo Primo*, *Saul*, *Scipione*, *Susanna*, *Samson*, *Ottone*, *Atalanta*, *Ariodante*, *Belshazzar*, *Ezio*, *Esther*, *Partenope*, *Serse*, *Giustino*, *Imeneo*, *Rodrigo*; since 1986: English Bach Festival at Covent Garden, *Orphée et Eurydice*; London Chamber Opera: *The Magic Flute*, *The Marriage of Figaro*; London Opera Players: *The Barber of Seville*, *L'Elisir d'Amore*, *La Cenerentola*, *Don Pasquale*.

RELATED PROFESSIONAL ACTIVITIES: Guest conductor with leading orchestras in the UK and abroad.

RECORDINGS INCLUDE: Handel, *Rodrigo*; Great Handel choruses (both EMI); Rameau, *Castor et Pollux* (ERAT).

AWARDS AND HONOURS INCLUDE: 1963, Fellow, Royal Academy of Music; 1971, Gold Medal of the Friends of

Drottningholm; 1972, Honorary Fellow, Royal Swedish Academy; 1977, Commander, Order of the British Empire (CBE); 1982, Knight Commander, Order of the North Star (Sweden); 1991, Karlsruhe Gold Commemorative Medal; Honorary Doctorates of Music: City University, London; Yankton College, South Dakota; Capital University, Columbus, Ohio.

ADDRESS: c/o Norman McCann International Artists Ltd, The Coach House, 56 Lawrie Park Gardens, London SE26 6XJ.

Palestrina; Wexford Festival, Giulietta, *Un Giorno di Regno*.

RELATED PROFESSIONAL ACTIVITIES: Numerous concerts, recitals and broadcasts in the UK and abroad.

RECORDINGS INCLUDE: Egk, *Peer Gynt* (ORFE); Albert, *Tiefland* (RCA).

AWARDS INCLUDE: 1978, John McCormack Award (Dublin); 1979, Munich City Scholarship Award.

ADDRESS: c/o Dr Germinal Hilbert, Maximilianstrasse 22, D-8000 Munich 22, Germany.

FEENEY ANGELA   Soprano

PERSONAL DETAILS: b. 19 October 1954, Belfast; m. 1980, Nikolaus Gruger (musician and professor of french horn), one child.

EDUCATION/TRAINING: 1974–1975, Belfast School of Music, with Douglas Armstrong; 1975–1978, Dublin College of Music, with Veronica Dunne; 1978–1980, Richard Strauss Konservatorium, Munich, with Ken Neate; 1980–1982, Munich State Opera School, with Heinrich Bender.

PROFESSIONAL DEBUT: 1977, Irish National Opera, Cherubino, *Le Nozze di Figaro*.

MAJOR DEBUTS INCLUDE: 1983, Cork City Opera, Leonora, *Il Trovatore*; 1985, title role, *Madama Butterfly*: Opera Northern Ireland and Deutsche Oper, Berlin; 1986: English National Opera, Donna Elvira, *Don Giovanni*; Dublin Grand Opera, Euridice, *Orfeo ed Euridice*.

CAREER INCLUDES: Since 1978: English National Opera: Mařenka, *The Bartered Bride*; Micaëla, *Carmen*; Nedda, *Pagliacci*; Bavarian State Opera, Munich (1983–1986, Principal Soprano): Echo, *Ariadne auf Naxos*; Papagena, *Die Zauberflöte*; Woglinde, *Götterdämmerung*; Gretel, *Hänsel und Gretel*; Ingrid, *Peer Gynt*; Cork City Opera, Mimi, *La Bohème*; Dublin Grand Opera: Maddalena, *Rigoletto*; Adalgisa, *Norma*; Frankfurt Opera, Flower Maiden, *Parsifal*; Hamburg State Opera, Angel,

FIELD HELEN   Soprano

PERSONAL DETAILS: b. 14 May 1951, Clwyd.

EDUCATION/TRAINING: Royal Northern College of Music; Royal College of Music, with Ruth Packer.

PROFESSIONAL DEBUT: 1976, Welsh National Opera, Eurydice, *Orpheus in the Underworld*.

EARLY CAREER INCLUDED: 1976–1984, Principal Soprano, Welsh National Opera: Rowan, *Let's Make an Opera*; Marzelline, *Fidelio*; Kristina, *The Makropoulos Case*; First Lady, *The Magic Flute*; Terinka, *The Jacobin* (1980, British stage première); Gilda, *Rigoletto*; Katerina, *The Greek Passion* (1981, British première); Mařenka, *The Bartered Bride*; Tatyana, *Eugene Onegin*; Micaëla, *Carmen*; Mimi, *La Bohème*; title roles: *The Coronation of Poppea*, *The Cunning Little Vixen*, *Jenůfa*.

MAJOR DEBUTS INCLUDE: 1980: Glyndebourne Touring Opera, Mimi, *La Bohème*; Scottish Opera at the Edinburgh Festival, title role, *The Cunning Little Vixen*; 1981, Opera North, Gilda, *Rigoletto*; 1982: Covent Garden, Emma, *Khovanshchina*; Netherlands Opera at the Holland Festival, Governess, *The Turn of the Screw*; 1983, English National Opera, Gilda, *Rigoletto* (also 1984, USA tour, including Metropolitan Opera, New York); 1984: Cologne Opera, Mařenka, *The Bartered Bride*; Wiesbaden Festival, Mimi, *La Bohème*; 1987, La Monnaie, Brussels, Desdemona, *Otello*; 1990,

Glyndebourne Festival Opera, Jo Ann, *New Year* (British première).
OPERATIC WORLD PREMIERES INCLUDE: 1989, Houston Grand Opera, Jo Ann, *New Year* by Michael Tippett; 1993, English National Opera, Elspeth, *Inquest of Love* by Jonathan Harvey.
CAREER IN THE UK INCLUDES: Since 1984: English National Opera: Jenifer, *The Midsummer Marriage*; Marguérite, *Faust*; Nedda, *Pagliacci*; Pamina, *The Magic Flute*; Violetta, *La Traviata*; Duchess of Parma/Helen of Troy, *Doctor Faust*; Donna Anna, *Don Giovanni*; Opera North: Violetta, *La Traviata*; Susanna, *The Marriage of Figaro*; Donna Anna, *Don Giovanni*; title roles: *The Cunning Little Vixen*, Daphne (1987, British stage première), *Manon*; Welsh National Opera: Desdemona, *Otello*; Mila, *Osud*; title role, *Madam Butterfly*.
RELATED PROFESSIONAL ACTIVITIES: Numerous concerts, recitals, broadcasts and television appearances in the UK and abroad.
RECORDINGS INCLUDE: Coleridge-Taylor, *Hiawatha's Wedding Feast* (ARGO); Delius, *A Village Romeo and Juliet* (DECC); Janáček, *Osud* (EMI); Martinů, *The Greek Passion* (SUPR); Rossini, *Stabat Mater* (CHAN); Verdi, *Rigoletto* (EMI).
AWARDS INCLUDE: 1976, Young Welsh Singers' Competition.
ADDRESS: c/o Lies Askonas Ltd, 186 Drury Lane, London WC2B 5RY.

FIELDING DAVID   Designer

PERSONAL DETAILS: b. 8 September 1948, Cheshire.
EDUCATION/TRAINING: Central School of Art and Design.
PROFESSIONAL DEBUT: 1969, Nottingham Playhouse, *The Homecoming* by Harold Pinter.
OPERATIC DEBUT: 1974, Scottish Opera, *The Magic Flute*.
CAREER: Since 1970, freelance designer for leading theatre and opera companies in the UK and abroad.

MAJOR OPERATIC DEBUTS: 1974, Wexford Festival, *Medea in Corinto*; 1975, Kent Opera, *Ruddigore*; 1976, Welsh National Opera, *Il Trovatore*; 1982, Netherlands Opera, *The Rake's Progress*; 1983: English National Opera, *Rienzi*; Opera North, *Beatrice and Benedict*; 1984, Long Beach Opera, California, *Don Carlos*; 1986, Covent Garden, *Der Fliegende Holländer*; 1987: Paris Opera, *Giulio Cesare*; Vienna State Opera, *Idomeneo*; 1988, Los Angeles Music Center Opera, *Wozzeck*; 1989/1990, English National Opera/Netherlands Opera co-production, *A Masked Ball*; 1991, Glyndebourne Festival Opera, *La Clemenza di Tito*.
OPERATIC WORLD PREMIERES INCLUDE: 1990: Almeida Festival, *The Intelligence Park* by Gerald Barry; English National Opera, *Clarissa* by Robin Holloway.
OPERA DESIGNS IN THE UK INCLUDE: Since 1974: English National Opera: *Mazeppa*, *Xerxes*, *Simon Boccanegra*, *Don Carlos*; Kent Opera: *The Marriage of Figaro*, *King Priam*; Scottish Opera: *Die Fledermaus*, *The Seraglio*, *Rigoletto*, *Wozzeck*, *The Rise and Fall of the City of Mahagonny*; Welsh National Opera, *The Turn of the Screw*; Scottish Opera/English National Opera co-production, *Street Scene*.
VIDEOS INCLUDE: Handel, *Xerxes* (English National Opera); Tippett, *King Priam* (Kent Opera).
ADDRESS: c/o Harriet Cruickshank, 97 Old South Lambeth Road, London SW8 1XU.

FIELDSEND DAVID
Tenor and Teacher

PERSONAL DETAILS: b. 16 April 1947, Barnsley; m. 1971, Joyce Boden (répétiteur); m. 1982, Jane Cardew (stage manager), one child.
EDUCATION/TRAINING: 1964–1967, Huddersfield School of Music, with Eugene Everest; 1967–1971, Guildhall School of Music and Drama, with Duncan Robertson; privately with Alexander Young and Richard Lewis.

PROFESSIONAL DEBUT: 1972, Wexford Festival, Vanya, *Katya Kabanova*.
EARLY CAREER INCLUDED: 1973–1978, Principal Tenor, Scottish Opera: Prologue, *The Turn of the Screw*; Shepherd, *Tristan und Isolde*; Page, *The Coronation of Poppea*; Jacquino, *Fidelio*; Arturo, *Lucia di Lammermoor*; Count, *The Barber of Seville*; Scaramuccio, *Ariadne auf Naxos*; Guidon, *The Golden Cockerel*; Moser, *Die Meistersinger von Nürnberg*; Toni, *Elegy for Young Lovers*; Bardolph, *Falstaff*; Monostatos, *The Magic Flute*.
MAJOR DEBUTS INCLUDE: 1983, Covent Garden, Struhan, *Der Rosenkavalier*; 1985, Théâtre des Champs Elysées, Paris, Bardolph, *Falstaff*; 1990, D'Oyly Carte Opera, Nanki-Poo, *The Mikado*.
CAREER IN THE UK INCLUDES: Since 1979: Craig-y-nos: Thomas, *Thomas and Sally*; Sailor, *Dido and Aeneas*; D'Oyly Carte Opera: Ralph Rackstraw, *HMS Pinafore*; Marco, *The Gondoliers*; Fairfax, *The Yeomen of the Guard*; Opera North, Fox, *The Cunning Little Vixen*; Travelling Opera: Ferrando, *Così fan tutte* (also at Anchorage Civic Opera); Count, *The Barber of Seville*; Ernesto, *Don Pasquale*; title role, *Orpheus in the Underworld*.
RELATED PROFESSIONAL ACTIVITIES: Numerous concerts, broadcasts and television appearances in the UK and abroad including *Top Cs and Tiaras* (Channel Four); teacher, Gresham's School, Norfolk and privately.
RECORDINGS INCLUDE: Lehár, *The Merry Widow* (EMI); Sullivan, *The Gondoliers* (TER).
ADDRESS: c/o Musicmakers, Little Easthall Farmhouse, St Paul's Walden, Nr Hitchin, Herts SG4 8DH.

FIFIELD CHRISTOPHER
Conductor and Writer

POSITION: Music Director, Central Festival Opera, Northampton.
PERSONAL DETAILS: b. 4 September 1945, Croydon; m. 1972, two children.

EDUCATION/TRAINING: 1965–1968, University of Manchester; 1965–1969, Royal Manchester College of Music; 1969–1970, Guildhall School of Music and Drama; 1970–1972, Hochschule für Musik, Cologne.
PROFESSIONAL AND OPERATIC DEBUT: 1973, Cape Town Opera, *The Merry Widow*.
CAREER: 1971–1972 and 1977–1986, member, music staff, Glyndebourne Festival Opera; 1973–1976, Assistant Music Director, Cape Town Opera; 1977, member, music staff, Wexford Festival; 1980–1990, Director of Music, University College Opera; since 1991, Music Director, Central Festival Opera, Northampton.
OPERA PERFORMANCES IN THE UK INCLUDE: Since 1980: Central Festival Opera, Northampton, *Macbeth*; University College Opera: *Hérodiade*; *Oberto, Conte di San Bonifacio* (1982, British première); *Gwendoline* (1983, British première); *Faust* (Spohr); *Le Villi/Edgar*; *Die Loreley* (1986, British première); *The Devil's Wall* (1987, British première); *Il Corsaro*; *Giovanna d'Arco*; *Un Giorno di Regno*.
PUBLICATIONS INCLUDE: *Max Bruch* (Gollancz), *Hans Richter* (Oxford University Press).
AWARDS INCLUDE: 1971, British Council Conducting Scholarship.
ADDRESS: c/o Music International, 13 Ardilaun Road, London N5 2QR.

FINDLAY PAUL
Administrator

POSITION: Managing Director, Royal Philharmonic Orchestra.
PERSONAL DETAILS: b. 1943, Dunedin, New Zealand; m., two children.
EDUCATION/TRAINING: Balliol College, Oxford, studied Greats.
CAREER: 1966–1967, Production Manager, New Opera Company and Cambridge University Opera; 1967–1968, stage manager, English Opera Group and Glyndebourne Touring Opera; Royal

Opera House, Covent Garden: 1968–1972, press officer; 1972–1976, personal assistant to General Director; 1976–1987, Assistant Director; 1987–1993, Opera Director; particularly responsible for British and overseas tours of The Royal Opera, The Royal Ballet and Sadler's Wells Royal Ballet, visiting companies to the Royal Opera House and all radio and television broadcasts; created Covent Garden Video Productions and Covent Garden Records in association with Conifer Records; since 1993, Managing Director, Royal Philharmonic Orchestra.

OTHER PROFESSIONAL ACTIVITIES INCLUDE: Board member: English Touring Opera, London Sinfonietta.

ADDRESS: c/o Royal Philharmonic Orchestra Ltd, 16 Clerkenwell Green, London EC1R 0DP.

FINLEY GERALD   Baritone

PERSONAL DETAILS: b. 30 January 1960, Montreal, Canada; m. 1990, Louise Winter (mezzo-soprano), one child.

EDUCATION/TRAINING: 1978–1979, Ottawa University, studied music with Gary Relyea; 1979–1980, Royal College of Music, with John York Skinner; 1980–1983: King's College, Cambridge, studied French and Italian; privately with Lyndon van der Pump; 1983–1986, Royal College of Music; 1987–1988, National Opera Studio.

PROFESSIONAL DEBUT: 1986, Mecklenburgh Opera, title role, The Marriage of Figaro.

MAJOR DEBUTS INCLUDE: 1991: Aix-en-Provence Festival, Demetrius, A Midsummer Night's Dream; Canadian Opera Company, Toronto, Sid, Albert Herring; 1992: Glyndebourne Festival Opera, Guglielmo, Così fan tutte; title role, The Marriage of Figaro: Opera North, Vancouver Opera.

CAREER IN THE UK INCLUDES: Since 1987: Covent Garden, Flemish Deputy, Don Carlos; Glyndebourne Festival and Touring Opera: Dominik, Arabella; Kuligin, Katya Kabanova; Sid, Albert Herring; Fiorello and title role, Il Barbiere di Siviglia; English Clerk, Death in Venice; Papageno, Die Zauberflöte; Mecklenburgh Opera, Papageno, The Magic Flute.

RELATED PROFESSIONAL ACTIVITIES: Numerous concerts, recitals and broadcasts in the UK and abroad.

RECORDINGS INCLUDE: Berlioz, L'Enfance du Christ; Mozart, Don Giovanni (both EMI); Purcell, King Arthur (ARCH).

VIDEOS INCLUDE: Britten, Death in Venice (Glyndebourne Touring Opera).

AWARDS INCLUDE: 1985, Countess of Munster Award; 1987, Walther Gruner International Lieder Competition; 1989, John Christie Award.

ADDRESS: c/o Harrison/Parrott Ltd, 12 Penzance Place, London W11 4PA.

FINNIE LINDA   Mezzo-soprano

PERSONAL DETAILS: b. 9 May 1952, Paisley.

EDUCATION/TRAINING: Royal Scottish Academy of Music and Drama, with Winifred Busfield.

PROFESSIONAL DEBUT: 1975, Scottish Opera, appeared in Hermiston by Robin Orr (world première).

MAJOR DEBUTS INCLUDE: 1978: Covent Garden, Grimgerde and Second Norn, Der Ring des Nibelungen; English National Opera, Giovanna, Rigoletto; Grand Théâtre, Bordeaux, Ozias, Juditha Triumphans; 1980: Welsh National Opera, Madame Larina, Eugene Onegin; Ludwigsburg, Marcellina, Le Nozze di Figaro; Paris Opera, Mary, Der Fliegende Holländer; 1985, La Monnaie, Brussels, Marcellina, Le Nozze di Figaro; Amneris, Aida: 1986, Opera North, 1987, Frankfurt Opera; 1988: Bayreuth Festival, Fricka, Siegrune and Second Norn, Der Ring des Nibelungen; Théâtre des Champs Elysées, Paris, Waltraute, Der Ring des Nibelungen.

OPERATIC WORLD PREMIERES INCLUDE: 1976, Scottish Opera at the York Festival, Woman, Confessions of a Justified Sinner by Thomas Wilson.

CAREER IN THE UK INCLUDES: Since 1976: Covent Garden: Madame Larina, *Eugene Onegin*; Waltraute, *Der Ring des Nibelungen*; English National Opera: Brangäne, *Tristan and Isolde*; Eboli, *Don Carlos*; Amneris, *Aida*; Madame Arvidson, *A Masked Ball*; Spitalfields Festival, Phénice, *Armide*.

RELATED PROFESSIONAL ACTIVITIES: Regular concerts, recitals and broadcasts with leading conductors and orchestras in the UK and abroad.

RECORDINGS INCLUDE: Bliss, vocal and orchestral works; Diepenbrock, *Die Nacht*; Elgar, *Sea Pictures*; Mendelssohn, *Elijah*; Prokofiev: *Alexander Nevsky, Ivan the Terrible*; Schumann and Brahms, lieder; Walton, vocal works (all CHAN); Beethoven, Symphony No. 9 (CHAN/EMI); Handel, *Messiah* (PICK); Puccini, *La Rondine* (CBS); Ravel, *L'Enfant et les Sortilèges* (EMI); Vivaldi, sacred choral music (PHIL).

AWARDS INCLUDE: 1974, Kathleen Ferrier Memorial Scholarship; 1977, International Vocal Competition, s'Hertogenbosch (Netherlands).

ADDRESS: c/o Christopher Tennant Artists' Management, Unit 2, 39 Tadema Road, London SW10 0PY.

FINNISSY MICHAEL
Composer, Librettist, Pianist and Teacher

POSITIONS: Research Fellow, University of Sussex; Teacher of Composition: Royal Academy of Music, Winchester College.

PERSONAL DETAILS: b. 17 March 1946, London.

EDUCATION/TRAINING: 1965–1968, Royal College of Music, composition with Bernard Stevens and Humphrey Searle, piano with Edwin Benbow and Ian Lake.

FIRST PROFESSIONAL PERFORMANCE OF A COMPOSITION: 1965, *Le Dormeur du Val* for mezzo-soprano and ensemble.

CAREER: Compositions include dance, instrumental, ensemble and vocal works; 1969–1974, member, Music Department, London School of Contemporary Dance; 1972–1980, work with various dance companies including: Ballet Rambert, Junction Dance Company, London Contemporary Dance Theatre, Strider; 1980–1981, Teacher of Composition, Dartington Hall Summer School; 1982–1983, Composer in Residence, Victorian College of Arts, Melbourne; since 1987, Research Fellow, University of Sussex; Teacher of Composition: since 1986, Winchester College; since 1991, Royal Academy of Music.

OPERATIC WORLD PREMIERES: 1973, Rotterdam, *Tsuru-Kame*; 1978, Queen Elizabeth Hall, *Mr Punch*; 1984, Victorian College of Arts, Melbourne, *Soda Fountain*; 1988, Théâtre de la Bastille, Paris (co-production with the Almeida Festival), *The Undivine Comedy*, opera in 17 scenes, libretto by the composer after the play by Zygmunt Krasinski, conductor the composer, director Pierre Audi, designer Kate Blacker; 1993, Royal Opera Garden Venture, *Thérèse Raquin*, opera in seven scenes, libretto by the composer after Zola.

RELATED PROFESSIONAL ACTIVITIES: Director: 1982–1987, Suoraan Ensemble; 1987–88, Exposé Ensemble; member: since 1985, BBC Reading Panel and Society for the Promotion of New Music Reading Panel; since 1988, Opera Studio Steering Committee, English National Opera; since 1989, conductor, Ixion Ensemble and Cambridge New Music Players; since 1990, Musical Adviser, Royal Opera Garden Venture; 1991–1993, President, International Society for Contemporary Music; as librettist: 1992, Music Theatre Wales at the Cardiff Festival of Music, libretto with Andrew Toovey, *Ubu* by Andrew Toovey (world première).

RECORDINGS INCLUDE: English Country Tunes (ETCE/FACT), String Trio, *Câtana*, *Contretänze* (all HARM), *Reels, Autumnall, Short But...*, *Kemp's Morris, Freightrain Bruise, Stanley Stokes East Street 1836* (all NMC), *Fast Dances, Slow Dances* (both MSCA), Gershwin arrangements (LDR).

PUBLICATIONS INCLUDE: Vocal scores:
1978, *Mr Punch* (Universal Edition); 1988,
The Undivine Comedy (Oxford University
Press).

ADDRESS: c/o Oxford University Press,
Walton Street, Oxford OX2 6DP.

FOLWELL NICHOLAS
Baritone

PERSONAL DETAILS: b. 11 July 1953,
Middlesex; m. 1981, Anne-Marie Ives
(soprano and teacher), two children.

EDUCATION/TRAINING: 1971–1976, Royal
Academy of Music; 1976–1978, London
Opera Centre; privately with Raimund
Herincx.

PROFESSIONAL DEBUT: 1978, Welsh
National Opera, Bosun, *Billy Budd*.

EARLY CAREER INCLUDED: 1978–1987,
Principal Baritone, Welsh National Opera:
Melot, *Tristan und Isolde*; Ottone, *The
Coronation of Poppea*; Fiorello, *The
Barber of Seville*; Leporello, *Don
Giovanni*; Klingsor, *Parsifal*; Don Pizarro,
Fidelio; Schaunard, *La Bohème*;
Alberich, *The Ring of the Nibelung*;
Escamillo, *Carmen*; Harašta, *The
Cunning Little Vixen*; title role, *The
Marriage of Figaro*.

MAJOR DEBUTS INCLUDE: 1985: Opera
North, *The Mastersingers of Nuremberg*;
Scottish Opera, Lindorf/Coppelius/
Dapertutto/Dr Miracle, *The Tales of
Hoffmann*; 1986, English National Opera,
Tonio, *Pagliacci*; 1988, Frankfurt Opera,
Marullo, *Rigoletto*; 1990: Covent Garden,
Harašta, *The Cunning Little Vixen*;
Glyndebourne Touring Opera, Don
Pizarro, *Fidelio*; 1991, Opera Zuid,
Holland, title role, *Le Nozze di Figaro*.

OPERATIC WORLD PREMIERES INCLUDE:
1989, Paris Opera, Koroviev, *Der Meister
und Margarita* by York Höller; 1991,
English National Opera, Mutius, *Timon of
Athens* by Stephen Oliver.

CAREER IN THE UK INCLUDES: Since 1987:
English National Opera: Papageno, *The
Magic Flute*; Harašta, *The Cunning Little
Vixen*; Chief of Police, *Lady Macbeth of

Mtsensk*; Falke, *Die Fledermaus*;
Glyndebourne Touring Opera, title role,
Le Nozze di Figaro; Scottish Opera:
Creon, *Oedipus Rex*; Melitone, *La Forza
del Destino*; Alberich, *Das Rheingold*;
Melot, *Tristan und Isolde*; title role, *Le
Nozze di Figaro*.

RELATED PROFESSIONAL ACTIVITIES:
Numerous concerts, recitals and
television appearances in the UK and
abroad.

RECORDINGS INCLUDE: Janáček, *The
Cunning Little Vixen* (EMI); Rimsky-
Korsakov, *Christmas Eve* (BBC); Sullivan,
The Mikado (TELA); Wagner: *Parsifal* (EMI),
Tristan und Isolde (DECC); Zemlinsky, *Der
Zwerg* (BBC).

HONOURS INCLUDE: 1990, Associate, Royal
Academy of Music.

ADDRESS: c/o Robert Gilder & Company,
Enterprise House, 59–65 Upper Ground,
London SE1 9PQ.

FRASER MALCOLM
Director, Teacher and Translator

POSITIONS: Associate Director, Buxton
Festival; J. Ralph Corbett Distinguished
Professor of Opera, University of
Cincinatti, Ohio.

PERSONAL DETAILS: b. 1 August 1939,
Kingston-upon-Thames; m. 1963, Fay
Conway (designer), four children.

CAREER: 1966–1967, Associate Director,
Theatre Royal, Lincoln; 1967–1975,
Resident Director, Welsh National Opera;
1968–1976, Senior Lecturer, Royal
Northern College of Music; Buxton
Festival: 1979–1986, founder and Artistic
Director; since 1986, Associate Director;
since 1987, J. Ralph Corbett Distinguished
Professor of Opera, University of
Cincinatti, Ohio; since 1987, Permanent
Opera Director, Wildwood Centre,
Arkansas; guest director with leading
opera companies in the UK and North
America.

OPERATIC WORLD PREMIERES INCLUDE:
1976, Portland Opera, Oregon, *Wuthering
Heights* by Bernard Herrmann; 1992,

College-Conservatory of Music, Cincinatti, *Zaide* by Mozart/John Mortimer (also Lincoln Center, New York).

OPERA PRODUCTIONS IN THE UK INCLUDE: Since 1979, Buxton Festival: *Lucia di Lammermoor, Hamlet, Il Matrimonio Segreto, Háry János, The Spinning Room* (1982, British première), *Griselda* (1983, first modern performance), *Médée, Il Filosofo di Campagna, King Arthur, L'Occasione fa il Ladro, Torquato Tasso, Il Pittor Parigino, Tancredi, Il Sogno di Scipione*.

RELATED PROFESSIONAL ACTIVITIES: Translator of several operas for Buxton Festival.

AWARDS INCLUDE: 1969, Churchill Fellowship; 1974, Prague International Television Festival Prize; 1982, Kodály Medal (Hungary); 1989, *Manchester Evening News* Award, *Médée* (Buxton Festival); National Opera Association (USA), Best College Opera Production: 1987, *The Magic Flute*; 1989, *The Chalk Circle*.

ADDRESS: c/o College-Conservatory of Music, University of Cincinatti, Cincinatti, OH 45221–0003, USA.

FREEMAN DAVID
Director, Editor, Librettist and Translator

POSITION: Artistic Director, Opera Factory.
PERSONAL DETAILS: b. 1 May 1952, Sydney, Australia; m. 1985, Marie Angel (soprano), one child.
EDUCATION/TRAINING: 1970–1973, University of Sydney, studied German, Italian and drama.
OPERATIC DEBUT: 1972, Opera Factory Sydney, *Orfeo* (also sang title role).
CAREER: Since 1972, freelance opera and theatre director in the UK and abroad; founder and Artistic Director: 1973–1976, Opera Factory Sydney; since 1976, Opera Factory Zurich; since 1982: Opera Factory London; Associate Director, English National Opera; 1991, founder, Opera Factory Films.

MAJOR OPERATIC DEBUTS INCLUDE: 1981, English National Opera, *Orfeo*; 1984, *Akhnaten*: Houston Grand Opera, New York City Opera; 1986, Opera North, *La Bohème*; 1990, Opéra Comique, Paris, *Manon Lescaut*; 1991/1992, Kirov Opera/Covent Garden co-production, *The Fiery Angel* (also 1992, Metropolitan Opera, New York).

OPERATIC WORLD PREMIERES INCLUDE: 1986: English National Opera, *The Mask of Orpheus* by Harrison Birtwistle; Opera Factory: *Hell's Angels* by Nigel Osborne; *Yan Tan Tethera* by Harrison Birtwistle; 1991, Opera Factory Zurich, *Julia* by Rudolf Kelterborn.

OPERA PRODUCTIONS IN THE UK INCLUDE: Since 1981: English National Opera: *Akhnaten* (1985, British première), *The Return of Ulysses*; Opera Factory: *Punch and Judy, The Beggar's Opera, The Knot Garden, La Calisto, Così fan tutte, Eight Songs for a Mad King/ Aventures et Nouvelles Aventures/ Mahagonny Songspiel, Iphigenias, The Ghost Sonata* (1989, British première), *Don Giovanni, The Marriage of Figaro, The Coronation of Poppea*; Opera Factory Zurich at the Queen Elizabeth Hall, *Julia* (1991, British première).

RELATED PROFESSIONAL ACTIVITIES: Opera Factory productions directed for Channel Four Television include: *The Marriage of Figaro, Così fan tutte, Don Giovanni*; 1986, editor with Brenton Langbein, *Iphigenias* (abridged version of *Iphigenia in Aulis* and *Iphigenia in Tauris*); librettist: *Hell's Angels, Julia* (with Rudolf Kelterborn); translator, *The Ghost Sonata*; theatre productions include *Faust* and *Morte d'Arthur* (both Lyric Theatre, Hammersmith).

HONOURS INCLUDE: 1985, Chevalier de l'Ordre des Arts et des Lettres (France).
ADDRESS: c/o Allied Artists, 42 Montpelier Square, London SW7 1JZ.

FRIEND LIONEL   Conductor

POSITIONS: Music Director, New Sussex
Opera and Nexus Opera.
PERSONAL DETAILS: b. 13 March 1945; m.
1969, Jane Hyland (cellist), three children.
EDUCATION/TRAINING: 1963–1967, Royal
College of Music, with Adrian Boult;
1967–1968, London Opera Centre.
PROFESSIONAL AND OPERATIC
DEBUT: 1969, Welsh National Opera, *La
Traviata*.
CAREER: 1969–1972, member, music staff:
Glyndebourne Festival Opera, Welsh
National Opera; 1971–1972, Conductor,
Glyndebourne Touring Opera; 1972–1975,
Second Kapellmeister, Cassel; English
National Opera: 1976–1978, member,
music staff; 1978–1989, staff conductor;
Music Director: since 1981, Nexus Opera;
since 1989, New Sussex Opera.
OPERATIC WORLD PREMIERES INCLUDE:
BBC Radio 3: 1981, *The Chakravaka Bird*
by Anthony Gilbert; 1983, *The Tigers* by
Havergal Brian; 1989, English National
Opera, *The Plumber's Gift* by David
Blake; 1992, Aldeburgh Festival, *Mary of
Egypt* by John Tavener.
OPERA PERFORMANCES IN THE UK
INCLUDE: Since 1970: English National
Opera: *The Seven Deadly Sins*, *The Turn
of the Screw*, *Toussaint*, *Tristan and
Isolde*, *Rusalka*, *The Queen of Spades*,
The Midsummer Marriage, *The Rape of
Lucretia*, *Hansel and Gretel*, *The
Makropoulos Case*, *Beatrice and
Benedict*, *Falstaff*, *Ariadne auf Naxos*,
Wozzeck, *Fennimore and Gerda*;
Glyndebourne Touring Opera: *Il Turco in
Italia*, *Die Entführung aus dem Serail*;
New Sussex Opera: *The Flying Dutchman*,
Tannhäuser, *Lost in the Stars*, *The Rake's
Progress*; Nexus Opera, *Curlew River*;
Opera Northern Ireland, *Un Ballo in
Maschera*; Welsh National Opera: *The
Barber of Seville*, *La Bohème*, *The Magic
Flute*.
RELATED PROFESSIONAL ACTIVITIES:
Guest conductor with numerous
companies and orchestras including The
Royal Ballet, BBC Symphony Orchestra,
City of Birmingham Symphony Orchestra,
Nash Ensemble; pianist, Meridian
Ensemble.
VIDEOS INCLUDE: Britten, *The Rape of
Lucretia* (English National Opera).
ADDRESS: c/o Allied Artists, 42 Montpelier
Square, London SW7 1JZ.

FRYATT JOHN   Tenor

PERSONAL DETAILS: b. 1927, York.
EDUCATION/TRAINING: 1950, privately with
Frank Titterton; further studies with
Joseph Hislop.
PROFESSIONAL DEBUT: 1952, D'Oyly Carte
Opera.
EARLY CAREER INCLUDED: Principal Tenor:
1952–1958, D'Oyly Carte Opera:
Defendant, *Trial by Jury*; Luiz, *The
Gondoliers*; Sergeant Meryll, *The
Yeomen of the Guard*; Nanki-Poo, *The
Mikado*; Frederic, *The Pirates of
Penzance*; 1958–1974, Sadler's Wells
Opera: Pedrillo, *The Seraglio*; Guillot,
Manon; Spalanzani, *The Tales of
Hoffmann*; Ringmaster, *The Bartered
Bride*; Menelaus, *La Belle Hélène*; Hauk-
Šendorf, *The Makropoulos Case* (1964,
British première); Blind, *Die Fledermaus*;
Don Basilio, *The Marriage of Figaro*;
Monostatos, *The Magic Flute*; Brazilian,
La Vie Parisienne; title role, *Orpheus in
the Underworld*; also New Opera
Company, Mephisto/Jacob Glock, *The
Fiery Angel* (1965, British stage
première).
MAJOR DEBUTS INCLUDE: 1970: Covent
Garden, Dancing Master, *Ariadne auf
Naxos*; Glyndebourne Festival Opera,
Albazar, *Il Turco in Italia*; Adelaide
Festival, Madwoman, *Curlew River* and
Nebuchadnezzar, *The Burning Fiery
Furnace*; 1974, Flanders Opera, Ghent,
Sir Philip Wingrave, *Owen Wingrave*;
1978, La Monnaie, Brussels, Don Basilio,
Le Nozze di Figaro; 1980, Opera North,
Trim, *The Mines of Sulphur*; 1984, Lyric
Opera, Chicago, Monsieur Triquet,
Eugene Onegin; 1985, Paris Opera, Idiot,
Wozzeck; 1986, Grand Théâtre, Geneva,

Sellem, *The Rake's Progress*; 1987, Netherlands Opera, Goro, *Madama Butterfly*; 1989: Santa Fe Opera, Duke, *Chérubin*; Vancouver Opera, Sellem, *The Rake's Progress*.

OPERATIC WORLD PREMIERES INCLUDE: 1964, English Opera Group at the Aldeburgh Festival, Dr Graham, *English Eccentrics* by Malcolm Williamson; Sadler's Wells Opera: 1965, Trim, *The Mines of Sulphur* by Richard Rodney Bennett; 1966, Henri Joubert, *The Violins of St Jacques* by Malcolm Williamson; 1967, Sir Timothy Belboys, *A Penny for a Song* by Richard Rodney Bennett; 1974, Caesar, *The Story of Vasco* by Gordon Crosse; 1970, Glyndebourne Festival Opera, Lillywhite, *The Rising of the Moon* by Nicholas Maw.

CAREER IN THE UK INCLUDES: Since 1971: Covent Garden, Dancing Master, *Manon Lescaut*; English Music Theatre, Don Anchise, *La Finta Giardiniera*; English National Opera: Valzacchi, *Der Rosenkavalier*; Bunthorne, *Patience*; Njegus, *The Merry Widow*; Don Basilio, *The Marriage of Figaro*; Glyndebourne Festival Opera: Brighella, *Ariadne auf Naxos*; Pisandro, *Il Ritorno d'Ulisse in Patria*; Don Basilio, *Le Nozze di Figaro*; Mercury, *La Calisto*; High Priest, *Idomeneo*; Sellem, *The Rake's Progress*; Dr Caius, *Falstaff*; Monostatos, *Die Zauberflöte*; Valzacchi, *Der Rosenkavalier*; Reverend Adams, *Peter Grimes*; New Sadler's Wells Opera, Duke of Plaza-Toro, *The Gondoliers*.

RECORDINGS INCLUDE: Mozart: *Le Nozze di Figaro*, *Die Entführung aus dem Serail*; Offenbach: *La Belle Hélène*, *La Vie Parisienne* (all EMI); Puccini, *Manon Lescaut* (DG); Stravinsky, *Pulcinella* (EMI).

VIDEOS INCLUDE: Monteverdi, *Il Ritorno d'Ulisse in Patria*; Mozart: *Idomeneo*, *Le Nozze di Figaro*, *Die Zauberflöte*; Stravinsky, *The Rake's Progress*; Verdi, *Falstaff* (all Glyndebourne Festival Opera); Puccini, *Manon Lescaut* (Covent Garden); Sullivan: *Cox and Box*, *Patience* (both Walker).

ADDRESS: c/o Music International, 13 Ardilaun Road, London N5 2QR.

* * * *

GADD STEPHEN Bass-baritone

PERSONAL DETAILS: b. 18 September 1964, Berkshire; m. 1992, Margaret Richardson (soprano).

EDUCATION/TRAINING: 1983–1986, Choral Scholar, St John's College, Cambridge, studied engineering; 1986–1990, Royal Northern College of Music, with Patrick McGuigan.

PROFESSIONAL DEBUT: 1990, Opera North, Herald, *Jérusalem* (British stage première).

CAREER IN THE UK INCLUDES: Since 1990: Covent Garden (1991, debut), Angelotti, *Tosca*; Opera North, Shchelkalov, *Boris Godunov*; Scottish Opera (1991, debut), Colline, *La Bohème*; Welsh National Opera (1990, debut): Don Juan, *From the House of the Dead*; Colline, *La Bohème*.

RELATED PROFESSIONAL ACTIVITIES: Concerts and recitals in the UK and abroad.

AWARDS INCLUDE: 1990, Kathleen Ferrier Memorial Scholarship.

ADDRESS: c/o Harrison/Parrott Ltd, 12 Penzance Place, London W11 4PA.

GALE ELIZABETH   Soprano

PERSONAL DETAILS: b. 8 November 1948, Sheffield.

EDUCATION/TRAINING: 1966–1969, Guildhall School of Music and Drama, with Winifred Radford.

PROFESSIONAL DEBUT: 1970, English Opera Group, Cupid, *King Arthur*.

EARLY CAREER INCLUDED: 1970–1973, appearances with English Opera Group, Glyndebourne Touring Opera, Kent Opera, Sadler's Wells Opera; roles included: Flora, *The Turn of the Screw*; Blonde, *Die Entführung aus dem Serail*; Susanna, *Le Nozze di Figaro*; Belinda, *Dido and Aeneas*; Zerlina, *Don Giovanni*; Amor, *The Coronation of Poppea*.

MAJOR DEBUTS INCLUDE: 1973, Glyndebourne Festival Opera, Barbarina, *Le Nozze di Figaro*; 1974, Covent Garden, Jano, *Jenůfa*; 1975, Grand Théâtre, Geneva, Zerlina, *Don Giovanni*; 1976: Welsh National Opera, Blonde, *The Seraglio*; Cologne Opera, Arsena, *Der Zigeunerbaron*; 1977, Scottish Opera, Queen of Shemakha, *The Golden Cockerel*; 1978, Wexford Festival, Karolina, *The Two Widows*; 1979, Opera North, Gretel, *Hansel and Gretel*; 1980: Frankfurt Opera, Télaire, *Castor et Pollux*; Zurich Opera, Adina, *L'Elisir d'Amore*; 1981, Netherlands Opera, Anna, *Intermezzo*; 1982, Paris Opera, Marzelline, *Fidelio*; 1986, Glyndebourne Festival Opera at the Hong Kong Arts Festival, Tytania, *A Midsummer Night's Dream*; 1987, Teatro San Carlo, Naples, Marzelline, *Fidelio*; 1991, Canadian Opera Company, Toronto, Despina, *Così fan tutte*.

CAREER IN THE UK INCLUDES: Since 1974: Covent Garden: Xenia, *Boris Godunov*; Zerlina, *Don Giovanni*; Naiad, *Ariadne auf Naxos*; Lisa, *La Sonnambula*; Adele, *Die Fledermaus*; Miss Wordsworth, *Albert Herring*; English National Opera, Despina, *Così fan tutte*; Glyndebourne Festival and Touring Opera: Susanna and Countess, *Le Nozze di Figaro*; Anna, *Intermezzo*; Nannetta, *Falstaff*; Zerlina, *Don Giovanni*; Drusilla, *L'Incoronazione di Poppea*; Marzelline, *Fidelio*; Amor, *Orfeo ed Euridice*; Tytania, *A Midsummer Night's Dream*; Miss Wordsworth, *Albert Herring*; Opera North: Despina, *Così fan tutte*; Queen of Shemakha, *The Golden Cockerel*; Blonde, *The Seraglio*; Scottish Opera, Despina, *Così fan tutte*.

RELATED PROFESSIONAL ACTIVITIES: Regular concerts and recitals in the UK and abroad.

RECORDINGS INCLUDE: Handel: *Israel in Egypt* (DECC), *Jephtha*, *Messiah* (both TELD); Mozart, *Don Giovanni* (EMI); Puccini, *La Rondine* (CBS); Purcell, *Dido and Aeneas* (PHIL).

VIDEOS INCLUDE: Beethoven, *Fidelio*; Britten, *Albert Herring*; Gluck, *Orfeo ed Euridice*; Monteverdi, *L'Incoronazione di Poppea*; Mozart: *Don Giovanni*, *Le Nozze di Figaro*; R. Strauss, *Intermezzo*; Verdi, *Falstaff* (all Glyndebourne Festival Opera); Sullivan, *The Yeomen of the Guard* (Walker).

AWARDS INCLUDE: 1974, John Christie Award.

ADDRESS: Not available.

GARDINER JOHN ELIOT
Conductor and Editor

POSITIONS: Artistic Director: Monteverdi Choir and Orchestra, English Baroque Soloists, L'Orchestre Révolutionnaire et Romantique; Principal Conductor, North German Radio Symphony Orchestra.

PERSONAL DETAILS: b. 20 April 1943, Dorset; m. Elizabeth Wilcock, three children.

EDUCATION/TRAINING: 1962–1965, King's College, Cambridge, studied history; 1965–1966, King's College, London, with Thurston Dart; 1966–1968, with Nadia Boulanger in Paris.

PROFESSIONAL DEBUT: 1966, Wigmore Hall, concert with the Monteverdi Choir.

OPERATIC DEBUT: 1969, Sadler's Wells Opera, *The Magic Flute*.

96

CAREER: Founder and Artistic Director: 1964, Monteverdi Choir; 1968, Monteverdi Orchestra; 1978, English Baroque Soloists; 1990, L'Orchestre Révolutionnaire et Romantique; 1980–1983, Principal Conductor, CBC Vancouver Orchestra; 1981–1990, Artistic Director, Göttingen Handel Festival; Lyons Opera: 1983–1988, Music Director; since 1988, Chef Fondateur (Honorary Conductor); since 1991, Principal Conductor, North German Radio Symphony Orchestra; leading exponent of baroque music.

MAJOR OPERATIC DEBUTS INCLUDE: 1973, Covent Garden, *Iphigénie en Tauride*; 1982, Aix-en-Provence Festival, *Les Boréades* by Jean-Philippe Rameau (world stage première); 1983, Lyons Opera, *Iphigénie en Tauride*; 1990, Salzburg Festival, *Orfeo*; as conductor and co-director: 1992, Teatro São Carlos, Lisbon/Théâtre du Châtelet, Paris co-production, *Cosi fan tutte* (also at Teatro Comunale, Ferrara).

OPERA PERFORMANCES INCLUDE: Since 1970: Aix-en-Provence Festival: *Hippolyte et Aricie*, *Le Nozze di Figaro*; English National Opera, *Orfeo*; Göttingen Handel Festival, *Jephtha*; Innsbruck Festival, *Acis and Galatea*; Lyons Opera: *Tamerlano*, *L'Etoile*, *Pelléas et Mélisande*, *Fortunio*, *Le Comte Ory*; Orange Festival, *Die Zauberflöte*; Théâtre du Châtelet, Paris, *La Damnation de Faust*; Phoenix Opera, *The Barber of Seville*.

RELATED PROFESSIONAL ACTIVITIES: Guest conductor with leading British and international orchestras; regular broadcasts and television performances worldwide; editor: *The Beggar's Opera*, *Les Boréades*, *Orfeo*.

RECORDINGS INCLUDE: More than 100 works including: Bach, *St Matthew Passion* (ARCH); Berlioz, *La Damnation de Faust*; Chabrier, *L'Etoile*; Gluck: *Iphigénie en Tauride* (all EMI), *Iphigénie en Aulide* (ERAT); Handel: *Acis and Galatea* (ARCH), *Dixit Dominus*, *L'Allegro, il Penseroso ed il Moderato*, *Tamerlano*

(all ERAT), *Jephtha*, *Semele* (both PHIL); Leclair, *Scylla et Glaucus* (ERAT); Monteverdi: *Orfeo*, *Vespers* (both DG); Mozart: *La Clemenza di Tito*, *Die Entführung aus dem Serail*, *Idomeneo* (all ARCH), Mass in C Minor (PHIL); Purcell: *The Fairy Queen* (ARCH), *King Arthur*; Rameau, *Les Boréades* (both ERAT); Rossini, *Le Comte Ory* (EMI).

VIDEOS INCLUDE: Monteverdi, *Vespers* (DG).

AWARDS AND HONOURS INCLUDE: Numerous international awards for recordings including *Gramophone*: 1978: *Acis and Galatea*, *Dixit Dominus*; 1980, *L'Allegro, il Penseroso ed il Moderato*; 1988, *Scylla et Glaucus*; 1989, *Jephtha*; 1990, *St Matthew's Passion*; 1991: *Idomeneo*, *Missa Solemnis* (Record of the Year); 1987, Honorary Doctorate, Lyons University; 1988, Officier de L'Ordre des Arts et des Lettres (France); 1989, Commander, Order of the British Empire (CBE).

ADDRESS: c/o IMG Artists, Media House, 3 Burlington Lane, Chiswick, London W4 2TH.

GARRETT ERIC   Bass-baritone

POSITION: Member, The Royal Opera, Covent Garden.

PERSONAL DETAILS: b. 10 June 1934, Yorkshire; m. Jean Povey (formerly Children's Organizer, The Royal Opera, Covent Garden), two children.

EDUCATION/TRAINING: Royal College of Music; further studies with Eva Turner, Joseph Plaut and Tito Gobbi.

PROFESSIONAL DEBUT: 1956, chorus member, Covent Garden.

EARLY CAREER INCLUDED: 1956–1959, chorus member, Covent Garden; 1960–1961, Carl Rosa Opera Company: Lindorf/Coppelius/Dapertutto/Dr Miracle, *The Tales of Hoffmann*; title role, *Don Giovanni*.

MAJOR DEBUTS INCLUDE: 1962, Covent Garden, Benoit, *La Bohème*; 1968, Welsh National Opera, Zuniga, *Carmen*; 1975,

Wexford Festival, Macrobio, *La Pietra del Paragone*; 1977, Scottish Opera, Baron Zeta, *The Merry Widow*; 1978, La Monnaie, Brussels, Swallow, *Peter Grimes*; 1980: Opera North, Sherrin, *The Mines of Sulphur*; Liège Opera, Mayor, *The Hero*; Flanders Opera, Antwerp/Ghent: 1979, Michonnet, *Adriana Lecouvreur*; 1980, title role, *Falstaff*; 1981, Baron Ochs, *Der Rosenkavalier*; 1982, Leporello, *Don Giovanni*; 1984: Los Angeles Opera Theater, Baron Ochs, *Der Rosenkavalier*; San Francisco Opera, Sacristan, *Tosca*; 1991, Bavarian State Opera, Munich, Mustafa, *L'Italiana in Algeri*.
OPERATIC WORLD PREMIERES INCLUDE: New Opera Company at Sadler's Wells Theatre: 1964, Orgon, *Tartuffe* by Arthur Benjamin; 1967, Pit Manager, *The Decision* by Thea Musgrave; 1969, New Opera Company at the Camden Festival, Grisha, *Under Western Eyes* by John Joubert; 1970, Covent Garden, Koen, *Victory* by Richard Rodney Bennett.
CAREER IN THE UK INCLUDES: Since 1962, member, Covent Garden, more than 50 roles including: Sacristan, *Tosca*; Priest, *Moses and Aaron* (1965, British première); Police Commissar, *Der Rosenkavalier*; Don Fernando, *Fidelio*; Nightwatchman, *Die Meistersinger von Nürnberg*; Polonius/Gildenstern, *Hamlet* (Searle, 1969, British première); Bartolo, *Il Barbiere di Siviglia* and *Le Nozze di Figaro*; Mayor, *Jenůfa*; José Castro, *La Fanciulla del West*; Frank, *Die Fledermaus*; Portly Gentleman/Fezziwig, *A Christmas Carol* (1981, British première at Sadler's Wells Theatre); Luther, *Les Contes d'Hoffmann*; First Officer, *The Carmelites*; Schmidt, *Andrea Chénier*; Geronte, *Manon Lescaut*; Snug, *A Midsummer Night's Dream*; Truffaldino, *Ariadne auf Naxos*; Burgher of Calais, *The King Goes Forth to France* (1987, British première); Lawyer, *Un Re in Ascolto* (1989, British première); Mustafa, *L'Italiana in Algeri*; Swallow, *Peter Grimes*; Skula, *Prince Igor*; Varlaam, *Boris Godunov*; Ceprano, *Rigoletto*; Don Magnifico, *La Cenerentola*; Alcindoro, *La Bohème*; title roles: *Gianni Schicchi*, *Don Pasquale*; also: Opera North and Scottish Opera, Kecal, *The Bartered Bride*; Welsh National Opera: Animal Tamer/Schigolch, *Lulu* (1971, British première); Dulcamara, *L'Elisir d'Amore*; Geronte, *Manon Lescaut*.
RECORDINGS INCLUDE: Donizetti, *La Fille du Régiment* (DECC); Puccini, *La Fanciulla del West* (DG).
VIDEOS INCLUDE: Giordano, *Andrea Chénier*; Offenbach, *Les Contes d'Hoffmann*; Puccini, *La Fanciulla del West* (all Covent Garden).
ADDRESS: c/o Kaye Artists Management Ltd, Barratt House, 7 Chertsey Road, Woking, Surrey GU21 5AB.

GARRETT LESLEY   Soprano

POSITION: Principal Soprano, English National Opera.
PERSONAL DETAILS: b. 10 April 1955, Yorkshire; m. 1991, Peter Christian, one child
EDUCATION/TRAINING: Royal Academy of Music, with Flora Nielsen, Henry Cummings and Joy Mammen; National Opera Studio.
PROFESSIONAL DEBUT: 1979, Batignano Festival, Amor, *Orontea*.
MAJOR DEBUTS INCLUDE: 1980, English National Opera, Alice, *Count Ory*; Wexford Festival: 1980, Dorinda, *Orlando*; 1981, title role, *Zaide*; 1982, Opera North, Sophie, *Werther*; 1984, Glyndebourne Festival Opera, Damigella, *L'Incoronazione di Poppea*; 1987, Grand Théâtre, Geneva, Servilia, *La Clemenza di Tito*; 1990, English National Opera Soviet Union tour (Bolshoi and Kiev), Atalanta, *Xerxes*.
OPERATIC WORLD PREMIERES INCLUDE: 1981, Welsh National Opera, Nicola, *The Journey* by John Metcalf.
CAREER IN THE UK INCLUDES: Since 1981: Buxton Festival: Carolina, *Il Matrimonio Segreto*; Isifile, *Jason*; English National Opera (since 1984, Principal Soprano):

Potboy/Wonderchild/Student, *The Adventures of Mr Brouček*; Atalanta, *Xerxes*; Bella, *The Midsummer Marriage*; Despina, *Così fan tutte*; Zerlina, *Don Giovanni*; Papagena, *The Magic Flute*; Valencienne, *The Merry Widow*; Yum-Yum, *The Mikado*; Eurydice, *Orpheus in the Underworld*; Alsi, *The Making of the Representative for Planet 8* (1988, British première); Oscar, *A Masked Ball*; Ninetta, *The Love for Three Oranges*; Susanna, *The Marriage of Figaro*; Musetta, *La Bohème*; Adele, *Die Fledermaus*; Rose Maurrant, *Street Scene*; Dalinda, *Ariodante*; title role, *The Cunning Little Vixen*; Glyndebourne Festival and Touring Opera: Zerlina, *Don Giovanni*; Despina, *Così fan tutte*; Opera North, Susanna, *The Marriage of Figaro*; Welsh National Opera, Esmeralda, *The Bartered Bride*.

RELATED PROFESSIONAL ACTIVITIES: Numerous concerts and recitals with leading conductors and orchestras in the UK and abroad.

RECORDINGS INCLUDE: Sullivan, *The Mikado* (TER); Taylor, *Wuthering Heights*; Diva! A Soprano at the Movies (both SILV).

VIDEOS INCLUDE: Handel, *Xerxes* (English National Opera); Monteverdi, *L'Incoronazione di Poppea* (Glyndebourne Festival Opera); Sullivan, *The Mikado* (English National Opera).

AWARDS INCLUDE: 1979: Countess of Munster Award, Decca-Kathleen Ferrier Prize.

ADDRESS: c/o Allied Artists, 42 Montpelier Square, London SW7 1JZ.

GELIOT MICHAEL
Director and Translator

PERSONAL DETAILS: b. 27 September 1933, London; m., two children.

EDUCATION/TRAINING: University of Cambridge.

PROFESSIONAL AND OPERATIC DEBUT: 1958, Cambridge University Opera, *The School for Wives/Catulli Carmina* (both British premières).

CAREER: Freelance opera and theatre director in the UK and abroad; Welsh National Opera: 1965–1968, Resident Director; 1969–1978, Director of Productions; 1979–1983, Principal Director and Artistic Consultant.

MAJOR OPERATIC DEBUTS INCLUDE: 1961: New Opera Company, *Volpone* (British première); Sadler's Wells Opera, *Rigoletto*; 1965, Scottish Opera, *Boris Godunov*; 1966, Welsh National Opera, *Don Giovanni*; 1970, Wexford Festival, *Albert Herring*; 1973, Netherlands Opera, *Wozzeck*; 1974, Munich Festival, *Fidelio*; 1978: Lyons Opera, *L'Ormindo*; Teatro Colón, Buenos Aires, *Dido and Aeneas*; 1980, Royal Opera, Copenhagen, *The Mikado*.

OPERATIC WORLD PREMIERES INCLUDE: 1968, Scottish Opera, *Full Circle* by Robin Orr; 1969, New Opera Company at the Camden Festival, *Under Western Eyes* by John Joubert; 1972, Covent Garden, *Taverner* by Peter Maxwell Davies; 1974, Welsh National Opera, *The Beach of Falesá* by Alun Hoddinott; 1976, Scottish Opera at the York Festival, *Confessions of a Justified Sinner* by Thomas Wilson; 1979, Cassel, *Commedia* by Edward Cowie.

OPERA PRODUCTIONS IN THE UK INCLUDE: Since 1959: Buxton Festival, *Don Quixote in Sierra Morena*; Covent Garden, *Carmen*; Handel Opera Society, *Saul*; New Opera Company: *Boulevard Solitude* (1962, British première), *Cardillac* (1970, British stage première); Opera North, *Macbeth*; Sadler's Wells Opera/English National Opera: *Don Pasquale, The Rise and Fall of the City of Mahagonny, The Damnation of Faust, The Seven Deadly Sins*; Scottish Opera, *Tristan und Isolde*; Welsh National Opera: *Nabucco, Così fan tutte* (two productions), *Aida, Die Fledermaus, The Magic Flute, Lulu* (1971, British première), *Turandot, Billy Budd, Don Carlos, Idomeneo, L'Elisir d'Amore, Otello, The Seraglio, The Marriage of Figaro, Monsieur Choufleuri's at Home/The Song of Fortunio, The Coronation of Poppea, The*

Greek Passion (1981, British première),
Don Giovanni, Andrea Chénier.
RELATED PROFESSIONAL ACTIVITIES:
Translations include: *The Chalk Circle,
The Magic Flute, Monsieur Choufleuri's at
Home, The Rise and Fall of the City of
Mahagonny, The Song of Fortunio*.
ADDRESS: Not available.

GELLHORN PETER
Conductor, Chorus Master and Répétiteur

POSITION: Music Director, London Opera
Players.
PERSONAL DETAILS: b. 24 October 1912,
Breslau, Germany; m. 1943, Olive Shirley
(soprano), four children.
EDUCATION/TRAINING: 1927–1934, Berlin
Music Academy; 1929–1932, University of
Berlin, piano with Richard Rössler,
conducting with Julius Prüwer and
Clemens Schmalstich.
OPERATIC DEBUT: 1939, Toynbee Hall
Theatre, London, *Orfeo ed Euridice*.
CAREER: 1935–1939, Music Director,
Toynbee Hall Theatre, London; 1941–
1943, Assistant Conductor, Sadler's Wells
Opera; 1943–1945, Conductor, Royal Carl
Rosa Opera (115 performances); 1946–
1953, conductor and Head of Music Staff,
The Royal Opera, Covent Garden (over
260 performances); 1954–1961 and 1974–
1975, conductor and Chorus Director,
Glyndebourne Festival Opera; 1961–1972,
Director, BBC Chorus; 1974–1979,
Conductor, Morley Opera; since 1950,
Music Director, Opera Players/London
Opera Players; since 1982, Associate
Conductor, London Chamber Opera.
RELATED PROFESSIONAL ACTIVITIES:
Numerous concerts, recitals and
broadcasts in the UK and abroad; 1973–
1978, member, music staff, London Opera
Centre; 1980–1988, visiting conductor and
répétiteur, Royal College of Music; since
1981, vocal coach, Guildhall School of
Music and Drama.
HONOURS INCLUDE: 1989, Fellow, Guildhall
School of Music and Drama.

ADDRESS: 33 Leinster Avenue, East Sheen,
London SW14 7JW.

GIBSON, SIR ALEXANDER
Conductor

POSITION: Conductor Laureate, Scottish
Opera.
PERSONAL DETAILS: b. 11 February 1926,
Lanarkshire; m. 1959, Anne Veronica
Waggett, four children.
PREVIOUS OCCUPATION: 1944–1948, served
with the Royal Signals.
EDUCATION/TRAINING: Royal Scottish
Academy of Music and Drama; University
of Glasgow; Royal College of Music;
Mozarteum, Salzburg, with Igor
Markevich; Accademia Chigiana, Siena,
with Paul van Kempen.
PROFESSIONAL AND OPERATIC DEBUT:
1952, Sadler's Wells Opera, *The Bartered
Bride*.
CAREER: Sadler's Wells Opera: 1951–1952,
répétiteur and Assistant Conductor; 1954–
1957, staff conductor; 1957–1959, Music
Director (conducted more than 25
operas); 1952–1954, Assistant Conductor,
BBC Scottish Orchestra; 1957–1958, Guest
Conductor, Covent Garden; Scottish
National Orchestra: 1959–1984, Principal
Conductor and Music Director; since
1984, Honorary President; Scottish Opera:
1962–1985, founder and Artistic Director;
1985–1987, Music Director; since 1987,
Conductor Laureate (conducted more
than 40 new productions including 1969,
first complete British performance of *The
Trojans* and 1971, first German language
production in Scotland of *Der Ring des
Nibelungen*); 1981–1983, Principal Guest
Conductor, Houston Symphony Orchestra;
guest conductor with leading orchestras
and opera companies worldwide.
OPERATIC WORLD PREMIÈRES INCLUDE:
Sadler's Wells Opera: 1957, *The Moon
and Sixpence* by John Gardner; 1961, *The
Ledge* by Richard Rodney Bennett;
Scottish Opera: 1968, *Full Circle* by Robin
Orr; 1974, *The Catiline Conspiracy* by Iain
Hamilton; 1975, *Hermiston* by Robin Orr.

RELATED PROFESSIONAL ACTIVITIES:
Since 1991, President, Royal Scottish
Academy of Music and Drama.

RECORDINGS INCLUDE: Elgar, *The Dream of
Gerontius* (CRD); Classic Opera (DECC); The
complete symphonies of Sibelius (CHAN);
excerpts: Berlioz: *Béatrice et Bénédict*,
La Damnation de Faust, *Les Troyens* (all
EMI).

RELEVANT PUBLICATIONS INCLUDE: 1972,
Scottish Opera: the First Ten Years by
Conrad Wilson (Collins); 1987, *It is a
Curious Story: The Tale of Scottish Opera
1962–1987* by Cordelia Oliver
(Mainstream).

AWARDS AND HONOURS INCLUDE: 1959,
Arnold Bax Prize; 1967, Commander,
Order of the British Empire (CBE); 1969,
Honorary Member, Royal Academy of
Music; 1973, Fellow: Royal College of
Music, Royal Scottish Academy of Music
and Drama; 1976, Incorporated Society of
Musicians, Musician of the Year Award;
1977, Knighthood; 1978: Fellow, Royal
Society of Edinburgh; Sibelius Medal
(Finland); 1980, Fellow, Royal Society of
Arts; Honorary Doctorates: Universities of
Aberdeen, Glasgow, Stirling, Newcastle,
York and Open University.

ADDRESS: 15 Cleveden Gardens, Glasgow
G12 0PU.

GILLETT CHRISTOPHER
Tenor

PERSONAL DETAILS: b. 16 May 1958,
London; m. 1984, Julia Holmes
(clarinettist), two children.

EDUCATION/TRAINING: 1976–1979, Choral
Scholar, King's College, Cambridge;
1979–1981, Royal College of Music, with
Robert Tear and Edgar Evans; 1982–1983,
National Opera Studio; currently with
Rudolf Piernay.

PROFESSIONAL DEBUT: 1981, New Sadler's
Wells Opera, Edwin, *The Gipsy Princess*.

MAJOR DEBUTS INCLUDE: 1983, Kent Opera,
Toby, *Robinson Crusoe*; 1984, Covent
Garden, Flute, *A Midsummer Night's
Dream*; 1986, Glyndebourne Touring

Opera, title role, *Albert Herring*; Nooni,
*The Making of the Representative for
Planet 8*: 1988, English National Opera
(British première); 1989, Netherlands
Opera; 1990, Music Theatre Wales, title
role, *The Martyrdom of St Magnus*; 1991,
Aix-en-Provence Festival, Flute, *A
Midsummer Night's Dream*.

OPERATIC WORLD PREMIÈRES INCLUDE:
1989, Royal Opera Garden Venture, title
role, *Caedmon* by Edward Lambert.

CAREER IN THE UK INCLUDES: Since 1982:
Buxton Festival: Sumers, *L'Italiana in
Londra*; Peregrine, *Le Huron*; Covent
Garden: Roderigo, *Otello*; Dov, *The Knot
Garden*; Pang, *Turandot*; Arbace,
Idomeneo; Glassmaker, *Death in Venice*;
Glyndebourne Touring Opera: Ferrando,
Così fan tutte; Tichon, *Katya Kabanova*;
Kent Opera: Hermes, *King Priam*; Don
Basilio, *The Marriage of Figaro*; New
Sadler's Wells Opera: Nanki-Poo, *The
Mikado*; Luiz/Marco, *The Gondoliers*;
Opera 80: Alfred, *Die Fledermaus*; Don
Basilio, *The Marriage of Figaro*; Opera
Northern Ireland, Vašek, *The Bartered
Bride*.

RELATED PROFESSIONAL ACTIVITIES:
Numerous concerts and recitals in the UK
and abroad.

RECORDINGS INCLUDE: Elgar, *The Kingdom*
(RCA); Maxwell Davies, *The Martyrdom of
St Magnus* (UNIC); Sullivan, *HMS Pinafore*
(TER).

VIDEOS INCLUDE: Tippett, *King Priam* (Kent
Opera).

ADDRESS: c/o Magenta Music International
Ltd, 64 Highgate High Street, London N6
5HX.

GLOVER JANE   Conductor

POSITIONS: Music Director, London Choral
Society; Principal Conductor,
Huddersfield Choral Society.

PERSONAL DETAILS: b. 13 May 1949,
Yorkshire.

EDUCATION/TRAINING: St Hugh's College,
Oxford.

PROFESSIONAL AND OPERATIC DEBUT:
1975, Wexford Festival, *Eritrea* (first
modern performance).

CAREER: Freelance conductor in the UK and
abroad; 1980–1985, Chorus Director,
Glyndebourne Festival Opera; 1982–1985,
Music Director, Glyndebourne Touring
Opera; Artistic Director: 1984–1991,
London Mozart Players; 1993, Buxton
Festival; since 1983, Music Director,
London Choral Society; since 1989,
Principal Conductor, Huddersfield Choral
Society.

MAJOR OPERATIC DEBUTS INCLUDE: 1982,
Glyndebourne Festival Opera, *Don
Giovanni*; 1986, Glyndebourne Festival
Opera at the Hong Kong Arts Festival, *A
Midsummer Night's Dream*; 1988, Covent
Garden, *Die Entführung aus dem Serail*;
1989, English National Opera, *Don
Giovanni*; 1991, Canadian Opera
Company, Toronto, *Le Nozze di Figaro*;
1992, Buxton Festival, *The Italian Girl in
Algiers*.

OPERATIC WORLD PREMIERES INCLUDE:
1977, Batignano Festival, *Il Giardino* by
Stephen Oliver.

OPERA PERFORMANCES IN THE UK
INCLUDE: Since 1976: English National
Opera: *The Magic Flute*, *Princess Ida*;
Glyndebourne Festival and Touring
Opera: *Il Barbiere di Siviglia*, *Die
Entführung aus dem Serail*, *Idomeneo*,
Così fan tutte, *Fidelio*, *Where the Wild
Things Are*, *A Midsummer Night's Dream*,
Albert Herring; Musica nel Chiostro (also
at Batignano Festival): *Tamerlano*, *Lo
Speziale*, *Orontea*, *Il Combattimento di
Tancredi e Clorinda*, *Il Ballo delle
Ingrate*; Phoenix Opera at the Camden
Festival, *Eritrea* (1982, British première).

RELATED PROFESSIONAL ACTIVITIES:
Numerous concerts and broadcasts with
leading orchestras in the UK and abroad;
writer and presenter of music
programmes for television; Oxford: St
Hugh's College: 1973–1975, Junior
Research Fellow; since 1982, Senior
Research Fellow; lecturer: 1976–1980, St
Anne's College; 1976–1984, St Hugh's
College; 1979–1984, Pembroke College;

1986–1987, member, Music Advisory
Panel, Arts Council of Great Britain; 1985–
1990, Governor, Royal Academy of Music;
BBC: 1981–1985, member, Central Music
Advisory Committee; since 1990,
Governor; Council member, British Youth
Opera.

RECORDINGS INCLUDE: Handel, *Water
Music* (CIRR); Mozart, *Requiem*; Walton,
Façade (both ASV).

PUBLICATIONS INCLUDE: 1978, *Cavalli*
(Batsford); contributor, numerous literary
and music journals.

AWARDS AND HONOURS INCLUDE: 1990,
Association for Business Sponsorship of
the Arts/Daily Telegraph Arts Award;
Honorary Doctorates: Universities of
Exeter, Loughborough, Council for
National Academic Awards and Open
University.

ADDRESS: c/o Lies Askonas Ltd, 186 Drury
Lane, London WC2B 5RY.

GOEHR ALEXANDER
Composer

POSITION: Professor of Music: University of
Cambridge and Trinity Hall, Cambridge.

PERSONAL DETAILS: b. 10 August 1932,
Berlin, Germany.

EDUCATION/TRAINING: 1952–1955, Royal
Manchester College of Music; 1955–1956,
Paris Conservatoire, masterclasses with
Olivier Messiaen.

FIRST PROFESSIONAL PERFORMANCE OF A
COMPOSITION: First Professional
Performance of a Composition: 1952,
Morley College, London, Sonata for
piano.

CAREER: Since 1952, compositions in all
genres including two operas, one ballet,
numerous orchestral, ensemble,
instrumental, vocal and choral works and
the music theatre work *Triptych* (*Naboth's
Vineyard*, *Shadowplay*, *Sonata about
Jerusalem*); 1956–1957, lecturer, Morley
College; 1960–1967, producer and
broadcaster, BBC; 1968, Tokyo, Winston
Churchill Trust Fellowship; 1968–1969,
Composer in Residence, New England

Conservatory, Boston; 1969–1970, Associate Professor of Music, Yale University; 1970–1971, Visiting Lecturer, University of Southampton; 1971–1976, West Riding Professor of Music, University of Leeds; since 1976, Professor of Music, Trinity Hall, Cambridge; 1980, Visiting Professor, Peking Conservatory of Music; 1990, Composer in Residence, Aldeburgh Festival.

OPERATIC WORLD PREMIERES: 1967, Hamburg State Opera, *Arden Muss Sterben (Arden Must Die)*, opera in two acts, libretto by Erich Fried after the anonymous 16th-century play *Arden of Faversham*, conductor Charles Mackerras, director Egon Monk; 1985, Deutsche Oper am Rhein, Duisburg, *Die Wiedertäufer (Behold the Sun)*, opera in three acts, libretto by John McGrath and the composer, conductor Hiroshi Wakasugi, director Bohumil Herlischka.

RELATED PROFESSIONAL ACTIVITIES: 1975, Artistic Director, Leeds Music Festival; 1982–1987, member, Board of Directors, Royal Opera House, Covent Garden; 1987, BBC Reith Lecture, The Survival of the Symphony.

RECORDINGS INCLUDE: *Metamorphosis/ Dance* for orchestra, *Romanza* for cello and orchestra, *Behold the Sun* concert aria, *Lyric Pieces*, *Sinfonia and Sing*, *Ariel* (all UNIC), Concerto for violin and orchestra, Three Pieces for piano (both HMV).

RELEVANT PUBLICATIONS INCLUDE: *The Music of Alexander Goehr: Interviews and Articles*, editor Bayan Northcott (Schott); *New Sounds, New Personalities: British Composers of the 1980s*, editor Paul Griffiths (Faber).

HONOURS INCLUDE: Honorary Member, American Academy and Institute of Arts and Letters; Honorary Fellow, Royal Academy of Music; Fellow: Royal College of Music, Royal Northern College of Music and Trinity Hall, Cambridge; Honorary Doctorates of Music: Universities of Southampton and Manchester.

ADDRESS: c/o Schott & Co. Ltd, 48 Great Marlborough Street, London W1V 2BN.

GOMEZ JILL   Soprano

PERSONAL DETAILS: b. 21 September 1942, New Amsterdam, Guyana.

EDUCATION/TRAINING: Royal Academy of Music; Guildhall School of Music and Drama, with Walther Gruner.

PROFESSIONAL DEBUT: 1968, Glyndebourne Touring Opera, Adina, *L'Elisir d'Amore*.

MAJOR DEBUTS INCLUDE: 1969, Glyndebourne Festival Opera, Mélisande, *Pelléas et Mélisande*; 1974, Wexford Festival, title role, *Thaïs*; 1976, Welsh National Opera, Jenifer, *The Midsummer Marriage*; 1977, Kent Opera, Tatyana, *Eugene Onegin*; 1978, Ludwigsburg Festival, Donna Elvira, *Don Giovanni*; 1979, Grand Théâtre, Bordeaux, Fiordiligi, *Così fan tutte*; 1981: Frankfurt Opera, Cleopatra, *Giulio Cesare*; Grand Théâtre, Geneva, Governess, *The Turn of the Screw*; Zurich Opera, Cinna, *Lucio Silla*; 1982, Berlioz Festival, Lyons, Teresa, *Benvenuto Cellini*; 1985, Frankfurt Opera, Donna Anna, *Don Giovanni*.

OPERATIC WORLD PREMIERES INCLUDE: 1970, Covent Garden, Flora, *The Knot Garden* by Michael Tippett; 1974, English Opera Group at the Aldeburgh Festival, Countess, *The Voice of Ariadne* by Thea Musgrave; BBC Radio 3, title roles: 1977, *Miss Julie* by William Alwyn; 1979, *Maddalena* by Sergei Prokofiev.

CAREER IN THE UK INCLUDES: Since 1970: Covent Garden: Lisa, *La Sonnambula*; Tytania, *A Midsummer Night's Dream*; Lauretta, *Gianni Schicchi*; English National Opera, Governess, *The Turn of the Screw*; English Opera Group: Ilia, *Idomeneo*; Governess, *The Turn of the Screw*; Glyndebourne Festival Opera: Anne Trulove, *The Rake's Progress*; Helena, *A Midsummer Night's Dream*; title role, *La Calisto*; Kent Opera: Violetta, *La Traviata*; Aminta, *Il Rè Pastore*; Donna Anna, *Don Giovanni*; Opera London, Helena, *A Midsummer Night's Dream*;

103

Scottish Opera: Elisabeth, *Elegy for Young Lovers*: Pamina, *The Magic Flute*; Anne Trulove, *The Rake's Progress*; Leïla, *Les Pecheurs de Pêrles*.

RELATED PROFESSIONAL ACTIVITIES: Numerous concerts, recitals, broadcasts, masterclasses and television appearances in the UK and abroad; leading interpreter of Spanish and French music; consultant for BBC Wales Cardiff Singer of the Year Competition; adjudicator for leading British music colleges.

RECORDINGS INCLUDE: Alwyn, *Miss Julie* (LYRI); Canteloube, *Songs of the Auvergne* (EMI); Handel, *Acis and Galatea* (ARGO); Mozart, *Don Giovanni* (EMI); Poulenc, *Dialogue des Carmélites* (Dutch Label); Rameau, *Hippolyte et Aricie* (L'OI); Tippett, *The Knot Garden* (PHIL); Cabaret Classics with John Constable (UNIC); *South of the Border down Mexico Way* (HYPE).

PUBLICATIONS INCLUDE: 1985, contributor, *Peter Pears: A Tribute on his 75th Birthday* (Faber).

AWARDS AND HONOURS INCLUDE: 1967 and 1968, John Christie Award; Fellow, Royal Academy of Music.

ADDRESS: Not available.

GRAHAM COLIN
Director, Designer, Librettist, Teacher and Translator

POSITION: Artistic Director, Opera Theatre of St Louis.

PERSONAL DETAILS: b. 22 September 1931, Sussex.

EDUCATION/TRAINING: Royal Academy of Dramatic Art.

PROFESSIONAL AND OPERATIC DEBUT: 1958, English Opera Group at the Aldeburgh Festival, *Noye's Fludde* by Benjamin Britten (world première).

CAREER: Over 300 productions for opera, theatre and television worldwide; Associate Director: 1963–1967, English Opera Group; 1966–1975, Sadler's Wells Opera/English National Opera; 1978–1983, Opera Theatre of St Louis; 1978–1984,

English National Opera; Artistic Director: 1966–1990, Aldeburgh Festival; 1968–1979, English Opera Group/English Music Theatre; 1984–1991, Banff Festival Opera, Alberta; since 1984, Opera Theatre of St Louis; since 1990, Vice-President, Aldeburgh Festival.

MAJOR OPERATIC DEBUTS INCLUDE: 1958, New Opera Company, *The Soldier's Tale*; 1961: Covent Garden, *Orfeo ed Euridice*; Sadler's Wells Opera, *The Cunning Little Vixen*; 1968, Scottish Opera at the Edinburgh Festival, *Peter Grimes*; 1974: Metropolitan Opera, New York, *Death in Venice*; Santa Fe Opera, *Owen Wingrave*; 1978, Opera Theatre of St Louis, *The Tree of Chastity*; 1984, Banff Festival Opera, Alberta, *A Midsummer Night's Dream*.

OPERATIC WORLD PREMIERES INCLUDE: English Opera Group at the Aldeburgh Festival: 1964, *Curlew River*; 1966, *The Burning Fiery Furnace*; 1967, *The Golden Vanity* (children's vaudeville); 1968, *The Prodigal Son*; 1973, *Death in Venice*; 1971, BBC Television, *Owen Wingrave* (all by Benjamin Britten); Sadler's Wells Opera: 1965, *The Mines of Sulphur*; 1967, *A Penny for a Song*; 1970, Covent Garden, *Victory* (all by Richard Rodney Bennett); English Opera Group at the Aldeburgh Festival: 1967, *The Bear* by William Walton; 1969, *The Grace of Todd* by Gordon Crosse; 1970, Glyndebourne Festival Opera, *The Rising of the Moon* by Nicholas Maw; 1967, New Opera Company at the Sadler's Wells Theatre, *The Decision*; 1974, English Opera Group at the Aldeburgh Festival, *The Voice of Ariadne*; 1977, Scottish Opera, *Mary, Queen of Scots* (all by Thea Musgrave); English National Opera: 1977, *The Royal Hunt of the Sun*; 1981, *Anna Karenina* (both by Iain Hamilton); 1976, English Music Theatre at the Aldeburgh Festival, *Tom Jones*; 1983, Banff Festival Opera, Alberta, *Sasha* (both by Stephen Oliver); 1979, English Music Theatre at the Old Vic Theatre, *An Actor's Revenge* by Minoru Miki; Opera Theatre of St Louis: 1979, *The Village Singer*; 1982, *The Postman Always Rings Twice*; 1985, *The*

Woodlanders (all by Stephen Paulus);
1983, Opera North, *Rebecca* by Wilfred
Josephs; 1991, Metropolitan Opera, New
York, *The Ghosts of Versailles* by John
Corigliano; 1992, Lyric Opera, Chicago,
The Song of Majnun by Bright Sheng.
OPERA PRODUCTIONS IN THE UK
INCLUDE: Since 1963: Covent Garden: *Owen
    Wingrave* by Benjamin Britten (1973,
    world stage première), *Troilus and
    Cressida*, *Death in Venice* (also
    designer); English Opera Group/English
    Music Theatre: *The Rape of Lucretia*, *The
    Beggar's Opera*, *Albert Herring*, *A
    Midsummer Night's Dream*, *Peter Grimes*,
    King Arthur, *The Turn of the Screw*, *Paul
    Bunyan* by Benjamin Britten (1976, world
    stage première), *Sandrina's Secret*, *The
    Fairy Queen*, *La Cubana* (1978, British
    première); Opera North, *Peter Grimes*;
    Sadler's Wells Opera/English National
    Opera: *Madam Butterfly*, *From the House
    of the Dead*, *Gloriana* (also co-designer),
    Don Pasquale, *The Force of Destiny*, *The
    Tales of Hoffmann*, *Lohengrin*, *The
    Coronation of Poppea*, *War and Peace*
    (1972, British stage première), *Don
    Carlos*, *Boris Godunov*, *The Adventures
    of Mr Brouček*, *Romeo and Juliet*, *Louise*,
    Gloriana; Scottish Opera: *Cinderella*,
    Pelléas et Mélisande.
RELATED PROFESSIONAL ACTIVITIES:
    1984–1991, Head of Opera Programme,
    Banff Festival Opera, Alberta; since 1988,
    teacher, Yale University Opera
    Department; recent designs include: 1990,
    Opera Theatre of St Louis, *Peter Grimes*;
    1991, Washington Opera, *King Arthur*.
VIDEOS INCLUDE: Britten, *Gloriana* (English
    National Opera).
PUBLICATIONS INCLUDE: Librettos: *The
    Golden Vanity*, new version of *King
    Arthur* (both Faber), *A Penny for a Song*
    (Universal Edition), *The Postman Always
    Rings Twice*, *The Woodlanders* (both
    European American Music); production
    notes for Britten's three Church Parables
    (Faber).
AWARDS AND HONOURS INCLUDE: 1972,
    Orpheus Award (Germany), *War and
    Peace* (Sadler's Wells Opera); 1979,

Churchill Fellowship; 1986, Honorary
    Doctorate of Arts, Webster University, St
    Louis; 1988, Opera America Production
    Prize, *Albert Herring*.
ADDRESS: c/o Opera Theatre of St Louis,
    PO Box 191910, St Louis, MO 63119, USA.

GRAHAM-HALL JOHN   Tenor

PERSONAL DETAILS: b. 23 November 1955,
    Middlesex; m. 1990, Helen Williams
    (soprano), one child.
PREVIOUS OCCUPATION: 1977–1980,
    Management Accounts Department,
    Royal Opera House, Covent Garden.
EDUCATION/TRAINING: 1974–1977, Choral
    Scholar, King's College, Cambridge;
    1980–1983, Royal College of Music, with
    Edward Brooks; privately with Rupert
    Bruce-Lockhart, Peter Harrison and David
    Harper.
PROFESSIONAL DEBUT: 1983, Opera North,
    Ferrando, *Così fan tutte*.
MAJOR DEBUTS INCLUDE: 1984, Lyons
    Opera, Lensky, *Eugene Onegin*; 1985,
    Glyndebourne Festival Opera, title role,
    Albert Herring; 1986, Welsh National
    Opera, Cassio, *Otello*; 1989, Covent
    Garden, title role, *Albert Herring*; 1990:
    Scottish Opera, Eisenstein, *Die
    Fledermaus*; Canadian Opera Company,
    Toronto, Lensky, *Eugene Onegin*; 1991:
    English National Opera, Don Basilio, *The
    Marriage of Figaro*; Aix-en-Provence
    Festival, Lysander, *A Midsummer Night's
    Dream*.
OPERATIC WORLD PREMIÈRES INCLUDE:
    1983, Royal College of Music, Phaethon,
    Metamorphoses by Richard Blackford.
CAREER IN THE UK INCLUDES: Since 1984:
    English National Opera, Cyril, *Princess
    Ida*; Glyndebourne Festival and Touring
    Opera: Flute, *A Midsummer Night's
    Dream*; Aschenbach, *Death in Venice*;
    Vanya, *Katya Kabanova*; Bob Boles,
    Peter Grimes; Kent Opera, Pedrillo, *The
    Seraglio*; Scottish Opera, Schoolmaster,
    The Cunning Little Vixen.

RELATED PROFESSIONAL ACTIVITIES:
Numerous concerts and recitals in the UK
and abroad.

RECORDINGS INCLUDE: Britten, *A
Midsummer Night's Dream*; Monteverdi,
L'Incoronazione di Poppea (both VIRG);
Orff, *Carmina Burana* (IMP).

VIDEOS INCLUDE: Britten, *Albert Herring*;
Janáček, *Katya Kabanova* (both
Glyndebourne Festival Opera).

ADDRESS: c/o Kaye Artists Management
Ltd, Barratt House, 7 Chertsey Road,
Woking, Surrey GU21 5AB.

GREENFIELD EDWARD
Critic, Broadcaster and Writer

POSITION: Chief Music Critic, *The Guardian*.

PERSONAL DETAILS: b. 30 July 1928,
Westcliff-on-Sea.

EDUCATION/TRAINING: Trinity Hall,
Cambridge.

CAREER: *The Guardian*: since 1953, staff
writer; since 1955, record critic; 1964–
1977, music critic; since 1977, Chief Music
Critic; since 1957, broadcaster on music
and recordings for BBC Radio; since
1960, member, Critics' Panel,
Gramophone.

PUBLICATIONS INCLUDE: 1958, *Puccini:
Keeper of the Seal* (Hutchinson); 1972,
Joan Sutherland; 1973, *André Previn*
(both Ian Allan); editor with Robert Layton
and Ivan March: 1960–1974, *Stereo
Record Guide* (nine volumes, Long
Playing Record Library); 1975–1984,
Penguin Stereo Record Guide (four
volumes); 1986–1991, *Penguin Guide to
Compact Discs, Cassettes and LPs* (five
volumes).

AWARDS AND HONOURS INCLUDE: 1981,
Goldener Verdienstzeichen (Salzburg);
1991, Honorary Member, Guildhall School
of Music and Drama.

ADDRESS: 16 Folgate Street, London E1
6BX.

GREENWOOD ANDREW
Conductor and Chorus Master

PERSONAL DETAILS: b. 21 July 1954, West
Yorkshire.

EDUCATION/TRAINING: 1972–1975, Clare
College, Cambridge, studied music, piano
and french horn; 1975–1976, London
Opera Centre; conducting with Edward
Downes.

PROFESSIONAL DEBUT: 1976, pianist, Opera
for All.

OPERATIC DEBUT: 1980, Opera 80, *The
Barber of Seville*.

CAREER: 1976–1977, pianist, Opera for All;
1977–1984, répétiteur, Covent Garden;
1979–1983, Music Director, Nonsuch
Opera, Epsom; 1984–1990, conductor and
Chorus Master, Welsh National Opera;
since 1990, freelance.

MAJOR OPERATIC DEBUTS INCLUDE: 1984,
Welsh National Opera, *Don Giovanni*;
1989, Cologne Opera, *The Bartered
Bride*; 1990, English National Opera, *The
Magic Flute*.

OPERA PERFORMANCES IN THE UK
INCLUDE: Since 1990: Chelsea Opera
Group, *Manon Lescaut*; English National
Opera: *Madam Butterfly*, *Don Giovanni*,
Don Pasquale; Welsh National Opera:
Der Rosenkavalier, *Carmen*.

RELATED PROFESSIONAL ACTIVITIES:
Since 1981, Associate/Guest Chorus
Master, Philharmonia Chorus.

RECORDINGS INCLUDE: Lesley Garrett,
Diva! A Soprano at the Movies (SILV).

ADDRESS: c/o Kaye Artists Management
Ltd, Barratt House, 7 Chertsey Road,
Woking, Surrey GU21 5AB.

GRIFFITHS PAUL
Critic, Librettist and Writer

POSITION: Music Critic, *The Times*.

PERSONAL DETAILS: b. 24 November 1947,
Glamorgan; m. 1977, Rachel Cullen, two
children.

EDUCATION/TRAINING: Lincoln College,
Oxford, studied biochemistry.

CAREER: 1973–1976, Area Editor, *The New Grove Dictionary of Music and Musicians*, sixth edition; *The Times*: 1979–1982, Assistant Music Critic; since 1982, Music Critic.

OPERATIC WORLD PREMIÈRES INCLUDE: 1991, Opera North, compiler and librettist, *The Jewel Box*, opera in two acts using material by Mozart, conductor Elgar Howarth, director Francisco Negrin, designer Anthony Baker.

PUBLICATIONS INCLUDE: 1978: *Boulez* (Oxford University Press), *A Concise History of Modern Music*; 1979, *A Guide to Electronic Music* (both Thames & Hudson); 1980, *Modern Music* (Dent); 1981, *Cage* (Oxford University Press); 1982: *Peter Maxwell Davies* (Robson), *Igor Stravinsky: The Rake's Progress* (Cambridge University Press); 1983: *György Ligeti* (Robson), *The String Quartet* (Thames & Hudson); 1984, *Bartók* (Dent); 1985: *New Sounds, New Personalities: British Composers of the 1980s*; *Olivier Messiaen and the Music of Time* (both Faber); 1986, *The Thames and Hudson Encyclopaedia of Twentieth Century Music*; 1989, *Myself and Marco Polo*; 1991: *The Lay of Sir Tristram*, *The Jewel Box* (all Chatto & Windus).

ADDRESS: The Old Bakery, Lower Heyford, Oxford OX5 3NS.

GUNTER JOHN   Designer

POSITION: Associate Designer, Royal National Theatre.

PERSONAL DETAILS: b. 31 October 1938, Essex; m. Micheline McKnight (dancer), two children.

EDUCATION/TRAINING: 1958–1961, Central School of Art and Design.

CAREER: Since 1962, freelance theatre and opera designer with leading companies in the UK and abroad including: Royal Shakespeare Company, Royal Court Theatre (1965–1966, Resident Designer), Zurich Playhouse (1970–1973, Resident Designer), Royal National Theatre (1988–1990, Head of Design; currently Associate Designer).

MAJOR OPERATIC DEBUTS INCLUDE: *Falstaff*: 1974, Hamburg State Opera; 1976, Cologne Opera; 1979, Teatro Colón, Buenos Aires, *Peter Grimes*; 1981, Welsh National Opera, *The Greek Passion* (British première); 1985: English National Opera, *Faust*; Glyndebourne Festival Opera, *Albert Herring*; Australian Opera, Sydney, *Un Ballo in Maschera*; 1986, Maggio Musicale, Florence, *Die Meistersinger von Nürnberg*; 1987, San Francisco Opera, *Fidelio*; 1988, La Scala, Milan, *Der Fliegende Holländer*; 1989: Covent Garden, *Albert Herring*; Los Angeles Music Center Opera, *Tosca*; 1991, Salzburg Festival, *Le Nozze di Figaro*; 1993, Scottish Opera, *Norma*.

OPERA DESIGNS IN THE UK INCLUDE: Since 1980: Buxton Festival, *Hamlet*; Covent Garden: *Der Fliegende Holländer*, *Porgy and Bess*; Glyndebourne Festival Opera: *Porgy and Bess*, *Simon Boccanegra*, *La Traviata*, *Falstaff*, *Le Nozze di Figaro*, *Peter Grimes*; Opera North: *Macbeth* (two productions), *Die Fledermaus*, *Attila*.

RELATED PROFESSIONAL ACTIVITIES: 1974–1982, Head of Theatre Department, Central School of Art and Design.

VIDEOS INCLUDE: Britten, *Albert Herring*; Mozart, *Le Nozze di Figaro*; Verdi, *La Traviata* (all Glyndebourne Festival Opera).

ADDRESS: c/o Curtis Brown Group Ltd, 162–168 Regent Street, London W1R 5TB.

GUY-BROMLEY PHILLIP
Baritone

PERSONAL DETAILS: b. Shropshire; m. Rosamund Podger (violinist), three children.

EDUCATION/TRAINING: 1973–1977, Birmingham School of Music, with Keith Darlington.

PROFESSIONAL DEBUT: 1978, Glyndebourne Touring Opera, Speaker, *Die Zauberflöte*.

EARLY CAREER INCLUDED: 1978–1984, appearances with Glyndebourne Touring Opera and Welsh National Opera; roles included: Don Fernando, *Fidelio*; Masetto, *Don Giovanni*; Christian, *Un Ballo in Maschera*; Mathieu, *Andrea Chénier*; Morales, *Carmen*; Sergeant, *La Bohème*.

MAJOR DEBUTS INCLUDE: 1980, Welsh National Opera, Innkeeper, *The Cunning Little Vixen*; 1984, Opera 80, Mustafa, *The Italian Girl in Algiers*; 1988: English National Opera, First Soldier, *Salome*; Wexford Festival, Gatekeeper of Hell, *The Devil and Kate*; 1989, Opera North, Tchelio, *The Love for Three Oranges*; 1991, Earls Court, Sciarrone, *Tosca*.

OPERATIC WORLD PREMIERES INCLUDE: 1981, Welsh National Opera, Old Man, *The Journey* by John Metcalf.

CAREER IN THE UK INCLUDES: Since 1985: English National Opera: Mr Flint, *Billy Budd*; Leporello, *Don Giovanni*; Ortel, *The Mastersingers of Nuremberg*; Farfarello, *The Love for Three Oranges*; Levis/Student from Cracow/Theology Student, *Doctor Faust*; Opera 80: Masetto/Commendatore, *Don Giovanni*; Monterone, *Rigoletto*; Alidoro, *Cinderella*; Park Lane Opera, Cassandro, *La Finta Semplice*; Pavilion Opera: Dulcamara, *L'Elisir d'Amore*; Leporello, *Don Giovanni*.

RECORDINGS INCLUDE: A Hundred Years of Italian Opera (OPRA).

VIDEOS INCLUDE: Britten, *Billy Budd* (English National Opera).

ADDRESS: c/o Opera and Concert Artists, 75 Aberdare Gardens, London NW6 3AN.

*　　*　　*　　*

HACKER ALAN
Conductor, Clarinettist, Editor and Teacher

PERSONAL DETAILS: b. 30 September 1938, Surrey; m. 1959, two children; m. 1977, Karen Evans (m. diss.), one child.

EDUCATION/TRAINING: Royal Academy of Music, studied clarinet with Jack Brymer and Reginald Kell.

PROFESSIONAL DEBUT: As clarinettist: 1957, London Philharmonic Orchestra.

OPERATIC DEBUT: 1986, Norrlands Opera, Umeå, *Den Bergtagna*.

CAREER: 1957–1966, clarinettist, London Philharmonic Orchestra; co-founder: 1967, Pierrot Players; 1970, The Fires of London; 1971, Matrix; 1972, Music Party for authentic performances of classical music; 1977, Classical Orchestra; 1957–1976, professor, Royal Academy of Music; 1970–1976, Artistic Director, York Early Music Festival; 1972–1973, Sir Robert Mayer Lecturer, University of Leeds; 1976–1986, Senior Lecturer in Music, University of York; Guest Conductor: 1981–1984, Orchestra La Fenice, Venice; 1990, Dublin Grand Opera.

OPERATIC WORLD PREMIERES INCLUDE: 1990, Scottish Opera, *The Vanishing Bridegroom* by Judith Weir.

OPERA PERFORMANCES INCLUDE: Since 1989: Opera North: *La Finta Giardiniera* (British operatic debut), *Così fan tutte*; Stuttgart State Opera, *Don Giovanni*.

RELATED PROFESSIONAL ACTIVITIES: Regular concerts as a conductor and clarinettist giving many first authentic performances of works by Bach, Beethoven, Haydn, Mozart (also editor); teacher, School of Fine Arts, Banff Centre, Alberta.

RECORDINGS INCLUDE: As clarinettist: Brahms, chamber works; Mendelssohn, chamber and orchestral works; Mozart, clarinet quintets (all AMON).

PUBLICATIONS INCLUDE: Editor, reconstruction of Clarinet Concerto by Mozart (Schott).

HONOURS INCLUDE: 1988, Officer, Order of the British Empire (OBE); Fellow, Royal Academy of Music.

ADDRESS: c/o Haydn Rawstron International Management, PO Box 654, London SE26 4DZ.

HAGLEY ALISON   Soprano

PERSONAL DETAILS: b. 1961, London.
EDUCATION/TRAINING: 1979–1984, Guildhall School of Music and Drama; 1983, masterclasses with Elisabeth Schwarzkopf; 1987–1988, National Opera Studio.
PROFESSIONAL DEBUT: 1985, Aldeburgh Festival, title role, *Rodelinda*.
MAJOR DEBUTS INCLUDE: 1985, Batignano Festival, Emilia, *Flavio*; 1987: Glyndebourne Festival Opera, Little Owl, *L'Enfant et les Sortilèges*; Glyndebourne Touring Opera, Despina, *Così fan tutte*; 1989: Covent Garden, Flower Maiden, *Parsifal*; English National Opera, Gretel, *Hansel and Gretel*; Scottish Opera, Musetta, *La Bohème*; 1991: Glyndebourne Festival Opera, Susanna, *Le Nozze di Figaro*; Grand Théâtre, Geneva, Second Niece, *Peter Grimes*; 1992: Welsh National Opera, Mélisande, *Pelléas et Mélisande*; Teatro La Fenice, Venice, Susanna, *Le Nozze di Figaro*.
CAREER IN THE UK INCLUDES: Since 1986: Covent Garden, Second Niece, *Peter Grimes*; English National Opera: Lauretta, *Gianni Schicchi*; Nannetta, *Falstaff*; Glyndebourne Festival and Touring Opera: Varvara, *Katya Kabanova*; Barbarina and Susanna, *Le Nozze di Figaro*; Karolka, *Jenůfa*; Nannetta, *Falstaff*; Papagena, *Die Zauberflote*; Opera 80, Clorinda, *Cinderella*; Park Lane Opera at the Camden Festival, Sandrina, *La Finta Giardiniera*; Scottish Opera, Adele, *Die Fledermaus*.
RECORDINGS INCLUDE: Elgar, *The Starlight Express* (CHAN); Mendelssohn, *A Midsummer Night's Dream* (COLL).
VIDEOS INCLUDE: Debussy, *Pelléas et Mélisande* (Welsh National Opera); Janáček, *Jenůfa* (Glyndebourne Festival Opera).

ADDRESS: c/o Harrison/Parrott Ltd, 12 Penzance Place, London W11 4PA.

HAITINK BERNARD
Conductor

POSITION: Music Director, The Royal Opera, Covent Garden.
PERSONAL DETAILS: b. 4 March 1929, Amsterdam, Netherlands; m. 1956, Marjolein Snyder, five children; m. 1991, Kirsti Goedhart.
EDUCATION/TRAINING: Amsterdam Conservatory of Music, studied violin and conducting under Felix Hupka; 1954 and 1955, attended annual summer conductors' course organized by Netherlands Radio Union under conductor Ferdinand Leitner.
PROFESSIONAL DEBUT: As violinist: 1953, Netherlands Radio Philharmonic; as conductor: 1956, Netherlands Radio Philharmonic at the Holland Festival, *Requiem in C Minor* (Cherubini).
OPERATIC DEBUT: 1966, Netherlands Opera at the Holland Festival, *Der Fliegende Holländer*.
CAREER: Netherlands Radio Philharmonic: 1954–1955, Second Conductor (co-responsibility for four radio orchestras); 1955–1956, Permanent Conductor; 1957–1961, Principal Conductor; Concertgebouw Orchestra, Amsterdam: 1961–1964, Joint Principal Conductor (with Eugen Jochum); 1964–1988, Artistic Director and Principal Conductor; London Philharmonic Orchestra: 1964–1967, Guest Conductor; 1967–1979, Artistic Director and Principal Conductor; since 1990, President; Music Director: 1978–1988, Glyndebourne Festival Opera; since 1987, Covent Garden.
MAJOR OPERATIC DEBUTS INCLUDE: 1972, Glyndebourne Festival Opera, *Die Entführung aus dem Serail*; 1977, Covent Garden, *Don Giovanni*; 1982, Metropolitan Opera, New York, *Fidelio*; 1991, Salzburg Festival, *Le Nozze di Figaro*.

OPERA PERFORMANCES IN THE UK
INCLUDE: Since 1972: Covent Garden:
*Lohengrin, Un Ballo in Maschera, Don
Carlos, Peter Grimes, Arabella, Jenůfa,
Der Rosenkavalier, Le Nozze di Figaro*
(also 1992, Japan tour), *Parsifal, Il
Trovatore, Prince Igor, Der Ring des
Nibelungen, Don Giovanni* (also 1992,
Japan tour), *Die Frau ohne Schatten, The
Cunning Little Vixen*; Glyndebourne
Festival Opera: *Die Zauberflöte, The
Rake's Progress, Pelléas et Mélisande,
Don Giovanni, Così fan tutte, Fidelio, La
Fedeltà Premiata, Der Rosenkavalier, A
Midsummer Night's Dream, L'Amour des
Trois Oranges, Idomeneo, Le Nozze di
Figaro, Arabella, Carmen, Albert Herring,
Simon Boccanegra, La Traviata,
Capriccio, Falstaff.*
RELATED PROFESSIONAL ACTIVITIES:
Regular appearances with leading
orchestras worldwide.
RECORDINGS INCLUDE: Beethoven, *Fidelio*
(PHIL); Britten, *Peter Grimes*; Mozart: *Così
fan tutte, Don Giovanni, Le Nozze di
Figaro, Die Zauberflöte*; R. Strauss:
Daphne, Der Rosenkavalier; Wagner:
*Götterdämmerung, Das Rheingold,
Siegfried, Tannhäuser, Die Walküre* (all
EMI); Verdi, *Don Carlos*; complete
symphonies of Beethoven, Bruckner and
Mahler (all PHIL).
VIDEOS INCLUDE: Beethoven, *Fidelio*; Bizet,
Carmen; Britten: *Albert Herring, A
Midsummer Night's Dream*; Mozart: *Don
Giovanni, Idomeneo, Die Zauberflöte*;
Prokofiev, *L'Amour des Trois Oranges*; R.
Strauss, *Arabella*; Verdi: *La Traviata* (all
Glyndebourne Festival Opera), *Don
Carlos* (Covent Garden).
RELEVANT PUBLICATIONS INCLUDE: 1987,
Bernard Haitink: A Working Life by Simon
Mundy (Robson).
AWARDS AND HONOURS INCLUDE: 1970,
Bruckner Medal of Honour (USA); 1971,
Gold Medal, International Gustav Mahler
Society; 1972, Chevalier de l'Ordre des
Arts et des Lettres (France); 1973,
Honorary Member, Royal Academy of
Music; 1977: Honorary Knight
Commander, Order of the British Empire
(KBE); Officer, Order of the Crown
(Belgium); 1984, Fellow, Royal College of
Music; 1988, Commander, Order of
Orange Nassau (Netherlands); 1990, Gold
Medal, Royal Philharmonic Society; 1991,
Erasmus Prize (Netherlands); Honorary
Doctorates of Music, Universities of
Oxford and Leeds; 1985, *Gramophone*
Operatic Award, *Don Giovanni*;
Gramophone Orchestral Award: 1986,
Sinfonia Antartica; 1990, *A Sea
Symphony* (both by Vaughan Williams).
ADDRESS: c/o Harold Holt Ltd, 31 Sinclair
Road, London W14 ONS.

HALL JOHN   Bass-baritone

PERSONAL DETAILS: b. 14 May 1956,
Brecon, South Wales; m. 1985, Julie
Crocker (Senior Stage Manager,
Glyndebourne Festival Opera), three
children.
EDUCATION/TRAINING: 1974–1979, Royal
College of Music, with Frederick Sharp.
PROFESSIONAL DEBUT: 1979, English Bach
Festival, Neptune, *Hippolyte et Aricie*.
MAJOR DEBUTS INCLUDE: 1981,
Glyndebourne Festival Opera, Lackey,
Ariadne auf Naxos; Afron, *Le Coq d'Or*;
1984, Théâtre du Châtelet, Paris; 1985,
Nancy Opera; 1986, Opera North, Priam,
The Capture of Troy; 1989, Kent Opera,
Antinöo, *The Return of Ulysses*; 1991,
Covent Garden, Mityukha, *Boris
Godunov*; 1992, English National Opera,
Antinöo/Time, *The Return of Ulysses*.
OPERATIC WORLD PREMIERES INCLUDE:
1988, Queen Elizabeth Hall, Cardinal
Camillo, *Beatrice Cenci* by Berthold
Goldschmidt; 1989, Almeida Festival, title
role, *Golem* by John Casken.
CAREER IN THE UK INCLUDES: Since 1980:
Buxton Festival, Goliath, *David and
Goliath*; Covent Garden, Sciarrone,
Tosca; Glyndebourne Festival and
Touring Opera: Masetto, *Don Giovanni*;
Leander, *The Love for Three Oranges*;
Grenville, *La Traviata*; Rocco, *Fidelio*;
Trulove, *The Rake's Progress*; title role,
Le Nozze di Figaro; Opera 80: Don

Basilio, *The Barber of Seville*; Bartolo,
The Marriage of Figaro; Opera North:
Zuniga, *Carmen*; Sacristan, *Tosca*;
Master of the Masquerade, *Masquerade*
(1990, British première); Siroco, *L'Etoile*;
Leporello, *Don Giovanni*; Bonze, *Madama
Butterfly*; Scottish Opera, Harašta, *The
Cunning Little Vixen*; University College
Opera: Creonte, *Orfeo ed Euridice*
(Haydn); Beneš, *The Devil's Wall* (1987,
British première).

RECORDINGS INCLUDE: Casken, *Golem*
(VIRG).

VIDEOS INCLUDE: R. Strauss, *Arabella*;
Verdi, *La Traviata* (both Glyndebourne
Festival Opera).

AWARDS INCLUDE: 1982, Glyndebourne
Touring Opera Singers' Award; 1983,
John Christie Award.

ADDRESS: c/o Korman International
Management, Crunnells Green Cottage,
Preston, Hertfordshire SG4 7UQ.

HALL, SIR PETER Director

PERSONAL DETAILS: b. 22 November 1930,
Suffolk; m. 1956, Leslie Caron (actress),
two children; m. 1965, Jacqueline Taylor,
two children; m. 1982, Maria Ewing
(soprano), one child; m. 1990, Nicky Frei,
one child.

EDUCATION/TRAINING: 1949–1952, St
Catharine's College, Cambridge.

PROFESSIONAL DEBUT: 1953, Theatre
Royal, Windsor, *The Letter* by Somerset
Maugham.

OPERATIC DEBUT: 1957, Sadler's Wells
Opera, *The Moon and Sixpence* by John
Gardner (world première).

CAREER: Associate Director: 1954–1955,
Oxford Playhouse; 1955–1956, Arts
Theatre, London; 1957, founder,
International Playwrights' Theatre; Royal
Shakespeare Company: 1960–1968,
Managing Director; 1968–1973, Co-
Director; Artistic Director: 1973–1988,
Royal National Theatre; 1984–1990,
Glyndebourne Festival Opera; since 1988,
founder and Director, The Peter Hall

Company; director of films for cinema and
television.

MAJOR OPERATIC DEBUTS INCLUDE: 1965,
Covent Garden, *Moses and Aaron* (British
première); 1970, Glyndebourne Festival
Opera, *La Calisto*; 1982, Metropolitan
Opera, New York, *Macbeth*; 1983:
Bayreuth Festival, *Der Ring des
Nibelungen*; Grand Théâtre, Geneva, *Le
Nozze di Figaro*; 1987, Lyric Opera,
Chicago, *Le Nozze di Figaro*; Los
Angeles Music Center Opera: 1986,
Salome; 1992, *The Magic Flute*.

OPERATIC WORLD PREMIERES INCLUDE:
1970, Covent Garden, *The Knot Garden*;
1989, Houston Grand Opera, *New Year*
(both by Michael Tippett).

OPERA PRODUCTIONS IN THE UK
INCLUDE: Since 1966: Covent Garden: *Die
Zauberflöte, Eugene Onegin, Tristan und
Isolde, Salome*; Glyndebourne Festival
Opera: *Il Ritorno d'Ulisse in Patria, Le
Nozze di Figaro, Don Giovanni, Così fan
tutte, Fidelio, A Midsummer Night's
Dream, Orfeo ed Euridice,
L'Incoronazione di Poppea, Carmen,
Albert Herring, Simon Boccanegra, La
Traviata, Falstaff, New Year* (1990, British
première).

RELATED PROFESSIONAL ACTIVITIES:
Since 1966, Associate Professor of
Drama, University of Warwick; 1975–1977,
Presenter, Aquarius (LWT); 1983, founder
member, Theatre Directors' Guild of
Great Britain.

VIDEOS INCLUDE: Bizet, *Carmen*; Britten:
*Albert Herring, A Midsummer Night's
Dream*; Gluck, *Orfeo ed Euridice*;
Monteverdi: *Il Ritorno d'Ulisse in Patria,
L'Incoronazione di Poppea*; Mozart: *Don
Giovanni, Le Nozze di Figaro*; Verdi, *La
Traviata* (all Glyndebourne Festival
Opera).

PUBLICATIONS INCLUDE: 1983, *Peter Hall's
Diaries*, editor John Goodwin (Hamish
Hamilton).

AWARDS AND HONOURS INCLUDE: 1963,
Commander, Order of the British Empire
(CBE); 1964, Honorary Fellow, St
Catharine's College, Cambridge; 1965,
Chevalier de l'Ordre des Arts et des

111

Lettres (France); 1977: Knighthood; Society of West End Theatre Award, Glyndebourne Festival Opera production of *Don Giovanni*; 1981, *Evening Standard Award*, *A Midsummer Night's Dream* (Glyndebourne Festival Opera); Honorary Doctorates of Literature: Universities of Leicester, Liverpool, Reading, York.

ADDRESS: c/o Peter Hall Company Ltd, The Albery Theatre, St Martin's Lane, London WC2N 4AH.

HALSEY SIMON
Conductor and Chorus Master

POSITIONS: Co-Music Director, City of Birmingham Touring Opera; Chorus Master, Flanders Opera, Antwerp.

PERSONAL DETAILS: b. 8 March 1958, Kingston-upon-Thames; m. 1986.

EDUCATION/TRAINING: 1976–1979, King's College, Cambridge; 1979–1980, Royal College of Music.

PROFESSIONAL DEBUT: 1980, Scottish Opera Go Round, *The Quest of the Hidden Moon*.

CAREER: 1980–1981, Conductor, Scottish Opera Go Round; 1981–1988, Director of Music, University of Warwick (also conductor, English Touring Opera); 1982, Chorus Master, City of Birmingham Symphony Orchestra; 1985, Associate Director, Philharmonia Chorus; 1988, Artistic Director, Salisbury Festival; since 1987, Co-Music Director, City of Birmingham Touring Opera; since 1991, Chorus Master, Flanders Opera, Antwerp.

OPERA PERFORMANCES IN THE UK
INCLUDE: Since 1981: Cambridge Opera Group: *Curlew River*, *The Tales of Hoffmann*, *The Burning Fiery Furnace*, *The Prodigal Son*; English Touring Opera/City of Birmingham Touring Opera: *Cinderella*, *La Bohème*, *Falstaff*, *The Ring Saga*, *Beauty and the Beast*, *Zaide*, *Les Boréades*.

ADDRESS: c/o Magenta Music International Ltd, 64 Highgate High Street, London N6 5HX.

HAMILTON IAIN   Composer

PERSONAL DETAILS: b. 6 June 1922, Glasgow.

PREVIOUS OCCUPATION: 1939–1946, engineer, Handley Page Ltd.

EDUCATION/TRAINING: 1947–1951, Scholar, Royal Academy of Music, studied composition with William Alwyn and piano with Harold Craxton; 1951, University of London.

FIRST WORK TO ACHIEVE PROMINENCE: 1952, Royal Philharmonic Society at the Royal Festival Hall, Concerto for clarinet and orchestra.

CAREER: Since 1952, numerous compositions in all genres including symphonies, concertos, string quartets, vocal and choral works and incidental music for film and theatre; lecturer: 1952–1958, Morley College; 1956–1960, University of London; 1962, Composer in Residence, Berkshire Music Center, Tanglewood, Massachusetts; 1962–1978, Mary Duke Biddle Professor of Music, Duke University, North Carolina (1966–1967, Chairman of the Department).

OPERATIC WORLD PREMIERES: 1969, Music Theatre Ensemble at the Edinburgh International Festival, *Pharsalia*, a dramatic commentary in one act after Lucan, conductor David Atherton, director John Cox; 1974, Scottish Opera, *The Catiline Conspiracy*, opera in two acts after Jonson, conductor Alexander Gibson, director Anthony Besch, designer Luciana Arrighi; 1977: English National Opera, *The Royal Hunt of the Sun*, opera in two acts after the play by Peter Shaffer, conductor David Lloyd-Jones, director Colin Graham, designer David Collis; BBC Radio 3, *Tamburlaine*, lyric drama for radio after Marlowe, conductor David Atherton; 1981, English National Opera, *Anna Karenina*, opera in three acts after Tolstoy, conductor Howard Williams, director Colin Graham, designer Ralph Koltai; 1984, Duke University, North Carolina, *Raleigh's Dream*, opera in one act; 1985, Arundel Festival, *Lancelot*, opera in two acts after Malory, conductor

Chris Nance, director Aidan Lang, designer Peter Farmer; unperformed opera (1967–1969), *Agamemnon*, opera in one act after Aeschylus (all librettos by the composer).

RELATED PROFESSIONAL ACTIVITIES: Chairman: 1958, Composers' Guild of Great Britain; 1958–1960, Music Committee, Institute of Contemporary Arts; founding member: American Society of University Composers, International Webern Society.

AWARD AND HONOURS INCLUDE: 1951: Royal Academy of Music Dove Prize, Royal Philharmonic Society Prize, Koussevitsky Prize (USA); 1954, Butterworth Award; 1956, Arnold Bax Prize; 1958, Fellow, Royal Academy of Music; 1970, Honorary Doctorate of Music, University of Glasgow; 1975, Ralph Vaughan Williams Award.

ADDRESS: c/o Universal Edition (London) Ltd, 2/3 Fareham Street, London W1V 4DU.

HANNAN EILENE   Soprano

PERSONAL DETAILS: b. Melbourne, Australia; m. 1980, Phillip Thomas (accompanist and répétiteur).

EDUCATION/TRAINING: Privately with Jean Stewart and Bettine McCaughan in Melbourne.

PROFESSIONAL DEBUT: 1971, Australian Opera, Sydney, Peep-Bo, *The Mikado*.

MAJOR DEBUTS INCLUDE: 1973, Australian Opera, Sydney (opening of Sydney Opera House), Natasha, *War and Peace*; 1977: Glyndebourne Festival Opera, title role, *The Cunning Little Vixen*; Wexford Festival, Salome, *Hérodiade*; 1978, English National Opera, Pamina, *The Magic Flute*; 1984, English National Opera USA tour (including Metropolitan Opera, New York), Natasha, *War and Peace*; 1987, Covent Garden, Nice Caroline, *The King Goes Forth to France* (British première).

CAREER INCLUDES: Since 1971, Australian Opera, Sydney: Barbarina, *The Marriage of Figaro*; Mimi, *La Bohème*; Oscar, *Un Ballo in Maschera*; Marzelline, *Fidelio*; Lauretta, *Gianni Schicchi*; Cherubino and Susanna, *The Marriage of Figaro*; Zerlina, *Don Giovanni*; Sophie, *Der Rosenkavalier*; Pamina, *The Magic Flute*; Adina, *The Elixir of Love*; Blanche, *The Carmelites*; Venus, *Tannhäuser*; Marschallin, *Der Rosenkavalier*; Pat Nixon, *Nixon in China*; title roles: *The Cunning Little Vixen*, *Jenůfa*; since 1978, English National Opera: Mila, *Osud* (1984, British stage première); Susanna, *The Marriage of Figaro*; Mélisande, *Pelléas and Mélisande*; Marzelline, *Fidelio*; Mimi, *La Bohème*; Micaëla, *Carmen*; Lauretta, *Gianni Schicchi*; Governess, *The Turn of the Screw*; title roles: *Katya Kabanova*, *Rusalka*, *The Merry Widow*, *The Coronation of Poppea*.

RECORDINGS INCLUDE: Delius, *Irmelin*; Tchaikovsky, *Eugene Onegin* (both EMI).

VIDEOS INCLUDE: Dvořák, *Rusalka* (English National Opera).

ADDRESS: c/o Ingpen & Williams Ltd, 14 Kensington Court, London W8 5DN.

HAREWOOD, THE EARL OF (George Henry Hubert Lascelles) Administrator

POSITIONS: Chairman, Board of Directors: English National Opera, Opera Factory.

PERSONAL DETAILS: b. 7 February 1923, London; m. 1949, Maria Donata Stein (musician), three children; m. 1967, Patricia Tuckwell (musician), one child.

EDUCATION/TRAINING: 1947–1949, King's College, Cambridge; (education interrupted by World War Two).

OPERATIC CAREER: 1950–1953, founder and Editor, *Opera*; Covent Garden: 1951–1953 and 1969–1972, member, Board of Directors; 1953–1960, staff member (including 1959–1960, Controller of Opera Planning); Managing Director: 1972–1985, Sadler's Wells Opera/English National Opera; 1978–1981, Opera North;

113

Chairman, Board of Directors: since 1982, Opera Factory; since 1986, English National Opera.

OTHER PROFESSIONAL ACTIVITIES INCLUDE: 1956–1966, Chairman, Music Advisory Committee, British Council; Artistic Director: 1958–1974, Leeds Music Festival; 1961–1965, Edinburgh International Festival; 1988, Adelaide Festival; 1963–1967, Chancellor, University of York; 1966–1976, Artistic Adviser, New Philharmonia Orchestra; 1966–1972, Chairman, Music Advisory Panel, Arts Council of Great Britain; BBC: 1969–1977, member, General Advisory Council; 1985–1987, Governor; since 1985, President, British Board of Film Classification.

PUBLICATIONS INCLUDE: 1981, auto-biography, *The Tongs and the Bones* (Weidenfeld & Nicholson); Editor: *Kobbé's Complete Opera Book*, *Kobbé's Illustrated Opera Book* (both Bodley Head).

AWARDS AND HONOURS INCLUDE: Honorary Doctorates of Law: 1959, University of Leeds; 1960, University of Aberdeen; 1962, Honorary Doctorate of Music, University of Hull; 1978, Janáček Medal (Czechoslovakia); 1982, Honorary Doctorate, University of York; 1983, Honorary Member, Royal Academy of Music; 1984, Honorary Fellow, King's College, Cambridge; 1985, *Evening Standard* Special Award; 1986, Knight Commander, Order of the British Empire (KBE); Honorary Member, Royal Northern College of Music.

ADDRESS: c/o English National Opera, London Coliseum, St Martin's Lane, London WC2N 4ES.

HARGREAVES GLENVILLE
Baritone

PERSONAL DETAILS: b. 26 July 1950, Bradford; m. 1984, Erica Stanton (choreographer).

EDUCATION/TRAINING: 1971–1974, Royal Northern College of Music, with Patrick McGuigan and Frederic Cox; 1974, London Opera Centre, with Frederic Cox; 1975, University of Liverpool, with Basil Smallman and Frederic Cox.

PROFESSIONAL DEBUT: 1981, Limburg, title role, *Il Barbiere di Siviglia*.

MAJOR DEBUTS INCLUDE: 1982: Covent Garden, Hermann, *Les Contes d'Hoffmann*; English National Opera, Second Priest, *The Magic Flute*; 1984, Opera North, Angelotti, *Tosca*; 1987, Marcello, *La Bohème*: Welsh National Opera, Scottish Opera.

OPERATIC WORLD PREMIERES INCLUDES: 1990, Welsh National Opera, Sir Charles Keighley, *Tornrak* by John Metcalf.

CAREER IN THE UK INCLUDES: Since 1982: Bloomsbury Theatre, London, Father, *Hansel and Gretel*; City of Birmingham Touring Opera, title role, *Falstaff*; English National Opera: Rayevsky, *War and Peace*; First Soldier, *Salome*; Mecklenburgh Opera, title role, *The Emperor of Atlantis*; Midsummer Opera, Don Parmenione, *L'Occasione fa il Ladro*; Opera North: Krušina, *The Bartered Bride*; Dark Fiddler, *A Village Romeo and Juliet*; Opera Northern Ireland: Belcore, *L'Elisir d'Amore*; Schaunard, *La Bohème*; Regency Opera: Count di Luna, *Il Trovatore*; Scarpia, *Tosca*; Scottish Opera, Priam, *The Trojans* (also 1990, at Covent Garden); University College Opera, Vok, *The Devil's Wall* (1987, British première); Volte Face, Mittenhofer, *Elegy for Young Lovers*; Welsh National Opera, title role, *Don Pasquale*.

RELATED PROFESSIONAL ACTIVITIES: Regular concerts, recitals and broadcasts in the UK.

RECORDINGS INCLUDE: Crosse, *Purgatory* (DECC).

ADDRESS: c/o Korman International Management, Crunnells Green Cottage, Preston, Hertfordshire SG4 7UQ.

HARPER EDWARD
Composer, Conductor and Pianist

POSITION: Reader in Music, University of Edinburgh.

PERSONAL DETAILS: b. 17 March 1941, Taunton; m. 1984, Dorothy Shanks, two children.

EDUCATION/TRAINING: 1959–1963, Christ Church, Oxford; 1958 and 1964, Royal College of Music.

FIRST PROFESSIONAL PERFORMANCE OF A COMPOSITION: 1965, BBC Scottish Symphony Orchestra, Violin Concerto.

CAREER: University of Edinburgh: 1964–1990, Lecturer in Music; since 1990, Reader in Music.

OPERATIC WORLD PREMIERES: 1975, Edinburgh University Opera, *Fanny Robin*, chamber opera, libretto by the composer after Thomas Hardy, conductor the composer, director Roger Savage; 1985, Scottish Opera, *Hedda Gabler*, opera in a prologue and three acts, libretto by the composer after Ibsen, conductor Diego Masson, director Graham Vick, designer Russell Craig; 1988, Edinburgh University Opera, *The Mellstock Quire*, chamber opera, libretto by Roger Savage after Thomas Hardy, conductor the composer, director Roger Savage.

RELATED PROFESSIONAL ACTIVITIES: 1973–1990, Director, New Music Group of Scotland, active as conductor and pianist; conductor of own compositions with Scottish Chamber Orchestra, BBC Scottish and BBC Welsh Orchestras.

ADDRESS: c/o Oxford University Press, 7–8 Hatherley Street, London SW1P 2QT.

HARRHY EIDDWEN   Soprano

PERSONAL DETAILS: b. 14 April 1949, Wiltshire; m. Greg Strange (journalist and broadcaster), one child.

EDUCATION/TRAINING: Royal Manchester College of Music, with Ena Mitchell; further studies with Paul Hamburger in London and André Vessières in Paris.

PROFESSIONAL DEBUT: 1969, Manchester, 'Requiem' (Fauré).

EARLY CAREER INCLUDED: Chorus member: 1970–1971, Welsh National Opera; 1971–1973, Glyndebourne Festival Opera.

MAJOR DEBUTS INCLUDE: 1974, Covent Garden, Wellgunde, *Das Rheingold*; 1975, English National Opera, Adele, *Count Ory*; 1979, Opera North, Octavian, *Der Rosenkavalier*; 1980: Glyndebourne Festival Opera, Diana, *La Fedeltà Premiata*; Welsh National Opera, title role, *The Coronation of Poppea*; 1985, Scottish Opera, Angelica, *Orlando*; 1986, Los Angeles Music Center Opera, Morgana, *Alcina*; 1987, Opéra du Rhin, Strasbourg, Marie, *Wozzeck*; 1989, Nancy Opera, Octavian, *Der Rosenkavalier*.

OPERATIC WORLD PREMIERES INCLUDE: 1980, Welsh National Opera, Oriane, *The Servants* by William Mathias; 1989, English National Opera, Marian Singleton, *The Plumber's Gift* by David Blake.

CAREER IN THE UK INCLUDES: Since 1974: Covent Garden: Echo, *Ariadne auf Naxos*; Sister Mathilde, *The Carmelites*; English Bach Festival, title role, *Dido and Aeneas*; English National Opera: Micaëla, *Carmen*; Countess and Marcellina, *The Marriage of Figaro*; Mimi, *La Bohème*; Pamina, *The Magic Flute*; title role, *Madam Butterfly*; Glyndebourne Touring Opera: Donna Anna, *Don Giovanni*; Fiordiligi, *Così fan tutte*; Handel Opera Society: Armida, *Rinaldo*; Anastasio, *Giustino*; title role, *Alcina*; Kent Opera: Pamina, *The Magic Flute*; title role, *Iphigenia in Tauris*; New Sadler's Wells Opera: Angèle, *The Count of Luxembourg*; title role, *The Merry Widow*; Opera North: Pamina, *The Magic Flute*; Mařenka, *The Bartered Bride*; Donna Elvira, *Don Giovanni*; Fiordiligi, *Così fan tutte*; Jenny, *The Threepenny Opera*; Adalgisa, *Norma*; Hecuba, *King Priam*; title role, *Katya Kabanova*; Scottish Opera, Rosina, *The Barber of Seville*; Welsh National Opera: Gilda, *Rigoletto*;

115

Asteria, *Tamburlaine* (Handel); Marie, *Wozzeck*; title role, *Madam Butterfly*.

RELATED PROFESSIONAL ACTIVITIES: Numerous concerts, recitals, broadcasts and television appearances in the UK and abroad.

RECORDINGS INCLUDE: Donizetti, *Ugo, Conte di Parigi* (OPRA); Handel: *Alcina* (EMI), *Amadigi* (ERAT); Lehár, *Die Lustige Witwe* (TER); Purcell, *The Fairy Queen* (DG); Smyth, *Mass in D* (VIRG); A Hundred Years of Italian Opera (OPRA).

AWARDS INCLUDE: 1972, Miriam Licette Scholarship.

ADDRESS: c/o Ron Gonsalves Personal Artists & Concert Management, 10 Dagnan Road, London SW12 9LQ.

HARRHY PAUL   Tenor

PERSONAL DETAILS: b. 6 September 1957, South Wales.

EDUCATION/TRAINING: 1979–1980, Royal Northern College of Music; 1980–1984, Guildhall School of Music; currently with Rudolf Piernay.

PROFESSIONAL DEBUT: 1985, Opera 80, Alfredo, *La Traviata*.

MAJOR DEBUTS INCLUDE: 1985, Opera North, title role, *The Rake's Progress*; 1987: English National Opera, High Priest, *Akhnaten*; Opera Factory, Pylade, *Iphigenias*; Scottish Opera, Pedrillo, *The Seraglio*; 1989: Batignano Festival, Timante, *Lo Schiavo di sua Moglie*; Wexford Festival: Bracy, *Der Templer und die Jüdin*; Marzio, *Mitridate, Rè di Ponto*; 1990: City of Birmingham Touring Opera, Loge and Mime, *The Ring Saga*; Dublin Grand Opera, Edmondo, *Manon Lescaut*; 1991, Covent Garden at Wembley Arena, Pong, *Turandot*; 1992, New Israeli Opera, Tel Aviv, Truffaldino, *L'Amour des Trois Oranges*.

OPERATIC WORLD PREMIERES INCLUDE: Almeida Festival: 1989, Stump, *Golem* by John Casken; 1990, Henri d'Esparaudieu, *The Intelligence Park* by Gerald Barry; 1991, Batignano Festival, Calandrino,

L'Oca del Cairo by Mozart/Stephen Oliver.

CAREER IN THE UK INCLUDES: Since 1985: Early Opera Project, Shepherd/Spirit, *Orfeo*; English National Opera: Valzacchi, *Der Rosenkavalier*; Janek, *The Makropoulos Case*; Truffaldino, *The Love for Three Oranges*; Mecklenburgh Opera, Pierrot, *The Emperor of Atlantis*; Northern Stage, Stump, *Golem*; Opera 80, title role, *The Rake's Progress*; Opera Factory, Lucano, *The Coronation of Poppea*; Opera North, Truffaldino, *The Love for Three Oranges*; Scottish Opera: Remendado, *Carmen*; Novice, *Billy Budd*; Mime, *Das Rheingold*.

RELATED PROFESSIONAL ACTIVITIES: Concerts, recitals and broadcasts in the UK and abroad.

RECORDINGS INCLUDE: Casken, *Golem* (VIRG); Milhaud, *Les Malheurs d'Orphée*; Stravinsky, *Renard* (both ASV).

AWARDS INCLUDE: BP Peter Pears Award.

ADDRESS: c/o Athole Still International Management Ltd, Greystoke House, 80–86 Westow Street, London SE19 3AF.

HARRIES KATHRYN
Soprano

PERSONAL DETAILS: b. 1951, Surrey.

EDUCATION/TRAINING: 1969–1974, Royal Academy of Music, with Flora Nielsen and Constance Shacklock (Graduate, Royal Schools of Music).

EARLY CAREER INCLUDED: 1974–1983: leading concert performer, repertoire ranging from Monteverdi to the 20th century; Presenter, *Music Time* (BBC Television).

MAJOR DEBUTS INCLUDE: 1983: Welsh National Opera, Flower Maiden, *Parsifal* (operatic debut); English National Opera, Irene, *Rienzi*; 1984, Scottish Opera, Leonore, *Fidelio*; 1986: Opera North, Donna Elvira, *Don Giovanni*; Metropolitan Opera, New York, Kundry, *Parsifal*; 1987, Berlioz Festival, Lyons, Dido, *Les Troyens*; 1988: Metropolitan Opera, New York, Gutrune, *Der Ring des Nibelungen*;

Théâtre des Champs Elysées, Paris, Sieglinde, *Der Ring des Nibelungen*; 1989: Covent Garden, Protagonista, *Un Re in Ascolto* (British première); Netherlands Opera, Ariane, *Ariane et Barbe-bleue*; 1990, St Etienne, title role, *Cléopâtre*; 1991, Théâtre du Châtelet, Paris, Giulietta, *Les Contes d'Hoffmann*; 1992: La Monnaie, Brussels, Dido, *Les Troyens*; Stuttgart State Opera, Donna Elvira, *Don Giovanni*.
OPERATIC WORLD PREMIERES INCLUDE: 1985, Scottish Opera, title role, *Hedda Gabler* by Edward Harper.
CAREER IN THE UK INCLUDES: Since 1983: Buxton Festival, Sylvie, *La Colombe*; Covent Garden, Gutrune, *Götterdämmerung*; English National Opera: Female Chorus, *The Rape of Lucretia*; Eva, *The Mastersingers of Nuremberg*; Donna Anna, *The Stone Guest* (1987, British stage première); Leonore, *Fidelio*; title role, *Katya Kabanova*; Opera North, title role, *The Merry Widow*; Scottish Opera: Senta, *Der Fliegende Holländer*; Judith, *Duke Bluebeard's Castle*; Dido, *The Trojans* (also 1990, at Covent Garden); Emilia Marty, *The Makropoulos Case*; Welsh National Opera: Leonore, *Fidelio*; Adalgisa, *Norma*; Sieglinde and Gutrune, *The Ring of the Nibelung*.
RELATED PROFESSIONAL ACTIVITIES: Regular concerts, recitals and broadcasts in the UK and abroad; 1970–1983, teacher of singing and piano, Kingston Polytechnic; 1976–1983, Professor of Singing, Royal Academy of Music.
RECORDINGS INCLUDE: Janáček, *Osud* (EMI); Massenet, *Cléopâtre* (French label); Wagner, *Parsifal* (EMI).
VIDEOS INCLUDE: Britten, *The Rape of Lucretia* (English National Opera).
HONOURS INCLUDE: 1990, Fellow, Royal Academy of Music.
ADDRESS: c/o Ingpen & Williams Ltd, 14 Kensington Court, London W8 5DN.

HARRIS JOHN   Tenor

PERSONAL DETAILS: b. 5 December 1944; m. 1984, Patricia Batho-Davies (actress, dancer and choreographer); two children from previous marriage.
PREVIOUS OCCUPATION: 1964–1970, industrial scientist.
EDUCATION/TRAINING: 1970–1973, Birmingham School of Music, with Linda Vaughan; since 1973, privately with John Mitchinson and Patrick McGuigan.
PROFESSIONAL DEBUT: 1973, Phoenix Opera, Goro, *Madam Butterfly*.
EARLY CAREER INCLUDED: 1974–1984, Principal Tenor, Welsh National Opera: Mr Upfold, *Albert Herring*; Incredibile, *Andrea Chénier*; Simpleton, *Boris Godunov*; Lensky, *Eugene Onegin*; Monostatos, *The Magic Flute*; Snout, *A Midsummer Night's Dream*; Esquire, *Parsifal*; Spoletta, *Tosca*; Young Sailor, *Tristan und Isolde*.
MAJOR DEBUTS INCLUDE: 1987, English National Opera, Don José, *Carmen*; Bardolph, *Falstaff*. 1989–1990, Welsh National Opera in Milan, New York and Tokyo; 1991, Théâtre des Champs Elysées, Paris.
OPERATIC WORLD PREMIERES INCLUDE: 1985, Arundel Festival, title role, *Lancelot* by Iain Hamilton; 1990, Welsh National Opera, Billy/Molecatcher, *Tornrak* by John Metcalf; 1992, Channel Four Television, Forecast, *Camera* by Anthony Moore.
CAREER IN THE UK INCLUDES: Since 1985: English National Opera, Goro, *Madam Butterfly*; Opera North, Tichon, *Katya Kabanova*; Welsh National Opera: Mime, *Siegfried* (also at Covent Garden); Normanno, *Lucia di Lammermoor*; Bardolph, *Falstaff*; Skuratov, *From the House of the Dead*; Goro, *Madam Butterfly*.
RELATED PROFESSIONAL ACTIVITIES: Regular concerts and recitals in the UK and abroad.

RECORDINGS INCLUDE: Martinů, *The Greek Passion* (SUPR); Verdi, *I Masnadieri* (DECC); Wagner: *Parsifal* (EMI), *Tristan und Isolde* (DECC).
ADDRESS: c/o M & M Lyric Artists, 6 Princess Road, London NW1 7JJ.

HARVEY JONATHAN
Composer

POSITION: Professor of Music, University of Sussex.
PERSONAL DETAILS: b. 3 May 1939, Sutton Coldfield; m. 1960, Rosaleen Barry, two children.
EDUCATION/TRAINING: 1957–1961, St John's College, Cambridge, with Erwin Stein and Hans Keller; 1961–1963, University of Glasgow.
FIRST PROFESSIONAL PERFORMANCE OF A COMPOSITION: 1962, *Triptych* for wind quintet and piano.
CAREER: Since 1964, compositions include orchestral, chamber, instrumental, vocal and choral works; 1964–1977, Lecturer in Music, University of Southampton; 1969–1970, Harkness Fellow, Princeton University; University of Sussex: 1977–1980, Reader; since 1980, Professor of Music.
OPERATIC WORLD PREMIERES: 1981, Winchester Cathedral, *Passion and Resurrection*, church opera, libretto from Bendictine Latin liturgical dramas translated by Michael Wadsworth, conductor Martin Neary, director Bishop John Taylor; 1993, English National Opera (co-production with La Monnaie, Brussels), *Inquest of Love*, opera in two acts, libretto by the composer with David Rudkin, conductor Mark Elder, director David Pountney, designer Nigel Lowery.
RECORDINGS INCLUDE: *Correspondences* – song cycle (UNIC), *I Love the Lord* – anthem (ASV), *Come Holy Ghost* – anthem (HYPE), *From Silence* for soprano and electronic ensemble (BRID), *Song Offerings* for soprano and ensemble (NIMB), *Serenade in Homage to Mozart* for wind ensemble,

based on *The Magic Flute* (EMI), Cello Concerto (Italian label).
PUBLICATIONS INCLUDE: 1975, *The Music of Stockhausen* (Faber).
HONOURS INCLUDE: Doctorate of Music, University of Cambridge; Honorary Doctorate of Music, University of Southampton.
ADDRESS: c/o Faber Music Ltd, 3 Queen Street, London WC1N 3AU.

HAWKES TOM
Director and Teacher

POSITIONS: Director of Productions: English Bach Festival, Lyric Theatre of Singapore.
PERSONAL DETAILS: b. 21 June 1938, London.
EDUCATION/TRAINING: 1959–1962, Royal Academy of Music, studied speech and drama.
PROFESSIONAL DEBUT: As actor: 1964, Derby Playhouse.
OPERATIC DEBUT: As director: 1965, Sadler's Wells Opera, *A Masked Ball*.
CAREER: Opera and theatre director in the UK and abroad; 1962–1964, Lecturer in Drama, Royal Manchester College of Music; 1964–1965, actor and stage director, Derby Playhouse; 1965–1968, staff director, Sadler's Wells Opera; 1974–1983, Artistic Director, Phoenix Opera; Director of Productions: 1979–1985, Handel Opera Society; 1986–1988, Morley Opera; since 1984, English Bach Festival.
MAJOR OPERATIC DEBUTS INCLUDE: 1968: Welsh National Opera, *Rigoletto*; La Monnaie, Brussels, *Dido and Aeneas*; 1969, Sadler's Wells Opera, *Madam Butterfly*; 1971, Opera Northern Ireland, *Tosca*; 1975, Dublin Grand Opera, *I Puritani*; 1977, English National Opera, *La Vie Parisienne*; 1981: English Bach Festival at Covent Garden, *Castor et Pollux*; New Sadler's Wells Opera, *Hansel and Gretel*; 1982, Guelph Spring Festival, Ontario, *The Two Widows*; 1983, Opera Theatre of St Louis, *Die Fledermaus*; 1990, Lyric Theatre of Singapore, *Carmen*.

OPERA PRODUCTIONS IN THE UK
INCLUDE: Since 1970: English Bach Festival: *Teseo, Orfeo ed Euridice, Alceste, Dido and Aeneas, Idomeneo, Riccardo Primo, Platée*; Handel Opera Society: *Ezio, Hercules, Partenope, Serse, Radamisto, Rodrigo*; Keynote Opera, *Wat Tyler* (1974, British stage première); Phoenix Opera: *Madam Butterfly, La Vie Parisienne, Dido and Aeneas, Pyramus and Thisbe, Don Quixote* (1979, British première), *Eritrea* (1982, British première), *The School for Fathers*; Royal Academy of Music, *Il Matrimonio Segreto*.
RELATED PROFESSIONAL ACTIVITIES: Lecturer in music theatre and theatre design: Birmingham School of Music, Guildhall School of Music and Drama, Royal Academy of Music, Royal College of Music, Central School of Art, Wimbledon School of Art, Hong Kong Academy for Performing Arts.
HONOURS INCLUDE: 1982, Honorary Member, Guildhall School of Music and Drama; 1990, Associate, Royal Academy of Music.
ADDRESS: c/o Music International, 13 Ardilaun Road, London N5 2QR.

HAYES QUENTIN   Baritone

PERSONAL DETAILS: b. 27 November 1958, Southend.
EDUCATION/TRAINING: 1977–1978, Dartington Arts College; 1979–1984, Guildhall School of Music and Drama, with Arthur Reckless and Rudolf Piernay; 1987–1988, National Opera Studio.
PROFESSIONAL DEBUT: 1985, Welsh National Opera, Morales, *Carmen*.
EARLY CAREER INCLUDED: 1985–1987, Welsh National Opera: Yamadori, *Madam Butterfly*; Herald, *Otello*; Fiorello, *The Barber of Seville*; Second Apprentice, *Wozzeck*.
MAJOR DEBUTS INCLUDE: 1987, City of Birmingham Touring Opera, Ford, *Falstaff*; 1989: English National Opera, Ford, *Falstaff*; Glyndebourne Touring Opera, title role, *Il Barbiere di Siviglia*.

OPERATIC WORLD PREMIERES INCLUDE:
1988, Munich Biennale, Eddy, *Greek* by Mark-Anthony Turnage; 1990, Welsh National Opera, Helmsman/Collinson/Sailor/Bearkeeper, *Tornrak* by John Metcalf; 1991: English National Opera, Flaminius, *Timon of Athens* by Stephen Oliver; Opera North, Pantalone, *The Jewel Box* by Mozart/Paul Griffiths; 1992, Womens Playhouse Trust, Leonardo, *Blood Wedding* by Nicola LeFanu.
CAREER IN THE UK INCLUDES: Since 1988: Edinburgh International Festival, Eddy, *Greek* (1988, British première); English National Opera: Kuligin, *Katya Kabanova*; Eddy, *Greek*.
RELATED PROFESSIONAL ACTIVITIES: Concerts, recitals (including performances at the Almeida Festival) and television appearances.
RECORDINGS INCLUDE: Britten, *Rejoice in the Lamb* (HYPE).
AWARDS INCLUDE: 1987, Countess of Munster Award.
ADDRESS: Not available.

HAYWARD ROBERT
Bass-baritone

PERSONAL DETAILS: b. November 1956, Surrey; m. Tamsin Dives (mezzo-soprano), two children.
EDUCATION/TRAINING: 1983–1985, Guildhall School of Music and Drama, with Rudolf Piernay; 1985–1986, National Opera Studio; currently with Audrey Langford.
PROFESSIONAL DEBUT: 1986, Glyndebourne Touring Opera, title role, *Don Giovanni*.
MAJOR DEBUTS INCLUDE: 1987, English National Opera, Tomsky/Plutus, *The Queen of Spades*; title role, *Le Nozze di Figaro*: 1987: Opera North, Welsh National Opera; 1988, Houston Grand Opera; 1989, Glyndebourne Festival Opera, Theseus, *A Midsummer Night's Dream*; 1990, Bavarian State Opera at Gran Teatre del Liceu, Barcelona, title role, *Don Giovanni*; 1992, Covent Garden, Spirit Messenger, *Die Frau ohne Schatten*.

CAREER IN THE UK INCLUDES: Since 1987: Glyndebourne Festival and Touring Opera: Major-Domo, *Capriccio*; Count, *Le Nozze di Figaro*; Opera North: Malatesta, *Don Pasquale*; Escamillo, *Carmen*; Guglielmo, *Così fan tutte*; Count, *The Marriage of Figaro*; Robert, *Yolande*; Marcello, *La Bohème*; title role, *Don Giovanni*; Welsh National Opera: Marcello, *La Bohème*; Sharpless, *Madam Butterfly*; title role, *Don Giovanni*.
RELATED PROFESSIONAL ACTIVITIES: Regular concerts and recitals with leading conductors and orchestras in the UK.
ADDRESS: c/o Ingpen & Williams Ltd, 14 Kensington Court, London W8 5DN.

HEGARTY MARY   Soprano

PERSONAL DETAILS: b. Cork.
EDUCATION/TRAINING: 1979–1985, Cork School of Music, with Maeve Coughlan; 1985, masterclasses with Elisabeth Schwarzkopf; 1986–1987, National Opera Studio; since 1986, privately with Josephine Veasey.
PROFESSIONAL DEBUT: 1984, Cork City Opera, Micaëla, *Carmen*.
EARLY CAREER INCLUDED: 1985–1986, appearances with Cork City Opera, Opera Northern Ireland; roles included: Nedda, *Pagliacci*; Nannetta, *Falstaff*.
MAJOR DEBUTS INCLUDE: 1987: City of Birmingham Touring Opera, Nannetta, *Falstaff*; Batignano Festival, Marzelline, *Leonore*; 1988, Covent Garden, Flower Maiden, *Parsifal*; 1989: English National Opera, Nannetta, *Falstaff*; Opera Factory, Eternity, *La Calisto*; 1990, Opera North, Leonora, *Masquerade* (British première); 1992, Dublin Grand Opera: Elvira, *L'Italiana in Algeri*; Adele, *Die Fledermaus*.
OPERATIC WORLD PREMIERES INCLUDE: 1991, Opera North, Colombina, *The Jewel Box* by Mozart/Paul Griffiths.
CAREER IN THE UK INCLUDES: Since 1987: Buxton Festival, Costanza, *Il Sogno di Scipione*; Covent Garden, Pousette,

Manon; English National Opera: Naiad, *Ariadne auf Naxos*; Papagena, *The Magic Flute*; New Sussex Opera, Anne Trulove, *The Rake's Progress*; Opera Factory, Cherubino, *The Marriage of Figaro*; Opera North: Ygraine, *Ariane and Bluebeard*; Frasquita, *Carmen*; Princess Laoula, *L'Etoile*.
RELATED PROFESSIONAL ACTIVITIES: Numerous concerts, recitals and broadcasts in the UK, Ireland and USA.
AWARDS INCLUDE: 1984, Golden Voice of Ireland Competition.
ADDRESS: c/o Magenta Music International Ltd, 64 Highgate High Street, London N6 5HX.

HELLINGS JANE
Administrator

POSITION: Administrator, Opera Factory.
PERSONAL DETAILS: b. 4 May 1962, London; m. 1985, Jonathan Holloway (theatre director), three children.
EDUCATION/TRAINING: 1981–1984, University of York, studied English and related literature.
CAREER: Administrator: 1984–1987, Red Shift Theatre Company; 1987–1988, Royal Court Young People's Theatre; since 1989, Opera Factory.
ADDRESS: c/o Opera Factory, 8A The Leathermarket, Weston Street, London SE1 3ER.

HERBERT KATHARINE
Administrator

POSITION: Administrator, English Touring Opera.
PERSONAL DETAILS: b. 11 June 1956, Hertford.
EDUCATION/TRAINING: 1974–1977, Ealing College, London, studied music and history of art.
CAREER: 1978–1980, secretary to the music director, English National Opera; English National Ballet: 1982–1985, Ballet and Music Co-ordinator; 1985–1988, Company

Manager; 1989–1991, Assistant General Administrator; since 1991, Administrator, Opera 80/English Touring Opera.

OTHER PROFESSIONAL ACTIVITIES INCLUDE: Since 1991, member, Board of Directors, Siobhan Davies Dance Company.

ADDRESS: c/o English Touring Opera, 121 West Block, Westminster Business Square, Durham Street, London SE11 5JH.

HERBERT PAUL   Conductor

POSITION: Co-Music Director, City of Birmingham Touring Opera.

PERSONAL DETAILS: b. 30 January 1946, Rugby; m. Jennifer Mock (actress).

PREVIOUS OCCUPATION: 1968–1973, school teacher.

EDUCATION/TRAINING: 1963–1967, Birmingham School of Music; 1967–1968, University of York; 1978, Accademia Chigiana, Siena.

CAREER: Music Director and Conductor: 1973–1989, Cannon Hill Children's Opera; 1981–1987, Birmingham Music Theatre; 1985–1990, Buxton and Cheltenham Festivals; since 1987, Co-Music Director, City of Birmingham Touring Opera.

OPERATIC WORLD PREMIERES INCLUDE: Cannon Hill Children's Opera: 1982, *The Ram King* by Christopher Brown; 1984, *Gawain and Ragnall* by Richard Blackford.

OPERA PERFORMANCES IN THE UK INCLUDE: Since 1980: Buxton Festival: *Robin Hood, David and Goliath, Sir Gawain and the Green Knight, Master Peter's Puppet Show, Help! Help! The Globolinks!*; Birmingham Music Theatre/ City of Birmingham Touring Opera: *The Seraglio, Don Pasquale, Trouble in Tahiti, La Bohème, The Magic Flute*; Cannon Hill Children's Opera: *Orlando Paladino, The Turn of the Screw*; Cheltenham Festival: *The Soldier's Tale, What the Old Man Does is Always Right.*

RELATED PROFESSIONAL ACTIVITIES: Since 1976, Director of Music, Midland Arts Centre.

ADDRESS: 11 Clarence Road, Moseley, Birmingham B13 9SX.

HERFORD HENRY
Baritone and Teacher

PERSONAL DETAILS: b. 24 February 1947, Edinburgh; m. 1982, Lindsay John (mezzo-soprano), three children.

EDUCATION/TRAINING: King's College, Cambridge, studied classics and English; Royal Northern College of Music, with Patrick McGuigan and Frederic Cox.

PROFESSIONAL DEBUT: 1977, Glyndebourne Touring Opera, Forester, *The Cunning Little Vixen.*

MAJOR DEBUTS INCLUDE: 1979, Batignano Festival: Creonte, *Orontea*; Narrator, *Il Combattimento di Tancredi e Clorinda*; 1980, Nancy Opera, Speaker, *Die Zauberflöte*; 1983: Covent Garden, Flemish Deputy, *Don Carlos*; Carnegie Hall, New York, Panatellas, *La Périchole*; 1989, Teatro São Luiz, Lisbon, Roderick, *La Chute de la Maison Usher.*

OPERATIC WORLD PREMIERES INCLUDE: 1987, Glyndebourne Touring Opera, Pasternak, *The Electrification of the Soviet Union* by Nigel Osborne; 1988, Queen Elizabeth Hall, Cenci, *Beatrice Cenci* by Berthold Goldschmidt.

CAREER IN THE UK INCLUDES: Since 1978: English Bach Festival, Satyr/Jupiter, *Platée*; Glyndebourne Festival and Touring Opera: Pasternak, *The Electrification of the Soviet Union*; Speaker, *Die Zauberflöte*; Demetrius, *A Midsummer Night's Dream*; Handel Opera Society, Priest of Jupiter, *Hercules*; Musica nel Chiostro, Merchant, *Beauty and the Beast* (1985, British première); Opera 80, Count, *The Marriage of Figaro*; Northern Stage, Smirnov, *The Bear*; Opera London, Demetrius, *A Midsummer Night's Dream*; Scottish Opera, Falke, *Die Fledermaus*; Spitalfields Festival, Roderick, *La Chute*

121

de la Maison Usher (1986, British première).

RELATED PROFESSIONAL ACTIVITIES: Regular concerts, recitals, broadcasts and television appearances in the UK and abroad; private teacher.

RECORDINGS INCLUDE: Bridge, *The Christmas Rose* (PEAR); Britten, *A Midsummer Night's Dream* (VIRG); Rameau, *Castor et Pollux* (ERAT).

AWARDS INCLUDE: 1980, Benson and Hedges Gold Award; 1982, International American Music Competition.

ADDRESS: c/o Ron Gonsalves Personal Artists & Concert Management, 10 Dagnan Road, London SW12 9LQ.

HERNON PAUL
Designer, Director and Translator

PERSONAL DETAILS: 17 May 1947, Northumberland.

PROFESSIONAL AND OPERATIC DEBUT: 1977, Opera Viva, *Zampa*.

CAREER: Since 1977, freelance opera and theatre designer and director in the UK and abroad; 1982–1984, co-founder, director and designer, London Music Theatre Group,

MAJOR OPERATIC DEBUTS INCLUDE: 1986, *Jenůfa*: Covent Garden, Zurich Opera; 1987, Bonn Opera, *Eugene Onegin*; 1988, Stuttgart State Opera, *Tannhäuser*.

OPERA PRODUCTIONS IN THE UK

INCLUDE: Since 1978: as designer: Covent Garden, *Das Rheingold*; Opera Northern Ireland: *Hansel and Gretel*, *La Belle Hélène*, *Il Tabarro*, *Gianni Schicchi*; as director or as director and designer: Abbey Opera: *A Midsummer Night's Dream*, *The Crucible* (1984, British première); Castleward Festival: *Così fan tutte*, *Don Giovanni*, *Die Zauberflöte*; English Bach Festival, *Acis and Galatea*; London Music Theatre Group: *Le Vin Herbé* (1982, British première), *Juditha Triumphans* (1984, British première); Opera Northern Ireland, *Le Nozze di Figaro*; Opera Viva, *Prima la Musica e*

poi le Parole (1979, British première; also 1981, Perth Festival, Western Australia).

RELATED PROFESSIONAL ACTIVITIES: Translations: *Prima la Musica e poi le Parole*, *Juditha Triumphans*, *Hansel and Gretel*; since 1990, Lecturer in Performance Technology, North East Wales Institute.

ADDRESS: c/o Music International, 13 Ardilaun Road, London N5 2QR.

HETHERINGTON HUGH
Tenor

EDUCATION/TRAINING: Royal Northern College of Music; currently with Audrey Langford.

PROFESSIONAL DEBUT: 1978, chorus member, Glyndebourne Festival Opera.

EARLY CAREER INCLUDED: 1979–1984, appearances with Chelsea Opera Group, Glyndebourne Festival and Touring Opera, New Sadler's Wells Opera, New Sussex Opera, University College Opera; roles included: Major-Domo, *Der Rosenkavalier*; Officer, *Ariadne auf Naxos*; Dr Caius, *Falstaff*; Master of Ceremonies and Truffaldino, *L'Amour des Trois Oranges*; Ralph Rackstraw, *HMS Pinafore*; Bob Boles, *Peter Grimes*; Armel, *Gwendoline*; Franz, *Faust* (Spohr).

MAJOR DEBUTS INCLUDE: 1984: Opera North, Luiz, *The Gondoliers*; Scottish Opera, Pang, *Turandot*; 1985, Covent Garden, Young Guard, *King Priam*; 1991: English National Opera, Prince, *The Love for Three Oranges*; Opera Factory, Don Basilio, *The Marriage of Figaro*.

OPERATIC WORLD PREMIERES INCLUDE: 1984, Glyndebourne Touring Opera, Moishe/Goat, *Where the Wild Things Are* by Oliver Knussen; 1987, Endymion Music Theatre, Tenor, *Vital Statistics* by Michael Nyman.

CAREER IN THE UK INCLUDES: Since 1984: D'Oyly Carte Opera, Tolloller, *Iolanthe*; Endymion Music Theatre, Narrator, *Il Combattimento di Tancredi e Clorinda*; English National Opera: Villager, *Orfeo*; Pisandro, *The Return of Ulysses*; Scottish

Opera: Dema, *L'Egisto*; Don Basilio, *Le Nozze di Figaro*; Tolloller, *Iolanthe*; Marquis/Prince/Manservant, *Lulu*; Raoul, *La Vie Parisienne*; Monsieur Triquet, *Eugene Onegin.*

RECORDINGS INCLUDE: Knussen, *Where the Wild Things Are* (UNIC); Stravinsky, *Renard* (ASV).

VIDEOS INCLUDE: Prokofiev, *L'Amour des Trois Oranges* (Glyndebourne Festival Opera).

AWARDS INCLUDE: 1980, Glyndebourne Touring Opera Singers' Award.

ADDRESS: c/o Korman International Management, Crunnells Green Cottage, Preston, Hertfordshire SG4 7UQ.

HICKOX RICHARD
Conductor

POSITIONS: Music Director: City of London Sinfonia, Bradford Festival Choral Society, London Symphony Chorus; Associate Conductor, London Symphony Orchestra; Principal Guest Conductor: Bournemouth Symphony Orchestra, Northern Sinfonia.

PERSONAL DETAILS: b. 5 March 1948, Buckinghamshire; m. 1976, Frances Sheldon-Williams, one child.

EDUCATION/TRAINING: Royal Academy of Music (Licentiate), studied organ, piano and composition; Organ Scholar, Queen's College, Cambridge.

PROFESSIONAL DEBUT: 1971, St John's Smith Square.

OPERATIC DEBUT: 1979, English National Opera, *Dido and Aeneas.*

CAREER: Since 1971, founder and Music Director, City of London Sinfonia; Music Director: 1972–1982, St Margaret's Church, Westminster; since 1976, London Symphony Chorus; since 1978, Bradford Festival Choral Society; 1980–1985, Principal Guest Conductor, Dutch Radio Orchestra; Associate Conductor: 1983–1984, San Diego Orchestra; since 1985, London Symphony Orchestra; Northern Sinfonia: 1982–1990, Artistic Director; since 1990, Principal Guest Conductor; since 1992, Principal Guest Conductor, Bournemouth Symphony Orchestra.

MAJOR OPERATIC DEBUTS INCLUDE: 1982, Opera North, *The Marriage of Figaro*; 1985: Covent Garden, *Die Zauberflöte*; Scottish Opera, *Orlando*; 1986, Los Angeles Music Center Opera, *Alcina*; 1991, Australian Opera, Sydney, *Julius Caesar.*

OPERA PERFORMANCES IN THE UK INCLUDE: Since 1985: Opera North, *Troilus and Cressida*; Royal Festival Hall, *Mozart and Salieri*; Scottish Opera, *The Barber of Seville*; Spitalfields Festival: *Alcina*, *Iphigénie en Aulide*, *L'Incoronazione di Poppea.*

RELATED PROFESSIONAL ACTIVITIES: Regular concerts, broadcasts and recordings with leading orchestras in the UK and abroad; artistic director of numerous music festivals including Spitalfields Festival; co-founder, Collegium Musicum 90, specializing in baroque choral repertory.

RECORDINGS INCLUDE: Britten: *A Midsummer Night's Dream*, *Noye's Fludde* (both VIRG), *War Requiem* (CHAN); Gluck, *Armide*; Handel, *Alcina* (both EMI); Monteverdi, *L'Incoronazione di Poppea* (VIRG); Walton, *Troilus and Cressida* (CHAN).

AWARDS AND HONOURS INCLUDE: First recipient, Sir Charles Groves Prize for services to British Music; Fellow, Royal College of Organists.

ADDRESS: c/o Intermusica Artists' Management, 16 Duncan Terrace, London N1 8BZ.

HILL MARTYN
Tenor

PERSONAL DETAILS: b. 14 September 1944, Kent; m. 1984, Marleen Marie de Maesschalck; four children.

EDUCATION/TRAINING: King's College, Cambridge; Royal College of Music; privately with Audrey Langford.

PROFESSIONAL DEBUT: 1972, Barber Institute, Birmingham, Grimoaldo, *Rodelinda*.

CAREER INCLUDES: Since 1972, numerous appearances with leading opera companies including: City of London Sinfonia at the Royal Festival Hall, Mozart, *Mozart and Salieri*; Glyndebourne Touring Opera: Belmonte, *Die Entführung aus dem Serail*; title role, *Idomeneo*; Kent Opera, Alessandro, *Il Rè Pastore*; Scottish Opera, Prologue/Peter Quint, *The Turn of the Screw*; roles in France and USA include: Flamand, *Capriccio*; Ferrando, *Così fan tutte*; title role, *The Rake's Progress*.

RELATED PROFESSIONAL ACTIVITIES: Regular concerts, recitals and broadcasts in the UK and abroad.

RECORDINGS INCLUDE: Britten, Vocal Works (VIRG); Delius, *Hassan* (EMI); Finzi, Song Cycles to words by Thomas Hardy (HYPE); Hahn, songs (HYPE); Handel: *Acis and Galatea* (ARCH), *Partenope* (DHM); Purcell: *The Fairy Queen* (ARCH), *The Indian Queen* (ERAT); Shostakovich, *Lady Macbeth of Mtsensk* (EMI); Stravinsky, *Pulcinella* (VIRG).

ADDRESS: c/o Ron Gonsalves Personal Artists & Concert Management, 10 Dagnan Road, London SW12 9LQ.

HILL SMITH MARILYN
Soprano

PERSONAL DETAILS: b. 9 February 1952, Surrey; m. 1974, Peter Kemp (music researcher and broadcaster).

EDUCATION/TRAINING: 1970–1974, Guildhall School of Music and Drama, with Arthur Reckless.

PROFESSIONAL DEBUT: 1978, English National Opera, Adele, *Die Fledermaus*.

MAJOR DEBUTS INCLUDE: 1981, Covent Garden, First Niece, *Peter Grimes*; 1984, Canadian Opera Company, Toronto, Cunegonde, *Candide*; 1987, Welsh National Opera, Musetta, *La Bohème*; 1988, Scottish Opera, Cunnegonde,

Candide; 1990, D'Oyly Carte Opera, Mabel, *The Pirates of Penzance*.

CAREER IN THE UK INCLUDES: Since 1978: English Bach Festival: Aricie, *Hippolyte et Aricie*; Almirena, *Rinaldo*; Télaire, *Castor et Pollux*; Belinda, *Dido and Aeneas*; Eurydice, *Orphée et Eurydice*; Costanza, *Riccardo Primo*; English National Opera: Papagena, *The Magic Flute*; Woodbird and Woglinde, *The Ring of the Nibelung*; Susanna, *The Marriage of Figaro*; Despina, *Così fan tutte*; Fiakermilli, *Arabella*; Blonde, *The Seraglio*; Venus/ Chief of Police, *Le Grand Macabre* (1982, British première); Olympia, *The Tales of Hoffmann*; Zerbinetta, *Ariadne auf Naxos*; Handel Opera Society, Rosmene, *Imeneo*; New Sadler's Wells Opera: Angèle, *The Count of Luxembourg*; Lady Harriet, *Martha*; Rose, *Ruddigore*; title roles: *The Gipsy Princess*, *Countess Maritza*; Opera Rara at the Camden Festival, Clotilde Talbot, *Maria Tudor*; Welsh National Opera, Constanze, *The Seraglio*.

RELATED PROFESSIONAL ACTIVITIES: Regular broadcasts and television appearances including *Top Cs and Tiaras* (Channel Four).

RECORDINGS INCLUDE: Bernstein, *Candide* (TER); Meyerbeer, *Dinorah* (OPRA); Rameau, *La Princesse de Navarre* (ERAT); Treasures of Operetta, Vols 1–3 (CHAN); Is It Really Me? (TER).

VIDEOS INCLUDE: Britten, *Peter Grimes* (Covent Garden).

ADDRESS: c/o Music International, 13 Ardilaun Road, London N5 2QR.

HILLMAN DAVID   Tenor

PERSONAL DETAILS: b. London; m. Jennifer Caron (soprano and teacher).

PREVIOUS OCCUPATION: 1957–1962, quantity surveyor.

EDUCATION/TRAINING: 1960–1963, National Opera School, with Joan Cross; privately with Antony Benskin and Otakar Kraus.

PROFESSIONAL DEBUT: 1962, Welsh National Opera, Arvino, *I Lombardi*.

EARLY CAREER INCLUDED: 1962–1969, appearances with Sadler's Wells Opera and Welsh National Opera; roles included: Nanki-Poo, *The Mikado*; Belmonte, *The Seraglio*; Paris, *La Belle Hélène*; Don Basilio, *The Marriage of Figaro*; Essex, *Gloriana*; Herman, *The Queen of Spades*; Rodolfo, *La Bohème*; Alfredo, *La Traviata*; Tamino, *The Magic Flute*.

MAJOR DEBUTS INCLUDE: Tamino, *Die Zauberflöte*: 1969, Bonn Opera; 1970, Scottish Opera; 1972, Netherlands Opera, title role, *The Rake's Progress*; 1974, Santa Fe Opera, Fritz, *The Grand Duchess of Gérolstein*; 1976, Covent Garden, Malcolm, *Macbeth*; 1979, Opera Theatre of St Louis, Tenor/Bacchus, *Ariadne auf Naxos*; 1985, Glyndebourne Festival Opera, Elemer, *Arabella*.

OPERATIC WORLD PREMIERES INCLUDE: Sadler's Wells Opera: 1965, Fenney, *The Mines of Sulphur* by Richard Rodney Bennett; 1966, Sosthène, *The Violins of St Jacques* by Malcolm Williamson; Scottish Opera: 1974, Quintus, *The Catiline Conspiracy* by Iain Hamilton; 1977, Darnley, *Mary, Queen of Scots* by Thea Musgrave; 1979, Opera Theatre of St Louis, Wilson Ford, *The Village Singer* by Stephen Paulus.

CAREER IN THE UK INCLUDES: Since 1970: Glyndebourne Festival Opera, Gaston, *La Traviata*; Kent Opera, Duke, *Rigoletto*; New Opera Company, Shepherd, *King Roger* (1975, British stage première); New Sadler's Wells Opera, Richard, *Ruddigore*; Opera North: Sinon, *The Capture of Troy*; title role, *The Tales of Hoffmann*; Regency Opera: Cavaradossi, *Tosca*; Calaf, *Turandot*; Sadler's Wells Opera/English National Opera: Janek, *The Makropoulos Case*; Eisenstein, *Die Fledermaus*; Vronsky, *Anna Karenina*; title role, *The Tales of Hoffmann*; Scottish Opera: Count, *The Barber of Seville*; Nero, *The Coronation of Poppea*; Edgardo, *Lucia di Lammermoor*; Eisenstein, *Die Fledermaus*; Cassio, *Otello*; Macduff, *Macbeth*; Demetrius, *A Midsummer Night's Dream*; Daniel Buchanan, *Street Scene*; University College Opera, David, *Saul and David* (1977, British stage première).

RELATED PROFESSIONAL ACTIVITIES: Film and television appearances as singer and actor.

VIDEOS INCLUDE: Sullivan: *Iolanthe*, *The Yeomen of the Guard* (both Walker).

ADDRESS: c/o Music International, 13 Ardilaun Road, London N5 2QR.

HODDINOTT ALUN
Composer

PERSONAL DETAILS: b. 11 August 1929, Glamorgan; m. 1953, Rhiannon Huws (music teacher), one child.

EDUCATION/TRAINING: 1946–1951, University College, Cardiff, studied viola, then composition with Arthur Benjamin.

FIRST PROFESSIONAL PERFORMANCE OF A COMPOSITION: 1949, BBC Welsh Orchestra, Nocturne for orchestra.

CAREER: Numerous compositions in all genres including seven symphonies; lecturer: 1951–1959, Welsh College of Music and Drama; 1959–1966, University College, Cardiff; 1966–1967, Reader, University of Wales; 1967–1987, Professor of Music and Head of Department, University College, Cardiff.

OPERATIC WORLD PREMIERES: 1974, Welsh National Opera, *The Beach of Falesá*, libretto by Glyn Jones after Robert Louis Stevenson, conductor Richard Armstrong, director Michael Geliot, designer Alexander McPherson; 1976, HTV, *The Magician*, opera for television, libretto by John Morgan (1976, world stage première, Sherman Theatre, Cardiff); 1977, Fishguard Festival, *What the Old Man Does is Always Right*, opera for children; 1979, BBC, *The Rajah's Diamond*, opera for television; 1981, Royal Northern College of Music, *The Trumpet Major* (all librettos by Myfanwy Piper).

125

RELATED PROFESSIONAL ACTIVITIES:
1967–1990, founder and Artistic Director,
Cardiff Festival of Music; often conducts
performances of own compositions.

RECORDINGS INCLUDE: *Laterne des Morts*
for orchestra, *A Contemplation upon
Flowers* for soprano and orchestra, *Scena*
for string orchestra, Symphony No. 6 (all
CHAN), *Lady and Unicorn* for chorus and
piano (LIBR).

PUBLICATIONS INCLUDE: Vocal scores:
1974, *The Beach of Falesá*; 1978, *The
Magician*; 1980, *What the Old Man Does
is Always Right*; 1981, *The Trumpet Major*
(all Oxford University Press).

AWARDS AND HONOURS INCLUDE: John
Edwards Memorial Award, Arnold Bax
Prize, Walford Davies Prize; 1983,
Commander, Order of the British Empire
(CBE); Hopkins Medal (St David's Society
of New York); Honorary Member, Royal
Academy of Music; Fellow: Royal
Northern College of Music, Welsh College
of Music and Drama, University College,
Cardiff.

ADDRESS: c/o Lengnick & Co. Ltd, 7–8
Greenland Place, London NW1 OAP.

HOLDEN AMANDA
Translator, Editor, Pianist and Accompanist, Teacher and Writer

PERSONAL DETAILS: b. 19 January 1948,
London.

EDUCATION/TRAINING: 1966–1969, Lady
Margaret Hall, Oxford; 1969–1971,
Guildhall School of Music and Drama;
1979–1981, American University,
Washington D.C.

CAREER: 1973–1986, pianist, accompanist
and teacher, Guildhall School of Music
and Drama; currently General Editor, *The
Penguin Opera Guide* and freelance
translator; translations include: *Armida*,
L'Italiana in Londra (both Buxton
Festival), *Les Boréades* (City of
Birmingham Touring Opera), *Falstaff* (City
of Birmingham Touring Opera, English
National Opera, English Touring Opera),
Ariodante, *Beatrice and Benedict*,

Lohengrin (all English National Opera),
La Finta Giardiniera, *The Marriage of
Figaro* (both Opera North), *Idomeneo*
(Oxford University Opera), *La Clemenza
di Tito* (Scottish Opera); translations with
Anthony Holden include: *The Barber of
Seville* (English National Opera, Scottish
Opera), *Don Giovanni* (English National
Opera), *La Bohème* (Opera North).

PUBLICATIONS INCLUDE: Children's book,
The Magic Flute (Faber); translation: *Don
Giovanni* (André Deutsch); contributor,
Mozart's operas and journeys in *The
Mozart Compendium* (Thames & Hudson);
surtitles and subtitles for several opera
productions at Covent Garden and on
BBC Television.

ADDRESS: 107 Sotheby Road, London N5
2UT.

HOLLAND MARK   Baritone

PERSONAL DETAILS: b. 19 September 1960,
Salford; m. Jennifer Rutland
(percussionist, m. diss.), two children.

EDUCATION/TRAINING: 1979–1983, Royal
Northern College of Music, with John
Cameron; 1984 and 1985, with Roberto
Benaglio in Italy.

PROFESSIONAL DEBUT: 1984, Welsh
National Opera, Duphol, *La Traviata*.

CAREER IN THE UK INCLUDES: Since 1984:
Buxton Festival, Mengotto, *La Buona
Figliuola*; City of Birmingham Touring
Opera: Marcello, *La Bohème*; Allazim,
Zaide; Opera Northern Ireland, Falke, *Die
Fledermaus*; Welsh National Opera
(1984–1990, Principal Baritone):
Schaunard, *La Bohème*; Don Carlo,
Ernani; Marullo, *Rigoletto*; Sacristan,
Tosca; Guglielmo, *Così fan tutte*; Enrico,
Lucia di Lammermoor; Panthée, *The
Trojans*; Count, *Le Nozze di Figaro*;
Leporello, *Don Giovanni*; Ford, *Falstaff*;
Sonora, *La Fanciulla del West*; title roles:
The Barber of Seville, *Eugene Onegin*.

OPERATIC WORLD PREMIERES INCLUDE:
Basle: 1991, title role, *Faust* by Luca
Lombardi; 1992, Alexander, *Die
Menschen* by Detlev Müller-Siemens.

126

RELATED PROFESSIONAL ACTIVITIES:
Concerts and recitals in the UK and
abroad.
RECORDINGS INCLUDE: Janáček, *Osud*
(EMI).
ADDRESS: c/o Robert Gilder & Company,
Enterprise House, 59–65 Upper Ground,
London SE1 9PQ.

HOLLOWAY ROBIN
Composer, Librettist, Teacher and Writer

POSITION: Lecturer in Music, University of
Cambridge.
PERSONAL DETAILS: b. 19 October 1943,
Warwickshire.
EDUCATION/TRAINING: King's College,
Cambridge; New College, Oxford.
FIRST PROFESSIONAL PERFORMANCE OF A
COMPOSITION: 1964, Garden Music for
ensemble.
CAREER: Numerous compositions in all
genres; since 1969, Fellow, Gonville and
Caius College, Cambridge; 1975–1980,
Assistant Lecturer in Music and since
1980, Lecturer in Music, University of
Cambridge.
OPERATIC WORLD PREMIERES: 1990,
English National Opera, *Clarissa*, opera
in two acts (composed in 1976), libretto by
the composer after the novel by Samuel
Richardson, conductor Oliver Knussen,
director David Pountney, designer David
Fielding; (a second opera commissioned
by English National Opera is currently in
progress, provisional title, *Boys and Girls
Come Out to Play*, scenario by the
composer, libretto by Gavin Ewart).
RECORDINGS INCLUDE: Romanza for violin
and small orchestra, *Sea Surface Full of
Clouds* (both CHAN), Brass Quintet (SAYD).
PUBLICATIONS INCLUDE: 1978, *Debussy
and Wagner* (Eulenburg); contributor:
Opera on Record 1 & 2 (Hutchinson); *The
Britten Companion* (Faber); Opera
Guides: *Parsifal, Twilight of the Gods*
(both Calder); opera companions to
Salome and *Elektra* (both Cambridge
University Press).

ADDRESS: c/o Boosey & Hawkes Ltd, 295
Regent Street, London W1R 8JH.

HOLMAN PETER
Conductor, Editor, Harpsichordist and Writer

POSITION: Music Director, Opera Restor'd.
PERSONAL DETAILS: b. 19 October 1946,
London; m. 1970, two children.
EDUCATION/TRAINING: 1967–1971, King's
College, London, with Thurston Dart.
PROFESSIONAL DEBUT: 1969, Ars Nova
concert.
OPERATIC DEBUT: 1979, Holme Pierrepont
Opera Trust, *Cupid and Death*.
CAREER: 1972–1983, professor, Royal
Academy of Music (medieval course and
performance practice); 1981–1982,
Visiting Professor of Musicology,
Washington University, St Louis; since
1971, lecturer, Colchester Institute Music
School (baroque and classical history);
since 1985, Music Director, Opera
Restor'd.
OPERA PERFORMANCES IN THE UK
INCLUDE: Since 1980: Holme Pierrepont
Opera Trust: *Venus and Adonis*, *The
Death of Dido* (1981, first modern
performance), *Thomas and Sally*, *Dido
and Aeneas*, *Phoebe* (1984, first modern
performance), *Pyramus and Thisbe*;
Opera Restor'd: *The Ephesian Matron*,
The Brickdust Man, *The Grenadier*,
Peleus and Thetis, *The Portrait* (1990, first
modern performance), *Lo Speziale*, *La
Serva Padrona*.
RELATED PROFESSIONAL ACTIVITIES:
Since 1979, continuo player and Director,
The Parley of Instruments; since 1988,
founder and Director, Essex Baroque
Orchestra.
PUBLICATIONS INCLUDE: *Four and Twenty
Fiddlers: The Violin at the English Court,
1540–1690* (Oxford University Press);
contributor, numerous music journals.
HONOURS INCLUDE: Honorary Associate,
Royal Academy of Music.
ADDRESS: c/o Opera Restor'd, 54 Astonville
Street, London SW18 5AJ.

127

HOSE ANTHONY
Conductor and Translator

POSITIONS: Artistic Director: Welsh Chamber Orchestra and Beaumaris Festival, Wales.

PERSONAL DETAILS: b. 24 May 1944, London; m. 1968, Beverley Bergen, one child; m. 1977, Moira Griffiths, one child.

EDUCATION/TRAINING: 1955–1966, Royal College of Music; 1966, Mozarteum, Salzburg; 1966–1968, privately with Rafael Kubelik.

PROFESSIONAL AND OPERATIC DEBUT: 1969, Bremen Opera, The Rake's Progress.

CAREER: 1966–1968, répétiteur, Glyndebourne Festival Opera; 1968–1969, répétiteur and assistant conductor, Bremen Opera; Welsh National Opera: 1969–1974, Chorus Master; 1974–1983, Head of Music; Buxton Festival: 1979–1987, Music Director; 1988–1991, Artistic Director; since 1986, Artistic Director: Welsh Chamber Orchestra and Beaumaris Festival, Wales.

OPERATIC WORLD PREMIERES INCLUDE: Welsh National Opera: 1980, The Servants by William Mathias; 1981, The Journey by John Metcalf.

OPERA PERFORMANCES IN THE UK INCLUDE: Since 1979, Buxton Festival: Lucia di Lammermoor, Hamlet, Beatrice and Benedict, Il Matrimonio Segreto, Háry János, Griselda (1983, first modern performance), La Colombe, Médée, Jason, La Buona Figliuola, Il Filosofo di Campagna, King Arthur, Ariodante, Il Pigmalione, L'Occasione fa il Ladro, Don Quixote in Sierra Morena, Armida, L'Italiana in Londra, Tancredi, The Seraglio.

RELATED PROFESSIONAL ACTIVITIES: Translations: Ariodante, Don Quixote in Sierra Morena, Elektra, Le Huron.

ADDRESS: Fairfield House, Brondeg, Aberdare, Mid-Glamorgan CF44 7PL.

HOWARD ANN   Mezzo-soprano

PERSONAL DETAILS: b. 22 July 1936, London; m. Keith Giles, one child.

EDUCATION/TRAINING: 1956–1962, privately with Topliss Green and Rodolpha Lhombino in London; 1962–1963, with Dominic Modesti in Paris (Covent Garden Scholarship).

PROFESSIONAL DEBUT: 1961, Covent Garden, Kate Pinkerton, Madama Butterfly.

EARLY CAREER INCLUDED: 1961–1963, chorus member, Covent Garden; 1964–1973, Principal Mezzo-soprano, Sadler's Wells Opera: Delilah, Samson and Delilah; Fricka, The Rhinegold; Ortrud, Lohengrin; Lilli Vanessi, Kiss Me Kate; Witch, Hansel and Gretel; also, Scottish Opera, Brangäne, Tristan und Isolde.

MAJOR DEBUTS INCLUDE: 1964: Sadler's Wells Opera, Czipra, The Gipsy Baron; Welsh National Opera, Azucena, Il Trovatore; 1969, Scottish Opera, Cassandra, The Trojans; title role, Carmen: 1970, Sadler's Wells Opera; 1971, New Orleans Opera; 1972, New York City Opera; 1973, Covent Garden, Amneris, Aida; 1974, Santa Fe Opera, title role, The Grand Duchess of Gérolstein; 1976, Amneris, Aida: Fort Worth and Canadian Opera Company, Toronto; 1977: Baltimore Opera Company, title role, The Italian Girl in Algiers; Grand Théâtre, Bordeaux, Amneris, Aida; 1978: Opera North, Dalila, Samson et Dalila; Baltimore Opera Company, Eboli, Don Carlos; 1979, Teatro San Carlo, Naples, Fricka, Das Rheingold; 1980, Nice Opera, Dulcinée, Don Quichotte; 1981, Fort Worth, Klytemnestra, Elektra; 1982, St Etienne, title role, Hérodiade; 1983, New Orleans Opera, Brangäne, Tristan und Isolde; 1984, Santiago Opera, Dalila, Samson et Dalila.

OPERATIC WORLD PREMIERES INCLUDE: 1965, Sadler's Wells Opera, Leda, The Mines of Sulphur by Richard Rodney Bennett; 1983, Opera North, Mrs Danvers, Rebecca by Wilfred Josephs; 1985, Santa Fe Opera, Caliban, The Tempest by John

Eaton; 1989, English National Opera, Elsie Worthing, *The Plumber's Gift* by David Blake.

CAREER IN THE UK INCLUDES: Since 1974: English National Opera: Secretary, *The Consul*; Fricka, *The Rhinegold*; Mescalina, *Le Grand Macabre* (1982, British première); Grandmother, *The Gambler*; Taven, *Mireille*; Hélène, *War and Peace*; Jezibaba, *Rusalka*; Kabanicha, *Katya Kabanova*; Azucena, *Il Trovatore*; Katisha, *The Mikado*; Auntie, *Peter Grimes*; Prince Orlofsky, *Die Fledermaus*; title role, *Carmen*; Opera North: Witch, *Hansel and Gretel*; Leda, *The Mines of Sulphur*; Hostess, *Boris Godunov*; Scottish Opera: Venus, *Orion*; Old Lady, *Candide*; Marcellina, *The Marriage of Figaro*; Welsh National Opera, title role, *The Grand Duchess of Gérolstein*.

RELATED PROFESSIONAL ACTIVITIES: Numerous concerts, recitals, broadcasts and television appearances in the UK and abroad; 1989, West End, Stepmother, *Into the Woods*.

RECORDINGS INCLUDE: Bernstein, *Candide* (TER); Humperdinck, *Hänsel und Gretel* (EMI); Sondheim, *Into the Woods* (RCA); Wagner, *The Valkyrie* (EMI).

VIDEOS INCLUDE: Dvořák, *Rusalka* (English National Opera); Sullivan, *Ruddigore* (Walker).

ADDRESS: c/o Stafford Law Associates, 26 Mayfield Road, Weybridge, Surrey KT13 8XB.

HOWARD JASON   Baritone

PERSONAL DETAILS: b. 8 September 1959, Merthyr Tydfil.

PREVIOUS OCCUPATION: 1977–1984, fireman.

EDUCATION/TRAINING: 1984–1987, Trinity College of Music, with John Wakefield; 1987–1988, Royal College of Music, with Norman Bailey; masterclasses with Carlo Bergonzi in Busseto and Alfredo Kraus in London.

PROFESSIONAL DEBUT: 1988, Scottish Opera, Guglielmo, *Così fan tutte*.

MAJOR DEBUTS INCLUDE: 1990, Opera North, Gaylord Ravenal, *Show Boat*; 1991: English National Opera, Ned Keene, *Peter Grimes*; Opéra Comique, Paris, Alfonso, *La Favorite*; 1992, Seattle Opera, title role, *Il Barbiere di Siviglia*; 1993, Welsh National Opera, Marcello, *La Bohème*.

CAREER IN THE UK INCLUDES: 1987, British Youth Opera, title role, *Don Giovanni*; since 1988: Opera North: Ramiro, *L'Heure Espanole*; Ezio, *Attila*; Escamillo, *Carmen*; title role, *Billy Budd*; Scottish Opera (1988–1989, Principal Baritone): Duphol and Germont, *La Traviata*; Sharpless, *Madama Butterfly*; title roles: *Don Giovanni*, *The Marriage of Figaro*; Welsh National Opera, title role, *Eugene Onegin*.

RELATED PROFESSIONAL ACTIVITIES: Concerts and oratorios in the UK; Council member, British Youth Opera.

RECORDINGS INCLUDE: Janáček, *The Makropoulos Case* (DECC); Romberg, *The Student Prince*; Sondheim, *A Little Night Music* (both TER).

AWARDS INCLUDE: 1987, Ricordi Opera Prize; 1988, John Scott Award (Scottish Opera); 1992, finalist, Opera Company of Philadelphia/Luciano Pavarotti International Voice Competition (USA).

ADDRESS: c/o John Coast, 31 Sinclair Road, London W14 ONS.

HOWARD YVONNE
Mezzo-soprano

PERSONAL DETAILS: b. 1 March 1958, Stafford.

EDUCATION/TRAINING: Royal Northern College of Music, with David Johnston and Joseph Ward.

PROFESSIONAL DEBUT: 1983, Glyndebourne Festival Opera, Fanny, *Intermezzo*.

MAJOR DEBUTS INCLUDE: 1990, City of Birmingham Touring Opera, Fricka and Waltraute, *The Ring Saga*; 1991: Covent Garden, Mercédès, *Carmen*; Scottish Opera, Suzuki, *Madama Butterfly*; 1992:

English National Opera, Amastre, *Xerxes*; Opera North, Maddalena, *Rigoletto*.

CAREER IN THE UK INCLUDES: Since 1984: Birmingham Music Theatre, Suzuki, *Madam Butterfly*; Covent Garden: Kate Pinkerton, *Madama Butterfly*; Karolka, *Jenůfa*; English National Opera, Meg Page, *Falstaff*; English Touring Opera (City of Birmingham Touring Opera), title role, *Cinderella*; Glyndebourne Touring Opera, Marcellina, *Le Nozze di Figaro*.

RELATED PROFESSIONAL ACTIVITIES: Concerts at the Wigmore Hall.

AWARDS INCLUDE: 1987, Elsie Sykes Memorial Fellowship.

ADDRESS: c/o Robert Gilder & Company, Enterprise House, 59–65 Upper Ground, London SE1 9PQ.

HOWARTH ELGAR
Conductor

PERSONAL DETAILS: b. 4 November 1935, Staffordshire; m. 1958, Mary Neary, three children.

EDUCATION/TRAINING: 1953–1956: University of Manchester, studied music; Royal Manchester College of Music.

PROFESSIONAL DEBUT: As trumpeter: 1958, Royal Opera House Orchestra, Covent Garden; as conductor: 1969, London Sinfonietta at the Venice Biennale.

OPERATIC DEBUT: 1973, Royal Northern College of Music, *The Rake's Progress*.

CAREER: 1958–1963, member, Royal Opera House Orchestra, Covent Garden; Principal Trumpeter: 1964–1970, Royal Philharmonic Orchestra; 1968–1972, London Sinfonietta; since 1972, freelance conductor with leading British orchestras and opera companies including 1985–1988, Principal Guest Conductor, Opera North.

MAJOR OPERATIC DEBUTS INCLUDE: 1978, Hamburg State Opera, *Le Grand Macabre*; 1979, Gothenburg, *Peter Grimes*; 1980: Opera North, *Nabucco*; Australian Opera, Sydney, *Boris Godunov*; 1981: Glyndebourne Festival Opera, *Il Barbiere di Siviglia*; Paris Opera, *Le Grand Macabre*; 1982, English National Opera, *Boris Godunov*; 1985, Covent Garden, *King Priam* (also at the Athens Festival).

OPERATIC WORLD PREMIERES INCLUDE: 1978, Royal Opera, Stockholm, *Le Grand Macabre* by György Ligeti; 1983, Opéra Comique, Paris, *Erzsebet* by Charles Chaynes; 1986: English National Opera, *The Mask of Orpheus*; Opera Factory, *Yan Tan Tethera* (both by Harrison Birtwistle); 1987, Glyndebourne Touring Opera, *The Electrification of the Soviet Union* by Nigel Osborne; 1991: Covent Garden, *Gawain* by Harrison Birtwistle; Opera North, *The Jewel Box* by Mozart/ Paul Griffiths.

OPERA PERFORMANCES IN THE UK INCLUDE: Since 1980: English National Opera, *Le Grand Macabre* (1982, British première); Glyndebourne Festival and Touring Opera: *The Electrification of the Soviet Union*, *Falstaff*; Opera North: *A Midsummer Night's Dream*, *La Bohème*, *Katya Kabanova*, *The Marriage of Figaro*, *Masquerade* (1990, British première), *Billy Budd*.

RELATED PROFESSIONAL ACTIVITIES: Arrangements and compositions primarily for brass instruments (several published by Chester Music and Novello).

RECORDINGS INCLUDE: Birtwistle: *Endless Parade* (PHIL), *Secret Theatre*, *Silbury Air*, *Carmen Arcadiae Mechanicae Perpetuum* (all ETCE); Ligeti: *Le Grand Macabre*, orchestral works (both WERG).

HONOURS INCLUDE: Royal Manchester College of Music: 1956, Associate; 1970, Fellow.

ADDRESS: c/o Allied Artists, 42 Montpelier Square, London SW7 1JZ.

HOWARTH JUDITH   Soprano

POSITION: Member, The Royal Opera, Covent Garden.

PERSONAL DETAILS: b. 11 September 1962, Ipswich; m. 1986.

EDUCATION/TRAINING: Royal Scottish Academy of Music and Drama, with Patricia McMahon; masterclass with Luciano Pavarotti.

PROFESSIONAL DEBUT: 1985, Covent Garden, First Maid, *The Birthday of the Infanta* (British première).

MAJOR DEBUTS INCLUDE: 1989: Covent Garden, Gilda, *Rigoletto*; Opera North, Susanna, *The Marriage of Figaro*; Scottish Opera, Zerlina, *Don Giovanni*; 1991: Aix-en-Provence Festival, Susanna, *Le Nozze di Figaro*; Salzburg Festival, Madame Silberklang, *Der Schauspieldirektor*.

CAREER IN THE UK INCLUDES: Since 1985: member, Covent Garden: Siebel, *Faust*; Teacher, *The Boy Who Grew Too Fast* (1986, British première at Sadler's Wells Theatre); Barbarina, *Le Nozze di Figaro* (also 1992, Japan tour); Giannetta, *L'Elisir d'Amore*; Frasquita, *Carmen*; Papagena, *Die Zauberflöte*; Elvira, *L'Italiana in Algeri*; Oscar, *Un Ballo in Maschera*; Musetta, *La Bohème*; Adele, *Die Fledermaus*; Woglinde, *Der Ring des Nibelungen*; Marguérite, *Les Huguenots*; Liù, *Turandot*; Norina, *Don Pasquale*; Marzelline, *Fidelio*; Guardian of the Threshold, *Die Frau ohne Schatten*; Morgana, *Alcina*; also, Opera North, Norina, *Don Pasquale*.

RELATED PROFESSIONAL ACTIVITIES: Concerts with BBC, English Chamber and Boston Symphony Orchestras including 1991, Proms.

RECORDINGS INCLUDE: Mozart, *Requiem* (ASV); Puccini, *Madama Butterfly* (DG).

VIDEOS INCLUDE: Bizet, *Carmen*; J. Strauss, *Die Fledermaus* (both Covent Garden); Mozart at Buckingham Palace (EMI).

AWARDS INCLUDE: 1985, Decca-Kathleen Ferrier Prize.

ADDRESS: c/o Lies Askonas Ltd, 186 Drury Lane, London WC2B 5RY.

HOWELL GWYNNE   Bass

POSITION: Member, The Royal Opera, Covent Garden.

PERSONAL DETAILS: b. 13 June 1938, Gorseinon, South Wales; m. 1968, Mary Morris, two children.

PREVIOUS OCCUPATION: Town planner.

EDUCATION/TRAINING: University of Wales, studied geography; University of Manchester, studied town planning; part time studies at Royal Manchester College of Music with Gwilym Jones; 1968–1972, privately with Otakar Kraus.

PROFESSIONAL DEBUT: 1968, Sadler's Wells Opera, Monterone, *Rigoletto*.

EARLY CAREER INCLUDED: 1968–1970, Principal Bass, Sadler's Wells Opera: Commendatore, *Don Giovanni*; Grenville, *La Traviata*; Bonze, *Madam Butterfly*; Ballad-Singer, *Gloriana*; Private Willis, *Iolanthe*; Colline, *La Bohème*.

MAJOR DEBUTS INCLUDE: 1970: Covent Garden, First Nazarene, *Salome*; Welsh National Opera, King, *Aida*; 1971, Gran Teatre del Liceu, Barcelona, Padre Guardiano, *La Forza del Destino*; 1977, Lyric Opera, Chicago, Pogner, *Die Meistersinger von Nürnberg*; 1978, San Francisco Opera, Heinrich, *Lohengrin*; 1979, Santa Fe Opera, Raimondo, *Lucia di Lammermoor*; 1980, Hamburg State Opera, Ramfis, *Aida*; 1981, Grand Théâtre, Geneva, Pimen, *Boris Godunov*; Lodovico, *Otello*: 1983, Paris Opera; 1985, Metropolitan Opera, New York; 1986, Canadian Opera Company, Toronto, title role, *Boris Godunov*; 1991: Glyndebourne Festival Opera, Sarastro, *The Magic Flute*; Cologne Opera, Fiesco, *Simon Boccanegra*.

OPERATIC WORLD PREMIERES INCLUDE: 1972, Covent Garden, Richard Taverner, *Taverner* by Peter Maxwell Davies.

CAREER IN THE UK INCLUDES: Since 1971: member, Covent Garden: King, *Aida*; Timur, *Turandot*; Prince Gremin, *Eugene Onegin*; Commendatore, *Don Giovanni*; Count Ribbing, *Un Ballo in Maschera*; Padre Guardiano, *La Forza del Destino*; Hobson, *Peter Grimes*; Truffaldino,

Ariadne auf Naxos; Count Walter, *Luisa Miller*; Crespel, *Les Contes d'Hoffmann*; Jack Wallace, *La Fanciulla del West*; Ghost of Hector, *The Trojans at Carthage*; Angelotti, *Tosca*; Grand Inquisitor, *Don Carlos*; Hermit, *Der Freischütz*; Titurel, *Parsifal*; Fasolt, *Das Rheingold*; Colline, *La Bohème*; Pimen, *Boris Godunov*; Old Hebrew, *Samson et Dalila*; Sparafucile, *Rigoletto*; King Marke, *Tristan und Isolde*; Fiesco, *Simon Boccanegra*; Pogner, *Die Meisteringer von Nürnberg*; Dosifei, *Khovanshchina*; Somnus, *Semele*; Emperor Phorcas, *Esclarmonde* (1983, British première); Sarastro, *Die Zauberflöte*; Capellio, *I Capuleti e i Montecchi*; Raimondo, *Lucia di Lammermoor*; Rocco, *Fidelio*; Badger/Priest, *The Cunning Little Vixen*; Marcel, *Les Huguenots*; Daland, *Der Fliegende Holländer*; Bartolo, *Le Nozze di Figaro* (also 1992, Japan tour); Jorg, *Stiffelio*; also: English National Opera: Philip II, *Don Carlos*; Hans Sachs, *The Mastersingers of Nuremberg*; Sarastro, *The Magic Flute*; Wanderer, *Siegfried*; Don Basilio, *The Barber of Seville*; Gurnemanz, *Parsifal*; title role, *Duke Bluebeard's Castle*; Opera North, King René, *Yolande*; Welsh National Opera: Colline, *La Bohème*; King Marke, *Tristan und Isolde*.

RELATED PROFESSIONAL ACTIVITIES: Regular concerts, recitals and broadcasts with leading conductors and orchestras in the UK and abroad.

RECORDINGS INCLUDE: Bach: *St John Passion, Mass in B Minor*; Beethoven: *Fidelio, Missa Solemnis* (all DECC), Symphony No. 9 (DECC/PICK); Elgar, *The Dream of Gerontius* (CHAN); Handel, *Messiah* (DECC/ARGO); Haydn, *Die Schöpfung* (ERAT); Janáček, *The Cunning Little Vixen* (EMI); Mahler, Symphony No. 8 (PHIL); Puccini, *La Fancuilla del West* (DG); Rossini, *Stabat Mater* (EMI); Verdi: *Un Ballo in Maschera* (PHIL), *Luisa Miller* (DG); Wagner, *Tristan und Isolde* (EMI).

VIDEOS INCLUDE: Offenbach, *Les Contes d'Hoffmann*; Puccini: *La Bohème, La Fanciulla del West*; Saint-Saëns, *Samson et Dalila* (all Covent Garden).

HONOURS INCLUDE: 1986, Honorary Fellow, University of Wales.

ADDRESS: c/o Ingpen & Williams Ltd, 14 Kensington Court, London W8 5DN.

HOWELLS ANNE
Mezzo-soprano

PERSONAL DETAILS: b. 12 January 1941, Lancashire; m. 1966, Ryland Davies (tenor); m. 1981, Stafford Dean (bass-baritone), two children.

EDUCATION/TRAINING: Royal Manchester College of Music, with Frederic Cox; privately with Vera Rozsa.

PROFESSIONAL DEBUT: 1964, chorus member, Glyndebourne Festival Opera.

EARLY CAREER INCLUDED: 1964–1966, chorus member and small roles, Glyndebourne Festival Opera.

MAJOR DEBUTS INCLUDE: Flora, *La Traviata*: 1965, Welsh National Opera; 1967, Covent Garden; Erisbe, *L'Ormindo*: 1967, Glyndebourne Festival Opera; 1971, Netherlands Opera; 1972, La Monnaie, Brussels; 1972, Lyric Opera, Chicago, Dorabella, *Così fan tutte*; 1973: Scottish Opera, Ottavia, *The Coronation of Poppea*; Grand Théâtre, Geneva, Octavian, *Der Rosenkavalier*; Lyons Opera, Dido, *Dido and Aeneas*; 1975: English National Opera, title role, *La Belle Hélène*; Metropolitan Opera, New York, Dorabella, *Così fan tutte*; 1976, Salzburg Festival, Annio, *La Clemenza di Tito*; 1977, Nantes Opera, title role, *Carmen*; 1979, San Francisco Opera, Dorabella, *Così fan tutte*; 1981, Deutsche Oper, Berlin, Idamante, *Idomeneo*; 1985, Covent Garden at the Athens Festival, Helen, *King Priam*; 1988, Los Angeles Music Center Opera, Despina, *Così fan tutte*.

OPERATIC WORLD PREMIERES INCLUDE: 1970: Covent Garden, Lena, *Victory* by Richard Rodney Bennett; Glyndebourne

Festival Opera, Cathleen, *The Rising of the Moon* by Nicholas Maw; 1987, Grand Théâtre, Geneva, Régine, *La Fôret* by Rolf Liebermann.

CAREER IN THE UK INCLUDES: Since 1967: Covent Garden (1969–1971, Principal Mezzo-soprano): Annina, *Der Rosenkavalier*; Ophelia, *Hamlet* (Searle, 1969, British première); Rosina, *Il Barbiere di Siviglia*; Cherubino, *Le Nozze di Figaro*; Hermia, *A Midsummer Night's Dream*; Annio, *La Clemenza di Tito* (also 1976, at La Scala, Milan); Siebel, *Faust*; Ascanio, *Benvenuto Cellini*; Zerlina, *Don Giovanni*; Dorabella, *Cosi fan tutte*; Mélisande, *Pelléas et Mélisande*; Maffio Orsini, *Lucrezia Borgia*; Cook, *The Nightingale* and Squirrel, *L'Enfant et les Sortilèges*; Meg Page, *Falstaff*; Helen, *King Priam*; Olga, *Eugene Onegin*; Thea, *The Knot Garden*; Magdalene, *Die Meistersinger von Nürnberg*; Adelaide, *Arabella*; Despina, *Cosi fan tutte* (also 1992, Japan tour); Clairon, *Capriccio*; Giulietta, *Les Contes d'Hoffmann*; English National Opera, title role, *The Merry Widow*; Glyndebourne Festival Opera: Dorabella, *Cosi fan tutte*; Composer, *Ariadne auf Naxos*; Minerva, *Il Ritorno d'Ulisse in Patria*; Diana, *La Calisto*; Clairon, *Capriccio*; Meg Page, *Falstaff*; Baba the Turk, *The Rake's Progress*; Scottish Opera: Octavian, *Der Rosenkavalier*; Mélisande, *Pelléas et Mélisande*; Diana, *Orion*; Clairon, *Capriccio*; Welsh National Opera, Prince Orlofsky, *Die Fledermaus*.

RELATED PROFESSIONAL ACTIVITIES: Regular concerts, recitals and broadcasts in the UK and abroad.

RECORDINGS INCLUDE: Berlioz, *Les Troyens* (PHIL); R. Strauss, *Der Rosenkavalier* (DECC); Sullivan, *The Mikado* (TELA); Wagner, *Parsifal* (DECC).

VIDEOS INCLUDE: Monteverdi, *Il Ritorno d'Ulisse in Patria* (Glynebourne Festival Opera); R. Strauss, *Der Rosenkavalier* (Covent Garden).

ADDRESS: c/o Harrison/Parrott Ltd, 12 Penzance Place, London W11 4PA.

HOWLETT NEIL
Baritone and Teacher

POSITION: Head of Vocal Studies, Royal Northern College of Music.

PERSONAL DETAILS: b. 24 July 1934, Surrey; m. 1962, Elizabeth Robson (soprano), two children; m. 1988, Carolyn Hawthorn (mezzo-soprano).

EDUCATION/TRAINING: 1954–1957, King's College, Cambridge; 1957–1958, with Tino Pattiera in Vienna; 1958–1959, Hochschule für Musik, Stuttgart.

PROFESSIONAL DEBUT: 1960, chorus member, Glyndebourne Festival Opera.

EARLY CAREER INCLUDED: 1961–1971, appearances with English Opera Group, Glyndebourne Touring Opera, Sadler's Wells Opera, Camden and Aix-en-Provence Festivals; roles included: Ferryman, *Curlew River*; Junius, *The Rape of Lucretia*; Agamemnon, *La Belle Hélène*; Amida, *L'Ormindo*; Ford, *Falstaff*; Masetto, *Don Giovanni*; title role, *Macbeth*.

MAJOR DEBUTS INCLUDE: 1970, Covent Garden, Silvio, *Pagliacci*; 1971, Hamburg State Opera, Masetto, *Don Giovanni*; 1972, Sadler's Wells Opera, Tonio, *Pagliacci*; 1985, Frankfurt Opera, Lindorf/Coppelius/Dapertutto/Dr Miracle, *Les Contes d'Hoffmann*; 1986, Teatro Colón, Buenos Aires, Amfortas, *Parsifal*.

OPERATIC WORLD PREMIERES INCLUDE: Sadler's Wells Opera/English National Opera: 1974, Mirador, *The Story of Vasco* by Gordon Crosse; 1977, title role, *Toussaint*; 1989, Commander, *The Plumber's Gift* (both by David Blake).

CAREER IN THE UK INCLUDES: Since 1972, Sadler's Wells Opera/English National Opera (1974–1989, Principal Baritone): Count di Luna, *Il Trovatore*; Amonasro, *Aida*; Don Pizarro, *Fidelio*; Don Alfonso, *Cosi fan tutte*; Golaud, *Pelléas and Mélisande*; Iago, *Otello*; Jokanaan, *Salome*; Mountjoy, *Gloriana*; Amfortas, *Parsifal*; Scarpia, *Tosca*; Mr Redburn, *Billy Budd*; title roles: *The Flying Dutchman*, *Simon Boccanegra*.

RELATED PROFESSIONAL ACTIVITIES: Numerous concerts and recitals in the UK and abroad; 1974–1992, teacher, Guildhall School of Music and Drama; since 1992, Head of Vocal Studies, Royal Northern College of Music.

RECORDINGS INCLUDE: Verdi, *Otello* (EMI).

VIDEOS INCLUDE: Britten, *Billy Budd* (English National Opera); Sullivan, *Princess Ida* (Walker).

AWARDS INCLUDE: 1957, Kathleen Ferrier Memorial Scholarship.

ADDRESS: c/o Ingpen & Williams Ltd, 14 Kensington Court, London W8 5DN.

HUDSON RICHARD   Designer

PERSONAL DETAILS: b. 9 June 1954, Zimbabwe.

EDUCATION/TRAINING: 1973–1975, Wimbledon School of Art.

PROFESSIONAL AND OPERATIC DEBUT: 1983, Warwick Arts Centre, *The Wreckers*.

CAREER: Freelance opera and theatre designer in the UK and abroad including Old Vic Theatre, Royal National Theatre, Royal Shakespeare Company, West End and Broadway.

MAJOR OPERATIC DEBUTS INCLUDE: 1985: Opera Northern Ireland, *Don Pasquale*; Scottish Opera, *La Vie Parisienne*; 1986, Wexford Festival, *Mignon*; 1987/1989, Royal Northern College of Music/ Opera North co-production, *Manon*; 1989, Zurich Opera, *Lucia di Lammermoor*; 1991, English National Opera, *The Marriage of Figaro*; 1992, Glyndebourne Festival Opera, *The Queen of Spades*.

OPERATIC WORLD PREMIERES INCLUDE: 1987, Kent Opera, *A Night at the Chinese Opera*; 1990, Scottish Opera, *The Vanishing Bridegroom* (both by Judith Weir).

OPERA DESIGNS IN THE UK INCLUDE: Since 1984: English National Opera, *The Force of Destiny*; Kent Opera, *Count Ory*; London Sinfonietta at the Queen Elizabeth Hall, *Elegy for Young Lovers*; Royal College of Music, *Il Matrimonio Segreto*;

Scottish Opera, *Candide*; Warwick Arts Centre, *The Dragon of Wantley*.

ADDRESS: c/o Kate Lewthwaite Associates, 6 Windmill Street, London W1P 1HF.

HULSE EILEEN   Soprano

PERSONAL DETAILS: b. London.

PREVIOUS OCCUPATION: Physical education teacher.

EDUCATION/TRAINING: 1981–1982, National Opera Studio; privately with Mary Makower.

PROFESSIONAL DEBUT: 1983, Oxford University Opera, Genio, *Orfeo ed Euridice* (Haydn).

MAJOR DEBUTS INCLUDE: 1983, Kent Opera, Suzanne, *Robinson Crusoe*; 1984, Glyndebourne Festival Opera, Fiakermilli, *Arabella*; 1985: English National Opera, Neferneferuaten, *Akhnaten* (British première); Scottish Opera, Papagena, *The Magic Flute*; 1989: City of Birmingham Touring Opera, Pamina, *The Magic Flute*; Welsh National Opera, Naiad, *Ariadne auf Naxos*; 1990: English National Opera Soviet Union tour (Bolshoi, Kirov and Kiev), Flora, *The Turn of the Screw*; Frankfurt Opera, Wood Nymph, *Rusalka*; 1991: Los Angeles Music Center Opera, Flora, *The Turn of the Screw*; Lucerne, Constanze, *Die Entführung aus dem Serail*; Théâtre du Châtelet, Paris, Shepherdess/Bat, *L'Enfant et les Sortilèges*; 1992, Teatro La Fenice, Venice, Flora, *The Turn of the Screw*; 1993, Nantes Opera, Constanze, *Die Entführung aus dem Serail*.

OPERATIC WORLD PREMIERES INCLUDE: 1984, Glyndebourne Touring Opera, Rhoda, *Higglety Pigglety Pop!* preliminary version by Oliver Knussen; 1990, Munich Biennale, Bella/Mrs Parkhearst, *63: Dream Palace* by Hans-Jürgen von Bose.

CAREER IN THE UK INCLUDES: Since 1984: Almeida Festival, Friedericka, *Jacob Lenz* (1987, British première); Alte Oper, Frankfurt at the Edinburgh International Festival, Miss Crisp, *The English Cat* (1987, British stage première); Buxton

Festival: Cupid, *King Arthur*; Madame Euterpova, *Help! Help! The Globolinks!*; English National Opera: Wood Nymph, *Rusalka*; Flora, *The Turn of the Screw*; Papagena, *The Magic Flute*; Glyndebourne Touring Opera: Max, *Where the Wild Things Are*; Queen of the Night, *Die Zauberflöte*; Kent Opera: Blonde, *The Seraglio*; Drusilla, *The Coronation of Poppea*; Queen of the Night, *The Magic Flute*; Zerlina, *Don Giovanni*.

RELATED PROFESSIONAL ACTIVITIES: Regular concerts, recitals and broadcasts in the UK, particularly of work by contemporary composers.

VIDEOS INCLUDE: Dvořák, *Rusalka* (English National Opera).

ADDRESS: c/o Robert Gilder & Company, Enterprise House, 59–65 Upper Ground, London SE1 9PQ.

HUTCHINSON STUART
Conductor, Pianist and Accompanist

PERSONAL DETAILS: b. 3 March 1956, London.

EDUCATION/TRAINING: 1974–1979, Royal Academy of Music: studied piano with John Streets and Alexander Kelly, opera course with Norman Feasey; 1979, masterclasses with Leonard Bernstein and John Pritchard.

PROFESSIONAL DEBUT: 1979, concert at the Purcell Room, London.

OPERATIC DEBUT: 1983, New Sadler's Wells Opera, *The Mikado*.

CAREER: 1975–1989, freelance répétiteur: English National Opera, New Sadler's Wells Opera, Opera 80, Opera North, Wexford Festival; 1976–1989, Music Director, University of London Chaplaincy; Guest Conductor: 1987 and 1988, London Opera Festival; 1990, Scottish Opera; Guest Music Director: 1988, New Sadler's Wells Opera; 1991, Scottish Ballet; 1986–1990, Artistic and Music Director, Morley Opera.

MAJOR OPERATIC DEBUTS INCLUDE: 1990, Scottish Opera, *The Threepenny Opera*; 1992, English National Opera, *Carmen*.

OPERA PERFORMANCES IN THE UK INCLUDE: Since 1986, Morley Opera: *Gianni Schicchi*, *Dido and Aeneas*, *Il Matrimonio Segreto*, *Owen Wingrave*, *The Turn of the Screw*, *The Rape of Lucretia*, *Die Zauberflöte*, *Così fan tutte*, *La Clemenza di Tito*, *Idomeneo*, *Paul Bunyan*, *Les Deux Journées*, *La Rappresentazione di Anima e di Corpo*, *Our Man in Havana*, *The Rise and Fall of the City of Mahagonny*, *Le Vin Herbé*, *Il Mondo della Luna*.

RELATED PROFESSIONAL ACTIVITIES: 1986–1987, Guest Music Director, Royal Shakespeare Company; Music Director: 1983–1985, Northcott Theatre, Exeter; 1988–1989, Old Vic Theatre; West End: 1984, *On Your Toes*; 1989, *Aspects of Love*.

AWARDS INCLUDE: 1984, Sony Radio Award.

ADDRESS: c/o Music International, 13 Ardilaun Road, London N5 2QR.

HYTNER NICHOLAS
Director

POSITION: Associate Director, Royal National Theatre.

PERSONAL DETAILS: b. 7 May 1956, Manchester.

EDUCATION/TRAINING: Trinity Hall, Cambridge.

PROFESSIONAL AND OPERATIC DEBUT: 1979, Kent Opera, *The Turn of the Screw*.

CAREER: Since 1979, freelance opera and theatre director in the UK and abroad; Associate Director: 1985–1988, Royal Exchange, Manchester, productions included: *As You like It*, *Edward II*, *Don Carlos*; since 1989, Royal National Theatre, productions include: *Ghetto*, *The Wind in the Willows*, *The Madness of George III*, *Carousel*; also: Royal Shakespeare Company: *Measure for Measure*, *The Tempest*, *King Lear*; West End and Broadway, *Miss Saigon*.

135

MAJOR OPERATIC DEBUTS INCLUDE: 1983,
English National Opera, *Rienzi*; 1987:
Covent Garden, *The King Goes Forth to
France* (British première); Paris Opera,
Giulio Cesare; 1988, English National
Opera/Netherlands Opera co-production,
The Magic Flute; 1989: Grand Théâtre,
Geneva, *Le Nozze di Figaro*; Houston
Grand Opera, *Giulio Cesare*; 1991,
Glyndebourne Festival Opera, *La
Clemenza di Tito*; 1993, Bavarian State
Opera, Munich, *Don Giovanni*.
OPERA PRODUCTIONS IN THE UK
INCLUDE: Since 1979: Covent Garden, *The
Knot Garden*; English National Opera:
Xerxes, *The Force of Destiny*; Kent
Opera: *The Marriage of Figaro*, *King
Priam*; New Sussex Opera: *Peter Grimes*,
The Queen of Spades.
VIDEOS INCLUDE: Handel, *Xerxes* (English
National Opera); Tippett, *King Priam*
(Kent Opera).
AWARDS INCLUDE: 1985: *Evening Standard*
Award, *Xerxes* (English National Opera);
Olivier Award, English National Opera
production of *Xerxes*.
ADDRESS: c/o Royal National Theatre,
South Bank, London SE1 9PX.

*   *   *   *

ISAACS JEREMY
Administrator

POSITION: General Director, Royal Opera
House, Covent Garden.
PERSONAL DETAILS: b. 28 September 1932,
Glasgow; m. 1958, Tamara Weinreich (d.
1986), two children; m. 1988, Gillian
Widdicombe (music critic and writer).
EDUCATION/TRAINING: Merton College,
Oxford.
CAREER: As television producer: 1955,
Granada (*What the Papers Say, All our
Yesterdays*); 1958, Associated-Rediffusion
(*This Week*); 1963, BBC (*Panorama*);
1967, Controller of Features, Associated-
Rediffusion; Thames Television: 1968–
1974, Controller of Features (producer,
The World at War); 1974–1978, Director of
Programmes; 1981–1987, first Chief
Executive, Channel Four; Covent Garden:
since 1985, member, Board of Directors;
since 1988, General Director.
OTHER PROFESSIONAL ACTIVITIES
INCLUDE: Since 1979, Governor, British Film
Institute (1979–1981), Chairman,
Production Board); since 1987, Director,
Open College.
PUBLICATIONS INCLUDE: 1989, *Storm over
Four: A Personal Account* (Weidenfeld &
Nicholson).

AWARDS AND HONOURS INCLUDE: Fellow:
1983, Royal Society of Arts; 1985, British
Academy of Film and Television Arts;
1986, British Film Institute; 1989: Guildhall
School of Music and Drama, Royal
Northern College of Music, Royal Scottish
Academy of Music and Drama; Honorary
Doctorates of Literature: 1984, University
of Strathclyde; 1987, Council for National
Academic Awards; 1988, University of
Bristol; 1988, Commandeur de l'Ordre des
Arts et des Lettres (France); several
awards for outstanding contribution to
television.
ADDRESS: c/o Royal Opera House, Covent
Garden, London WC2E 9DD.

ISEPP MARTIN
**Pianist and Accompanist,
Conductor, Harpsichordist
and Teacher**

POSITIONS: Head of Music Studies, National
Opera School; Head of Academy of
Singing (Lieder), School of Fine Arts,
Banff Centre, Alberta.
PERSONAL DETAILS: b. 30 September 1930,
Vienna, Austria; m. 1966, Rose Harris,
two children.

EDUCATION/TRAINING: 1939–1952, studied piano with Leonie Gombrich; 1949–1952, Lincoln College, Oxford; 1952, Royal College of Music.

CAREER: 1954–1957, member, English Opera Group (1954, premièred piano part, *The Turn of the Screw* by Benjamin Britten); Glyndebourne Festival Opera: 1957–1973, member, music staff; 1973–1993, Head of Music Staff; 1973–1977, Head of Opera Training, Juilliard School of Music, New York; since 1978, Head of Music Studies, National Opera Studio; since 1982, Head of Academy of Singing (Lieder), School of Fine Arts, Banff Centre, Alberta; guest coach: 1983 and 1984, Peking Opera and Peking Conservatory of Music (for Mozart roles); since 1984: Canadian Opera Ensemble, Toronto; L'Atelier Lyrique, Montreal Opera; Metropolitan Opera Studio, New York; conductor: Glyndebourne Touring Opera: 1984, *Le Nozze di Figaro*; 1986, *Don Giovanni*; 1987, Washington Opera, *Die Entführung aus dem Serail*; continuo player: Handel Opera Society, New York; Glyndebourne Festival Opera series of Mozart/da Ponte operas.

RELATED PROFESSIONAL ACTIVITIES: Since 1960, accompanist for many leading singers including Janet Baker, Elisabeth Schwarzkopf, John Shirley-Quirk and Elisabeth Söderström; frequent masterclasses for singers and pianists at the Britten-Pears School for Advanced Musical Sudies, as well as in Europe and North America.

RECORDINGS INCLUDE: As harpsichordist: Mozart: *Così fan tutte, Don Giovanni, Le Nozze di Figaro* (all EMI); as pianist: English and German songs with Janet Baker and John Shirley-Quirk (SAGA), French songs with Hugues Cuenod (NIMB); as conductor: Walton, *The Bear* (CHAN).

AWARDS AND HONOURS INCLUDE: 1952, Associate, Royal College of Music; 1965, Carroll Donner Stuchell Medal for Accompanists.

ADDRESS: c/o Glyndebourne Festival Opera, Lewes, East Sussex BN8 5UU or National Opera Studio, Morley College, 61 Westminster Bridge Road, London SE1 7HT.

* * * *

JACOBS ARTHUR
Critic, Translator and Writer

PERSONAL DETAILS: b. 14 June 1922, Manchester; m. 1953, Betty Upton Hughes (journalist), two children.

EDUCATION/TRAINING: Merton College, Oxford.

CAREER: 1947–1952, Music Critic, *Daily Express*; since 1952, freelance critic for various publications including *Financial Times* and *Musical Times*; since 1962, member, Editorial Board, *Opera*; 1968–1989, record reviewer, *Sunday Times*; 1971–1979, Editor, *British Music Yearbook*; 1964–1979, professor, Royal Academy of Music; 1979–1984, Head of Music Department, Huddersfield

Polytechnic; 1991–1992, Visiting Scholar, Wolfson College, Oxford; since 1967, visiting professor at universities in Australia, Canada and USA; translations include: *Aida, The Barber of Baghdad, Benvenuto Cellini, Cinderella, The Comedy of Errors, The Coronation of Poppea, Don Carlos, Expectation, Iphigenia in Aulis, The Italian Girl in Algiers, The Love Potion, Lulu, Medea, The Musical Director, Paris and Helen, The Queen of Spades, Richard I, Silent Night, The Silent Woman, The Spectacle of the Soul and the Body, The Touchstone, Trial by Tea Party, The Tsarina's Shoes, The Turk in Italy, Upstage and Downstage.*

OPERATIC WORLD PREMIERES INCLUDE: 1964, Jeanetta Cochrane Theatre, London, librettist, *One Man Show* by Nicholas Maw.

PUBLICATIONS INCLUDE: 1951, *Gilbert and Sullivan* (Parrish); 1958, *The Penguin Dictionary of Music*; 1964, *One Man Show* (Boosey & Hawkes); 1966, with Stanley Sadie, *The Pan Book of Opera*; 1972, *A Short History of Western Music* (Penguin); 1984, *Arthur Sullivan, A Victorian Musician* (Oxford University Press; 2nd edition 1992, Scolar Press); 1990, *The Penguin Dictionary of Musical Performers*; translations: *The Coronation of Poppea* (Novello), *Cinderella, The Italian Girl in Algiers, The Love Potion, The Touchstone* (all Ricordi), *Expectation, Lulu* (both Universal).

HONOURS INCLUDE: 1969, Honorary Member, Royal Academy of Music.

ADDRESS: 7 Southdale Road, Oxford OX2 7SE.

JAMES EIRIAN   Mezzo-soprano

PERSONAL DETAILS: b. 7 September 1952, Cardigan, Wales; m. 1975, one child.

EDUCATION/TRAINING: Royal College of Music, with Ruth Packer; privately with Rupert Bruce-Lockhart.

PROFESSIONAL DEBUT: 1977, Kent Opera, Olga, *Eugene Onegin*.

EARLY CAREER INCLUDED: 1978–1984: Buxton Festival, Medea, *Jason*; English National Opera: Chambermaid, *The Makropoulos Case*; Kitchen Boy, *Rusalka*; Kent Opera: Melanto, *The Return of Ulysses*; Annina, *La Traviata*; Meg Page, *Falstaff*; Venus, *Il Ballo delle Ingrate*; Cherubino, *The Marriage of Figaro*; Friday, *Robinson Crusoe*; New Sadler's Wells Opera, Nancy, *Martha*; Singers Company: Dorabella, *Così fan tutte*; title role, *La Périchole*.

MAJOR DEBUTS INCLUDE: 1985, English National Opera, Cupid, *Orpheus in the Underworld*; 1986, Lyons Opera, Fatima, *Oberon*; 1987: Alte Oper, Frankfurt at the Edinburgh International Festival, Babette,

The English Cat (British stage première); Covent Garden, Annina, *Der Rosenkavalier*; Houston Grand Opera, Cupid, *Orpheus in the Underworld*; Grand Théâtre, Geneva: 1987, Olga, *Eugene Onegin*; 1988, Hänsel, *Hänsel und Gretel*; 1988, Aix-en-Provence Festival, Dorabella, *Così fan tutte*; 1991: Welsh National Opera, Prince Orlofsky, *Die Fledermaus*; Netherlands Opera, Ascanio, *Benvenuto Cellini*; 1992: Scottish Opera, Sesto, *Julius Caesar*; Despina, *Così fan tutte*: Teatro São Carlos, Lisbon; Teatro Comunale, Ferrara; Théâtre du Châtelet, Paris.

CAREER IN THE UK INCLUDES: Since 1985: Buxton Festival, title role, *Ariodante*; Covent Garden: Javotte, *Manon*; Smeton, *Anna Bolena*; Nancy, *Albert Herring*; Tisbe, *La Cenerentola*; English National Opera: Flora, *La Traviata*; Rosina, *The Barber of Seville*; Kent Opera: Nero, *Agrippina*; Dido, *Dido and Aeneas*; Rosina, *The Barber of Seville*; title role, *The Coronation of Poppea*.

RELATED PROFESSIONAL ACTIVITIES: Numerous concerts, recitals and broadcasts in the UK and abroad and five series for Welsh Television.

RECORDINGS INCLUDE: Bridge, *Christmas Rose* (PEAR); Handel, *Teseo* (ERAT) Mozart, *Die Zauberflöte* (EMI).

ADDRESS: c/o Lies Askonas Ltd, 186 Drury Lane, London WC2B 5RY.

JARMAN RICHARD
Administrator

POSITION: Managing Director, Scottish Opera.

PERSONAL DETAILS: b. 24 April 1949, Hertfordshire.

EDUCATION/TRAINING: Trinity College, Oxford, studied English.

CAREER: 1971–1976, publicity officer and Assistant to Administrative Director, Sadler's Wells Opera/English National Opera; 1977–1978, Advance Manager, Opera North; 1978–1984, Artistic Assistant to Festival Administrator, Edinburgh

International Festival; 1984–1990, General
Administrator, English National Ballet/
London Festival Ballet; since 1991,
Managing Director, Scottish Opera.
PUBLICATIONS INCLUDE: *History of the
London Coliseum, 1901–1981; History of
the Sadler's Wells Opera* (both English
National Opera).
ADDRESS: c/o Scottish Opera, 39 Elmbank
Crescent, Glasgow G2 4PT.

JEFFES PETER   Tenor

PERSONAL DETAILS: b. 2 August 1948,
London; m., four children.
EDUCATION/TRAINING: Royal College of
Music, with Mark Raphael; further studies
with Paolo Silveri in Rome.
PROFESSIONAL DEBUT: 1977, English
National Opera on tour, Caramello, *A
Night in Venice*.
MAJOR DEBUTS INCLUDE: 1979, Scottish
Opera, Vanya, *Katya Kabanova*; 1980,
Welsh National Opera, Tamino, *The
Magic Flute*; 1981: English Bach Festival,
Castor, *Castor et Pollux*; Avignon, Nicias,
Thaïs; 1982: Covent Garden, Nathanael,
Les Contes d'Hoffmann; Grand Théâtre,
Geneva, Elvino, *La Sonnambula*; Nantes
Opera, Narciso, *Il Turco in Italia*; 1983,
Aix-en-Provence Festival, Marzio,
Mitridate, Rè di Ponto; 1984, Opera North,
Romeo, *A Village Romeo and Juliet*;
1987, Peralada Festival, Mozart, *Mozart
and Salieri*; 1990, St Etienne, title role,
Faust; 1992, New Israeli Opera, Tel Aviv,
Prince, *L'Amour des Trois Oranges*.
OPERATIC WORLD PREMIERES INCLUDE:
1985, Paris Opera, Hans, *Docteur Faustus*
by Konrad Boehmer.
CAREER IN THE UK INCLUDES: Since 1977:
Buxton Festival, Arturo, *Lucia di
Lammermoor*; English Bach Festival:
Mercury, *Platée*; Acis, *Acis and Galatea*;
title role, *Idomeneo*; Glyndebourne
Touring Opera: Lysander, *A Midsummer
Night's Dream*; title role, *The Rake's
Progress*; Handel Opera Society: Damon,
Acis and Galatea; Hyllus, *Hercules*; Kent
Opera, Tamino, *The Magic Flute*; New

Sadler's Wells Opera, Paris, *La Belle
Hélène*; Opera North: Jack, *A Midsummer
Marriage*; Leukippos, *Daphne* (1987,
British stage première); Prince, *The Love
for Three Oranges*; Steersman, *The
Flying Dutchman*; Opera Northern
Ireland, Ferrando, *Così fan tutte*; Scottish
Opera, Apollo, *Orion*; Welsh National
Opera, Nero, *The Coronation of Poppea*.
RELATED PROFESSIONAL ACTIVITIES:
Regular concerts, recitals, broadcasts
and television appearances in the UK and
abroad.
RECORDINGS INCLUDE: Chabrier, *Le Roi
Malgré Lui*; Franck, *Les Béatitudes*;
Rameau, *Castor et Pollux* (all ERAT);
Rossini, opera arias (ARAB).
ADDRESS: c/o Music International, 13
Ardilaun Road, London N5 2QR.

JENKINS GRAEME
Conductor

POSITION: Music Director, Dallas Civic
Opera.
PERSONAL DETAILS: b. 31 December 1958,
London; m. 1986, Joanna Bridge, one
child.
EDUCATION/TRAINING: 1978–1981, Gonville
and Caius College, Cambridge; 1981–
1983, Royal College of Music, with David
Willcocks and Norman Del Mar.
PROFESSIONAL AND OPERATIC DEBUT:
1982, Kent Opera, *The Beggar's Opera*.
CAREER: 1982–1984, Assistant Conductor,
Kent Opera; 1985, assistant conductor to
Bernard Haitink, Glyndebourne Festival
Opera; 1986–1991, Music Director,
Glyndebourne Touring Opera; 1991–1993,
Artistic Director, Arundel Festival; since
1993, Music Director, Dallas Civic
Opera.
MAJOR OPERATIC DEBUTS INCLUDE: 1986,
Scottish Opera, *Il Trovatore*; 1987:
Glyndebourne Festival Opera, *Carmen*;
Grand Théâtre, Geneva, *Hänsel und
Gretel*; 1988, English National Opera,
Così fan tutte; 1989: Opera North, *Show
Boat*; Netherlands Opera, *Simon

Boccanegra; 1990: Australian Opera, Sydney, *La Bohème*; Canadian Opera Company, Toronto: *Carmen*, *La Rondine*; 1992, Australian Opera, Melbourne, *Der Rosenkavalier*.

OPERATIC WORLD PREMIERES INCLUDE: 1991, English National Opera, *Timon of Athens* by Stephen Oliver.

OPERA PERFORMANCES IN THE UK INCLUDE: Since 1982: English National Opera, *A Masked Ball*; Glyndebourne Festival and Touring Opera: *A Midsummer Night's Dream*, *Simon Boccanegra*, *Capriccio*, *L'Heure Espagnole/L'Enfant et les Sortilèges*, *Falstaff*, *Arabella*, *Death in Venice*, *Albert Herring*, *Fidelio*, *Idomeneo*, *Jenůfa*; Kent Opera: *The Seraglio*, *The Marriage of Figaro*; Musica nel Chiostro: *La Dori*, *Beauty and the Beast* (1985, British première); Scottish Opera: *The Marriage of Figaro*, *Così fan tutte*, *Oedipus Rex*.

VIDEOS INCLUDE: Britten, *Death in Venice* (Glyndebourne Touring Opera).

ADDRESS: c/o Harold Holt Ltd, 31 Sinclair Road, London W14 ONS.

JENKINS NEIL   Tenor

PERSONAL DETAILS: b. 9 April 1945, Sussex; m. 1969, Sandra Wilkes; m. 1982, Penny Maxwell; five children.

EDUCATION/TRAINING: 1963–1966, Choral Scholar, King's College, Cambridge; 1966–1968, Royal College of Music; further studies with John Carol Case, Gerald English, Helga Mott, Robert Bowman.

PROFESSIONAL DEBUT: 1968, Israel Festival, Nika Magadoff, *The Consul*.

EARLY CAREER INCLUDED: 1969–1974, Kent Opera: Don Ottavio, *Don Giovanni*; Ferrando, *Così fan tutte*; Young Prince, *The Patience of Socrates*.

MAJOR DEBUTS INCLUDE: 1974, Welsh National Opera, Count, *The Barber of Seville*; 1976, English Music Theatre at the Aldeburgh Festival, Johnny Inkslinger, *Paul Bunyan* by Benjamin Britten (world stage première); 1981,

Scottish Opera, Nadir, *The Pearl Fishers*; 1984, Opera North, Schoolmaster, *The Cunning Little Vixen*; 1985, Glyndebourne Festival Opera, Cat/Milkman, *Higglety Pigglety Pop!* (provisional complete version) and Moishe/Goat, *Where the Wild Things Are*; 1986, Grand Théâtre, Geneva, Young Servant, *Elektra*; title role, *Oberon*: 1986, Lyons Opera; 1987, Teatro La Fenice, Venice; 1989, Wexford Festival, Don Jerome, *The Duenna* (Prokofiev); 1992, English National Opera, Apollo, *Orfeo*.

OPERATIC WORLD PREMIERES INCLUDE: 1986, Royal Academy of Arts, Elderly Gentleman, *Exposition of a Picture* by Stephen Oliver.

CAREER IN THE UK INCLUDES: Since 1975: Alte Oper, Frankfurt at the Edinburgh International Festival, Lord Puff, *The English Cat* (1987, British stage première); English Music Theatre: Belfiore, *Sandrina's Secret*; Ramiro, *Cinderella*; Quint, *The Turn of the Screw*; Minstrel/Phoebus, *The Fairy Queen*; English National Opera, Eumete, *The Return of Ulysses*; Glyndebourne Touring Opera: Monostatos, *Die Zauberflöte*; Don Basilio, *Le Nozze di Figaro*; Kent Opera: Quint, *The Turn of the Screw*; Achilles, *King Priam*; title roles: *The Return of Ulysses*, *Robinson Crusoe*, *Count Ory*; New Sussex Opera, title role, *Peter Grimes*; Opera North, Podestà, *La Finta Giardiniera*; Scottish Opera, Goro, *Madama Butterfly*; Welsh National Opera, Herod, *Salome*.

RELATED PROFESSIONAL ACTIVITIES: Numerous television appearances; 1975–1976, Professor of Singing, Royal College of Music; since 1989, teacher at various summer schools; Vice-president, Huntingdon Philharmonic and Brighton Music Festival; President, Grange Choral Society, Hampshire.

RECORDINGS INCLUDE: Bernstein, *Candide* (DG); Lehár, *The Count of Luxembourg* (TER); Mozart, *Le Nozze di Figaro* (PHIL); Romberg, *The Student Prince* (TER); Rossini, *Elisabetta, Regina d'Inghilterra* (PHIL).

VIDEOS INCLUDE: Knussen, *Higglety Pigglety Pop!/Where the Wild Things Are* (Glyndebourne Festival Opera); Tippett, *King Priam* (Kent Opera).

AWARDS INCLUDE: 1967, Tankard Lieder Prize; 1972, National Federation of Music Societies' Award.

ADDRESS: c/o Music International, 13 Ardilaun Road, London N5 2QR.

JENKINS TERRY   Tenor

POSITION: Principal Tenor, English National Opera.

PERSONAL DETAILS: b. 9 October 1941, Hertfordshire; m. 1965, two children.

EDUCATION/TRAINING: 1951–1955, Westminster Abbey Choir School; 1961–1964, University College, London, studied engineering; 1964–1966, Guildhall School of Music and Drama, with Fabian Smith; 1967–1968, London Opera Centre.

PROFESSIONAL DEBUT: 1966, Opera for All, Nemorino, *The Elixir of Love*.

EARLY CAREER INCLUDED: 1969–1971, appearances with Basilica Opera, Dublin Grand Opera, Glyndebourne Touring Opera; roles included: Monsieur Triquet, *Eugene Onegin*; Malcolm, *Macbeth*; Schmidt, *Werther*; Scaramuccio, *Ariadne auf Naxos*.

MAJOR DEBUTS INCLUDE: 1971, Glyndebourne Festival Opera, Master of Ceremonies, *The Queen of Spades*; 1972, Sadler's Wells Opera, Duke, *Patience*; 1983, Seattle Opera, Loge, *Das Rheingold*; 1991, Aix-en-Provence Festival, Snout, *A Midsummer Night's Dream*.

OPERATIC WORLD PREMIERES INCLUDE: 1976, Covent Garden, Officer/Victim, *We Come to the River* by Hans Werner Henze; 1977, English National Opera, Brother Marcos, *The Royal Hunt of the Sun* by Iain Hamilton.

CAREER IN THE UK INCLUDES: Since 1972: Principal Tenor, Sadler's Wells Opera/English National Opera, more than 60 roles including: Eisenstein, *Die Fledermaus*; Borsa, *Rigoletto*; Gaston, *La Traviata*; Dr Caius, *Falstaff*; Pedrillo, *The Seraglio*; Don Basilio, *The Marriage of Figaro*; Spoletta, *Tosca*; Tchekalinsky, *The Queen of Spades*; Jack, *The Midsummer Marriage*; several roles, *Pacific Overtures*; First Guest, *The Stone Guest* (1987, British stage première); Schoolmaster, *The Cunning Little Vixen*; Abraham Kaplan, *Street Scene*; Schmidt, *Werther*; Devil, *Christmas Eve*; Goro, *Madam Butterfly*; Dancaïro, *Carmen*; title role, *Orpheus in the Underworld*; also Covent Garden at Sadler's Wells Theatre, Bob Cratchit, *A Christmas Carol* (1981, British première).

RELATED PROFESSIONAL ACTIVITIES: Numerous concerts and recitals in the UK and abroad.

RECORDINGS INCLUDE: Sondheim, *Pacific Overtures* (TER); Vaughan Williams, *Sir John in Love*; Verdi, *Rigoletto* (both EMI); Weill, *Street Scene* (TER).

VIDEOS INCLUDE: Sullivan, *Patience* (Walker); Verdi, *Rigoletto* (English National Opera).

PUBLICATIONS INCLUDE: Contributor, *The Musician's Handbook* (Rhinegold).

ADDRESS: c/o Music International, 13 Ardilaun Road, London N5 2QR.

JOHN NICHOLAS
Dramaturg and Writer

POSITION: Dramaturg, English National Opera.

PERSONAL DETAILS: b. 18 August 1952, London.

EDUCATION/TRAINING: University College, Oxford.

CAREER: Since 1976: Box Office Manager, Harrogate Festival; Company Secretary, New Opera Company; English National Opera: Editorial Assistant, Editorial Co-ordinator and since 1986, Dramaturg.

OTHER PROFESSIONAL ACTIVITIES INCLUDE: Since 1980, founder and Editor, *Opera Guides* (Calder); currently compiling *Blue Guide to Operatic Europe*.

PUBLICATIONS INCLUDE: 1984, *Oxford Topic Book on Opera* (Oxford University Press); Editor: 1992, *Power House: The English National Opera Experience* (Lime Tree); 1993, *Violetta and her Sisters* (Faber); many articles for programmes and academic publications on Mozart, Puccini and Verdi.

ADDRESS: c/o English National Opera, London Coliseum, St Martin's Lane, London WC2N 4ES.

JOLL PHILLIP   Bass-baritone

PERSONAL DETAILS: b. 14 March 1954, Merthyr Tydfil; m. Penelope Walker (mezzo-soprano), two children.

EDUCATION/TRAINING: 1975–1978, Royal Northern College of Music, with Frederic Cox; 1978–1979, National Opera Studio, with Hans Hotter and Reginald Goodall.

PROFESSIONAL DEBUT: 1978, English National Opera, Bonze, *Madam Butterfly*.

MAJOR DEBUTS INCLUDE: 1979: Opera North, Duphol, *La Traviata*; Welsh National Opera, Orest, *Elektra*; 1980, Scottish Opera at the Edinburgh International Festival, Forester, *The Cunning Little Vixen*; 1982: Covent Garden, Second Nazarene, *Salome*; English National Opera, title role, *The Flying Dutchman*; 1983, Frankfurt Opera, Amfortas, *Parsifal*; 1987, Metropolitan Opera, New York, Donner, *Das Rheingold*; 1989: Bregenz Festival, title role, *Der Fliegende Holländer*; Lyric Opera of Queensland, Jokanaan, *Salome*; 1990, Saarbrücken: Wotan, *Das Rheingold*; Gunther, *Götterdämmerung*; 1991, Klagenfurt, title role, *Jonny Spielt Auf*.

OPERATIC WORLD PREMIERES INCLUDE: 1980, Welsh National Opera, Patrice/ General Klein, *The Servants* by William Mathias.

CAREER IN THE UK INCLUDES: Since 1979: Cheltenham Festival, Head Reaper, *Ruth*; Covent Garden: Ottokar, *Der Freischütz*; Donner, *Das Rheingold*; Spirit Messenger, *Die Frau ohne Schatten*;

English National Opera, Donner, *The Rhinegold*; Opera North: Jokanaan, *Salome*; King Fisher, *The Midsummer Marriage*; Opera Northern Ireland, Kecal, *The Bartered Bride*; Welsh National Opera: Stage Hand, *The Makropoulos Case*; Kurwenal, *Tristan und Isolde*; Adolf, *The Jacobin* (1980, British stage première); Monterone, *Rigoletto*; Forester, *The Cunning Little Vixen*; Kostandis, *The Greek Passion* (1981, British première); Don Fernando, *Fidelio*; Amfortas, *Parsifal*; Wotan, *The Ring of the Nibelung*; Riccardo, *I Puritani*; Chorèbe, *The Trojans*; Jokanaan, *Salome*; Barak, *Die Frau ohne Schatten*; title roles: *Eugene Onegin*, *Wozzeck*, *Macbeth*.

RELATED PROFESSIONAL ACTIVITIES: Numerous concerts and oratorios in the UK.

RECORDINGS INCLUDE: Martinů, *The Greek Passion* (SUPR); Wagner: *Parsifal* (EMI), *Tristan und Isolde* (DECC).

ADDRESS: c/o Robert Gilder & Company, Enterprise House, 59–65 Upper Ground, London SE1 9PR.

JONAS PETER   Administrator

POSITION: Intendant (General Director), Bavarian State Opera, Munich.

PERSONAL DETAILS: b. 14 October 1946, London; m. 1989, Lucy Hull (concert and opera agent).

EDUCATION/TRAINING: 1965–1968, University of Sussex; 1968–1971, Royal Northern College of Music (Licentiate, Royal Academy of Music); 1971–1973, Royal College of Music (Certificate of Advanced Musical Study); 1973–1974, Eastman School of Music, University of Rochester, New York.

CAREER: Chicago Symphony Orchestra: 1974–1976, assistant to Music Director; 1976–1985, Artistic Administrator; 1977–1985, Director of Artistic Administration, Orchestral Association of Chicago (Chicago Symphony Orchestra, Chicago Civic Orchestra, Chicago Symphony

142

Chorus, Allied Arts Association and Orchestra Hall); 1985–1993, General Director, English National Opera; since 1993/1994 season, Intendant (General Director), Bavarian State Opera, Munich.

OTHER PROFESSIONAL ACTIVITIES INCLUDE: Since 1985, member, Board of Management, National Opera Studio; since 1989, Council member, Royal College of Music.

RELEVANT PUBLICATIONS INCLUDE: 1992, *Power House: The English National Opera Experience* (Lime Tree).

HONOURS INCLUDE: 1989, Fellow: Royal College of Music, Royal Society of Arts; 1993, Commander, Order of The British Empire (CBE).

ADDRESS: c/o Bavarian State Opera, Maximilanstrasse 11, D–8000, Munich, Germany.

JONES DELLA   Mezzo-soprano

PERSONAL DETAILS: b. Neath, South Wales; m. Paul Vigars, one child.

EDUCATION/TRAINING: 1964–1968, Royal College of Music; 1968–1970, Centre Lyrique, Geneva, with Maria Carpi; privately with Denis Dowling.

PROFESSIONAL DEBUT: 1970, Grand Théâtre, Geneva, Fyodor, *Boris Godunov.*

EARLY CAREER INCLUDED: 1970–1977, appearances with Grand Théâtre, Geneva, English Music Theatre, Handel Opera Society, Park Lane Opera, Phoenix Opera; roles included: Olga, *Eugene Onegin*; Clytemnestra, *Iphigénie en Aulide*; Bradamante, *Alcina*; Tamiris, *Il Rè Pastore*; Jenny, *The Threepenny Opera*; title role, *Cinderella.*

MAJOR DEBUTS INCLUDE: 1972, Grand Théâtre, Bordeaux, Suzuki, *Madama Butterfly*; 1973, Sadler's Wells Opera, Ninon, *The Devils of Loudun* (British première); 1977, Welsh National Opera, Rosina, *The Barber of Seville*; 1978, Scottish Opera, Hansel, *Hansel and Gretel*; 1980, Opera North, Isolier, *Count Ory*; 1983: Covent Garden, Cat, *L'Enfant et les Sortilèges*; Flanders Opera, Antwerp/Ghent, Adalgisa, *Norma*; Grand Théâtre, Geneva, Sesto, *Giulio Cesare*;

1986: Los Angeles Music Center Opera, Ruggiero, *Alcina*; Teatro La Fenice, Venice, Baba the Turk, *The Rake's Progress*; 1989, Paris Opera, Dido, *Dido and Aeneas*; 1990, Théâtre du Châtelet, Paris, Ruggiero, *Alcina.*

OPERATIC WORLD PREMIERES INCLUDE: 1976, English Music Theatre at the Aldeburgh Festival, Jenny, *Tom Jones* by Stephen Oliver; 1977, BBC Radio 3, Kristin, *Miss Julie* by William Alwyn; 1981, English National Opera, Dolly, *Anna Karenina* by Iain Hamilton.

CAREER IN THE UK INCLUDES: Since 1977: Covent Garden: Rosina, *Il Barbiere di Siviglia*; Marquise Melibea, *Il Viaggio a Reims*; English National Opera (1977–1982, Principal Mezzo-soprano): Suzuki, *Madam Butterfly*; Rosina, *The Barber of Seville*; La Ciesca, *Gianni Schicchi*; Isolier, *Count Ory*; Ninetta, *The Thieving Magpie*; Voice on the Record, *The Consul*; Cherubino, *The Marriage of Figaro*; Sesto, *Julius Caesar*; Valencienne, *The Merry Widow*; Ottavia, *The Coronation of Poppea*; Dorabella, *Così fan tutte*; Messenger, *Orfeo*; Preziosilla, *The Force of Destiny*; title roles: *Cinderella, Carmen, The Italian Girl in Algiers*; Opera London: Nero, *L'Incoronazione di Poppea*; Hermia, *A Midsummer Night's Dream*; Opera North: Herodias, *Salome*; Magdalene, *The Mastersingers of Nuremberg*; Jocasta, *Oedipus Rex*; Scottish Opera: Clori, *L'Egisto*; Preziosilla, *La Forza del Destino*; Donna Elvira, *Don Giovanni*; Welsh National Opera: Dido, *The Trojans*; Herodias, *Salome*; Brangäne, *Tristan und Isolde* (also 1993, at Covent Garden).

RELATED PROFESSIONAL ACTIVITIES: Regular concerts, recitals, broadcasts and festival appearances in the UK and abroad.

RECORDINGS INCLUDE: Boito, *Mefistofele* (DECC); Donizetti: *L'Assedio di Calais* and *Ugo, Conte di Parigi* (both OPRA); Handel: *Alcina, Giulio Cesare* (both EMI); Meyerbeer, *Il Crociato in Egitto* (OPRA); Monteverdi, *L'Incoronazione di Poppea* (VIRG); Mozart: *Don Giovanni, Le Nozze di*

143

Figaro (both L'OI); Purcell, *Dido and Aeneas* (PHIL); Rossini: *Guillaume Tell* (DECC), opera arias (CHAN).

VIDEOS INCLUDE: Handel, *Julius Caesar* (English National Opera); Sullivan, *HMS Pinafore* (Walker).

AWARDS INCLUDE: 1969, Kathleen Ferrier Memorial Scholarship.

ADDRESS: c/o Music International, 13 Ardilaun Road, London N5 2QR.

JONES, DAME GWYNETH
Soprano

PERSONAL DETAILS: b. 7 November 1936, Pontnewynydd, Wales; m. Till Haberfeld, one child.

EDUCATION/TRAINING: Royal College of Music, with Arnold Smith and Ruth Packer; Accademia Chigiana, Siena; International Opera Centre, Zurich; further studies with Maria Carpi in Geneva.

PROFESSIONAL DEBUT: Zurich Opera: 1962, as mezzo-soprano: Annina, *Der Rosenkavalier*; 1963, as soprano: Amelia, *Un Ballo in Maschera*.

MAJOR DEBUTS INCLUDE: Covent Garden: 1964: Leonore, *Fidelio*; Leonora, *Il Trovatore*; 1965, Sieglinde, *Die Walküre*; 1966: Dallas Civic Opera, Lady Macbeth, *Macbeth*; Deutsche Oper, Berlin, Leonora, *Il Trovatore*; Grand Théâtre, Geneva, Desdemona, *Otello*; Leonore, *Fidelio*: Bavarian State Opera, Munich and Vienna State Opera; 1967, La Scala, Milan, Leonora, *Il Trovatore*; 1970, Hamburg State Opera, title role, *Salome*; 1972, Metropolitan Opera, New York, Sieglinde, *Die Walküre*; 1975, Lyric Opera, Chicago, Leonore, *Fidelio*; 1978: Paris Opera, title role, *L'Incoronazione di Poppea*; Salzburg Festival, Marschallin, *Der Rosenkavalier*; Bayreuth Festival: 1966, Sieglinde, *Die Walküre*; 1968, *Eva, Die Meistersinger von Nürnberg*; 1969: Kundry, *Parsifal*; Senta, *Der Fliegende Holländer*; 1972, Elisabeth/Venus, *Tannhäuser*; 1974, Brünnhilde, *Götterdämmerung*; 1975 and 1976

(centenary production), Brünnhilde, *Der Ring des Nibelungen*.

CAREER INCLUDES: Principal Dramatic Soprano: since 1963, Covent Garden (debut 1963, Wellgunde, *Götterdämmerung*); since 1966: Deutsche Oper, Berlin and Vienna State Opera; since 1967, Bavarian State Opera, Munich; roles include: Leonore, *Fidelio*; Leonora, *Il Trovatore*; Senta, *Der Fliegende Holländer*; Sieglinde and Brünnhilde, *Der Ring des Nibelungen*; Desdemona, *Otello*; Lady Macbeth, *Macbeth*; Elisabeth de Valois, *Don Carlos*; Kundry, *Parsifal*; Isolde, *Tristan und Isolde*; Ortrud, *Lohengrin*; Marschallin, *Der Rosenkavalier*; Elisabeth, *Tannhäuser*; Dyer's Wife, *Die Frau ohne Schatten*; Elle, *La Voix Humaine*; Woman, *Erwartung*; title roles: *Aida, Tosca, Médée, La Fanciulla del West, Salome, Elektra, Turandot.*

RELATED PROFESSIONAL ACTIVITIES: Regular broadcasts and television appearances.

RECORDINGS INCLUDE: Beethoven, *Fidelio* (DG); R. Strauss, *Der Rosenkavalier* (CBS); Verdi, *Otello* (EMI); Wagner: *Der Fliegende Holländer, Lohengrin, Parsifal* (all DG), *Die Walküre, Siegfried, Götterdämmerung* (all PHIL), Wagner Recital (CHAN); Famous Operatic Scenes (DG).

VIDEOS INCLUDE: Wagner, *Der Ring des Nibelungen* (Bayreuth Festival).

AWARDS AND HONOURS INCLUDE: 1976, Commander, Order of the British Empire (CBE); 1977, Kammersängerin (Austria and Bavaria); 1986, Dame Commander, Order of the British Empire (DBE); 1987, Shakespeare Prize (Hamburg); 1988, Commander's Cross of the Order of Merit (Federal Republic of Germany); 1989, Honorary Member, Vienna State Opera; 1992, Commandeur de l'Ordre des Arts et des Lettres (France); Fellow, Royal College of Music; Honorary Doctorate of Music, University of Wales.

ADDRESS: P.O. Box 8037, Zurich, Switzerland.

JONES RICHARD   Director

PERSONAL DETAILS: b. 7 June 1953, London.

PREVIOUS OCCUPATION: Jazz musician.

EDUCATION/TRAINING: Universities of Hull and London.

CAREER: 1982–1983, trainee director, Scottish Opera; since 1983, freelance opera and theatre director in the UK and abroad.

MAJOR OPERATIC DEBUTS INCLUDE: 1984, Batignano Festival, *Apollo et Hyacinthus*; 1985, Opera Northern Ireland, *Don Pasquale*; 1986: Opera 80, *The Rake's Progress*; Wexford Festival, *Mignon*; 1987, Opera North, *Carmen*; 1988, Scottish Opera, *Così fan tutte*; 1991: Bregenz Festival/Netherlands Opera co-production, *Mazeppa*; Teatro São Carlos, Lisbon, *L'Amour des Trois Oranges*.

OPERATIC WORLD PREMIERES: 1987, Kent Opera, *A Night at the Chinese Opera* by Judith Weir; 1989, English National Opera, *The Plumber's Gift* by David Blake.

OPERA PRODUCTIONS IN THE UK

INCLUDE: Since 1984: English National Opera, *Die Fledermaus*; Kent Opera, *Count Ory*; Opera 80, *Rigoletto*; Royal College of Music, *Il Matrimonio Segreto*; Scottish Opera: *Das Rheingold*, *Die Walküre*; Scottish Opera Go Round, *Macbeth*; co-productions: Opera North/ English National Opera, *The Love for Three Oranges*; Royal Northern College of Music/Opera North, *Manon*.

ADDRESS: c/o Judy Daish Associates Ltd, 83 Eastbourne Mews, London W2 6LQ.

JOSEPHS WILFRED
Composer

PERSONAL DETAILS: b. 24 July 1927, Newcastle upon Tyne; m. 1956, Valerie Wisbey, two children.

PREVIOUS OCCUPATION: 1951–1964, dental surgeon.

EDUCATION/TRAINING: 1947, musical studies with Arthur Milner; 1951, qualified in dental surgery, University of Durham (at Newcastle); 1954–1956, Guildhall School of Music and Drama, with Alfred Nieman; 1958–1959, with Max Deutsch in Paris.

CAREER: Numerous compositions in all genres including 10 symphonies and extensive work for film and television; 1970, Composer in Residence, University of Wisconsin, Milwaukee; 1972, Visiting Professor in Composition and Composer in Residence, Roosevelt University, Chicago.

OPERATIC WORLD PREMIERES: 1983, Opera North, *Rebecca*, opera in three acts, libretto by Edward Marsh after Daphne du Maurier, conductor David Lloyd-Jones, director Colin Graham, designer Stefanos Lazaridis; 1990, Norrlands Opera, Umeå, *Pathelin*, opera in one act (completed in 1963), libretto by Edward Marsh; children's operas at the Harrogate International Festival: 1978, *Through the Looking Glass and What Alice Found There*, conductor Michael Grady, director Sheila Rix; 1990, *Alice in Wonderland*, conductor Wayne Marshall, director Lynne Schey (both librettos by the composer after Lewis Carroll).

RELATED PROFESSIONAL ACTIVITIES: Since 1988, Music Consultant, London International Film School; Council and executive member, Composers' Guild of Great Britain; Council member, Performing Right Society.

RECORDINGS INCLUDE: *Requiem*, 5th Symphony, Beethoven variations (all UNIC), Concerto for brass (TRAX), Fanfare for orchestra (CALA), Doubles for two pianos (NOVE), 14 Studies for piano (NOVE).

AWARDS AND HONOURS INCLUDE: 1956, Cobbett Prize, String Quartet No. 1; 1963, International Composing Competition (Milan), *Requiem*; 1969, Guardian/Arts Council Prize, *King of the Coast* (children's musical); 1978, Honorary Doctorate of Music, University of Newcastle.

ADDRESS: 15 Douglas Court, Quex Road, London NW6 4PT.

JOSHUA ROSEMARY
Soprano

PERSONAL DETAILS: b. 16 October 1964, Cardiff.
EDUCATION/TRAINING: 1983–1985, Welsh College of Music and Drama, with April Cantelo; 1988–1990, Royal College of Music Opera School, with Graziella Sciutti; masterclasses with Thomas Allen and Claudio Desderi.
PROFESSIONAL DEBUT: 1989, English National Opera, First Graduate, *Street Scene*.
MAJOR DEBUTS INCLUDE: 1989, Koblenz, Woodbird, *Siegfried*; 1990, Opera Northern Ireland, Pamina, *The Magic Flute*; 1991, Buxton Festival, Blonde, *The Seraglio*; 1992, Scottish Opera, Susanna, *The Marriage of Figaro*; English National Opera: 1992, title role, *Princess Ida*; 1993, Norina, *Don Pasquale*.
CAREER IN THE UK INCLUDES: 1987–1988, member, British Youth Opera, roles included: Zerlina, *Don Govanni*; Susanna, *The Marriage of Figaro*; since 1989: English National Opera: Barbarina, *The Marriage of Figaro*; Ingrid, *Fennimore and Gerda*; Flora, *The Turn of the Screw*; Yum-Yum, *The Mikado*; Adele, *Die Fledermaus*; Sophie, *Der Rosenkavalier*; Zerlina, *Don Giovanni*; Travelling Opera: Babarina and Susanna, *The Marriage of Figaro*; Despina, *Così fan tutte*.
RELATED PROFESSIONAL ACTIVITIES: Concerts and oratorios in the UK.
AWARDS INCLUDE: 1986, Countess of Munster Award; 1990, Tagore Gold Medal, Royal College of Music; 1992, Royal Philharmonic Society Debut Award.
ADDRESS: c/o Harrison/Parrott Ltd, 12 Penzance Place, London W11 4PA.

JUDD WILFRED
Director and Translator

POSITION: Artistic Director, Royal Opera Garden Venture, Covent Garden.

PERSONAL DETAILS: b. 1952, Hertford; m. Felicity Hayes-McCoy (actress and writer).
EDUCATION/TRAINING: 1970–1973, St Edmund Hall, Oxford, studied English; London Opera Centre.
PROFESSIONAL AND OPERATIC DEBUT: 1979, Northern Opera, *Faust*.
CAREER: 1979–1987, freelance opera director in the UK; 1988–1991, Director of Productions, Opera 80; Covent Garden: 1984–1991, staff director, staging revivals; since 1988, Artistic Director, Royal Opera Garden Venture.
OPERATIC WORLD PREMIERES INCLUDE: Royal Opera Garden Venture: 1989: *Soap Opera* by Kenneth Chalmers, *Survival Song* by Priti Paintal; 1990, *Etain* by Edward Maguire; 1991: *Beyond Men and Dreams* by Bennett Hogg, *Echoes* by John Hawkins; 1992 (co-production with Birmingham Repertory Company), *Biko* by Priti Paintal.
OPERA PRODUCTIONS INCLUDE: Since 1979: Guildhall School of Music and Drama: *The Magic Flute*, *Falstaff*, *L'Etoile*; Northern Opera: *Lohengrin*, *Don Carlos*; Opera East, *La Bohème*; Opera 80: *Cinderella* (also translation), *Eugene Onegin*, *The Merry Widow*; Wexford Festival, *Orlando*.
ADDRESS: c/o Royal Opera House, Covent Garden, London WC2E 9DD.

JUDGE IAN   Director

PERSONAL DETAILS: b. 21 July 1946, Lancashire.
PREVIOUS OCCUPATIONS: 1964–1969, commercial artist; 1971–1974, actor.
EDUCATION/TRAINING: 1969–1971, Guildhall School of Music and Drama.
PROFESSIONAL DEBUT: 1975, Royal Shakespeare Company, assistant director, *Henry V*.

OPERATIC DEBUT: 1985, English National Opera, *Faust*.

CAREER: Since 1975, freelance opera and theatre director; numerous productions with Royal Shakespeare Company and at leading British theatres including *The Wizard of Oz*, *The Comedy of Errors*, *A Little Night Music*, *Merrily We Roll Along*.

MAJOR OPERATIC DEBUTS INCLUDE: 1986, Opera North, *Faust*; 1988, Hesse State Opera, Wiesbaden, *Lohengrin*; 1989, Los Angeles Music Center Opera, *Tosca*; 1990, Victoria State Opera, Melbourne, *Faust*; 1991, Scottish Opera, *Falstaff*; 1992: Covent Garden, *Der Fliegende Holländer*; Cologne Opera, *Macbeth*; Victoria State Opera, Melbourne/Houston Grand Opera co-production, *The Tales of Hoffmann*.

OPERA PRODUCTIONS IN THE UK INCLUDE: Since 1986: Buxton Festival, *Ariodante*; English National Opera: *The Merry Widow*, *Cavalleria Rusticana/Pagliacci*; New Sadler's Wells Opera: *Ruddigore*, *Bitter Sweet*; Opera North: *Macbeth*, *Tosca*, *Acis and Galatea*, *Boris Godunov*, *Attila*; Scottish Opera: *Turandot*, *Norma*; Opera North/Royal Shakespeare Company co-production, *Show Boat*.

ADDRESS: c/o Simpson Fox Associates Ltd, 52 Shaftesbury Avenue, London W1V 7DE.

* * * *

KALE STUART   Tenor

PERSONAL DETAILS: b. 27 October 1944, Neath, South Wales; m. 1989, two children.

EDUCATION/TRAINING: 1963–1968, Guildhall School of Music and Drama; 1969–1970, London Opera Centre (both with Joyce Newton).

EARLY CAREER INCLUDED: 1971–1976, Principal Tenor, Welsh National Opera: Don Ottavio, *Don Giovanni*; Red Whiskers, *Billy Budd*; Goro, *Madam Butterfly*; Prince Paul, *The Grand Duchess of Gérolstein*; John Styx, *Orpheus in the Underworld*; title role, *Albert Herring*.

MAJOR DEBUTS INCLUDE: 1971, Welsh National Opera, Prince, *Lulu* (British première); 1972, Sadler's Wells Opera, Beppe, *Pagliacci*: 1983, Bucharest, title role, *Siegfried*; 1987, Captain, *Wozzeck*: Opéra du Rhin, Strasbourg and Nancy Opera; 1988: Covent Garden, Guillot, *Manon*; Adelaide Festival, Mephisto, *The Fiery Angel*; Royal Court Theatre, Drottningholm, Don Anchise, *La Finta Giardiniera*; 1989: Teatro Valli, Reggio Emilia, Captain, *Wozzeck*; Théâtre du Châtelet, Paris, Lucano, *L'Incoronazione di Poppea*; 1990: English National Opera Soviet Union tour (Bolshoi, Kirov and Kiev), Quint, *The Turn of the Screw*; Captain, *Wozzeck*: San Francisco Opera and Canadian Opera Company, Toronto,

OPERATIC WORLD PREMIERES INCLUDE: Sadler's Wells Opera/English National Opera: 1974, Lieutenant Barbaris, *The Story of Vasco* by Gordon Crosse; 1977: Don Miguel, *The Royal Hunt of the Sun* by Iain Hamilton; Bayon de Libertat/Sothonax/Leclerc, *Toussaint* by David Blake; 1981, Landau, *Anna Karenina* by Iain Hamilton; 1988, Queen Elizabeth Hall, Orsino, *Beatrice Cenci* by Berthold Goldschmidt.

CAREER IN THE UK INCLUDES: Since 1976: Covent Garden: Bob Boles, *Peter Grimes*; High Priest, *Idomeneo*; English National Opera (1976–1987, Principal Tenor): Menelaus, *La Belle Hélène*; Valzacchi, *Der Rosenkavalier*; Spalanzani, *The Tales of Hoffmann*; Gherardo, *Gianni Schicchi*; Nika Magadoff, *The Consul*; Don Basilio, *The Marriage of Figaro*; Composer/Harper/Miroslav, *The Adventures of Mr Brouček*; Don Ottavio, *Don Giovanni*; Prologue and Quint, *The*

Turn of the Screw; Simpleton, *Boris Godunov*; Shepherd, *Tristan and Isolde*; Hauk-Šendorf, *The Makropoulos Case*; Tchaplitsky, *The Queen of Spades*; Marquis/Rash Gambler, *The Gambler*; Dancing Master, *Ariadne auf Naxos*; Vogelgesang, *The Mastersingers of Nuremberg*; Spirit of the Masque, *Gloriana*; Hrazda, *Osud* (1984, British stage première); Alfred, *Die Fledermaus*; Beelzebub/Student from Cracow, *Doctor Faust* (1986, British stage première); Nanki-Poo, *The Mikado*; Spoletta, *Tosca*; Zinovy, *Lady Macbeth of Mtsensk* (1987, British stage première); Herod, *Salome*; Truffaldino, *The Love for Three Oranges*; title role, *Orpheus in the Underworld*; New Opera Company, Michel, *Julietta* (1978, British première).

RELATED PROFESSIONAL ACTIVITIES: Numerous concerts and broadcasts in the UK.

RECORDINGS INCLUDE: Janáček, *Osud*; Offenbach, *The Tales of Hoffmann*; Verdi, *Otello* (all EMI).

VIDEOS INCLUDE: Mozart: *La Finta Giardiniera*, *Idomeneo* (both Drottningholm).

ADDRESS: c/o Athole Still International Management Ltd, Greystoke House, 80–86 Westow Street, London SE19 3AF.

KATONA PETER MARIO
Administrator

POSITION: Artistic Administrator, The Royal Opera, Covent Garden.

PERSONAL DETAILS: b. 20 September 1945, Berlin, Germany.

EDUCATION/TRAINING: 1965–1968, Free University, Berlin, studied German literature, theatre history and journalism.

CAREER: Administrator and Assistant to Artistic Director (Christoph von Dohnányi): 1968–1977, Frankfurt Opera, 1977–1983, Hamburg State Opera; since 1983, Artistic Administrator, Covent Garden.

OTHER PROFESSIONAL ACTIVITIES INCLUDE: 1964–1976, contributor, numerous operatic journals.

ADDRESS: c/o Royal Opera House, Covent Garden, London WC2E 9DD.

KEENLYSIDE SIMON
Baritone

PERSONAL DETAILS: b. 3 August 1959, London.

EDUCATION/TRAINING: 1980–1983, St John's College, Cambridge, studied zoology; 1983–1987, Royal Northern College of Music, with John Cameron.

PROFESSIONAL DEBUT: 1987, Hamburg State Opera, Count, *Le Nozze di Figaro* (1987–1988, Principal Baritone).

MAJOR DEBUTS INCLUDE: 1989: Scottish Opera, Marcello, *La Bohème* (British debut); Covent Garden, Silvio, *Pagliacci*; 1990, English National Opera, Guglielmo, *Così fan tutte*; 1991, Welsh National Opera, Falke, *Die Fledermaus*; 1992, Grand Théâtre, Geneva, Papageno, *Die Zauberflöte*; 1993: Glyndebourne Touring Opera, title role, *Don Giovanni*; La Monnaie, Brussels, Mercury, *La Calisto*; San Fransisco Opera, Olivier, *Capriccio*.

CAREER IN THE UK INCLUDES: Since 1989: Covent Garden, Ping, *Turandot*; Scottish Opera: Danilo, *The Merry Widow*; Guglielmo, *Così fan tutte*; Schaunard, *La Bohème*; Pagageno, *The Magic Flute*; title roles: *The Barber of Seville*, *Billy Budd*; Welsh National Opera: Oreste, *Iphigénie en Tauride*; title role, *The Barber of Seville*.

RELATED PROFESSIONAL ACTIVITIES: Numerous concerts and lieder recitals in the UK and abroad.

RECORDINGS INCLUDE: Britten, *Peter Grimes* (EMI); Schubert, lieder (COLL).

AWARDS INCLUDE: 1986: Frederic Cox Award, Royal Northern College of Music; Richard Tauber Memorial Prize; 1987, Walther Gruner International Lieder Competition; 1990, Elly Ameling Lieder Prize.

ADDRESS: c/o Lies Askonas Ltd, 186 Drury Lane, London WC2B 5RY.

KELLY JANIS   Soprano

PERSONAL DETAILS: b. 30 December 1954, Glasgow; m. Ward Veazey (designer and artist).

EDUCATION/TRAINING: 1972–1976, Royal Scottish Academy of Music and Drama; 1976–1979, Royal College of Music; 1980–1983: with Elisabeth Grummer in Paris and Frankfurt; with Janice Chapman and David Keren in London; currently with Audrey Langford.

PROFESSIONAL DEBUT: 1979, Musical Theatre Company, London, Yum-Yum, *The Mikado*.

MAJOR DEBUTS INCLUDE: 1980, English National Opera, Damigella, *The Coronation of Poppea*; 1982, Anchorage Civic Opera, Despina, *Così fan tutte*; 1989, Scottish Opera, Rose Maurrant, *Street Scene*; 1991, Opera North, Serpetta, *La Finta Giardiniera*.

OPERATIC WORLD PREMIERES INCLUDE: 1981, English National Opera, Kitty, *Anna Karenina* by Iain Hamilton; 1986: English National Opera, First Woman/Fury, *The Mask of Orpheus* by Harrison Birtwistle; Opera Factory, several roles, *Hell's Angels* by Nigel Osborne.

CAREER IN THE UK INCLUDES: Since 1979: English National Opera: Flora, *The Turn of the Screw*; Barbarina, *The Marriage of Figaro*; Bekhetaten, *Akhnaten* (1985, British première); Dew Fairy and Gretel, *Hansel and Gretel*; Venus, *Orpheus in the Underworld*; Papagena, *The Magic Flute*; Rose Maurrant, *Street Scene*; Yum-Yum, *The Mikado*; Opera Factory: Flora, *The Knot Garden*; Despina, *Così fan tutte*; Zerlina, *Don Giovanni*; Susanna, *The Marriage of Figaro*; Fortune/Ottavia, *The Coronation of Poppea*; title role, *La Calisto*; Opera North, Magnolia, *Show Boat*; Park Lane Opera at the Camden Festival: Serpetta, *La Finta Giardiniera*; Ninetta, *La Finta Semplice*; Scottish Opera, Polly, *The Beggar's Opera*.

RELATED PROFESSIONAL ACTIVITIES: Numerous concerts, recitals, broadcasts and television appearances in the UK and abroad; operatic excerpts for *Inspector Morse* television series.

RECORDINGS INCLUDE: Weill, *Street Scene* (TER).

VIDEOS INCLUDE: Sullivan, *The Pirates of Penzance* (Walker).

ADDRESS: c/o Ron Gonsalves Personal Artists & Concert Management, 10 Dagnan Road, London SW12 9LQ.

KENNEDY MICHAEL
Critic and Writer

POSITION: Associate Northern Editor and Staff Music Critic, *Daily Telegraph*; Music Critic, *Sunday Telegraph*.

PERSONAL DETAILS: b. 19 February 1926, Manchester; m. 1947, Eslyn Durdle.

EDUCATION/TRAINING: Berkhamsted School.

CAREER: *Daily Telegraph*: 1941–1960, editorial staff member; since 1950, staff music critic (1987–1989, Joint Chief Critic); 1960–1986, Northern Editor; since 1986, Associate Northern Editor; since 1989, Music Critic, *Sunday Telegraph*.

PUBLICATIONS INCLUDE: 1964, *The Works of Ralph Vaughan Williams*; 1968, *Portrait of Edward Elgar*; 1989, *Portrait of William Walton* (all Oxford University Press); 1974, *Gustav Mahler*; 1976, *Richard Strauss*; 1981, *Benjamin Britten* (all Dent); 1987, *Adrian Boult* (Hamish Hamilton); Editor: 1980, *The Concise Oxford Dictionary of Music*; 1985, *The Oxford Dictionary of Music* (both Oxford University Press); contributor: *Penguin Opera Guide*, *The New Grove Dictionary of Opera* (Macmillan).

HONOURS INCLUDE: 1971, Honorary Member, Royal Manchester College of Music; 1975, Honorary Master of Arts, University of Manchester; 1981: Officer, Order of the British Empire (OBE); Fellow, Royal Northern College of Music.

ADDRESS: c/o *Sunday Telegraph*, 181 Marsh Wall, London E14 9SR.

KENNEDY RODERICK
Bass-baritone

PERSONAL DETAILS: b. 7 May 1951,
Birmingham; m. 1983, Jane Randall
(stage manager), four children.
PREVIOUS OCCUPATION: 1969–1974,
advertising executive.
EDUCATION/TRAINING: Guildhall School of
Music and Drama; privately with Otakar
Kraus.
PROFESSIONAL DEBUT: 1976, Covent
Garden, Spinelloccio, *Gianni Schicchi*.
MAJOR DEBUTS INCLUDE: 1978: English
National Opera, Monk, *Don Carlos*; Welsh
National Opera, Theseus, *A Midsummer
Night's Dream*; 1979, Wexford Festival,
Grand Pontiff, *La Vestale*; 1980:
Aldeburgh Festival, Bottom, *A
Midsummer Night's Dream*; Scottish
Opera at the Edinburgh Festival, Doctor,
Wozzeck; 1981: Glyndebourne Festival
Opera, Don Fernando, *Fidelio*; San
Francisco Opera, Doctor, *Wozzeck*; 1983,
Gran Teatre del Liceu, Barcelona,
Phanuel, *Hérodiade*; 1984, Deutsche
Oper, Berlin, Arkel, *Pelléas et Mélisande*;
1985: Lyric Opera, Chicago, Capellio, *I
Capuleti e i Montecchi*; Vienna Festival,
Tolomeo, *Giulio Cesare*; 1986: Théâtre du
Châtelet, Paris, Alidoro, *La Cenerentola*;
Zurich Opera, Tolomeo, *Giulio Cesare*;
1987: Grand Théâtre, Geneva, Publio, *La
Clemenza di Tito*; Netherlands Opera,
Don Basilio, *Il Barbiere di Siviglia*; 1988,
Maggio Musicale, Florence, Swallow,
Peter Grimes; 1990: Rome Opera, Tutor,
Le Comte Ory; Teatro La Fenice, Venice,
Rodrigo, *Lulu*; 1991, Aix-en-Provence
Festival, Bottom, *A Midsummer Night's
Dream*.
OPERATIC WORLD PREMIERES INCLUDE:
1977, Covent Garden, Lieutenant, *The Ice
Break* by Michael Tippett.
CAREER IN THE UK INCLUDES: Since 1976:
Covent Garden (member, 1977–1980): Wig
Maker, *Ariadne auf Naxos*; Mr Ratcliffe,
Billy Budd; Cuno, *Der Freischütz*;
Nobleman, *Lohengrin*; Larkens and
Ashby, *La Fanciulla del West*; Astolfo,
Lucrezia Borgia; Angelotti, *Tosca* (also

1979, Far East tour); Zuniga, *Carmen*;
Timur, *Turandot* (also 1986, Far East
tour); Fasolt, *Das Rheingold*; Créon,
Médée; Melcthal, *Guillaume Tell*; English
Bach Festival, Pluto, *Hippolyte et Aricie*;
English National Opera: Podestà, *The
Thieving Magpie*; Tutor, *Count Ory*;
Fasolt, *The Rhinegold*; Angelotti, *Tosca*;
Glyndebourne Festival Opera: Rocco,
Fidelio; Theseus, *A Midsummer Night's
Dream*; Seneca, *L'Incoronazione di
Poppea*; Alidoro, *La Cenerentola*; Voice
of Neptune, *Idomeneo*; Scottish Opera:
Night, *L'Egisto*; Prince Gremin, *Eugene
Onegin*; Sparafucile, *Rigoletto*; Colline,
La Bohème; Pogner, *Die Meistersinger
von Nürnberg*; Collatinus, *The Rape of
Lucretia*; Prologue/Acrobat, *Lulu*.
RELATED PROFESSIONAL ACTIVITIES:
Television appearances in the UK and
abroad; 1987, designed new logo for
Scottish Opera (25th anniversary) and the
programme used throughout the 1987–
1988 season.
RECORDINGS INCLUDE: Bantock, *The
Immortal Hour* (HYPE); Handel, *The
Messiah* (TELD); Verdi: *La Forza del
Destino* (BBC), *La Traviata* (EMI); Weill, *Die
Sieben Todsünden* (CBS).
VIDEOS INCLUDE: Monteverdi,
L'Incoronazione di Poppea; Mozart,
Idomeneo; Rossini, *La Cenerentola* (all
Glyndebourne Festival Opera); Sullivan,
Patience (Walker).
ADDRESS: Not available.

KENNY YVONNE   Soprano

POSITION: Member, The Royal Opera,
Covent Garden.
PERSONAL DETAILS: b. 25 November 1950,
Sydney, Australia.
EDUCATION/TRAINING: Sydney
Conservatorium of Music; Scuola della
Scala, Milan; further studies with Erich
Vietheer and David Harper in London.
PROFESSIONAL DEBUT: 1975, concert at the
Queen Elizabeth Hall, title role,
Rosmonda d'Inghilterra.
EARLY CAREER INCLUDED: 1975–1976,

appearances at Camden, Edinburgh International and Spitalfields Festivals; roles included: Amy, *Il Castello di Kenilworth*; Frasquita and Micaëla, *Carmen*; Giunia, *Lucio Silla*.
MAJOR DEBUTS INCLUDE: 1976, Scottish Opera, Pamina, *The Magic Flute*; 1977: English National Opera, Sophie, *Der Rosenkavalier*; Victoria State Opera, Melbourne, Mélisande, *Pelléas et Mélisande*; 1979, Covent Garden Far East tour (Korea), Pamina, *Die Zauberflöte*; 1980: Glyndebourne Touring Opera, Constanze, *Die Entführung aus dem Serail*; Australian Opera, Sydney, Leïla, *Les Pêcheurs de Perles*; Hamburg State Opera, Oscar, *Un Ballo in Maschera*; 1981: Australian Opera, Sydney: Susanna, *Le Nozze di Figaro*; Gilda, *Rigoletto*; Théâtre du Châtelet, Paris, Leïla, *Les Pêcheurs de Perles*; 1983: Glyndebourne Festival Opera, Ilia, *Idomeneo*; Opéra Comique, Paris, Micaëla, *Carmen*; Aspasia, *Mitridate, Rè di Ponto*: Schwetzingen Festival, Aix-en-Provence Festival; 1984, Salzburg Festival, Ilia, *Idomeneo*; 1985, Zurich Opera, title role, *Manon*; 1986: La Scala, Milan, Pamina, *Die Zauberflöte*; Mozart Festival, Paris, Donna Elvira, *Don Giovanni*; 1987, Australian Opera, Sydney, title role, *Alcina*; 1989, Teatro La Fenice, Venice, title role, *Semele*; 1990, English National Opera Soviet Union tour (Bolshoi and Kiev), Romilda, *Xerxes*.
OPERATIC WORLD PREMIERES INCLUDE: 1976, Covent Garden (debut), Young Lady 2/Young Girl 2/Victim 1, *We Come to the River* by Hans Werner Henze; 1984, Lyons Opera, title role, *Medea* by Gavin Bryars.
CAREER IN THE UK INCLUDES: Since 1976: member, Covent Garden: Barena, *Jenůfa*; High Priestess, *Aida*; Barbarina, *Le Nozze di Figaro*; Echo, *Ariadne auf Naxos*; Ilia, *Idomeneo*; Woodbird, *Siegfried*; Oscar, *Un Ballo in Maschera*; Giannetta, *L'Elisir d'Amore*; Pamina, *Die Zauberflöte*; Servilia, *La Clemenza di Tito*; Ännchen, *Der Frieschütz*; Sophie, *Der Rosenkavalier*; Micaëla, *Carmen*; Sophie, *Werther*; Helena, *A Midsummer Night's Dream*; Susanna, *Le Nozze di Figaro*; Marzelline, *Fidelio*; Adina, *L'Elisir d'Amore*; Liù, *Turandot*; Aspasia, *Mitridate, Rè di Ponto*; title roles: *Semele*, *Alcina*; also: English National Opera, Romilda, *Xerxes*; Glyndebourne Festival Opera, Alice Ford, *Falstaff*; Donna Anna, *Don Giovanni*; Scottish Opera, Constanze, *The Seraglio*.
RELATED PROFESSIONAL ACTIVITIES: Regular concerts, recitals, broadcasts and television appearances in the UK and abroad.
RECORDINGS INCLUDE: Bizet, *Carmen* (DG); Britten, Folksongs (ETCE); Donizetti: *Emilia di Liverpool* and *Ugo, Conte di Parigi* (both OPRA); Elgar, *The Kingdom* (RCA); Meyerbeer, *Il Crociato in Egitto* (OPRA); Mozart: *Die Entführung aus dem Serail*, *Lucio Silla* (both TELD), *Le Nozze di Figaro* (DECC), *Die Zauberflöte* (PHIL); Live at the Wigmore Hall (ETCE).
VIDEOS INCLUDE: Mozart: *Idomeneo* (Glyndebourne Festival Opera); *Mitridate, Rè di Ponto* (film by Jean-Pierre Ponnelle); Mozart at Buckingham Palace (EMI).
AWARDS AND HONOURS INCLUDE: 1975, Kathleen Ferrier Memorial Scholarship; 1989, Member, Order of Australia (AM).
ADDRESS: c/o Lies Askonas Ltd, 186 Drury Lane, London WC2B 5RY.

KENYON NICHOLAS
Administrator, Broadcaster, Critic and Writer

POSITION: Controller, BBC Radio 3.
PERSONAL DETAILS: b. 23 February 1951, Cheshire; m. 1976, Marie-Ghislaine Latham-Koenig, four children.
EDUCATION/TRAINING: Balliol College, Oxford, studied modern history.
CAREER: 1973–1976, English Bach Festival; 1976–1979, BBC Music Division; music critic: 1979–1982, *The New Yorker*; 1982–1985, *The Times*; 1985–1992, *The Observer* (1987–1992, Chief Music Critic); 1982–1987, Music Editor, *The Listener*; 1983–1992, Editor, *Early Music*; 1991,

151

Artistic Consultant, Mozart Now Festival, South Bank Centre; since 1992, Controller, BBC Radio 3; regular radio broadcaster and contributor, numerous journals.

PUBLICATIONS INCLUDE: 1981, *The BBC Symphony Orchestra, The First Fifty Years, 1930–1980* (BBC); 1987, *Simon Rattle: The Making of a Conductor* (Faber); 1988, Editor, *Authenticity and Early Music* (Oxford University Press).

ADDRESS: c/o BBC Radio, Broadcasting House, Portland Place, London W1A 1AA.

KERR VIRGINIA   Soprano

PERSONAL DETAILS: b. Dublin.

EDUCATION/TRAINING: 1974–1976, Royal Irish Academy of Music, Dublin; 1976–1982, Guildhall School of Music and Drama, with Rudolf Piernay.

PROFESSIONAL DEBUT: 1982, Birmingham Music Theatre, Fiordiligi, *Così fan tutte.*

EARLY CAREER INCLUDED: 1983–1988: Birmingham Music Theatre, Governess, *The Turn of the Screw*; Dublin Grand Opera: Micaëla, *Carmen*; Governess, *The Turn of the Screw*; Musetta, *La Bohème*; Liù, *Turandot*; Leïla, *Les Pêcheurs de Perles*; Donna Elvira, *Don Giovanni.*

MAJOR DEBUTS INCLUDE: 1988, Batignano Festival, Aspasia, *Temistocle*; 1990: Glyndebourne Festival Opera, Glasha, *Katya Kabanova*; Scottish Opera, title role, *Salome*; 1992: Opera North, Grete, *Der Ferne Klang* (British première); Manoel Theatre, Malta, Countess, *Le Nozze di Figaro.*

OPERATIC WORLD PREMIERES INCLUDE: 1990, Scottish Opera, Bride/Wife/Mother, *The Vanishing Bridegroom* by Judith Weir.

CAREER IN THE UK INCLUDES: Since 1988: Scottish Opera: Donna Elvira, *Don Giovanni*; Helmwige, *Die Walküre*; Scottish Opera Go Round, title role, *Jenůfa.*

RELATED PROFESSIONAL ACTIVITIES: Regular concerts, recitals and broadcasts in the UK and abroad.

ADDRESS: c/o Robert Gilder & Company, Enterprise House, 59–65 Upper Ground, London SE1 9PQ.

KIMM FIONA   Mezzo-soprano

PERSONAL DETAILS: b. 24 May 1952, Ipswich.

EDUCATION/TRAINING: 1970–1974, Royal College of Music, with Meriel St Clair; privately: 1974–1978, with Lyndon van der Pump; since 1978, with Peter Harrison.

PROFESSIONAL DEBUT: 1978, Glyndebourne Touring Opera, Third Lady, *Die Zauberflöte.*

MAJOR DEBUTS INCLUDE: 1980: English National Opera, Fyodor, *Boris Godunov*; Glyndebourne Festival Opera, Third Lady, *Die Zauberflöte*; Opera North, Hansel, *Hansel and Gretel*; 1981, Berlioz Festival, Lyons, Ursula, *Béatrice et Bénédict*; 1983, Covent Garden, Fyodor, *Boris Godunov*; 1984: Scottish Opera, Clori, *L'Egisto*; English National Opera USA tour (including Metropolitan Opera, New York), Sonya, *War and Peace*; Grand Théâtre, Geneva, Smeraldina, *L'Amour des Trois Oranges.*

OPERATIC WORLD PREMIERES INCLUDE: 1988, Munich Biennale, Wife/Doreen/Waitress/Sphinx, *Greek* by Mark-Anthony Turnage.

CAREER IN THE UK INCLUDES: Since 1979: Covent Garden, Page, *Salome*; Edinburgh International Festival, Wife/Doreen/Waitress/Sphinx, *Greek* (1988, British première); English National Opera: Page, *Salome*; Prince Orlofsky, *Die Fledermaus*; Sonya, *War and Peace*; Kitchen Boy, *Rusalka*; Diana, *Orpheus in the Underworld*; Lola, *Cavalleria Rusticana*; Siebel, *Faust*; Wife/Doreen/Waitress/Sphinx, *Greek*; Smeraldina, *The Love for Three Oranges*; Glyndebourne Festival and Touring Opera: Dryad, *Ariadne auf Naxos*; Smeraldina, *L'Amour des Trois Oranges*; Mother/Cat, *L'Enfant et les Sortilèges*; Sesto, *La Clemenza di Tito*; Celia, *La Fedeltà Premiata*; Baba the Turk, *The Rake's Progress*; New Opera

Company, Countess, *Commedia* (1982, British première); Opera North: Mercédès, *Carmen*; Rosalind, *The Mines of Sulphur*; Julie Le Verne, *Show Boat*; Woman/Spanish Girl/Waitress, *Der Ferne Klang* (1992, British première); Scottish Opera: Olga, *Eugene Onegin*; Flosshilde, *Das Rheingold*; Olga Olsen, *Street Scene*; Meg Page, *Falstaff*.

RELATED PROFESSIONAL ACTIVITIES: Numerous concerts and recitals in the UK and abroad including several world premières of works by Mark-Anthony Turnage and other contemporary composers.

RECORDINGS INCLUDE: Berlioz, *L'Enfance du Christ* (ASV); Weill, *Street Scene* (DECC).

VIDEOS INCLUDE: Dvořák, *Rusalka* (English National Opera); Mozart, *Die Zauberflöte*; Prokofiev, *L'Amour des Trois Oranges* (both Glyndebourne Festival Opera); Sullivan, *The Gondoliers* (Walker).

AWARDS INCLUDE: 1978, John Christie Award.

ADDRESS: c/o Ron Gonsalves Personal Artists & Concert Management, 10 Dagnan Road, London SW12 9LQ.

KING MARY   Mezzo-soprano

PERSONAL DETAILS: 16 June 1952, Tunbridge Wells.

PREVIOUS OCCUPATION: 1974–1976, teacher of humanities.

EDUCATION/TRAINING: 1970–1973, University of Birmingham; 1973–1974, University of Oxford; 1976–1978, Guildhall School of Music and Drama.

PROFESSIONAL DEBUT: 1980, Glyndebourne Touring Opera, Baba the Turk, *The Rake's Progress*.

MAJOR DEBUTS INCLUDE: 1985, Minnesota Opera, Mama/Tzippie, *Where the Wild Things Are*; 1987, Opera Factory, Blind Mary, *The Martyrdom of St Magnus*; 1990, Covent Garden, Cockerel, *The Cunning Little Vixen*.

OPERATIC WORLD PREMIERES INCLUDE: 1984, Glyndebourne Touring Opera, Mama/Tzippie, *Where the Wild Things*

Are by Oliver Knussen; 1985, Arundel Festival, Morgan le Fay, *Lancelot* by Iain Hamilton; 1987, Pompidou Centre, Paris, Linda Lampton, *Valis* by Tod Machover; 1988, Almeida Festival, Muse, *The Undivine Comedy* by Michael Finnissy; 1992, Womens Playhouse Trust, Maid, *Blood Wedding* by Nicola LeFanu.

CAREER IN THE UK INCLUDES: Since 1981: Almeida Festival, Agni, *Kopernikus* (1985, British première); Glyndebourne Touring Opera, Marcellina, *Le Nozze di Figaro*; Kent Opera, Mrs Peachum, *The Beggar's Opera*; Music Theatre Wales, Blind Mary, *The Martyrdom of St Magnus*; New Sussex Opera, Baba the Turk, *The Rake's Progress*.

RELATED PROFESSIONAL ACTIVITIES: Regular concerts, recitals and broadcasts in the UK and abroad; teacher, Guildhall School of Music and Drama.

RECORDINGS INCLUDE: Janáček, *The Cunning Little Vixen* (EMI); Knussen, *Where the Wild Things Are* (UNIC); Machover, *Valis* (BRID).

VIDEOS INCLUDE: Knussen, *Where the Wild Things Are* (Glyndebourne Festival Opera).

AWARDS INCLUDE: 1976, Countess of Munster Award; 1978, Glyndebourne Touring Opera Singers' Award.

ADDRESS: c/o Gillian Clench International Artists' Management, 1 Mount Pleasant Cottages, Rhiwbina Hill, Cardiff CF4 6UP.

KITCHEN LINDA   Soprano

PERSONAL DETAILS: b. 20 March 1960, Lancashire; m. 1990, Aidan Lang (director).

EDUCATION/TRAINING: 1978–1983, Royal Northern College of Music, with Nicholas Powell; 1983–1984, National Opera Studio; privately: 1977–1978, with Barbara Robotham; 1983–1989, with David Keren; since 1990, with Audrey Langford.

PROFESSIONAL DEBUT: 1981, Buxton Festival, Juliet, *Let's Make an Opera*.

MAJOR DEBUTS INCLUDE: 1983: Covent Garden, Noble Orphan, *Der Rosen-*

kavalier; Glyndebourne Festival Opera,
Blonde, *Die Entführung aus dem Serail*;
1985, English National Opera, Sotopenre,
Akhnaten (British première); 1986, Opera
North, Zerlina, *Don Giovanni*; 1991: Welsh
National Opera, Adele, *Die Fledermaus*;
Grand Théâtre, Geneva, Jemmy,
Guillaume Tell.
OPERATIC WORLD PREMIERES INCLUDE:
1985, Arundel Festival, Elaine, *Lancelot*
by Iain Hamilton.
CAREER IN THE UK INCLUDES: Since 1983:
Covent Garden: Barbarina, *Le Nozze di
Figaro*; Maid, *The Birthday of the Infanta*
(1985, British première); Jano, *Jenůfa*;
Iris, *Semele*; Echo, *Ariadne auf Naxos*;
Sophie, *Werther*; Shepherd, *Tannhäuser*;
Giannetta, *L'Elisir d'Amore*; Flower
Maiden, *Parsifal*; Flora, *The Knot
Garden*; Oscar, *Un Ballo in Maschera*;
Xenia, *Boris Godunov*; Javotte, *Manon*;
Nurse, *Un Re in Ascolto* (1989, British
première); Jemmy, *Guillaume Tell*;
Papagena, *Die Zauberflöte*; Countess
Ceprano, *Rigoletto*; Strawberry Seller,
Death in Venice; Glyndebourne Festival
Opera, Amor, *L'Incoronazione di Poppea*;
Opera Factory, Satirino/Destiny, *La
Calisto*; Opera North: Cherubino and
Susanna, *Le Nozze di Figaro*; Serpetta,
La Finta Giardiniera; Niece, *Peter
Grimes*; Magnolia, *Show Boat*; Polly, *The
Threepenny Opera*; Eurydice, *Orpheus in
the Underworld.*
RELATED PROFESSIONAL ACTIVITIES:
Regular concerts, recitals and broadcasts
in the UK.
RECORDINGS INCLUDE: Haydn and
Schubert Masses (MERI); Meyerbeer, *Il
Crociato in Egitto* (OPRA); Vaughan
Williams, *Serenade to Music* (HYPE).
VIDEOS INCLUDE: Monteverdi,
L'Incoronazione di Poppea
(Glyndebourne Festival Opera).
AWARDS INCLUDE: 1986, Heinz Bursary
(Covent Garden).
ADDRESS: c/o Lies Askonas Ltd, 186 Drury
Lane, London WC2B 5RY.

KITCHINER JOHN   Baritone

PERSONAL DETAILS: b. 2 December 1933,
Bedford.
EDUCATION/TRAINING: London Opera
Centre, with Joan Cross; privately with
Otakar Kraus and Ellis Keeler.
MAJOR DEBUTS INCLUDE: 1965:
Glyndebourne Festival Opera, Count, *Le
Nozze di Figaro*; Sadler's Wells Opera,
Zuniga, *Carmen*; 1967: Scottish Opera,
Guglielmo, *Così fan tutte*; Welsh National
Opera, Count, *The Marriage of Figaro*;
1970, Wexford Festival, Mr Gedge, *Albert
Herring.*
OPERATIC WORLD PREMIERES INCLUDE:
1964: English Opera Group at the
Aldeburgh Festival, Pilgrim, *Curlew River*
by Benjamin Britten; Jeanetta Cochrane
Theatre, London, Denys Feather, *One
Man Show* by Nicholas Maw; English
National Opera: 1977: Salinas, *The Royal
Hunt of the Sun* by Iain Hamilton;
Mirbeck/Saint-Remy/Spanish General/
French Officer, *Toussaint* by David Blake;
1986, Troupe of Ceremony/Judge, *The
Mask of Orpheus* by Harrison Birtwistle.
CAREER IN THE UK INCLUDES: Since 1965:
Handel Opera Society: Fenice, *Deidamia*;
Ariodate, *Serse*; Sadler's Wells Opera/
English National Opera: Cuffe, *Gloriana*;
Falke, *Die Fledermaus*; Yeletsky, *The
Queen of Spades*; Agamemnon, *La Belle
Hélène*; Count di Luna, *Il Trovatore*; First
Officer, *From the House of the Dead*;
Andrei, *War and Peace*; Faninal, *Der
Rosenkavalier*; Barbaruccio, *A Night in
Venice*; Schlemil, *The Tales of Hoffmann*;
Mars, *Orpheus in the Underworld*; Mr
Kofner, *The Consul*; Giorgio, *The
Thieving Magpie*; Father, *The Nose*;
Escamillo, *Carmen*; Major Murgatroyd,
Patience; Curio, *Julius Caesar*; Cascada
and Count Danilo, *The Merry Widow*;
Dominik, *Arabella*; Mitiukha/Krushchov,
Boris Godunov; Sharpless, *Madam
Butterfly*; Count Lerma, *Don Carlos*;
Second Guest, *The Stone Guest*;
Steward, *Lady Macbeth of Mtsensk* (both
1987, British stage premières); Lord Abe,
Pacific Overtures; d'Obigny, *La Traviata*;

Pedug, *The Making of the Representative for Planet 8* (1988, British première); Marcello, *La Bohème*; George Jones, *Street Scene*; Wig Maker, *Ariadne auf Naxos*; Sciarrone, *Tosca*; Brandy Distiller, *Fennimore and Gerda*; title role, *The Barber of Seville*; Welsh National Opera: Zuniga and Escamillo, *Carmen*; d'Obigny, *La Traviata*; Don Alfonso, *Così fan tutte*; Bartolo, *The Barber of Seville*; title role, *Macbeth*.

RELATED PROFESSIONAL ACTIVITIES: Concerts and broadcasts in the UK.

RECORDINGS INCLUDE: Sondheim, *Pacific Overtures* (TER); Verdi, *La Traviata* (EMI).

VIDEOS INCLUDE: Handel, *Julius Caesar* (English National Opera).

ADDRESS: Not available.

KNAPP PETER
Baritone, Director and Translator

POSITION: Artistic Director, Travelling Opera.

PERSONAL DETAILS: b. 4 August 1947, Buckinghamshire; m. 1984, Maryanne Tennyson, two children.

EDUCATION/TRAINING: St John's College, Cambridge; Graduate School of Fine Arts, Florence.

PROFESSIONAL DEBUT: 1973, Glyndebourne Touring Opera, Count, *Le Nozze di Figaro*.

CAREER INCLUDES: Since 1973, appearances in the UK and abroad include: English National Opera: Count, *The Marriage of Figaro*; title role, *Don Giovanni*; Glyndebourne Festival Opera, Foreman, *Jenůfa*; Kent Opera: Germont, *La Traviata*; Don Pizarro, *Fidelio*; title roles: *Don Giovanni, Eugene Onegin, Orfeo*; New Opera Company, title role, *King Roger* (1975, British stage première); Opera North, Mr Redburn, *Billy Budd*; Opera Northern Ireland, Ford, *Falstaff*; Scottish Opera: Mr Redburn, *Billy Budd*; Baron Zeta, *The Merry Widow*; Travelling Opera: Alfonso, *Così fan tutte*; Pluto, *Orpheus in the Underworld*; title roles: *The Barber of Seville, The Marriage of Figaro, Rigoletto*; Batignano Festival, Aeneas, *Dido and Aeneas*; Florence, title role, *Orfeo*; France: Tarquinius, *The Rape of Lucretia*; Count, *The Marriage of Figaro*; Frankfurt Opera, Count di Luna, *Il Trovatore*; Hong Kong, title role, *Rigoletto*; Venice, Claudio, *Agrippina*; Zurich Opera, Marcello, *La Bohème*; since 1978, founder and Artistic Director, Travelling Opera.

OPERATIC WORLD PREMIÈRES INCLUDE: 1983, Opera North, Maxim de Winter, *Rebecca* by Wilfred Josephs.

RELATED PROFESSIONAL ACTIVITIES: Concerts in the UK and abroad; director and/or translator: *The Barber of Seville, La Bohème, Carmen, Così fan tutte, Don Giovanni, Don Pasquale, The Marriage of Figaro, Orpheus in the Underworld, La Périchole, Rigoletto*, (all Travelling Opera).

RECORDINGS INCLUDE: Falla, *Master Peter's Puppet Show* (DECC); Monteverdi, *Vespers* (EMI).

AWARDS INCLUDE: 1977, Benson & Hedges Gold Award.

ADDRESS: c/o Kaye Artists Management Ltd, Barratt House, 7 Chertsey Road, Woking, Surrey GU21 5AB.

KNIGHT GILLIAN
Mezzo-soprano

PERSONAL DETAILS: b. 1 November 1939, Worcestershire; one child.

EDUCATION/TRAINING: Royal Academy of Music (Licentiate), with May Blyth and Roy Henderson; 1988, Open University degree.

PROFESSIONAL DEBUT: 1958, D'Oyly Carte Opera.

EARLY CAREER INCLUDED: 1958–1971: Principal Mezzo-soprano, D'Oyly Carte Opera, then Sadler's Wells Opera; roles included: Katisha, *The Mikado*; Ruth, *The Pirates of Penzance*; Lady Jane, *Patience*; Suzuki, *Madam Butterfly*; Ragonde, *Count Ory*; Juno/Ino, *Semele*; Maddalena, *Rigoletto*; title roles: *Carmen, The Italian Girl in Algiers*; also: Camden Festival,

Malcolm, *La Donna del Lago*; Handel Opera Society, Amastre, *Serse*.

MAJOR DEBUTS INCLUDE: Title role, *Carmen*: 1970: Covent Garden, Welsh National Opera; 1975: Saragossa, Valencia; 1975, Wexford Festival, Margared, *Le Roi d'Ys*; 1977, Paris Opera, Second Lady, *Die Zauberflöte*; 1977, Grand Théâtre, Tours, Dulcinée, *Don Quichotte*; 1978, Rouen, Charlotte, *Werther*; 1981: Opera North, title role, *Carmen*; Dallas Civic Opera, title role, *La Périchole*; Grand Théâtre, Geneva, Maddalena, *Rigoletto*; 1984, Frankfurt Opera, Madame Arvidson, *Un Ballo in Maschera*; 1986, Pittsburgh Opera, Gertrude, *Hamlet*; 1986, Scottish Opera, Queen of the Fairies, *Iolanthe*; 1991, Teatro La Fenice, Venice, Madame Larina, *Eugene Onegin*.

OPERATIC WORLD PREMIERES INCLUDE: Covent Garden: 1972, Rose Parrowe, *Taverner* by Peter Maxwell Davies; 1976, Young Lady 6/Young Girl 6/Victim 6, *We Come to the River* by Hans Werner Henze; 1991: Royal Opera Garden Venture, Mother, *Echoes* by John Hawkins; Basle, Mephistofele 1, *Faust* by Luca Lombardi.

CAREER IN THE UK INCLUDES: Since 1971: Covent Garden (1971–1977, member): Page, *Salome*; Maddalena, *Rigoletto*; Fenena, *Nabucco*; Lola, *Cavalleria Rusticana*; Annina, *Der Rosenkavalier*; Olga, *Eugene Onegin*; Meg Page, *Falstaff*; Helen, *King Priam*; Suzuki, *Madama Butterfly*; Inez, *Il Trovatore*; Erda, Flosshilde, Siegrune and Waltraute, *Der Ring des Nibelungen*; Maid, *The Birthday of the Infanta* (1985, British première); Fortune Teller, *Arabella*; Spirit of Antonia's Mother, *Les Contes d'Hoffmann*; Madame Larina, *Eugene Onegin*; Third Maid, *Elektra*; Juno/Ino, *Semele*; Zulma, *L'Italiana in Algeri*; Emilia, *Otello*; Magdalene, *Die Meistersinger von Nürnberg*; Forester's Wife/Owl, *The Cunning Little Vixen*; Fortune Teller, *The Fiery Angel*; Herodias, *Salome*; Voice from Above, *Die Frau ohne Schatten*; English National Opera, Spirit of Antonia's Mother, *The Tales of Hoffmann*; Handel Opera Society, title role, *Rinaldo*; Opera North, title role, *The Duenna* (1992, British stage première); Welsh National Opera, Nurse, *Die Frau ohne Schatten*.

RELATED PROFESSIONAL ACTIVITIES: Regular concerts and recitals with leading orchestras and conductors in the UK and abroad.

RECORDINGS INCLUDE: Berlioz, *La Damnation de Faust* (PHIL); Janáček, *The Cunning Little Vixen* (EMI); Puccini: *Madama Butterfly, La Rondine, Suor Angelica, Il Tabarro* (all CBS); Purcell, *Dido and Aeneas* (PHIL); Schoenberg, *Moses und Aron* (CBS); Sullivan: *The Gondoliers, HMS Pinafore, Iolanthe, Patience, Ruddigore, The Yeomen of the Guard* (all DECC); Verdi: *La Forza del Destino* (RCA), *Rigoletto* (DECC); Wagner, *Twilight of the Gods* (EMI).

VIDEOS INCLUDE: Sullivan: *The Gondoliers, HMS Pinafore, Iolanthe, Patience, Ruddigore, The Yeomen of the Guard* (all Walker).

ADDRESS: c/o Kaye Artists Management Ltd, Barratt House, 7 Chertsey Road, Woking, Surrey GU21 5AB.

KNUSSEN OLIVER
Composer and Conductor

POSITIONS: Co-Artistic Director, Aldeburgh Festival; Head of Contemporary Music, Berkshire Music Center, Tanglewood, Massachusetts.

PERSONAL DETAILS: b. 12 June 1952, Glasgow.

EDUCATION/TRAINING: 1963–1969, privately with John Lambert; 1965–1970, Purcell School; 1970–1973, Berkshire Music Center, Tanglewood, with Gunther Schuller.

FIRST PROFESSIONAL PERFORMANCE OF A COMPOSITION: 1968, London Symphony Orchestra, Symphony No. 1 (also conductor).

CAREER: Since 1968, compositions in all genres including two operas, orchestral, chamber, instrumental, choral and vocal works; 1974, Koussevitzky Centennial Commission, USA; Composer in Residence: 1976, Aspen Festival, Colorado; 1978, Arnolfini Gallery, Bristol; 1977–1982, Instructor in Composition, Royal College of Music Junior Department; Berkshire Music Center, Tanglewood: 1981, Guest Teacher; 1986–1990, Co-ordinator of Contemporary Music Activities; since 1990, Head of Contemporary Music; 1986–1990, Director, Almeida Ensemble; 1990–1992, Stoeger Composer in Residence, Chamber Music Society of Lincoln Center, New York; since 1983, Co-Artistic Director, Aldeburgh Festival.

OPERATIC WORLD PREMIERES: 1980, La Monnaie, Brussels, *Max and the Maximonsters (Where the Wild Things Are)*, fantasy opera in two acts, libretto by Maurice Sendak and the composer after the book by Sendak, conductor Ronald Zollman, director Rhoda Levine, designer Sendak; 1984, Glyndebourne Touring Opera, *Where the Wild Things Are* (definitive one act version), conductor the composer, director Frank Corsaro, designer Maurice Sendak; *Higglety Pigglety Pop!* fantasy opera in one act: 1984, Glyndebourne Touring Opera (preliminary version), conductor the composer; 1985, Glyndebourne Festival Opera (provisional complete version), conductor the composer; 1990, Los Angeles Music Center Opera (revised version), conductor Randall Behr (all three versions: libretto by Maurice Sendak and the composer after the book by Sendak, director Frank Corsaro, designer Sendak).

RELATED PROFESSIONAL ACTIVITIES: Since 1981, Guest Conductor: London Sinfonietta, Philharmonia Orchestra, ensembles and opera companies in the UK and abroad including 1990, English National Opera, *Clarissa* by Robin Holloway (world première).

RECORDINGS INCLUDE: *Where the Wild Things Are*, *Ophelia Dances*, Symphony No. 2 for soprano and chamber orchestra,

Symphony No. 3, Cantata for oboe and string trio, *Coursing* for chamber orchestra, *Trumpets* for soprano and three clarinets (all UNIC); as conductor: Britten, *The Prince of the Pagodas* (VIRG) and works by Carter (VIRG), Goehr (UNIC), Saxton (EMI).

VIDEOS INCLUDE: *Higglety Pigglety Pop!/ Where the Wild Things Are* (Glyndebourne Festival Opera).

AWARDS INCLUDE: 1969, Watney-Sargent Award for Young Conductors; 1971, Margaret Grant Composition Prize, Berkshire Music Center, Tanglewood (USA); 1982, first winner, Park Lane Group Composer Award.

ADDRESS: c/o Faber Music Ltd, 3 Queen Square, London WC1N 3AU or Virgil Blackwell Management, 808 West End Avenue, New York, NY 10025, USA.

KOLTAI RALPH   Designer

PERSONAL DETAILS: b. 31 July 1924; m. 1956, Annena Stubbs (m. diss.).

EDUCATION/TRAINING: Central School of Art and Design.

PROFESSIONAL AND OPERATIC DEBUT: 1950, London Opera Club, *Angélique*.

CAREER: Since 1950, more than 170 productions as freelance opera, theatre and ballet designer in the UK and abroad; 1963–1966 and since 1976, Associate Designer, Royal Shakespeare Company; 1965–1972, Head of Theatre Design, Central School of Art.

MAJOR OPERATIC DEBUTS INCLUDE: 1951, English Opera Group, *The Wandering Scholar*; 1952, Sadler's Wells Opera, *Samson and Delilah*; 1955, Covent Garden, *Tannhäuser*; 1959, New Opera Company, *The Prisoner* (British première); 1960, Handel Opera Society, *Hercules*; 1962, Teatro Colón, Buenos Aires, *A Midsummer Night's Dream*; 1963, Scottish Opera, *Otello*; 1965, Los Angeles Music Center Opera, *Don Giovanni*; 1971, Welsh National Opera, *Lulu* (British première); 1973: Australian Opera, Sydney, *Tannhäuser*; Cassel, *Lulu*;

Netherlands Opera, *Wozzeck*; 1974, Bavarian State Opera, Munich, *Fidelio*; 1979, Aalborg, *Die Dreigroschenoper*; 1983, Lyons Opera, *Die Soldaten*; 1984, Grand Théâtre, Geneva, *L'Italiana in Algeri*; 1992, Norwegian Opera, Oslo, *The Makropoulos Case*.

OPERATIC WORLD PREMIÈRES INCLUDE: Covent Garden: 1972, *Taverner* by Peter Maxwell Davies; 1977, *The Ice Break* by Michael Tippett; 1981, English National Opera, *Anna Karenina* by Iain Hamilton.

OPERA DESIGNS IN THE UK INCLUDE: Since 1953: New Opera Company: *Erwartung* (1960, British première), *Volpone* (1961, British première), *Boulevard Solitude* (1962, British première); Phoenix Opera, *Don Quixote* (1979, British première); Sadler's Wells Opera/English National Opera: *Carmen, Il Tabarro, Murder in the Cathedral* (1962, British première), *The Rise and Fall of the City of Mahagonny, Attila, From the House of the Dead, The Ring of the Nibelung, Duke Bluebeard's Castle, The Seven Deadly Sins, Pacific Overtures*; Scottish Opera: *Volo di Notte* (1963, British première), *Don Giovanni, Boris Godunov, The Rake's Progress, Elegy for Young Lovers, Tristan and Isolde, Macbeth*; Welsh National Opera: *The Midsummer Marriage, Don Giovanni*.

RELATED PROFESSIONAL ACTIVITIES: As director and designer: Hong Kong Arts Festival: 1987, *The Flying Dutchman*; 1990, *La Traviata*.

AWARDS AND HONOURS INCLUDE: 1975, 1979 and 1991, co-winner, Gold Medal, International Exhibition of Stage Design, Prague Quadriennale; 1983, Commander, Order of the British Empire (CBE); 1984, Royal Designer for Industry (RDI), Royal Society of Arts.

ADDRESS: c/o London Management, 235/241 Regent Street, London W1R 7AG.

* * * *

LALANDI LINA   Administrator

POSITION: Director, English Bach Festival.
PERSONAL DETAILS: b. Athens, Greece; m. Ralph Emery.
EDUCATION/TRAINING: Athens Conservatory, studied harpsichord and piano.
CAREER: International career as harpsichordist; since 1962, founder and Director, English Bach Festival.
HONOURS INCLUDE: 1975, Officer, Order of the British Empire (OBE); 1979, Officier de l'Ordre des Arts et des Lettres (France).
ADDRESS: c/o English Bach Festival, 15 South Eaton Place, London SW1W 9ER.

LANG AIDAN   Director

POSITIONS: Director of Productions, Glyndebourne Touring Opera; Artistic Director, Opera Zuid, Holland.
PERSONAL DETAILS: b. 9 October 1957, Kingston-upon-Thames; m. 1990, Linda Kitchen (soprano).
EDUCATION/TRAINING: 1977–1980, University of Birmingham, studied English and drama.
CAREER: Staff director: 1984–1985, Glyndebourne Festival Opera; 1985–1991, Welsh National Opera; since 1990, Artistic Director, Opera Zuid, Holland; since 1991, Director of Productions, Glyndebourne Touring Opera.
MAJOR OPERATIC DEBUTS INCLUDE: 1985, Göttingen Handel Festival, *Tamerlano*; 1990, Canadian Opera Company, Toronto, *Carmen*; 1990/1991, Welsh National Opera/Opera Northern Ireland co-production, *Hansel and Gretel*; 1991, Opera Zuid, Holland, *Werther*.
OPERATIC WORLD PREMIERES INCLUDE: 1985, Arundel Festival, *Lancelot* by Iain Hamilton.

OPERA PRODUCTIONS IN THE UK
INCLUDE: Since 1990: Glyndebourne
    Touring Opera, *La Bohème*; Welsh
    National Opera, *Count Ory*.
ADDRESS: c/o Lies Askonas Ltd, 186 Drury
    Lane, London WC2B 5RY.

LANGFORD AUDREY
Teacher (formerly Soprano)

PERSONAL DETAILS: b. 28 June 1912,
    Rochdale; m. Frederick Riddle; m.
    Andrew Field.
EDUCATION/TRAINING: Royal College of
    Music.
PROFESSIONAL DEBUT: 1936, Covent
    Garden, Flower Maiden, *Parsifal*.
CAREER INCLUDES: 1936–1950: member,
    Covent Garden; numerous concerts,
    recitals and broadcasts in the UK and
    abroad; 1950, founder, Cantica Voice
    Studio.
STUDENTS HAVE INCLUDED: Marie Angel,
    Josephine Barstow, Jeffrey Black, Susan
    Bullock, Christine Bunning, Teresa Cahill,
    Robert Hayward, Hugh Hetherington,
    Martyn Hill, Janis Kelly, Linda Kitchen,
    Sally Langford, Maureen Morelle, Arwel
    Huw Morgan, Ashley Putnam, Elizabeth
    Ritchie, Joan Rodgers, Russell Smythe,
    Gillian Sullivan, Stephen Varcoe,
    Josephine Veasey, Wendy Verco.
ADDRESS: 55 Hayes Road, Bromley, Kent
    BR2 9AE.

LANGFORD SALLY
Director (formerly Mezzo-soprano)

POSITION: Director of Productions, Kentish
    Opera.
PERSONAL DETAILS: b. 9 July 1938,
    London; m. 1962, three children.
EDUCATION/TRAINING: 1959–1962, National
    Opera School; privately with Audrey
    Langford and Andrew Field.
PROFESSIONAL DEBUT: 1962, English
    Opera Group at Drottningholm Festival,
    appeared in *Dido and Aeneas*.
CAREER: 1962–1966, appearances with
    English Opera Group, Handel Opera

Society, Kentish Opera; since 1967,
    Director of Productions, Kentish Opera.
OPERA PRODUCTIONS IN THE UK
INCLUDE: Since 1967, Kentish Opera, more
    than 25 productions including: *Aida*,
    Eugene Onegin, *Macbeth*, *Manon
    Lescaut*, *Peter Grimes*.
ADDRESS: Watermede, Wickhurst Road,
    Sevenoaks Weald, Kent TN14 6LX.

LANGRIDGE PHILIP   Tenor

PERSONAL DETAILS: b. 16 December 1939,
    Kent; m. 1981, Ann Murray (mezzo-
    soprano), one child (three children from
    previous marriage).
EDUCATION/TRAINING: Royal Academy of
    Music: 1958–1961, studied violin; 1962–
    1964, vocal studies with Bruce Boyce;
    privately with Celia Bizony.
PROFESSIONAL DEBUT: 1964,
    Glyndebourne Festival Opera,
    Manservant, *Capriccio*.
CAREER INCLUDES: Since 1965: Buxton
    Festival (1980, debut), Benedict, *Beatrice
    and Benedict*; Covent Garden (1983,
    debut): Fisherman, *The Nightingale* and
    Teapot, *L'Enfant et les Sortilèges*; Prince
    Shuisky, *Boris Godunov*; Laca, *Jenůfa*;
    Aschenbach, *Death in Venice*; title roles:
    Idomeneo, *Peter Grimes*; English
    National Opera (1984, debut): Peter Quint,
    The Turn of the Screw; Živný, *Osud* (1984,
    British stage première); Captain Vere,
    Billy Budd; Gregor, *The Makropoulos
    Case*; Benedict, *Beatrice and Benedict*;
    title roles: *Peter Grimes*, *Oedipus Rex*;
    English Opera Group (1974, debut): Male
    Chorus, *The Rape of Lucretia*; Satyavan,
    Sāvitri; Glyndebourne Festival and
    Touring Opera: Don Ottavio, *Don
    Giovanni*; Florestan, *Fidelio*; Laca,
    Jenůfa; Pelegrin, *New Year* (1990, British
    première); title roles: *Idomeneo*, *La
    Clemenza di Tito*; Handel Opera Society
    (1967, debut): Lélio and title role,
    Scipione; Lurcanio, *Ariodante*; Aminta,
    Atalanta; Scottish Opera, Aschenbach,
    Death in Venice; Welsh National Opera
    (1979, debut), Prologue, *The Turn of the*

Screw; Netherlands Opera, Nero,
L'Incoronazione di Poppea (1971,
European debut); Lyric Opera, Chicago,
title role, *Oedipus Rex* (1981, US debut);
Aix-en-Provence Festival, Oronte, *Alcina*;
Angers, title role, *Idomeneo*; Bavarian
State Opera, Munich, title role, *The Diary
of One who Disappeared*; Frankfurt
Opera, Castor, *Castor et Pollux*; La Scala,
Milan, Andrès, *Wozzeck*; Metropolitan
Opera, New York, Ferrando, *Così fan
tutte*; Salzburg Festival, Aron, *Moses und
Aron*; Teatro Massimo Bellini, Palermo,
title role, *Otello* (Rossini); Théâtre des
Champs Elysées, Paris, Don Ottavio, *Don
Giovanni*; Vienna State Opera, Andrès,
Wozzeck; Wexford Festival, Eurimedonte,
Eritrea (1975, first modern performance);
Zurich Opera, Nero, *L'Incoronazione di
Poppea.*
OPERATIC WORLD PREMIERES INCLUDE:
1969, Music Theatre Ensemble at the
Edinburgh International Festival,
Narrator, *Pharsalia* by Iain Hamilton;
1976, Scottish Opera (debut) at the York
Festival, title role, *Confessions of a
Justified Sinner* by Thomas Wilson; 1986,
English National Opera, Orpheus the
Man, *The Mask of Orpheus* by Harrison
Birtwistle.
RELATED PROFESSIONAL ACTIVITIES:
Regular concerts, recitals and broadcasts
with leading conductors and orchestras in
the UK and abroad; 1983–1986, member,
Music Advisory Panel, Arts Council of
Great Britain.
RECORDINGS INCLUDE: Berg, *Wozzeck*
(DG); Birtwistle, *Punch and Judy* (ETCE);
Handel, *Messiah* (RPO); Holst, *Sāvitri*
(HYPE); Janáček: *The Diary of One who
Disappeared* (DG), *Osud*; Massenet,
Werther (both EMI); Monteverdi, *Vespers*;
Mozart, *Le Nozze di Figaro*; Schoenberg,
Moses und Aron; Stravinsky, *The Rake's
Progress*; Tippett, *King Priam* (all DECC).
VIDEOS INCLUDE: Berg, *Wozzeck* (Vienna
State Opera); Britten, *Billy Budd* (English
National Opera); Mozart, *Idomeneo*
(Glyndebourne Festival Opera).
AWARDS AND HONOURS INCLUDE: Royal
Academy of Music: 1977, Associate; 1985,

Fellow; 1984, Olivier Award, *Osud*
(English National Opera); 1985, Grammy
Award (USA), *Moses und Aron*; 1989,
Royal Philharmonic Society/Charles
Heidsieck Award.
ADDRESS: c/o Allied Artists, 42 Montpelier
Square, London SW7 1JZ.

LATHAM KEITH   Baritone

PERSONAL DETAILS: b. 27 January 1954,
Lancashire; m. 1977.
PREVIOUS OCCUPATION: 1970–1980,
clerical work.
EDUCATION/TRAINING: Royal Northern
College of Music, with Patrick McGuigan.
PROFESSIONAL DEBUT: 1984, Scottish
Opera, Titon, *Orion.*
MAJOR DEBUTS INCLUDE: 1985, Opera
North, Speaker, *The Magic Flute*; 1989,
English National Opera, Zurga, *The Pearl
Fishers*; 1990: City of Birmingham
Touring Opera, Alberich, *The Ring Saga*;
Dublin Grand Opera, Balstrode, *Peter
Grimes*; 1991, Opera Theatre Company,
Dublin, title role, *Falstaff.*
OPERATIC WORLD PREMIERES INCLUDE:
1991, English National Opera, Apemantus,
Timon of Athens by Stephen Oliver.
CAREER IN THE UK INCLUDES: Since 1984:
Chelsea Opera Group, Lescaut, *Manon
Lescaut*; Opera North: Amonasro, *Aida*;
Sonora, *La Fanciulla del West*; Valentin,
Faust; Creon, *Oedipus Rex*; Germont, *La
Traviata*; Kuligin, *Katya Kabanova*;
Scarpia, *Tosca*; Enrico, *Lucia di
Lammermoor*; Zurga, *Les Pêcheurs de
Perles*; Count di Luna, *Il Trovatore*;
Sharpless, *Madama Butterfly*; Donald,
Billy Budd; Barnaba, *La Gioconda*; title
roles: *Macbeth, Rigoletto*; Scottish Opera:
Krušina, *The Bartered Bride*; Marullo,
Rigoletto; Fiorello, *Il Barbiere di Siviglia*;
University College Opera, Nilakantha,
Lakmé.
AWARDS INCLUDE: 1982, Ostend Opera
Concours, Duet Prize.
ADDRESS: c/o Gillian Clench International
Artists' Management, 1 Mount Pleasant
Cottages, Rhiwbina Hill, Cardiff CF4 6UP.

LAURENCE ELIZABETH
Mezzo-soprano and Clarinettist

PERSONAL DETAILS: b. 22 November 1949, Harrogate.
PREVIOUS OCCUPATION Music teacher.
EDUCATION/TRAINING: 1969–1970, Colchester School of Art; 1970–1974, Trinity College of Music; 1974–1975, Trent Park Training College.
PROFESSIONAL DEBUT: 1982, Musée de l'Art Moderne, Paris, *La Nuit des Soupliantes* by Nicos Cornelios (world première).
MAJOR DEBUTS INCLUDE: 1986, Teatro La Zarzuela, Madrid, Jocasta, *Oedipus Rex*; 1988, Glyndebourne Festival Opera, Anna, *The Electrification of the Soviet Union*; 1989, Covent Garden, Mezzo-soprano, *Un Re in Ascolto* (British première).
OPERATIC WORLD PREMIERES INCLUDE: 1987, Glyndebourne Touring Opera, Anna, *The Electrification of the Soviet Union* by Nigel Osborne; 1989, Paris Opera, Behemoth, *Der Meister und Margarita* by York Höller; 1991, Covent Garden, Lady de Hautdesert, *Gawain* by Harrison Birtwistle; 1992, Almeida Opera, Duchess of Alba, *Terrible Mouth* by Nigel Osborne.
CAREER INCLUDES: Since 1983: Glyndebourne Touring Opera, Nancy, *Albert Herring*; Angers Opera, Dido, *Dido and Aeneas*; Bonn Opera, Erda, *Das Rheingold*; Monte Carlo Opera, Mallika, *Lakmé*; Opéra Bastille, Paris, Mezzo-soprano, *Un Re in Ascolto*; Théâtre du Châtelet, Paris, Cherubino, *Le Nozze di Figaro*.
RELATED PROFESSIONAL ACTIVITIES: Regular concerts, recitals, broadcasts and television appearances in the UK and abroad; extensive post romantic and contemporary repertoire includes works by Berio, Boulez, Mahler, Nono, Reger, Schoenberg and Wagner.
RECORDINGS INCLUDE: Bartók, *Duke Bluebeard's Castle*; Boulez, *Le Visage Nuptial* (both ERAT).

ADDRESS: c/o Ingpen & Williams Ltd, 14 Kensington Court, London W8 5DN.

LAVENDER JUSTIN   Tenor

PERSONAL DETAILS: b. 4 June 1951, Bedford; m. 1990, Louise Crane (mezzo-soprano); two children from previous marriage.
EDUCATION/TRAINING: 1971–1975, Guildhall School of Music and Drama; privately with William McAlpine.
PROFESSIONAL DEBUT: 1976, English Music Theatre, First Armed Man, *The Magic Flute*.
EARLY CAREER INCLUDED: 1976–1983, appearances with English Music Theatre, New Opera Company, Opera North; roles included: Chief of Police, *Julietta* (1978, New Opera Company, British première); Nemorino, *The Elixir of Love*; Camille, *The Merry Widow*; Vašek, *The Bartered Bride*.
MAJOR DEBUTS INCLUDE: 1980: Victoria State Opera, Melbourne, title role, *Count Ory*; Victoria State Opera at Sydney Opera House, Nadir, *The Pearl Fishers*; Western Australian Opera, Belmonte, *Die Entführung aus dem Serail*; 1981, Lyric Opera of Queensland, Paris, *La Belle Hélène*; 1984, Karlsruhe, Jupiter, *Semele*; 1985, Rome Opera, Don Ottavio, *Don Giovanni*; 1988, Teatro La Zarzuela, Madrid, Pylade, *Ermione*; 1990: Covent Garden, Arnold, *Guillaume Tell*; National Theatre, Prague, Don Ottavio, *Don Giovanni*; Tamino, *Die Zauberflöte*; Vienna State Opera, Vienna Volksoper; 1991: Essen Opera, Ferrando, *Così fan tutte*; La Scala, Milan, title role, *Le Comte Ory*; Opéra Comique, Paris, Fernand, *La Favorite*; Pittsburgh Opera, Count, *Il Barbiere di Siviglia*; 1992, Mannheim, Don Ottavio, *Don Giovanni*.
OPERATIC WORLD PREMIERES INCLUDE: 1985, Grand Théâtre, Geneva, Lorenzi, *Il Ritorno di Casanova* by Girolamo Arrigo; 1989, Nancy Opera, Montezuma, *La Noche Triste* by Jean Prodomidès; 1990,

English National Opera, Brother, *Clarissa* by Robin Holloway.

CAREER IN THE UK INCLUDES: Since 1984: Buxton Festival, Lindoro, *The Italian Girl in Algiers*; Covent Garden, Count, *Il Barbiere di Siviglia*; Opera North, Astrologer, *The Golden Cockerel*; Scottish Opera: Painter/Negro, *Lulu*; Alfred, *Die Fledermaus*; Froh, *Das Rheingold*.

RELATED PROFESSIONAL ACTIVITIES: Numerous concerts with leading conductors and orchestras in the UK and abroad.

RECORDINGS INCLUDE: Prodomidès, *La Noche Triste* (French label).

ADDRESS: c/o Athole Still International Management Ltd, Greystoke House, 80–86 Westow Street, London SE19 3AF.

LAWLESS STEPHEN   Director

CAREER: 1979–1985, staff director: Covent Garden, Glyndebourne Festival and Touring Opera; 1986–1990: Principal Associate Director, Glyndebourne Festival Opera; Director of Productions, Glyndebourne Touring Opera; since 1990, freelance opera director in the UK and abroad.

MAJOR OPERATIC DEBUTS INCLUDE: 1982, Opera 80, *Die Fledermaus*; 1988, Scottish Opera, *The Pearl Fishers*; 1989, Glyndebourne Touring Opera, *Death in Venice*; 1990: Canadian Opera Company, Toronto, *Der Rosenkavalier*; 1992, Glyndebourne Festival Opera, *Death in Venice*.

OPERA PRODUCTIONS IN THE UK INCLUDE: Since 1981: Buxton Festival: *David and Goliath, Sir Gawain and the Green Knight*; Guildhall School of Music and Drama, *Le Nozze di Figaro*; Opera Rara at the Camden Festival, *Gli Orazi ed i Curiazi*; Royal Academy of Music, *Les Boréades* (1985, British stage première).

ADDRESS: c/o Lies Askonas Ltd, 186 Drury Lane, London WC2B 5RY.

LAWLOR THOMAS
Bass-baritone

PERSONAL DETAILS: b. 17 June 1938, Dublin; m. 1971, Pauline Wales (mezzo-soprano); m. 1982, Ghislaine Labour.

EDUCATION/TRAINING: 1956–1959, University College, Dublin, studied philosophy, politics and English; 1960–1963, Guildhall School of Music and Drama.

PROFESSIONAL DEBUT: 1963, member, D'Oyly Carte Opera.

EARLY CAREER INCLUDED: 1963–1971, Principal Bass-baritone, D'Oyly Carte Opera, singing all the leading Gilbert and Sullivan bass-baritone roles in the UK and abroad.

OPERATIC WORLD PREMIERES INCLUDE: 1983, Opera North, Giles Lacy, *Rebecca* by Wilfred Josephs.

CAREER IN THE UK INCLUDES: Since 1971: Covent Garden, Benoit, *La Bohème*; Glyndebourne Festival and Touring Opera: Lackey, *Ariadne auf Naxos*; Don Alfonso, *Cosi fan tutte*; Major Domo, *Capriccio*; Benoit and Schaunard, *La Bohème*; Osmin; *Die Entführung aus dem Serail*; Antonio and Bartolo, *Le Nozze di Figaro*; Zaretsky, *Eugene Onegin*; Lawyer, *Intermezzo*; Harašta, *The Cunning Little Vixen*; Keeper of the Madhouse, *The Rake's Progress*; Kent Opera: Sir Joseph Porter, *HMS Pinafore*; Pasha Selim, *The Seraglio*; Time, *The Return of Ulysses*; Sparafucile, *Rigoletto*; Rocco, *Fidelio*; Leporello, *Don Giovanni*; New Sadler's Wells Opera: Pooh-Bah, *The Mikado*; Dick Deadeye, *HMS Pinafore*; Sir Roderick, *Ruddigore*; Opera North: Sacristan, *Tosca*; Geronte, *Manon Lescaut*; Magistrate, *Werther*; Somarone, *Beatrice and Benedict*; Cuno, *Der Freischütz*; Parson, *The Cunning Little Vixen*; Kecal, *The Bartered Bride*; Artists' Manager, *Johnny Strikes Up* (1984, British première); Grand Inquisitor, *The Gondoliers*; Polkan, *The Golden Cockerel*; Baron Zeta, *The Merry Widow*.

RELATED PROFESSIONAL ACTIVITIES: Faculty member and stage director, Bay

View Summer Conservatory of Music, Michigan; adjudicator, British Federation of Music Festivals; 1991, teacher, Royal Academy of Music and Trinity College of Music.

RECORDINGS INCLUDE: Sullivan: *HMS Pinafore*, *Ruddigore*, *The Yeomen of the Guard* (all DECC).

VIDEOS INCLUDE: Mozart, *Le Nozze di Figaro*; Stravinsky, *The Rake's Progress* (both Glyndebourne Festival Opera); Sullivan: *Cox and Box* (Walker), *The Mikado* (Warner Brothers).

ADDRESS: c/o Music International, 13 Ardilaun Road, London N5 2QR.

LAWTON JEFFREY   Tenor

PERSONAL DETAILS: b. 11 December 1941, Oldham; m. 1962, Ann Whitehead, three children.

PREVIOUS OCCUPATIONS: 1964–1975, buyer for several companies; 1975–1980, Head of Operations, mail order company.

EDUCATION/TRAINING: Vocal studies with Patrick McGuigan.

PROFESSIONAL DEBUT: 1981, Welsh National Opera, Florestan, *Fidelio*.

MAJOR DEBUTS INCLUDE: Title role, *Otello*: 1986, Welsh National Opera; 1987, Nancy Opera; 1990: Covent Garden and La Monnaie, Brussels; 1990, Netherlands Opera, Radamès, *Aida*; 1991, English National Opera, Edmund, *Lear*; 1992, Opera North, Prince Shuisky, *Boris Godunov*.

CAREER IN THE UK INCLUDES: Since 1981, Welsh National Opera: Ringmaster, *The Bartered Bride*; Tichon, *Katya Kabanova*; Judge, *Un Ballo in Maschera*; Laca, *Jenůfa*; Siegfried, *Götterdämmerung*; Don José, *Carmen*; Emperor, *Die Frau ohne Schatten*; Aegisth, *Elektra*; Tristan, *Tristan und Isolde* (also 1993, at Covent Garden).

RELATED PROFESSIONAL ACTIVITIES: Numerous concerts and recitals in the UK and abroad.

RECORDINGS INCLUDE: Martinů, *The Greek Passion* (SUPR).

ADDRESS: c/o Music International, 13 Ardilaun Road, London N5 2QR.

LAZARIDIS STEFANOS
Designer and Director

POSITION: Associate Artist, English National Opera.

PERSONAL DETAILS: b. 28 July 1942, Ethiopia.

EDUCATION/TRAINING: 1960–1963: Ecole Internationale, Geneva; Central School of Speech and Drama.

PROFESSIONAL DEBUT: 1967, Yvonne Arnaud Theatre, Guildford, *Eccentricities of a Nightingale* by Tennessee Williams.

OPERATIC DEBUT: 1970, Sadler's Wells Opera, *Carmen*.

CAREER: Since 1967, freelance opera, ballet and theatre designer in the UK and abroad; since 1990, also opera director.

MAJOR OPERATIC DEBUTS INCLUDE: 1971, Covent Garden, *Le Nozze di Figaro*; 1977, Australian Opera, Sydney, *Macbeth*; 1978: Scottish Opera at the Aix-en-Provence Festival, *Dido and Aeneas*; Netherlands Opera, *Tannhäuser*; 1980, Opera North, *Nabucco*; 1983, Teatro Comunale, Bologna, *Tristan und Isolde*; 1984: Houston Grand Opera, *Der Fliegende Holländer*; Maggio Musicale, Florence, *Rigoletto*; 1985, Stuttgart State Opera, *Fidelio*; 1986: Krefeld/Mönchengladbach, *Ariane et Barbe-Bleu*; San Francisco Opera, *Don Carlos*; 1986/1987: English National Opera/Deutsche Oper, Berlin co-production, *Doctor Faust* (British stage première); Maggio Musicale, Florence/English National Opera co-production, *Tosca*; 1988: Los Angeles Music Center Opera, *The Mikado*; Nice Opera, *Pelléas et Mélisande*; 1989: Earls Court, *Carmen*; Bregenz Festival, *Der Fliegende Holländer*; Paris Opera, *Doktor Faust*; 1990: Scottish Opera, *Oedipus Rex/Duke Bluebeard's Castle* (director and designer); Frankfurt Opera, *Rusalka*; 1991: La Scala, Milan, *La Fanciulla del West*; Teatro La Fenice, Venice, *Hänsel und Gretel*; 1992/1993, English National

Opera/Bavarian State Opera, Munich co-production, *The Adventures of Mr Brouček*; 1993: Australian Opera, Sydney, *Orphée et Eurydice* (director and designer); Bregenz Festival, *Nabucco*.

OPERATIC WORLD PREMIERES INCLUDE: 1983, Opera North, *Rebecca* by Wilfred Josephs.

OPERA DESIGNS IN THE UK INCLUDE: Since 1970: Covent Garden: *Don Giovanni*, *Idomeneo*, *Werther*; English Music Theatre, *The Threepenny Opera*; New Sadler's Wells Opera, *Martha*; Opera North: *Oedipus Rex*, *The Bartered Bride*, *Prince Igor*, *Katya Kabanova*; Sadler's Wells Opera/English National Opera: *The Seraglio*, *Il Trovatore*, *Katya Kabanova*, *Dalibor*, *Werther* (two productions), *Euryanthe*, *The Two Foscari*, *Aida*, *The Flying Dutchman*, *Rusalka*, *Madam Butterfly*, *Osud* (1984, British stage première), *The Midsummer Marriage*, *The Mikado*, *Lady Macbeth of Mtsensk* (1987, British stage première), *Hansel and Gretel*, *La Traviata*, *Macbeth*, *Wozzeck*; Scottish Opera: *Les Pêcheurs de Perles*, *Don Giovanni*.

VIDEOS INCLUDE: Bizet, *Carmen* (Earls Court); Dvořák, *Rusalka* (English National Opera); Puccini, *La Fanciulla del West* (La Scala, Milan); Sullivan, *The Mikado* (English National Opera).

ADDRESS: c/o English National Opera, London Coliseum, St Martin's Lane, London WC2N 4ES.

LECCA MARIE-JEANNE
Designer

PERSONAL DETAILS: b. 31 January 1959, Bucharest, Romania; m. 1982, Dan-Mihai Sandru.

EDUCATION/TRAINING: 1977–1981, Grigorescu Art Institute, Bucharest.

PROFESSIONAL DEBUT: 1981, Piatra Neamt Youth Theatre, Romania, *The Dragon* by Evgheni Schwartz.

OPERATIC DEBUT: 1985, John Lewis Partnership Music Society, *Le Pré aux Clercs*.

CAREER: 1981–1984, theatre designer in Romania; since 1985, opera, television and theatre designer in the UK and abroad.

MAJOR OPERATIC DEBUTS INCLUDE: 1985, Wexford Festival, *La Wally*; 1986: English National Opera, *Moses*; Scottish Opera, *Iolanthe*; 1987, Hesse State Opera, Wiesbaden, *Carmen*; 1989, Dortmund, *Il Trovatore*; 1991, Minnesota Opera, *Carmen*.

OPERA DESIGNS IN THE UK INCLUDE: Since 1986: Brighton Festival, *Noye's Fludde*; D'Oyly Carte Opera, *The Pirates of Penzance*; English National Opera: *The Stone Guest* (1987, British stage première), *Pacific Overtures* (costumes only), *Falstaff*, *Pelléas and Mélisande*; English Touring Opera (City of Birmingham Touring Opera), *La Bohème*; Scottish Opera Go Round, *Tosca*.

RELATED PROFESSIONAL ACTIVITIES: Poster and programme designer, exhibitions in Romania, Bulgaria and Germany; 1991, costume designer, *The Big One* (Channel Four).

ADDRESS: c/o Performing Arts, 6 Windmill Street, London W1P 1HF.

LEGGATE ROBIN   Tenor

POSITION: Member, The Royal Opera, Covent Garden.

PERSONAL DETAILS: b. 18 April 1946, Cheshire.

PREVIOUS OCCUPATION: 1970–1972, production manager, asbestos cement manufacturer.

EDUCATION/TRAINING: 1964–1967, The Queen's College, Oxford, studied engineering; 1970–1971, Cranfield Business School; 1973–1975, Royal Northern College of Music; privately with David Keren.

PROFESSIONAL DEBUT: 1974, Keynote Opera, Herald, *Wat Tyler* (British stage première).

MAJOR DEBUTS INCLUDE: 1975, Kent Opera, Tamino, *The Magic Flute*; 1976, English National Opera, Nero, *The*

Coronation of Poppea; Cassio, *Otello*: 1977, Covent Garden; 1978, Hamburg State Opera; 1979, Scottish Opera, Don Ottavio, *Don Giovanni*; Tamino, *Die Zauberflöte*: 1979, Netherlands Opera; 1983, Théâtre du Châtelet, Paris; 1984, Welsh National Opera, Camille, *The Merry Widow*; 1991, Glyndebourne Festival Opera, Arbace, *Idomeneo*; 1992: Salzburg Festival, Second Jew, *Salome*; Teatro La Zarzuela, Madrid, Father Paul, *The Duenna* by Roberto Gerhard (world stage première).

OPERATIC WORLD PREMIERES INCLUDE: 1986, La Monnaie, Brussels, Teacher, *Das Schloss* by André Laporte.

CAREER IN THE UK INCLUDES: Since 1976, member, Covent Garden, more than 30 roles including: Joe, *La Fanciulla del West*; Elemer, *Arabella*; Nobleman, *Lohengrin*; Don Alvar, *L'Africaine*; Narraboth, *Salome*; Tamino, *Die Zauberflöte*; Novice, *Billy Budd*; Liverotto, *Lucrezia Borgia*; Arturo, *Lucia di Lammermoor*; Painter/Negro, *Lulu* (1981, British première, three act version); Bob Cratchit, *A Christmas Carol* (1981, British première at Sadler's Wells Theatre); Chevalier, *The Carmelites*; Paris, *King Priam*; Malcolm, *Macbeth*; Pang, *Turandot* (also 1986, Far East tour); Singer, *Un Re in Ascolto* (1989, British première); Ruiz, *Il Trovatore*; Ovlur, *Prince Igor*; Simpleton, *Boris Godunov*; Apparition of a Youth, *Die Frau ohne Schatten*; Yamadori, *Madama Butterfly*; Schoolmaster, *The Cunning Little Vixen*.

RECORDINGS INCLUDE: Boito, *Mefistofele* (DECC); Haydn, *Armida* (PHIL); Puccini, *La Fanciulla del West* (DG); Verdi: *Un Ballo in Maschera, Il Trovatore* (both PHIL).

VIDEOS INCLUDE: Puccini: *La Fanciulla del West, Manon Lescaut* (both Covent Garden).

AWARDS INCLUDE: 1975, Richard Tauber Memorial Prize.

ADDRESS: c/o Harrison/Parrott Ltd, 12 Penzance Place, London W11 4PA.

LEIFERKUS SERGEI
Baritone

POSITION: Principal Baritone, Kirov Opera.

PERSONAL DETAILS: b. 4 April 1946, Leningrad, Soviet Union; m. 1968, one child.

EDUCATION/TRAINING: 1965–1972, Leningrad State Conservatoire, with Yuri Barsov and Sergei Shaposhnikov.

PROFESSIONAL DEBUT: 1972, Maly Theatre, Leningrad, King, *Die Kluge*.

EARLY CAREER INCLUDED: 1972–1978, Principal Baritone, Maly Theatre, Leningrad: Germont, *La Traviata*; Robert, *Iolanta*; title roles: *Il Barbiere di Siviglia, Don Giovanni*.

MAJOR DEBUTS INCLUDE: 1977, Kirov Opera, Andrei, *War and Peace*; 1982, Wexford Festival, Marquis, *Grisélidis* (western debut); 1985: Scottish Opera, title role, *Don Giovanni* (British debut); Théâtre du Châtelet, Paris, Germont, *La Traviata*; 1987: English National Opera, Zurga, *The Pearl Fishers*; Kirov Opera at Covent Garden: Tomsky/Plutus, *The Queen of Spades*; title role, *Eugene Onegin*; 1988, Opera North, Scarpia, *Tosca*; 1989: Covent Garden, Count di Luna, *Il Trovatore*; San Francisco Opera, Telramund, *Lohengrin*; 1990: Canadian Opera Company, Toronto, title role, *Eugene Onegin*; Dallas Civic Opera, title role, *Prince Igor*; Salzburg Easter Festival, Don Pizarro, *Fidelio*; 1991: title role, *Mazeppa*: Bregenz Festival, Netherlands Opera; Opéra Bastille, Paris, Tomsky/Plutus, *The Queen of Spades*; Teatro Colón, Buenos Aires, Count di Luna, *Il Trovatore*; Vienna State Opera, title role, *Eugene Onegin*; 1992, Glyndebourne Festival Opera, Tomsky/Plutus, *The Queen of Spades*.

CAREER INCLUDES: Since 1978: Principal Baritone, Kirov Opera: Rangoni, *Boris Godunov*; Ruprecht, *The Fiery Angel*; Gryaznoi, *The Tsar's Bride*; Amonasro, *Aida*; Count di Luna, *Il Trovatore*; Rodrigo, *Don Carlos*; Ernesto, *Il Pirata*; Don Carlos, *Il Forza del Destino*; Valentin, *Faust*; Marcello, *La Bohème*; Sharpless,

Madama Butterfly; title role, *Prince Igor*; also: Covent Garden: Ruprecht, *The Fiery Angel*; Iago, *Otello*; title roles: *Prince Igor, Eugene Onegin*; English National Opera, Escamillo, *Carmen*; Opera North, Zurga, *The Pearl Fishers*; Scottish Opera: Escamillo, *Carmen*; title role, *Eugene Onegin*; Wexford Festival: Boniface, *Le Jongleur de Notre-Dame*; Fiddler, *Königskinder*; title role, *Hans Heiling*.

RELATED PROFESSIONAL ACTIVITIES: Regular concerts and recitals with leading conductors and orchestras worldwide.

RECORDINGS INCLUDE: Janáček, *Glagolitic Mass* (DECC); Mussorgsky, songs and dances (RCA); Rachmaninov, *The Bells* and *Spring Cantata* (DECC); Shostakovich, Symphony No. 14; Tchaikovsky, *The Queen of Spades* (RCA).

ADDRESS: c/o Allied Artists, 42 Montpelier Square, London SW7 1JZ.

LEWIS KEITH   Tenor

PERSONAL DETAILS: b. 6 October 1950, Methven, New Zealand.

EDUCATION/TRAINING: London Opera Centre.

EARLY CAREER INCLUDED: 1976–1978, appearances with Chelsea Opera Group, English Bach Festival, Glyndebourne Touring Opera, Park Lane Opera; roles included: Don Ottavio, *Don Giovanni*; Ferrando, *Così fan tutte*.

MAJOR DEBUTS INCLUDE: 1978: Glyndebourne Festival Opera, Don Ottavio, *Don Giovanni*; Nantes Opera, title role, *L'Ormindo*; 1979: Kent Opera, Alfredo, *La Traviata*; Lyons Opera, Hylas, *Ercole Amante*; 1980, Victoria State Opera, Melbourne, Nadir, *Les Pêcheurs de Perles*; 1981, Opera North, Escamillo, *Carmen*; 1982, English National Opera, Tamino, *The Magic Flute*; 1983, Paris Opera, Amenophis, *Mosè in Egitto*; 1984, San Francisco Opera, Don Ottavio, *Don Giovanni*; 1985, Deutsche Oper, Berlin, errando, *Così fan tutte*; 1987, Frankfurt Opera, Pylade, *Iphigénie en Tauride*;

1991, San Diego Opera, Don Ottavio, *Don Giovanni*.

OPERATIC WORLD PREMIERES INCLUDE: 1979, Covent Garden (debut), Christ/Father, *Thérèse* by John Tavener.

CAREER IN THE UK INCLUDES: Since 1978: Covent Garden: Tebaldo, *I Capuleti e i Montecchi*; Count, *Il Barbiere di Siviglia*; Tamino, *Die Zauberflöte*; English National Opera, Count, *The Barber of Seville*; Glyndebourne Festival and Touring Opera: Jove, *Il Ritorno d'Ulisse in Patria*; Belmonte, *Die Entführung aus dem Serail*; Lucano, *L'Incoronazione di Poppea*; Matteo, *Arabella*; title role, *Idomeneo*.

RELATED PROFESSIONAL ACTIVITIES: Regular concerts, recitals and broadcasts with leading conductors and orchestras in the UK and abroad.

RECORDINGS INCLUDE: Beethoven, Symphony No. 9 (RCA); Berlioz: *Lélio, Requiem, Te Deum* (all DENO); Gluck, *Alceste* (EMI); Handel, *Messiah* (DECC); Mozart: *Don Giovanni* (EMI), *Requiem* (SONY); Schumann, *Das Paradies und die Peri* (SUPR); R. Strauss, *Salome* (SONY); Verdi, *Otello* (PHIL).

VIDEOS INCLUDE: Monteverdi, *L'Incoronazione di Poppea*; R. Strauss, *Arabella* (both Glyndebourne Festival Opera).

AWARDS INCLUDE: 1976, Kathleen Ferrier Memorial Scholarship; 1979, John Christie Award.

ADDRESS: c/o Lies Askonas Ltd, 186 Drury Lane, London WC2B 5RY.

LLOYD HUGH   Administrator

POSITION: Administrator, National Opera Studio.

PERSONAL DETAILS: b. 18 May 1958, London; m. 1984, Alma Sheehan (soprano).

EDUCATION/TRAINING: 1977–1980, University of Durham.

CAREER: 1981–1982, assistant to press officer and box office accountant, Glyndebourne Festival Opera; National Opera Studio: 1982–1986, Assistant

Administrator; since 1986, Administrator and Company Secretary.

ADDRESS: c/o National Opera Studio, Morley College, 61 Westminster Bridge Road, London SE1 7HT.

LLOYD MICHAEL
Conductor and Répétiteur

POSITION: Assistant Music Director, English National Opera.

PERSONAL DETAILS: b. 5 August 1946, Worcestershire; m. 1976, Patricia Rianne (dancer, m. diss.), two children.

EDUCATION/TRAINING: 1965–1968, University of East Anglia; 1969–1971, Royal College of Music, studied piano with David Parkhouse.

PROFESSIONAL DEBUT: 1973, Scottish Ballet.

CAREER: 1972–1976, company pianist and conductor, Scottish Ballet; Cassel: 1976–1977, ballet conductor; 1978–1980, Assistant Music Director; 1980–1984, conductor and répétiteur, Stuttgart State Opera; English National Opera: 1984–1990, member, music staff and conductor; since 1990, Assistant Music Director.

MAJOR OPERATIC DEBUTS INCLUDE: 1979, Cassel, Tosca; 1983, Stuttgart State Opera, Albert Herring; 1986, English National Opera, Madam Butterfly.

OPERA PERFORMANCES IN THE UK INCLUDE: Since 1987, English National Opera: Don Giovanni, Cavalleria Rusticana/Pagliacci, La Bohème, A Masked Ball, The Turn of the Screw, The Cunning Little Vixen, Christmas Eve, Don Carlos, Rigoletto, Don Pasquale, Macbeth.

ADDRESS: c/o English National Opera, London Coliseum, St Martin's Lane, London WC2N 4ES.

LLOYD ROBERT   Bass

PERSONAL DETAILS: b. 2 March 1940, Essex; m. 1964, Sandra Watkins (m. diss), four children.

PREVIOUS OCCUPATIONS: 1963–1966, Instructor Lieutenant, Royal Navy; 1966–1968, civilian tutor, Bramshill Police College.

EDUCATION/TRAINING: 1959–1962, Keble College, Oxford, studied modern history; 1968–1969, London Opera Centre; privately with Otakar Kraus.

PROFESSIONAL DEBUT: 1969, University College Opera, Don Fernando, Leonore.

EARLY CAREER INCLUDED: 1969–1972: Principal Bass, Sadler's Wells Opera: Grenville, La Traviata (debut); Sparafucile, Rigoletto; Zuniga, Carmen; King, The Love for Three Oranges; Masetto, Don Giovanni; Don Fernando, Fidelio; Brander, The Damnation of Faust; Crespel, The Tales of Hoffmann; Fasolt, The Rhinegold; also: Barber Institute, Birmingham, Ralph, La Jolie Fille de Perth; Phoenix Opera, Superintendent Budd, Albert Herring.

MAJOR DEBUTS INCLUDE: 1972: Covent Garden, Second Strelyets, Khovanshchina; Glyndebourne Festival Opera, Neptune, Il Ritorno d'Ulisse in Patria; Welsh National Opera, Sarastro, The Magic Flute; 1974: Scottish Opera, Sarastro, The Magic Flute; Aix-en-Provence Festival, Publio, La Clemenza di Tito; 1975, San Francisco Opera, Sarastro, Die Zauberflöte; 1977: Canadian Opera Company, Toronto, Sarastro, The Magic Flute; Paris Opera, Commendatore, Don Giovanni; 1978, Netherlands Opera, Fiesco, Simon Boccanegra; 1979, Bavarian State Opera, Munich, Ramfis, Aida; 1979, Covent Garden Far East tour: Hobson, Peter Grimes; Angelotti, Tosca; 1982: Deutsche Oper, Berlin, Padre Guardiano, La Forza del Destino; Hamburg State Opera, Banquo, Macbeth; La Scala, Milan, Narbal, Les Troyens; 1985, Grand Théâtre, Geneva, Procida, I Vespri Siciliani; 1987, Teatro Comunale, Florence, title role, Boris Godunov; 1988, Metropolitan Opera, New York, Don Basilio, Il Barbiere di Siviglia; 1989, Vienna State Opera, Padre Guardiano, La

167

Forza del Destino; 1990, Kirov Opera, title role, *Boris Godunov*.

OPERATIC WORLD PREMIERES INCLUDE: 1969, New Opera Company at the Camden Festival, Mikulim, *Under Western Eyes* by John Joubert.

CAREER IN THE UK INCLUDES: Since 1972: Covent Garden (1972–1982, member): Masetto, *Don Giovanni*; Banquo, *Macbeth*; Horaste, *Troilus and Cressida*; Hermit, *Der Freischütz*; Ashby, *La Fanciulla del West*; Bartolo, *Le Nozze di Figaro*; Heinrich, *Lohengrin*; Monterone and Sparafucile, *Rigoletto*; Biterolf, *Tannhäuser*; Arkel, *Pélleas et Mélisande*; Fasolt, *Das Rheingold*; Sarastro, *Die Zauberflote*; Trulove, *The Rake's Progress*; Raimondo, *Lucia di Lammermoor*; Fiesco, *Simon Boccanegra*; Oroveso, *Norma*; Lindorf, *Les Contes d'Hoffmann*; Philip II, *Don Carlos*; Timur, *Turandot*; Daland, *Der Fliegende Holländer*; Don Basilio, *Il Barbiere di Siviglia*; Bonze, *Madama Butterfly*; Count des Grieux, *Manon*; Gurnemanz, *Parsifal*; Osmin, *Die Entführung aus dem Serail*; Créon, *Médée*; Walter, *Guillaume Tell*; Commendatore, *Don Giovanni* (also 1992, Japan tour); Rocco, *Fidelio*; Giorgio, *I Puritani*; title role, *Boris Godunov*; Glyndebourne Festival Opera: Sarastro, *Die Zauberflöte*; Seneca, *L'Incoronazione di Poppea*; Fiesco, *Simon Boccanegra*; Scottish Opera: Fiesco, *Simon Boccanegra*; Arkel, *Pelléas et Mélisande*; title role, *Don Giovanni*.

RELATED PROFESSIONAL ACTIVITIES: Regular concerts, recitals, broadcasts and television appearances in the UK and abroad including *Six Foot Cinderella: A Guide to the Bass Voice* (BBC); President, British Youth Opera.

RECORDINGS INCLUDE: Berlioz: *Béatrice et Bénédict, Benvenuto Cellini* (both PHIL), *La Damnation de Faust, Roméo et Juliette* (both DENO); Massenet: *Esclarmonde* (DECC), *Werther* (PHIL); Mozart: *La Clemenza di Tito, Don Giovanni, Die Entführung aus dem Serail* (all PHIL), *Die Zauberflöte* (TELA); Puccini: *La Bohème*

(PHIL), *La Fanciulla del West* (DG), *Manon Lescaut* (EMI); Rossini, *Il Barbiere di Siviglia* (PHIL); Verdi: *Un Ballo in Maschera* (DECC/PHIL), *Giovanna d'Arco* (EMI), *Macbeth, Rigoletto, Il Trovatore* (all PHIL); Wagner, *Parsifal* (ERAT).

VIDEOS INCLUDE: Beethoven, *Fidelio* (Covent Garden); Monteverdi: *L'Incoronazione di Poppea, Il Ritorno d'Ulisse in Patria* (both Glyndebourne Festival Opera); Puccini, *La Fanciulla del West* (Covent Garden); Wagner, *Lohengrin* (Vienna State Opera).

HONOURS INCLUDE: 1991, Commander, Order of the British Empire (CBE).

ADDRESS: c/o Harrison/Parrott Ltd, 12 Penzance Place, London W11 4PA.

LLOYD-DAVIES MARY
Soprano

PERSONAL DETAILS: b. 16 July 1951, Llanuwchllyn, Wales; m. 1983, Hugh M. Roberts, one child.

EDUCATION/TRAINING: 1970–1974, Royal College of Music, with Ruth Packer and Gordon Stewart; 1975, with Pierre Bernac in Paris.

PROFESSIONAL DEBUT: 1976, Vermont Opera Theater, several roles, *L'Enfant et les Sortilèges*.

MAJOR DEBUTS INCLUDE: Welsh National Opera: 1987, Leonore, *Fidelio*; 1988, title role, *Tosca*; 1991, Pocket Opera Company, Nuremberg, Brünnhilde, *Der Ring des Nibelungen*.

CAREER IN THE UK INCLUDES: Since 1977: primarily a concert performer; opera performances include: Chelsea Opera Group, Elisabeth, *Tannhäuser*; Mid Wales Opera: Desdemona, *Otello*; title role, *Tosca*; New Sussex Opera, Venus, *Tannhäuser*; Scottish Opera Go Round, Lady Macbeth, *Macbeth*; Welsh National Opera: Gerhilde, *The Valkyrie*; Lady Macbeth, *Macbeth*.

RELATED PROFESSIONAL ACTIVITIES: Regular concerts, recitals, broadcasts and television appearances in the UK and abroad; 1984, 1987 and 1991, adjudicator:

National Eisteddfod of Wales, Youth
Eisteddfod of Wales.
RECORDINGS INCLUDE: Solo album (SAIN).
AWARDS AND HONOURS INCLUDE: 1972,
Associate, Royal College of Music; 1973:
Blue Riband, National Eisteddfod of
Wales; Princeps Cantorum, International
Eisteddfod, Llangollen.
ADDRESS: c/o Harlequin Agency Ltd, 1
University Place, Cardiff CF2 2JU.

LLOYD-JONES DAVID
Conductor, Editor and Translator

PERSONAL DETAILS: b. 19 November 1934,
London; m. 1964, Carol Whitehead, three
children.
EDUCATION/TRAINING: 1955–1959,
Magdalen College, Oxford, studied
Russian, German and music; further
studies with Iain Hamilton and John
Pritchard.
PROFESSIONAL DEBUT: 1961, Liverpool
Philharmonic Orchestra.
OPERATIC DEBUT: 1962, New Opera
Company at Sadler's Wells Theatre, *The
Wager* by Buxton Orr (world première).
CAREER: 1959–1960, répétiteur, Covent
Garden; 1961–1964, Chorus Master and
Assistant Conductor, New Opera
Company; 1966–1970, conductor at Bath,
Camden, City of London and Wexford
Festivals including 1968, Camden
Festival, *Yolande* (British première);
1972–1978, Assistant Music Director,
Sadler's Wells Opera/English National
Opera; Opera North: 1978–1981, founder
and Music Director; 1981–1990, Artistic
Director; guest conductor at leading
international opera houses in Europe and
North America including Amsterdam,
Karlsruhe, Paris, St Petersburg and
Toronto.
MAJOR OPERATIC DEBUTS INCLUDE: 1967:
Scottish Opera, *Boris Godunov*; Welsh
National Opera, *Carmen*; 1969, Sadler's
Wells Opera, *The Love for Three
Oranges*; 1971, Covent Garden, *Boris
Godunov*; 1978, Opera North, *Samson et
Dalila*.

OPERATIC WORLD PREMIERES INCLUDE:
1977, English National Opera, *The Royal
Hunt of the Sun* by Iain Hamilton; 1983,
Opera North, *Rebecca* by Wilfred
Josephs.
OPERA PERFORMANCES IN THE UK
INCLUDE: 1972–1978, Sadler's Wells Opera/
English National Opera: *War and Peace*
(1972, British stage première), *Katya
Kabanova*, *Carmen*, *La Bohème*, *Tosca*,
Count Ory; since 1978, Opera North, more
than 50 productions including: *Hansel and
Gretel*, *Peter Grimes*, *The Marriage of
Figaro*, *Rigoletto*, *Der Fliegende
Holländer*, *Der Rosenkavalier*, *A Village
Romeo and Juliet*, *The Tales of Hoffmann*,
Macbeth, *The Bartered Bride*, *Così fan
tutte*, *Prince Igor*, *Madama Butterfly*,
Beatrice and Benedict, *Cavalleria
Rusticana/Pagliacci*, *Orfeo ed Euridice*,
Johnny Strikes Up (1984, British
première), *The Mastersingers of
Nuremberg*, *The Midsummer Marriage*,
Aida, *La Fanciulla del West*, *Don
Giovanni*, *The Trojans*, *Daphne* (1987,
British stage première), *Fidelio*, *Acis and
Galatea*, *The Love for Three Oranges*,
Faust, *Salome*, *Yolande*.
RELATED PROFESSIONAL ACTIVITIES:
Regular concerts, broadcasts and
television performances with leading
orchestras in the UK and abroad;
translations include: *Boris Godunov*,
Eugene Onegin, *The Love for Three
Oranges*, *The Queen of Spades*, *Yolande*.
RECORDINGS INCLUDE: Massenet,
Hérodiade (RODO).
PUBLICATIONS INCLUDE: *Boris Godunov*:
1968, translation and vocal score; 1975,
critical edition of original full score (all
Oxford University Press); 1971, *Eugene
Onegin*, translation (Schauer); 1975, *The
Gondoliers*, study score (Eulenburg);
contributor: 1980, *The New Grove
Dictionary of Music and Musicians*
(Macmillan); numerous music and literary
journals.
HONOURS INCLUDE: 1986, Honorary
Doctorate of Music, University of Leeds.
ADDRESS: c/o Allied Artists, 42 Montpelier
Square, London SW7 1JZ.

169

LOCKHART JAMES
Conductor, Pianist and Accompanist and Teacher

POSITION: Director of Opera Department, London Royal Schools' Vocal Faculty.
PERSONAL DETAILS: b. 16 October 1930, Edinburgh; m. 1954, Sheila Grogan (cellist), three children.
EDUCATION/TRAINING: University of Edinburgh; Royal College of Music.
PROFESSIONAL DEBUT: 1954, Yorkshire Symphony Orchestra.
OPERATIC DEBUT: 1958, University of Texas at Austin, *Il Matrimonio Segreto*.
CAREER: 1946–1954: Assistant Organist and Choirmaster, St Giles Cathedral, Edinburgh; Organist and Choirmaster: St John the Divine, Kennington, London; All Souls, Langham Place, London; assistant conductor: 1954–1955, Yorkshire Symphony Orchestra; 1955–1956, Münster Opera; 1956–1957, Bavarian State Opera, Munich; 1957–1959, Glyndebourne Festival Opera; 1960–1961, BBC Scottish Symphony Orchestra; 1957–1959, Director of Opera Workshop, University of Texas at Austin; 1959–1960 and 1962–1968, assistant conductor and coach, Covent Garden; conductor: 1960–1961, Scottish Opera; 1961–1962, Sadler's Wells Opera; 1961–1972, Professor of Repertoire, Royal College of Music; Music Director: 1968–1973, Welsh National Opera; 1972–1980, Cassel; 1981–1988, Koblenz; 1981–1991, The Rhine Philharmonic, Koblenz; 1986–1992, Director of Opera, Royal College of Music; since 1992, Director of Opera Department, London Royal Schools' Vocal Faculty; regular appearances as guest conductor at opera houses in Europe and the USA.
MAJOR OPERATIC DEBUTS INCLUDE: *The Marriage of Figaro*: 1960, Sadler's Wells Opera; 1963, Covent Garden; 1974: Cassel, *Der Ring des Nibelungen*; Hamburg State Opera, *I Vespri Siciliani*; 1975: Bavarian State Opera, Munich, *Aida*; Stuttgart State Opera, *Albert Herring*; 1984, English National Opera

USA tour (including Metropolitan Opera, New York), *War and Peace*.
OPERATIC WORLD PREMIERES INCLUDE: 1967, English Opera Group at the Aldeburgh Festival, *The Bear* by William Walton; 1979, Cassel, *Commedia* by Edward Cowie; 1989, Royal College of Music, *The Fisherman* by Paul Max Edlin.
OPERA PERFORMANCES IN THE UK INCLUDE: Since 1967: Buxton Festival: *Il Sogno di Scipione*, *The Impresario*; Covent Garden: *Boris Godunov*, *Tosca*; Royal College of Music: *Cendrillon*, *Paul Bunyan*, *Eugene Onegin*; Sadler's Wells Opera/English National Opera: *The Bear*, *Il Trovatore*, *Madam Butterfly*; Welsh National Opera: *Boris Godunov*, *Fidelio*, *Falstaff*, *Aida*, *Lulu* (1971, British première), *Billy Budd*, *Don Carlos*, *Otello*.
RELATED PROFESSIONAL ACTIVITIES: Numerous concerts and broadcasts with leading British orchestras; internationally known as accompanist particularly with Margaret Price.
RECORDINGS INCLUDE: Dittersdorf, *Doktor und Apotheker* (German label); Smetana, *The Bartered Bride*; Verdi, *Rigoletto* (both EMI).
HONOURS INCLUDE: 1987, Fellow, Royal College of Music.
ADDRESS: c/o Royal College of Music, Prince Consort Road, London SW7 2BS.

LOPPERT MAX   Critic

PERSONAL DETAILS: b. 24 August 1946, Johannesburg, South Africa.
CAREER: Since 1980, Chief Music Critic, *Financial Times*; *Opera*: 1978–1986, member, Editorial Board; since 1986, Associate Editor.
ADDRESS: c/o *Financial Times*, 1 Southwark Bridge, London SE1 9HL.

LOTT FELICITY   Soprano

PERSONAL DETAILS: b. 8 May 1947, Cheltenham; m. 1973, Robin Golding (Registrar, Royal Academy of Music); m.

1984, Gabriel Woolf (actor and broadcaster), one child.

EDUCATION/TRAINING: 1965–1969, Royal Holloway College, London, studied French; 1969–1973, Royal Academy of Music, with Olive Groves and Flora Nielsen.

PROFESSIONAL DEBUT: 1973, Unicorn Opera, Abingdon, Seleuce, *Tolomeo*.

MAJOR DEBUTS INCLUDE: 1975, English National Opera, Pamina, *The Magic Flute*; 1977, Glyndebourne Festival Opera, Anne Trulove, *The Rake's Progress*; 1979, La Monnaie, Brussels, title role, *L'Incoronazione di Poppea*; 1980, Paris Opera, Donna Elvira, *Don Giovanni*; 1987, Lyric Opera, Chicago, Countess, *Le Nozze di Figaro*; 1988, Bavarian State Opera, Munich, Christine, *Intermezzo*; 1990, Metropolitan Opera, New York, Marschallin, *Der Rosenkavalier*; 1991, Vienna State Opera, title role, *Arabella*; 1992: La Scala, Milan, title role, *Arabella*; Salzburg Festival, Countess, *Le Nozze di Figaro*.

OPERATIC WORLD PREMIERES INCLUDE: 1976, Covent Garden (debut), Lady 3/Girl 3, *We Come to the River* by Hans Werner Henze.

CAREER IN THE UK INCLUDES: Since 1975: Covent Garden: Anne Trulove, *The Rake's Progress*; Countess, *Le Nozze di Figaro*; Blanche, *The Carmelites*; Helena, *A Midsummer Night's Dream*; Eva, *Die Meistersinger von Nürnberg*; Ellen Orford, *Peter Grimes*; Marschallin, *Der Rosenkavalier*; English National Opera: Roxane, *King Roger*; Natasha, *War and Peace*; Fiordiligi, *Così fan tutte*; Donna Elvira, *Don Giovanni*; Glyndebourne Festival and Touring Opera: Pamina, *Die Zauberflöte*; Octavian, *Der Rosenkavalier*; Countess, *Le Nozze di Figaro*; Helena, *A Midsummer Night's Dream*; Christine, *Intermezzo*; Countess, *Capriccio*; Elle, *La Voix Humaine*; Fiordiligi, *Così fan tutte*; Scottish Opera: Mařenka, *The Bartered Bride*; Euridice, *Orfeo ed Euridice*; Welsh National Opera: Countess, *The Marriage of Figaro*; Jenifer, *The Midsummer Marriage*; Governess, *The Turn of the Screw*; Pamina, *The Magic Flute*.

RELATED PROFESSIONAL ACTIVITIES: Numerous concerts, recitals, broadcasts and television appearances in the UK and abroad; founder member, Songmakers' Almanac.

RECORDINGS INCLUDE: Charpentier, *Louise* (ERAT); Delius, orchestral and vocal works (UNIC); Handel, *Messiah* (RPO); Mozart, *Le Nozze di Figaro* (EMI); Schubert, lieder (IMP); R. Strauss: *Four Last Songs*, orchestral and vocal works; Wolf, lieder; English songs (all CHAN), *Sweet Power of Song*, *On Wings of Song* (both EMI).

VIDEOS INCLUDE: Britten, *A Midsummer Night's Dream*; Mozart, *Die Zauberflöte*; R. Strauss, *Intermezzo*; Stravinsky, *The Rake's Progress* (all Glyndebourne Festival Opera).

HONOURS INCLUDE: 1989, Honorary Doctorate, University of Sussex; 1990, Commander, Order of the British Empire (CBE).

ADDRESS: c/o Lies Askonas Ltd, 186 Drury Lane, London WC2B 5RY.

LOWERY NIGEL   Designer

PERSONAL DETAILS: b. London.

EDUCATION/TRAINING: 1979–1982, Central School of Art and Design.

OPERATIC DEBUT: 1984, Batignano Festival, *Apollo et Hyacinthus*.

CAREER: Since 1983, freelance opera and theatre designer in the UK and abroad.

OPERATIC WORLD PREMIÈRES INCLUDE: 1989, English National Opera, *The Plumber's Gift* by David Blake; 1990, Glyndebourne Education on Hastings Pier, *Hastings Spring* by Jonathan Dove; 1991: Royal Opera Garden Venture, *The Judgement of Paris* by John Woolrich; Batignano Festival, *L'Oca del Cairo* by Mozart/Stephen Oliver; 1992: Almeida Opera, *Terrible Mouth* by Nigel Osborne; English National Opera Contemporary Opera Studio, *Soundbites*, a triple bill: *Pig* by Jonathan Dove/ *The Rebuilding of*

Waterloo Bridge by Giles Chaundy/*Nevis* by Kenneth Dempster; 1993, English National Opera, *Inquest of Love* by Jonathan Harvey.

OPERA DESIGNS INCLUDE: Since 1985: Almeida Opera, *Mario and the Magician* (1992, British première); Batignano Festival: *Ba-ta-clan, Lo Schiavo di sua Moglie*; D'Oyly Carte Opera, *The Gondoliers*; English National Opera: *Oedipus Rex/Duke Bluebeard's Castle*, *Die Fledermaus*, *The Duel of Tancredi and Clorinda*; Opera North, *Carmen*; Scottish Opera: *Così fan tutte, Das Rheingold, Die Walküre*; Scottish Opera Go Round, *Macbeth*; Nice Opera, *Werther*; Teatro São Carlos, Lisbon, *La Chute de la Maison Usher*.

AWARDS INCLUDE: 1982, Arts Council Designer Award; 1991, joint winner, International Exhibition of Stage Design, Prague Quadriennale.

ADDRESS: c/o Harriet Cruickshank, 97 Old South Lambeth Road, London SW8 1XU.

LUXON BENJAMIN   Baritone

PERSONAL DETAILS: b. 24 March 1937, Cornwall; m. 1969, Sheila Amit, three children.

PREVIOUS OCCUPATION: Physical education teacher.

EDUCATION/TRAINING: Guildhall School of Music and Drama; further studies with Walther Gruner in London.

PROFESSIONAL DEBUT: 1963, English Opera Group, Tarquinius, *The Rape of Lucretia.*

EARLY CAREER INCLUDED: 1963–1971, appearances with English Opera Group, Handel Opera Society, Morley Opera, St Pancras Festival; roles included: Sid, *Albert Herring*; Demetrius, *A Midsummer Night's Dream*; Elder Son, *The Prodigal Son*; Argante, *Rinaldo*; title roles: *Il Turco in Italia, King Arthur.*

MAJOR DEBUTS INCLUDE: 1972, Glyndebourne Festival Opera, title role, *Il Ritorno d'Ulisse in Patria*; 1974, English National Opera, Rodrigo, *Don Carlos*;

1980: Scottish Opera, title role, *Wozzeck*; Metropolitan Opera, New York, title role, *Eugene Onegin*; 1981: La Monnaie, Brussels, Rodrigo, *Don Carlos*; Paris Opera, Balstrode, *Peter Grimes*; 1984, Opera Company of Boston, title role, *Don Giovanni*; 1985, Vienna Festival, title role, *Giulio Cesare*; 1986: Edinburgh International Festival, Sherasmin, *Oberon*; title role, *Eugene Onegin*: Grand Théâtre, Geneva and La Scala, Milan; 1987, Opera Company of Philadelphia, Balstrode, *Peter Grimes*; 1988, Los Angeles Music Center Opera, title role, *Wozzeck.*

OPERATIC WORLD PREMIERES INCLUDE: 1971, BBC Television, title role, *Owen Wingrave* by Benjamin Britten; 1972, Covent Garden (debut), Jester, *Taverner* by Peter Maxwell Davies; 1977, BBC Radio 3, Jean, *Miss Julie* by William Alwyn.

CAREER IN THE UK INCLUDES: Since 1972: Covent Garden: Marcello, *La Bohème*; Wolfram, *Tannhäuser*; Demetrius, *A Midsummer Night's Dream*; Diomede, *Troilus and Cressida*; Ford, *Falstaff*; Falke, *Die Fledermaus*; Escamillo, *Carmen*; Guglielmo, *Così fan tutte*; title roles: *Owen Wingrave* by Benjamin Britten (1973, world stage première), *Eugene Onegin*; English National Opera: Papageno, *The Magic Flute*; title roles: *Falstaff, Gianni Schicchi*; Glyndebourne Festival Opera: Count, *Le Nozze di Figaro*; Forester, *The Cunning Little Vixen*; Ford, *Falstaff*; Papageno, *Die Zauberflöte*; title role, *Don Giovanni*; Scottish Opera, Papageno, *The Magic Flute.*

RELATED PROFESSIONAL ACTIVITIES: Extensive lieder repertoire; regular concerts, recitals, broadcasts and television appearances with leading orchestras and conductors in the UK and abroad.

RECORDINGS INCLUDE: Berlioz, *L'Enfance du Christ* (ASV); Britten: *The Rape of Lucretia* (DECC), *War Requiem* (TELA); Elgar: *The Dream of Gerontius* (CRD), *The Kingdom* (RCA); Fauré, *Requiem* (EMI);

172

Mahler, Symphony No. 8 (PHIL); Schubert: *Die Schöne Müllerin*, *Schwanengesang*, *Winterreise* (all CHAN); Stravinsky, *Oedipus Rex* (DECC).

VIDEOS INCLUDE: Monteverdi, *Il Ritorno d'Ulisse in Patria*; Mozart: *Don Giovanni*, *Le Nozze di Figaro*, *Die Zauberflöte*; Verdi, *Falstaff* (all Glyndebourne Festival Opera); J. Strauss, *Die Fledermaus* (Covent Garden).

HONOURS INCLUDE: 1970, Fellow, Guildhall School of Music and Drama; 1974, Bard of the Cornish Gorsedd; 1980: Honorary Member, Royal Academy of Music; Honorary Doctorate of Music, University of Exeter; 1986, Commander, Order of the British Empire (CBE).

ADDRESS: c/o Harold Holt Ltd, 31 Sinclair Road, London W14 0NS.

*　*　*　*

MACKAY PENELOPE
Soprano and Teacher

PERSONAL DETAILS: b. 6 April 1943, Bradford.

PREVIOUS OCCUPATION: 1963–1965, bilingual secretary.

EDUCATION/TRAINING: 1961–1963, secretarial college, French Lycée, London; 1965–1969, Guildhall School of Music and Drama, with Winifred Radford.

PROFESSIONAL DEBUT: 1971, Glyndebourne Touring Opera, Zaida, *Il Turco in Italia*.

EARLY CAREER INCLUDED: 1972–1979: English Opera Group/English Music Theatre: Brigitte, *Iolanta*; Second Lady, *Die Zauberflöte*; Goose, *Paul Bunyan* by Benjamin Britten (1976, world stage première); Helena, *The Fairy Queen*; Rachel, *La Cubana* (1978, British première); Arminda, *La Finta Giardiniera*; Glyndebourne Touring Opera, Destiny, *La Calisto*.

MAJOR DEBUTS INCLUDE: 1980, English National Opera, title role, *Manon*; 1982, Liège Opera, Donna Elvira, *Don Giovanni*; 1984: New Sadler's Wells Opera, title role, *Countess Maritza*; Opera North, Anita, *Johnny Strikes Up* (British première); 1985: Handel Opera Society, title role, *Rodrigo*; Graz, title role, *Angelica Vincitrice di Alcina* (first modern performance); Flanders Opera, Antwerp: 1985, Anne Trulove, *The Rake's Progress*; 1987, Mimi, *La Bohème*; 1990, Covent Garden, Fox, *The Cunning Little Vixen*.

OPERATIC WORLD PREMIERES INCLUDE: 1972, New Opera Company at Sadler's Wells Theatre, Lover, *Time Off? Not a Ghost of a Chance!* by Elisabeth Lutyens; 1973, English Opera Group at the Aldeburgh Festival, Strolling Player, *Death in Venice* by Benjamin Britten; 1986, Opera Factory, Virgin Mary/ Agrippina/Vanozza, *Hell's Angels* by Nigel Osborne; 1987, Buxton Festival, commissioned and performed *Waiting* by Stephen Oliver.

CAREER IN THE UK INCLUDES: Since 1980, English National Opera: Frasquita, *Carmen*; Pauline, *La Vie Parisienne*; Drusilla, *The Coronation of Poppea*; Musetta, *La Bohème*; First Lady, *The Magic Flute*; Rosalinde, *Die Fledermaus*; Miranda, *Le Grand Macabre* (1982, British première); Flower Maiden, *Parsifal*; title roles: *The Merry Widow*, *La Belle Hélène*, *Mireille*.

RELATED PROFESSIONAL ACTIVITIES: Regular concerts and recitals; since 1989, teacher: Guildhall School of Music and Drama and Royal Academy of Music.

ADDRESS: c/o Jeffrey & White Management, 5 Richmond Mews, London W1V 5AG.

MACKENZIE JANE LESLIE
Soprano

PERSONAL DETAILS: b. 15 May 1956, British Columbia, Canada; m. 1983, two children.

EDUCATION/TRAINING: 1974–1978, University of Victoria, British Columbia, with Frances James Adaskin; 1978–1980, Else Mayer-Lismann Workshop, London; 1979–1981, Britten-Pears School for Advanced Musical Studies, masterclasses with Peter Pears, Galina Vishnevskaya, Elisabeth Schwarzkopf; currently with Morag Noble.

PROFESSIONAL DEBUT: 1983, Kent Opera, Donna Elvira, *Don Giovanni*.

MAJOR DEBUTS INCLUDE: 1983, Guelph Spring Festival, Ontario, Amor, *Orfeo ed Euridice*; 1984: English National Opera, Marzelline, *Fidelio*; Opera North, Pamina, *The Magic Flute*; Batignano Festival, Dafne, *Apollo e Dafne*; 1986: Scottish Opera, Micaëla, *Carmen*; Pamina, *Die Zauberflöte*: Edmonton Opera, Manitoba Opera, Vancouver Opera; 1987: Welsh National Opera, Mimi, *La Bohème*; Grand Théâtre, Geneva, First Lady, *Die Zauberflöte*; 1988, Vancouver Opera, Governess, *The Turn of the Screw*.

CAREER IN THE UK INCLUDES: Since 1984: City of Birmingham Touring Opera, Alphise, *Les Boréades*; English National Opera, Countess, *The Marriage of Figaro*; Harrogate International Festival, Governess, *The Turn of the Screw*; Opera North: Anne Trulove, *The Rake's Progress*; Euridice, *Orfeo ed Euridice*; Fiordiligi, *Così fan tutte*; Donna Elvira, *Don Giovanni*; Countess, *The Marriage of Figaro*; Mimi, *La Bohème*; Scottish Opera: Pamina, *The Magic Flute*; Countess, *The Marriage of Figaro*.

RELATED PROFESSIONAL ACTIVITIES: Concerts, recitals and broadcasts in the UK and Canada.

AWARDS INCLUDE: 1982, National Vocal Competition, Guelph Spring Festival (Canada).

ADDRESS: c/o Music International, 13 Ardilaun Road, London N5 2QR.

MACKERRAS, SIR CHARLES
Conductor and Editor

POSITIONS: Conductor Emeritus, Welsh National Opera; Principal Guest Conductor: Royal Philharmonic Orchestra, San Francisco Opera, Scottish Chamber Orchestra.

PERSONAL DETAILS: b. 17 November 1925, Schenectady, USA; m. 1947, Judith Wilkins (clarinettist), two children.

EDUCATION/TRAINING: 1939–1944, New South Wales State Conservatorium of Music, Sydney, piano with R. Pennicuick, oboe with J. Brinkman, composition with E. L. Bainton; 1947–1948, Prague Academy of Music, with Václav Talich.

PROFESSIONAL DEBUT: 1945, Sydney Symphony Orchestra.

OPERATIC DEBUT: 1948, Sadler's Wells Opera, *Die Fledermaus*.

CAREER: 1943–1946, Principal Oboist, Sydney Symphony Orchestra; 1949–1954, staff conductor, Sadler's Wells Opera; 1954–1956, Principal Conductor, BBC Concert Orchestra; 1957–1966, freelance conductor with leading British and European orchestras; 1966–1969, First Conductor, Hamburg State Opera; 1970–1977, Music Director, Sadler's Wells Opera/English National Opera; 1976–1979, Chief Guest Conductor, BBC Symphony Orchestra; 1982–1985, Chief Conductor, Sydney Symphony Orchestra; 1986–1988, Principal Guest Conductor, Royal Liverpool Philharmonic Orchestra; Welsh National Opera: 1987–1992, Music Director; since 1992, Conductor Emeritus; Principal Guest Conductor: since 1992: San Francisco Opera, Scottish Chamber Orchestra; since 1993, Royal Philharmonic Orchestra; world authority on Janáček (British premières, Sadler's Wells Opera: 1951, *Katya Kabanova*; 1964, *The Makropoulos Case*).

MAJOR OPERATIC DEBUTS INCLUDE: 1962, Deutsche Staatsoper, East Berlin, *Fidelio*; 1964, Covent Garden, *Katerina Ismailova*; 1965, Hamburg State Opera, *Il Trovatore*; 1969, San Francisco Opera, *Die Zauberflöte*; 1972, Metropolitan Opera,

New York, *Orfeo*; 1973: Australian Opera, Sydney (opening season of Sydney Opera House), *Die Zauberflöte*; Deutsche Oper, Berlin, *Don Carlos*; Paris Opera, *Il Trovatore*; 1980, Vienna State Opera, *Jenůfa*; 1984, Teatro La Fenice, Venice, *Orlando*; 1987, Welsh National Opera, *The Trojans*; 1991, Stavovské Theatre, Prague, *Don Giovanni* (opening production of restored opera house).
OPERATIC WORLD PREMIERES INCLUDE: 1956, English Opera Group at the Scala Theatre, London, *Ruth* by Lennox Berkeley; 1958, English Opera Group at the Aldeburgh Festival, *Noye's Fludde* by Benjamin Britten; 1967, Hamburg State Opera, *Arden Muss Sterben* by Alexander Goehr.
OPERA PERFORMANCES IN THE UK INCLUDE: Since 1987: Covent Garden, *Semele*; English National Opera: *The Pearl Fishers*, *The Makropoulos Case*, *Xerxes*, *Katya Kabanova*, *Fennimore and Gerda/Gianni Schicchi*, *The Cunning Little Vixen*, *The Adventures of Mr Brouček*; Glyndebourne Festival Opera, *Falstaff*; Welsh National Opera: *The Trojans*, *La Bohème*, *Le Nozze di Figaro*, *The Cunning Little Vixen*, *Salome*, *La Traviata*, *Die Frau ohne Schatten*, *Die Entführung aus dem Serail*, *Ariadne auf Naxos*, *Lucia di Lammermoor*, *The Bartered Bride*, *Così fan tutte*, *Idomeneo*, *Der Rosenkavalier*, *Iphigénie en Tauride*, *Tristan und Isolde* (also 1993, at Covent Garden).
RELATED PROFESSIONAL ACTIVITIES: Numerous concerts and television performances; ballet arrangements: 1951, *Pineapple Poll* by Sullivan; 1954, *Lady and the Fool* by Verdi; 1986, reconstruction of Sullivan's lost Cello Concerto; editor of works by Handel and Janáček for publication and performance.
RECORDINGS INCLUDE: Delius, *A Village Romeo and Juliet* (ARGO); Donizetti: *Mary Stuart*, *Roberto Devereux*; Handel, *Julius Caesar* (all EMI); Janáček: *The Cunning Little Vixen*, *From the House of the Dead*, *Jenůfa*, *Katya Kabanova*, *The Makropoulos Case* (all DECC), *Osud* (EMI),

Glagolitic Mass; Martinů, *The Greek Passion* (both SUPR); Mozart, *Die Zauberflöte*; Sullivan, *The Mikado* (both TELA); Verdi, *La Traviata* (EMI).
VIDEOS INCLUDE: Donizetti, *Mary Stuart*; Handel: *Julius Caesar*, *Xerxes* (all English National Opera).
PUBLICATIONS AND RELEVANT PUBLICATIONS INCLUDE: 1987, *Charles Mackerras: A Musicians' Musician* by Nancy Phelan (Gollancz); contributor, numerous music journals.
AWARDS AND HONOURS INCLUDE: 1969, Honorary Member, Royal Academy of Music; 1974, Commander, Order of the British Empire (CBE); 1977, *Evening Standard* Award; *Gramophone* Record of the Year: 1977, *Katya Kabanova*; 1980, *From the House of the Dead*; 1978, Janáček Medal (Czechoslovakia); 1979, Knighthood; 1981, Grammy Award (USA), *From the House of the Dead*; 1983, Prix Fondation Jacques Ibert (France); *Gramophone* Operatic Award: 1983, *The Cunning Little Vixen*; 1984, *Jenůfa*; 1986, *Gramophone* Choral Award, *Glagolitic Mass*; 1987, Fellow, Royal College of Music; Honorary Doctorates: 1990, University of Hull; 1991, University of Nottingham; 1991, Martinů Medal (Czechoslovakia).
ADDRESS: c/o S.A. Gorlinsky Ltd, 34 Dover Street, London W1X 4NJ.

MACKIE WILLIAM   Bass

PERSONAL DETAILS: b. 16 August 1954, Ayr.
EDUCATION/TRAINING: 1976–1980, Royal Scottish Academy of Music, with Neilson Taylor.
PROFESSIONAL DEBUT: 1980, Scottish Opera, Antonio, *Le Nozze di Figaro*.
EARLY CAREER INCLUDED: Principal Bass: 1980–1981, Scottish Opera; 1982–1983, Welsh National Opera; roles included: Alidoro, *La Cenerentola*; Raimondo, *Lucia di Lammermoor*; d'Obigny, *La Traviata*; Theseus, *A Midsummer Night's Dream*; Count Horn, *Un Ballo in Maschera*; Bonze, *Madam Butterfly*; Don

175

Juan, *From the House of the Dead*; Second Knight, *Parsifal*.

MAJOR DEBUTS INCLUDE: 1982, Welsh National Opera, Commendatore, *Don Giovanni*; 1983: Covent Garden, Lavitsky, *Boris Godunov*; English National Opera, Truffaldino, *Ariadne auf Naxos*; 1985: Kent Opera, Don Basilio, *The Barber of Seville*; Opera North, Ferrando, *Il Trovatore*; 1989: Aix-en-Provence Festival, Second Priest/Second Armed Man, *Die Zauberflöte*; Netherlands Opera, Pietro, *Simon Boccanegra*; 1990, Opéra du Rhin, Strasbourg, Father, *Hänsel und Gretel*; 1991, Pocket Opera Company, Nuremberg, Assur, *Semiramide*.

OPERATIC WORLD PREMIERES INCLUDE: 1981, Royal Scottish Academy of Music and Drama, title role, *Columba* by Kenneth Leighton.

CAREER IN THE UK INCLUDES: Since 1984: English National Opera, King of France, *Lear* (1989, British première); Kent Opera, Tutor, *Count Ory*; Opera Northern Ireland, Bartolo, *Le Nozze di Figaro*; Welsh National Opera: Fotis, *The Greek Passion*; Ramfis, *The Drama of Aida*; Colline, *La Bohème*; Angelotti, *Tosca*; Don Basilio, *The Barber of Seville*; Fasolt, *The Rhinegold*; Lodovico, *Otello*.

RELATED PROFESSIONAL ACTIVITIES: Numerous oratorios, recitals and broadcasts in the UK and abroad.

RECORDINGS INCLUDE: Wagner, *Parsifal* (EMI).

HONOURS INCLUDE: 1981, Silver Medal, Worshipful Company of Musicians.

ADDRESS: c/o Preston Management: 74 New Bond Street, London W1Y 9DD or North Barrow, Somerset BA22 7LZ.

MANNION ROSA   Soprano

POSITION: Principal Soprano, English National Opera.

PERSONAL DETAILS: b. 29 January 1962, Lancashire; m. 1985, Gerard McQuade, two children.

EDUCATION/TRAINING: 1980–1983, Royal Scottish Academy of Music and Drama, with Patricia Boyer Kelly.

PROFESSIONAL DEBUT: 1984, Scottish Opera, Adina, *L'Elisir d'Amore*.

EARLY CAREER INCLUDED: 1984–1986, Principal Soprano, Scottish Opera: Amor, Orion; Dorinda, *Orlando*; Pamina, *The Magic Flute*; Barbarina, *The Marriage of Figaro*; Sophie, *Werther*; Gilda, *Rigoletto*.

MAJOR DEBUTS INCLUDE: 1988: English National Opera, Sophie, *Der Rosenkavalier*; Glyndebourne Festival Opera, Constanze, *Die Entführung aus dem Serail*; 1990, Opera North, Magnolia, *Show Boat*; 1991, New Israeli Opera, Tel Aviv, Pamina, *Die Zauberflöte*; 1992,· Dorabella, *Così fan tutte*: Teatro São Carlos, Lisbon; Teatro Comunale, Ferrara; Théâtre du Châtelet, Paris.

OPERATIC WORLD PREMIERES INCLUDE: 1990, English National Opera, Anna Howe, *Clarissa* by Robin Holloway.

CAREER IN THE UK INCLUDES: Since 1986: Buxton Festival: Ginevra, *Ariodante*; Dorotea, *Don Quixote in Sierra Morena*; English National Opera (since 1989, Principal Soprano): Cordelia, *Lear* (1989, British première); First Niece, *Peter Grimes*; Ninetta, *The Love for Three Oranges*; Sophie, *Werther*; Oscar, *A Masked Ball*; Atalanta, *Xerxes*; Gretel, *Hansel and Gretel*; Gilda, *Rigoletto*; Opera North, Gilda, *Rigoletto*; Scottish Opera, Susanna, *The Marriage of Figaro*.

RELATED PROFESSIONAL ACTIVITIES: Numerous concerts and recitals in the UK and abroad.

RECORDINGS INCLUDE: Mozart: *Ascanio in Alba* (ADDA), *Così fan tutte* (DG).

AWARDS INCLUDE: Countess of Munster Award, Shell-Scottish Opera Award, John Scott Award (Scottish Opera).

ADDRESS: c/o John Coast, 31 Sinclair Road, London W14 ONS.

MANSON ANNE   Conductor

POSITION: Music Director, Mecklenburgh Opera.

PERSONAL DETAILS: b. 28 September 1961, Boston, USA.

EDUCATION/TRAINING: 1980–1983, Harvard University; 1985, King's College, London; 1985–1987, Royal College of Music; 1987–1989, Royal Northern College of Music.

PROFESSIONAL AND OPERATIC DEBUT: 1988, Mecklenburgh Opera, *The Emperor of Atlantis*.

CAREER: Since 1988, Music Director, Mecklenburgh Opera; 1991, music assistant, Vienna State Opera.

OPERATIC WORLD PREMIERES INCLUDE: 1991, Royal Opera Garden Venture, *Echoes* by John Hawkins; 1992, Womens Playhouse Trust, *Blood Wedding* by Nicola LeFanu.

OPERA PERFORMANCES INCLUDE: Since 1989: Mecklenburgh Opera: *Die Weisse Rose* (1989, British première), *Mannekins* (1990, British première), *The Soldier's Tale*, *Petrified* (1992, British première); ; Opera 80: *Don Pasquale*, *Don Giovanni*; Leipzig Opera, *My Fair Lady*.

RELATED PROFESSIONAL ACTIVITIES: 1992, concert series, Vienna Chamber Orchestra.

AWARDS INCLUDE: Marshall Scholarship (USA); Tagore Gold Medal, Royal College of Music; 1991, Mecklenburgh Opera, Prudential Award for Opera.

ADDRESS: c/o Mecklenburgh Opera, 55 Marmora Road, London SE22 0RY.

MARKS DENNIS
Administrator and Director

POSITION: General Director, English National Opera.

PERSONAL DETAILS: b. 2 July 1948; m. 1992, Sally Groves (music publisher); two children.

EDUCATION/TRAINING: Trinity College, Cambridge.

CAREER: BBC Television: 1970–1981, director/producer, arts documentaries; 1985–1988, editor, music features; 1988–1991, Assistant Head of Music and Arts; 1991–1993, Head of Music Programmes; 1981–1985, co-founder and director/producer of music programmes, Third Eye (independent television production company); 1987–1991, responsible for all BBC Television opera productions including: as director: *The Electrification of the Soviet Union*, *New Year* (both BBC); as producer: *Duke Bluebeard's Castle* (BBC), *Boris Godunov*, *Così fan tutte*, *Prince Igor* (all Covent Garden), *Billy Budd*, *Hansel and Gretel*, *Lady Macbeth of Mtsensk*, *Wozzeck* (all English National Opera), *La Clemenza di Tito*, *Death in Venice*, *L'Heure Espagnole/L'Enfant et les Sortilèges* (all Glyndbourne Festival Opera), *A Night at the Chinese Opera* (Kent Opera), *The Love for Three Oranges* (Opera North), *Falstaff*, *Otello* (both Welsh National Opera); since 1993/1994 season, General Director, English National Opera.

OTHER PROFESSIONAL ACTIVITIES INCLUDE: Freelance author and journalist.

AWARDS INCLUDE: 1989, Royal Philharmonic Society/Charles Heidsieck Award, Prix Italia: BBC Television production of *Duke Bluebeard's Castle*.

ADDRESS: c/o English National Opera, London Coliseum, St Martin's Lane, London WC2N 4ES.

MARSHALL MARGARET
Soprano

PERSONAL DETAILS: b. 4 January 1949, Stirling; m. 1970, Graeme Davidson, two children.

EDUCATION/TRAINING: Royal Scottish Academy of Music and Drama; privately with Ena Mitchell and Hans Hotter.

PROFESSIONAL DEBUT: 1977, Teatro Comunale, Florence, Euridice, *Orfeo ed Euridice*.

177

MAJOR DEBUTS INCLUDE: 1980, Covent Garden, Countess, *Le Nozze di Figaro*; 1982: Hamburg State Opera, Fiordiligi, *Così fan tutte*; La Scala, Milan, Countess, *Le Nozze di Figaro*; Salzburg Festival, Fiordiligi, *Così fan tutte*; 1983, Glyndebourne Festival Opera, Ilia, *Idomeneo*; 1988: Vienna State Opera, Countess, *Le Nozze di Figaro*; Zurich Opera, Marschallin, *Der Rosenkavalier*; 1991: Canadian Opera Company, Toronto, Vitellia, *La Clemenza di Tito*; Deutsche Oper, Berlin, Countess, *Le Nozze di Figaro*.

CAREER IN THE UK INCLUDES: Since 1977: Covent Garden, Fiordiligi, *Così fan tutte*; English National Opera, Donna Elvira, *Don Giovanni*; Scottish Opera: Euridice, *Orfeo ed Euridice*; Pamina, *The Magic Flute*; Ilia, *Idomeneo*; Countess, *Capriccio*; Countess, *Le Nozze di Figaro*.

RECORDINGS INCLUDE: Gluck, *Orfeo ed Euridice*; Mozart, *Così fan tutte*; Salieri, *Les Danaïdes* (all EMI).

AWARDS INCLUDE: 1974, Munich International Competition; 1992, Gulliver Award (Scotland).

ADDRESS: c/o Harold Holt Ltd, 31 Sinclair Road, London W14 0NS.

MARTIN ADRIAN   Tenor

PERSONAL DETAILS: b. Oxford; m., two children.

EDUCATION/TRAINING: London Opera Centre.

PROFESSIONAL DEBUT: 1971, chorus member, D'Oyly Carte Opera.

EARLY CAREER INCLUDED: 1971–1974, member, D'Oyly Carte Opera, appearances in *Patience*, *The Gondoliers*, *Ruddigore*, *The Mikado*, *Iolanthe*, *The Pirates of Penzance*; 1975–1977, Opera for All: Don Ramiro, *Cinderella*; Tonio, *The Daughter of the Regiment*; Judge, *A Masked Ball*.

MAJOR DEBUTS INCLUDE: 1978, Glyndebourne Touring Opera, Tamino, *Die Zauberflöte*; 1979, Opera North, Camille, *The Merry Widow*; 1981: English National Opera, Camille, *The Merry Widow*; Hamburg State Opera, title role, *Les Contes d'Hoffmann*; 1982, Welsh National Opera, Lensky, *Eugene Onegin*; 1986: Covent Garden, Pong, *Turandot*; Lyric Opera of Queensland, Rodolfo, *La Bohème*; Paris Opera, Tybalt, *Roméo et Juliette*.

CAREER IN THE UK INCLUDES: Since 1979: Buxton Festival, Normanno, *Lucia di Lammermoor*; Covent Garden: First Priest, *Die Zauberflöte*; Esquire, *Parsifal*; Dancing Master, *Ariadne auf Naxos*; English National Opera: Young Sailor, *Tristan and Isolde*; Cassio, *Otello*; Alfred, *Die Fledermaus*; Steersman, *The Flying Dutchman*; Anatol, *War and Peace*; Rodolfo, *La Bohème*; Simpleton, *Boris Godunov*; Don Ottavio, *Don Giovanni*; Vincent, *Mireille*; Ferrando, *Così fan tutte*; Nadir, *The Pearl Fishers*; Janek, *The Makropoulos Case*; Erik, *Fennimore and Gerda*; Shepherd, *Orfeo*; Ernesto, *Don Pasquale*; Glyndebourne Touring Opera, Idamante, *Idomeneo*; Opera North: Ismaele, *Nabucco*; Sali, *A Village Romeo and Juliet*; Alfredo, *La Traviata*; Rodolfo, *La Bohème*; Jacquino, *Fidelio*; Ernesto, *Don Pasquale*.

ADDRESS: c/o Athole Still International Management Ltd, Greystoke House, 80–86 Westow Street, London SE19 3AF.

MASON ANNE   Mezzo-soprano

PERSONAL DETAILS: b. Lincolnshire; m. Geoffrey Moses (bass).

EDUCATION/TRAINING: Royal Academy of Music, with Marjorie Thomas; National Opera Studio; currently with Peter Harrison.

PROFESSIONAL DEBUT: 1977, Welsh National Opera, Second Girl, *The Marriage of Figaro*.

EARLY CAREER INCLUDED: 1977–1982: Abbey Opera, Silla, *Palestrina* (1981, British stage première); Opera North: Fenena, *Nabucco*; Second Lady, *The Magic Flute*; Welsh National Opera:

Second Maid, *Elektra*; Second Lady, *The Magic Flute*.

MAJOR DEBUTS INCLUDE: 1983: English National Opera, Grimgerde, *The Valkyrie*; Glyndebourne Festival Opera, Linetta, *L'Amour des Trois Oranges*; Innsbruck Festival, Celso, *Il Tito*; 1986, Covent Garden Far East tour, Mercédès, *Carmen*; 1987: Glyndebourne Touring Opera, Dorabella, *Così fan tutte*; Netherlands Opera, Suzuki, *Madama Butterfly*; 1988, Aix-en-Provence Festival, Annio, *La Clemenza di Tito*; Teatro La Zarzuela, Madrid: 1989, Marcellina, *Le Nozze di Figaro*; 1992, Dona Clara, *The Duenna* by Roberto Gerhard (world stage première).

OPERATIC WORLD PREMIERES INCLUDE: 1984, Batignano Festival, Beauty, *La Bella e la Bestia* by Stephen Oliver; 1985, Scottish Opera, Mrs Elvsted, *Hedda Gabler* by Edward Harper.

CAREER IN THE UK INCLUDES: Since 1983: Covent Garden: Annina, *La Traviata*; Emilia, *Otello*; Louis XV Chair, *L'Enfant et les Sortilèges*; Zulma, *L'Italiana in Algeri*; Page, *Salome*; Wellgunde and Waltraute, *Der Ring des Nibelungen*; Annio, *La Clemenza di Tito*; Second Lady, *Die Zauberflöte*; Suzuki, *Madama Butterfly*; Annina, *Der Rosenkavalier*; Enrichetta, *I Puritani*; English National Opera, Dorabella, *Così fan tutte*; Kent Opera, Helen, *King Priam*; Musica nel Chiostro, title role, *La Dori*; New Sussex Opera, Ascanio, *Benvenuto Cellini*; Opera North: various roles, *Peace*; Suzuki, *Madam Butterfly*; Park Lane Opera at the Camden Festival: Ramiro, *La Finta Giardiniera*; title role, *Margot la Rouge*; Scottish Opera: Sesto, *La Clemenza di Tito*; Cornelia, *Julius Caesar*.

RELATED PROFESSIONAL ACTIVITIES: Numerous concerts, recitals and broadcasts in the UK and abroad.

RECORDINGS INCLUDE: Donizetti, *Emilia di Liverpool* (OPRA); Mozart, *Le Nozze di Figaro* (EMI); A Hundred Years of Italian Opera (OPRA).

VIDEOS INCLUDE: Sullivan, *HMS Pinafore* (Walker); Tippett, *King Priam* (Kent Opera).

AWARDS AND HONOURS INCLUDE: Countess of Munster Award; Honorary Associate, Royal Academy of Music.

ADDRESS: c/o Ron Gonsalves Personal Artists & Concert Management, 10 Dagnan Road, London SW12 9LQ.

MASTERSON VALERIE
Soprano

PERSONAL DETAILS: b. Birkenhead; m. 1965, Andrew March, two children.

EDUCATION/TRAINING: Royal College of Music, with Gordon Clinton; further studies with Adelaide Saraceni in Milan and with Eduardo Asquez in London.

PROFESSIONAL DEBUT: 1963, Landestheater, Salzburg, Frasquita, *Carmen*.

EARLY CAREER INCLUDED: 1963–1964, Contract Soprano, Landestheater, Salzburg: Nannetta, *Falstaff*; Fiorella, *Il Turco in Italia*; 1966–1970, Principal Soprano, D'Oyly Carte Opera: Mabel, *The Pirates of Penzance*; Casilda, *The Gondoliers*; Yum-Yum, *The Mikado*; title role, *Princess Ida*; 1971–1972: Camden Festival, Amenaide, *Tancredi*; Handel Opera Society, Berenice, *Scipione*.

MAJOR DEBUTS INCLUDE: 1971, Sadler's Wells Opera, Constanze, *The Seraglio*; 1972, Glyndebourne Touring Opera, Constanze, *Die Entführung aus dem Serail*; 1974, Covent Garden, Woglinde, *Das Rheingold*; 1975: Aix-en-Provence Festival, Mathilde, *Elisabetta, Regina d'Inghilterra*; Toulouse, title role, *Manon*; 1978, Paris Opera, Marguérite, *Faust*; 1980: Glyndebourne Festival Opera, Constanze, *Die Entführung aus dem Serail*; National Theatre, Prague, Countess, *Le Nozze di Figaro*; San Francisco Opera, Violetta, *La Traviata*; 1981: Grand Théâtre, Geneva, Gilda, *Rigoletto*; Lyric Opera, Chicago, Antonia, *Les Contes d'Hoffmann*; 1982: La Piccola Scala, Milan, Ginevra, *Ariodante*; Teatro

179

Colón, Buenos Aires, Countess Adele, *Le Comte Ory*; 1983, Gran Teatre del Liceu, Barcelona, Marguérite, *Faust*.
OPERATIC WORLD PREMIERES INCLUDE: 1976, Covent Garden, Second Soldier's Wife, *We Come to the River* by Hans Werner Henze.
CAREER IN THE UK INCLUDES: Since 1972: Covent Garden: Woglinde, *Götter-dämmerung*; Marzelline, *Fidelio*; Violetta, *La Traviata*; Madame Lidoine, *The Carmelites*; Marguérite, *Faust*; Micaëla, *Carmen*; Anne who Steals, *The King Goes Forth to France* (1987, British première); title role, *Semele*; English Bach Festival, Ilia, *Idomeneo*; Sadler's Wells Opera/English National Opera (1972–1980, Principal Soprano): Countess Adele, *Count Ory*; Adele, *Die Fledermaus*; Woodbird, *Siegfried*; Violetta, *La Traviata*; Oscar, *A Masked Ball*; Sophie, *Der Rosenkavalier*; Pamina, *The Magic Flute*; Susanna and Countess, *The Marriage of Figaro*; Cleopatra, *Julius Caesar*; Gilda, *Rigoletto*; Mimi, *La Bohème*; Juliet, *Roméo and Juliet*; Romilda, *Xerxes*; Leïla, *The Pearl Fishers*; Marschallin, *Der Rosenkavalier*; Governess, *The Turn of the Screw*; title roles: *The Merry Widow*, *Manon*, *Louise*, *Mireille*; Welsh National Opera, Fiordiligi, *Così fan tutte*.
RELATED PROFESSIONAL ACTIVITIES: Numerous concerts, recitals, broadcasts and television appearances in the UK and abroad; Vice-president, British Youth Opera; since 1972, professor, London Royal Schools' Vocal Faculty.
RECORDINGS INCLUDE: Handel, *Julius Caesar* (EMI); Rossini, *Elisabetta, Regina d'Inghilterra* (PHIL); Sullivan: *The Mikado*, *Princess Ida* (both DECC); Verdi, *La Traviata*, Wagner: *The Rhinegold, Twilight of the Gods* (all EMI).
VIDEOS INCLUDE: Handel, *Julius Caesar* (English National Opera); Mozart, *Die Entführung aus dem Serail* (Glyndebourne Festival Opera); Sullivan, *The Mikado* (D'Oyly Carte Opera).

AWARDS AND HONOURS INCLUDE: 1983, Society of West End Theatre Award, *Semele* (Covent Garden); 1988, Commander, Order of the British Empire (CBE).
ADDRESS: c/o Music International, 13 Ardilaun Road, London N5 2QR.

MASTERTON-SMITH SIMON
Bass-baritone and Teacher

PERSONAL DETAILS: b. 19 November 1945, Middlesex; m. 1976, Sarah Hillary (ballet dancer and teacher), two children.
PREVIOUS OCCUPATIONS: Management trainee and commodity broker.
EDUCATION/TRAINING: 1969–1972, Guildhall School of Music and Drama, with Arthur Reckless; 1972–1974, London Opera Centre, with Pieter van der Stolk; privately with Gustav Sacher and Josephine Veasey.
PROFESSIONAL DEBUT: 1974, La Monnaie, Brussels, First Soldier, *Salome*.
CAREER INCLUDES: Since 1974: Bryanston Festival: Polyphemus, *Acis and Galatea*; Adonis, *Venus and Adonis*; D'Oyly Carte Opera: Sergeant Meryll, *The Yeomen of the Guard*; Sergeant of Police, *The Pirates of Penzance*; English National Opera: Mars, *Orpheus in the Underworld*; Lillas Pastia, *Carmen*; Wagner, *Faust*; Shogun's Mother, *Pacific Overtures*; Marl, *The Making of the Representative for Planet 8* (1988, British première); Alcindoro, *La Bohème*; Harry Easter, *Street Scene*; Opera for All: Dandini, *Cinderella*; Sulpice, *The Daughter of the Regiment*; Count Horn, *A Masked Ball*; University College Opera, Abner, *Saul and David* (1977, British stage première); Opera Omaha, Nebraska, Colonel Pickering, *My Fair Lady*.
RELATED PROFESSIONAL ACTIVITIES: Concerts and recitals in the UK; teacher: 1981–1983, London Studio Centre; since 1981, privately.

RECORDINGS INCLUDE: Offenbach, *Orpheus in the Underworld*; Sondheim, *Pacific Overtures*; Sullivan, *The Pirates of Penzance*; Weill, *Street Scene* (all TER).
ADDRESS: c/o J.G.A., 2 Silver Place, London W1R 3LL.

MATHESON-BRUCE GRAEME
Tenor

PERSONAL DETAILS: b. 19 July 1945, Dundee; m. 1969, Anne-Marie Ives (soprano, m. diss.), one son.
PREVIOUS OCCUPATION: 1970–1972, civil servant.
EDUCATION/TRAINING: 1963–1964, University of St Andrews; 1965–1969, Royal Scottish Academy of Music and Drama; 1969–1970, Royal Manchester College of Music (both with Ena Mitchell); 1973–1974, London Opera Centre; since 1970, privately with Nicholas Powell.
PROFESSIONAL DEBUT: 1973, Sadler's Wells Opera, Blind, *Die Fledermaus*.
EARLY CAREER INCLUDED: 1973–1982, appearances with Abbey Opera, English Opera Group, Glyndebourne Festival and Touring Opera, Sadler's Wells Opera/ English National Opera; roles included: Gaston, *La Traviata*; Prunier, *La Rondine*; Gnat/Cock, *The Cunning Little Vixen*; Sellem, *The Rake's Progress*; Dr Caius, *Falstaff*; Mercury, *Orpheus in the Underworld*; title role, *Palestrina* (1981, Abbey Opera, British stage première).
MAJOR DEBUTS INCLUDE: 1982, Bremen Opera, Macduff, *Macbeth*; 1987, Houston Grand Opera, Herod, *Salome*; 1988, Nantes Opera, title role, *Otello*; 1992, Pittsburgh Opera, Tristan, *Tristan and Isolde*.
OPERATIC WORLD PREMIERES INCLUDE: 1980, Roundhouse, London, appeared in *The Pig Organ* by Richard Blackford; English National Opera: 1990, Lovelace, *Clarissa* by Robin Holloway; 1992, Pentheus, *Bakxai* by John Buller.
CAREER IN THE UK INCLUDES: Since 1982: English National Opera: Eisslinger, *The Mastersingers of Nuremberg*; Drunken Cossack, *Mazeppa*; Florestan, *Fidelio*; High Priest, *Akhnaten* (1985, British première); Prince, *Rusalka*; Bob Boles and title role, *Peter Grimes*; Tenor/ Bacchus, *Ariadne auf Naxos*; Herman, *The Queen of Spades*; Glyndebourne Festival Opera, Tchekalinsky, *The Queen of Spades*; Kent Opera, Don Basilio, *The Marriage of Figaro*; New Sussex Opera, title role, *Tannhäuser*; Opera North: Don Basilio, *The Marriage of Figaro*; Skula, *Prince Igor*.
ADDRESS: Not available.

MAUCERI JOHN   Conductor

POSITION: Chief Conductor, Hollywood Bowl Orchestra, Los Angeles.
PERSONAL DETAILS: b. 12 September 1945, New York City, USA; m. 1968, Betty Weiss, one child.
EDUCATION/TRAINING: Yale University; Berkshire Music Center, Tanglewood, Massachusetts.
PROFESSIONAL AND OPERATIC DEBUT: 1973, Wolf Trap Opera, Virginia, *The Saint of Bleecker Street*.
CAREER: Music Department, Yale University: 1968–1974, Faculty member; 1974–1984, Associate Professor; Music Director: 1968–1974, Yale Symphony Orchestra; 1979–1982, Washington Opera; 1985–1987, American Symphony Orchestra; 1986, Leonard Bernstein Festival; 1987–1993, Scottish Opera; since 1979, Kennedy Center, Washington D.C. (1982–1990, Music Theatre consultant); since 1990, Chief Conductor, Hollywood Bowl Orchestra.
MAJOR OPERATIC DEBUTS INCLUDE: 1974: Welsh National Opera, *Don Carlos* (British debut); Santa Fe Opera, *Lulu*; 1976: Scottish Opera, *Otello*; Metropolitan Opera, New York, *Fidelio*; 1977: New Orleans Opera, *The Barber of Seville*; New York City Opera, *Mefistofele*; 1979, Kennedy Center, Washington D.C., *Der Schauspieldirektor*; 1980, Washington Opera, *Lucia di Lammermoor*; 1983: Covent Garden in Manchester, *Madama*

Butterfly; English National Opera, *The Force of Destiny*; 1984, La Scala, Milan, *A Quiet Place*; 1987, Lyric Opera, Chicago, *La Bohème*.

OPERATIC WORLD PREMIERES INCLUDE: 1974, Spoleto Festival, *Tamu-Tamu* by Gian Carlo Menotti; 1976, San Franisco Opera, *Angle of Repose* by Andrew Imbrie.

OPERA PERFORMANCES IN THE UK INCLUDE: Since 1983: Covent Garden: *La Bohème, La Fanciulla del West*; English National Opera: *Madam Butterfly, Rigoletto*; Scottish Opera: *Carmen, Billy Budd, Aida, La Bohème, Candide* (revised version), *Das Rheingold, Don Giovanni, Street Scene, La Traviata, La Forza del Destino, Salome, Madama Butterfly, The Trojans, Falstaff, Regina* (1991, British première), *Die Walküre, Norma, The Makropoulos Case*.

RELATED PROFESSIONAL ACTIVITIES: Concerts and broadcasts with leading orchestras worldwide; 1983, Broadway, co-producer, *On Your Toes*; since 1986: trustee, National Institute for Opera and Music Theatre, USA; member, Advisory Panel: American Institute for Verdi Studies, Charles Ives Society.

RECORDINGS INCLUDE: Bernstein, *Candide* (NEW); Blitzstein, *Regina* (DECC); Gershwin: *Girl Crazy, Strike up the Band* (both NONE); Weill: *Aufstieg und Fall der Stadt Mahagonny, Mahagonny-Gesänge, Die Sieben Todsünden, Street Scene* (all DECC).

AWARDS INCLUDE: 1985, Alumni Award in Arts, Yale University; 1987, Grammy Award (USA), *Candide*; 1989, Wavenden All Music Award, Conductor of the Year; 1991: Stereo Review Record of the Year (USA), *Girl Crazy*; Record Critics' Prize (Germany), *Mahagonny-Gesänge* and *Die Sieben Todsünden*.

ADDRESS: c/o Columbia Artists Management Inc., 165 West 57th Street, New York, NY 10019, USA.

MAW NICHOLAS Composer

POSITION: Professor of Music, Milton Avery Graduate School of the Arts, Bard College, Annandale-on-Hudson, New York.

PERSONAL DETAILS: b. 5 November 1935, Grantham.

EDUCATION/TRAINING: 1955–1958, Royal Academy of Music, with Paul Steinitz and Lennox Berkeley; 1958–1959, with Nadia Boulanger and Max Deutsch in Paris.

FIRST PROFESSIONAL PERFORMANCE OF A COMPOSITION: 1958, London, Requiem Mass for women's voices and string orchestra.

CAREER: Since 1958, compositions in all genres including two operas, numerous orchestral, chamber, choral and vocal works; 1964–1966, lecturer, Royal Academy of Music; 1966–1970, first Fellow Commoner in Creative Arts, Trinity College, Cambridge; 1972–1974, Visiting Lecturer, University of Exeter; Visiting Professor of Composition: 1984, 1985 and 1989, Yale University; 1986, Boston University; currently Professor of Music, Milton Avery Graduate School of the Arts, Bard College, Annandale-on-Hudson, New York.

OPERATIC WORLD PREMIERES: 1964, Jeanetta Cochrane Theatre, London, *One Man Show*, comic opera in two acts, libretto by Arthur Jacobs, conductor Norman Del Mar, director William Chappell; 1970, Glyndebourne Festival Opera, *The Rising of the Moon*, opera in three acts, libretto by Beverley Cross, conductor Raymond Leppard, director Colin Graham, designer Osbert Lancaster.

RELATED PROFESSIONAL ACTIVITIES: Founder member and first Chairman, Association of Professional Composers.

RECORDINGS INCLUDE: *Balulalow, Chamber Music, Our Lady's Song, Scenes and Arias, Sinfonia*, Sonata for strings and two horns, String Quartet (all ARGO), *Life Studies* (CONT), *Odyssey* (EMI), *La Vita Nuova, The Voice of Love* (both CHAN).

AWARDS AND HONOURS INCLUDE: 1980,
Midsummer Prize, Corporation of London;
Fellow, Royal Academy of Music.
ADDRESS: c/o Faber Music Ltd, 3 Queen
Square, London WC1N 3AU.

MAXWELL DONALD
Baritone

PERSONAL DETAILS: b. 12 December 1948,
Perth.
PREVIOUS OCCUPATION: 1971–1976,
geography teacher.
EDUCATION/TRAINING: University of
Edinburgh, studied geography; vocal
studies with Joseph Hislop.
PROFESSIONAL DEBUT: 1977, Scottish
Opera, Morton, *Mary, Queen of Scots.*
EARLY CAREER INCLUDED: 1977–1982,
Scottish Opera: Figaro, *The Barber of
Seville*; Sharpless, *Madama Butterfly*;
Enrico, *Lucia di Lammermoor*; Zurga, *Les
Pêcheurs de Perles.*
MAJOR DEBUTS INCLUDE: 1982, Welsh
National Opera, Anckarström, *Un Ballo in
Maschera*; 1983, English National Opera,
Yeletsky, *The Queen of Spades*; 1986,
Teatro Colón, Buenos Aires, Balstrode,
Peter Grimes; 1987, Covent Garden,
English Archer, *The King Goes Forth to
France* (British première); 1989–1990,
Welsh National Opera in Milan, New York
and Tokyo, title role, *Falstaff*; 1990, Paris
Opera, Iago, *Otello.*
CAREER IN THE UK INCLUDES: Since 1982:
Covent Garden, Donner and Gunther, *Der
Ring des Nibelungen*; English Bach
Festival, Thoas, *Iphigénie en Tauride*;
English National Opera: Baron Prus, *The
Makropoulos Case*; Leander, *The Love
for Three Oranges*; Father, *Hansel and
Gretel*; Eisenstein, *Die Fledermaus*; title
roles: *The Barber of Seville, Wozzeck*;
Opera London, Bottom, *A Midsummer
Night's Dream*; Opera North: Don Pizarro,
Fidelio; Escamillo, *Carmen*; title role, *Der
Fliegende Holländer*; Scottish Opera,
Baron Prus, *The Makropoulos Case*;
Welsh National Opera: Shishkov, *From
the House of the Dead*; Ned Keene, *Peter
Grimes*; Marcello, *La Bohème*; Don
Alfonso, *Così fan tutte*; Iago, *Otello*;
Count, *Le Nozze di Figaro*; Rance,
La Fanciulla del West; Golaud,
Pelléas et Mélisande; title roles:
Rigoletto, Falstaff.
RELATED PROFESSIONAL ACTIVITIES:
Numerous concerts, broadcasts, recitals
and television appearances in the UK and
abroad particularly as member of Music
Box (with Linda Ormiston and pianist);
private teacher.
RECORDINGS INCLUDE: Britten: *A
Midsummer Night's Dream, Noye's
Fludde* (both VIRG); Menotti, *Amahl and
the Night Visitors* (TER); Mozart, *Le Nozze
di Figaro* (PHIL); Orff, *Carmina Burana*
(IMP); Tippett, *The Ice Break* (VIRG).
VIDEOS INCLUDE: Debussy, *Pelléas et
Mélisande* (Welsh National Opera).
AWARDS INCLUDE: 1977, John Noble Opera
Award.
ADDRESS: c/o Music International, 13
Ardilaun Road, London N5 2QR.

MAXWELL DAVIES,
SIR PETER
Composer and Conductor

PERSONAL DETAILS: b. 8 September 1934,
Salford.
EDUCATION/TRAINING: Royal Manchester
College of Music; University of
Manchester; 1957, with Goffredo Petrassi
in Rome; 1962–1964, Harkness Fellow,
Graduate Music School, Princeton
University, with Roger Sessions, Milton
Babbitt, Earl Kim.
FIRST WORK TO ACHIEVE PROMINENCE:
1955, Sonata for trumpet and piano.
CAREER: 170 published works in all genres
including four symphonies, seven
concertos, six operas, 11 music theatre
works (including: 1969, *Eight Songs for a
Mad King*; 1984, *The No. 11 Bus* and six
for performance by children) and many
other works for performance by non
specialist children; 1959–1962, Director of
Music, Cirencester Grammar School;
1966, Visiting Composer, University of
Adelaide; co-founder: 1967, Pierrot

Players; 1970, The Fires of London (1970–1987, Artistic Director); 1977–1986, founder and Artistic Director, St Magnus Festival, Orkney Islands; 1975–1980, Professor of Composition, Royal Northern College of Music; 1985, Visiting Fromm Professor of Composition, Harvard University; Artistic Director: 1979–1984, Dartington Hall Summer School of Music; since 1989, Hoy Summer School, Orkney Islands; since 1985, Associate Composer and Conductor, Scottish Chamber Orchestra; since 1992, Conductor/Composer: BBC Philharmonic Orchestra, Royal Philharmonic Orchestra.

OPERATIC WORLD PREMIERES: 1972, Covent Garden, *Taverner*, opera in two acts, after 16th-century letters and documents, conducter Edward Downes, director Michael Geliot, designer Ralph Koltai; St Magnus Festival: 1977, *The Martyrdom of St Magnus*, chamber opera in one act, after the novel by George Mackay Brown, conductor the composer, director Murray Melvin; 1978, *The Two Fiddlers*, opera in two acts for children to play and sing, after George Mackay Brown, conductor Norman Mitchell, director Jack Ridgway; 1980, *Cinderella*, pantomine opera in two acts for children to play and sing, conductor Glenys Hughes, director Marlene Mainland; 1980, Edinburgh International Festival, *The Lighthouse*, chamber opera in one act with prologue, conductor Richard Dufallo, director David William; 1988, Darmstadt, *Resurrection*, opera in one act with prologue, conductor Hans Drewanz, director Peter Brenner, designer Waltraud Engelbert (all librettos by the composer).

RELATED PROFESSIONAL ACTIVITIES: Guest conductor with leading British and international orchestras; numerous television apppearances as composer and conductor; President: since 1983, Schools Music Association; since 1986: St Magnus Festival, Composers' Guild of Great Britain; since 1989, National Federation of Music Societies.

RECORDINGS INCLUDE: *Eight Songs for a Mad King*, *The Martydom of St Magnus*, *Miss Donnithorne's Maggot*, *The Two Fiddlers*, *Sinfonia*, *Sinfonia concertante*, *Sinfonietta Accademica* (all UNIC), Symphony No. 3 (BBC), Symphony No. 4 (COLL), Concerto for trumpet and orchestra (COLL/PHIL), *Strathclyde Concerto* for cello and orchestra, *Strathclyde Concerto* for oboe and orchestra (both UNIC), *Strathclyde Concerto* for horn, trumpet and orchestra, *Strathclyde Concerto* for clarinet and orchestra (both COLL), Concerto for violin and orchestra (CBS).

RELEVANT PUBLICATIONS INCLUDE: 1979, *Peter Maxwell Davies: Studies from Two Decades* by Stephen Pruslin (Boosey & Hawkes); 1982, *Peter Maxwell Davies* by Paul Griffiths (Robson).

AWARDS AND HONOURS INCLUDE: 1978, Fellow, Royal Northern College of Music; Honorary Member: 1979, Royal Academy of Music; 1981, Guildhall School of Music and Drama; 1981: Commander, Order of the British Empire (CBE); Honorary Doctorate of Law, University of Aberdeen; 1987: Knighthood; Honorary Member, Royal Philharmonic Society; 1988, Officier de l'Ordre des Arts et des Lettres (France); 1989, Cobbett Medal for Chamber Music; 1991, first award, Association of British Orchestras; Honorary Doctorates of Music: Universities of Edinburgh, Manchester, Bristol and Open University.

ADDRESS: c/o Judy Arnold, 50 Hogarth Road, London SW5 0PU.

MEDCALF STEPHEN
Director

POSITIONS: Director of Productions, English Touring Opera; Associate Director of Productions, Opera School, Guildhall School of Music and Drama.

PERSONAL DETAILS: b. Buckinghamshire.

EDUCATION/TRAINING: University of Nottingham, studied economic and social history; London Drama Studio.

CAREER: 1982–1988: staff director: Glyndebourne Festival and Touring Opera, Opera North, Aldeburgh, Buxton, Camden and Wexford Festivals; since 1991: Director of Productions, Opera 80/ English Touring Opera; Associate Director of Productions, Opera School, Guildhall School of Music and Drama.

MAJOR OPERATIC DEBUTS INCLUDE: 1988, Buxton Festival, *Il Combattimento di Tancredi e Clorinda*; 1989, Opera North, *The Flying Dutchman*; 1991, Opera 80, *The Magic Flute*; 1992: Teatro São Carlos, Lisbon/Théâtre du Châtelet, Paris co-production, *Così fan tutte* (also at Teatro Comunale, Ferrara); Wexford Festival, *Il Piccolo Marat*.

OPERA PRODUCTIONS IN THE UK INCLUDE: Since 1985: Birmingham Conservatoire, *Manon*; Guildhall School of Music and Drama: *Angélique*, *La Vida Breve*, *Betrothal in a Monastery*; Harrogate International Festival, *The Turn of the Screw*; Mid Wales Opera: *Tosca*, *Otello*, *Madama Butterfly*; New Sussex Opera, *Aida*; Opera East, *The Barber of Seville*; Opera Viva: *The Magic Flute*, *The Carmelites*; Opera 80/English Touring Opera, *Don Giovanni*.

ADDRESS: c/o Performing Arts, 6 Windmill Street, London W1R 5HX.

MEE ANTHONY   Tenor

PERSONAL DETAILS: b. 9 September 1951, Lancashire; m. 1984, Heather Anthony (soprano).

PREVIOUS OCCUPATION: Motor mechanic.

EDUCATION/TRAINING: 1968–1972, Leigh Technical College, studied motor vehicle engineering; 1980–1984, Royal Northern College of Music, with Patrick McGuigan.

PROFESSIONAL DEBUT: 1984, Welsh National Opera, title role, *Ernani*.

MAJOR DEBUTS INCLUDE: 1985, Opera North, Arturo, *I Puritani*; 1986, English National Opera, Gabriele, *Simon Boccanegra*; 1989, Scottish Opera, Lippo Fiorentino, *Street Scene*; 1990, English National Opera Soviet Union tour (Bolshoi and Kirov), Malcolm, *Macbeth*.

CAREER IN THE UK INCLUDES: Since 1984: Chelsea Opera Group, Des Grieux, *Manon Lescaut*; Craig-y-nos, Rodolfo, *La Bohème*; English National Opera: Cavaradossi, *Tosca*; Nadir, *The Pearl Fishers*; Beppe, *Pagliacci*; Lippo Fiorentino, *Street Scene*; Malcolm, *Macbeth*; Megaros/Student, *Doctor Faust*; Alfred, *Die Fledermaus*; Herald, *Don Carlos*; Dancing Master, *Ariadne auf Naxos*; First Armed Man, *The Magic Flute*; Opera North, King Ouf I, *L'Etoile*; Scottish Opera: Trabucco, *La Forza del Destino*; Dr Caius, *Falstaff*; Welsh National Opera, Panait, *The Greek Passion*.

RELATED PROFESSIONAL ACTIVITIES: Concerts at major venues in the UK.

RECORDINGS INCLUDE: Weill, *Street Scene* (DECC).

ADDRESS: c/o Stafford Law Associates, 26 Mayfield Road, Weybridge, Surrey KT13 8XB.

METCALF JOHN   Composer

POSITIONS: Artistic Director, Vale of Glamorgan Festival; Associate Artistic Director and Composer in Residence, School of Fine Arts, Banff Centre, Alberta, Canada.

PERSONAL DETAILS: b. 13 August 1946, Swansea; m. Gillian Alexander (artist and designer), three children.

EDUCATION/TRAINING: 1964–1967, University College, Cardiff, with Alun Hoddinott; 1970–1971, Goldsmith's College, University of London, electronic music with Hugh Davies.

FIRST PROFESSIONAL PERFORMANCE OF A COMPOSITION: 1970, BBC Welsh Symphony Orchestra, Sinfonia.

CAREER: Since 1970, compositions in all genres including four music theatre/ operas, numerous orchestral, chamber, choral and vocal works; commissions from Gulbenkian Foundation, BBC, London Sinfonietta, Welsh National Opera

185

and Bath, Cardiff, Cheltenham, Frankfürt
Festivals.

OPERATIC WORLD PREMIÈRES: 1972,
Gwent, *PTOC*, multi-media work for
children; 1981, Welsh National Opera, *The
Journey*, opera in two acts, libretto by
John Hope Mason, conductor Anthony
Hose, director John Eaton, designer Peter
Mumford; 1984, St Donat's Music Theatre
Ensemble, *The Crossing*, music theatre
work in five scenes, conductor David
Seaman; 1990, Welsh National Opera,
Tornrak, opera in two acts; libretto by
Michael Wilcox, conductor Richard
Armstrong, director Mike Ashman,
designer Bernard Culshaw.

RELATED PROFESSIONAL ACTIVITIES:
1971–1981, Director of Music, United
World College of the Atlantic, South
Wales; 1975–1985, Artistic Director, St
Donat's Arts Centre, South Wales; School
of Fine Arts, Banff Centre, Alberta: since
1986, Associate Artistic Director; since
1991, Composer in Residence; since 1990,
Artistic Director, Vale of Glamorgan
Festival.

AWARDS AND HONOURS INCLUDE: 1973,
Gulbenkian Dance Fellow; Arts Fellow:
1977, UK/USA Bicentennial; 1984,
University of Wales.

ADDRESS: c/o Gillian Clench International
Artists' Management, 1 Mount Pleasant
Cottages, Rhiwbina Hill, Cardiff CF4 6UP.

MICHAELS-MOORE ANTHONY
Baritone

POSITION: Member, The Royal Opera,
Covent Garden.

PERSONAL DETAILS: b. 8 April 1957, Essex;
m. Ewa Bozena Migocki, one child.

PREVIOUS OCCUPATIONS: 1975–1978,
Second Lieutenant, Second Royal Tank
Regiment; 1979–1984, primary school
teacher.

EDUCATION/TRAINING: 1975–1978,
University of Newcastle; 1978–1979,
Teacher Training College, Newcastle;
1984–1985, Royal Scottish Academy of
Music and Drama, with Neilsen Taylor;
since 1981, privately with Eduardo
Asquez.

PROFESSIONAL DEBUT: 1982, English Bach
Festival, chorus member, *Castor et
Pollux*.

EARLY CAREER INCLUDED: 1982–1984,
chorus member: English Bach Festival,
World of Gilbert and Sullivan; 1985–1986:
Opera North, Messenger, *Oedipus Rex*;
Scottish Opera Go Round, Scarpia, *Tosca*.

MAJOR DEBUTS INCLUDE: 1987: Covent
Garden, Nightwatchman, *Die Frau ohne
Schatten*; English National Opera, Zurga,
The Pearl Fishers; 1988, Opera Company
of Philadelphia, Guglielmo, *Così fan tutte*;
1990, Welsh National Opera, title role, *Il
Barbiere di Siviglia*; 1991: Canadian
Opera Company, Toronto, Guglielmo,
Così fan tutte; Gran Teatre del Liceu,
Barcelona, title role, *Il Barbiere di
Siviglia*; 1992, Teatro La Zarzuela,
Madrid, Don Ferdinand, *The Duenna* by
Roberto Gerhard (world stage première).

CAREER IN THE UK INCLUDES: Since 1987:
member, Covent Garden: Shchelkalov,
Boris Godunov; Ping, *Turandot*; Marullo,
Rigoletto; Marcello, *La Bohème*; Silvio,
Pagliacci; Ned Keene, *Peter Grimes*;
Ottokar, *Der Freischütz*; Dominik,
Arabella; Speaker, *Die Zauberflöte*;
Falke, *Die Fledermaus*; Sonora, *La
Fanciulla del West*; Belcore, *L'Elisir
d'Amore*; Malatesta, *Don Pasquale*;
Forester, *The Cunning Little Vixen*; title
role, *Il Barbiere di Siviglia*; also: Buxton
Festival, Mendo, *Don Quixote in Sierra
Morena*; English National Opera: Count,
The Marriage of Figaro; Yeletsky, *The
Queen of Spades*; Opera North:
Escamillo, *Carmen*; Germont, *La
Traviata*; Rodrigo, *Don Carlos*; title role,
The Marriage of Figaro.

RELATED PROFESSIONAL ACTIVITIES:
Numerous concerts and broadcasts in the
UK and abroad.

VIDEOS INCLUDE: Strauss, *Die Fledermaus*
(Covent Garden).

AWARDS INCLUDE: 1986, finalist, Opera
Company of Philadelphia/Luciano
Pavarotti International Voice Competition
(USA).

ADDRESS: c/o John Coast, 31 Sinclair Road, London W14 ONS.

MILES ALASTAIR   Bass

PERSONAL DETAILS: b. 11 July 1961, Middlesex.

PREVIOUS OCCUPATIONS: 1982–1985, freelance orchestral flautist and teacher.

EDUCATION/TRAINING: 1979–1983, Guildhall School of Music and Drama: flute with Trevor Wye and Peter Lloyd, vocal studies with Richard Standen; privately: 1984–1985, with Bruce Boyce; 1986–1987, with Rudolf Piernay.

PROFESSIONAL DEBUT: 1985, Opera 80, Trulove, *The Rake's Progress.*

MAJOR DEBUTS INCLUDE: 1986, Glyndebourne Touring Opera, Pietro, *Simon Boccanegra*; 1987, Vancouver Opera, Colline, *La Bohème*; 1988: Covent Garden, Second Knight, *Parsifal*; English National Opera, Harašta, *The Cunning Little Vixen*; 1989, Welsh National Opera, Spirit Messenger, *Die Frau ohne Schatten*; 1990, Glyndebourne Festival Opera, Speaker, *Die Zauberflöte*; 1991: Deutsche Oper, Berlin, Giorgio, *I Puritani*; Lyons Opera, Colline, *La Bohème*; 1992, Edinburgh International Festival, Priest, *Moses and Aaron* (concert performance); 1993: Netherlands Opera, title role, *Le Nozze di Figaro*; San Francisco Opera, Giorgio, *I Puritani.*

CAREER IN THE UK INCLUDES: Since 1986: Covent Garden: Lord Sidney, *Il Viaggio a Reims*; Lorenzo, *I Capuleti e i Montecchi*; Don Fernando, *Fidelio*; Glyndebourne Touring Opera, Dikoy, *Katya Kabanova*; Welsh National Opera: Colline, *La Bohème*; Raimondo, *Lucia di Lammermoor*; Don Basilio, *Il Barbiere di Siviglia*; Sparafucile, *Rigoletto*; Da Silva, *Ernani.*

RELATED PROFESSIONAL ACTIVITIES: Numerous concerts with leading conductors and orchestras in the UK.

RECORDINGS INCLUDE: Beethoven: *Mass in C, Missa Solemnis* (both ARCH); Handel, *Saul* (PHIL); Monteverdi, *Vespers* (ARCH);

Mozart, *Don Giovanni* (EMI); Verdi, *Ernani* (DECC).

AWARDS INCLUDE: 1986: Decca-Kathleen Ferrier Prize, Esso/Glyndebourne Touring Opera Award; 1987, John Christie Award.

ADDRESS: c/o Lies Askonas Ltd, 186 Drury Lane, London WC2 5RY.

MILLER JONATHAN   Director

PERSONAL DETAILS: b. 21 July 1934, London; m. 1956, Helen Collet, three children.

EDUCATION/TRAINING: St John's College, Cambridge, studied natural sciences.

PROFESSIONAL DEBUT: 1961, London and New York, performed and co-wrote, Beyond the Fringe.

OPERATIC DEBUT: 1974, New Opera Company, *Arden Must Die* (British première).

CAREER: Freelance opera and theatre director, television presenter and producer, author and lecturer; 1973–1975, Associate Director, Royal National Theatre; 1979–1981, Producer, BBC Television Shakespeare series; 1978–1987, Associate Director, English National Opera; 1988–1990, Artistic Director, Old Vic Theatre.

MAJOR OPERATIC DEBUTS INCLUDE: 1975: Glyndebourne Festival Opera, *The Cunning Little Vixen*; Kent Opera, *Cosi fan tutte*; 1977, *The Cunning Little Vixen*: Australian Opera, Sydney and Frankfurt Opera; 1978, English National Opera, *The Marriage of Figaro*; 1982, Opera Theatre of St Louis, *Cosi fan tutte*; 1983, Scottish Opera, T*he Magic Flute*; 1986/1987, Maggio Musicale, Florence/English National Opera co-production, *Tosca*; 1988, Los Angeles Music Center Opera, *The Mikado*; 1989: Glimmerglass Opera, New York, *La Traviata*; Houston Grand Opera, *The Mikado*; 1991: La Scala, Milan, *La Fanciulla del West*; Metropolitan Opera, New York, *Katya Kabanova*; Tel Aviv, *Die Zauberflöte*; Vienna State Opera, *Le Nozze di Figaro*;

1992, Opera Omaha, Nebraska, *Ermione* (also designer).

OPERA PRODUCTIONS IN THE UK INCLUDE: Since 1975: English National Opera: *The Turn of the Screw, Arabella, Otello, Rigoletto, Don Giovanni, The Magic Flute, The Mikado, The Barber of Seville*; Kent Opera: *Rigoletto, Orfeo, Eugene Onegin, La Traviata, Falstaff, Fidelio*; Scottish Opera, *Candide*.

RELATED PROFESSIONAL ACTIVITIES: Since 1959, Doctor of Medicine; Research Fellow: 1970–1973, History of Medicine, University College, London; since 1984, Neuro-psychology, University of Sussex; since 1977, Visiting Professor in Drama, Westfield College, London.

VIDEOS INCLUDE: Sullivan, *The Mikado*; Verdi, *Rigoletto* (both English National Opera).

PUBLICATIONS AND RELEVANT PUBLICATIONS INCLUDE: 1972, editor, *Freud: The Man, His World, His Influence* (Weidenfeld & Nicholson); 1978, *The Body in Question* (Cape); 1983: *States of Mind* (BBC), *The Human Body*; 1984, *The Facts of Life* (both Cape); 1986, *Subsequent Performances*; 1990, editor, *The Don Giovanni Book: Myths of Seduction and Betrayal* (both Faber); 1992, *A Profile of Jonathan Miller* by Michael Romain (Cambridge University Press).

AWARDS AND HONOURS INCLUDE: 1981: Honorary Doctorate of Literature, University of Leicester; Silver Medal, Royal Television Society; 1982: Honorary Fellow, St John's College, Cambridge; *Evening Standard* Award, *Rigoletto* (English National Opera); Society of West End Theatre Award, English National Opera production of *Rigoletto*; 1983, Commander, Order of the British Empire (CBE); 1990, Albert Medal, Royal Society of Arts; 1991, Honorary Fellow, Royal Academy of Arts.

ADDRESS: c/o IMG Artists, Media House, 3 Burlington Lane, Chiswick, London W4 2TH.

MILLS BEVERLEY
Mezzo-soprano

PERSONAL DETAILS: b. Kent; m., one child.

EDUCATION/TRAINING: Trinity College of Music, with James Gaddarn; 1978–1979, National Opera Studio, with Nancy Evans.

PROFESSIONAL DEBUT: 1980, Batignano Festival, Alessandro, *Tolomeo*.

MAJOR DEBUTS INCLUDE: 1981, Glyndebourne Touring Opera, Cherubino, *Le Nozze di Figaro*; 1982: Welsh National Opera, Bersi, *Andrea Chénier*; Venus/ Autumn, *L'Egisto*: Scottish Opera, Schwetzingen Festival and Teatro La Fenice, Venice; 1984, Opera North, Page, *Salome*.

CAREER IN THE UK INCLUDES: Since 1981: Aldeburgh Festival: Nancy, *Albert Herring*; title role, *The Rape of Lucretia*; Buxton Festival: Alinda, *Jason*; Eleonora di Scandiano, *Torquato Tasso*; Opera North: Polly, *The Threepenny Opera*; Tessa, *The Gondoliers*; Siebel, *Faust*; Rosina, *The Barber of Seville*; Cherubino, *The Marriage of Figaro*; Selysette, *Ariane and Bluebeard*; Dorabella, *Così fan tutte*; Scottish Opera: Prince Orlofsky, *Die Fledermaus*; Fatima, *Oberon*; Baroness, *La Vie Parisienne*; Cherubino, *The Marriage of Figaro*; title role, *La Cenerentola*; Welsh National Opera: Amneris, *The Drama of Aida*; Mercédès, *Carmen*; Valencienne, *The Merry Widow*; Zerlina, *Don Giovanni*; Cherubino, *Le Nozze di Figaro*; Page, *Salome*; Suzuki, *Madam Butterfly*; Teresa, *La Sonnambula*; Isolier, *Count Ory*.

RELATED PROFESSIONAL ACTIVITIES: Numerous concerts, recitals, television and festival appearances in the UK.

VIDEOS INCLUDE: Sullivan, *Iolanthe* (Walker).

ADDRESS: c/o Gillian Clench International Artists' Management, I Mount Pleasant Cottages, Rhiwbina Hill, Cardiff CF4 6UP.

MILLS BRONWEN   Soprano

PERSONAL DETAILS: m. Malcolm Hunter (director), two children.
EDUCATION/TRAINING: University of London, studied music; Guildhall School of Music and Drama, with Rudolf Piernay.
PROFESSIONAL DEBUT: 1980, Kent Opera, Miss Jessel, *The Turn of the Screw*.
EARLY CAREER INCLUDED: 1981–1984, appearances with Cambridge University Opera, Handel Opera Society, Opera 80, Opera Restor'd, Batignano Festival; roles included: Lina, *Stiffelio*; Tigrane, *Radamisto*; Fiordiligi, *Così fan tutte*; Violetta, *La Traviata*; Aeneas, *The Death of Dido* (1981, Opera Restor'd, first modern performance); Dido, *Dido and Aeneas*; Governess, *The Turn of the Screw*.
MAJOR DEBUTS INCLUDE: 1985: Opera North, title role, *The Golden Cockerel*; Teatro Municipale, Reggio Emilia, Almirena, *Rinaldo*; 1989: Volte-Face at the Queen Elizabeth Hall, Elisabeth, *Elegy for Young Lovers*; New Israeli Opera, Tel Aviv, Violetta, *La Traviata*; 1990, Dublin Grand Opera, Violetta, *La Traviata*.
CAREER IN THE UK INCLUDES: Since 1985: Craig-y-nos: Norina, *Don Pasquale*; Countess, *Count Ory*; Music Theatre Wales: Madeline, *The Fall of the House of Usher* (1989, British première); Mrs P, *The Man who Mistook his Wife for a Hat*; Opera North: Queen of Shemakha, *The Golden Cockerel*; Blonde, *The Seraglio*; title role, *Daphne*; Opera Restor'd, Cupid, *The Death of Dido*.
RECORDINGS INCLUDE: Boyce, *Solomon*; Gay, *The Beggar's Opera* (both HYPE).
ADDRESS: c/o Magenta Music International Ltd, 64 Highgate High Street, London N6 5HX.

MILNER HOWARD   Tenor

PERSONAL DETAILS: b. Oxford.
PREVIOUS OCCUPATION: 1977–1980, jazz musician.
EDUCATION/TRAINING: 1972–1975, Pembroke College, Cambridge, studied English; Guildhall School of Music and Drama: 1975–1976, studied clarinet; 1983–1985, vocal studies with Rudolph Piernay; currently with Janice Chapman.
PROFESSIONAL DEBUT: 1986, Glyndebourne Touring Opera, Mr Upfold, *Albert Herring*.
MAJOR DEBUTS INCLUDE: 1987, Scottish Opera, Pedrillo, *The Seraglio*; 1988, English National Opera, Squeak, *Billy Budd*; 1991: Covent Garden, First Servant, *Capriccio*; Théâtre Municipal, Aix-en-Provence, Mengone, *Lo Speziale*.
OPERATIC WORLD PREMIERES INCLUDE: 1990, London Opera Festival, Tommy, *Albergo Empedocle* by Paul Barker.
CAREER IN THE UK INCLUDES: Since 1987: Covent Garden, Apprentice, *Die Meistersinger von Nürnberg*; English National Opera, Spoletta, *Tosca*; Kent Opera: Jacquino, *Fidelio*; Eumete, *The Return of Ulysses*; title role, *Count Ory*; Opera Factory: Don Curzio, *The Marriage of Figaro*; Arnalta/Freed Slave, *The Coronation of Poppea*; Scottish Opera, Camille, *The Merry Widow*.
RECORDINGS INCLUDE: Bach, *Mass in B Minor* (DG); Beethoven, *Choral Fantasia* (EMI); Finzi, *Intimations of Immortality*; Monteverdi: *L'Incoronazione di Poppea* (both BBC), *Orfeo* (DG); Mozart, *Ascanio in Alba* (ADDA).
VIDEOS INCLUDE: Britten, *Billy Budd* (English National Opera).
ADDRESS: c/o Korman International Management, Crunnells Green Cottage, Preston, Hertfordshire, SG4 7UQ.

MILNES RODNEY
Critic and Translator

POSITIONS: Editor, *Opera*; Chief Opera Critic, *The Times*.
PERSONAL DETAILS: b. 26 July 1936.
EDUCATION/TRAINING: Christ Church, Oxford, studied history.
CAREER: 1966–1968, Editorial Director, Rupert Hart-Davis Ltd; 1968–1987, Music Critic, *Harpers and Queen* Magazine;

1970–1990, Opera Critic, *The Spectator*; 1988–1990, President, Critics' Circle; 1990–1992, Opera Critic, *Evening Standard*; since 1992, Chief Opera Critic, *The Times*; *Opera*: since 1971, contributor; since 1973, member, Editorial Board; 1976–1986, Associate Editor; since 1986, Editor; translations include: *Don Quixote* (Phoenix Opera), *The Jacobin* (Welsh National Opera), *Osud*, *Rusalka* (both English National Opera).

HONOURS INCLUDE: Knight, Order of White Rose (Finland).

ADDRESS: c/o *Opera*, 1a Mountgrove Road, London N5 2LU.

MINTON YVONNE
Mezzo-soprano

PERSONAL DETAILS: b. 4 December 1938, Sydney, Australia; m. 1965, William Barclay, two children.

EDUCATION/TRAINING: 1951–1960, privately with Marjorie Walker; 1957–1960, Elsa Strahlia Scholar, Sydney Conservatorium of Music; further studies with Henry Cummings and Joan Cross in London.

PROFESSIONAL DEBUT: 1964, City Literary Institute, London, title role, *The Rape of Lucretia*.

MAJOR DEBUTS INCLUDE: 1965, Covent Garden, Lola, *Cavalleria Rusticana*; 1969, Cologne Opera, Sesto, *La Clemenza di Tito*; Octavian, *Der Rosenkavalier*: 1970, Lyric Opera, Chicago; 1971, Paris Opera; 1972, Australian Opera, Melbourne; 1973, Metropolitan Opera, New York; 1974, Brangäne, *Tristan und Isolde*: Bayreuth Festival, San Francisco Opera; 1975, Frankfurt Opera, Octavian, *Der Rosenkavalier*; 1976: Covent Garden at La Scala, Milan: Sesto, *La Clemenza di Tito*; Ascanio, *Benvenuto Cellini*; Bayreuth Festival (centenary production), Waltraute, *Der Ring des Nibelungen*; 1977, Munich Festival, Composer, *Ariadne auf Naxos*; 1978, Salzburg Festival, Octavian, *Der Rosenkavalier*; 1980, Grand Théâtre, Geneva, Composer, *Ariadne auf Naxos*; 1990, Maggio Musicale, Florence, Begbick, *Aufstieg und Fall der Stadt Mahagonny*; 1991, State Opera of South Australia, Adelaide, Klytemnestra, *Elektra*.

OPERATIC WORLD PREMIERES INCLUDE: 1964, Jeanetta Cochrane Theatre, London, Maggie Dempster, *One Man Show* by Nicholas Maw; 1970, Covent Garden, Thea, *The Knot Garden* by Michael Tippett; 1979, Paris Opera, Countess Geschwitz, three act version of *Lulu* by Alban Berg.

CAREER IN THE UK INCLUDES: Since 1965: Covent Garden (1965–1971, member): Mistress of the Novices, *Suor Angelica*; Virgin, *Moses and Aaron* (1965, British première); Marina, *Boris Godunov*; Nicklausse, *Les Contes d'Hoffmann*; Annina and Octavian, *Der Rosenkavalier*; Second Lady, *Die Zauberflöte*; Ascanio, *Benvenuto Cellini*; Mercédès, *Carmen*; Helen, *King Priam*; Voice from Above, *Die Frau ohne Schatten*; Cherubino, *Le Nozze di Figaro*; Meg Page, *Falstaff*; Dorabella, *Così fan tutte*; Orfeo, *Orfeo ed Euridice*; Geneviève, *Pelléas et Mélisande*; Olga, *Eugene Onegin*; Marfa, *Khovanshchina*; Sesto, *La Clemenza di Tito*; Composer, *Ariadne auf Naxos*; Dido, *The Trojans at Carthage*; Kundry, *Parsifal*; Brangäne, *Tristan und Isolde*; Waltraute and Fricka, *Der Ring des Nibelungen*; Charlotte, *Werther*; Handel Opera Society, title role, *Rinaldo*; New Opera Company, Hostess/Mother Superior, *The Fiery Angel* (1965, British stage première).

RELATED PROFESSIONAL ACTIVITIES: Numerous concerts, recitals, broadcasts and television appearances in the UK and abroad.

RECORDINGS INCLUDE: Bellini, *Norma* (DECC); Berg, *Lulu* (DG); Bizet, *Carmen* (DECC); Mozart: *La Clemenza di Tito*, *Le Nozze di Figaro* (both PHIL), *Die Zauberflöte*; R. Strauss: *Elektra*, *Der Rosenkavalier*; Tippett, *King Priam* (all DECC); Wagner: *Parsifal* (ERAT), *Das Rheingold*, *Die Walküre* (both EURO), *Tristan und Isolde* (PHIL).

AWARDS AND HONOURS INCLUDE: 1960, Opera Aria Competition (Canberra); 1961, Kathleen Ferrier Contralto Prize, s'Hertogenbosch (Netherlands); 1975, Honorary Member, Royal Academy of Music; 1980, Commander, Order of the British Empire (CBE).

ADDRESS: c/o Ingpen & Williams Ltd, 14 Kensington Court, London W8 5DN.

MITCHINSON JOHN
Tenor and Teacher

POSITION: Head of Vocal Studies, Welsh College of Music and Drama, Cardiff.

PERSONAL DETAILS: b. 31 March 1932, Lancashire; m. 1958, Maureen Guy (mezzo-soprano), two children.

EDUCATION/TRAINING: 1950–1953, Royal Manchester College of Music, with Frederic Cox and Heddle Nash; privately with Boriska Gereb.

PROFESSIONAL DEBUT: 1952, *Music For You*, television series with Eric Robinson.

EARLY CAREER INCLUDED: 1952–1971, international concerts, recitals and broadcasts (particularly of rare operas) with leading conductors and orchestras.

MAJOR DEBUTS INCLUDE: 1972, Sadler's Wells Opera, title role, *Oedipus Rex*; 1978, Welsh National Opera, Aegisth, *Elektra*; 1981, title role, *Peter Grimes*: Basle and National Theatre, Prague; 1983: Buxton Festival, Gualtiero, *Griselda* (first modern performance); Opera North, Max, *Der Freischütz*; 1987, Scottish Opera, Morozov, *From the House of the Dead*.

OPERATIC WORLD PREMIERES INCLUDE: 1973, Israel Festival, Poet, *Masada 967* by Josef Tal.

CAREER IN THE UK INCLUDES: Since 1972: Sadler's Wells Opera/English National Opera: A Vision of the Author, *The Adventures of Mr Brouček*; title roles: *Dalibor*, *Idomeneo*; Welsh National Opera: Tristan, *Tristan und Isolde*; Manolios, *The Greek Passion* (1981, British première); Morozov, *From the*

House of the Dead; title role, *Peter Grimes*.

RELATED PROFESSIONAL ACTIVITIES: Regular concerts and broadcasts in the UK and abroad; 1988–1992, Senior Tutor, School of Vocal Studies, Royal Northern College of Music; since 1992, Head of Vocal Studies, Welsh College of Music and Drama, Cardiff.

RECORDINGS INCLUDE: Berlioz, *Béatrice et Bénédict* (L'OI); Elgar, *The Dream of Gerontius* (EMI); Janáček, *Glagolitic Mass* (PHIL); Martinů, *The Greek Passion* (SUPR); Mahler: Symphony No. 8 (CBS), *Das Lied von der Erde* (CFP); Purcell, *Dido and Aeneas* (L'OI); Wagner, *Tristan und Isolde* (DECC).

AWARDS AND HONOURS INCLUDE: 1957, Kathleen Ferrier Memorial Scholarship; Associate and Fellow, Royal Manchester College of Music.

ADDRESS: c/o Music International, 13 Ardilaun Road, London N5 2QR.

MOLL MARIA   Soprano

EDUCATION/TRAINING: Royal Academy of Music, with Marjorie Thomas; London Opera Centre.

PROFESSIONAL DEBUT: 1978, chorus member, Glyndebourne Festival Opera.

MAJOR DEBUTS INCLUDE: 1979, Glyndebourne Touring Opera, Leonore, *Fidelio*; 1980, Glyndebourne Festival Opera, Second Lady, *Die Zauberflöte*; 1982, Welsh National Opera, Leonora, *La Forza del Destino*; 1983: Covent Garden, Solo Voice, The Nightingale and Shepherdess, *L'Enfant et les Sortilèges*; Opera North, Musetta, *La Bohème*; 1985, Scottish Opera, Italian Soprano, *Capriccio*; 1987: English National Opera, Aksinya/Convict, *Lady Macbeth of Mtsensk* (British stage première); Batignano Festival, title role, *Leonore*.

CAREER IN THE UK INCLUDES: Since 1980: English National Opera: Mother/Witch, *Hansel and Gretel*; Regan, *Lear*; Innkeeper's Daughter, *Königskinder*; Frasquita, *Carmen*; Glyndebourne

Touring Opera, Musetta, *La Bohème*;
Opera North: Abigaille, *Nabucco*; Berta,
The Barber of Seville; Fata Morgana, *The
Love for Three Oranges*; Opera Northern
Ireland: Lady in Waiting, *Macbeth*; Donna
Anna, *Don Giovanni*; Scottish Opera, title
role, *Tosca*; Welsh National Opera, Lady
Macbeth, *Macbeth*.

RELATED PROFESSIONAL ACTIVITIES:
Several television appearances including
Moll of Kintyre (Scottish Television);
Carlotta, *The Phantom of the Opera* (West
End).

AWARDS INCLUDE: 1984, Shell-Scottish
Opera Award.

ADDRESS: c/o Korman International
Management, Crunnells Green Cottage,
Preston, Hertfordshire SG4 7UQ.

MONTAGUE DIANA
Mezzo-soprano

PERSONAL DETAILS: b. 1954, Winchester.

EDUCATION/TRAINING: Royal Manchester
School of Music, with Ronald Stear,
Frederic Cox and Rupert Bruce-Lockhart.

PROFESSIONAL DEBUT: 1977, Glyndebourne
Touring Opera, Zerlina, *Don Giovanni*.

MAJOR DEBUTS INCLUDE: 1978, Batignano
Festival, Dido, *Dido and Aeneas*; 1981,
English National Opera, Proserpina,
Orfeo; 1982, Covent Garden, Nicklausse,
Les Contes d'Hoffmann; 1983: Bayreuth
Festival, Wellgunde and Siegrune, *Der
Ring des Nibelungen*; La Monnaie,
Brussels, Isolier, *Le Comte Ory*; 1984,
Lyons Opera, title role, *Iphigénie en
Tauride*; Cherubino, *Le Nozze di Figaro*:
1985, Aix-en-Provence Festival; 1986:
Scottish Opera, Salzburg Festival; 1987:
Frankfurt Opera, Dorabella, *Così fan
tutte*; Metropolitan Opera, New York,
Sesto, *La Clemenza di Tito*; 1989,
Glyndebourne Festival Opera, Orfeo,
Orfeo ed Euridice; 1990: Idamante,
Idomeneo: Salzburg Festival and Teatro
La Zarzuela, Madrid; Vienna State Opera,
Cherubino, *Le Nozze di Figaro*; 1991,
Teatro la Fenice, Venice, Romeo, *I
Capuleti e i Montecchi*; 1992: Welsh

National Opera, title role, *Iphigénie en
Tauride*; Cherubino, *Le Nozze di Figaro*:
Opéra Bastille, Paris and Teatro Colón,
Buenos Aires.

CAREER IN THE UK INCLUDES: Since 1978:
Covent Garden: Second Lady, *Die
Zauberflöte* (also 1979, Far East tour);
Kate Pinkerton, *Madama Butterfly*;
Tebaldo, *Don Carlos*; Flower Maiden,
Parsifal; Page, *Lohengrin*; Lady Artist,
Lulu (1981, British première, three act
version); Laura, *Luisa Miller*; Annio, *La
Clemenza di Tito*; Cherubino, *Le Nozze di
Figaro*; Parséïs, *Esclarmonde*; Fox, *The
Cunning Little Vixen*; Dorabella, *Così fan
tutte* (also 1992, Japan tour); English
National Opera, Emilia, *Otello*;
Glyndebourne Festival Opera: Human
Frailty, *Il Ritorno d'Ulisse in Patria*;
Sesto, *La Clemenza di Tito*; Opera Rara
at the Camden Festival, Curiazio, *Gli
Orazi ed i Curiazi*; Scottish Opera, Prince
Orlofsky, *Die Fledermaus*.

RELATED PROFESSIONAL ACTIVITIES:
Numerous concerts, recitals, broadcasts
and television appearances in the UK and
abroad.

RECORDINGS INCLUDE: Bellini: *I Capuleti e
i Montecchi* (NUOV), *Norma* (DECC); Gluck,
Iphigénie en Tauride (PHIL); Handel, arias
(DG); Janáček, *The Cunning Little Vixen*
(EMI); Meyerbeer, *Il Crociato in Egitto*
(OPRA); Monteverdi: *Orfeo* (DG), *Il Ritorno
d'Ulisse in Patria* (CBS); A Hundred Years
of Italian Opera (OPRA).

ADDRESS: c/o Harrison/Parrott Ltd, 12
Penzance Place, London W11 4PA.

MONTGOMERY KENNETH
Conductor

POSITION: Artistic Director, Opera Northern
Ireland.

PERSONAL DETAILS: b. 28 October 1943,
Belfast.

EDUCATION/TRAINING: 1961–1965, Royal
College of Music, with Adrian Boult; 1963,
with Sergiu Celibidache in Siena; 1965–
1967, with Hans Schmidt-Isserstedt in
Hamburg.

PROFESSIONAL AND OPERATIC DEBUT: 1967, Glyndebourne Festival Opera, *L'Elisir d'Amore*.

CAREER: 1966, apprentice conductor, BBC Northern Symphony Orchestra; 1967–1968, Assistant Chorus Master and staff conductor, Glyndebourne Festival Opera; 1970–1973, Assistant Conductor, Bournemouth Sinfonietta and Bournemouth Symphony Orchestra; Music Director: 1973–1975, Bournemouth Sinfonietta; 1975–1976, Glyndebourne Touring Opera; Chief Conductor: 1976–1980, Netherlands Radio Orchestra; 1980–1990, Large Broadcasting Choir, Netherlands; 1983–1989, Radio Symphony Orchestra, Netherlands; since 1985, Artistic Director, Opera Northern Ireland.

MAJOR OPERATIC DEBUTS INCLUDE: 1967, Sadler's Wells Opera, *Così fan tutte*; 1970: Netherlands Opera, *L'Ormindo*; Wexford Festival, Oberon; 1975, Covent Garden, *Le Nozze di Figaro*; 1977: Canadian Opera Company, Toronto, *Die Zauberflöte*; Houston Grand Opera, *L'Incoronazione di Poppea*; 1982, Santa Fe Opera, *Mignon*; 1985, Paris Opera, *Iphigénie en Tauride*; 1986, Scottish Opera, *Werther*; 1990, Vancouver Opera, *Alcina*; 1991, San Diego Opera, *The Passion of Jonathan Wade*.

OPERA PERFORMANCES IN THE UK INCLUDE: Since 1985, Opera Northern Ireland: *Falstaff, Ariadne auf Naxos, La Traviata, La Bohème, The Seraglio, Don Giovanni, The Magic Flute, Le Nozze di Figaro, Così fan tutte, Rigoletto*.

RELATED PROFESSIONAL ACTIVITIES: Guest conductor with leading international orchestras; Artistic Director, Opera Class, Royal Conservatory, The Hague; masterclasses, Utrecht Conservatory.

RECORDINGS INCLUDE: J.C. Bach, Six Symphonies, Op. 6 (CFP).

AWARDS INCLUDE: Tagore Gold Medal, Royal College of Music; Silver Medal, Worshipful Company of Musicians.

ADDRESS: c/o Robert Gilder & Company, Enterprise House, 59–65 Upper Ground, London SE1 9PQ.

MORA BARRY   Baritone

PERSONAL DETAILS: b. 1940, Palmerston North, New Zealand.

EDUCATION/TRAINING: Privately with Otakar Kraus and John Matheson in London.

PROFESSIONAL DEBUT: 1976, Gelsenkirchen, Anckerström, *Un Ballo in Maschera*.

CAREER INCLUDES: Principal Baritone: 1976–1980, Gelsenkirchen; 1980–1987, Frankfurt Opera; roles included: Tamare, *Die Gezeichneten*; Rodrigo, *Don Carlos*; Count di Luna, *Il Trovatore*; Speaker, *Die Zauberflöte*; Father, *Hänsel und Gretel*; Harlequin, *Ariadne auf Naxos*; Dandini, *La Cenerentola*; Sharpless, *Madama Butterfly*; Major Mary, *Die Soldaten*; Lescaut, *Manon Lescaut*; Malatesta, *Don Pasquale*; Marcello, *La Bohème*; Ford, *Falstaff*; Donner and Gunther, *Der Ring des Nibelungen*; title roles: Rigoletto, *Il Ritorno d'Ulisse in Patria*.

MAJOR DEBUTS INCLUDE: 1980, Covent Garden, Donner and Gunther, *Der Ring des Nibelungen*; 1983, Scottish Opera at the Edinburgh International Festival, Traveller, *Death in Venice*; 1984, Deutsche Oper, Berlin, Major Mary, *Die Soldaten*; 1985, Zurich Opera, Malatesta, *Don Pasquale*; 1986, Welsh National Opera, Donner, *The Rhinegold*; 1989, Vancouver Opera, Germont, *La Traviata*; 1990: Welsh National Opera in Tokyo, Ford, *Falstaff*; Gran Teatre del Liceu, Barcelona, Music Master, *Ariadne auf Naxos*; 1991, Netherlands Opera, Fieramosca, *Benvenuto Cellini*; 1992, Australian Opera, Sydney, Faninal, *Der Rosenkavalier*.

CAREER IN THE UK INCLUDES: Since 1981: Covent Garden: Kothner, *Die Meistersinger von Nürnberg*; De Brétigny, *Manon*; Scottish Opera, Filotero, *Orion*; Welsh National Opera: Donner and Gunther, *The Ring of the Nibelung* (also at Covent Garden); Forester, *The Cunning Little Vixen*; Germont, *La Traviata*; Music Master, *Ariadne auf Naxos*; Faninal, *Der*

Rosenkavalier; Don Alfonso, *Così fan tutte*; Frank, *Die Fledermaus*.

RELATED PROFESSIONAL ACTIVITIES INCLUDE: Numerous concerts and recitals in the UK and abroad.

RECORDINGS INCLUDE: Delius, *A Village Romeo and Juliet* (ARGO); Janáček, *Osud* (EMI).

ADDRESS: c/o Haydn Rawstron International Management, PO Box 654, London SE26 4DZ.

MORELLE MAUREEN
Mezzo-soprano

PERSONAL DETAILS: b. 1934, Hampshire.

EDUCATION/TRAINING: Guildford School of Music, piano with Rose Keen; Royal College of Music: piano with Eric Harrison, vocal studies with Arnold Matters; further studies with Andrew Field, Audrey Langford and Nina Walker.

PROFESSIONAL DEBUT: 1955, Opera for All, Tisbe, *Cinderella*.

EARLY CAREER INCLUDED: 1955–1965, appearances with English Opera Group, Opera for All, Sadler's Wells Opera, Welsh National Opera; roles included: Rosina, *The Barber of Seville*; Dorabella, *Così fan tutte*; Cherubino, *The Marriage of Figaro*; Sandman, *Hansel and Gretel*; title role, *L'Enfant et les Sortilèges*.

MAJOR DEBUTS INCLUDE: 1965: Covent Garden, *Il Trittico* (Frugola, *Il Tabarro*; Infirmary Sister, *Suor Angelica*; La Ciesca, *Gianni Schicchi*); Glyndebourne Festival Opera, Smeton, *Anna Bolena*; 1977, Spoleto Festival, Donato's Mother, *Maria Golovin*.

OPERATIC WORLD PREMIERES INCLUDE: 1968, English Opera Group at the Aldeburgh Festival, Judy, *Punch and Judy* by Harrison Birtwistle.

CAREER IN THE UK INCLUDES: Since 1966: Covent Garden: Third Maid, *Elektra*; Mayor's Wife, *Jenůfa*; English Opera Group, Hermia, *A Midsummer Night's Dream*; Handel Opera Society, Arsamene, *Serse*; Glyndebourne Touring Opera: Marcellina, *Le Nozze di Figaro*;

Madame Larina, *Eugene Onegin*; Opera North: Suzuki, *Madam Butterfly*; Háta, *The Bartered Bride*; Madame Larina, *Eugene Onegin*; Mamma Lucia, *Cavalleria Rusticana*; Sadler's Wells Opera/English National Opera: Isolier, *Count Ory*; Ottavia, *The Coronation of Poppea*; Maria, *War and Peace* (1972, British première); Prince Orlofsky, *Die Fledermaus*; Mercédès, *Carmen*; Fricka, Flosshilde and Waltraute, *The Ring of the Nibelung*; Azucena, *Il Trovatore*; title role, *Iolanthe*; Scottish Opera, Azucena, *Il Trovatore*; Welsh National Opera: Fenena, *Nabucco*; Suzuki, *Madam Butterfly*.

RELATED PROFESSIONAL ACTIVITIES: Masterclasses at Morley College.

AWARDS INCLUDE: 1963, Queen's Prize for Women Singers.

ADDRESS: c/o Korman International Management, Crunnells Green Cottage, Preston, Hertfordshire SG4 7UQ.

MORGAN ARWEL HUW
Bass-baritone

POSITION: Principal Bass-baritone, English National Opera.

PERSONAL DETAILS: b. 18 June 1948, Neath, South Wales; m. 1975, Sarah Mair, two children.

PREVIOUS OCCUPATIONS: 1969–1978, analytical chemist, teacher and laboratory assistant.

EDUCATION/TRAINING: 1966–1969, Imperial College of Science and Technology; 1971–1973, University College of Wales, Aberystwyth, Soil Science Department; 1984–1988, vocal studies with Ingrid Surgenor; since 1990, with Audrey Langford.

PROFESSIONAL DEBUT: 1978, chorus member, Welsh National Opera.

EARLY CAREER INCLUDED: 1978–1987, Welsh National Opera: Lictor, *The Coronation of Poppea*; Steersman, *Tristan und Isolde*; Ladas, *The Greek Passion* (1981, British première); Count Ribbing, *Un Ballo in Maschera*; Don

Fernando, *Fidelio*; Hobson, *Peter Grimes*; Angelotti, *Tosca*.

MAJOR DEBUTS INCLUDE: 1987, English National Opera, Priest, *Lady Macbeth of Mtsensk* (British stage première); 1991, Aix-en-Provence Festival, Snug, *A Midsummer Night's Dream*.

CAREER IN THE UK INCLUDES: Since 1987: Principal Bass-baritone, English National Opera: Parson, *The Cunning Little Vixen*; Sacristan, *Tosca*; Duphol, *La Traviata*; Carl Olsen, *Street Scene*; Pish-Tush, *The Mikado*; Kothner, *The Mastersingers of Nuremberg*; Tchelio, *The Love for Three Oranges*; Panas, *Christmas Eve* (1988, British stage première); Speaker, *The Magic Flute*; Leporello, *Don Giovanni*; Antonio, *The Marriage of Figaro*; Sacristan/Lunobor/Domšík, *The Adventures of Mr Brouček*; Doctor, *Macbeth*; title role, *Don Pasquale*; also: Opera 80, Osmin, *The Seraglio*; Opera North, Fabrizio, *The Thieving Magpie*.

RELATED PROFESSIONAL ACTIVITIES: Concerts and oratorios in the UK.

RECORDINGS INCLUDE: Thomas, *Hamlet* (DECC); Weill, *Street Scene* (TER).

AWARDS INCLUDE: 1977, National Eisteddfod of Wales, Bass Competition.

ADDRESS: c/o Ingpen & Williams Ltd, 14 Kensington Court, London W8 5DN.

MOSES GEOFFREY Bass

PERSONAL DETAILS: b. 24 September 1952, Abercynon, South Wales; m. Anne Mason (mezzo-soprano).

EDUCATION/TRAINING: Emmanuel College, Cambridge, studied history; Guildhall School of Music and Drama; privately with Otakar Kraus and Peter Harrison.

PROFESSIONAL DEBUT: 1977, Welsh National Opera, Don Basilio, *The Barber of Seville*.

EARLY CAREER INCLUDED: 1978–1982, Principal Bass, Welsh National Opera: Colline, *La Bohème*; Bonze, *Madam Butterfly*; Nourabad, *The Pearl Fishers*; Jago, *Ernani*; Sarastro, *The Magic Flute*; Seneca, *The Coronation of Poppea*;

Angelotti, *Tosca*; Sparafucile, *Rigoletto*; King Marke, *Tristan und Isolde*; Harašta, *The Cunning Little Vixen*; Spirit Messenger, *Die Frau ohne Schatten*; Fotis, *The Greek Passion* (1981, British première); Giorgio, *I Puritani*.

MAJOR DEBUTS INCLUDE: 1982: Covent Garden, Lindorf, *Les Contes d'Hoffmann*; Glyndebourne Touring Opera, Commendatore, *Don Giovanni*; Opera North, Bonze, *Madam Butterfly*; 1983: English National Opera, Cecco, *Rienzi*; Kent Opera, Commendatore, *Don Giovanni*; 1984, Glyndebourne Festival Opera, Starveling, *A Midsummer Night's Dream*; 1985: Scottish Opera, Don Basilio, *Il Barbiere di Siviglia*; La Monnaie, Brussels, Crespel, *Les Contes d'Hoffmann*; 1986, Hamburg State Opera, Don Basilio, *Il Barbiere di Siviglia*; 1988, Netherlands Opera, First Nazarene, *Salome*.

CAREER IN THE UK INCLUDES: Since 1983: Covent Garden: Foltz and Ortel, *Die Meistersinger von Nürnberg*; Cleomer, *Esclarmonde*; Dumas, *Andrea Chénier*; Montano, *Otello*; Pistol, *Falstaff*; Fifth Jew, *Salome*; English National Opera: Méphistophélès, *Faust*; Vaudemont, *The Sicilian Vespers*; Angelotti, *Tosca*; Glyndebourne Festival and Touring Opera: Don Basilio, *Il Barbiere di Siviglia*; Lamoral, *Arabella*; Bartolo, *Le Nozze di Figaro*; Voice of Neptune, *Idomeneo*; Pietro and Fiesco, *Simon Boccanegra*; Major-Domo, *Capriccio*; Hobson, *Peter Grimes*; Opera North, Sarastro, *The Magic Flute*; Welsh National Opera: Pistol, *Falstaff*; Rodolfo, *La Sonnambula*; Hermit/Samiel, *Der Freischütz*; Zuniga, *Carmen*; Bartolo, *Le Nozze di Figaro*; Baldassare, *La Favorita* (also 1993, at Covent Garden); Prince Gremin, *Eugene Onegin*.

RELATED PROFESSIONAL ACTIVITIES: Regular concerts in the UK and Europe.

RECORDINGS INCLUDE: Martinů, *The Greek Passion* (SUPR); Verdi, *Rigoletto* (PHIL); Wagner, *Tristan und Isolde* (DECC).

VIDEOS INCLUDE: R. Strauss, *Arabella* (Glyndebourne Festival Opera).

ADDRESS: c/o Harrison/Parrott Ltd, 12
Penzance Place, London W11 4PA.

MOSHINSKY ELIJAH
Director

POSITION: Associate Director, The Royal
Opera, Covent Garden.
PERSONAL DETAILS: b. 8 January 1946,
Melbourne, Australia; m. 1970, Ruth
Dyttman, two children.
EDUCATION/TRAINING: University of
Melbourne; St Antony's College, Oxford,
studied history.
PROFESSIONAL DEBUT: 1973, Oxford and
Cambridge Shakespeare Company, *As
You Like It*.
OPERATIC DEBUT: 1975, Covent Garden,
Peter Grimes.
CAREER: Since 1973, freelance opera,
theatre and television director in the UK
and abroad; Covent Garden: 1973–1975,
Associate Resident Director; 1975–1979,
Principal Guest Director; since 1979,
Associate Director; 1984, Artistic Director,
Adelaide Festival.
MAJOR OPERATIC DEBUTS INCLUDE: 1976:
Adelaide Festival, *Wozzeck*; Dallas Civic
Opera, *Salome*; 1978: Kent Opera, *The
Seraglio*; Australian Opera, Sydney, *A
Midsummer Night's Dream*; Gothenburg,
The Cunning Little Vixen; 1979, Welsh
National Opera, *Ernani*; 1980,
Metropolitan Opera, New York, *Un Ballo
in Maschera*; 1981, Paris Opera, *Peter
Grimes*; 1982, English National Opera, *Le
Grand Macabre* (British première); 1985/
1986, Covent Garden and Lyric Opera,
Chicago/Metropolitan Opera, New York
co-production, *Samson*; 1985, Grand
Théâtre, Geneva, *I Vespri Siciliani*; 1987,
Maggio Musicale, Florence, *Benvenuto
Cellini*; 1988, Scottish Opera, *La Bohème*.
OPERATIC WORLD PREMIERES INCLUDE:
1979, Netherlands Opera, *Winter Cruise*
by Hans Henkemans.
OPERA PRODUCTIONS IN THE UK
INCLUDE: Since 1976: Covent Garden:
Lohengrin, *The Rake's Progress*,
Macbeth, *Samson et Dalila*, *Tannhäuser*,
Otello, *Die Entführung aus dem Serail*,
Attila, *Simon Boccanegra*, *Stiffelio*;
English National Opera: *The
Mastersingers of Nuremberg*, *The
Bartered Bride*.
VIDEOS INCLUDE: Britten, *Peter Grimes*;
Saint-Saëns, *Samson et Dalila*; Verdi,
Simon Boccanegra (all Covent Garden).
AWARDS INCLUDE: Society of West End
Theatre Award: 1978, Covent Garden
production of *Lohengrin*; 1979, Covent
Garden production of *The Rake's
Progress*.
ADDRESS: c/o Judy Daish Associates Ltd, 83
Eastbourne Mews, London W2 6LQ.

MOSLEY GEORGE   Baritone

PERSONAL DETAILS: b. 28 April 1959,
London.
EDUCATION/TRAINING: 1980–1984, Guildhall
School of Music and Drama, with Laura
Sarti; 1984–1986, Hochschule für Musik,
Munich, with Joseph Loibl; 1985–1986,
National Opera Studio, with David Mason.
PROFESSIONAL DEBUT: 1987, Opera 80,
Dandini, *Cinderella*.
EARLY CAREER INCLUDED: 1987–1989,
appearances with Opera West, Pavilion
Opera; roles included: Guglielmo, *Così
fan tutte*; Count, *Le Nozze di Figaro*;
Malatesta, *Don Pasquale*; title role, *Don
Giovanni*.
MAJOR DEBUTS INCLUDE: 1989: Opera 80,
title role, *Eugene Onegin*; Scottish Opera,
Prince Orlofsky, *Die Fledermaus*; 1990,
English National Opera, Marco, *Gianni
Schicchi*; 1991: Modena, Count, *Le Nozze
di Figaro*; Pisa, Malatesta, *Don Pasquale*;
title role, *Don Giovanni*: Livorno, *Lucca*;
1992, Flanders Opera, Antwerp,
Patroclus, *King Priam*.
CAREER INCLUDES: Since 1990: English
National Opera: Duke of Albany, *Lear*;
Yamadori, *Madam Butterfly*; Opera North,
Patroclus, *King Priam*; Pisa: Count, *Le
Nozze di Figaro*; Guglielmo, *Così fan
tutte*; Dandini, *La Cenerentola*; Nick
Shadow, *The Rake's Progress*.

RELATED PROFESSIONAL ACTIVITIES:
Concerts and recitals in the UK.
RECORDINGS INCLUDE: Handel, *Agrippina*;
Purcell, *Dido and Aeneas* (both PHIL);
Schumann, *Dichterliebe* and *Liederkreis*
(COLL).
AWARDS INCLUDE: 1988, International
Mozart Prize (Salzburg).
ADDRESS: c/o Robert Gilder & Company,
Enterprise House, 59–65 Upper Ground,
London SE1 9PQ.

MOYLE JULIAN   Baritone

PERSONAL DETAILS: b. 4 February 1927,
Melbourne, Australia.
PREVIOUS OCCUPATIONS: 1945–1956:
farmer, music store salesman and
selector for music wholesalers.
EDUCATION/TRAINING: 1940–1944, Geelong
College, Australia; 1955–1956, Royal
College of Music, with Arnold Matters;
further studies with Boriska Gereb,
Gerald Davies and Betty Bannerman in
London and Ettore Campogalliani in
Mantua.
PROFESSIONAL DEBUT: 1956, Opera for All,
Malatesta, *Don Pasquale*.
EARLY CAREER INCLUDED: 1956–1959,
Opera for All: Germont, *La Traviata*;
Guglielmo, *Così fan tutte*; Count, *The
Marriage of Figaro*; Michele, *Il Tabarro*;
Peachum, *The Beggar's Opera*; title role,
The Barber of Seville; 1959–1970,
appearances with Chelsea Opera Group,
Handel Opera Society, Sadler's Wells
Opera (1960–1970, Principal Baritone);
roles included: Ford, *Falstaff*; Zebul,
Jephtha; Kulegin, *Katya Kabanova*;
Papageno, *The Magic Flute*; Dandini,
Cinderella; Raimbaud, *Count Ory*;
Taddeo, *The Italian Girl in Algiers*; title
role, *The Barber of Seville*.
OPERATIC WORLD PREMIERES INCLUDE:
1957, New Opera Company at Sadler's
Wells Theatre, Jacques 1, *A Tale of Two
Cities* by Arthur Benjamin; Welsh
National Opera: 1980, Hans Joseph, *The
Servants* by William Mathias; 1981,
Storyteller, *The Journey* by John Metcalf.

CAREER IN THE UK INCLUDES: Since 1971:
New Sadler's Wells Opera: Prince Basil,
The Count of Luxembourg; Duke of Plaza-
Toro, *The Gondoliers*; Prince Popolescu,
Countess Maritza; Baron Zeta, *The Merry
Widow*; Welsh National Opera (1971–1984,
Principal Baritone): Count, *The Marriage
of Figaro*; Baron Prus, *The Makropoulos
Case*; Sharpless, *Madam Butterfly*;
Sacristan, *Tosca*; Badger, *The Cunning
Little Vixen*; Krušina, *The Bartered Bride*;
Patriarcheas, *The Greek Passion* (1981,
British première); Krušina, *The Bartered
Bride*; Chekunov, *From the House of the
Dead*; Bartolo, *The Marriage of Figaro*.
RECORDINGS INCLUDE: Kálmán, *Countess
Maritza*; Lehár, *The Merry Widow* (both
TER).
ADDRESS: Not available.

MURPHY SUZANNE   Soprano

PERSONAL DETAILS: b. Limerick.
EDUCATION/TRAINING: 1973–1976, Dublin
College of Music, with Veronica Dunne.
PROFESSIONAL DEBUT: 1976, Welsh
National Opera, Constanze, *The Seraglio*.
EARLY CAREER INCLUDED: 1976–1981,
Principal Soprano, Welsh National Opera:
Amalia, *I Masnadieri*; Gilda, *Rigoletto*;
Helena, *A Midsummer Night's Dream*;
Leonora, *Il Trovatore*; Elisabeth de
Valois, *Don Carlos*; Queen of the Night,
The Magic Flute; Jenifer, *The Midsummer
Marriage*; Violetta, *La Traviata*; Elvira,
Ernani; Julie, *The Jacobin* (1980, British
stage première); title role, *Rodelinda*.
MAJOR DEBUTS INCLUDE: 1980, Welsh
National Opera at Komische Oper, East
Berlin, Elvira, *Ernani*; 1981, English
National Opera, Constanze, *The Seraglio*;
1983, Opera North, Olympia/Giulietta/
Antonia/Stella, *The Tales of Hoffmann*;
1985: New York City Opera, title role,
Norma; Vancouver Opera, Amelia, *Un
Ballo in Maschera*; 1986: Aix-en-Provence
Festival, Donna Anna, *Don Giovanni*;
Lyons Opera, Reiza, *Oberon*; Pittsburgh
Opera, Fiordiligi, *Così fan tutte*; 1987,
Vienna State Opera, Elettra, *Idomeneo*;

1989: Scottish Opera, title role, *The Merry Widow*; Welsh National Opera in Milan and New York, Alice Ford, *Falstaff*; Cologne Opera, Elettra, *Idomeneo*.

CAREER IN THE UK INCLUDES: Since 1982: English National Opera, Donna Anna, *Don Giovanni*; Opera North: Elvira, *I Puritani*; Donna Anna, *Don Giovanni*; Welsh National Opera: Amelia, *Un Ballo in Maschera*; Elvira, *I Puritani*; Musetta, *La Bohème*; Rosalinde, *Die Fledermaus*; Alice Ford, *Falstaff*; Elvira, *Ernani*; title roles: *The Merry Widow*, *Lucia di Lammermoor*, *La Fanciulla del West*, *Tosca*.

RELATED PROFESSIONAL ACTIVITIES: Numerous concerts and recitals in the UK and abroad.

RECORDINGS INCLUDE: Beethoven, Symphony No. 9 (CBS); works by Rachmaninov and Tchaikovsky (CHAN).

ADDRESS: c/o Ingpen & Williams Ltd, 14 Kensington Court, London W8 5DN.

MURRAY ANN Mezzo-soprano

PERSONAL DETAILS: b. 27 August 1949, Dublin; m. 1981, Philip Langridge (tenor), one child.

EDUCATION/TRAINING: University College, Dublin; Royal Northern College of Music, with Frederic Cox; 1972–1974, London Opera Centre.

PROFESSIONAL DEBUT: 1974, Scottish Opera at the Maltings, Snape, title role, *Alceste*.

CAREER INCLUDES: Since 1974: Buxton Festival (1980, debut), Beatrice, *Beatrice and Benedict*; Covent Garden (1976, debut): Cherubino, *Le Nozze di Figaro*; Ascagne, *The Trojans at Carthage*; Dorabella, *Così fan tutte*; Composer, *Ariadne auf Naxos*; Rosina, *Il Barbiere di Siviglia*; Octavian, *Der Rosenkavalier*; Idamante, *Idomeneo*; Sifare, *Mitridate, Rè di Ponto*; Ruggiero, *Alcina*; Donna Elvira, *Don Giovanni*; title role, *L'Enfant et les Sortilèges*; English Music Theatre (1976, debut): Ramiro, *Sandrina's Secret*; title role, *Cinderella*; English National

Opera (1975, debut): Isolier, *Count Ory*; Fricka, *The Valkyrie*; Rosina, *The Barber of Seville*; Charlotte, *Werther*; Beatrice, *Beatrice and Benedict*; title roles: *Xerxes* (also 1990, Soviet Union tour, Bolshoi and Kiev), *Ariodante*; Glyndebourne Festival Opera (1979, debut), Minerva, *Il Ritorno d'Ulisse in Patria*; Opera North (1978, debut), Dido, *Dido and Aeneas*; Scottish Opera: Zerlina, *Don Giovanni*; Prince Orlofsky, *Die Fledermaus*; Concertgebouw, Amsterdam (1974, European debut), Annio, *La Clemenza di Tito* (concert performance); New York City Opera (1979, US debut), Sesto, *La Clemenza di Tito*; Aix-en-Provence Festival, Bradamante, *Alcina*; Cologne Opera: Dorabella, *Così fan tutte*; title roles: *La Cenerentola*, *La Périchole*, *Cendrillon*; Hamburg State Opera, Cherubino, *Le Nozze di Figaro*; La Monnaie, Brussels, Prince, *Cendrillon*; La Scala, Milan, Dorabella, *Così fan tutte*; Metropolitan Opera, New York, Sesto, *La Clemenza di Tito*; Salzburg Festival: Nicklausse, *Les Contes d'Hoffmann*; Dorabella, *Così fan tutte*; Minerva, *Il Ritorno d'Ulisse in Patria* (new version by Henze); title role, *La Cenerentola*; Schwetzingen Festival, Sifare, *Mitridate, Rè di Ponto*; Vienna State Opera, Composer, *Ariadne auf Naxos*; Wexford Festival, Laodicea, *Eritrea* (1975, first modern performance); Zurich Opera, Cecilio, *Lucio Silla*.

RELATED PROFESSIONAL ACTIVITIES: Regular concerts, recitals, broadcasts and television appearances with leading conductors and orchestras in the UK and abroad.

RECORDINGS INCLUDE: Berlioz, *L'Enfance du Christ* (EMI); Mozart: *Così fan tutte* (DG), *Lucio Silla* (RICE), *Le Nozze di Figaro*; Offenbach, *Les Contes d'Hoffmann* (both EMI); Purcell, *Dido and Aeneas* (TELD); Schubert, Complete Lieder, Vol. 3 (HYPE); English Songs, *Sweet Power of Song, On Wings of Song* (all EMI).

VIDEOS INCLUDE: Handel, *Xerxes* (English National Opera); Mozart, *Don Giovanni* (La Scala, Milan); *Mitridate, Rè Di Ponto* (film by Jean-Pierre Ponnelle); Rossini, *La Cenerentola* (Salzburg Festival).

ADDRESS: c/o Lies Askonas Ltd, 186 Drury Lane, London WC2B 5RY.

MUSGRAVE THEA   Composer

PERSONAL DETAILS: b. 27 May 1928, Edinburgh; m. 1971, Peter Mark (General Director, Virginia Opera).

EDUCATION/TRAINING: 1947–1950, University of Edinburgh, with Hans Gal and Mary Grierson; 1950–1954, with Nadia Boulanger in Paris.

FIRST PROFESSIONAL PERFORMANCE OF A COMPOSITION: 1951, Paris, Two Songs.

CAREER: Since 1951, compositions in all genres including seven operas, numerous orchestral, chamber, choral and vocal works; 1958–1965, lecturer, Extramural Department, University of London; 1970, Guest Professor, University of California, Santa Barbara; currently, Distinguished Professor, Queen's College, City University of New York.

OPERATIC WORLD PREMIERES: 1962, Morley College, *The Abbot of Drimock*, chamber opera in one act, libretto by Maurice Lindsay, conductor Lawrence Leonard, director Anthony Besch (1958, Park Lane Opera, concert performance); 1967, New Opera Company at Sadler's Wells Theatre, *The Decision*, opera in three acts, libretto by Maurice Lindsay, conductor Leon Lovett, director Colin Graham, designer Peter Whiteman; 1974, English Opera Group at the Aldeburgh Festival, *The Voice of Ariadne*, chamber opera in three acts, libretto by Amalia Elguera after *The Last of the Valerii* by Henry James, conductor the composer, director Colin Graham, designer Peter Whiteman; 1977, Scottish Opera at the Edinburgh International Festival, *Mary, Queen of Scots*, opera in three acts, librettist and conductor the composer, director Colin Graham, designers Robin Don and Colin Graham; 1979, Virginia Opera, *A Christmas Carol*, libretto by the composer after Dickens, conductor Peter Mark, director David Farrar, designer Miguel Romero; 1981, BBC Radio 3, *An Occurance at Owl Creek Bridge*, libretto by the composer after short story by Ambrose Bierce, conductor the composer; 1985, Virginia Opera, *Harriet, The Woman Called Moses*, opera in two acts, libretto by the composer, conductor Peter Mark, director Gordon Davidson, designer Jeffrey Beecroft.

RECORDINGS INCLUDE: *A Christmas Carol* (MMG), *Mary, Queen of Scots* (NOVE), Clarinet Concerto, *Night Music* (both ARGO), Concerto for orchestra, Horn Concerto (both DECC), Impromptu No. 1 for flute and oboe (BBC), Four Madrigals (LEON), *Rorate Coeli* (LEON/LIBR), *Verses of Love* (LIBR).

AWARDS AND HONOURS INCLUDE: 1976, Honorary Doctorate, Council for National Academic Awards; USA: 1974, Koussevitzky Prize; 1974–1975 and 1982–1983, Guggenheim Fellowship; Honorary Doctorates: 1979, Smith College, Massachusetts; 1980, Old Dominion University, Norfolk, Virginia.

ADDRESS: c/o Novello & Co. Ltd, 3 Primrose Mews, 1A Sharpeshall Street, London NW1 8YL.

McCARTHY MICHAEL
Director

POSITION: Co-artistic Director, Music Theatre Wales.
PERSONAL DETAILS: b. 29 September 1959, Kingston-upon-Thames.
EDUCATION/TRAINING: University of Birmingham.
PROFESSIONAL AND OPERATIC DEBUT: 1982, Cardiff New Opera Group, *The Lighthouse*.
CAREER: 1982–1987, freelance director with several small-scale music theatre companies; since 1988, Co-artistic Director, Music Theatre Wales.
MAJOR OPERATIC DEBUTS INCLUDE: 1987, Kent Opera, *Il Rè Pastore*; 1988: Opera 80, *The Seraglio*; Opera North, *Fidelio*; 1991, Glyndebourne Touring Opera, *Così fan tutte* (revival director).
OPERA PRODUCTIONS IN THE UK INCLUDE: Since 1983: Cardiff New Opera Group: *The Duel of Tancredi and Clorinda/The Garden/The Impresario*, *The Turn of the Screw*, *The Diary of One who Disappeared*, *Sāvitri*; Music Theatre Wales: *The Martyrdom of St Magnus*, *The Fall of the House of Usher* (1989, British première), *Euridice*, *The Four Note Opera*, *The Man Who Mistook his Wife for a Hat*; Scottish Chamber Orchestra, *The Soldier's Tale*.
RELATED PROFESSIONAL ACTIVITIES: 1992, Co-director, The Valleys Festival, South Wales.
ADDRESS: 19 Wilson Street, Splott, Cardiff CF2 2NZ.

McCORMACK ELIZABETH
Mezzo-soprano

PERSONAL DETAILS: b. 18 October 1964, Dunfermline, Fife; m. 1990, Douglas Vipond (musician).
EDUCATION/TRAINING: 1982–1988, Royal Scottish Academy of Music and Drama, studied music performance and with Duncan Robertson and Leonard Hancock;

1988–1989, National Opera Studio; currently with Patricia McMahon.
PROFESSIONAL DEBUT: 1988, Scottish Opera, title role, *Iolanthe*.
MAJOR DEBUTS INCLUDE: 1988, Banff Festival Opera, Alberta, Nancy, *Albert Herring*; 1990: Buxton Festival, title role, *Tancredi*; English National Opera, Pitti-Sing, *The Mikado*; 1992, Opera North, Pippo, *The Thieving Magpie*; 1993, Théâtre du Châtelet, Paris, Flora, *La Traviata*.
OPERATIC WORLD PREMIERES INCLUDE: 1988, Royal Scottish Academy of Music and Drama, Mrs Fischer, *On the Razzle* by Robin Orr; 1990, Scottish Opera, Daughter, *The Vanishing Bridegroom* by Judith Weir.
CAREER IN THE UK INCLUDES: Since 1988: English National Opera, Cherubino, *The Marriage of Figaro*; Scottish Opera: Cherubino, *The Marriage of Figaro*; Dorabella, *Così fan tutte*.
RELATED PROFESSIONAL ACTIVITIES: Concerts in London, France and Spain.
RECORDINGS INCLUDE: Hasse, *Requiem* (ADDA).
AWARDS INCLUDE: 1987: John Noble Opera Award, Decca-Kathleen Ferrier Prize, Royal Over-Seas League Music Competition; 1988 and 1989, Countess of Munster Award.
ADDRESS: c/o John Coast, 31 Sinclair Road, London W14 ONS.

McDONALD ANTONY
Designer

PERSONAL DETAILS: b. 11 September 1950.
EDUCATION/TRAINING: 1970–1973, Central School of Speech and Drama; 1973–1974, School of Theatre, Manchester Polytechnic; 1976–1977, Theatre Design School, English National Opera.
PROFESSIONAL DEBUT: 1978, Avon Touring Theatre Company, *Face Value* by A.C.H. Smith.
OPERATIC DEBUT: 1978, Welsh National Opera, *Let's Make an Opera*.

CAREER: Since 1979, freelance designer for numerous dance, opera and theatre companies including Ballet Rambert, Second Stride Dance Theatre, London Contemporary Dance Theatre, Old Vic Theatre, Royal Court Theatre, Royal National Theatre and Royal Shakespeare Company.

OPERATIC WORLD PREMIERES INCLUDE: Second Stride: 1989, *Heaven Ablaze in his Breast* by Judith Weir; 1991, *Lives of the Great Prisoners*; 1992, Almeida Theatre, *The Chance* (both by Orlando Gough).

OPERA DESIGNS INCLUDE: Since 1979: Australian Opera, Sydney, *Le Nozze di Figaro*; Batignano Festival, *The Turn of the Screw*; Opera Northern Ireland, *The Daughter of the Regiment*; Scottish Opera, *Orlando*; co-designs with Tom Cairns: English National Opera: *Billy Budd*, *Beatrice and Benedict*; Opera North, *The Midsummer Marriage*; Opera North/Scottish Opera/Welsh National Opera co-production, *The Trojans* (also 1990, at Covent Garden); Netherlands Opera, *Benvenuto Cellini*.

RELATED PROFESSIONAL ACTIVITIES: Associate Director, Second Stride Dance Theatre; teacher: Almeida Theatre Design School, Central School of Art and Design.

VIDEOS INCLUDE: Britten, *Billy Budd* (English National Opera).

ADDRESS: 34 The Colonnades, 105 Wilton Way, London E8 1BH.

McDONNELL TOM
Bass-baritone

PERSONAL DETAILS: b. 27 April 1940, Melbourne, Australia; m. Jennie Smith, two children.

EDUCATION/TRAINING: Melbourne University, studied law and arts; Melba Conservatorium, Melbourne, with Lennox Brewer.

PROFESSIONAL DEBUT: 1965, Sutherland-Williamson Opera Company, Australia tour, Belcore, *L'Elisir d'Amore*.

EARLY CAREER INCLUDED: 1966–1975, Principal Bass-baritone, Sadler's Wells Opera/English National Opera: Strephon, *Iolanthe*; Ottone, *The Coronation of Poppea*; Escamillo, *Carmen*; Germont, *La Traviata*; Schaunard, *La Bohème*; Andrei, *War and Peace* (1972, British stage première); Papageno, *The Magic Flute*; Grosvenor, *Patience*; Masetto, *Don Giovanni*; Captain, *The Bassarids* (1974, British stage première); Count and title role, *The Marriage of Figaro*.

MAJOR DEBUTS INCLUDE: 1969, Glyndebourne Touring Opera, title role, *Eugene Onegin*; 1973, Australian Opera, Sydney (opening of Sydney Opera House), Andrei, *War and Peace*; 1975, Netherlands Opera, Count, *Capriccio*; 1978, State Opera of South Australia, Adelaide, Count, *The Marriage of Figaro*; 1980: Scottish Opera, Theseus, *A Midsummer Night's Dream*; Adelaide Festival, Traveller, *Death in Venice*; 1981, Opera North, title role, *Don Giovanni*; 1983, Wexford Festival, Don Alvaro, *La Vedova Scaltra*; 1984, Opera Factory, Faber, *The Knot Garden*.

OPERATIC WORLD PREMIERES INCLUDE: 1974, Sadler's Wells Opera, Lieutenant September, *The Story of Vasco* by Gordon Crosse; 1976, Covent Garden (debut), Officer 3/Minister 2, *We Come to the River* by Hans Werner Henze; 1977: Covent Garden, Yuri, *The Ice Break* by Michael Tippett; English National Opera, Atahuallpa, *The Royal Hunt of the Sun* by Iain Hamilton; 1979, English Music Theatre at the Old Vic Theatre, Heima, *An Actor's Revenge* by Minoru Miki; 1985, Arundel Festival, King Arthur, *Lancelot* by Iain Hamilton; 1986: English National Opera, Aristaeus the Man, *The Mask of Orpheus* by Harrison Birtwistle; Opera Factory: several roles, *Hell's Angels* by Nigel Osborne; Ram, *Yan Tan Tethera* by Harrison Birtwistle.

CAREER IN THE UK INCLUDES: Since 1976: Buxton Festival, Don Pedro, *Beatrice and Benedict*; Covent Garden: Bello, *La Fanciulla del West*; Fiorello, *Il Barbiere di Siviglia*; Flemish Deputy, *Don Carlos*;

New Sussex Opera, title role, *Boris Godunov*; Opera Factory: Jove/Silvano, *La Calisto*; Don Alfonso, *Così fan tutte*; Håkon, *The Martyrdom of St Magnus*; Commendatore, *Don Giovanni*; Seneca's Friend/Lictor, *The Coronation of Poppea*; Antonio, *The Marriage of Figaro*; Opera North, Galitsky, *Prince Igor*; Scottish Opera: Don Alfonso, *Così fan tutte*; Apollo and Lidio, *L'Egisto*; University College Opera, Saul, *Saul and David* (1977, British stage première).

RELATED PROFESSIONAL ACTIVITIES: Numerous concerts, recitals, broadcasts and television appearances in the UK.

RECORDINGS INCLUDE: Handel, *Israel in Egypt* (DECC); Puccini, *La Fanciulla del West* (DG).

VIDEOS INCLUDE: Puccini, *La Fanciulla del West* (Covent Garden); Sullivan, *The Gondoliers* (Walker).

ADDRESS: 25 Talbot Road, London N6 4QS.

McGUIGAN PATRICK
Teacher, Baritone and Director

POSITION: Senior Tutor, School of Vocal Studies, Royal Northern College of Music.

PERSONAL DETAILS: b. 8 February 1933, Dublin; m. 1966, Caroline Crawshaw (soprano and teacher), two children.

EDUCATION/TRAINING: 1953–1957, Royal Irish Academy of Music, with Adelio Vianni; 1957–1960, further studies with Tino Pattiera in Vienna and E. Herbert Caesari in London; 1960–1964, Royal Manchester College of Music, with Frederic Cox.

PROFESSIONAL DEBUT: As baritone: 1965, St Pancras Festival, Golaud, *Pelléas et Mélisande*.

CAREER INCLUDES: Early career as an actor with leading Irish theatre companies and with the English Stage Company at the Royal Court Theatre; 1964–1973, Principal Baritone, Sadler's Wells Opera and appearances with Kent Opera, Welsh National Opera, Holland and Wexford Festivals; 1965–1973, visiting teacher and opera director, Royal Manchester College of Music; since 1973, Senior Tutor, School of Vocal Studies, Royal Northern College of Music.

STUDENTS HAVE INCLUDED Matthew Best, John Connell, Stephen Gadd, Glenville Hargreaves, John Harris, Henry Herford, Keith Latham, Jeffrey Lawton, Anthony Mee, Stephen Richardson, Nigel Robson, Andrew Shore, Gwion Thomas, John Tomlinson.

HONOURS INCLUDE: 1986, Fellow, Royal Northern College of Music.

ADDRESS: c/o Royal Northern College of Music, 124 Oxford Road, Manchester M13 9RD.

McINTYRE, SIR DONALD
Bass-baritone

PERSONAL DETAILS: b. 22 October 1934, Auckland, New Zealand; m. 1961, Jill Redington, three children.

PREVIOUS OCCUPATION: 1956–1957, school teacher.

EDUCATION/TRAINING: 1954–1956, Auckland Teachers' Training College; 1957–1959, Guildhall School of Music and Drama.

PROFESSIONAL DEBUT: 1959, Welsh National Opera, Zaccaria, *Nabucco*.

EARLY CAREER INCLUDED: 1960–1967, Principal Bass, Sadler's Wells Opera: Guglielmo, *Così fan tutte*; Méphistophélès, *Faust*; title roles: *Attila*, *The Marriage of Figaro*, *The Flying Dutchman*.

MAJOR DEBUTS INCLUDE: 1960, Sadler's Wells Opera, Biterolf, *Tannhäuser*; 1967, Covent Garden, Don Pizarro, *Fidelio*; Bayreuth Festival: 1967, Telramund, *Lohengrin*; 1968, Klingsor, *Parsifal*; 1969, title role, *Der Fliegende Holländer*; 1973, Amfortas, *Parsifal*; 1974, Kurwenal, *Tristan und Isolde*; 1973 and 1976 (centenary production), Wotan, *Der Ring des Nibelungen*; 1972, Vienna State Opera, title role, *Der Fliegende Holländer*; 1974, Metropolitan Opera,

New York, Wotan, *Der Ring des Nibelungen*; 1975, Lyric Opera, Chicago, Gunther, *Götterdämmerung*; 1984, Zurich Opera, Hans Sachs, *Die Meistersinger von Nürnberg*.

OPERATIC WORLD PREMIERES INCLUDE: 1964, Sadler's Wells Opera at Bath Festival, Stranger, *Martin's Lie* by Gian Carlo Menotti; 1970, Covent Garden, Heyst, *Victory* by Richard Rodney Bennett.

CAREER IN THE UK INCLUDES: Since 1968, Covent Garden (1968–1975, member): Barak, *Die Frau ohne Schatten*; Jokanaan, *Salome*; Golaud, *Pelléas et Mélisande*; Escamillo, *Carmen*; Wotan, *Das Rheingold*; Caspar and Ottokar, *Der Freischütz*; Orest, *Elektra*; Kurwenal, *Tristan und Isolde*; Telramund, *Lohengrin*; Nick Shadow, *The Rake's Progress*; Shaklovity, *Khovanshchina*; Doctor, *Wozzeck*; Monterone, *Rigoletto*; Balstrode, *Peter Grimes*; Prospero, *Un Re in Ascolto* (1989, British première); Sarastro, *Die Zauberflöte*.

RELATED PROFESSIONAL ACTIVITIES: Numerous concerts, recitals, broadcasts, television appearances and masterclasses in the UK and abroad.

RECORDINGS INCLUDE: Berlioz, *La Damnation de Faust* (DG); Debussy, *Pelléas et Mélisande* (CBS); Stravinsky, *Oedipus Rex* (DECC); Wagner, *Parsifal* (EMI).

VIDEOS INCLUDE: Wagner, *Der Ring des Nibelungen* (Bayreuth Festival).

HONOURS INCLUDE: 1975, Officer, Order of the British Empire (OBE); 1985, Commander, Order of the British Empire (CBE); 1989, Fidelio Medal, Association of International Opera Directors; 1990, New Zealand Commemoration Medal; 1992, Knighthood.

ADDRESS: c/o Ingpen & Williams Ltd, 14 Kensington Court, London W8 5DN.

McLAUGHLIN MARIE
Soprano

PERSONAL DETAILS: b. 2 November 1954, Lanarkshire; m., two children.

EDUCATION/TRAINING: London Opera Centre/National Opera Studio; since 1976, privately with Joan Anderson in Glasgow.

PROFESSIONAL DEBUT: 1978, Musica nel Chiostro, Grilletta, *Lo Speziale*.

MAJOR DEBUTS INCLUDE: 1978: English National Opera, Anna Gomez, *The Consul*; Scottish Opera, Amor, *Orfeo ed Euridice*; 1979, Aldeburgh Festival, Tatyana, *Eugene Onegin*; 1980, Covent Garden, Barbarina, *Le Nozze di Figaro*; 1981, Welsh National Opera, Susanna, *The Marriage of Figaro*; 1982: English National Opera, Gilda, *Rigoletto*; Aix-en-Provence Festival, First Lady, *Die Zauberflöte*; Paris Opera, Stephano, *Roméo et Juliette*; Rome Opera, Ilia, *Idomeneo*; Santa Fe Opera, Susanna, *Le Nozze di Figaro*; 1983: Bonn Opera, Marzelline, *Fidelio*; Grand Théâtre, Geneva, Valencienne, *Die Lustige Witwe*; Hamburg State Opera, Zdenka, *Arabella*; 1984: Deutsche Oper, Berlin, Marzelline, *Fidelio*; Susanna, *Le Nozze di Figaro*: Munich Festival, Washington Opera; 1985, Glyndebourne Festival Opera, Micaëla, *Carmen*; 1986, Metropolitan Opera, New York, Marzelline, *Fidelio*; 1987: Lyric Opera, Chicago, Despina, *Così fan tutte*; Salzburg Festival, Susanna, *Le Nozze di Figaro*; Vienna State Opera, Ilia, *Idomeneo*; 1988, La Scala, Milan, Adina, *L'Elisir d'Amore*; 1992, Grand Théâtre, Geneva, Jenny, *Aufstieg und Fall der Stadt Mahagonny*.

CAREER IN THE UK INCLUDES: Since 1978: Aldeburgh Festival, Tytania, *A Midsummer Night's Dream*; Covent Garden: Zerlina, *Don Giovanni*; Iris, *Semele*; Susanna, *Le Nozze di Figaro* (also 1992, Japan tour); Marzelline, *Fidelio*; Tytania, *A Midsummer Night's Dream*; High Priestess, *Aida*; Nannetta, *Falstaff*; Israelite/Philistine Woman, *Samson*; Norina, *Don Pasquale*; Adina, *L'Elisir d'Amore*; Zdenka, *Arabella*;

Micaëla, *Carmen*; English National Opera: Belinda, *Dido and Aeneas*; Annina, *A Night in Venice*; Stephano, *Romeo and Juliet*; Tatyana, *Eugene Onegin*; Glyndebourne Festival Opera, Violetta, *La Traviata*.

RELATED PROFESSIONAL ACTIVITIES: Numerous concerts, recitals, broadcasts and television appearances in the UK and abroad.

RECORDINGS INCLUDE: Handel, *L'Allegro il penseroso ed il moderato* (ERAT); Mozart: *Cosi fan tutte* (DG), *Die Zauberflöte*; Purcell, *Dido and Aeneas* (both PHIL); Schubert, lieder (HYPE); Sullivan, *The Mikado* (TELA).

VIDEOS INCLUDE: Beethoven, *Fidelio* (Covent Garden); Bizet, *Carmen* (Glyndebourne Festival Opera); Verdi: *Rigoletto* (English National Opera), *La Traviata* (Glyndebourne Festival Opera).

ADDRESS: c/o Harrison/Parrott Ltd, 12 Penzance Place, London W11 4PA.

McLEOD LINDA   Soprano

PERSONAL DETAILS: b. 29 November 1952, Indiana, USA; m. 1985, Albert Pullen (theatre technician).

EDUCATION/TRAINING: 1970–1974, Western Washington University, studied French and music; 1977–1978, Guildhall School of Music and Drama, with Mary Makower; since 1988, privately with Rudolf Piernay.

PROFESSIONAL DEBUT: 1978, Opera for All, Flora, *La Traviata*.

EARLY CAREER INCLUDED: 1978–1988, as mezzo-soprano: English National Opera: Sonya, *War and Peace*; Dryad, *Ariadne auf Naxos*; Ninetta, *The Sicilian Vespers*; Chambermaid, *The Makropoulos Case*; Javotte, *Manon*; Opera for All: Rosina, *The Barber of Seville*; Lady Pamela, *Fra Diavolo*; Opera North, Mercédès, *Carmen*; Scottish Opera Go Round, Kostelnička, *Jenůfa*; since 1988, soprano.

MAJOR DEBUTS INCLUDE: 1983: English National Opera, Wood Nymph, *Rusalka*; Glyndebourne Touring Opera, Clarissa, *The Love for Three Oranges*; 1984, Opera

North, Second Lady, *The Magic Flute*; 1988, Scottish Opera, Jenifer, *The Midsummer Marriage*; 1992: Flanders Opera, Antwerp, Andromache, *King Priam*; Washington Opera, Senta, *Der Fliegende Holländer*.

OPERATIC WORLD PREMIERES INCLUDE: 1984, Batignano Festival, Fairy, *La Bella e la Bestia* by Stephen Oliver; 1993, English National Opera, Ann, *Inquest of Love* by Jonathan Harvey.

CAREER IN THE UK INCLUDES: Since 1988: City of Birmingham Touring Opera, Brünnhilde and Wellgunde, *The Ring Saga*; English National Opera: Donna Elvira, *Don Giovanni*; title role, *Rusalka*; New Sussex Opera, Elisabeth, *Tannhäuser*; Opera North: Andromache, *King Priam*; Elisabeth de Valois, *Don Carlos*; Scottish Opera: Ortlinde, *Die Walküre*; Donna Anna, *Don Giovanni*.

RECORDINGS INCLUDE: Verdi: *Ernani* (DECC), *Rigoletto* (EMI).

VIDEOS INCLUDE: Dvořák, *Rusalka* (English National Opera).

ADDRESS: c/o Ingpen & Williams Ltd, 14 Kensington Court, London W8 5DN.

McMASTER BRIAN
Administrator

POSITION: Artistic Director, Edinburgh International Festival.

PERSONAL DETAILS: b. 9 May 1943, Hertfordshire.

EDUCATION/TRAINING: University of Bristol.

CAREER: 1968–1973, International Artists' Department, EMI Ltd; 1973–1976, Controller of Opera Planning, English National Opera; 1976–1991, General Administrator and then Managing Director, Welsh National Opera; since 1991, Artistic Director, Edinburgh International Festival.

OTHER PROFESSIONAL ACTIVITIES INCLUDE: 1984–1989, Artistic Director, Vancouver Opera.

HONOURS INCLUDE: 1987, Commander, Order of the British Empire (CBE).

ADDRESS: c/o Edinburgh International Festival, 21 Market Street, Edinburgh EH1 1BW.

McMURRAY JOHN
Administrator, Dramaturg, Librettist and Writer

POSITION: Administrator, City of Birmingham Touring Opera.

PERSONAL DETAILS: b. 10 August 1953, Manchester; m. 1987.

EDUCATION/TRAINING: 1972–1975, University of Leeds; 1975–1976, Centre for Journalism Studies, University College, Cardiff.

CAREER: 1976–1980, reporter, then Education Correspondent, *Yorkshire Post*; 1980–1983, Assistant Editor, *Classical Music* Magazine; 1984–1989, Publications Editor, Royal Opera House, Covent Garden; since 1989, Administrator, City of Birmingham Touring Opera.

OPERATIC WORLD PREMIERES INCLUDE: 1989, Royal Opera Garden Venture, librettist, *The Standard Bearer* by Michael Christie.

OTHER PROFESSIONAL ACTIVITIES INCLUDE: 1986–1988, editorial consultant, *The Illustrated Opera Libretto* series (ROH/Simon & Schuster/Pagoda); contributor, numerous literary and music journals.

AWARDS INCLUDE: 1992, Wagner Society's Sir Reginald Goodall Award, City of Birmingham Touring Opera production of *The Ring Saga*.

ADDRESS: c/o City of Birmingham Touring Opera, 205 The Argent Centre, 60 Frederick Street, Birmingham B1 3HS.

* * * *

NEWMAN HENRY   Baritone

PERSONAL DETAILS: b. 20 May 1938, Birmingham; m. 1965, Peggy Troman (mezzo-soprano), two children.

PREVIOUS OCCUPATION: 1961–1972, teacher and lecturer in arts and crafts.

EDUCATION/TRAINING: 1956–1960, Birmingham College of Arts and Crafts, studied silversmithing; 1960–1961, Birmingham Art Teachers' Training College; 1963–1967, vocal studies with Winifred Tandy as a member of the Joy McArden Singers.

PROFESSIONAL DEBUT: 1971, chorus member, Covent Garden.

EARLY CAREER: 1972–1982, Welsh National Opera (1977–1982, Principal Baritone): Monterone, *Rigoletto* (debut); Yamadori and Sharpless, *Madam Butterfly*; Zurga, *The Pearl Fishers*; Bosun, *Billy Budd*; Schaunard, *La Bohème*; Shchelkalov/Lavitsky, *Boris Godunov*; Sid, *Albert Herring*; Tomsky/Plutus, *The Queen of Spades*; Donald, *Billy Budd*; Demetrius, *A Midsummer Night's Dream*; Marcello, *La Bohème*; Speaker, *The Magic Flute*; Germont, *La Traviata*; Scarpia, *Tosca*; Count, *The Marriage of Figaro*; Papageno, *The Magic Flute*.

MAJOR DEBUTS INCLUDE: 1982, Buxton Festival, Lover, *The Spinning Room* (British première); 1983, Covent Garden, Morales, *Carmen*; 1984: Opera North, Manz, *A Village Romeo and Juliet*; Scottish Opera, Tobias Mill, *The Marriage Contract*; 1986, English National Opera, Asmodus/Student/Brother, *Doctor Faust* (British stage première).

OPERATIC WORLD PREMIERES INCLUDE: Welsh National Opera: 1980, Peter Jack, *The Servants* by William Mathias; 1981, Craig, *The Journey* by John Metcalf.

CAREER IN THE UK INCLUDES: Since 1982: Barber Institute, Birmingham, Mikeli, *Les Deux Journées*; English National Opera: Sharpless, *Madam Butterfly*; Flemish Deputy, *Don Carlos*; Welsh National

Opera: Don Fernando, *Fidelio*; Escamillo, *Carmen*; Roucher, *Andrea Chénier*; Falke, *Die Fledermaus*; Father, *Hansel and Gretel*; Don Alfonso, *Così fan tutte*; title roles: *Don Giovanni, Don Pasquale*.
RELATED PROFESSIONAL ACTIVITIES: Regular concerts, recitals, broadcasts and television appearances in the UK.
RECORDINGS INCLUDE: Donizetti, *Don Pasquale*; Vaughan Williams, *Hugh the Drover*; Verdi, *La Traviata* (all EMI).
ADDRESS: 100 Stanwell Road, Penarth, South Glamorgan CF6 2LP.

NICOLL HARRY   Tenor

PERSONAL DETAILS: b. 9 April 1952, Perthshire.
EDUCATION/TRAINING: Royal Scottish Academy of Music and Drama, with Marjorie Blakeston; privately with Lyndon van der Pump; currently with Edward Brooks.
PROFESSIONAL DEBUT: 1978, Scottish Opera Go Round, Nemorino, *The Elixir of Love*.
EARLY CAREER INCLUDED: 1978–1979, Scottish Opera Go Round: Alfredo, *La Traviata*; Ferrando, *Così fan tutte*.
MAJOR DEBUTS INCLUDE: 1980, Welsh National Opera, Page, *The Coronation of Poppea*; 1983: English National Opera, Scaramuccio, *Ariadne auf Naxos*; Batignano Festival, Prologue/Quint, *The Turn of the Screw*; 1984: Berlin Kammeroper, Sandy, *The Lighthouse*; Cologne Opera, Vašek, *The Bartered Bride*; 1985, Teatro La Fenice, Venice, Soliman, *Zaide*; 1986, Opera North, Count, *The Barber of Seville*; 1988: Glyndebourne Touring Opera, Pedrillo, *Die Entführung aus dem Serail*; Frankfurt Opera, Roderigo, *Otello*.
OPERATIC WORLD PREMIERES INCLUDE: 1988, Berlin Kammeroper, King, *Europa und der Stier* by Helge Jörns; 1990, Scottish Opera, Lover/Friend/Preacher, *The Vanishing Bridegroom* by Judith Weir.

CAREER IN THE UK INCLUDES: Since 1980: English Bach Festival, Thespis/Mercury, *Platée*; English National Opera: French Admiral, *Pacific Overtures*; Nanki-Poo, *The Mikado*; Daniel Buchanan, *Street Scene*; Mecklenburgh Opera, Tenor, *Mannekins* (1990, British première); New Sadler's Wells Opera, Brissard, *The Count of Luxembourg*; Opera Factory, Bad'Un/Piper, *Yan Tan Tethera*; Opera North: Nanki-Poo, *The Mikado*; Baron Lummer, *Intermezzo*; Gonzalve, *L'Heure Espagnole*; title role, *Orpheus in the Underworld*; Scottish Opera: Count, *The Barber of Seville*; Bardolph, *Falstaff*; Welsh National Opera: Vašek, *The Bartered Bride*; Brigella, *Ariadne auf Naxos*; Simpleton, *Wozzeck*.
RECORDINGS INCLUDE: Lehár, *The Count of Luxembourg*; Sondheim, *Pacific Overtures* (both TER); A Hundred Years of Italian Opera (OPRA).
ADDRESS: c/o Ron Gonsalves Personal Artists & Concert Management, 10 Dagnan Road, London SW12 9LQ.

NILON PAUL   Tenor

PERSONAL DETAILS: b. 23 December 1961, West Yorkshire.
EDUCATION/TRAINING: 1980–1985, Royal Northern College of Music, with Frederic Cox.
PROFESSIONAL DEBUT: 1984, Buxton Festival, Volano, *Jason*.
MAJOR DEBUTS INCLUDE: 1986, Teatro La Fenice, Venice, Sellem, *The Rake's Progress*; 1987, Opera North, Hylas, *The Trojans*; 1990, New Israeli Opera, Tel Aviv, Ferrando, *Così fan tutte*; 1991, English National Opera, Narraboth, *Salome*.
OPERATIC WORLD PREMIERES INCLUDE: 1988, Batignano Festival, Citizen, *Mario ed il Mago* by Stephen Oliver.
CAREER IN THE UK INCLUDES: Since 1985: Aldeburgh Festival, Grimoaldo, *Rodelinda*; Almeida Opera, Citizen, *Mario and the Magician* (1992, British première); Buxton Festival, Capocchio, *Il Filosofo di*

Campagna; City of Birmingham Touring Opera, Fenton, *Falstaff*; English National Opera: Telemaco, *The Return of Ulysses*; Tamino, *The Magic Flute*; Narrator, *The Duel of Tancredi and Clorinda*; Lurcanio, *Ariodante*; Opera 80: Don Ottavio, *Don Giovanni*; Duke, *Rigoletto*; Opera North: Belfiore, *La Finta Giardiniera*; Leander, *Masquerade* (1990, British première); Ferrando, *Così fan tutte*; Don Ottavio, *Don Giovanni*; Opera Northern Ireland, Scaramuccio, *Ariadne auf Naxos*.

RELATED PROFESSIONAL ACTIVITIES: Concerts and recitals in the UK and Spain.

RECORDINGS INCLUDE: Donizetti, *L'Assedio di Calais* (OPRA).

ADDRESS: c/o Harrison/Parrott Ltd, 12 Penzance Place, London W11 4PA.

NORRINGTON ROGER
Conductor

POSITIONS: Joint Artistic Director, Early Opera Project; Music Director: London Baroque Players, London Classical Players, Schütz Choir of London and Orchestra of St Luke's, New York City.

PERSONAL DETAILS: b. 16 March 1934, Oxford; m. 1964, two children; m. 1986, Kay Lawrence.

EDUCATION/TRAINING: Choral Scholar, Clare College, Cambridge, studied English; Royal College of Music, with Adrian Boult.

PROFESSIONAL DEBUT: 1962, concert with Schütz Choir of London.

OPERATIC DEBUT: 1966, Chelsea Opera Group, *The Rake's Progress*.

CAREER: 1962–1969, freelance tenor and conductor; Principal Conductor: 1969–1984, Kent Opera; 1985–1989, Bournemouth Sinfonietta; 1986–1988, Chief Guest Conductor, Jerusalem Symphony Orchestra; Music Director: since 1962, Schütz Choir of London; since 1975, London Baroque Players; since 1978, London Classical Players; since 1990, Orchestra of St Luke's, New York City; since 1984, founder and Joint Artistic

Director (with Kay Lawrence), Early Opera Project.

MAJOR OPERATIC DEBUTS INCLUDE: 1969, Kent Opera, *L'Incoronazione di Poppea*; 1971, Sadler's Wells Opera, *The Barber of Seville*; 1982, La Piccola Scala, Milan, *Ariodante*; 1983, Teatro La Fenice, Venice, *The Turn of the Screw*; 1984, Maggio Musicale, Florence, *Orfeo*; 1986, Covent Garden, *Samson*.

OPERA PERFORMANCES IN THE UK INCLUDE: 1969–1984, Kent Opera, more than 30 productions including: *Idomeneo, Così fan tutte, Orfeo, Rigoletto, Iphigenia in Tauris, La Traviata, Eugene Onegin, The Seraglio, The Return of Ulysses, The Turn of the Screw, The Magic Flute, Falstaff, Venus and Adonis, Il Ballo delle Ingrate, The Marriage of Figaro, Fidelio, King Priam*; since 1985: Covent Garden: *Albert Herring, Peter Grimes*; English National Opera, *Don Giovanni*.

RELATED PROFESSIONAL ACTIVITIES: Regular concerts and festival appearances in the UK and abroad; editor, *L'Incoronazione di Poppea* (Kent Opera).

RECORDINGS INCLUDE: Beethoven: complete symphonies, piano concertos; Berlioz, *Symphonie Fantastique*; Brahms, Symphony No. 1; Mendelssohn, Symphonies Nos 3 & 4; Mozart: *Don Giovanni, Die Zauberflöte*; Schubert, Symphonies Nos 5, 8 & 9; Schumann, Symphonies Nos 3 & 4 (all EMI).

VIDEOS INCLUDE: Tippett, *King Priam* (Kent Opera).

HONOURS INCLUDE: 1980, Officer, Order of the British Empire (OBE); 1981, Cavaliere Ufficiali dell'ordine al merito della Repubblica Italiana; 1990: Commander, Order of the British Empire (CBE); Honorary Fellow, Clare College, Cambridge.

ADDRESS: c/o Allied Artists, 42 Montpelier Square, London SW7 1JZ.

NUNN TREVOR   Director

PERSONAL DETAILS: b. 14 January 1940, Ipswich; m. 1969, Janet Suzman (actress, m. diss.); m. 1986, Sharon Lee Hill (actress, m. diss.); four children.

EDUCATION/TRAINING: Downing College, Cambridge, studied English.

PROFESSIONAL DEBUT: 1962, Belgrade Theatre, Coventry, *The Caucasian Chalk Circle* by Bertolt Brecht.

OPERATIC DEBUT: 1983, Glyndebourne Festival Opera, *Idomeneo*.

CAREER: As theatre director: 1962–1964, Belgrade Theatre, Coventry; Royal Shakespeare Company: 1965–1968, Associate Director; 1968–1978, Artistic Director and Chief Executive; 1978–1987, Joint Artistic Director and Chief Executive; since 1987, Director Emeritus; currently freelance theatre and opera director in the UK and abroad.

OPERA PRODUCTIONS IN THE UK INCLUDE: Since 1983: Covent Garden, *Porgy and Bess*; Glyndebourne Festival Opera: *Porgy and Bess*, *Così fan tutte*, *Peter Grimes*.

RELATED PROFESSIONAL ACTIVITIES: Numerous productions for film and television.

VIDEOS INCLUDE: Mozart, *Idomeneo* (Glyndebourne Festival Opera).

HONOURS INCLUDE: 1978, Commander, Order of the British Empire (CBE); Honorary Master of Arts, Universities of Newcastle and Warwick.

ADDRESS: c/o Homevale Ltd, 140a Gloucester Mansions, Cambridge Circus, London WC2H 8HD.

NYMAN MICHAEL   Composer

PERSONAL DETAILS: b. 23 March 1944; m. 1970, two children.

EDUCATION/TRAINING: 1961–1965, Royal Academy of Music, composition with Alan Bush; 1964–1967, King's College, London, musicology with Thurston Dart; 1965–1966, Conservatorum Ciprian Porumbescu, Bucharest, folk music with Emilia Comisel.

CAREER: Since 1967: numerous compositions in all genres including three operas, works for ballet, television, theatre and scores for 16 films directed by Peter Greenaway; founder and Director, Michael Nyman Band (formerly Campiello Band).

OPERATIC WORLD PREMIERES: 1986, ICA Theatre, London, *The Man Who Mistook his Wife for a Hat*, adapted by Michael Morris and Christopher Rawlence after Oliver Sacks; 1987, Endymion Music Theatre, *Vital Statistics*; 1988, Rotterdam, *Orpheus' Daughter*; 1991, *Hérouville, La Princesse de Milan*, opera-ballet with the choreographer Karine Japorta.

RELATED PROFESSIONAL ACTIVITIES: 1965–1968, musicologist; 1968–1978, music critic; 1965–1980, lecturer in music at art colleges.

RECORDINGS INCLUDE: *The Man who Mistook his Wife for a Hat* (CBS), String Quartets, *Prospero's Books* (both DECC), *The Draughtman's Contract*, *A Zed and Two Noughts*, *Drowning by Numbers* and *The Cook, the Thief, his Wife and her Lover* (all VIRG).

RELEVANT PUBLICATIONS INCLUDE: *Experimental Music: Cage and Beyond* (Studio Vista/Schirmer).

HONOURS INCLUDE: 1991, Fellow, Royal Academy of Music.

ADDRESS: Not available.

*   *   *   *

O'BRIEN TIMOTHY   Designer

PERSONAL DETAILS: b. 8 March 1929, Assam, India.

EDUCATION/TRAINING: 1949–1952, Corpus Christi College, Cambridge; 1952–1953, Henry Fellowship, Yale University.

PROFESSIONAL DEBUT: 1956, Arts Theatre, London, *The Bald Prima Donna/The New Tenant* by Eugene Ionesco.

OPERATIC DEBUT: 1958, Sadler's Wells Opera, *The Flying Dutchman*.

CAREER: Since 1956, opera, television and theatre designer for leading companies in the UK and abroad; 1956–1966, Head of Design, ABC Television; 1966–1988, Associate Artist, Royal Shakespeare Company.

MAJOR OPERATIC DEBUTS INCLUDE: Co-designs with Tazeena Firth: 1972, Norwegian Opera, Oslo, *La Cenerentola*; *The Bassarids*: 1974, English National Opera (British première); 1975, Frankfurt Opera; 1977, Deutsche Oper, Berlin, *Falstaff*; 1978: Australian Opera, Sydney, *A Midsummer Night's Dream*; Gothenburg, *The Cunning Little Vixen*; 1983, Vienna State Opera, *Turandot*; sole designs: 1985: Cologne Opera, *Lucia di Lammermoor*; Grand Théâtre, Geneva, *Les Vêpres Siciliennes*; 1985/1986, Covent Garden and Lyric Opera, Chicago/ Metropolitan Opera, New York co-production, *Samson*; 1986, Netherlands Opera, *Die Meistersinger von Nürnberg*; 1991, Kirov Opera, *War and Peace*.

OPERATIC WORLD PREMIERES INCLUDE: 1961, Sadler's Wells Opera, *The Ledge* by Richard Rodney Bennett; 1970, Covent Garden, *The Knot Garden* by Michael Tippett.

OPERA DESIGNS IN THE UK INCLUDE: Since 1962: City of Birmingham Touring Opera, *Beauty and the Beast*; Covent Garden: *Peter Grimes, The Rake's Progress* (both with Tazeena Firth), *Lulu* (1981, British première, three act version), *Tannhäuser, Otello, Die Entführung aus dem Serail*; Sadler's Wells Opera/English National Opera: *The Bartered Bride, The Girl of the Golden West, Le Grand Macabre*

(1982, British première), *The Mastersingers of Nuremberg*.

RELATED PROFESSIONAL ACTIVITIES: Since 1984, Chairman, Society of British Theatre Designers; since 1988, Honorary Associate Artist, Royal Shakespeare Company.

VIDEOS INCLUDE: Britten, *Peter Grimes*; Mozart, *Die Entführung aus dem Serail* (both Covent Garden); Puccini, *Turandot* (Vienna State Opera).

AWARDS INCLUDE: 1976, co-winner, Gold Medal, International Exhibition of Stage Design, Prague Quadriennale.

ADDRESS: 33 Lansdowne Gardens, London SW8 2EQ.

O'NEILL DENNIS   Tenor

PERSONAL DETAILS: b. 25 February 1948, South Wales; m. 1970, Ruth Collins, two children; m. 1988, Ellen Folkestad.

EDUCATION/TRAINING: Private studies with Frederic Cox in Manchester, Ettore Campogalliani in Mantua, Luigi Ricci in Rome.

PROFESSIONAL DEBUT: 1971, Scottish Opera for All, Ramiro, *Cinderella*.

EARLY CAREER INCLUDED: 1975–1979: Principal Tenor: 1975–1977, State Opera of South Australia, Adelaide; 1977–1979, Scottish Opera; roles included: Ferrando, *Così fan tutte*; Rodolfo, *La Bohème*; Fenton, *Falstaff*; Duke, *Rigoletto*; Belmonte, *Die Entführung aus dem Serail*; also: Perth Festival, Australia, Paolino, *Il Matrimonio Segreto*; Wexford Festival, Cecco, *Il Mondo della Luna*.

MAJOR DEBUTS INCLUDE: 1979: Covent Garden, Flavio, *Norma*; Welsh National Opera, Alfredo, *La Traviata*; 1980, Glyndebourne Festival Opera, Italian Tenor, *Der Rosenkavalier*; 1981, Alfredo, *La Traviata*: Hamburg State Opera, Vienna State Opera; 1984, San Francisco Opera, Elvino, *La Sonnambula*; 1985, Lyric Opera, Chicago, Tebaldo, *I Capuleti e i Montecchi*; 1986, Metropolitan Opera, New York, Alfredo, *La Traviata*; 1991,

Bavarian State Opera, Munich, Manrico, *Il Trovatore*.

CAREER IN THE UK INCLUDES: Since 1980: Covent Garden: Pinkerton, *Madama Butterfly*; Matteo, *Arabella*; Elvino, *La Sonnambula*; Beppe, *Pagliacci*; Macduff, *Macbeth*; Alfred, *Die Fledermaus*; Duke, *Rigoletto*; Italian Tenor, *Der Rosenkavalier*; Edgardo, *Lucia di Lammermoor*; Gustavus, *Un Ballo in Maschera*; Rodolfo, *La Bohème*; Foresto, *Attila*; Calaf, *Turandot*; title role, *Don Carlos*; Opera North, Don José, *Carmen*; Welsh National Opera: Rodolfo, *La Bohème*; Cavaradossi, *Tosca*; Dick Johnson, *La Fanciulla del West*; title roles: *Idomeneo*, *Ernani*.

RELATED PROFESSIONAL ACTIVITIES: Regular concerts, recitals, broadcasts and television appearances in the UK and abroad including *Dennis O'Neill Sings* (BBC) and *Caruso*, documentary series (HTV); 1988, founder, Dennis O'Neill Annual Bursary for Young Artists; President, The Friends of Welsh National Opera.

RECORDINGS INCLUDE: Puccini, *La Fanciulla del West* (RCA); Tosti, songs (MERI); Verdi: *Aida* (DG), *Requiem* (RCA); Dennis O'Neill Sings (BBC).

VIDEOS INCLUDE: J. Strauss, *Die Fledermaus*; R. Strauss, *Der Rosenkavalier* (both Covent Garden).

ADDRESS: c/o Ingpen & Williams Ltd, 14 Kensington Court, London W8 5DN.

O'NEILL PATRICIA   Soprano

PERSONAL DETAILS: b. 29 October 1950, South Wales; m. 1977, Peter Price; m. 1987, Patrick Wheatley (baritone), one child.

EDUCATION/TRAINING: Welsh National Opera Training Scheme, University College, Cardiff; Royal College of Music; 1979, National Opera Studio; since 1979, privately with Esther Salaman.

PROFESSIONAL DEBUT: 1974, Handel Opera Society, Dalinda, *Ariodante*.

EARLY CAREER INCLUDED: 1978, Scottish Opera Go Round: Adina, *The Elixir of Love*; Fiordiligi, *Così fan tutte*.

MAJOR DEBUTS INCLUDE: 1978, Scottish Opera, Gianetta, *The Elixir of Love*; 1979, Batignano Festival, Silandra, *Orontea*; 1980, English National Opera, Xenia, *Boris Godunov*; 1982, Flanders Opera, Antwerp, Mimi, *La Bohème*; 1984, English National Opera USA tour (including Metropolitan Opera, New York): Gilda, *Rigoletto*; title role, *Patience*; 1985, Opera North, Bella, *The Midsummer Marriage*; 1988, D'Oyly Carte Opera, Mabel, *The Pirates of Penzance*.

CAREER IN THE UK INCLUDES: Since 1980: City of Birmingham Touring Opera, Mimi, *La Bohème*; Craig-y-nos, title role, *Madam Butterfly*; English National Opera (1981–1986, Principal Soprano): Málinka/ Etherea/Kunka, *The Adventures of Mr Brouček*; Mimi, *La Bohème*; Zerlina, *Don Giovanni*; Marzelline, *Fidelio*; Kristina, *The Makropoulos Case*; Euridice, *Orfeo*; Chloë, *The Queen of Spades*; Gilda, *Rigoletto*; Antonia, *The Tales of Hoffmann*; title role, *Patience*; New Sussex Opera, Lisa, *The Queen of Spades*; Scottish Opera: Lidka, *The Two Widows*; Olympia/Giulietta/Antonia/ Stella, *The Tales of Hoffmann*; Bella, *The Midsummer Marriage*; Phyllis, *Iolanthe*.

RELATED PROFESSIONAL ACTIVITIES: Numerous concerts, broadcasts and television appearances in the UK and abroad.

AWARDS INCLUDE: 1973, Young Welsh Singers Competition; 1979, Peter Stuyvesant Award; 1981, Bel Canto Competition (Belgium).

ADDRESS: c/o Harlequin Agency Ltd, 1 University Place, Cardiff, CF2 2JU.

OKE ALAN   Baritone

PERSONAL DETAILS: b. 27 February 1954, London; m. 1977, Fiona Milne (mezzo-soprano), two children.

EDUCATION/TRAINING: 1971–1975, Royal Scottish Academy of Music and Drama, with Lilian Liddell; further studies with Joan Alexander in Glasgow and Hans Hotter in Munich.

PROFESSIONAL DEBUT: 1978, Scottish Opera Go Round, Belcore, *The Elixir of Love*.

EARLY CAREER INCLUDED: 1978–1984, Scottish Opera: Germont, *La Traviata*; Dandini, *Cinderella*; Marullo, *Rigoletto*; Schaunard, *La Bohème*; Demetrius, *A Midsummer Night's Dream*; Captain, *Manon Lescaut*; Zurga, *The Pearl Fishers*; English Clerk, *Death in Venice*; Papageno, *The Magic Flute*; Ping, *Turandot*.

MAJOR DEBUTS INCLUDE: 1983, Covent Garden, Jester, *Taverner*; 1984, English National Opera, Grosvenor, *Patience*; 1986, Opera Company of Boston, Jester, *Taverner*.

OPERATIC WORLD PREMIERES INCLUDE: 1987, Kent Opera, Actor, *A Night at the Chinese Opera* by Judith Weir.

CAREER IN THE UK INCLUDES: Since 1984: D'Oyly Carte Opera: Giuseppe, *The Gondoliers*; Corcoran, *HMS Pinafore*; Ko-Ko, *The Mikado*; Kent Opera: Count, *The Marriage of Figaro*; Escamillo, *Carmen*; New Sadler's Wells Opera, Count Danilo, *The Merry Widow*; Opera North: Albert, *Werther*; Ko-Ko, *The Mikado*; Pantaloon, *The Love for Three Oranges*; Macheath, *The Threepenny Opera*; Hérrison de Porc Epic, *L'Etoile*; Pluto, *Orpheus in the Underworld*; Scottish Opera: Olivier, *Capriccio*; Bobinet, *La Vie Parisienne*; Harry Easter, *Street Scene*; Cascada, *The Merry Widow*.

RECORDINGS INCLUDE: Lehár, *The Merry Widow*; Sullivan, *The Gondoliers* (both TER).

AWARDS INCLUDE: 1975, Countess of Munster Award.

ADDRESS: c/o M & M Lyric Artists, 6 Princess Road, London NW1 7JJ.

OLIVER ALEXANDER   Tenor

PERSONAL DETAILS: b. 27 June 1944, Bridge of Allan, Scotland.

EDUCATION/TRAINING: Royal Scottish Academy of Music and Drama, with Margaret Dick; Vienna State Academy, with Anton Dermota.

PROFESSIONAL DEBUT: 1967, Vienna Chamber Opera, appeared in *La Molinara*.

MAJOR DEBUTS INCLUDE: 1968, Glyndebourne Touring Opera, Don Ottavio, *Don Giovanni*; 1969, Scottish Opera, Jacquino, *Fidelio*; 1970, Welsh National Opera, Alfred, *Die Fledermaus*; 1971, Covent Garden, *Die Meistersinger von Nürnberg*; Arnalta, *L'Incoronazione di Poppea*: 1971, Netherlands Opera; 1977, Zurich Opera; 1982, La Monnaie, Brussels, Arbace, *Idomeneo*; 1988, English National Opera, Monostatos, *The Magic Flute*.

OPERATIC WORLD PREMIERES INCLUDE: 1970, Glyndebourne Festival Opera, Brother Timothy, *The Rising of the Moon* by Nicholas Maw; 1976, Covent Garden, Soldier/Madman, *We Come to the River* by Hans Werner Henze; La Monnaie, Brussels: 1983, Prelati, *La Passion de Gilles* by Philippe Boesmans; 1986, Bürgel, *Das Schloss* by André Laporte; 1987, La Scala, Milan, Edoardo, *Riccardo III* by Flavio Testi.

CAREER IN THE UK INCLUDES: Since 1968: Covent Garden: Monsieur Triquet, *Eugene Onegin*; Don Basilio and Don Curzio, *Le Nozze di Figaro*; Abbé, *Andrea Chénier*; Idiot, *Wozzeck*; Flute, *A Midsummer Night's Dream*; Mr Upfold, *Albert Herring*; Mime, *Siegfried*; English National Opera, Iro, *The Return of Ulysses*; Glyndebourne Festival and Touring Opera: Monostatos, *Die Zauberflöte*; Pedrillo, *Die Entführung aus dem Serail*; Ferrando, *Così fan tutte*; Narciso, *Il Turco in Italia*; Dancing Master and Scaramuccio, *Ariadne auf Naxos*; Iro, *Il Ritorno d'Ulisse in Patria*; Arbace, *Idomeneo*; Baron Lummer, *Intermezzo*; Sellem, *The Rake's Progress*; Opera

North, Nemorino, *The Elixir of Love*;
Scottish Opera: Ernesto, *Don Pasquale*;
Lensky, *Eugene Onegin*; Vašek, *The
Bartered Bride*; Idiot, *Wozzeck*; Welsh
National Opera: Monostatos, *The Magic
Flute*; Pong, *Turandot*; Arbace,
Idomeneo; Pedrillo, *The Seraglio*.

RELATED PROFESSIONAL ACTIVITIES:
Numerous concerts, recitals and
masterclasses in the UK and abroad.

RECORDINGS INCLUDE: Verdi, *La Traviata*
(DECC).

VIDEOS INCLUDE: Britten, *Albert Herring*
(Glyndebourne Festival Opera); Giordano,
Andrea Chénier (Covent Garden);
Sullivan: *Iolanthe*, *The Pirates of
Penzance*, *The Sorcerer* (all Walker).

AWARDS INCLUDE: 1966, Richard Tauber
Memorial Prize.

ADDRESS: c/o Harrison/Parrott Ltd, 12
Penzance Place, London W11 4PA.

OPIE ALAN   Baritone

POSITION: Principal Baritone, English
National Opera.

PERSONAL DETAILS: b. 22 March 1945,
Cornwall; m. 1970, Kathleen Smales
(mezzo-soprano), two children.

EDUCATION/TRAINING: Choral Scholar,
Gonville and Caius College, Cambridge;
1965–1968, Guildhall School of Music,
with Arthur Reckless; 1968–1969, London
Opera Centre; 1970–1985, privately with
Vera Rozsa.

PROFESSIONAL DEBUT: 1969, Sadler's
Wells Opera, Papageno, *The Magic Flute*.

EARLY CAREER INCLUDED: 1969–1973:
Cambridge University Opera, Tomeš, *The
Kiss*; Covent Garden, Officer, *Il Barbiere
di Siviglia*; English Opera Group,
Demetrius, *A Midsummer Night's Dream*;
Glyndebourne Touring Opera, Guglielmo,
Così fan tutte; Kent Opera, title role, *Don
Giovanni*; New Opera Company,
Kovalyov, *The Nose* (1973, British stage
première); Phoenix Opera, title role, *The
Barber of Seville*.

MAJOR DEBUTS INCLUDE: 1970: Welsh
National Opera, Falke, *Die Fledermaus*;
Santa Fe Opera, Rochefort, *Anna Bolena*;
Wexford Festival, Sid, *Albert Herring*;
1976, Vienna Volksoper, Malatesta, *Don
Pasquale*; 1979, Lyric Opera, Chicago,
Roucher, *Andrea Chénier*; 1980, La
Monnaie, Brussels, title role, *Il Barbiere
di Siviglia*; 1982, Buxton Festival, title
role, *Háry János*; 1984, Paris Opera,
Faninal, *Der Rosenkavalier*; 1985: Covent
Garden, Hector, *King Priam*;
Glyndebourne Festival Opera, Sid, *Albert
Herring*; Beckmesser, *Der Meistersinger
von Nürnberg*: 1986, Netherlands Opera;
1987, Bayreuth Festival; 1989,
Glyndebourne Touring Opera, Traveller,
Death in Venice.

OPERATIC WORLD PREMIERES INCLUDE:
1978, Lyric Opera, Chicago, Messias,
Paradise Lost by Krzysztof Penderecki;
1981, English National Opera, Stiva, *Anna
Karenina* by Iain Hamilton.

CAREER IN THE UK INCLUDES: Since 1973:
Principal Baritone, Sadler's Wells Opera/
English National Opera: Major
Murgatroyd, *Patience*; Raimbaud, *Count
Ory*; Strephon, *Iolanthe*; Papageno, *The
Magic Flute*; Eisenstein and Falke, *Die
Fledermaus*; Guglielmo, *Così fan tutte*;
Beckmesser, *The Mastersingers of
Nuremberg*; Lescaut, *Manon*; Morales,
Carmen; Dandini, *Cinderella*; Cecil, *Mary
Stuart*; Denisov, *War and Peace*; Cecil,
Gloriana; Valentin, *Faust*; Junius, *The
Rape of Lucretia*; Tomsky/Plutus, *The
Queen of Spades*; Zurga, *The Pearl
Fishers*; Paolo, *Simon Boccanegra*;
Germont, *La Traviata*; Silvio, *Pagliacci*;
Marcello, *La Bohème*; Fiddler,
Königskinder; Melitone, *The Force of
Destiny*; Malatesta, *Don Pasquale*; title
roles: *The Barber of Seville*, *Doctor Faust*,
The Marriage of Figaro; also: Covent
Garden: Ping, *Turandot*; Mangus, *The
Knot Garden*; Paolo, *Simon Boccanegra*;
Traveller, *Death in Venice*; Glyndebourne
Festival Opera: Balstrode, *Peter Grimes*;
Traveller, *Death in Venice*; title role, *Le
Nozze di Figaro*; Scottish Opera: Baron,

La Vie Parisienne; Storch, *Intermezzo*;
Forester, *The Cunning Little Vixen*.
RELATED PROFESSIONAL ACTIVITIES:
Regular concerts, recitals, broadcasts
and television appearances in the UK and
abroad.
RECORDINGS INCLUDE: Donizetti, *Mary
Stuart* (EMI); Massenet, *Thérèse*;
Meyerbeer, *Les Huguenots*; (both DECC)
Vaughan Williams, *Serenade to Music*
(HYPE); Verdi: *Otello* (DECC), *Rigoletto* (EMI);
Weill, *Sieben Todsünden* (CBS).
VIDEOS INCLUDE: Britten: *Albert Herring*
(Glyndebourne Festival Opera), *Death in
Venice* (Glyndebourne Touring Opera),
Gloriana, *The Rape of Lucretia*; Donizetti,
Mary Stuart (both English National
Opera); Verdi, *Simon Boccanegra* (Covent
Garden).
HONOURS INCLUDE: Associate, Guildhall
School of Music and Drama.
ADDRESS: c/o Allied Artists, 42 Montpelier
Square, London SW7 1JZ.

ORMISTON LINDA
Mezzo-soprano

PERSONAL DETAILS: b. 15 January 1948,
Motherwell.
EDUCATION/TRAINING: 1965–1969,
University of Glasgow, studied music and
computing science; 1969–1972, Royal
Scottish Academy of Music and Drama,
with Winifred Busfield; 1972–1974, London
Opera Centre, with Joy Mammen.
PROFESSIONAL DEBUT: 1974, Opera for All,
title role, *Cinderella* (also student
performance at La Monnaie, Brussels).
EARLY CAREER INCLUDED: 1974–1984:
Buxton Festival: Marie-Louise, *Háry
János*; Mazet, *La Colombe*; Handel
Opera Society, Amastre, *Serse*; Opera for
All: Olga, *Eugene Onegin*; Zerlina, *Don
Giovanni*; Scottish Opera: Háta and
Ludmilla, *The Bartered Bride*; Olga,
Eugene Onegin; Hermia, *A Midsummer
Night's Dream*; Marcellina, *Le Nozze di
Figaro*; Climene, *L'Egisto*.
MAJOR DEBUTS INCLUDE: 1985, Opera
North, She-Ancient, *The Midsummer
Marriage*; 1986, Glyndebourne Touring
Opera, Mrs Herring, *Albert Herring*; 1988,
Glyndebourne Festival Opera, Feklusha,
Katya Kabanova; 1990, La Monnaie,
Brussels, Florry, *Stephen Climax*; Mother
Goose, *The Rake's Progress*: 1989,
Vancouver Opera; 1991, Monte Carlo
Opera.
OPERATIC WORLD PREMIERES INCLUDE:
1976, Scottish Opera at the York Festival,
Woman Accuser, *Confessions of a
Justified Sinner* by Thomas Wilson; 1977,
Scottish Opera at the Edinburgh
International Festival, Mary Seton, *Mary,
Queen of Scots* by Thea Musgrave; 1991,
Opera North, Mathilde, *Caritas* by Robert
Saxton.
CAREER IN THE UK INCLUDES: Since 1985:
Glyndebourne Festival Opera: Mayor's
Wife, *Jenůfa*; Mother Goose, *The Rake's
Progress*; New Sadler's Wells Opera:
Mad Margaret, *Ruddigore*; Little
Buttercup, *HMS Pinafore*; Opera North:
Marthe, *Faust*; Magdelone, *Masquerade*;
Grete's Mother/Milli, *Der Ferne Klang*
(1992, British première); Public Opinion,
Orpheus in the Underworld; Opera
Northern Ireland, Despina, *Così fan tutte*.
RELATED PROFESSIONAL ACTIVITIES:
Numerous concerts and recitals in the UK
and abroad; member, Music Box (with
Donald Maxwell and pianist).
RECORDINGS INCLUDE: Britten, *Noye's
Fludde* (VIRG); Saxton, *Caritas* (COLL);
Sullivan: *HMS Pinafore*, *Ruddigore* (both
TER).
VIDEOS INCLUDE: Janáček: *Jenůfa*, *Katya
Kabanova* (both Glyndebourne Festival
Opera).
ADDRESS: c/o Music International, 13
Ardilaun Road, London N5 2QR.

OSBORNE NIGEL
Composer, Broadcaster and Writer

POSITION: Professor of Music, University of Edinburgh.

PERSONAL DETAILS: b. 23 June 1948, Manchester.

EDUCATION/TRAINING: 1967–1970, St Edmund Hall, Oxford, studied composition with Kenneth Leighton and serial technique with Egon Wellesz; 1970–1971: Polish Radio Experimental Studio; Warsaw Academy of Music, with Witold Rudzinski.

FIRST WORK TO ACHIEVE PROMINENCE: 1971, *Seven Words* (cantata).

CAREER: Since 1971, compositions in all genres including three operas and numerous orchestral, instrumental, choral and vocal works; incidental music for ballet, radio, television and theatre including *Faust* and *Morte d'Arthur* (both Lyric Theatre, Hammersmith); 1978–1986, Lecturer in Music, University of Nottingham; since 1990, Professor of Music, University of Edinburgh.

OPERATIC WORLD PREMIERES: 1986, Opera Factory, *Hell's Angels*, chamber opera in two acts, libretto by David Freeman after *The Council of Love* by Oskar Panizza, conductor Diego Masson, director David Freeman, designer David Roger; 1987, Glyndebourne Touring Opera, *The Electrification of the Soviet Union*, opera in two acts, libretto by Craig Raine after *The Last Summer* and *Spektorsky* by Boris Pasternak, conductor Elgar Howarth, director Peter Sellars, designer George Tsypin; 1992, Almeida Opera, *Terrible Mouth*, libretto by Howard Barker, conductor David Parry, director David Pountney, designer Nigel Lowery.

RELATED PROFESSIONAL ACTIVITIES: Writer and broadcaster on new music and music in education; Editor-in-Chief, *Contemporary Music Review*.

RECORDINGS INCLUDE: *After Night* (BEDI), Piano Sonata (MERL), *Albanian Nights* for wind ensemble, based on *Cosi fan tutte* (EMI).

AWARDS INCLUDE: 1971, International Opera Prize, Radio Suisse Romande (Switzerland); 1973, Gaudeamus Prize (Netherlands); 1977, Radcliffe Award; 1982, Koussevitsky Foundation Grant (USA), for contribution to contemporary music.

ADDRESS: c/o Universal Edition (London) Ltd, 2/3 Fareham Street, London W1V 4DU.

OWENS ANNE-MARIE
Mezzo-soprano

POSITION: Principal Mezzo-soprano, English National Opera.

PERSONAL DETAILS: b. South Shields.

EDUCATION/TRAINING: 1971–1977, Newcastle School of Music, with Mary Bullock; 1977–1979, Guildhall School of Music and Drama, with Laura Sarti; 1980–1981, National Opera Studio.

PROFESSIONAL DEBUT: 1979, chorus member, Kent Opera.

MAJOR DEBUTS INCLUDE: 1981, Glyndebourne Touring Opera, Mistress Quickly, *Falstaff*; 1982, English National Opera, Rosina, *The Barber of Seville*; 1983, Aix-en-Provence Festival, Tisbe, *La Cenerentola*; 1984: Glyndebourne Festival Opera, Arnalta, *L'Incoronazione di Poppea*; Metz, Marcellina, *Le Nozze di Figaro*; 1985, Scottish Opera, Metella, *La Vie Parisienne*; 1987: Covent Garden, Clotilde, *Norma*; Opera North, Jocasta, *Oedipus Rex*; 1988, Wexford Festival, Kate, *The Devil and Kate*; 1991, Welsh National Opera, Ragonde, *Count Ory*; 1992: La Monnaie, Brussels, Baba the Turk, *The Rake's Progress*; Lausanne Opera, Fidalma, *Il Matrimonio Segreto*.

CAREER IN THE UK INCLUDES: Since 1981: Principal Mezzo-soprano, English National Opera: Marcellina, *The Marriage of Figaro*; Suzuki, *Madam Butterfly*; Hostess, *Boris Godunov*; Maddalena, *Rigoletto*; Fvolka, *The Marriage*; Suzanne, *Toussaint*; Waltraute, *The Valkyrie*; Bianca, *The Rape of Lucretia*; Annina, *Der Rosenkavalier*; Ragonde,

Count Ory; Háta, *The Bartered Bride*;
She-Ancient, *The Midsummer Marriage*;
Magdalene, *The Mastersingers of
Nuremberg*; Voice from Above, *Parsifal*;
Charlotte, *Werther*; Third Lady, *The
Magic Flute*; Solokha/Tsarina, *Christmas
Eve* (1988, British stage première);
Geneviève, *Pelléas and Mélisande*;
Preziosilla, *The Force of Destiny*; Lady
Psyche, *Princess Ida*; also: Covent
Garden: Nurse, *Boris Godunov*; Third
Lady, *Die Zauberflöte*; Rossweisse, *Die
Walküre*; Spirit of Antonia's Mother, *Les
Contes d'Hoffmann*; New Sussex Opera,
Pauline/Daphnis, *The Queen of Spades*;
Opera North, Ariane, *Ariane and
Bluebeard*; Scottish Opera: Suzuki,

Madama Butterfly; Jocasta, *Oedipus Rex*;
Welsh National Opera, Madame Arvidson,
Un Ballo in Maschera.
RELATED PROFESSIONAL ACTIVITIES:
Regular concerts in the UK and abroad.
RECORDINGS INCLUDE: Bruckner, sacred
choral works; Rossini, *Petite Messe
Solennelle* (both CONI).
VIDEOS INCLUDE: Britten, *The Rape of
Lucretia* (English National Opera);
Monteverdi, *L'Incoronazione di Poppea*
(Glyndebourne Festival Opera).
ADDRESS: c/o Athole Still International
Management Ltd, Greystoke House, 80–86
Westow Street, London SE19 3AF.

* * * *

PADMORE ELAINE
**Artistic Director, Administrator,
Broadcaster and Soprano**

entered Birmingham University, autumn 1962!

POSITIONS: Artistic Director: Royal Opera,
Copenhagen; Wexford Festival.
PERSONAL DETAILS: b. 3 February 1947 ?
West Yorkshire.
EDUCATION/TRAINING: University of
Birmingham, studied music; répétiteur's
scholarship, Guildhall School of Music
and Drama; private vocal studies with
Helen Isepp; Licentiate, Trinity College of
Music.
CAREER: Répétiteur, Barber Institute,
Birmingham; co-founder: Opera 70 and
Operabout (Opera East), sang leading
roles with both; BBC Radio 3: 1971, music
programmes producer; 1976–1982, Head
of Opera; 1982–1990, presenter; 1975–
1985, lecturer, Royal Academy of Music;
1989–1990, Guest Artistic Director, Dublin
Grand Opera; Artistic Director: 1982–1994,
Wexford Festival; 1990–1992, Classical
Productions (UK) Ltd (arena opera at
Earls Court); 1991–1993, Dublin Grand
Opera; 1991–1993, Artistic Consultant,
London Opera Festival; since 1993 Artistic
Director, Royal Opera, Copenhagen.

PUBLICATIONS INCLUDE: 1971, *Great
Composers: Wagner* (Faber); contributor:
Music in the Modern Age (Weidenfeld &
Nicholson), *New Grove Dictionary of
Music and Musicians* (Macmillan).
HONOURS INCLUDE: Honorary Associate,
Royal Academy of Music.
ADDRESS: c/o Royal Opera, Copenhagen,
PO Box 2185, 1017 Copenhagen K,
Denmark.

PAGE STEVEN Baritone

PERSONAL DETAILS: b. 24 March 1955,
Surrey.
PREVIOUS OCCUPATION: Trade-mark
attorney.
EDUCATION/TRAINING: 1981–1982, National
Opera Studio; privately with Margaret
Hyde.
PROFESSIONAL DEBUT: 1984, Opera 80, Don
Alfonso, *Così fan tutte*.
EARLY CAREER INCLUDED: 1984–1986:
Buxton Festival, Cold Genius, *King
Arthur*; Kent Opera, Zuniga, *Carmen*;
Opera 80, Nick Shadow, *The Rake's
Progress*.

215

MAJOR DEBUTS INCLUDE: 1986, English
National Opera, Morales, *Carmen*; 1988,
Scottish Opera, Guglielmo, *Così fan tutte*;
1992, Glyndebourne Touring Opera, Nick
Shadow, *The Rake's Progress*.
CAREER IN THE UK INCLUDES: Since 1987:
Buxton Festival: Martino, *L'Occasione fa
il Ladro*; Don Gherardo, *Torquato Tasso*;
Milord Arespingh, *L'Italiana in Londra*;
English National Opera: Albert, *Werther*;
Tarquinius, *The Rape of Lucretia*; Paolo,
Simon Boccanegra; Valentin, *Faust*;
Count, *The Marriage of Figaro*; title role,
Don Giovanni; Scottish Opera: Marcello,
La Bohème; Count, *Le Nozze di Figaro*;
Chorèbe, *Les Troyens*; Ford, *Falstaff*; title
role, *Don Giovanni*.
RELATED PROFESSIONAL ACTIVITIES:
Concerts and recitals in the UK.
AWARDS INCLUDE: 1981, Countess of
Munster Award.
ADDRESS: c/o Stafford Law Associates, 26
Mayfield Road, Weybridge, Surrey KT13
8XB.

PAINTAL PRITI   Composer

PERSONAL DETAILS: b. 1960, New Delhi,
India.
EDUCATION/TRAINING: 1977–1982, India,
studied ethnomusicology; 1982–1983,
University of York, with Neil Sorrell; 1983–
1985, Royal Northern College of Music,
with Anthony Gilbert.
FIRST PROFESSIONAL PERFORMANCE OF A
COMPOSITION: 1986, Huddersfield
Contemporary Music Festival, *Ayodhya*
(commissioned for dance by Lontano).
CAREER: Compositions include chamber,
instrumental and vocal works; since 1988,
founder and Artistic Director, Shiva Nova,
Euroasian ensemble touring the UK and
Europe.
OPERATIC WORLD PREMIERES: Royal
Opera Garden Venture: 1989, *Survival
Song*, opera in one act, libretto by
Richard Fawkes, conductor Robert
Ziegler, director Wilfred Judd, designer

Mark Dakin; 1992, *Biko*, opera in two acts,
libretto by Richard Fawkes and the
composer, conductor Timothy Lole,
director Wilfred Judd, designer David
Short.
ADDRESS: 73 Cromwell Avenue, London N6
7HS.

PALMER FELICITY
Mezzo-soprano

PERSONAL DETAILS: b. 6 April 1944,
Cheltenham.
EDUCATION/TRAINING: 1962–1967, Guildhall
School of Music and Drama; 1967–1968,
Hochschule für Musik, Munich.
PROFESSIONAL DEBUT: As soprano: 1971,
Kent Opera, Dido, *Dido and Aeneas*.
EARLY CAREER INCLUDED: As soprano:
1971–1983: Camden Festival, Ismene,
Mitridate, Rè di Ponto; English National
Opera: Donna Elvira, *Don Giovanni*;
Countess, *The Marriage of Figaro*;
Marguérite, *The Damnation of Faust*;
Brangäne, *Tristan and Isolde*; Spitalfields
Festival, title role, *Armide*; since 1983,
mezzo-soprano.
MAJOR DEBUTS INCLUDE: 1973, Houston
Grand Opera, Countess, *Le Nozze di
Figaro*; 1975, English National Opera,
Pamina, *The Magic Flute*; 1976, Scottish
Opera, Donna Elvira, *Don Giovanni*; 1977,
Berne, title role, *Alcina*; 1978: Frankfurt
Opera, Cleopatra, *Giulio Cesare*; Wexford
Festival, Anezka, *The Two Widows*; 1980,
Elettra, *Idomeneo*: Vienna Festival, Zurich
Opera; 1981, Opera North, Donna Elvira,
Don Giovanni; 1982, Kent Opera, title
role, *Agrippina*; 1985: Covent Garden,
Andromache, *King Priam*; Glyndebourne
Festival Opera, Florence Pike, *Albert
Herring*; Kabanicha, *Katya Kabanova*:
1986, Lyric Opera, Chicago; 1988,
Netherlands Opera; 1991, Leipzig Opera,
Klytemnestra, *Elektra*; 1992: Welsh
National Opera, Klytemnestra, *Elektra*;
Teatro La Zarzuela, Madrid, title role, *The

Duenna by Roberto Gerhard (world stage première).

OPERATIC WORLD PREMIERES INCLUDE: 1987, La Scala, Milan, Marguerita, *Riccardo III* by Flavio Testi.

CAREER IN THE UK INCLUDES: Since 1983: Covent Garden, Cook, *The Nightingale* and Cat/Squirrel, *L'Enfant et les Sortilèges*; Florence Pike, *Albert Herring*; English National Opera: Adriano, *Rienzi*; Liùbov, *Mazeppa*; Katisha, *The Mikado*; Herodias, *Salome*; Mother/Witch, *Hansel and Gretel*; Jezibaba, *Rusalka*; Glyndebourne Festival Opera: Kabanicha, *Katya Kabanova*; Mistress Quickly, *Falstaff*; Marcellina, *Le Nozze di Figaro*; Countess, *The Queen of Spades*; Opera North: Orpheus, *Orpheus and Eurydice*; title role, *Tamburlaine* (Handel); Scottish Opera: Widow Begbick, *The Rise and Fall of the City of Mahagonny*; Fricka, *Das Rheingold*.

RELATED PROFESSIONAL ACTIVITIES: Numerous concerts, broadcasts and television appearances in the UK and abroad; 1990–1991, teacher, Trinity College of Music; masterclasses in Sweden.

RECORDINGS INCLUDE: Britten, *Phaedra*; Gluck, *Armide* (both EMI); Holst, *Sāvitri* (HYPE); Mozart: *Idomeneo* (TELD), *Le Nozze di Figaro*; Offenbach, *Les Contes d'Hoffmann*; Rossini, *La Cenerentola* (all PHIL); Sullivan, *The Mikado* (TELA); Tippett: *A Child of Our Time* (RPO), *King Priam* (DECC).

VIDEOS INCLUDE: Britten, *Albert Herring*; Janáček, *Katya Kabanova* (both Glyndebourne Festival Opera); Sullivan, *The Mikado* (English National Opera).

AWARDS AND HONOURS INCLUDE: 1970, Kathleen Ferrier Memorial Scholarship; Fellow, Guildhall School of Music and Drama; 1993, Commander, Order of the British Empire (CBE).

ADDRESS: c/o Harrison/Parrott Ltd, 12 Penzance Place, London W11 4PA.

PARROTT ANDREW
Conductor

POSITIONS: Founder and Director: Taverner Choir, Taverner Consort, Taverner Players; Associate Conductor, London Mozart Players.

PERSONAL DETAILS: b. 10 March 1947, Walsall; m. 1986, Emily Van Evera (soprano).

EDUCATION/TRAINING: 1966–1971, Merton College, Oxford.

PROFESSIONAL DEBUT: 1973, Bath Festival, Taverner Choir concert.

OPERATIC DEBUT: 1987, Kent Opera, Pygmalion/Dido and Aeneas.

CAREER: 1969–1971: Director of Music, Merton College, Oxford; music assistant to Michael Tippett; since 1973, founder and Director, Taverner Choir, also Taverner Consort and Taverner Players; since 1989, Associate Conductor, London Mozart Players; guest conductor with leading orchestras in the UK, Europe and North America; specialist in pre-classical and 20th century music; concert performances of operas at Oslo Sommeropera and La Scala, Milan; English Bach Festival, Flanders Festival, since 1991, stage performances include: Opera North, *The Marriage of Figaro*; Opera Atelier, Toronto, *Die Zauberflöte*.

OPERATIC WORLD PREMIÈRES INCLUDE: 1987, Kent Opera, *A Night at the Chinese Opera* by Judith Weir; 1991, BBC Television, *Scipio's Dream* by Mozart/ Judith Weir.

RECORDINGS INCLUDE: More than 30 recordings including: Bach: *Mass in B Minor, St John Passion*; Handel: *Israel in Egypt, Messiah*; Monteverdi, *Vespers* (all EMI); Mozart: *Mass in C Minor, Requiem* (both DENO); Purcell, *Dido and Aeneas* (CHAN).

VIDEOS INCLUDE: *Una Stravaganza dei Medici* (Taverner).

AWARDS INCLUDE: 1990, Prix Italia; 1991, Golden Gate Award (USA).

ADDRESS: c/o Allied Artists, 42 Montpelier Square, London SW7 1JZ.

PARRY DAVID
Conductor and Translator

POSITION: Music Director, English National
Opera Contemporary Opera Studio.
PERSONAL DETAILS: b. 23 March 1949,
London.
EDUCATION/TRAINING: St John's College,
Cambridge; Royal Academy of Music,
piano with Gordon Green and
composition with Nicholas Maw; further
studies with Sergiu Celibidache.
OPERATIC DEBUT: 1976, English Music
Theatre, *Cinderella*.
CAREER: Conductor and répétiteur: 1976–
1977, English Music Theatre; 1977–1978,
Dortmund Opera; 1978–1980, Opera
North; Opera 80: 1981–1983, Associate
Music Director; 1984–1987, Music
Director; since 1989, Music Director,
English National Opera Contemporary
Opera Studio.
MAJOR OPERATIC DEBUTS INCLUDE: 1976,
Glyndebourne Touring Opera, *Falstaff*;
1979, Opera North, *Hansel and Gretel*;
1981: Opera 80, *The Barber of Seville*; La
Monnaie, Brussels, *Capriccio*; 1984,
Opera Northern Ireland, *Rigoletto*; 1985,
English National Opera, *Count Ory*; 1986:
Dublin Grand Opera, *Madama Butterfly*;
Icelandic Opera, *Il Trovatore*; 1988, San
Sebastian, *Il Barbiere di Siviglia*; 1990,
Earls Court Japan tour, *Carmen*; 1991:
Norrlands Opera, Umeå, *A Midsummer
Night's Dream*; Teatro La Zarzuela,
Madrid, *Peter Grimes*; 1992, Hong Kong
Arts Festival, *Tosca*.
OPERATIC WORLD PREMIERES INCLUDE:
Batignano Festival: 1988, *Mario ed il
Mago* by Stephen Oliver; 1991, *L'Oca del
Cairo* by Mozart/Stephen Oliver; 1992:
Almeida Opera, *Terrible Mouth* by Nigel
Osborne; English National Opera
Contemporary Opera Studio, *Soundbites*,
a triple bill: *Pig* by Jonathan Dove/*The
Rebuilding of Waterloo Bridge* by Giles
Chaundy/*Nevis* by Kenneth Dempster.
OPERA PERFORMANCES INCLUDE: Since
1977: English Music Theatre, *The Rape of
Lucretia*; English National Opera, *Così
fan tutte*; Opera 80: *Die Fledermaus, Così
fan tutte, La Traviata, The Italian Girl in
Algiers, A Masked Ball, Don Giovanni,
Rigoletto*; Opera North: *Die Fledermaus,
Rigoletto, Don Giovanni, Così fan tutte*;
Opera Northern Ireland: *Don Pasquale,
Die Fledermaus*; Opera Rara at the
Camden Festival: *Gli Orazi ed i Curiazi,
Francesca di Foix/La Romanziera* (both
1982, both British premières), *Maria
Tudor*; Batignano Festival: *La Finta
Semplice, The Turn of the Screw, Apollo
e Dafne, La Grotta di Trofonio, Il Re
Teodoro in Venezia, Ba-ta-clan*; Dublin
Grand Opera: *Don Pasquale, Il Trovatore,
La Traviata, Die Zauberflöte*; San
Sebastian, *Don Pasquale*.
RELATED PROFESSIONAL ACTIVITIES:
Translations include: *Così fan tutte, Don
Giovanni, Don Pasquale, Die Fledermaus,
Der Freischütz, The Italian Girl in Algiers,
Lucia di Lammermoor, Rigoletto, The
Seven Deadly Sins, La Traviata*.
RECORDINGS INCLUDE: Donizetti: *L'Assedio
di Calais, Emilia di Liverpool*; Meyerbeer,
Il Crociato in Egitto (all OPRA).
ADDRESS: Not available.

PARRY ELISABETH
Administrator (formerly Soprano)

POSITIONS: Managing Director: London
Chamber Opera, London Opera Players.
PERSONAL DETAILS: b. 3 September 1921,
Aberdeen.
EDUCATION/TRAINING: Accademia
Musicale Chigiana, Siena and private
studies in London and Rome.
PROFESSIONAL DEBUT: 1947, Glyndebourne
Festival Opera, Lucia, *The Rape of
Lucretia*.
CAREER: 1947–1949, English Opera Group,
roles included: Cis, *Albert Herring*;
Rowan, *Let's Make an Opera* by
Benjamin Britten (1949, world première);
1949–1975, appearances with leading
British opera companies and numerous
concerts, recitals and broadcasts in the
UK and abroad; 1975, retired from
singing; since 1950, co-founder and
Managing Director, Opera Players/

London Opera Players; since 1982,
Managing Director, London Chamber
Opera.

ADDRESS: c/o Opera Players Ltd,
Broadmeade Copse, Westwood Lane,
Wanborough, Surrey GU3 2JN.

PAYNE NICHOLAS
Administrator

POSITION: Opera Director, The Royal
Opera, Covent Garden.

PERSONAL DETAILS: b. 4 January 1945,
Kent; m. 1986, Linda Adamson, two
children.

EDUCATION/TRAINING: 1963–1966, Trinity
College, Cambridge.

CAREER: 1968–1970, finance assistant,
Royal Opera House, Covent Garden;
1970–1976, Subsidy Officer, Arts Council
of Great Britain; 1976–1982, Financial
Controller, Welsh National Opera; 1982–
1993, General Administrator, Opera
North; since 1993/1994 season, Opera
Director, The Royal Opera, Covent
Garden.

AWARDS INCLUDE: 1992, Prudential Award
for Opera to Opera North.

ADDRESS: c/o Royal Opera House, Covent
Garden, London WC2E 9DD.

PAYNE PATRICIA
Mezzo-soprano

PERSONAL DETAILS: b. 8 March 1942,
Dunedin, New Zealand; m. 1974, David
Galloway.

EDUCATION/TRAINING: Dunedin, New
Zealand: Teacher Training College and
University of Otago; privately with Dora
Drake and Valda McCracken; 1967–1968,
London Opera Centre; further studies
with Roy Henderson, Ruth Packer,
Elisabeth Puritz, Peter Harrison, Vera
Rozsa, Hans Hotter and Carlo Ricci.

PROFESSIONAL DEBUT: 1969, Llandudno,
Messiah.

EARLY CAREER INCLUDED: 1969–1974,
primarily a concert performer including
1973–1974, Principal Alto, Netherlands
Bach Society; 1974–1979, member,
Covent Garden: Erda and First Norn, *Der
Ring des Nibelungen*; Filipyevna, *Eugene
Onegin*; Madame Arvidson, *Un Ballo in
Maschera*; Azucena, *Il Trovatore*; Mrs
Sedley, *Peter Grimes*; Grandmother,
Jenůfa; Laura, *Luisa Miller*; Geneviève,
Pelléas et Mélisande; Mother Goose, *The
Rake's Progress*.

MAJOR DEBUTS INCLUDE: 1971, Handel
Opera Society, Joacim, *Susanna* (operatic
debut); 1974: Covent Garden,
Schwertleite, *Die Walküre*; Gran Teatro
del Liceu, Barcelona, La Cieca, *La
Gioconda*; 1976, Nice Opera, Madame
Arvidson, *Un Ballo in Maschera*; 1977:
Bayreuth Festival, Schwertleite and First
Norn, *Der Ring des Nibelungen*; Erda,
Das Rheingold: Frankfurt Opera, San
Francisco Opera; Madame Arvidson, *Un
Ballo in Maschera*: 1978, La Scala, Milan;
1979, Hamburg State Opera; 1980: Lyric
Opera, Chicago and Metropolitan Opera,
New York; La Cieca, *La Gioconda*: 1979,
Grand Théâtre, Geneva; 1980, Verona
Arena; 1981, Teatro Comunale, Florence,
First Norn, *Götterdämmerung*; 1985,
English National Opera, Ludmilla, *The
Bartered Bride*.

CAREER IN THE UK INCLUDES: Since 1980:
Covent Garden: Marcellina, *Le Nozze di
Figaro*; Mother Jeanne, *The Carmelites*;
English National Opera: Filipyevna,
Eugene Onegin; Third Lady, *The Magic
Flute*; Clarissa, *The Love for Three
Oranges*; Herodias, *Salome*; Countess,
The Queen of Spades; Opera North:
Azucena, *Il Trovatore*; Gaea, *Daphne*
(1987, British stage première); Clarissa,
The Love for Three Oranges; Scottish
Opera, Azucena, *Il Trovatore*; Welsh
National Opera: Nurse, *Die Frau ohne
Schatten*; Madame Arvidson, *Un Ballo in
Maschera*; Fricka and Waltraute, *The
Ring of the Nibelung*.

RELATED PROFESSIONAL ACTIVITIES:
Regular concerts, recitals and broadcasts
in the UK and abroad.

RECORDINGS INCLUDE: Beethoven, *Missa Solemnis*; Britten, *Peter Grimes*; Verdi, *Un Ballo in Maschera* (all PHIL); Puccini, *Suor Angelica* (CBS).

VIDEOS INCLUDE: Britten, *Peter Grimes* (Covent Garden).

AWARDS INCLUDE: 1966, *Sun* Aria Competition (Sydney); 1972, International Vocal Competition, s'Hertogenbosch (Netherlands).

ADDRESS: c/o Opera and Concert Artists, 75 Aberdare Gardens, London NW6 3AN.

PETERS JOHANNA
Teacher, Administrator and Mezzo-soprano

POSITION: Head of Vocal Studies, Guildhall School of Music and Drama.

PERSONAL DETAILS: b. 3 January 1932, Glasgow.

EDUCATION/TRAINING: 1952–1957, National School of Opera, with Anne Wood.

PROFESSIONAL DEBUT: 1959, Glyndebourne Festival Opera, Marcellina, *Le Nozze di Figaro*.

CAREER INCLUDES: Since 1959, appearances with Covent Garden, English Opera Group (including 1964, Soviet Union tour, Florence Pike, *Albert Herring*), Glyndebourne Festival Opera, Handel Opera Society, Sadler's Wells Opera, Scottish Opera, Welsh National Opera and leading opera houses and festivals in Europe and USA; roles include: Nurse, *Boris Godunov*; Annina, *La Traviata*; Theodosia, *Die Schweigsame Frau*; Baba the Turk, *The Rake's Progress*; Mrs Sedley, *Peter Grimes*; Marthe, *Faust*; First Norn, *Götterdämmerung*; Mistress Quickly, *Falstaff*; Public Opinion, *Orpheus in the Underworld*; numerous concerts, oratorios, recitals and broadcasts with leading conductors and orchestras, repertoire ranging from Monteverdi to Boulez; Guildhall School of Music and Drama: 1978–1986, Head of Opera Studies; since 1989, Head of Vocal Studies.

OPERATIC WORLD PREMIÈRES INCLUDE: 1960, English Opera Group at the Aldeburgh Festival, Hippolyta, *Midsummer Night's Dream* by Benjamin Britten; 1970, Glyndebourne Festival Opera, Widow Sweeney, *The Rising of the Moon* by Nicholas Maw; 1974, Scottish Opera, Sempronia, *The Catiline Conspiracy* by Iain Hamilton.

STUDENTS HAVE INCLUDED: Elen ap Robert, Maria Bovino, Isobel Bradshaw, Maureen Brathwaite, Alison Buchanan, Yvonne Burnett, Joseph Cornwell, Sophie Daneman, Julia Gooding, Julie Gossage, Richard Halton, Bernadette Lord, Helen Lothian, Sarah Pring, Sarah Rhodes, Valerie Seymour, Peter Snipp, Talitha Theobald, Rachel Tovey, Janice Watson, Annabelle Williams, Paul Scott Williams, Caroline Zygadlo.

RECORDINGS INCLUDE: Britten, *Albert Herring* (DECC).

VIDEOS INCLUDE: Sullivan, *Ruddigore* (Walker).

HONOURS INCLUDE: 1980, Fellow, Guildhall School of Music and Drama.

ADDRESS: c/o Guildhall School of Music and Drama, Barbican, London EC2Y 8DT.

PIMLOTT STEVEN   Director

PERSONAL DETAILS: b. 18 April 1953, Stockport; one child.

EDUCATION/TRAINING: 1971–1974, University of Cambridge, studied English.

PROFESSIONAL AND OPERATIC DEBUT: 1978, English National Opera, *The Seraglio* (touring production).

CAREER: 1976–1978, staff director, English National Opera, staging revivals; since 1978, freelance opera and theatre director in the UK and abroad; productions include: Crucible Theatre, Sheffield, *Carmen Jones*; Royal Exchange, Manchester, *Carousel*; Royal National Theatre: *Sunday in the Park with George, The Miser*; Royal Shakespeare Company, *Julius Caesar*.

MAJOR OPERATIC DEBUTS INCLUDE: 1978, Opera North, *La Bohème*; 1982, Scottish Opera, *The Pearl Fishers*; 1987, Jerusalem Festival, *La Traviata*; 1988, Bregenz Festival, *Samson et Dalila*; 1989, Earls Court, *Carmen*; 1992: Flanders Opera, Antwerp, *Un Ballo in Maschera*; New Israeli Opera, Tel Aviv, *Eugene Onegin*.

OPERA PRODUCTIONS IN THE UK INCLUDE: Since 1979: Opera 80, *Don Giovanni*; Opera North: *Tosca, Nabucco, The Bartered Bride, Werther, Cavalleria Rusticana/Pagliacci, Prince Igor*.

VIDEOS INCLUDE: Bizet, *Carmen* (Earls Court).

ADDRESS: c/o Harriet Cruickshank, 97 Old South Lambeth Road, London SW8 1XU.

PLATT NORMAN
Director, Administrator, Librettist, Teacher and Translator
(formerly Baritone)

PERSONAL DETAILS: b. 29 August 1920, Lancashire; m. 1942, Diana Clay, two children; m. 1963, Johanna Bishop (librettist and teacher), three children.

EDUCATION/TRAINING: 1939–1941, King's College, Cambridge.

OPERATIC DEBUT: As baritone: 1946, Sadler's Wells Opera, Ned Keene, *Peter Grimes*; as director: 1966, Swan Theatre, Worcester, *Pimpinone/Dido and Aeneas*.

CAREER: 1946–1948, member, Sadler's Wells Opera and English Opera Group; 1948–1972, freelance; 1969–1989, founder and Artistic Director, Kent Opera.

OPERATIC WORLD PREMIÈRES INCLUDE: Kent Opera: 1976, Schwetzingen Festival, director and librettist, *The Pardoner's Tale* by Alan Ridout; commissioned *A Night at the Chinese Opera* by Judith Weir (1987, first performance).

OPERA PRODUCTIONS IN THE UK INCLUDE: 1969–1989, Kent Opera: *The Coronation of Poppea, Dido and Aeneas, Venus and Adonis, The Magic Flute, Iphigenia in Tauris, The Return of Ulysses, Agrippina, Don Giovanni, Peter Grimes*.

RELATED PROFESSIONAL ACTIVITIES: Founder member, Deller Consort; co-founder, Canterbury Theatre and Festival Trust; 1984–1986, Chairman, Canterbury Festival Planning Committee; 1991, founder, Kent Opera concert series; translations: *Atalanta, The Coronation of Poppea, Don Giovanni, Fidelio, The Patience of Socrates*; teacher of singing and acting.

PUBLICATIONS INCLUDE: 1991, Series Editor, *Opera in Performance* (Bristol Classical Press).

HONOURS INCLUDE: 1981, Honorary Doctorate of Civil Law, University of Kent; 1985, Officer, Order of the British Empire (OBE).

ADDRESS: Pembles Cross Farmhouse, Egerton, Ashford, Kent TN27 9EN.

PLAYFAIR SARAH
Administrator

POSITIONS: Director of Artistic Administration, Glyndebourne Festival Opera; Administrator, Glyndebourne Touring Opera.

PERSONAL DETAILS: b. 16 January 1947, London.

EDUCATION/TRAINING: 1965–1968, University of Sussex; 1970–1971, Central London Polytechnic; 1972–1973, London Opera Centre.

CAREER: 1973, Stage Manager, Opera Rara; 1973–1974, Deputy Stage Manager, Welsh National Opera; 1974–1982, Assistant Controller of Planning, English National Opera; Controller of Planning: 1982–1986, Scottish Opera; 1986–1989, Welsh National Opera; since 1989: Director of Artistic Administration, Glyndebourne Festival Opera; Administrator, Glyndebourne Touring Opera.

ADDRESS: c/o Glyndebourne Festival Opera, Lewes, East Sussex BN8 5UU.

PLOWRIGHT ROSALIND
Soprano

PERSONAL DETAILS: b. 21 May 1949, Worksop; m. 1984, J. Anthony Kaye (concert and opera agent), two children.

EDUCATION/TRAINING: Royal Northern College of Music, with Frederic Cox; London Opera Centre, with Erich Vietheer and Roberto Benaglio.

PROFESSIONAL DEBUT: 1975, Glyndebourne Touring Opera, Agathe, *Der Freischütz*.

EARLY CAREER INCLUDED: 1975–1979: English National Opera, Helmvige, *The Valkyrie*; Glyndebourne Touring Opera: Countess, *Le Nozze di Figaro*; Donna Elvira, *Don Giovanni*; Kent Opera, Messenger, *Orfeo*; Welsh National Opera, Helena, *A Midsummer Night's Dream*.

MAJOR DEBUTS INCLUDE: 1979, English National Opera, Miss Jessel, *The Turn of the Screw*; 1980: Covent Garden, Ortlinde, *Die Walküre*; Berne, title roles: *Ariadne auf Naxos*, *Alceste*; 1981: Bavarian State Opera, Munich, Donna Anna, *Don Giovanni*; Frankfurt Opera: Leonora, *Il Trovatore*; title role, *Aida*; 1982: Paris Opera, Amelia, *Un Ballo in Maschera*; San Diego Opera, Medora, *Il Corsaro*; 1983: La Scala, Milan, title role, *Suor Angelica*; San Francisco Opera, title role, *Ariadne auf Naxos*; 1985: Deutsche Oper, Berlin, Leonora, *Il Trovatore*; Houston Grand Opera, title role, *Madama Butterfly*; Montpellier, title role, *Norma*; Verona Arena, Leonora, *Il Trovatore*; 1986, Teatro La Fenice, Venice, Lina, *Stiffelio*; 1988, Grand Théâtre, Geneva, Elisabeth de Valois, *Don Carlos*; 1990: Torre del Lago Puccini Festival, title role, *Tosca*; Vienna State Opera, Amelia, *Un Ballo in Maschera*.

CAREER IN THE UK INCLUDES: Since 1980: Buxton Festival, title role, *Médée*; Covent Garden: Donna Anna, *Don Giovanni*; Madeleine, *Andrea Chénier*; Senta, *Der Fliegende Holländer*; Desdemona, *Otello*; Leonora, *Il Trovatore*; title roles: *Aida*, *Ariadne auf Naxos*, *Médée*; English National Opera: Queen Elizabeth, *Mary Stuart*; Desdemona, *Otello*; Elena, *The Sicilian Vespers*; Elisabeth de Valois, *Don Carlos*; Opera North, title role, *La Gioconda*.

RELATED PROFESSIONAL ACTIVITIES: Numerous concerts, recitals, broadcasts and television appearances in the UK and abroad.

RECORDINGS INCLUDE: Donizetti, *Mary Stuart* (EMI); Mahler, Symphony No. 2 (DG); Mendelssohn, *Elijah* (CHAN); Offenbach, *Les Contes d'Hoffmann* (EMI); Verdi: *La Forza del Destino*, *Il Trovatore* (both DG).

VIDEOS INCLUDE: Donizetti, *Mary Stuart* (English National Opera); Verdi, *Il Trovatore* (Verona Arena).

AWARDS INCLUDE: 1979, Seventh International Competition for Opera Singers (Sofia); 1980, Society of West End Theatre Award, Miss Jessel, *The Turn of the Screw* (English National Opera).

ADDRESS: c/o Kaye Artists Management Ltd, Barratt House, 7 Chertsey Road, Woking, Surrey GU21 5AB.

POGSON GEOFFREY   Tenor

PERSONAL DETAILS: b. London; m., four children.

PREVIOUS OCCUPATION: International marketing.

EDUCATION/TRAINING: Choral Scholar, St Catharine's College, Cambridge, studied English; 1973–1976, Trinity College of Music; privately with Eduardo Asquez and Elisabeth Flemming.

PROFESSIONAL DEBUT: 1977, Edinburgh International Festival, Remendado, *Carmen*.

EARLY CAREER INCLUDED: 1977–1979, appearances with Chelsea Opera Group, Phoenix Opera, University College Opera; roles included: Ippolito, *La Spinalba*; Calafione, *Don Quixote*; King Charles, *The Maid of Orleans*.

MAJOR DEBUTS INCLUDE: 1978, Scottish Opera, Cethegus, *The Catiline Conspiracy*; 1979, English National Opera, Cavaradossi, *Tosca*; 1980, Opera North, Don José, *Carmen*; 1984, Dublin Grand Opera, Eisenstein, *Die*

Fledermaus; 1992, Glyndebourne Festival Opera, Master of Ceremonies, *The Queen of Spades*.

OPERATIC WORLD PREMIERES INCLUDE: 1981, English National Opera, Vronsky, *Anna Karenina* by Iain Hamilton; 1983, Opera North, Frank Crawley, *Rebecca* by Wilfred Josephs; 1988, Queen Elizabeth Hall, Judge, *Beatrice Cenci* by Berthold Goldschmidt; 1991, English National Opera, Lucullus, *Timon of Athens* by Stephen Oliver.

CAREER IN THE UK INCLUDES: Since 1979: English National Opera: Don José, *Carmen*; Des Grieux, *Manon*; Alfred, Eisenstein and Blind, *Die Fledermaus*; Count Danilo, *The Merry Widow*; Prologue and Quint, *The Turn of the Screw*; Jacquino, *Fidelio*; Nero, *The Coronation of Poppea*; Tybalt, *Romeo and Juliet*; Teacher, *Lady Macbeth of Mtsensk* (1987, British stage première); Gaston, *La Traviata*; Cornwall, *Lear* (1989, British première); Marquis/Rash Gambler, *The Gambler*; Monostatos, *The Magic Flute*; Opera North, Pinkerton, *Madam Butterfly*; Scottish Opera, Duke, *Rigoletto*.

RELATED PROFESSIONAL ACTIVITIES: Numerous concerts, recitals and broadcasts in the UK.

RECORDINGS INCLUDE: Bizet, *Carmen* (DG); Verdi, *La Traviata* (EMI).

ADDRESS: c/o M & M Lyric Artists, 6 Princess Road, London NW1 7JJ.

POLLOCK ADAM
Administrator, Designer and Translator

POSITION: Artistic Director and Administrator, Musica nel Chiostro.

PERSONAL DETAILS: b. 28 October 1936, London.

EDUCATION/TRAINING: 1958–1959, Bristol Old Vic Theatre School.

CAREER: Freelance designer in the UK and abroad; since 1974, founder, Artistic Director and Administrator, Musica nel Chiostro which performs rare operas at the Batignano Festival in Italy, also in the

UK and France and has premièred several works by Stephen Oliver.

OPERATIC WORLD PREMIERES INCLUDE: As designer: 1977, Batignano Festival, *Il Giardino*; 1980, King's Head, Islington, *A Man of Feeling*; 1988, Batignano Festival, *Mario ed il Mago* (all by Stephen Oliver).

OPERA DESIGNS INCLUDE: Since 1966: Musica nel Chiostro: *Dido and Aeneas, L'Ormindo, Tamerlano, Il Combattimento di Tancredi e Clorinda, La Serva Padrona, Lo Speziale, Bastien und Bastienne, Orontea, Il Ballo delle Ingrate, La Finta Semplice, La Dori, La Zingara, La Grotta di Trofonio, Il Ritorno d'Ulisse in Patria, Il Re Teodoro in Venezia, Leonore, Exposition of a Picture, King Priam* (1990, Italian première); Opera North, *Hansel and Gretel*; Scottish Opera, *Albert Herring*; Wexford Festival: *Oberon, L'Ajo nell'imbarazzo*.

RELATED PROFESSIONAL ACTIVITIES INCLUDE: Numerous English translations for Park Lane Opera and the BBC; several Italian translations with Luisa Saviori for Musica nel Chiostro.

HONOURS INCLUDE: 1981, Grifone d'Oro (Italy).

ADDRESS: c/o Musica nel Chiostro: 377 Liverpool Road, London N1 1NL or Santa Croce, 58041 Batignano GR, Italy.

POPE CATHRYN   Soprano

POSITION: Principal Soprano, English National Opera.

PERSONAL DETAILS: b. London.

EDUCATION/TRAINING: Royal College of Music, with Ruth Packer; National Opera Studio.

PROFESSIONAL DEBUT: 1982, English National Opera, Sophie, *Werther*.

MAJOR DEBUTS INCLUDE: 1984: Covent Garden, Giannetta, *L'Elisir d'Amore*; Opera North, Amor, *Orpheus and Eurydice*; 1989, Scottish Opera, Pamina, *The Magic Flute*; 1990, Netherlands Opera, Gretel, *Hansel and Gretel*.

223

CAREER IN THE UK INCLUDES: Since 1982: Covent Garden: Frasquita, *Carmen*; Naiad, *Ariadne auf Naxos*; English National Opera (since 1985, Principal Soprano): Wood Nymph, *Rusalka*; Lucia, *The Rape of Lucretia*; Venus, *Orpheus in the Underworld*; Voice from Heaven, *Don Carlos*; Anna, *Moses*; Flower Maiden, *Parsifal*; Zerlina, *Don Giovanni*; Gretel, *Hansel and Gretel*; Despina, *Così fan tutte*; Oksana, *Christmas Eve* (1988, British stage première); Leïla, *The Pearl Fishers*; Kristina, *The Makropoulos Case*; Papagena and Pamina, *The Magic Flute*; Mélisande, *Pelléas and Mélisande*; Donna Elvira, *Don Giovanni*; Susanna, *The Marriage of Figaro*; Goosegirl, *Königskinder*; Gilda, *Rigoletto*; Micaëla, *Carmen*; New Sussex Opera, Marguérite, *Faust*.

RELATED PROFESSIONAL ACTIVITIES: Numerous concerts and broadcasts in the UK and abroad.

RECORDINGS INCLUDE: Mozart, *Le Nozze di Figaro* (PHIL); Offenbach, *Orpheus in the Underworld* (TER); Stravinsky, *The Rake's Progress* (DECC).

VIDEOS INCLUDE: Britten, *The Rape of Lucretia*; Dvořák, *Rusalka*; (both English National Opera).

ADDRESS: c/o Stafford Law Associates, 26 Mayfield Road, Weybridge, Surrey KT13 8XB.

PORTER ANDREW
Critic, Director, Editor, Librettist and Translator

POSITIONS: Music Critic: *The Observer*, *The New Yorker*.

PERSONAL DETAILS: b. 26 August 1928, Cape Town, South Africa.

EDUCATION/TRAINING: 1947–1950, Organ Scholar, University College, Oxford, studied English.

CAREER: 1950–1952, freelance critic for various publications including *Daily Express, Daily Telegraph, Manchester Guardian, The Times; Opera*: 1953–1956, Associate Editor; since 1953, member,

Editorial Board; 1960–1967, Editor, *Musical Times*; Music Critic: 1952–1974, *Financial Times*; since 1972, *The New Yorker*; since 1992, *The Observer*; 1973–1974, Visiting Fellow, All Souls College, Oxford; 1980–1981, Ernest Bloch Professor, University of California, Berkeley; translations include: *La Bohème, Così fan tutte, Deceit Outwitted, Don Carlos, Don Giovanni, Falstaff, Figaro's Wedding, First Comes the Music, The Force of Destiny, Henry VIII, Idomeneo, The Impresario, Intermezzo, The Journey to Rheims, Lucio Silla, Macbeth, The Magic Flute, Nabucco, Orpheus and Eurydice, Otello, Ottone, Parsifal, Resurrection* (Alfano), *Rigoletto, The Ring of the Nibelung, The Seraglio, Tristan and Isolde, The Turk in Italy, The Unexpected Meeting*; editor, *Don Carlos* (responsible for rediscovering full version in the Paris Opera library).

OPERATIC WORLD PREMIÈRES INCLUDE: As librettist: 1985, Santa Fe Opera, *The Tempest* by John Eaton; 1992, Lyric Opera, Chicago, *The Song of Majnun* by Bright Sheng.

OPERA PRODUCTIONS INCLUDE: As director: Carnegie Hall: *Orlando Paladino, Semele, Intermezzo*; Indiana University Opera Theater, Bloomington: *Tamerlano, The Rake's Progress*; Seattle Opera, *La Forza del Destino*.

RECORDINGS OF TRANSLATIONS INCLUDE: Verdi, *Otello*; Wagner, *The Ring of the Nibelung – The Rhinegold, The Valkyrie, Siegfried, Twilight of the Gods* (all EMI).

PUBLICATIONS INCLUDE: 1974, *A Musical Season: An English Critic in New York* (Gollancz); 1978, *Music of Three Seasons* (Chatto & Windus); 1981, *Music of Three More Seasons* (Knopf, New York); 1984, *Verdi's Macbeth: A Sourcebook*, co-editor with David Rosen (Cambridge University Press); *Musical Events, A Chronicle: 1980–1983, 1983–1986, 1990* (all Grafton); translations: *The Magic Flute* (Faber), *Parsifal, The Ring of the Nibelung – The Rhinegold, The Valkyrie, Siegfried,*

224

Twilight of the Gods (all Calder), *Rigoletto* (Ricordi).

ADDRESS: c/o The Observer, Chelsea Bridge House, Queenstown Road, London SW8 4NN.

POULTON ROBERT   Baritone

PERSONAL DETAILS: b. 4 June 1957, Brighton; m. Philippa Smith (mezzo-soprano), one child.

EDUCATION/TRAINING: 1981–1986, Guildhall School of Music and Drama, with Rudolf Piernay; 1986–1987, National Opera Studio; 1987, masterclass with Thomas Allen.

PROFESSIONAL DEBUT: 1986, Nexus Opera at the Proms, Ferryman, *Curlew River*.

CAREER IN THE UK INCLUDES: Since 1986: English National Opera, Leander, *The Love for Three Oranges*; Glyndebourne Festival and Touring Opera: Ramiro, *L'Heure Espagnole* and Tom Cat/Clock, *L'Enfant et les Sortilèges*; Kuligin, *Katya Kabanova*; Duphol, *La Traviata*; Foreman, *Jenůfa*; Ned Keene, *Peter Grimes*; Lido Boatman/Hotel Waiter, *Death in Venice*; title role, *Le Nozze di Figaro*; Opera North, Leander, *The Love for Three Oranges*; Scottish Opera: Publio, *La Clemenza di Tito*; Morales, *Carmen*; title role, *The Marriage of Figaro*.

OPERATIC WORLD PREMIÈRES INCLUDE: 1990, Scottish Opera, Doctor/Policeman/Stranger, *The Vanishing Bridegroom* by Judith Weir; 1991, Netherlands Opera, title role, *Gassir the Hero* by Theo Loevendie.

RELATED PROFESSIONAL ACTIVITIES: Concerts and recitals in the UK and abroad.

VIDEOS INCLUDE: Janáček: *Jenůfa*, *Katya Kabanova* (both Glyndebourne Festival Opera).

AWARDS INCLUDE: 1987, Esso/Glyndebourne Touring Opera Award; 1988, John Christie Award.

ADDRESS: c/o Ron Gonsalves Personal Artists & Concert Management, 10 Dagnan Road, London SW12 9LQ.

POUNTNEY DAVID
Director and Translator

PERSONAL DETAILS: b. 10 September 1947, Oxford; m. 1980, Jane Henderson, two children.

EDUCATION/TRAINING: 1966–1969, St John's College, Cambridge.

PROFESSIONAL AND OPERATIC DEBUT: 1971, Scottish Opera, *The Rake's Progress*.

CAREER: Scottish Opera: 1970–1976, staff director; 1976–1980, Director of Productions; 1982–1993, Director of Productions, English National Opera.

MAJOR OPERATIC DEBUTS INCLUDE: 1972: Netherlands Opera, *The Rake's Progress*; Wexford Festival, *Katya Kabanova*; 1974: English Opera Group, *La Rondine*; Houston Grand Opera, *Macbeth*; 1975, Cassel, *The Queen of Spades*; 1976, San Francisco Opera, *The Makropoulos Case*; 1978, Australian Opera, Sydney, *Die Meistersinger von Nürnberg*; 1981: Komische Oper, East Berlin, *La Bohème*; Rome Opera, *Eugene Onegin*; 1982/1983, Netherlands Opera/English National Opera co-production, *The Queen of Spades*; 1986, Vancouver Opera, *From the House of the Dead*; 1988: Adelaide Festival, *The Fiery Angel*; Deutsche Oper, Berlin, *Doktor Faust*; Lyric Opera, Chicago, *Satyagraha*; 1989: Bregenz Festival, *Der Fliegende Holländer*; Paris Opera, *Doktor Faust*; 1991, Los Angeles Music Center Opera, *Elektra*; 1992/1993, English National Opera/Bavarian State Opera, Munich co-production, *The Adventures of Mr Brouček*.

OPERATIC WORLD PREMIERES INCLUDE: 1977, English National Opera, *Toussaint* by David Blake; 1978, Houston Grand Opera, *Bilby's Doll* by Carlisle Floyd; 1980, Netherlands Opera, *Satyagraha* by Philip Glass; 1990, English National Opera, *Clarissa* by Robin Holloway; 1992:

Almeida Opera, *Terrible Mouth* by Nigel Osborne; Metropolitan Opera, New York, *The Voyage* by Philip Glass; 1993, English National Opera (co-production with La Monnaie, Brussels), *Inquest of Love* by Jonathan Harvey

OPERA PRODUCTIONS IN THE UK INCLUDE: Since 1975: English National Opera: *The Flying Dutchman*, *The Makropoulos Case*, *Rusalka*, *The Gambler*, *The Valkyrie*, *Osud* (1984, British stage première), *Orpheus in the Underworld*, *The Midsummer Marriage*, *The Diary of One Who Disappeared*, *Doctor Faust* (both 1986, British stage premières), *Carmen*, *Lady Macbeth of Mtsensk* (1987, British stage première), *Hansel and Gretel*, *The Cunning Little Vixen*, *La Traviata*, *Christmas Eve* (1988, British stage première), *Falstaff*, *Macbeth*, *Wozzeck*, *Pelléas and Mélisande*, *Königskinder*, *Don Carlos*; Scottish Opera: *Eugene Onegin*, *Die Fledermaus*, *Die Meistersinger von Nürnberg*, *The Golden Cockerel*, *The Bartered Bride*, *The Seraglio*, *The Two Widows*; Welsh National Opera, *From the House of the Dead*; co-productions: Scottish Opera/English National Opera, *Street Scene*; Scottish Opera/Opera North, *Don Giovanni*; Scottish Opera/Welsh National Opera: *Jenůfa*, *The Makropoulos Case*, *Katya Kabanova*, *The Cunning Little Vixen*.

RELATED PROFESSIONAL ACTIVITIES: Translations include: *The Adventures of Mr Brouček*, *The Bartered Bride*, *Christmas Eve*, *Die Fledermaus*, *The Flying Dutchman*, *From the House of the Dead*, *The Gambler*, *Hansel and Gretel*, *The Kiss*, *Königskinder*, *Lady Macbeth of Mtsensk*, *The Seraglio*, *La Traviata*, *The Two Widows*.

VIDEOS INCLUDE: Dvořák, *Rusalka* (English National Opera).

RELEVANT PUBLICATIONS INCLUDE: 1992, *Power House: English National Opera Experience* (Lime Tree).

AWARDS AND HONOURS INCLUDE: Olivier Award: 1984, Welsh National Opera production of *From the House of the Dead*; 1986, English National Opera production of *Doctor Faust*; 1987, English National Opera production of *Lady Macbeth of Mtsenk*; 1992, Chevalier de l'Ordre des Arts et Lettres (France).

ADDRESS: c/o Harrison/Parrott Ltd, 12 Penzance Place, London W11 4PA.

POWELL CLAIRE
Mezzo-soprano

PERSONAL DETAILS: b. 7 April 1954, Dorset; m. 1988, Mark Ellidge.

EDUCATION/TRAINING: 1972–1976, Royal Academy of Music; 1976–1978, London Opera Centre; privately with Peter Harrison and Joy Mammen.

PROFESSIONAL DEBUT: 1978, Glyndebourne Touring Opera, Second Lady, *Die Zauberflöte*.

MAJOR DEBUTS INCLUDE: 1982: Frankfurt Opera, Madame Arvidson, *Un Ballo in Maschera*; Opéra Comique, Paris, Nicklausse, *Les Contes d'Hoffmann*; 1983, Rome Opera, Idamante, *Idomeneo*; 1984: Canadian Opera Company, Toronto, title role, *Carmen*; Madrid Festival, Cornelia, *Giulio Cesare*; 1986, La Monnaie, Brussels, Prince Orlofsky, *Die Fledermaus*; 1987, Teatro La Zarzuela, Madrid, Orfeo, *Orfeo ed Euridice*; 1988, Paris Opera, Varvara, *Katya Kabanova*; 1989, Bavarian State Opera, Munich, Eboli, *Don Carlos*; 1990: Hamburg State Opera, title role, *Carmen*; San Francisco Opera, Maddalena, *Rigoletto*; 1991: Opéra Bastille, Paris, Varvara, *Katya Kabanova*; Théâtre des Champs Elysées, Paris, Mistress Quickly, *Falstaff*; 1992: Gran Teatre del Liceu, Barcelona, Pauline/Daphnis, *The Queen of Spades*; Toulouse, Mistress Quickly, *Falstaff*.

OPERATIC WORLD PREMIERES INCLUDE: 1980, Welsh National Opera, Marina, *The Servants* by William Mathias.

CAREER IN THE UK INCLUDES: Since 1978: Covent Garden (1979–1985, member): Olga, *Eugene Onegin*; Prince Orlofsky, *Die Fledermaus*; Nicklausse, *Les Contes d'Hoffmann*; Schoolboy/Page, *Lulu* (1981,

British première, three act version); Hermia, *A Midsummer Night's Dream*; Bianca, *A Florentine Tragedy* (1985, British première); Mercédès, *Carmen*; Karolka, *Jenůfa*; Rosette, *Manon*; Maddalena, *Rigoletto*; Eboli, *Don Carlos*; Neris, *Médée*; Dalila, *Samson et Dalila*; Emilia, *Otello*; Glyndebourne Festival and Touring Opera: Amaranta, *La Fedeltà Premiata*; Juno, *Il Ritorno d'Ulisse in Patria*; Meg Page, *Falstaff*; Hippolyta, *A Midsummer Night's Dream*; Opera North: Hansel, *Hansel and Gretel*; Beatrice, *Beatrice and Benedict*; Eboli, *Don Carlos*; title role, *Carmen*; Welsh National Opera: Maddalena, *Rigoletto*; Rosina, *Il Barbiere di Siviglia*; Preziosilla, *La Forza del Destino*.

RECORDINGS INCLUDE: Falla, *El Amor Brujo* (VIRG); Monteverdi, *Il Ritorno D'Ulisse in Patria* (CBS); R. Strauss, *Der Rosenkavalier* (EMI).

VIDEOS INCLUDE: Britten, *A Midsummer Night's Dream* (Glyndebourne Festival Opera); Offenbach, *Les Contes d'Hoffmann* (Covent Garden).

AWARDS AND HONOURS INCLUDE: 1978, Richard Tauber Memorial Prize; 1990, Associate, Royal Academy of Music.

ADDRESS: c/o John Coast, 31 Sinclair Road, London W14 ONS.

POWER PATRICK
Tenor and Teacher

PERSONAL DETAILS: b. Wellington, New Zealand.

EDUCATION/TRAINING: Universities of Otago and Auckland, studied music and anthropology; Auckland Teachers College; L'Università per Stranieri, Perugia, studied Italian language.

PROFESSIONAL DEBUT: 1976, Norwegian Opera, Oslo, Don Ottavio, *Don Giovanni*.

EARLY CAREER INCLUDED: Principal Tenor: 1976–1979 and 1982–1983, Norwegian Opera, Oslo; 1979–1981, Gärtnerplatz, Munich; 1981–1982, Krefeld/ Mönchengladbach; roles included: Don Ottavio, *Don Giovanni*; Count, *Il Barbiere di Siviglia*; Rodolfo, *La Bohème*; Narraboth, *Salome*; Cassio, *Otello*; Idamante, *Idomeneo*; Lyonel, *Martha*; Lensky, *Eugene Onegin*; Tamino, *Die Zauberflöte*; Tonio, *La Fille du Régiment*; Ferrando, *Così fan tutte*; Rinuccio, *Gianni Schicchi*; Lorenzo, *Fra Diavolo*; title role, *Albert Herring*.

MAJOR DEBUTS INCLUDE: 1978, Bonn Opera, Count, *Il Barbiere di Siviglia*; 1979, Glyndebourne Festival Opera, Telemaco, *Il Ritorno d'Ulisse in Patria*; 1982, Covent Garden, Simpleton, *Boris Godunov*; 1984, Wexford Festival, title role, *Le Jongleur de Notre-Dame*; 1985: English National Opera, Vanya, *Katya Kabanova*; Scottish Opera, Count, *Il Barbiere di Siviglia*; Paris Opera, Evandre, *Alceste*; 1986, Canadian Opera Company, Toronto, Alfredo, *La Traviata*; 1987: Montreal Opera, Tamino, *Die Zauberflöte*; San Francisco Opera, Count, *Il Barbiere di Siviglia*; 1988, Nadir, *Les Pêcheurs de Perles*: Pisa and Victoria State Opera, Melbourne.

CAREER IN THE UK INCLUDES: Since 1980: Covent Garden: Marzio, *Mitridate, Rè di Ponto*; title role, *Les Contes d'Hoffmann*; Glyndebourne Festival Opera: Flute, *A Midsummer Night's Dream*; Jacquino, *Fidelio*; Opera North: Des Grieux, *Manon*; Opera Northern Ireland, Fenton, *Falstaff*; Scottish Opera: Steersman, *Der Fliegende Holländer*; Rodolfo, *La Bohème*.

RELATED PROFESSIONAL ACTIVITIES: Voice teacher: 1975–1976, New Zealand School of Music; 1976, Keri Keri Summer Music School, New Zealand.

RECORDINGS INCLUDE: Balfe, *The Bohemian Girl* (ARGO); Monteverdi, *Il Ritorno d'Ulisse in Patria* (CBS); Purcell, *Dido and Aeneas* (PHIL);

VIDEOS INCLUDE: Britten, *A Midsummer Night's Dream* (Glyndebourne Festival Opera).

ADDRESS: c/o Athole Still International Management Ltd, Greystoke House, 80–86 Westow Street, London SE19 3AF.

227

PRICE, DAME MARGARET
Soprano

PERSONAL DETAILS: b. 13 April 1941, Tredegar, Wales.

EDUCATION/TRAINING: Trinity College of Music.

PROFESSIONAL DEBUT: 1962, Welsh National Opera, Cherubino, *The Marriage of Figaro*.

MAJOR DEBUTS INCLUDE: 1963, Covent Garden, Cherubino, *Le Nozze di Figaro*; 1964, Scottish Opera, Zerlina, *Don Giovanni*; 1966, Glyndebourne Festival Opera, Angel, *Jephtha*; 1969, San Francisco Opera, Pamina, *Die Zauberflöte*; 1971, Cologne Opera, Donna Anna, *Don Giovanni*; 1972: Bavarian State Opera, Munich, Amelia, *Simon Boccanegra*; Lyric Opera, Chicago, Fiordiligi, *Così fan tutte*; 1973: Paris Opera, Countess, *Le Nozze di Figaro*; Vienna State Opera, Donna Anna, *Don Giovanni*; 1975, Salzburg Festival, Constanze, *Die Entführung aus dem Serail*; 1976, Paris Opera, Desdemona, *Otello*; Elisabeth de Valois, *Don Carlos*: 1977, Cologne Opera; 1978, La Scala, Milan; 1979: Bavarian State Opera, Munich, title role, *Aida*; Zurich Opera, title role, *Norma*; 1984, Bavarian State Opera, Munich, title roles: *Adriana Lecouvreur*, *Ariadne auf Naxos*; 1985, Metropolitan Opera, New York, Desdemona, *Otello*.

CAREER IN THE UK INCLUDES: Since 1963: Covent Garden: Pamina, *Die Zauberflöte*; Marzelline, *Fidelio*; Fiordiligi, *Così fan tutte*; Donna Anna, *Don Giovanni*; Desdemona, *Otello*; Amelia, *Un Ballo in Maschera*; title role, *Norma*; Glyndebourne Festival Opera: Constanze, *Die Entführung aus dem Serail*; Fiordiligi, *Così fan tutte*; Welsh National Opera: Nannetta, *Falstaff*; Amelia, *Simon Boccanegra*; Mimi, *La Bohème*; Pamina, *The Magic Flute*.

RELATED PROFESSIONAL ACTIVITIES: Extensive lieder repertoire; regular concerts, recitals, broadcasts and television appearances in the UK and abroad.

RECORDINGS INCLUDE: Brahms, *Ein Deutsches Requiem* (TELD); Elgar, *The Kingdom* (EMI); Handel, *Messiah* (PHIL); Mozart: *Così fan tutte*, *Le Nozze di Figaro* (both EMI), *Die Zauberflöte* (PHIL); Verdi, *Un Ballo in Maschera* (DECC); Wagner, *Tristan und Isolde* (DG); lieder: Brahms, Schubert, Schumann (all ORFE), R. Strauss (EMI).

VIDEOS INCLUDE: Verdi, *Requiem* (Edinburgh International Festival).

AWARDS AND HONOURS INCLUDE: 1961, Ricordi Opera Prize; 1965, Kathleen Ferrier Memorial Scholarship; 1967, Honorary Fellow, Trinity College of Music; 1981, Kammersängerin (Bavaria); 1982, Commander, Order of the British Empire (CBE); 1983, Honorary Doctorate of Music, University of Wales; 1993, Dame Commander, Order of the British Empire (DBE).

ADDRESS: c/o Dr Germinal Hilbert, Maximilianstrasse 22, D-8000, Munich 22, Germany.

PROWSE PHILIP
Director and Designer

POSITION: Director, Citizens Theatre, Glasgow.

PERSONAL DETAILS: b. 1937.

EDUCATION/TRAINING: Slade School of Art.

OPERATIC DEBUT: As designer: 1962, English Opera Group, *Dido and Aeneas*; as director and designer: 1982, Welsh National Opera, *Tamburlaine* (Handel).

CAREER: Opera, ballet and theatre director and designer in the UK and abroad; since 1970, Director, Citizens Theatre, Glasgow.

OPERA PRODUCTIONS IN THE UK INCLUDE: As designer: since 1963: Covent Garden: *Orfeo ed Euridice*, *Ariadne auf Naxos*; English National Opera, *Don Giovanni*; Scottish Opera, *The Magic Flute*; as director and designer: since 1982: Opera North: *Orpheus and Eurydice*, *The Threepennny Opera*, *Tamburlaine* (Handel), *Aida*, *Daphne* (1987, British stage première), *La Gioconda*; English National Opera/Opera North co-production, *The Pearl Fishers*.

ADDRESS: c/o Harriet Cruickshank, 97 Old South Lambeth Road, London SW8 1XU.

PRYCE-JONES JOHN
Conductor

PERSONAL DETAILS: b. 11 May 1946.
EDUCATION/TRAINING: Corpus Christi College, Cambridge.
PROFESSIONAL AND OPERATIC DEBUT: 1969, Welsh National Opera, *The Marriage of Figaro*.
CAREER: 1968, Assistant Chorus Master, Welsh National Opera; 1978–1987, founding Chorus Master and conductor, Opera North; 1987, Head of Music, Scottish Opera; 1988–1990, Artistic Director: Halifax Choral Society, John Currie Singers; 1990–1992, Music Director, D'Oyly Carte Opera.

OPERA PERFORMANCES IN THE UK INCLUDE: Since 1970: D'Oyly Carte Opera: *The Mikado*, *The Yeomen of the Guard*; Opera North: *The Marriage of Figaro*, *Rigoletto*, *The Merry Widow*, *The Threepenny Opera*, *Aida*, *Macbeth*, *La Traviata*; Scottish Opera: *The Midsummer Marriage*, *La Vie Parisienne*, *La Bohème*; Welsh National Opera: *The Barber of Seville*, *Aida*, *L'Elisir d'Amore*, *The Grand Duchess of Gérolstein*, *Rigoletto*, *La Bohème*.
RECORDINGS INCLUDE: Sullivan: *The Gondoliers*, *Iolanthe*, *The Mikado*, *The Pirates of Penzance* (all TER).
ADDRESS: c/o Stafford Law Associates, 26 Mayfield Road, Weybridge, Surrey KT13 8XB.

* * * *

RAFFERTY MICHAEL
Conductor

POSITION: Music Director, Music Theatre Wales.
PERSONAL DETAILS: b. 5 April 1956, Carlisle.
EDUCATION/TRAINING: 1975–1979, University of Lancaster, studied physics and music; 1979–1982, University College, Cardiff, studied musical acoustics.
PROFESSIONAL AND OPERATIC DEBUT: 1982, Cardiff New Opera Group, *The Lighthouse*.
CAREER: Music Director: 1982–1987, Cardiff New Opera Group; since 1988, Music Theatre Wales.
OPERATIC WORLD PREMIÈRES INCLUDE: 1992, Music Theatre Wales at the Cardiff Festival of Music, *Ubu* by Andrew Toovey.
OPERA PERFORMANCES INCLUDE: Since 1983: Cardiff New Opera Group: *The Duel of Tancredi and Clorindà/The Garden/The Impresario*, *The Turn of the Screw*, *The Diary of One who Disappeared*, *Sāvitri*;

Music Theatre Wales: *The Martyrdom of St Magnus*, *The Fall of the House of Usher* (1989, British première), *Euridice*, *The Four Note Opera*, *The Man Who Mistook his Wife for a Hat*; Banff Centre, Alberta, *Punch and Judy*.
RELATED PROFESSIONAL ACTIVITIES: 1987–1988, physicist, Research Fellow, University of Exeter.
RECORDINGS INCLUDE: Maxwell Davies, *The Martyrdom of St Magnus* (UNIC).
ADDRESS: c/o Music Theatre Wales, St Donat's Arts Centre, Llantwit Major, South Glamorgan CF6 9WF.

RATH JOHN   Bass-baritone

PERSONAL DETAILS: b. 10 June 1946, Manchester.
EDUCATION/TRAINING: 1965–1968, University of Manchester, studied music; 1970–1974, further studies with Elsa Cavelti in Basle and Max Lorenz in Salzburg; 1974–1975, Royal Northern College of Music.

PROFESSIONAL DEBUT: 1972, Basle, Calchas, *La Belle Hélène*.

MAJOR DEBUTS INCLUDE: 1977: Glyndebourne Touring Opera, Masetto, *Don Giovanni*; Opera Northern Ireland, Sparafucile, *Rigoletto*; 1978: Glyndebourne Festival Opera, Second Priest/Second Armed Man, *Die Zauberflöte*; Handel Opera Society, Argante, *Rinaldo*; 1981: Batignano Festival, Allazim, *Zaide*; Bouffes du Nord, Paris, Escamillo, *La Tragédie de Carmen*; La Monnaie, Brussels, Masetto, *Don Giovanni*; 1982, Lille Opera, Colline, *La Bohème*; 1984: English Bach Festival, Charon, *Alceste*; Théâtre du Châtelet, Paris, Don Alvar, *Les Indes Galantes*; 1986, Scottish Opera, Spalanzani/Crespel/Schlemil, *The Tales of Hoffmann*; 1987, Maggio Musicale, Florence, Sleep/Corydon/Winter/Hymen, *The Fairy Queen*; 1988, Kent Opera, Rocco, *Fidelio*; 1989, Stockholm Folkopera at the Edinburgh International Festival, Jokanaan, *Salome*; 1990: D'Oyly Carte Opera, Dick Deadeye, *HMS Pinafore*; Berlin Kammeroper, title role, *Il Barbiere di Siviglia* (Paisiello); 1992, Wexford Festival: Captain, *Il Piccolo Marat*; Angelo, *The Comedy of Errors*; 1993, Opera North, Doctor, *Wozzeck*.

CAREER IN THE UK INCLUDES: Since 1977: D'Oyly Carte Opera: Don Alhambra, *The Gondoliers*; Private Willis, *Iolanthe*; Shadbolt, *The Yeomen of the Guard*; title role, *The Mikado*; English Bach Festival: Polyphemus, *Acis and Galatea*; Aeneas, *Dido and Aeneas*; Mahomet, *Le Siège de Corinthe*; Glyndebourne Touring Opera: Guglielmo, *Così fan tutte*; Melibeo, *La Fedeltà Premiata*; Kent Opera, title role, *Don Giovanni*; Nexus Opera, Traveller, *Curlew River*.

RELATED PROFESSIONAL ACTIVITIES: Numerous concerts and oratorios in the UK and abroad.

RECORDINGS INCLUDE: Sullivan: *The Gondoliers*, *Iolanthe* (both TER).

ADDRESS: c/o Athole Still International Management Ltd, Greystoke House, 80–86 Westow Street, London SE19 3AF.

RATTLE SIMON   Conductor

POSITION: Principal Conductor and Artistic Adviser, City of Birmingham Symphony Orchestra.

PERSONAL DETAILS: b. 19th January 1955, Liverpool; m. 1980, Elise Ross (soprano), two children.

EDUCATION/TRAINING: 1971–1974, Royal Academy of Music.

PROFESSIONAL DEBUT: 1974, Bournemouth Sinfonietta.

OPERATIC DEBUT: 1975, Glyndebourne Touring Opera, *The Rake's Progress*.

CAREER: 1974–1977, Assistant Conductor, Bournemouth Symphony Orchestra and Sinfonietta; 1976, youngest conductor to appear at the Proms (with the London Sinfonietta); 1977–1980: Assistant Conductor, BBC Scottish Symphony Orchestra; Associate Conductor, Royal Liverpool Philharmonic Orchestra; 1981–1983, Artistic Director, South Bank Summer Music Festival; 1981–1984, Principal Guest Conductor, Rotterdam Philharmonic Orchestra; 1983–1986, Co-Artistic Director, Aldeburgh Festival; since 1980, Principal Conductor and Artistic Adviser, City of Birmingham Symphony Orchestra; Principal Guest Conductor: since 1981, Los Angeles Philharmonic Orchestra; since 1992, Orchestra of the Age of Enlightenment.

MAJOR OPERATIC DEBUTS INCLUDE: 1977, Glyndebourne Festival Opera, *The Cunning Little Vixen*; 1985, English National Opera, *Katya Kabanova*; 1988, Los Angeles Music Center Opera, *Wozzeck*; 1990, Covent Garden, *The Cunning Little Vixen*.

OPERA PERFORMANCES IN THE UK INCLUDE: Since 1976: Chelsea Opera Group, *Porgy and Bess*; English Music Theatre at the Aldeburgh Festival, *The Threepenny Opera*; Glyndebourne Festival and Touring Opera: *La Fedeltà Premiata*, *Ariadne auf Naxos*, *Der Rosenkavalier*, *L'Amour des Trois Oranges*, *Idomeneo*, *Porgy and Bess*, *L'Heure Espagnole/L'Enfant et les*

Sortilèges, Le Nozze di Figaro, Così fan tutte.

RELATED PROFESSIONAL ACTIVITIES: Regular guest appearances with the Berlin Philharmonic and other leading orchestras worldwide.

RECORDINGS INCLUDE: Britten, War Requiem; Elgar, The Dream of Gerontius; Gershwin, Porgy and Bess; Holst, The Planets; Janáček: The Cunning Little Vixen, Glagolitic Mass; Mahler, Symphonies Nos 2, 6 & 10; Maw, Odyssey; Nielsen, Symphony No. 4; Rachmaninov, Symphony No. 2; Shostakovich, Symphony No. 10; Stravinsky: Petrushka, Pulcinella, The Rite of Spring; complete symphonies of Sibelius; The Jazz Album (all EMI).

VIDEOS INCLUDE: Ravel, L'Enfant et les Sortilèges (Glyndebourne Festival Opera).

RELEVANT PUBLICATIONS INCLUDE: 1988, Simon Rattle: The Making of a Conductor by Nicholas Kenyon (Faber).

AWARDS AND HONOURS INCLUDE: 1974, John Player International Conducting Competition; 1987, Commander, Order of the British Empire (CBE); 1989: Royal Philharmonic Society/Charles Heidsieck Award; Gramophone Operatic Award, Porgy and Bess; Honorary Doctorates: University of Birmingham, City of Birmingham Polytechnic.

ADDRESS: c/o Harold Holt Ltd, 31 Sinclair Road, London W14 0NS.

RAWNSLEY JOHN   Baritone

PERSONAL DETAILS: b. 14 December 1949, Lancashire; m. Nuala Willis (mezzo-soprano).

EDUCATION/TRAINING: Royal Northern College of Music, with Ellis Keeler and Albert Haskayne; privately with Otakar Kraus.

PROFESSIONAL DEBUT: 1975, Glyndebourne Touring Opera, Kilian, Der Freischütz.

MAJOR DEBUTS INCLUDE: 1977: Glyndebourne Festival Opera, Masetto, La Bohème; Welsh National Opera, title role, The Marriage of Figaro; 1979: Covent Garden, Schaunard, La Bohème; Opera North, High Priest, Samson et Dalila; 1980, Nancy Opera, Tonio, Pagliacci; 1982: English National Opera, Amonasro, Aida; Théâtre du Châtelet, Paris, Ezio, Attila; 1983, La Monnaie, Brussels, Marcello, La Bohème; 1984: Grand Théâtre, Geneva, Taddeo, L'Italiana in Algeri; Marseilles Opera, Germont, La Traviata; 1987: La Scala, Milan, Tonio, Pagliacci; Vienna State Opera, Paolo, Simon Boccanegra; 1988, Gran Teatre del Liceu, Barcelona, Tonio, Pagliacci; 1990, Bonn Opera, title role, Macbeth; 1991, Baths of Caracalla, Rome, Tonio, Pagliacci; title role, Rigoletto: 1982, English National Opera; 1984: Scottish Opera, English National Opera USA tour (including Metropolitan Opera, New York); 1985, Macerata Festival; 1986, Teatro Verdi, Trieste; 1987: Canadian Opera Company, Toronto and San Diego Opera; 1989, Frankfurt Opera; 1992, Norwegian Opera, Oslo.

CAREER IN THE UK INCLUDES: Since 1976: Covent Garden: Sacristan, Tosca; Hermann, Les Contes d'Hoffmann; Sonora, La Fanciulla del West; Christian, Un Ballo in Maschera; Enrico, Lucia di Lammermoor; English National Opera, Papageno, The Magic Flute; Glyndebourne Festival and Touring Opera: Marcello, La Bohème; Perrucchetto, La Fedeltà Premiatà; Paolo, Simon Boccanegra; Ford, Falstaff; Nick Shadow, The Rake's Progress; title role, Il Barbiere di Siviglia; Opera North: Marcello, La Bohème; Father, Hansel and Gretel; title roles: Rigoletto, Macbeth; Opera Northern Ireland, Marcello, La Bohème.

RECORDINGS INCLUDE: Mozart, Don Giovanni; Verdi, Rigoletto (both EMI).

VIDEOS INCLUDE: Mozart, Don Giovanni; Rossini, Il Barbiere di Siviglia (both Glyndebourne Festival Opera); Puccini, La Fanciulla del West (Covent Garden); Verdi, Rigoletto (English National Opera).

231

AWARDS AND HONOURS INCLUDE: 1976,
John Christie Award; 1983, Fellow, Royal
Northern College of Music.
ADDRESS: c/o Ron Gonsalves Personal
Artists & Concert Management, 10
Dagnan Road, London SW12 9LQ.

REA SEAN   Bass

PERSONAL DETAILS: b. 13 January 1940,
Surrey.
PREVIOUS OCCUPATION: Cosmetic dentist.
EDUCATION/TRAINING: Guildhall School of
Music and Drama.
PROFESSIONAL DEBUT: 1976, Glyndebourne
Touring Opera, Pistol, *Falstaff.*
MAJOR DEBUTS INCLUDE: 1977, Welsh
National Opera, Superintendent Budd,
Albert Herring; 1980, English National
Opera, Lictor, *The Coronation of Poppea*;
1981, Covent Garden, Pietro, *Simon
Boccanegra*; 1987, Nice Opera,
Commendatore, *Don Giovanni*; 1989,
Dortmund Opera, Pimen, *Boris Godunov.*
CAREER IN THE UK INCLUDES: Since 1976:
English National Opera: Steersman,
Tristan and Isolde; Monterone and
Sparafucile, *Rigoletto*; Cardinal
Raimondo, *Rienzi*; Sarastro, *The Magic
Flute*; King, *Aida*; Pogner, *The
Mastersingers of Nuremberg*;
Commendatore, *Don Giovanni*;
Glyndebourne Touring Opera, Major-
Domo, *Ariadne auf Naxos*; Opera North:
Peneios, *Daphne* (1987, British stage
première); Pimen, *Boris Godunov*;
Commendatore, *Don Giovanni*; Opera
Northern Ireland: Angelotti, *Tosca*; Count
Ribbing, *The Masked Ball*; Welsh
National Opera: Sparafucile, *Rigoletto*;
Oroveso, *Norma*; Sarastro, *The Magic
Flute*; Narbal, *The Trojans*; Prince
Gremin, *Eugene Onegin*; Tutor, *Count
Ory*; Jago, *Ernani.*
RELATED PROFESSIONAL ACTIVITIES:
Numerous appearances in musical
theatre; since 1991, Artistic Director,
Island Opera, Isle of Man.
RECORDINGS INCLUDE: Mahler, *Das
Klagende Lied*; Verdi, *Otello* (both EMI).

VIDEOS INCLUDE: Verdi, *Rigoletto* (English
National Opera).
ADDRESS: c/o Stafford Law Associates, 26
Mayfield Road, Weybridge, Surrey KT13
8XB.

REED TIM   Designer

PERSONAL DETAILS: b. 11 February 1953,
Cirencester.
EDUCATION/TRAINING: 1972–1975,
University of Hull, studied drama; 1975–
1976, London Opera Centre, stage
management course.
PROFESSIONAL AND OPERATIC DEBUT:
1977, Wexford Festival, *Il Maestro di
Capella/La Serva Pedrona/La Serva e
l'Ussero.*
CAREER: Since 1977, opera, theatre and
ballet designer in the UK and abroad;
1986–1991, Head of Design, Opera
Northern Ireland.
OPERA DESIGNS INCLUDE: Since 1978:
Opera 80: *Così fan tutte, Albert Herring*;
Opera Northern Ireland: *Macbeth,
Falstaff, Ariadne auf Naxos, La Bohème,
Die Entführung aus dem Serail, La
Traviata, The Magic Flute*; Dublin Grand
Opera: *Così fan tutte, Die Fledermaus,
Der Rosenkavalier*; Madrid Opera
Festival, *Macbeth*; Marseilles Opera,
Falstaff; Monte Carlo Opera, *Falstaff*;
Netherlands Opera, *L'Ormindo*; New
Israeli Opera, Tel Aviv: *La Traviata, The
Turn of the Screw, Hänsel und Gretel*;
Norrlands Opera, Umeå, *Le Nozze di
Figaro*; Wexford Festival: *Il Mondo della
Luna* (costumes only), *Crispino e la
Comare, Un Giorno di Regno, La Vedova
Scaltra, Cendrillon.*
OPERATIC WORLD PREMIERES INCLUDE:
1985, Paris Opera, *Docteur Faustus* by
Konrad Boehmer.
ADDRESS: c/o MLR Ltd, 200 Fulham Road,
London SW10 9PN.

REMEDIOS ALBERTO   Tenor

PERSONAL DETAILS: b. 27 February 1935, Liverpool; m. 1965, Judith Hosken, three children.

EDUCATION/TRAINING: 1949–1951, privately with Edwin Francis in Liverpool; 1953–1956, Royal College of Music, with Joseph Hislop and Clive Carey.

PROFESSIONAL DEBUT: 1957, Sadler's Wells Opera, Tinca, *Il Tabarro*.

EARLY CAREER INCLUDED: Principal Tenor: 1958–1968, Sadler's Wells Opera; 1968–1970, Frankfurt Opera; roles included: Alfredo, *La Traviata*; Bacchus, *Ariadne auf Naxos*; Erik, *The Flying Dutchman*; Max, *Der Freischütz*; Tamino, *The Magic Flute*; Florestan, *Fidelio*; Duke, *Rigoletto*; title role, *The Damnation of Faust*.

MAJOR DEBUTS INCLUDE: 1965: Covent Garden, Grigory, *Boris Godunov*; Sutherland-Williamson Opera Company, Australia tour, Edgardo, *Lucia di Lammermoor*; 1968, Sadler's Wells Opera, Walther, *The Mastersingers of Nuremberg*; 1972, Cape Town Opera, Don Ottavio, *Don Giovanni*; 1973, San Francisco Opera, Grigory, *Boris Godunov*; 1974, San Diego Opera, title role, *Siegfried* (1977, *The Ring of the Nibelung*); 1975: Welsh National Opera, title role, *Otello*; Seattle Opera, title role, *Siegfried* (1978, *The Ring of the Nibelung*); Bacchus, *Ariadne auf Naxos*; 1976, Metropolitan Opera, New York; 1977, Scottish Opera; 1978: Dallas Civic Opera, Erik, *Der Fliegende Holländer*; Opera Company of Boston, title role, *The Damnation of Faust*; 1979, Teatro Colón, Buenos Aires, title role, *Peter Grimes*; 1981, Canadian Opera Company, Toronto, Erik, *Der Fliegende Holländer*; 1982, Rio de Janeiro, title role, *Peter Grimes*; 1983, Marseilles Opera, title role, *Lohengrin*; 1984, Australian Opera, Sydney: Siegmund, *Die Walküre*; title role, *Otello*; 1985: Kentucky Opera, Florestan, *Fidelio*; Victoria State Opera, Melbourne, title role, *Lohengrin*; 1986, State Opera of South Australia, Adelaide, Radamès,

Aida; 1990, Lyric Opera of Queensland, Erik, *Der Fliegende Holländer*.

CAREER IN THE UK INCLUDES: Since 1966: Covent Garden: Erik, *Der Fliegende Holländer*; Mark, *The Midsummer Marriage*; Florestan, *Fidelio*; Froh, *Das Rheingold*; Aeneas, *Les Troyens*; Bacchus, *Ariadne auf Naxos*; First Armed Man, *Die Zauberflöte* (also 1979, Far East tour); Siegfried, *Der Ring des Nibelungen*; Max, *Der Freischütz*; Sadler's Wells Opera/English National Opera: Siegmund and Siegfried, *The Ring of the Nibelung*; Don José, *Carmen*; Don Alvaro, *The Force of Destiny*; Des Grieux, *Manon*; Florestan, *Fidelio*; Tristan, *Tristan and Isolde*; A Vision of the Author, *The Adventures of Mr Brouček*; title role, *Lohengrin*; Scottish Opera: Walther, *The Mastersingers of Nuremberg*; Laca, *Jenůfa*; title role, *Oedipus Rex*.

RELATED PROFESSIONAL ACTIVITIES: Numerous concerts, recitals, broadcasts and television appearances in the UK and abroad.

RECORDINGS INCLUDE: Tippett, *The Midsummer Marriage* (PHIL); Wagner: *The Valkyrie, Siegfried, Twilight of the Gods* (all EMI).

AWARDS AND HONOURS INCLUDE: 1963, Union of Bulgarian Composers Award; 1981, Commander, Order of the British Empire (CBE).

ADDRESS: c/o Opera and Concert Artists, 75 Aberdare Gardens, London NW6 3AN.

REMEDIOS RAMON   Tenor

PERSONAL DETAILS: b. 9 May 1940, Liverpool; m. Jackie Bond.

EDUCATION/TRAINING: Guildhall School of Music and Drama, with Joseph Hislop and Parry Jones; National School of Opera/London Opera Centre, with Joan Cross and Anne Wood.

PROFESSIONAL DEBUT: 1965, Opera for All, Alfredo, *La Traviata*.

EARLY CAREER INCLUDED: 1965–1967, appearances with Morley Opera, Opera for All and Western Opera, Ireland; roles included: Pinkerton, *Madam Butterfly*; Fenton, *Falstaff*.

MAJOR DEBUTS INCLUDE: 1967, Scottish Opera, Froh, *Das Rheingold*; 1968, Welsh National Opera, Ismaele, *Nabucco*; 1973: Cologne Opera (1973–1975, Principal Tenor), Ernesto, *Don Pasquale*; Frankfurt Opera, Alfredo, *La Traviata*; 1975, English National Opera, Alfredo, *La Traviata*; 1976, Handel Opera Society, title role, *Belshazzar*; 1980, Marseilles Opera, Narraboth, *Salome*; 1981, Avignon, Cassio, *Otello*; 1982, Covent Garden, Narraboth, *Salome*; 1985: Jerusalem, Don José, *Carmen*; Monte Carlo Opera, Narraboth, *Salome*.

CAREER IN THE UK INCLUDES: Since 1968: Covent Garden: Second Jew, *Salome*; Uldino, *Attila*; Bruno, *I Puritani*; Roderigo, *Otello*; English National Opera (1975–1977, Principal Tenor): Janek, *The Makropoulos Case*; Narraboth, *Salome*; Paris, *La Belle Hélène*; David, *The Mastersingers of Nuremberg*; Vítek, *Dalibor*; Caramello, *A Night in Venice*; Lensky, *Eugene Onegin*; Vakula, *Christmas Eve*; New Sadler's Wells Opera: Fritz, *The Grand Duchess of Gérolstein*; Count Tassilo, *Countess Maritza*; Welsh National Opera (1968–1973, Principal Tenor): Grigory, *Boris Godunov*; Alfredo, *La Traviata*; Macduff, *Macbeth*; Count, *The Barber of Seville*; Tamino, *The Magic Flute*; Painter, *Lulu* (1971, British première); Don Ottavio, *Don Giovanni*; Novice, *Billy Budd*; Duke, *Rigoletto*; Radamès, *The Drama of Aida*; Skuratov, *From the House of the Dead*.

RELATED PROFESSIONAL ACTIVITIES INCLUDE: Numerous concerts, broadcasts and television appearances in the UK and abroad.

RECORDINGS INCLUDE: Kálmán, *Countess Maritza* (TER).

AWARDS INCLUDE: 1962, Ricordi Opera Prize; 1963, Countess of Munster Award.

ADDRESS: c/o Norman McCann International Artists Ltd, The Coach House, 56 Lawrie Park Gardens, London SE26 6XJ.

RENDALL DAVID   Tenor

PERSONAL DETAILS: b. 11 October 1948, London; m., four children.

EDUCATION/TRAINING: Royal Academy of Music, with Olive Groves and Alexander Young; Salzburg Mozarteum; privately with Helga Mott.

PROFESSIONAL DEBUT: 1975, Glyndebourne Touring Opera, Ferrando, *Così fan tutte*.

MAJOR DEBUTS INCLUDE: 1975, Covent Garden, Italian Tenor, *Der Rosenkavalier*; 1976, English National Opera, Leicester, *Mary Stuart*; Ferrando, *Così fan tutte*; 1976, Glyndebourne Festival Opera; 1977, Hamburg State Opera and Opéra du Rhin, Strasbourg; 1978: New York City Opera, Rodolfo, *La Bohème*; Don Ottavio, *Don Giovanni*: Paris Opera, San Francisco Opera; 1979: La Scala, Milan, title role, *The Rake's Progress*; Vienna State Opera, Don Ottavio, *Don Giovanni*; 1980, Metropolitan Opera, New York, Ernesto, *Don Pasquale*; 1981, Teatro Colón, Buenos Aires, Lindoro, *L'Italiana in Algeri*; 1982, Grand Théâtre, Geneva, Alfredo, *La Traviata*; 1983, Berlioz Festival, Lyons, title role, *La Damnation de Faust*; 1985, Welsh National Opera, Pinkerton, *Madam Butterfly*; title role, *La Clemenza di Tito*: 1988, Aix-en-Provence Festival; 1989, Zurich Opera; 1992, Teatro La Zarzuela, Madrid, Don Antonio, *The Duenna* by Roberto Gerhard (world stage première).

CAREER IN THE UK INCLUDES: Since 1975: Covent Garden: Duke, *Rigoletto*; Don Ottavio, *Don Giovanni*; Young Sailor, *Tristan und Isolde*; Count, *Il Barbiere di Siviglia*; Rodrigo, *La Donna del Lago*; Matteo, *Arabella*; Rodolfo, *La Bohème*; Des Grieux, *Manon*; Flamand, *Capriccio*; English National Opera: Rodolfo, *La Bohème*; Tamino, *The Magic Flute*; Alfredo, *La Traviata*; Pinkerton, *Madam Butterfly*; Duke, *Rigoletto*; Cavaradossi, *Tosca*; Glyndebourne Festival Opera: Belmonte, *Die Entführung aus dem Serail*; title role, *The Rake's Progress*.

RELATED PROFESSIONAL ACTIVITIES:
Numerous concerts, recitals, broadcasts
and television appearances in the UK and
abroad.
RECORDINGS INCLUDE: Beethoven: *Missa
Solemnis* (HARM), Symphony No. 9 (CHAN);
Bruckner, *Te Deum* (DG); Donizetti, *Mary
Stuart*; Mozart, *Requiem* (both EMI);
Puccini, *La Rondine* (CBS).
VIDEOS INCLUDE: Donizetti, *Mary Stuart*
(English National Opera).
ADDRESS: c/o Harrison/Parrott Ltd, 12
Penzance Place, London W11 4PA.

RICHARDSON MARK   Bass

POSITION: Principal Bass, English National
Opera.
PERSONAL DETAILS: b. Surrey; m. Christine
Thompson (soprano).
PREVIOUS OCCUPATION: Theatre
electrician.
EDUCATION/TRAINING: Royal Manchester
College of Music.
PROFESSIONAL DEBUT: 1979, chorus
member, English National Opera.
CAREER INCLUDES: Since 1980: Buxton
Festival, Mustafa, *The Italian Girl in
Algiers*; English National Opera (since
1983, Principal Bass): Paris, *Romeo and
Juliet*; Ceprano, *Rigoletto*; Gavrila/
Klausewitz/Berthier/Ramballe, *War and
Peace*; Ragman, *Louise*; Director, *The
Gambler*; Stefan, *The Marriage*;
Hermann, *The Tales of Hoffmann*; Maître
Ambroise/Ferryman, *Mireille*; Grenville,
La Traviata; Béthune, *The Sicilian
Vespers*; Second Guest, *Osud* (1984,
British stage première); Lamoral,
Arabella; Second Armed Man, *The Magic
Flute*; Steersman, *Tristan and Isolde*,
Indian, *The Bartered Bride*; Masetto, *Don
Giovanni*; Pish-Tush and Pooh-Bah, *The
Mikado*; King, *Aida*; Gaoler, *Tosca*;
Policeman, *Lady Macbeth of Mtsensk*
(1987, British stage première); Nourabad,
The Pearl Fishers; Surin, *The Queen of
Spades*; Pietro, *Simon Boccanegra*;
Donald, *Billy Budd*; Patsyuk, *Christmas
Eve* (1988, British stage première); Count

Ribbing, *A Masked Ball*; King of France,
Lear; Hobson, *Peter Grimes*; Parson, *The
Cunning Little Vixen*; Colline, *La
Bohème*; Frank Maurrant, *Street Scene*;
Flemish Deputy, *Don Carlos*; Bonze,
Madam Butterfly; Truffaldino, *Ariadne auf
Naxos*; also, Welsh National Opera: Don
Basilio, *The Barber of Seville*; Angelotti,
Tosca.
RELATED PROFESSIONAL ACTIVITIES:
Concerts and recitals in the UK.
RECORDINGS INCLUDE: Sullivan, *The
Mikado* (TER); Verdi, *Rigoletto* (EMI).
VIDEOS INCLUDE: Sullivan, *The Mikado*
(English National Opera).
ADDRESS: c/o English National Opera,
London Coliseum, St Martin's Lane,
London WC2N 4ES.

RICHARDSON STEPHEN
Bass

PERSONAL DETAILS: b. 20 June 1959,
Liverpool; m. Colleen Barsley (dancer),
one child.
EDUCATION/TRAINING: 1978–1981,
University of Manchester, studied music;
1981–1983, Royal Northern College of
Music, with Patrick McGuigan; currently
with David Keren.
PROFESSIONAL DEBUT: 1983, chorus
member, Glyndebourne Festival Opera.
MAJOR DEBUTS INCLUDE: 1984: English
National Opera, King, *Aida*; Welsh
National Opera, Colline, *La Bohème*;
1985, Opera North, Sarastro, *The Magic
Flute*; 1986, Scottish Opera, Private Willis,
Iolanthe; 1990, Banff Centre, Alberta,
Captain, *Tornrak*.
OPERATIC WORLD PREMIERES INCLUDE:
1984, Glyndebourne Touring Opera, Lion,
Higglety Pigglety Pop! preliminary
version by Oliver Knussen; 1990, Almeida
Festival, Sir Joshua Cramer, *The
Intelligence Park* by Gerald Barry; 1991,
Opera North, Father, *The Jewel Box* by
Mozart/Paul Griffiths.
CAREER IN THE UK INCLUDES: Since 1984:
Aldeburgh Festival, Doctor, *Punch and
Judy*; Chelsea Opera Group, Geronte,

235

Manon Lescaut; Glyndebourne Festival and Touring Opera: Lion, *Higglety Pigglety Pop!* and Bruno, *Where the Wild Things Are*; Don Fernando, *Fidelio*; Kent Opera: Mongolian Soldier, *A Night at the Chinese Opera*; Commendatore, *Don Giovanni*; New Sussex Opera, Trulove, *The Rake's Progress*; Northern Stage, title role, *Golem*; Opera Northern Ireland: Osmin, *The Seraglio*; Sarastro, *The Magic Flute*; Scottish Opera, Mr Ratcliffe, *Billy Budd*; Welsh National Opera: Oroveso, *Norma*; Priam, *The Trojans*.

RELATED PROFESSIONAL ACTIVITIES: Numerous concerts and recitals in the UK and abroad; private teacher.

RECORDINGS INCLUDE: Knussen, *Where the Wild Things Are* (UNIC); Mozart, *Requiem* (DENO); Purcell, *Odes for Queen Mary 1691* (DG).

VIDEOS INCLUDE: Knussen, *Higglety Pigglety Pop!/Where The Wild Things Are* (Glyndebourne Festival Opera).

ADDRESS: c/o M & M Lyric Artists, 6 Princess Road, London NW1 7JJ.

RIDLER ANNE   Translator

PERSONAL DETAILS: b. 30 July 1912, Rugby; m. 1938, Vivian Ridler, four children.

EDUCATION/TRAINING: King's College, London; further studies in Florence and Rome.

CAREER: Editorial assistant, Faber and Faber Ltd; six volumes of poetry and several verse plays published; translations include: *The Coronation of Poppea* (English National Opera and Opera Factory), *The Duel of Tancredi and Clorinda, Orfeo, The Return of Ulysses* (all English National Opera), *Agrippina* (Buxton Festival and Kent Opera), *Così fan tutte, Don Giovanni, The Marriage of Figaro* (all Opera Factory).

PUBLICATIONS INCLUDE: Translations: *Così fan tutte, The Marriage of Figaro* (both Perpetua Press), *Eritrea* (Oxford University Press), *Orfeo* (Faber).

ADDRESS: c/o English National Opera, London Coliseum, St Martin's Lane, London WC2N 4ES or Opera Factory, 8A The Leathermarket, Weston Street, London SE1 3ER.

RIGBY JEAN   Mezzo-soprano

PERSONAL DETAILS: b. Lancashire; m. 1987, Jamie Hayes (director), three children.

EDUCATION/TRAINING: 1973–1977, Birmingham School of Music, studied piano, viola and from 1976 singing; 1977–1981, Royal Academy of Music, with Patricia Clark (since 1981, privately); 1981–1982, National Opera Studio.

PROFESSIONAL DEBUT: 1982, English National Opera, Mercédès, *Carmen*.

MAJOR DEBUTS INCLUDE: English National Opera: 1983, title role, *The Rape of Lucretia*; 1987, title role, *Carmen*; 1989, Penelope, *The Return of Ulysses*; 1983, Covent Garden, Tebaldo, *Don Carlos*; 1984: English National Opera USA tour (including Metropolitan Opera, New York), Maddalena, *Rigoletto*; Glyndebourne Festival Opera, Hippolyta, *A Midsummer Night's Dream*; 1991, Scottish Opera, title role, *Carmen*.

OPERATIC WORLD PREMIÈRES INCLUDE: 1986, English National Opera, Eurydice, *The Mask of Orpheus* by Harrison Birtwistle.

CAREER IN THE UK INCLUDES: Since 1982: Buxton Festival: Ernestina, *L'Occasione fa il Ladro*; title role, *The Italian Girl in Algiers*; Covent Garden: Mercédès, *Carmen*; Olga, *Eugene Onegin*; Lola, *Cavalleria Rusticana* (at Kenwood); Nicklausse, *Les Contes d'Hoffmann*; English National Opera (1982–1990, Principal Mezzo-soprano): Armando, *Le Grand Macabre* (1982, British première); Pauline/Daphnis, *The Queen of Spades*; Marina, *Boris Godunov*; Blanche, *The Gambler*; Maddalena, *Rigoletto*; Magdalene, *The Mastersingers of Nuremberg*; Frances, *Gloriana*; Dorabella, *Così fan tutte*; Amastre, *Xerxes*; Cornelia, *Julius Caesar*; Pitti-

Sing, *The Mikado*; Zefka, *The Diary of One Who Disappeared* (1986, British stage première); Octavian, *Der Rosenkavalier*; Varvara, *Katya Kabanova*; Ursula, *Beatrice and Benedict*; Jocasta, *Oedipus Rex*; Glyndebourne Festival Opera: Mercédès, *Carmen*; Nancy, *Albert Herring*.

RECORDINGS INCLUDE: Bizet, *Carmen* (PHIL); Sullivan, *The Mikado*; (TER); Verdi, *Rigoletto* (EMI).

VIDEOS INCLUDE: Bizet, *Carmen* (Covent Garden); Britten: *Gloriana*, *The Rape of Lucretia*; Verdi, *Rigoletto* (all English National Opera).

AWARDS AND HONOURS INCLUDE: 1982, Royal Over-Seas League Music Competition; 1989, Fellow, Royal Academy of Music.

ADDRESS: c/o John Coast, 31 Sinclair Road, London W14 ONS.

RITCHIE ELIZABETH
Soprano

PERSONAL DETAILS: b. 24 November 1948, London; m. 1970, Ian Kinnell, two children.

PREVIOUS OCCUPATION: 1970–1974, school teacher.

EDUCATION/TRAINING: 1966–1969, Royal Academy of Music, with May Blyth and Joy Mammen; 1974–1976, London Opera Centre, with Audrey Langford.

PROFESSIONAL DEBUT: 1979, Glyndebourne Touring Opera, Diana, *La Fedeltà Premiata*.

MAJOR DEBUTS INCLUDE: 1983: Welsh National Opera, Flower Maiden, *Parsifal*; Théâtre du Châtelet, Paris, Hébé, *Les Indes Galantes*; 1984: New Sadler's Wells Opera, Josephine, *HMS Pinafore*; University College Opera, Kunigunde, *Faust* (Spohr); 1985, Opera North, First Lady, *The Magic Flute*; 1986, English National Opera, Flower Maiden, *Parsifal*; 1989, Scottish Opera, Woglinde, *Das Rheingold*.

CAREER IN THE UK INCLUDES: Since 1979, Glyndebourne Festival and Touring Opera: Fortune, *Il Ritorno d'Ulisse in Patria*; Echo, *Ariadne auf Naxos*; Countess, *Le Nozze di Figaro*.

RELATED PROFESSIONAL ACTIVITIES: Regular concerts, recitals and oratorios in the UK and Holland.

RECORDINGS INCLUDE: Sullivan, *HMS Pinafore* (TER); Wagner, *Parsifal* (EMI).

AWARDS INCLUDE: Countess of Munster Award.

ADDRESS: The Old Rectory, Little Birch, Hereford HR2 8BB.

RITCHIE IAN   Administrator

POSITION: General Administrator, Opera North.

PERSONAL DETAILS: b. 19 June 1953, London.

EDUCATION: 1971–1972, Royal College of Music, vocal studies; 1972–1975, Trinity College, Cambridge, studied law and music; 1975–1976, Guildhall School of Music and Drama, vocal studies.

CAREER: 1976–1979, Promotion Manager, Universal Edition (music publishers); 1979–1984, General Manager, City of London Sinfonia; 1983–1984, Artistic Director, City of London Festival; 1984–1993, Managing Director, Scottish Chamber Orchestra; 1989–1993, Co-artistic Director, St Magnus Festival, Orkney Islands; since 1993/1994 season, General Administrator, Opera North.

OTHER PROFESSIONAL ACTIVITIES INCLUDE: 1983–1986, member, Music Advisory Panel, Arts Council of Great Britain; 1990–1993, Chairman, Association of British Orchestras; 1992, member: Arts Council Working Party for small scale opera and music theatre, Scottish Arts Council Combined Arts Committee.

AWARDS INCLUDE: 1991, Prudential Award for the Arts to Scottish Chamber Orchestra.

ADDRESS: c/o Opera North, Grand Theatre, 46 New Briggate, Leeds LS1 6NU.

RIVERS MALCOLM
Baritone and Teacher

PERSONAL DETAILS: b. 19 April 1937, Ipswich; m., one child.
EDUCATION/TRAINING: 1957–1963, Royal College of Music.
PROFESSIONAL DEBUT: 1966, English Opera Group, Collatinus, *The Rape of Lucretia*.
EARLY CAREER INCLUDED: 1966–1969, member, English Opera Group; 1971–1979, Principal Baritone, Sadler's Wells Opera/English National Opera: Alfio, *Cavalleria Rusticana*; Dolokhov, *War and Peace* (1972, British stage première); Creon, *Oedipus Rex*; Escamillo, *Carmen*; Duphol, *La Traviata*.
MAJOR DEBUTS INCLUDE: 1975, Seattle Opera, Alberich, *Der Ring des Nibelungen*; 1976, Covent Garden, Antenor, *Troilus and Cressida*; 1981, Teatro San Carlo, Naples, Alberich, *Der Ring des Nibelungen*.
OPERATIC WORLD PREMIERES INCLUDE: English Opera Group at the Aldeburgh Festival: 1966, appeared in *The Burning Fiery Furnace*; 1968, Elder Son, *The Prodigal Son* (both by Benjamin Britten); English National Opera: 1977, Pedro, *The Royal Hunt of the Sun*; 1981, Prince Yashvin, *Anna Karenina* (both by Iain Hamilton); 1992, Opera Omaha, Nebraska, Tydeus, *Gardens of Adonis* by Hugo Weisgall.
CAREER IN THE UK INCLUDES: Since 1980: Covent Garden, Sid, *La Fanciulla del West*; D'Oyly Carte Opera: Pirate King, *The Pirates of Penzance*; Pooh-Bah, *The Mikado*; English National Opera: Montano, *Otello*; Orlik, *Mazeppa*; Melot, *Tristan and Isolde*; Marullo, *Rigoletto*; Kayama Yesaemon, *Pacific Overtures*; Bosun, *Billy Budd*.
RELATED PROFESSIONAL ACTIVITIES: Numerous concerts and recitals in the UK and abroad; several appearances in West End musicals; administrator and conceiver of *Being Alive*, an anthology of the works of Stephen Sondheim; since 1988, teacher of stage and vocal technique.

RECORDINGS INCLUDE: Britten, *The Burning Fiery Furnace* (LOND); Puccini, *La Fanciulla del West* (DG); Sondheim, *Pacific Overtures* (TER); Verdi, *Otello*; Walton, *Troilus and Cressida* (both EMI).
VIDEOS INCLUDE: Britten, *Billy Budd*; Verdi, *Rigoletto* (both English National Opera).
ADDRESS: c/o M & M Lyric Artists, 6 Princess Road, London NW1 7JJ.

RIZZI CARLO   Conductor

POSITION: Music Director, Welsh National Opera.
PERSONAL DETAILS: b. 19 July 1960, Milan.
EDUCATION/TRAINING: 1977–1982, Milan Conservatoire, studied conducting, composition and piano; 1983, with Vladimir Delman in Bologna; 1984, with Franco Ferrara in Siena.
PROFESSIONAL AND OPERATIC DEBUT: 1982, Milan Angelicum, *L'Ajo nell'imbarazzo*.
CAREER: 1985–1989, guest conductor at numerous Italian concert halls and opera houses, performances included: *Beatrice di Tenda*, *Don Giovanni*, *Falstaff*, *L'Italiana in Algeri*, *Norma*, *Rigoletto*, *Torquato Tasso*, *La Traviata*; since 1992, Music Director, Welsh National Opera.
MAJOR OPERATIC DEBUTS INCLUDE: 1988, Buxton Festival, *Torquato Tasso* (British debut); 1989: Opera North, *Tosca*; Australian Opera, Sydney, *Il Barbiere di Siviglia*; Netherlands Opera, *Don Pasquale*; 1990, Welsh National Opera, *Il Barbiere di Siviglia*; 1991: Covent Garden, *La Cenerentola*; Teatro Carlo Felice, Genoa, (opening production of restored opera house), *Il Trovatore*; 1992: Cologne Opera, *L'Occasione fa il Ladro*; Deutsche Oper, Berlin, *L'Italiana in Algeri*; Grand Théâtre, Geneva, *Luisa Miller*; 1993, Metropolitan Opera, New York, *La Bohème*.
OPERA PERFORMANCES IN THE UK INCLUDE: Since 1990: Covent Garden: *Il Barbiere di Siviglia*, *Così fan tutte*, *Il Viaggio a Reims*; Opera North, *La Traviata*; Welsh National Opera: *Count*

Ory, Rigoletto, Elektra, Tosca, La Favorita
(also 1993, at Covent Garden), La
Bohème, Un Ballo in Maschera, Eugene
Onegin.

RELATED PROFESSIONAL ACTIVITIES:
Regular concerts with leading orchestras
in the UK and abroad.

RECORDINGS INCLUDE: Cimarosa, L'Italiana
in Londra; Donizetti, Il Furioso all'isola di
San Domingo (both BONG); Rossini, Ciro in
Babilonia (AKAD); Verdi, La Traviata (TELD).

AWARDS INCLUDE: Toscanini Conductors
Competition (Parma).

ADDRESS: c/o Allied Artists, 42 Montpelier
Square, London SW7 1JZ.

ROBERTS STEPHEN
Baritone

PERSONAL DETAILS: b. 8 February 1949.

PREVIOUS OCCUPATION: 1972–1977, lay
cleric, Westminster Cathedral Choir.

EDUCATION/TRAINING: 1967–1972, Royal
College of Music, with Gerald English and
Redvers Llewelyn; privately with Helga
Mott and Erich Vietheer.

CAREER INCLUDES: Since 1977: primarily a
concert performer; operatic roles include:
Spitalfields Festival, Ubalde, Armide
(1982, operatic debut); London
Sinfonietta: Ramiro, L'Heure Espagnole;
Mittenhofer, Elegy for Young Lovers;
Opera North: Count, The Marriage of
Figaro; Falke, Die Fledermaus; New
Israeli Opera, Tel Aviv, Aeneas, Dido and
Aeneas.

RELATED PROFESSIONAL ACTIVITIES:
Regular concerts, oratorios, recitals,
radio and television broadcasts with
leading conductors and orchestras in the
UK and abroad.

RECORDINGS INCLUDE: Bach, St Matthew
Passion; Birtwistle, Punch and Judy (both
DECC); Elgar, The Apostles (CHAN); Fauré,
Requiem (RPO); Gluck, Armide (EMI); Orff,
Carmina Burana (DECC); Penderecki, St
Luke Passion (ARGO); Tippett, King Priam
(DECC); Vaughan Williams, Symphony No.
1 – A Sea Symphony (VIRG).

ADDRESS: c/o Harrison/Parrott Ltd, 12
Penzance Place, London W11 4PA.

ROBINSON ETHNA
Mezzo-soprano

POSITION: Principal Mezzo-soprano,
English National Opera.

PERSONAL DETAILS: b. 20 June 1956,
Dublin; m. Donald Cooper (opera and
theatre photographer), two children.

PREVIOUS OCCUPATION: 1977–1979,
primary school teacher.

EDUCATION/TRAINING: 1975–1978, Froebel
College of Primary Education, Dublin;
1977–1978, Trinity College, Dublin; 1979–
1981, Birmingham School of Music, with
Pamela Cook; 1981–1984, Guildhall
School of Music and Drama, with Noelle
Barker.

PROFESSIONAL DEBUT: 1984, English
National Opera, Rosette, Manon.

MAJOR DEBUTS INCLUDE: 1990, English
National Opera Soviet Union tour (Bolshoi
and Kiev), Amastre, Xerxes.

OPERATIC WORLD PREMIERES INCLUDE:
English National Opera: 1986, Eurydice
the Myth/Persephone, The Mask of
Orpheus by Harrison Birtwistle; 1993,
Philia, Inquest of Love by Jonathan
Harvey.

CAREER IN THE UK INCLUDES: Since 1984,
Principal Mezzo-soprano, English
National Opera: Kate Pinkerton, Madam
Butterfly; Countess Ceprano, Rigoletto;
Guest, Anna Karenina; Meretaten,
Akhnaten (1985, British première);
Tebaldo, Don Carlos; Miriam, Moses;
Cherubino, The Marriage of Figaro;
Mercédès, Carmen; Cupid, Orpheus in
the Underworld; Hansel, Hansel and
Gretel; Second Lady, The Magic Flute;
Olga, Eugene Onegin; Pitti-Sing, The
Mikado; Beatrice, Beatrice and Benedict;
Margret, Wozzeck; Dorabella, Così fan
tutte; Kitchen Boy, Rusalka; Fortune/
Juno/Melanto, The Return of Ulysses;
Dryad, Ariadne auf Naxos; Pauline/
Daphnis, The Queen of Spades.

239

RELATED PROFESSIONAL ACTIVITIES:
Concerts in the UK and abroad.

VIDEOS INCLUDE: Sullivan, *The Mikado*
(English National Opera).

AWARDS INCLUDE: 1979, John Player Vocal
Bursary; 1981, Ludlow Philharmonia
Prize; 1983, Royal Over-Seas League
Music Competition.

ADDRESS: c/o English National Opera,
London Coliseum, St Martin's Lane,
London WC2N 4ES.

ROBINSON PETER   Conductor

PERSONAL DETAILS: b. 24 June 1949,
Hartlepool.

EDUCATION/TRAINING: 1968–1971, Organ
Scholar, St John's College, Oxford.

PROFESSIONAL AND OPERATIC DEBUT:
1974, Australian Opera, Melbourne, *The
Barber of Seville*.

CAREER: 1967–1968, Assistant Organist,
Durham Cathedral; 1971–1973, member,
music staff and Chorus Master,
Glyndebourne Festival Opera; 1972,
Chorus Master, Wexford Festival; 1973–
1980, Head of Music Staff and Resident
Conductor, Australian Opera, Melbourne;
English National Opera: 1980–1981,
member, music staff; 1981–1989,
Assistant Music Director; since 1989,
freelance conductor in the UK and
abroad.

MAJOR OPERATIC DEBUTS INCLUDE: 1981,
English National Opera, *Così fan tutte*;
1982, Kent Opera, *The Beggar's Opera*;
1986, Batignano Festival, *Il Ritorno
d'Ulisse in Patria*; 1987, Victorian State
Opera, Melbourne, *Le Nozze di Figaro*;
1988, Scottish Opera, *The Pearl Fishers*;
1991: Opera Factory, *The Marriage of
Figaro*; State Opera of South Australia,
Adelaide, *Don Giovanni*.

OPERATIC WORLD PREMIERES INCLUDE:
1971, Oxford University Opera, *The
Duchess of Malfi* by Stephen Oliver.

OPERA PERFORMANCES IN THE UK
INCLUDE: Since 1981: English National
Opera: *Don Giovanni, Orfeo, Mireille,
Madam Butterfly, Otello, Così fan tutte,*

*The Marriage of Figaro, Orpheus in the
Underworld, Mary Stuart, The Mikado,
The Mastersingers of Nuremberg, Simon
Boccanegra, Hansel and Gretel, The Turn
of the Screw*; Kent Opera, *Don Giovanni*;
Opera Factory, *The Coronation of
Poppea*.

RELATED PROFESSIONAL ACTIVITIES:
Guest conductor: 1985 and 1989, Royal
Academy of Music; 1988, Guildhall School
of Music and Drama; since 1981, teacher
and coach, National Opera Studio.

RECORDINGS INCLUDE: Sullivan, *The
Mikado* (TER).

VIDEOS INCLUDE: Sullivan, *The Mikado*
(English National Opera).

ADDRESS: 69 Fordwych Road, London NW2
3TL.

ROBSON CHRISTOPHER
Counter-tenor

PERSONAL DETAILS: b. 9 December 1953,
Falkirk, Scotland; m. 1974, Laura Snelling
(m. diss).

EDUCATION/TRAINING: 1970–1972,
Cambridgeshire College of Arts and
Technology; 1973–1974, Trinity College of
Music; privately with Paul Esswood and
Helga Mott; masterclasses with Geoffrey
Parsons, Peter Pears, Laura Sarti,
Thomas Helmsley and John Shirley-
Quirk.

PROFESSIONAL DEBUT: 1976, Queen
Elizabeth Hall, concert performance,
Samson.

EARLY CAREER INCLUDED: 1979–1983:
Barber Institute, Birmingham, Argone,
Sosarme (1979, operatic debut); Abbey
Opera, Oberon, *A Midsummer Night's
Dream*; Handel Opera Society, Lichas,
Hercules; Kent Opera, Narciso,
Agrippina; Phoenix Opera at the Camden
Festival, Dione, *Eritrea* (1982, British
première).

MAJOR DEBUTS INCLUDE: 1981, English
National Opera, Shepherd, *Orfeo*; 1984:
Opera Factory, Endymion, *La Calisto*; title
role, *Akhnaten*: Houston Grand Opera,
New York City Opera; 1986: Frankfurt

Opera, Cupid, *Orpheus in the Underworld*; Innsbruck, Corindo, *Orontea*; 1988: Covent Garden, Athamas, *Semele*; Berlin Kammeroper, title role, *Orlando*; 1990, English National Opera Soviet Union tour (Bolshoi and Kiev), Arsamene, *Xerxes* (first counter-tenor to make stage debut in Soviet Union); 1991, Nancy Opera, Voice of Apollo, *Death in Venice*; 1992, Scottish Opera, Tolomeo, *Julius Caesar*.

OPERATIC WORLD PREMIERES INCLUDE: 1983, Opera Factory, Zurich, Gringoire, *Der Glöckner von Notre-Dame* by Howard Goodall; 1989, Almeida Festival, Ometh, *Golem* by John Casken.

CAREER IN THE UK INCLUDES: Since 1984: English National Opera: Arsamene, *Xerxes*; Edgar, *Lear* (1989, British première); Polinesso, *Ariodante*; title roles: *Akhnaten* (1985, British première), *Julius Caesar*; Opera Factory, Habinnas, *Satyricon* (1990, British première); Northern Stage, Ometh, *Golem*.

RELATED PROFESSIONAL ACTIVITIES: Regular concerts and recitals in the UK and abroad; member: 1974–1980, Brompton Oratory Choir; 1974–1985, Monteverdi Choir; 1980–1984, Westminster Cathedral Choir; 1981–1986, Kings Consort; since 1985, New London Consort; project work for Opera in Focus/ Baylis Programme at English National Opera; 1988, recorded Ariel's songs for Royal National Theatre's production of *The Tempest*.

RECORDINGS INCLUDE: Casken, *Golem* (VIRG); Handel, *Messiah* (CHAN); Monteverdi: *Orfeo, Vespers* (both DECC); Purcell, *Come Ye Sons of Art* (VIRG); Schütz, *Auferstehungs Historia* (SONY); Tippett, *The Ice Break* (VIRG); Vivaldi, *Nisi Dominus* (MERI).

VIDEOS INCLUDE: Handel, *Xerxes* (English National Opera).

AWARDS INCLUDE: 1979, Greater London Arts Association Young Musicians Prize.

ADDRESS: c/o Music International, 13 Ardilaun Road, London N5 2QR.

ROBSON NIGEL　　Tenor

PERSONAL DETAILS: b. Argyllshire.

EDUCATION/TRAINING: University of York; Royal Northern College of Music, with Alexander Young.

PROFESSIONAL DEBUT: 1977, chorus member, Glyndebourne Festival Opera.

EARLY CAREER INCLUDED: 1977–1983, appearances with Glyndebourne Touring Opera, New Opera Company, Oxford University Opera; roles included: Schoolmaster, *The Cunning Little Vixen*; Sellem, *The Rake's Progress*; Harlequin, *Commedia* (1982, New Opera Company, British première); Orfeo, *Orfeo ed Euridice*.

MAJOR DEBUTS INCLUDE: 1981, English National Opera, Apollo, *Orfeo*; 1982, Opera Factory, Lawyer, *Punch and Judy*; 1985, Lyons Opera, Bajazet, *Tamerlano*; 1988, Göttingen Handel Festival, title role, *Jephtha*; 1989, Opera North, Don Anchise, *La Finta Giardiniera*; 1990, Glyndebourne Festival Opera, Presenter, *New Year* (British première); 1991, Teatro La Zarzuela, Madrid, Arbace, *Idomeneo*; 1992, Scottish Opera, Captain Vere, *Billy Budd*.

OPERATIC WORLD PREMIERES INCLUDE: 1985, Arundel Festival, Mordred, *Lancelot* by Iain Hamilton; 1986: English National Opera, Orpheus the Myth/Hades, *The Mask of Orpheus* by Harrison Birtwistle; Opera Factory, several roles, *Hell's Angels* by Nigel Osborne; 1988, Théâtre de la Bastille, Paris, Leader, *The Undivine Comedy* by Michael Finnissy.

CAREER IN THE UK INCLUDES: Since 1984: Abbey Opera at the Camden Festival, title role, *The Protaganist* (1986, British stage première); Buxton Festival, Marchese, *La Buona Figliuola*; Opera Factory: Dov, *The Knot Garden*; Linfea and Pan, *La Calisto*; Colonel, *The Ghost Sonata* (1989, British première); Don Ottavio, *Don Giovanni*; Ferrando, *Così fan tutte*; Nero, *The Coronation of Poppea*; title role, *The Martyrdom of St Magnus*; Opera North, Captain Vere, *Billy Budd*; Scottish Opera, Gregor, *The Makropoulos Case*.

241

RELATED PROFESSIONAL ACTIVITIES: Regular concerts, recitals, broadcasts and television appearances in the UK and abroad; particularly associated with the Monteverdi Choir and Orchestra.
RECORDINGS INCLUDE: Handel: *Alexander's Feast, Jephtha* (both PHIL), *Tamerlano* (ERAT); Monteverdi: *Orfeo* (DG), *Vespers*; Mozart, *Idomeneo* (both ARCH); Tippett, *Songs for Dov* (VIRG).
ADDRESS: c/o Ingpen & Williams Ltd, 14 Kensington Court, London W8 5DN.

RODEN ANTHONY   Tenor

PERSONAL DETAILS: b. Adelaide, Australia; m. Doreen Cryer (mezzo-soprano).
PREVIOUS OCCUPATION: 1960–1968, insurance executive.
EDUCATION/TRAINING: 1965–1968, Elder Conservatorium of Music, Adelaide, with Arnold Matters; 1969–1970, London Opera Centre, with Alexander Young.
PROFESSIONAL DEBUT: 1971, Glyndebourne Touring Opera, Lensky, *Eugene Onegin*.
MAJOR DEBUTS INCLUDE: 1972, Krefeld/ Mönchengladbach, Ottavio, *Don Giovanni*; 1973: Glyndebourne Festival Opera, Tamino, *Die Zauberflöte*; Welsh National Opera, Idamante, *Idomeneo*; 1974, English National Opera, Ferrando, *Così fan tutte*; 1976, National Theatre, Prague, Tamino, *Die Zauberflöte*; 1977, Kent Opera, title role, *Idomeneo*; 1981, Opera North, Macduff, *Macbeth*; 1982, Victoria State Opera, Melbourne, Samson, *Samson et Dalila*; title role, *Peter Grimes*: 1988, Covent Garden; 1990, Freiburg.
OPERATIC WORLD PREMIERES INCLUDE: 1977, English National Opera, Diego, *The Royal Hunt of the Sun* by Iain Hamilton; 1984, Victoria State Opera, Melbourne, Lawrence Hargreave, *Fly* by Barry Conyngham.
CAREER IN THE UK INCLUDES: Since 1972: City of Birmingham Touring Opera, Soliman, *Zaide*; Covent Garden: First Armed Man, *Die Zauberflöte*; Hunchback Brother, *Die Frau ohne Schatten*; English

National Opera: Alfred, *Die Fledermaus*; Tamino, *The Magic Flute*; Camille, *The Merry Widow*; Italian Tenor, *Der Rosenkavalier*; Don Ottavio, *Don Giovanni*; Count, *The Barber of Seville*; Glyndebourne Festival and Touring Opera: Belmonte, *Die Entführung aus dem Serail*; High Priest, *Idomeneo*; Captain and Gabriele, *Simon Boccanegra*; Kent Opera, Pylade, *Iphigenia in Tauris*; Opera North: Tichon, *Katya Kabanova*; Ismaele, *Nabucco*; title role, *Oedipus Rex*; Scottish Opera: Don Ottavio, *Don Giovanni*; Lensky, *Eugene Onegin*; Welsh National Opera: Belmonte, *The Seraglio*; Florestan, *Fidelio*; title role, *Idomeneo*.
RECORDINGS INCLUDE: Conyngham, *Fly*; Handel, *Scipio* (both Australian labels).
VIDEOS INCLUDE: Mozart: *Die Entführung aus dem Serail, Idomeneo* (both Glyndebourne Festival Opera).
AWARDS INCLUDE: 1971, John Christie Award.
ADDRESS: c/o Patricia Greenan, 19B Belsize Park, London NW3 4DU.

RODGERS JOAN   Soprano

PERSONAL DETAILS: b. 4 November 1956, Cumbria; m. 1988, Paul Daniel (Music Director, Opera North), one child.
EDUCATION/TRAINING: University of Liverpool, studied Russian; Royal Northern College of Music, with Joseph Ward; currently with Audrey Langford.
PROFESSIONAL DEBUT: 1982, Aix-en-Provence Festival, Pamina, *Die Zauberflöte*.
MAJOR DEBUTS INCLUDE: 1983: Covent Garden, Princess, *L'Enfant et les Sortilèges*; English National Opera, Wood Nymph, *Rusalka*; Schwetzingen Festival, Arbate, *Mitridate, Rè di Ponto*; Tatyana, *Eugene Onegin*: 1984, Lyons Opera; 1985, Vancouver Opera; 1986: Teatro Regio, Turin, Ilia, *Idomeneo*; Théâtre des Champs Elysées, Paris (Mostly Mozart Festival), Despina, *Così fan tutte*; 1987: Scottish Opera, Susanna, *The Marriage of*

Figaro; Zurich Opera, Zerlina, *Don Giovanni*; 1988: Opera North, Mimi, *La Bohème*; Netherlands Opera, Zerlina, *Don Giovanni*; 1989, Glyndebourne Festival Opera, Susanna, *Le Nozze di Figaro*; 1990: Bavarian State Opera, Munich, Pamina, *Die Zauberflöte*; Opéra Bastille, Paris, Susanna, *Le Nozze di Figaro*; Maggio Musicale, Florence: 1991, Despina, *Cosi fan tutte*; 1992, Susanna, *Le Nozze di Figaro*.

CAREER IN THE UK INCLUDES: Since 1983: Covent Garden: Xenia, *Boris Godunov*; Echo, *Ariadne auf Naxos*; Zerlina, *Don Giovanni*; Servilia, *La Clemenza di Tito*; Pamina, *Die Zauberflöte*; English National Opera: Pamina, *The Magic Flute*; Gilda, *Rigoletto*; Nannetta, *Falstaff*; Countess, *The Marriage of Figaro*; Opera North, title role, *Yolande*; Scottish Opera, Cleopatra, *Julius Caesar*.

RELATED PROFESSIONAL ACTIVITIES: Numerous concerts, recitals, broadcasts and television appearances in the UK and abroad; 1987, translator with Paul Daniel, *The Stone Guest* (English National Opera).

RECORDINGS INCLUDE: Mozart: *Cosi fan tutte, Don Giovanni, Le Nozze di Figaro* (all ERAT).

VIDEOS INCLUDE: Mozart, *Mitridate, Rè di Ponto* (film by Jean-Pierre Ponnelle).

AWARDS INCLUDE: 1981, Kathleen Ferrier Memorial Scholarship.

ADDRESS: c/o Ingpen & Williams Ltd, 14 Kensington Court, London W8 5DN.

ROEBUCK JANINE
Mezzo-soprano

PERSONAL DETAILS: b. 5 January 1954, Barnsley.

EDUCATION/TRAINING: 1972–1976, University of Manchester, studied French; 1977–1981, Royal Northern College of Music, with Nicholas Powell and Frederic Cox; 1981–1982, Paris Conservatoire, with Régine Crespin; 1982–1983, National Opera Studio, with David Harper; currently with Edgar Evans.

PROFESSIONAL DEBUT: 1984, New Sadler's Wells Opera, Manja, *Countess Maritza*.

MAJOR DEBUTS INCLUDE: 1984, Opera 80, title role, *The Italian Girl in Algiers*; 1985: Buxton Festival, Paoluccia, *La Buona Figliuola*; Scottish Opera, Lucille, *The Silken Ladder* and Clarina, *The Marriage Contract*; 1989: Covent Garden, Coryphée, *Alceste*; Batignano Festival, Eduige, *Rodelinda*.

CAREER IN THE UK INCLUDES: Since 1984: Craig-y-nos, Suzuki, *Madam Butterfly*; Dorset Opera, Tebaldo, *Don Carlos*; D'Oyly Carte Opera: Pitti-Sing, *The Mikado*; Phoebe, *The Yeomen of the Guard*; English Bach Festival, First Witch, *Dido and Aeneas*; New Sadler's Wells Opera: Tessa, *The Gondoliers*; Hebe, *HMS Pinafore*; Pitti-Sing, *The Mikado*; Olga, *The Merry Widow*; Flora, *La Traviata*; Pavilion Opera: Dorabella, *Cosi fan tutte*; Maddalena, *Rigoletto*; Scottish Opera, Grimgerde, *Die Walküre*.

RELATED PROFESSIONAL ACTIVITIES: Numerous concerts, recitals and broadcasts in the UK.

RECORDINGS INCLUDE: Lehàr, *The Merry Widow*; Sullivan, *HMS Pinafore* (both TER).

ADDRESS: c/o Music International, 13 Ardilaun Road, London N5 2QR.

ROGER DAVID   Designer

POSITION: Associate Designer, Opera Factory, London and Zurich.

PERSONAL DETAILS: b. 23 February 1951, Edinburgh.

PREVIOUS OCCUPATION: 1975–1977, social worker.

EDUCATION/TRAINING: 1970–1973, University of Newcastle, studied German; 1973–1974, University of Bristol, studied modern German drama; 1977–1978, University of Vincennes, scenographic studies; 1979–1980, English National Opera, Theatre Design School.

PROFESSIONAL DEBUT: 1980, Lyric Theatre, Belfast, *A Yeats Cycle*.

OPERATIC DEBUT: 1984, Freiburg, *Le Grand Macabre*.

CAREER: Since 1980, freelance theatre and opera designer for numerous companies including Soho Poly, Royal Court Theatre and Theatre Royal, Stratford East; since 1984, Assocate Designer, Opera Factory London and Zurich.

MAJOR OPERATIC DEBUTS INCLUDE: 1984, Opera Factory, *The Knot Garden*; 1985, English National Opera, *Akhnaten* (British première); 1986, Opera North, *La Bohème*; 1991/1992, Kirov Opera/Covent Garden co-production, *The Fiery Angel* (also 1992, Metropolitan Opera, New York).

OPERATIC WORLD PREMIERES INCLUDE: 1986, Opera Factory: *Hell's Angels* by Nigel Osborne, *Yan Tan Tethera* by Harrison Birtwistle; 1991, Opera Factory Zurich, *Julia* by Rudolf Kelterborn.

OPERA DESIGNS IN THE UK INCLUDE: Since 1984: English National Opera, *The Return of Ulysses*; Opera Factory: *La Calisto*, *Così fan tutte*, *Eight Songs for a Mad King*, *Aventures et Nouvelles Aventures*, *Iphigenias*, *The Ghost Sonata* (1989, British première), *Don Giovanni*, *The Marriage of Figaro*, *The Coronation of Poppea*; Opera Factory Zurich at the Queen Elizabeth Hall, *Julia* (1991, British première).

RELATED PROFESSIONAL ACTIVITIES: Opera Factory productions designed for Channel Four Television include: *The Marriage of Figaro*, *Così fan tutte*, *Don Giovanni*.

ADDRESS: c/o Garricks, 7 Garrick Street, London WC2E 9AR.

ROLFE JOHNSON ANTHONY
Tenor

POSITIONS: Director of Vocal Studies, Britten-Pears School for Advanced Musical Studies; Artistic Director, Gregynog Festival, Wales.

PERSONAL DETAILS: b. 5 November 1940, Oxfordshire.

EDUCATION/TRAINING: Guildhall School of Music and Drama; privately with Vera Rozsa; currently with Diane Forlano in Chicago.

OPERATIC DEBUT: 1973, English Opera Group, Vaudemont, *Iolanta*.

EARLY CAREER INCLUDED: 1974–1977: English Opera Group/English Music Theatre: Tamino, *The Magic Flute*; title role, *Albert Herring*; Glyndebourne Touring Opera: Lensky, *Eugene Onegin*; Fenton, *Falstaff*; Handel Opera Society: Jupiter, *Semele*; Lurcanio, *Ariodante*; Acis, *Acis and Galatea*.

MAJOR DEBUTS INCLUDE: 1974, Glyndebourne Festival Opera, Stroh, *Intermezzo*; 1978, English National Opera, Don Ottavio, *Don Giovanni*; 1979: Scottish Opera, Lensky, *Eugene Onegin*; Welsh National Opera, Tamino, *The Magic Flute*; 1981, Karlsruhe, Jupiter, *Semele*; 1983: Grand Théâtre, Geneva, Aschenbach, *Death in Venice*; Netherlands Opera, title role, *La Clemenza di Tito*; Salzburg Mozart Week, Polidoro, *La Finta Semplice*; 1984: Aix-en-Provence Festival, Podestà, *La Finta Giardiniera*; La Monnaie, Brussels, Pelléas, *Pelléas et Mélisande*; La Scala, Milan, title role, *Lucio Silla*; 1986, Opera North, title role, *The Rake's Progress*; Hamburg State Opera, title role, *La Clemenza di Tito*; 1988, Covent Garden, Jupiter, *Semele*; 1991, title role, *Idomeneo*: Salzburg Festival, Vienna State Opera and Metropolitan Opera, New York.

CAREER IN THE UK INCLUDES: Since 1978: Covent Garden, Oronte, *Alcina*; English National Opera: Tamino, *The Magic Flute*; Belmonte, *The Seraglio*; Ferrando, *Così fan tutte*; Male Chorus, *The Rape of Lucretia*; Essex, *Gloriana*; Des Grieux, *Manon*; title roles: Orfeo, *The Return of Ulysses*; Scottish Opera at the Edinburgh International Festival, Aschenbach, *Death in Venice*; Spitalfields Festival, Renaud, *Armide*; Welsh National Opera: Lensky, *Eugene Onegin*; Bajazet, *Tamburlaine* (Handel).

RELATED PROFESSIONAL ACTIVITIES:
Regular concerts, recitals, broadcasts
and television appearances in the UK and
abroad.

RECORDINGS INCLUDE: Britten, *Peter
Grimes* (EMI); Handel: *Acis and Galatea*
(ORFE), *Athalia, Esther* (both L'OI), *Israel in
Egypt* (EMI), *Jephtha* (DECC), *Messiah*
(PHIL), *Saul* (TELD), *Solomon* (PHIL);
Monteverdi, *Orfeo* (ARCH); Mozart: *La
Clemenza di Tito, Idomeneo* (both ARCH),
La Finta Semplice (ORFE), *Lucio Silla*
(RICE), *Die Zauberflöte* (EMI); Stravinsky:
Oedipus Rex (EMI), *Pulcinella* (ERAT);
Sullivan, *The Mikado* (TELA).

VIDEOS INCLUDE: Britten: *Gloriana, The
Rape of Lucretia* (both English National
Opera).

AWARDS AND HONOURS INCLUDE: 1972,
The Friends of Covent Garden Dame Eva
Turner Award; 1975, John Christie Award;
1992, Commander, Order of the British
Empire (CBE).

ADDRESS: c/o Lies Askonas Ltd, 186 Drury
Lane, London WC2B 5RY.

ROOCROFT AMANDA
Soprano

PERSONAL DETAILS: b. 9 February 1966,
Lancashire.

EDUCATION/TRAINING: 1985–1989, Royal
Northern College of Music, with Barbara
Robotham.

PROFESSIONAL DEBUT: 1990, Welsh
National Opera, Sophie, Der
Rosenkavalier.

MAJOR DEBUTS INCLUDE: Pamina, *Die
Zauberflöte*: 1990, Glyndebourne Touring
Opera; 1991, Covent Garden; Fiordiligi,
Così fan tutte: 1991, Glyndebourne
Festival Opera; 1992: Netherlands Opera;
Teatro Comunale, Ferrara; Teatro São
Carlos, Lisbon; Théâtre du Châtelet,
Paris; 1992, Covent Garden, Giulietta, *I
Capuleti e i Montecchi*; 1993, English
National Opera, Ginevra, *Ariodante*.

RELATED PROFESSIONAL ACTIVITIES:
Television appearances include 1989 and
1991, *A Girl from Coppull* (documentary
for Granada).

RECORDINGS INCLUDE: Mozart, *Così fan
tutte* (ARCH); Vaughan Williams, *Serenade
to Music* (HYPE).

AWARDS INCLUDE: 1988: Frederic Cox
Award, Royal Northern College of Music;
Decca-Kathleen Ferrier Prize; 1990, Royal
Philharmonic Society/Charles Heidsieck
Debut Award.

ADDRESS: c/o Ingpen & Williams Ltd, 14
Kensington Court, London W8 5DN.

ROSE PETER   Bass

PERSONAL DETAILS: b. 27 March 1961,
Canterbury.

EDUCATION/TRAINING: 1979–1982,
University of East Anglia, studied music;
1982–1985, Guildhall School of Music and
Drama, with Ellis Keeler; 1985–1986,
National Opera Studio.

PROFESSIONAL DEBUT: 1986, Glyndebourne
Festival Opera at the Hong Kong Arts
Festival, Commendatore, *Don Giovanni*.

EARLY CAREER INCLUDED: 1986–1989:
Principal Bass, Welsh National Opera:
Bartolo, *Le Nozze di Figaro*; Angelotti,
Tosca; Prince Gremin, *Eugene Onegin*;
Osmin, *The Seraglio*; also, Glyndebourne
Touring Opera: Commendatore, *Don
Giovanni*; Don Inigo, *L'Heure Espagnole*;
Osmin, *The Seraglio*; Don Basilio, *Il
Barbiere di Siviglia*.

MAJOR DEBUTS INCLUDE: 1988: Covent
Garden, Rochefort, *Anna Bolena*; English
National Opera, Angelotti, *Tosca*; 1990:
Scottish Opera, Narbal, *The Trojans* (also
at Covent Garden); Maggio Musicale,
Florence, Commendatore, *Don Giovanni*;
1991: Netherlands Opera, Walter, *Luisa
Miller*; San Francisco Opera,
Commendatore, *Don Giovanni*; 1992:
Lyric Opera, Chicago, Kecal, *The
Bartered Bride*; Pittsburgh Opera,
Abimelech, *Samson et Dalila*; Salzburg
Festival, First Nazarene, *Salome*; 1992,

Aix-en-Provence Festival, Bottom, *A Midsummer Night's Dream*.

CAREER IN THE UK INCLUDES: Since 1989: Covent Garden: Lodovico, *Otello*; Orest's Tutor, *Elektra*; Nightwatchman, *Die Meistersinger von Nürnberg*; English National Opera, The King of Clubs, *The Love for Three Oranges*; Glyndebourne Festival Opera: Trulove, *The Rake's Progress*; Publio, *La Clemenza di Tito*; Commendatore, *Don Giovanni*; Welsh National Opera: Tutor, *Count Ory*; King Marke, *Tristan und Isolde* (also 1993, at Covent Garden); Baldassare, *La Favorita*.

RELATED PROFESSIONAL ACTIVITIES: Concerts with leading conductors and orchestras in the UK and abroad.

RECORDINGS INCLUDE: Mozart: *Don Giovanni* (SONY), *Le Nozze di Figaro* (ERAT).

AWARDS INCLUDE: 1985: Gold Medal, Guildhall School of Music and Drama; Kathleen Ferrier Memorial Scholarship; 1986, John Christie Award.

ADDRESS: c/o Harrison/Parrott Ltd, 12 Penzance Place, London W11 4PA.

ROZARIO PATRICIA   Soprano

PERSONAL DETAILS: b. Bombay, India; m. Mark Troop (pianist), one child.

EDUCATION/TRAINING: 1975–1979, Guildhall School of Music and Drama, with Walther Gruner; National Opera Studio; since 1980, privately with Vera Rozsa.

PROFESSIONAL DEBUT: 1979, Opera Viva, Rosina, *The Triumph of Honour.*

MAJOR DEBUTS INCLUDE: 1982, Netherlands Opera, Giulietta, *La Schiava Liberata*; 1983, Batignano Festival, Tolomeo, *La Dori*; 1984: Opera North, Eurydice, *Orpheus and Eurydice*; Innsbruck Festival, Florinda, *Rodrigo*; 1985, Glyndebourne Touring Opera, Ilia, *Idomeneo*; 1986: Kent Opera, Nero, *The Coronation of Poppea*; Aix-en-Provence Festival, Zerlina, *Don Giovanni*; Ismene, *Mitridate, Rè di Ponto*: 1986, Lyons Opera; 1989, Wexford Festival; 1992, Ludwigsburg, Pamina, *Die Zauberflöte*;

1993, English National Opera, Clorinda, *The Duel of Tancredi and Clorinda*.

OPERATIC WORLD PREMIÈRES INCLUDE: 1989, Almeida Festival, Miriam, *Golem* by John Casken; 1992, Aldeburgh Festival, title role, *Mary of Egypt* by John Tavener.

CAREER IN THE UK INCLUDES: Since 1985: Kent Opera: Statue, *Pygmalion* and Belinda, *Dido and Aeneas*; Pamina, *The Magic Flute*; Countess Adele, *Count Ory*; Marzelline, *Fidelio*; Mecklenburgh Opera, Hanka, *Petrified* (1992, British première); Northern Stage, Miriam, *Golem*; Opera North, Sophie, *Werther*; Park Lane Opera, Rosina, *La Finta Semplice*.

RELATED PROFESSIONAL ACTIVITIES: Regular concerts, recitals and broadcasts with leading conductors and orchestras in the UK and abroad.

RECORDINGS INCLUDE: Canteloube, *Songs of the Auvergne* (PICK); Casken, *Golem* (VIRG); Haydn, *Stabat Mater* (ARCH); Mahler, Symphony No. 4; Respighi, choral works (both COLL); Satie, *Socrate-drame symphonique* (FACT).

AWARDS INCLUDE: 1979, Maggie Teyte Prize.

ADDRESS: c/o Lies Askonas Ltd, 186 Drury Lane, London WC2B 5RY.

ROZSA VERA
Teacher (formerly Mezzo-soprano)

POSITION: Consultant Professor, Guildhall School of Music and Drama.

PERSONAL DETAILS: b. Budapest, Hungary; m. Ralph Nordell, one child.

EDUCATION/TRAINING: Franz Liszt Academy of Music, Budapest, diploma in performance and teaching; studied composition with Zoltán Kodály in Budapest; vocal studies with Sergio Nasor in Vienna.

PROFESSIONAL DEBUT: 1945, Budapest State Opera, Hänsel, *Hänsel und Gretel*.

CAREER INCLUDES: Appearances with Budapest State Opera, Vienna State Opera and at many international festivals; roles included: Rosina, *Il Barbiere di Siviglia*; Fyodor, *Boris Godunov*;

Mercédès, *Carmen*; Nicklausse, *Les Contes d'Hoffmann*; Prince Orlofsky, *Die Fledermaus*; Cherubino, *Le Nozze di Figaro*; Maddalena, *Rigoletto*; Azucena, *Il Trovatore*; concerts, oratorios, recitals and broadcasts with leading orchestras and conductors in Europe and USA; 1975, retired from singing; Senior Lecturer: 1965–1970, Royal Manchester College of Music; 1975–1980, Opera Studio, Paris; since 1980, Consultant Professor, Guildhall School of Music and Drama; masterclasses at festivals, music schools and universities worldwide including Aix-en-Provence, Aldeburgh, Centre de Musique Baroque (Versailles), European Opera Centre (Belgium), Jerusalem Music Academy, Stockholm Opera Studio, Sibelius Academy (Helsinki), universities in Arizona, Colorado, Indiana, San Francisco, Utah, Australia and New Zealand; coach for several choirs including City of Birmingham Symphony Orchestra and BRT Orchestra (Brussels).

STUDENTS HAVE INCLUDED: Nancy Argenta, Ingrid Attrot, Nan Christie, Helena Dose, Enid Hartle, Anne Howells, Karita Mattila, Alan Opie, Anne-Sofie von Otter, Anthony Rolfe Johnson, Patricia Rozario, Anna Steiger, Kiri Te Kanawa, Sarah Walker, Lillian Watson.

RELEVANT PUBLICATIONS INCLUDE: 1982, *Kiri* by David Fingleton (Collins).

HONOURS INCLUDE: 1989, Officer, Order of the British Empire (OBE); 1990, Fellow, Guildhall School of Music and Drama.

ADDRESS: c/o Guildhall School of Music and Drama, Barbican, London EC2Y 8DT.

* * * *

SADIE STANLEY
Critic and Writer

PERSONAL DETAILS: b. 30 October 1930, Middlesex; m. 1953, Adele Bloom (d. 1978), three children; m. 1978, Julie Anne Vertrees, (musician and writer), two children.

EDUCATION/TRAINING: 1950–1956, Gonville and Caius College, Cambridge, studied music.

CAREER: 1957–1965, professor, Trinity College of Music; 1964–1981, Music Critic, *The Times*; since 1981, freelance critic and writer; Editor: 1967–1987, *Musical Times*; since 1970, The New Grove Dictionaries; since 1976, *Master Musicians* series; 1984–1991, music consultant, *Man and Music* (Granada Television); Royal Musical Association: 1985–1989, Vice-president; since 1989, President; member: since 1955, International Musicological Society; since 1963, Critics' Circle; since 1970, American Musicological Society; since 1987, Directorium.

PUBLICATIONS INCLUDE: 1962, *Handel*; 1966, *Mozart* (both Calder); 1966, with Arthur Jacobs, *The Pan Book of Opera*; *The Great Composers*: 1967, *Beethoven*; 1968, *Handel* (both Faber); Editor: 1980, *The New Grove Dictionary of Music and Musicians*; 1982, *Mozart*, *The New Grove Biographies*; 1984, *The New Grove Dictionary of Musical Instruments*; 1986, with H. Wiley Hitchcock, *The New Grove Dictionary of American Music*; 1988, *The New Grove Concise Dictionary of Music*; 1989, The New Grove Handbook in Music series: *The History of Opera*; with H. M. Brown, *Performance Practice* (two vols); with D. W. Krummel, *Music Printing and Publishing*; 1992, *The New Grove Dictionary of Opera* (all Macmillan); 1985, with Alison Latham, *The Cambridge Music Guide* (Cambridge University Press); contributor: *Gramophone*, *Musical Times*, *Opera*.

HONOURS INCLUDE: 1981: Honorary Member, Royal Academy of Music; Honorary Doctorate of Literature, University of Leicester; 1982:

Commander, Order of the British Empire (CBE); Fellow, Royal Society of Arts.

ADDRESS: 12 Lyndhurst Road, London NW3 5NL.

SAMS JEREMY
Translator, Composer and Répétiteur

PERSONAL DETAILS: b. 12 January 1957, London.

EDUCATION/TRAINING: 1975–1978, Magdalene College, Cambridge; 1978–1979, Guildhall School of Music and Drama.

CAREER: Translator of plays and operas including: *Figaro's Wedding*, *The Force of Destiny*, *Macbeth*, *The Magic Flute* (all English National Opera), *Così fan tutte* (Kent Opera and English Touring Opera), *L'Etoile*, *Johnny Strikes Up*, *Orpheus in the Underworld*, *The Thieving Magpie* (all Opera North); composer of over 30 television and theatre scores notably for Royal National Theatre and Royal Shakespeare Company; freelance répétiteur in the UK and abroad.

PUBLICATIONS INCLUDE: Translation: *Macbeth* (Calder); contributor on French opera: *The New Grove Dictionary of Opera* (Macmillan), *The Penguin Opera Guide*.

ADDRESS: c/o Michael Imison Playwrights Ltd, 28 Almeida Street, London N1 1TD.

SANDISON GORDON
Baritone

PERSONAL DETAILS: b. 13 August 1949, Aberdeen; m. 1984, Yvonne Lea (mezzo-soprano), two children.

EDUCATION/TRAINING: 1967–1973, Royal Scottish Academy of Music and Drama, with David Kelly (diplomas in music and drama).

PROFESSIONAL DEBUT: 1973, Scottish Opera, Cascada, *The Merry Widow*.

EARLY CAREER INCLUDED: Principal Baritone: 1973–1979, Scottish Opera; 1979–1980, Aachen Opera; roles included: Schaunard, *La Bohème*; Malatesta, Don *Pasquale*; Belcore, *The Elixir of Love*; Harlequin, *Ariadne auf Naxos*; title roles: *The Barber of Seville*, *The Marriage of Figaro*, *Don Giovanni*.

MAJOR DEBUTS INCLUDE: 1981, Wexford Festival, Osmin, *Zaide*; 1982, Glyndebourne Festival Opera, Masetto, *Don Giovanni*; 1984, Covent Garden, Fléville, *Andrea Chénier*; 1986, Théâtre du Châtelet, Paris, title role, *Il Signor Bruschino*.

CAREER IN THE UK INCLUDES: Since 1980: Buxton Festival: Tagliaferro, *La Buona Figliuola*; Don Parmenione, *L'Occasione fa il Ladro*; Baron Cricca, *Il Pittor Parigino*; Covent Garden: Duphol, *La Traviata*; Starveling, *A Midsummer Night's Dream*; Mandarin, *Turandot* (also 1986, Far East tour); Morales, *Carmen*; Masetto, *Don Giovanni*; Burgher of Calais, *The King Goes Forth to France* (1987, British première); Zaretsky, *Eugene Onegin*; Benoit, *La Bohème*; Sciarrone, *Tosca*; English National Opera: Harlequin, *Ariadne auf Naxos*; Mayor, *Christmas Eve*; Glyndebourne Festival and Touring Opera: Dancaïro, *Carmen*; Duphol, *La Traviata*; Mayor, *Jenůfa*; title role, *Il Barbiere di Siviglia*; Kent Opera: Count, *The Marriage of Figaro*; Jim Cocks, *Robinson Crusoe*; title role, *The Barber of Seville*; New Sadler's Wells Opera: Sir Tristram Mickelford, *Martha*; Robin, *Ruddigore*; Corcoran, *HMS Pinafore*; Opera North, Belcore, *The Elixir of Love*; Scottish Opera: Papageno, *The Magic Flute*; Falke, *Die Fledermaus*; Mr Flint, *Billy Budd*; Don Alfonso, *Così fan tutte*; title role, *Falstaff*.

RELATED PROFESSIONAL ACTIVITIES: Numerous concerts, broadcasts and television appearances in the UK and abroad.

RECORDINGS INCLUDE: Bizet, *Carmen* (DG).

VIDEOS INCLUDE: Giordano, *Andrea Chénier* (Covent Garden); Bizet, *Carmen*; Janáček, *Jenůfa*; Mozart, *Don Giovanni*;

Verdi, *La Traviata* (all Glyndebourne
Festival Opera).
ADDRESS: c/o Lies Askonas Ltd, 186 Drury
Lane, London WC2B 5RY.

SAVIDGE PETER   Baritone

PERSONAL DETAILS: b. Essex; m., three
children.
EDUCATION/TRAINING: 1971–1974, Corpus
Christi College, Cambridge, studied
history; 1974–1975, Guildhall School of
Music and Drama.
PROFESSIONAL DEBUT: 1976, English Music
Theatre, Papageno, *The Magic Flute*.
EARLY CAREER INCLUDED: 1977–1979,
English Music Theatre: Mr Gedge, *Albert
Herring*; Dandini, *Cinderella*; Roberto/
Nardo, *Sandrina's Secret*; English Clerk,
Death in Venice (also at Covent Garden).
MAJOR DEBUTS INCLUDE: 1979, Covent
Garden, Novice's Friend, *Billy Budd*;
1982, Welsh National Opera, Leone,
Tamburlaine (Handel); 1984, Opera North,
Macheath, *The Threepenny Opera*; 1991,
Nancy Opera, Traveller, *Death in Venice*;
1992, Singapore Opera, title role, *The
Barber of Seville*.
CAREER IN THE UK INCLUDES: Since 1979:
Covent Garden: Flemish Deputy, *Don
Carlos*; Ned Keene, *Peter Grimes*; Opera
North: Giuseppe, *The Gondoliers*; Leone,
Tamburlaine (Handel); Storch,
Intermezzo; Count, *The Marriage of
Figaro*; Jack Favell, *Rebecca*; Count
Danilo, *The Merry Widow*; Marcello, *La
Bohème*; Nardo, *La Finta Giardiniera*;
Valentin, *Faust*; Ned Keene, *Peter
Grimes*; Gaylord Ravenal, *Show Boat*;
title roles: *Don Giovanni*, *The Barber of
Seville*; Welsh National Opera: Papageno,
The Magic Flute; Count Danilo, *The Merry
Widow*; Guglielmo, *Così fan tutte*;
Schaunard and Marcello, *La Bohème*;
Harlequin, *Ariadne auf Naxos*; Count, *The
Marriage of Figaro*; Eisenstein, *Die
Fledermaus*.

RELATED PROFESSIONAL ACTIVITIES:
Regular concerts, recitals, broadcasts
and festival appearances in the UK and
abroad.
RECORDINGS INCLUDE: Handel, *Hercules*
(ARCH).
VIDEOS INCLUDE: Sullivan: *The Gondoliers*,
Princess Ida, *The Yeomen of the Guard*
(all Walker).
AWARDS INCLUDE: 1980, International Vocal
Competition, s'Hertogenbosch
(Netherlands); 1982, Benson and Hedges
Gold Award.
ADDRESS: c/o Gillian Clench International
Artists' Management, 1 Mount Pleasant
Cottages, Rhiwbina Hill, Cardiff CF4 6UP.

SAXTON ROBERT   Composer

POSITION: Head of Composition, Guildhall
School of Music and Drama.
PERSONAL DETAILS: b. 8 October 1953,
London.
EDUCATION/TRAINING: 1970–1974, privately
with Elisabeth Lutyens; 1972–1975, St
Catharine's College, Cambridge, with
Robin Holloway; 1975–1976: Worcester
College, Oxford, with Robert Sherlaw
Johnson; privately with Luciano Berio.
FIRST WORK TO ACHIEVE PROMINENCE:
1972, Cockpit Theatre, London, *Ritornelli
and Intermezzi* for piano.
CAREER: Numerous compositions in all
genres including orchestral, chamber,
instrumental, vocal and choral works;
1984–1985, Lecturer in Music, University
of Bristol; 1985–1986, Fulbright Arts
Fellow, Princeton University; since 1990,
Head of Composition, Guildhall School of
Music and Drama.
OPERATIC WORLD PREMIERES: 1991, Opera
North (co-production with Huddersfield
Contemporary Music Festival), *Caritas*,
chamber opera in two acts, libretto by
Arnold Wesker after his play of the same
name, conductor Diego Masson, director
Patrick Mason, designer Joe Vaněk.
RECORDINGS INCLUDE: *Caritas*, Violin
Concerto, *In the Beginning*, *Music to
Celebrate the Resurrection of Christ*, *I will

Awake the Dawn (all COLL), Paraphrase on Mozart's *Idomeneo* for wind ensemble, Concerto for orchestra, *Ring of Eternity*, *Sentinel of the Rainbow*, *Circles of Light* (all EMI), *The Child of Light* (CONT), *Night Music* for guitar (BRID).
ADDRESS: c/o Chester Music Ltd, 8/9 Frith Street, London W1V 5TZ.

SCHMID PATRIC
Administrator, Editor, Record Producer and Teacher

POSITION: Artistic Director, Opera Rara.
PERSONAL DETAILS: b. 12 April 1944, Texas, USA.
CAREER: Since 1970, co-founder and Artistic Director with Don White, Opera Rara, presenting concerts and staged productions at the Camden Festival, Hong Kong Arts Festival, Queen Elizabeth Hall, Sadler's Wells Theatre and Ulster Hall, Belfast including: *L'Etoile du Nord*, *Francesca di Foix/La Romanziera*, *Maria Tudor*, *Gli Orazi ed i Curiazi*, *Robinson Crusoe*, *Torquato Tasso*, *Virginia*; since 1977, record producer, Opera Rara, with particular emphasis on Donizetti and Meyerbeer.
OPERATIC WORLD PREMIÈRES INCLUDE: Compiler and editor: 1976, Ulster Hall, Belfast, *Christopher Columbus*, a pastiche using material from 22 operettas by Jacques Offenbach, libretto by Don White, conductor Alun Francis, director Don White, designer Steven Gregory; 1978, Whitla Hall, Belfast, *Gabriella di Vergy* by Gaetano Donizetti (revised version), conductor Alun Francis.
OTHER PROFESSIONAL ACTIVITIES INCLUDE: Editor and vocal coach; contributor, numerous music journals.
RECORDINGS AS PRODUCER INCLUDE: Donizetti: *L'Assedio di Calais*, *Emilia di Liverpool*, *Maria Padilla* and *Ugo, Conte di Parigi*; Meyerbeer: *Il Crociato in Egitto*, *Dinorah*; A Hundred Years of Italian Opera, Vols 1–3 (all OPRA).

PUBLICATIONS INCLUDE: Editor, vocal scores: *Christopher Columbus*, *Robinson Crusoe* (both Weinberger).
ADDRESS: c/o Opera Rara, 25 Compton Terrace, London N1 2UN.

SHANNON RANDALL
Administrator

POSITION: Managing Director, Opera Northern Ireland.
PERSONAL DETAILS: b. 19 February 1953, Holywood, Northern Ireland; m. 1983, Jae Mussett (dancer).
EDUCATION/TRAINING: 1971–1974, University of Surrey.
CAREER: 1974–1984, freelance double bass player; 1980–1984, Orchestra Manager, Opera 80; 1984–1987, Manager, Irish Chamber Orchestra; 1985–1987, founder and Administrator, Opera Theatre Company, Dublin; since 1987, General Manager, then Managing Director, Opera Northern Ireland.
OTHER PROFESSIONAL ACTIVITIES INCLUDE: Since 1990, Council member, National Campaign for the Arts.
ADDRESS: c/o Opera Northern Ireland, 181a Stranmillis Road, Belfast BT9 5DU.

SHARPE TERENCE   Baritone

PERSONAL DETAILS: b. 30 August 1933, Sheffield; m., two children.
PREVIOUS OCCUPATION: 1956–1967, architect.
EDUCATION/TRAINING: 1951–1956, University of Sheffield, studied architecture; 1969–1972, Gulbenkian Fellowship, vocal studies with Luigi Ricci in Rome and Otakar Kraus in London.
PROFESSIONAL DEBUT: 1967, Cambridge University Opera, Sherasmin, *Oberon*.
MAJOR DEBUTS INCLUDE: 1972, title role, *Billy Budd*: Lausanne Opera, Zurich Opera; 1979, Teatro Colón, Buenos Aires, Balstrode, *Peter Grimes*; 1991: Icelandic Opera, title role, *Rigoletto*; Ljubljana, Amonasro, *Aida*.

CAREER IN THE UK INCLUDES: Since 1968: Covent Garden, Sid, *La Fanciulla del West*; D'Oyly Carte Opera, Sergeant Meryll, *The Yeomen of the Guard*; Opera North, Sharpless, *Madam Butterfly*; Opera Northern Ireland, title role, *Don Pasquale*; Sadler's Wells Opera/English National Opera, title roles: *The Barber of Seville*, *Rigoletto*; Scottish Opera: Bartolo, *The Barber of Seville*; Don Alfonso, *Così fan tutte*; Welsh National Opera: Escamillo, *Carmen*; Germont, *La Traviata*; Amonasro, *Aida*; Marcello, *La Bohème*; Rodrigo, *Don Carlos*; Belcore, *L'Elisir d'Amore*; Guglielmo, *Così fan tutte*; Count di Luna, *Il Trovatore*; Gerard, *Andrea Chénier*; title roles: *Rigoletto*, *The Barber of Seville*, *Nabucco*, *Simon Boccanegra*, *Billy Budd*, *Macbeth*.

RELATED PROFESSIONAL ACTIVITIES: Numerous concerts and recitals in the UK and abroad, repertoire includes works by Bach, Brahms, Handel, Mahler and Schubert; 1985–1987, tutor, Royal Northern College of Music; since 1984, private teacher.

RECORDINGS INCLUDE: Giordano, *Andrea Chénier* (RCA); Verdi: *La Traviata* (HMV), *I Vespri Siciliani* (RCA).

ADDRESS: c/o Musicmakers, Little Easthall Farmhouse, St Paul's Walden, Nr Hitchin, Hertfordshire SG4 8DH.

SHILLING ERIC
Baritone and Teacher

POSITION: Principal Baritone, English National Opera.

PERSONAL DETAILS: b. 12 October 1920, London; m. Erica Johns, two children.

EDUCATION/TRAINING: 1939–1944, Guildhall School of Music and Drama, with Walter Hyde; 1944–1948, Royal College of Music, with Dorothea Webb and Clive Carey.

PROFESSIONAL DEBUT: 1945, Sadler's Wells Opera, Marullo, *Rigoletto*.

EARLY CAREER INCLUDED: 1945–1958, appearances with Intimate Opera Company (1948–1958, Principal Baritone and Resident Director), London Opera Players, Sadler's Wells Opera; roles included: Schaunard, *La Bohème*; Dr Caius, *Sir John in Love*; Osmin, *The Seraglio*; title roles: *The Barber of Seville*, *Don Pasquale*.

OPERATIC WORLD PREMIERES INCLUDE: Sadler's Wells Opera/English National Opera: 1963, Hawthorne, *Our Man in Havana* by Malcolm Williamson; 1974, Major Braun, *The Story of Vasco* by Gordon Crosse; 1990, Screwtape, *Clarissa* by Robin Holloway.

CAREER IN THE UK INCLUDES: Since 1959, Principal Baritone, Sadler's Wells Opera/English National Opera: Frank, *Die Fledermaus*; Daland, *The Flying Dutchman*; Bartolo and title role, *The Marriage of Figaro*; Bartolo and title role, *The Barber of Seville*; Kolenatý, *The Makropoulos Case* (1964, British première); Papageno, *The Magic Flute*; Alberich, *Twilight of the Gods*; Zuniga, *Carmen*; Rostov, *War and Peace* (1972, British stage première); Mannoury, *The Devils of Loudun* (1973, British première); Baron Zeta, *The Merry Widow*; Lord Chancellor, *Iolanthe*; Leporello, *Don Giovanni*; Don Magnifico, *Cinderella*; Faninal, *Der Rosenkavalier*; Jupiter, *Orpheus in the Underworld*; Calchus, *La Belle Hélène*; Amantio and title role, *Gianni Schicchi*; Fool, *Lear*; Potapych, *The Gambler*; Sacristan, *Tosca*; Tax Collector, *Fennimore and Gerda*; Benoit/Alcindoro, *La Bohème*; Pish-Tush, *The Mikado*; Mayor, *Königskinder*; Wig Maker, *Ariadne auf Naxos*.

RELATED PROFESSIONAL ACTIVITIES: 1964–1971, Professor of Singing, Royal College of Music.

RECORDINGS INCLUDE: Berlioz, *Béatrice et Bénédict* (L'OI); Offenbach, *Orpheus in the Underworld* (HMV).

VIDEOS INCLUDE: Sullivan, *The Gondoliers* (Walker).

AWARDS AND HONOURS INCLUDE: Associate, Royal College of Music; 1990, Worshipful Company of Musicians, Sir Charles Santley Memorial Award.

ADDRESS: c/o Music International, 13 Ardilaun Road, London N5 2QR.

SHIMELL WILLIAM   Baritone

PERSONAL DETAILS: b. 23 September 1952, Essex.

EDUCATION/TRAINING: Guildhall School of Music and Drama, with Ellis Keeler; National Opera Studio.

PROFESSIONAL DEBUT: 1978, chorus member, Kent Opera.

EARLY CAREER INCLUDED: 1979–1985, appearances with English National Opera, Glyndebourne Festival and Touring Opera, Kent Opera, Scottish Opera and Welsh National Opera; roles included: Guglielmo, *Così fan tutte*; Papageno, *The Magic Flute*; Harašta, *The Cunning Little Vixen*; Dandini, *La Cenerentola*; Nick Shadow, *The Rake's Progress*; title roles: *Le Nozze di Figaro*, *Don Giovanni*.

MAJOR DEBUTS INCLUDE: 1986, Théâtre du Châtelet, Paris, Dandini, *La Cenerentola*; 1988, San Francisco Opera, Nick Shadow, *The Rake's Progress*; Count, *Le Nozze di Figaro*: 1987, La Scala, Milan; 1989, Grand Théâtre, Geneva; 1990, Vienna State Opera; 1991, Lyric Opera, Chicago; title role, *Don Giovanni*: 1988: Frankfurt Opera, Netherlands Opera; 1989, Santiago Opera; Malatesta, *Don Pasquale*: 1988, Frankfurt Opera; 1990, Netherlands Opera; 1991: La Scala, Milan, Doulinski, *Lodoïska*; Vienna State Opera, Marcello, *La Bohème*.

CAREER IN THE UK INCLUDES: Since 1985, Covent Garden: Schaunard (debut) and Marcello, *La Bohème*; Guglielmo, *Così fan tutte* (also 1992, Japan tour); Albert, *Werther*; Malatesta, *Don Pasquale*; Olivier, *Capriccio*.

RECORDINGS INCLUDE: Cherubini, *Lodoïska* (Italian label); Mozart, *Don Giovanni* (EMI).

AWARDS INCLUDE: 1983, Shell UK International Singing Prize.

ADDRESS: c/o Harrison/Parrott Ltd, 12 Penzance Place, London W11 4PA.

SHIRLEY-QUIRK JOHN
Bass-baritone

PERSONAL DETAILS: b. 28 August 1931, Liverpool; m. 1955, Patricia Hastie, two children; m. 1981, Sara Watkins (conductor and oboist), three children.

PREVIOUS OCCUPATIONS: Officer, RAF Education Branch; Assistant Lecturer in Chemistry, Acton Technical College.

EDUCATION/TRAINING: 1948–1953, University of Liverpool, studied chemistry; vocal studies with Roy Henderson.

PROFESSIONAL DEBUT: 1961, Glyndebourne Festival Opera, Mittenhofer, *Elegy for Young Lovers* (British première).

EARLY CAREER INCLUDED: 1961–1962, chorister, St Paul's Cathedral; 1963–1973, English Opera Group, created roles in all Britten operas from *Curlew River* to *Death in Venice*.

MAJOR DEBUTS INCLUDE: 1963, Scottish Opera, Golaud, *Pelléas et Mélisande*; Traveller, *Death in Venice*: 1973, Covent Garden; 1974, Metropolitan Opera, New York; 1980, La Scala, Milan, Rangoni, *Boris Godunov*.

OPERATIC WORLD PREMIERES INCLUDE: English Opera Group at the Aldeburgh Festival: 1964, Ferryman, *Curlew River*; 1966, Shadrach, *The Burning Fiery Furnace*; 1968, Father, *The Prodigal Son*; 1973, Traveller, *Death in Venice*; 1970, BBC Television, Mr Coyle, *Owen Wingrave* (all by Benjamin Britten); 1976, Scottish Opera at the York Festival, Gil-Martin, *Confessions of a Justified Sinner* by Thomas Wilson; 1977, Covent Garden, Lev, *The Ice Break* by Michael Tippett.

CAREER IN THE UK INCLUDES: Since 1973: Aldeburgh Festival, solo performer, *A Water Bird Talk* (1983, British première); Covent Garden: Mr Coyle, *Owen Wingrave* by Benjamin Britten (1973, world stage première); High Priest, *Alceste*; Rangoni, *Boris Godunov*; English Opera Group, Collatinus, *The Rape of Lucretia*; Glyndebourne Touring Opera, Don Alfonso, *Così fan tutte*; Scottish Opera: Mittenhofer, *Elegy for*

Young Lovers; Don Pizarro, *Fidelio*; Aeneas, *Dido and Aeneas* and Death, *Sāvitri*; title role, *Eugene Onegin*.

RELATED PROFESSIONAL ACTIVITIES: Wide concert repertoire ranging from Purcell to Tippett; frequent recitals, broadcasts and television appearances worldwide; since 1977, member, Court, Brunel University.

RECORDINGS INCLUDE: Berlioz: *Roméo et Juliette* (ORFE), vocal works (PHIL); Britten: *Billy Budd*, *The Burning Fiery Furnace*, *Curlew River*, *Death in Venice*, *A Midsummer Night's Dream*, *The Prodigal Son*, *The Rape of Lucretia*, *Canticles* (all DECC), *War Requiem* (CHAN), songs and instrumental works (MERI); Delius: *La Calinda*, *A Village Romeo and Juliet*, Elgar, *The Dream of Gerontius* (all EMI); Handel, *Messiah* (PHIL); Mozart: *Requiem Mass*, choral works (both DECC); Purcell, *Dido and Aeneas* (PHIL); Tippett: *A Child of our Time* (RPO), *The Vision of St Augustine* (RCA); Vaughan Williams, choral works (EMI); Walton, *Belshazzar's Feast* (EMI).

AWARDS AND HONOURS INCLUDE: 1969, Worshipful Company of Musicians, Sir Charles Santley Memorial Award; 1972, Honorary Member, Royal Academy of Music; 1975, Commander, Order of the British Empire (CBE); 1976, Honorary Doctorate of Music, University of Liverpool; 1981, Doctorate, Brunel University.

ADDRESS: c/o Harrison/Parrott Ltd, 12 Penzance Place, London W11 4PA.

SHORE ANDREW   Baritone

PERSONAL DETAILS: b. 1952, Oldham; m. Fiona Macdonald, three children.

EDUCATION/TRAINING: 1971–1974, University of Bristol, studied theology; 1975–1976, Royal Northern College of Music; 1976–1977, London Opera Centre.

PROFESSIONAL DEBUT: 1977, Opera for All, Fiorello, *The Barber of Seville*.

EARLY CAREER INCLUDED: 1977–1979, several roles with Opera for All; 1979–1981, chorus member, Kent Opera.

MAJOR DEBUTS INCLUDE: 1985, Opera North, Dodon, *The Golden Cockerel*; 1987, Scottish Opera, Baron, *La Vie Parisienne*; 1988, English National Opera, Don Alfonso, *Così fan tutte*; 1990, Glyndebourne Festival Opera, title role, *Falstaff*; 1991, Bartolo, *Il Barbiere di Siviglia*: Welsh National Opera, Vancouver Opera and National Arts Centre, Ottawa; 1992, Covent Garden, Baron Trombonok, *Il Viaggio a Reims*.

CAREER IN THE UK INCLUDES: Since 1981: English National Opera: Papageno, *The Magic Flute*; Doeg, *The Making of the Representative for Planet 8* (1988, British première); Bartolo, *The Barber of Seville*; Frank, *Die Fledermaus*; title roles: *Falstaff*, *Don Pasquale*; Glyndebourne Festival and Touring Opera: Mr Gedge, *Albert Herring*; Don Alfonso, *Così fan tutte*; Kent Opera: Antonio and title role, *The Marriage of Figaro*; Will Atkins, *Robinson Crusoe*; Bartolo, *The Barber of Seville*; Papageno, *The Magic Flute*; Pasha Selim, *The Seraglio*; Lesbo, *Agrippina*; Opera North: Leander, *The Love for Three Oranges*; Sacristan, *Tosca*; Podestà, *The Thieving Magpie*; Varlaam, *Boris Godunov*; Don Jerome, *The Duenna* (1992, British stage première); title roles: *Gianni Schicchi*, *Don Pasquale*, *King Priam*, *Wozzeck*; Scottish Opera: Mr Flint, *Billy Budd*; Don Alfonso, *Così fan tutte*; Welsh National Opera, Sacristan, *Tosca*.

ADDRESS: c/o Athole Still International Managament Ltd, Greystoke House, 80–86 Westow Street, London SE19 3AF.

SIDHOM PETER   Baritone

PERSONAL DETAILS: b. 23 September 1948, Ismailia, Egypt.

PREVIOUS OCCUPATION: 1971–1985, music studio manager, BBC Radio 3.

EDUCATION/TRAINING: 1967–1970, University of London, studied modern languages; 1972–1977, with Hervey Alan; since 1987, with Josephine Veasey.

PROFESSIONAL DEBUT: 1985, Wexford Festival, appeared in *Ariodante*.

MAJOR DEBUTS INCLUDE: 1986, Manoel Theatre, Malta: Germont, *La Traviata*; Scarpia, *Tosca*; 1987, English National Opera, Jupiter, *Orpheus in the Underworld*; 1990, Batignano Festival, title role, *King Priam*; 1991, Welsh National Opera, title role, *Rigoletto*; 1993, Covent Garden, Schaunard, *La Bohème*.

OPERATIC WORLD PREMIERES INCLUDE: 1989, Royal Opera Garden Venture: The Man, *The Menaced Assassin* by Jeremy Peyton Jones; Herod/Joe, *The Uranium Miners' Radio Orchestra Plays Scenes from Salome's Revenge* by Andrew Poppy; 1990, English National Opera, Uncle/Voice of Father, *Clarissa* by Robin Holloway.

CAREER IN THE UK INCLUDES: Since 1988: City of Birmingham Touring Opera, Donner and Gunther, *The Ring Saga*; English National Opera: Duphol, *La Traviata*; Messenger, *Oedipus Rex*; Tomsky/Plutus, *The Queen of Spades*; title role, *Macbeth*; Opera Factory, Bengtsson, *The Ghost Sonata* (1989, British première); Opera North, Dr Vigelius, *Der Ferne Klang* (1992, British première); Welsh National Opera: Thoas, *Iphigénie en Tauride*; Bonze, *Madam Butterfly*; Scarpia, *Tosca*.

ADDRESS: c/o Allied Artists, 42 Montpelier Square, London SW7 1JZ.

SLORACH MARIE   Soprano

PERSONAL DETAILS: b. 8 May 1951, Glasgow; m. 1977, Peter Bodenham (tenor), one child.

EDUCATION/TRAINING: 1971–1974, Royal Scottish Academy of Music and Drama, with David Kelly; privately with Erich Vietheer.

PROFESSIONAL DEBUT: 1974, Scottish Opera, Musetta, *La Bohème*.

EARLY CAREER INCLUDED: 1974–1981, Principal Soprano, Scottish Opera: Marzelline, *Fidelio*; Esmeralda and Mařenka, *The Bartered Bride*; Gretel, *Hansel and Gretel*; Zerlina, *Don Giovanni*; Mimi, *La Bohème*; Eva, *Die Meistersinger von Nürnberg*; Anezka, *The Two Widows*; Adina, *L'Elisir d'Amore*; Tatyana, *Eugene Onegin*; Leïla, *Les Pêcheurs de Perles*.

MAJOR DEBUTS INCLUDE: 1978, Aix-en-Provence Festival, First Witch, *Dido and Aeneas*; 1981: Opera North, Mařenka, *The Bartered Bride*; Wexford Festival, Maliella, *I Gioielli della Madonna*; 1982, Glyndebourne Touring Opera, Donna Anna, *Don Giovanni*; 1983, English National Opera, Lisa, *The Queen of Spades*; 1987, Australian Opera, Sydney, Amelia, *Simon Boccanegra*.

OPERATIC WORLD PREMIÈRES INCLUDE: 1979, English Music Theatre at the Old Vic Theatre, Nimiji, *An Actor's Revenge* by Minoru Miki.

CAREER IN THE UK INCLUDES: Since 1982: Dorset Opera: Elisabeth de Valois, *Don Carlos*; title role, *Giovanna d'Arco*; English National Opera: Donna Elvira, *Don Giovanni*; First Lady, *The Magic Flute*; Nella, *Gianni Schicchi*; Glyndebourne Touring Opera: Elettra, *Idomeneo*; Amelia, *Simon Boccanegra*; Handel Opera Society, Esilena, *Rodrigo*; Opera North: Fiordiligi, *Così fan tutte*; Eva, *The Mastersingers of Nuremberg*; Micaëla, *Carmen*; title role, *Katya Kabanova*; Scottish Opera: Liù, *Turandot*; Governess, *The Turn of the Screw*; Fiordiligi, *Così fan tutte*; Jenifer, *The Midsummer Marriage*; Ellen Orford, *Peter Grimes*; Spitalfields Festival, Melissa, *Armide*.

RELATED PROFESSIONAL ACTIVITIES: Numerous concerts and recitals in the UK.

AWARDS INCLUDE: 1979, second prize, Seventh International Competition for Opera Singers (Sofia).

ADDRESS: c/o Music International, 13 Ardilaun Road, London N5 2QR.

SMITH JULIAN   Conductor

POSITION: Head of Music, Welsh National
Opera.

PERSONAL DETAILS: b. 21 April 1944,
Surrey; m. Katherine Reed, two children.

EDUCATION/TRAINING: St Catharine's
College, Cambridge, studied music.

PROFESSIONAL AND OPERATIC DEBUT:
1973, Welsh National Opera, *Rigoletto*.

CAREER: Welsh National Opera: 1973, staff
conductor; 1974–1983, Chorus Master;
since 1983, Head of Music.

MAJOR OPERATIC DEBUTS INCLUDE: 1985:
Purchase, New York (Pepsico
Summerfare), *Tamerlano*; Vancouver
Opera, *I Puritani*.

OPERA PERFORMANCES IN THE UK
INCLUDE: Since 1973, Welsh National
Opera, more than 30 productions
including: *Idomeneo*, *The Magic Flute*,
Manon Lescaut, *L'Elisir d'Amore*, *La
Bohème*, *La Traviata*, *Tosca*, *I Puritani*,
The Merry Widow, *Norma*, *Lucia di
Lammermoor*, *La Sonnambula*, *La
Fanciulla del West*, *Ernani*, *Madam
Butterfly*, *La Favorita*; also,
Glyndebourne Touring Opera, *La
Bohème*.

RELATED PROFESSIONAL ACTIVITIES:
Editor, restored first version of *Madama
Butterfly* for Ricordi (performed 1982,
Teatro La Fenice, Venice); music adviser,
Cardiff Singer of the World Competition.

ADDRESS: c/o Welsh National Opera, John
Street, Cardiff CF1 4SP.

SMYTHE RUSSELL   Baritone

PERSONAL DETAILS: b. 19 December 1949,
Dublin.

EDUCATION/TRAINING: 1970–1974, Guildhall
School of Music and Drama; 1974–1975,
London Opera Centre (both with Arthur
Reckless); since 1987, with Audrey
Langford.

PROFESSIONAL DEBUT: 1976, English Music
Theatre at the Aldeburgh Festival, Ballad
Singer, *Paul Bunyan* by Benjamin Britten
(world stage première).

EARLY CAREER INCLUDED: 1977–1980,
Welsh National Opera: Yeletsky, *The
Queen of Spades*; Count, *The Marriage of
Figaro*; Papageno, *The Magic Flute*;
Ottone, *The Coronation of Poppea*; title
roles: *The Barber of Seville*, *Billy Budd*,
Eugene Onegin.

MAJOR DEBUTS INCLUDE: 1980, Hamburg
State Opera, Tony, *West Side Story*; 1981,
English National Opera, title role, *The
Barber of Seville*; 1983: Paris Opera,
Harlequin, *Ariadne auf Naxos*; Vienna
Volksoper, Eberbach, *Der Wildschütz*;
1984, Covent Garden, Ned Keene, *Peter
Grimes*; 1986: Lyons Opera, Sherasmin,
Oberon; Vancouver Opera, Papageno,
The Magic Flute; 1987: Dublin Grand
Opera, Malatesta, *Don Pasquale*; La
Monnaie, Brussels, Guglielmo, *Così fan
tutte*; 1989, Frankfurt Opera, Nardo, *La
Finta Giardiniera*; 1991: Basle, Oreste,
Iphigénie en Tauride; Teatro Lírico
Nacional, Madrid, Ned Keene, *Peter
Grimes*.

OPERATIC WORLD PREMIÈRES INCLUDE:
1976, English Music Theatre at the
Aldeburgh Festival, title role, *Tom Jones*
by Stephen Oliver.

CAREER IN THE UK INCLUDES: Since 1981:
Buxton Festival, title role, *Torquato
Tasso*; Covent Garden, Guglielmo, *Così
fan tutte*; English Bach Festival, Oreste,
Iphigénie en Tauride; English National
Opera: Pelléas, *Pelléas and Mélisande*;
Papageno, *The Magic Flute*; Tarquinius,
The Rape of Lucretia; Guglielmo, *Così
fan tutte*; Albert, *Werther*; Opera North,
title role, *The Barber of Seville*; Scottish
Opera, Falke, *Die Fledermaus*; Welsh
National Opera, Garibaldo, *Rodelinda*.

RELATED PROFESSIONAL ACTIVITIES:
Numerous concerts, recitals and
television appearances in the UK and
abroad.

RECORDINGS INCLUDE: Donizetti, *L'Assedio
di Calais* (OPRA); Mozart, *La Finta
Giardiniera* (RICE); A Hundred Years of
Opera (OPRA).

VIDEOS INCLUDE: Britten, *The Rape of
Lucretia* (English National Opera);
Sullivan, *Cox and Box* (Walker).

255

SOLTI

ADDRESS: c/o Athole Still International Management Ltd, Greystoke House, 80–86 Westow Street, London SE19 3AF.

SOLTI, SIR GEORG
Conductor

POSITIONS: Music Director Laureate, Chicago Symphony Orchestra and The Royal Opera, Covent Garden.
PERSONAL DETAILS: b. 21 October 1912, Budapest, Hungary; m. 1946, Hedwig Oeschli; m. 1967, Anne Valerie Pitts, two children.
EDUCATION/TRAINING: Liszt Academy of Music, Budapest, studied piano and composition with Belá Bartók, Ernö Dohnányi, Zoltan Kodály and Leo Weiner.
PROFESSIONAL DEBUT: 1930, as concert pianist and accompanist.
OPERATIC DEBUT: 1938, Budapest Opera, Le Nozze di Figaro.
CAREER: 1930–1939, répétiteur and conductor, Budapest Opera; 1936 and 1937, assistant to Toscanini at Salzburg Festival; 1939–1946, concert pianist in Switzerland (1942, first prize, Geneva International Piano Competition); 1946–1952, Music Director, Bavarian State Opera, Munich; 1952–1961, Music Director, Frankfurt Opera; The Royal Opera, Covent Garden: 1961–1971, Music Director, (more than 20 new productions including: Der Ring des Nibelungen, A Midsummer Night's Dream, Iphigénie en Tauride, Don Giovanni, Erwartung, La Forza del Destino, Le Nozze di Figaro, Rigoletto, Arabella, Der Fliegende Holländer, Die Zauberflöte, Cosi fan tutte, Die Meistersinger von Nürnberg, Orfeo ed Euridice, Salome, Eugene Onegin, Tristan und Isolde and 1965, British première, Moses and Aaron); since 1992, Music Director Laureate; 1972–1975, Music Director, L'Orchestre de Paris; Chicago Symphony Orchestra: 1969–1991, Music Director; since 1991, Music Director Laureate; London Philharmonic

Orchestra: 1979–1983, Principal Conductor and Artistic Director; 1983–1990, Conductor Emeritus; 1990–1993, Artistic Director, Salzburg Easter Festival and Whitsun Concerts; appearances as guest conductor with leading orchestras and opera houses worldwide.
BRITISH OPERATIC DEBUTS INCLUDE: 1952, Hamburg State Opera at the Edinburgh International Festival, Die Zauberflöte; 1954, Glyndebourne Festival Opera, Don Giovanni; 1959, Covent Garden, Der Rosenkavalier.
OPERA PERFORMANCES IN THE UK INCLUDE: Since 1972, Covent Garden: Elektra, Carmen, Die Frau ohne Schatten, Falstaff, Parsifal, Der Rosenkavalier, Die Entführung aus dem Serail, Simon Boccanegra, Otello.
RELATED PROFESSIONAL ACTIVITIES: Broadcasts and television appearances worldwide including 1991, Orchestra! with Dudley Moore (Channel Four).
RECORDINGS INCLUDE: Numerous orchestral works and 40 operas including: Beethoven, Fidelio; Bizet, Carmen; Gluck, Orfeo ed Euridice; Mozart: Die Entführung aus dem Serail, Le Nozze di Figaro, Die Zauberflöte; Puccini: La Bohème, Tosca; Schoenberg, Moses und Aron; R. Strauss: Ariadne auf Naxos, Elektra, Die Frau ohne Schatten, Der Rosenkavalier, Salome; Tchaikovsky, Eugene Onegin; Verdi: Aida, Un Ballo in Maschera, Don Carlos, Falstaff, Otello, Rigoletto, Simon Boccanegra; Wagner: Der Fliegende Holländer, Götterdämmerung, Lohengrin, Die Meistersinger von Nürnberg, Parsifal, Das Rheingold, Siegfried, Die Walküre; complete symphonies of Beethoven, Brahms and Mahler (all DECC).
VIDEOS INCLUDE: Berlioz, La Damnation de Faust (Chicago Symphony Orchestra); Humperdinck, Hänsel und Gretel (Polygram); R. Strauss: Arabella (Vienna State Opera), Der Rosenkavalier (Covent Garden); Tchaikovsky, Eugene Onegin (Polygram); Verdi, Simon Boccanegra (Covent Garden); Orchestra! Vols 1–3

256

(Channel Four); *The Maestro and the Diva* (Sony).

RELEVANT PUBLICATIONS INCLUDE: 1974, *A Season with Solti: A Year in the Life of The Chicago Symphony Orchestra* by William Barry Furlong (Macmillan); 1979, *Solti: The Art of The Conductor* by Paul Robinson (Macdonald & Jane's).

AWARDS AND HONOURS INCLUDE: 30 Grammy Awards (USA), including special Trustees award for Ring Cycle; 15 Grand Prixs du Disque (France); 1968, Honorary Commander, Order of the British Empire (CBE); 1971, Knight Commander, Order of the British Empire (KBE – 1972, adopted British nationality); 1987, Knight Commander's Cross, Order of Merit (Federal Republic of Germany); Honorary Fellow: 1980, Royal College of Music; 1990, Jesus College, Oxford; 1984, Evening Standard Award, *Der Rosenkavalier* (Covent Garden); 1989, Gold Medal, Royal Philharmonic Society; numerous honorary doctorates from British and foreign universities including Leeds, London, Oxford, Harvard and Yale.

ADDRESS: Chalet 'Le Haut Pré', 1884 Villars sur Ollon, Vaud, Switzerland.

SQUIRES SHELAGH
Mezzo-soprano

POSITION: Principal Mezzo-soprano, English National Opera.

PERSONAL DETAILS: b. 17 June 1936.

PREVIOUS OCCUPATION: 1953–1964, insurance clerk.

EDUCATION/TRAINING: Guildhall School of Music and Drama.

PROFESSIONAL DEBUT: 1968, Glyndebourne Touring Opera, Third Boy, *Die Zauberflöte*.

EARLY CAREER INCLUDED: 1968–1972, chorus member, Glyndebourne Festival Opera; 1969, Phoenix Opera, Cherubino, *The Marriage of Figaro*.

OPERATIC WORLD PREMIERES INCLUDE: 1990, English National Opera, Aunt, *Clarissa* by Robin Holloway.

CAREER IN THE UK INCLUDES: since 1972, Principal Mezzo-soprano, Sadler's Wells Opera/English National Opera: Annina, *Der Rosenkavalier*; Tisbe, *Cinderella*; Adelaide, *Arabella*; Maria, *War and Peace* (1972, British stage première); Sister Louise, *The Devils of Loudun* (1973, British première); Rosette, *Manon*; Kate Pinkerton, *Madam Butterfly*; Emilia, *Otello*; Miss Stuhla, *Osud* (1984, British stage première); Lady Saphir, *Patience*; Marcellina, *The Marriage of Figaro*; Public Opinion, *Orpheus in the Underworld*; Annina, *La Traviata*; Flower Maiden, *Parsifal*; Third Lady, *The Magic Flute*; Mamma Lucia, *Cavalleria Rusticana*; Housewife, *Gloriana*; Ludmilla, *The Bartered Bride*; Governess, *The Queen of Spades*; Woman with a Purple Nose, *Christmas Eve* (1988, British stage première); Nurse, *Eugene Onegin*; La Ciesca, *Gianni Schicchi*; Jezibaba, *Rusalka*; Mrs Sedley, *Peter Grimes*; Mrs Olsen, *Street Scene*; Margret, *Wozzeck*; Franči Novaková/Kedruta, *The Adventures of Mr Brouček*.

RECORDINGS INCLUDE: Verdi: *Otello*, *La Traviata*; Wagner: *The Rhinegold*, *The Valkyrie*, *Twilight of the Gods* (all EMI).

VIDEOS INCLUDE: Britten, *Gloriana* (English National Opera); Sullivan, *Patience* (Walker).

ADDRESS: c/o English National Opera, London Coliseum, St Martin's Lane, London WC2N 4ES.

STAPLETON ROBIN
Conductor

PERSONAL DETAILS: b. Surrey.

EDUCATION/TRAINING: Royal College of Music, London Opera Centre.

OPERATIC DEBUT: 1973, Glyndebourne Touring Opera, *La Bohème*.

CAREER: Covent Garden: 1968–1974, member, music staff; 1974–1977 and 1987–1991, Chorus Master; 1977–1987 and since 1991, freelance conductor in the UK and abroad.

MAJOR OPERATIC DEBUTS INCLUDE: 1976, Teheran Opera, *Rigoletto*; 1978: Mexico City, *Carmen*; Netherlands Opera, *La Traviata*; Wexford Festival, *Edgar*; 1981, Pretoria, *La Traviata*; 1982: Icelandic Opera, *Der Zigeunerbaron*; Johannesburg, *Norma*; 1983, Cork City Opera, *Madama Butterfly*; 1984, Dublin Grand Opera, *Die Fledermaus*.

OPERA PERFORMANCES IN THE UK INCLUDE: Since 1974: Covent Garden: *Cavalleria Rusticana/Pagliacci*, *La Bohème*, *Macbeth*, *Tosca* (also 1979, Japan tour), *Die Fledermaus*, *Der Freischütz*; Opera North, *Rigoletto*; Opera Northern Ireland: *La Bohème*, *Don Giovanni*; Scottish Opera: *Hansel and Gretel*, *La Bohème*.

RELATED PROFESSIONAL ACTIVITIES: Regular concerts and broadcasts with leading orchestras in the UK and abroad; numerous television performances including: *Placido Domingo's Christmas Choice*, *Kiri and Friends*, *Stuart Burrows Sings*.

RECORDINGS INCLUDE: Verdi, arias (CPF); Great Operatic Duets (DECC).

ADDRESS: c/o Stafford Law Associates, 26 Mayfield Road, Weybridge, Surrey KT13 8XB.

STEIGER ANNA   Soprano

PERSONAL DETAILS: b. 13 February 1960, Los Angeles, USA.

EDUCATION/TRAINING: 1977–1983, Guildhall School of Music and Drama, with Noelle Barker; 1985–1986, National Opera Studio; currently with Vera Rozsa.

PROFESSIONAL DEBUT: 1984, Opera 80, Dorabella, *Così fan tutte*.

MAJOR DEBUTS INCLUDE: 1986: Glyndebourne Festival Opera, title role, *L'Incoronazione di Poppea*; Lausanne Opera, Clorinda, *La Cenerentola*; 1988: Covent Garden, Flower Maiden, *Parsifal*; English National Opera, Kristina, *The Makropoulos Case*; 1989: Frankfurt Opera, Serpetta, *La Finta Giardiniera*; Grand Théâtre, Geneva, Concepcion,

L'Heure Espagnole; Los Angeles Music Center Opera, Jenny, *Aufstieg und Fall der Stadt Mahagonny*; 1990: Netherlands Opera, Despina, *Così fan tutte*; New York City Opera, Concepcion, *L'Heure Espagnole*; 1991: Opera Theatre of St Louis, Composer, *Ariadne auf Naxos*; Seattle Opera, Zerlina, *Don Giovanni*.

OPERATIC WORLD PREMIERES INCLUDE: 1987, Glyndebourne Touring Opera, Sashka, *The Electrification of the Soviet Union*; 1992, Almeida Opera, Hooded Figure, *Terrible Mouth* (both by Nigel Osborne).

CAREER IN THE UK INCLUDES: Since 1985: Covent Garden, Karolka, *Jenůfa*; Glyndebourne Festival and Touring Opera: Frasquita and Micaëla, *Carmen*; Squirrel, *L'Enfant et les Sortilèges* and Concepcion, *L'Heure Espagnole*; Miss Wordsworth, *Albert Herring*; Opera North, Musetta, *La Bohème*.

RELATED PROFESSIONAL ACTIVITIES: Numerous concerts, recitals, broadcasts and television appearances in the UK and abroad.

RECORDINGS INCLUDE: Milhaud, *Les Malheurs d'Orphée* (ASV); Mozart, *Così fan tutte* (TELD); Varèse, *Offrandes* (SONY).

AWARDS INCLUDE: 1985: John Christie Award, Richard Tauber Memorial Prize, Peter Stuyvesant Foundation Scholarship.

ADDRESS: c/o Harrison/Parrott Ltd, 12 Penzance Place, London W11 4PA.

STEPHENSON DONALD
Tenor

PERSONAL DETAILS: b. 15 February 1947, Leeds; m. 1971, Faith Wilson (mezzo-soprano), two children; m. 1987, Alison Truefitt (soprano and translator).

PREVIOUS OCCUPATION: 1964–1969, banker.

EDUCATION/TRAINING: 1969–1971, Royal Manchester College of Music, with Frederic Cox; 1975, privately with Otakar Kraus; 1982–1983, National Opera Studio.

EARLY CAREER INCLUDED: 1976–1982: Abbey Opera, Caesar, *Antony and Cleopatra*; English Music Theatre: Actor, *The Fairy Queen*; Alidoro, *Cinderella*.

MAJOR DEBUTS INCLUDE: 1983, Welsh National Opera, title role, *Parsifal*; 1984, Scottish Opera, Florestan, *Fidelio*; 1985, Opera North, Mark, *The Midsummer Marriage*; 1986, Freiburg, Alwa, *Lulu*; 1987, Regensburg, Florestan, *Fidelio*; 1988, Freiburg, Erik, *Der Fliegende Holländer*.

OPERATIC WORLD PREMIERES INCLUDE: 1984, Fires of London at Queen Elizabeth Hall, Preacher, *The No. 11 Bus* by Peter Maxwell Davies.

CAREER IN THE UK INCLUDES: Since 1983: Chelsea Opera Group, Sergei, *Lady Macbeth of Mtsensk*; English National Opera: First Jew, *Salome*; Bob Boles, *Peter Grimes*; Glyndebourne Festival Opera, Second Soldier, *L'Incoronazione di Poppea*; Kent Opera, Nebuchadnezzar, *The Burning Fiery Furnace*; Stockholm Folkopera at the Edinburgh International Festival, Herod, *Salome*; Welsh National Opera: *Radamès*, Aida; *Don José*, *Carmen*; Siegmund, *The Valkyrie*; Max, *Der Freischütz*.

RELATED PROFESSIONAL ACTIVITIES: Concerts, broadcasts and television appearances in the UK and abroad.

VIDEOS INCLUDE: Monteverdi, *L'Incoronazione di Poppea* (Glyndebourne Festival Opera).

ADDRESS: Not available.

STIRLING ANGUS
Administrator

POSITION: Chairman, Board of Directors, Royal Opera House, Covent Garden.

PERSONAL DETAILS: b. 10 December 1933; m. 1959, Armyne Schofield, three children.

EDUCATION/TRAINING: Trinity College, Cambridge; University of London, studied history of art.

CAREER: Covent Garden: 1981–1991, Chairman, The Friends of Covent Garden; Board of Directors: since 1979, member; since 1991, Chairman.

OTHER PROFESSIONAL ACTIVITIES INCLUDE: Paul Mellon Foundation for British Art: 1966–1969, Assistant Director; 1969–1970, Joint Director; 1971–1979, Deputy Secretary General, Arts Council of Great Britain; member: 1979–1989, Executive Committee, London Symphony Orchestra; 1980–1985, Crafts Council; 1981–1983, Management Committee, Courtauld Institute of Art; 1982–1989, Board of Governors, Live Music Now; 1983–1990, Board of Trustees, The Theatres Trust; 1988–1991, Deputy Chairman, Royal Ballet Board; since 1983, Director-General, The National Trust.

HONOURS INCLUDE: Companion, British Institute of Management; Fellow, Royal Society of Arts.

ADDRESS: c/o Royal Opera House, Covent Garden, London WC2E 9DD.

STOCKDALE FREDERICK
Administrator and Director

POSITION: General Manager, Pavilion Opera.

PERSONAL DETAILS: b. 20 May 1947, Northampton; three children.

EDUCATION/TRAINING: 1966–1969, Jesus College, Cambridge, studied law.

CAREER: Pavilion Opera: since 1981, founder and General Manager; since 1986, also director, productions include: *Rigoletto*, *Le Nozze di Figaro*, *Lucia di Lammermoor*, *Don Giovanni*, *Les Contes d'Hoffmann*.

PUBLICATIONS INCLUDE: 1990, with M. Dreyer, *The Opera Guide* (Collins & Brown); 1991, *Figaro here, Figaro there: Pavilion Opera, An Impresario's Diary* (John Murray).

ADDRESS: c/o Pavilion Opera, Thorpe Tilney Hall, Nr Lincoln, Lincolnshire LN4 3SL.

STUART-ROBERTS
DEBORAH   Soprano

PERSONAL DETAILS: b. 19 April 1959,
Aberystwyth; m. John Burgess (theatre
technician).

EDUCATION/TRAINING: 1977–1983, Royal
Northern College of Music, with Caroline
Crawshaw (since 1983, privately); 1984–
1985, National Opera Studio.

PROFESSIONAL DEBUT: As mezzo-soprano:
1984, Scottish Opera, Lucille, *The Silken
Ladder* and Clarina, *The Marriage
Contract*.

MAJOR DEBUTS INCLUDE: 1988,
Netherlands Opera, Page, *Salome*; 1989,
Paris, Mercédès, *Carmen*; 1992,
Brussels, Andromache, *King Priam* (since
1990, soprano).

CAREER IN THE UK INCLUDES: Since 1985:
Glyndebourne Festival Opera: Hippolyta,
A Midsummer Night's Dream; title role,
La Cenerentola; Scottish Opera,
Valencienne, *The Merry Widow*; Welsh
National Opera (1985–1988, Principal
Mezzo-soprano): Dorabella, *Così fan
tutte*; Rosina, *The Barber of Seville*; Dido,
The Trojans; Wellgunde, *The Ring of the
Nibelung*; title role, *Carmen*.

RELATED PROFESSIONAL ACTIVITIES:
Numerous concerts with leading
conductors in the UK.

RECORDINGS INCLUDE: Cilea, *Adriana
Lecouvreur* (DECC).

ADDRESS: Not available.

SUART RICHARD   Baritone

PERSONAL DETAILS: b. 5 September 1951,
Blackpool; m. 1981, Susan Cook (pianist),
three children.

EDUCATION/TRAINING: 1971–1974, St John's
College, Cambridge; 1974–1977, Royal
Academy of Music, with Henry
Cummings.

PROFESSIONAL DEBUT: 1977, member,
English Music Theatre.

OPERATIC WORLD PREMIERES INCLUDE:
1979, English Music Theatre at the Old
Vic Theatre, Horimiya, *An Actor's

Revenge by Minoru Miki; 1986: English
National Opera, Troupe of Ceremony/
Judge, *The Mask of Orpheus* by Harrison
Birtwistle; Opera Factory: several roles,
Hell's Angels by Nigel Osborne; Caleb
Raven, *Yan Tan Tethera* by Harrison
Birtwistle; 1988, Munich Biennale, Dad/
Café Manager, *Greek* by Mark-Anthony
Turnage.

CAREER IN THE UK INCLUDES: Since 1977:
Aldeburgh Festival, title role, *Naboth's
Vineyard*; Buxton Festival, Taddeo, *The
Italian Girl in Algiers*; D'Oyly Carte
Opera: Lord Chancellor, *Iolanthe*; The
Duke of Plaza Toro, *The Gondoliers*;
Edinburgh International Festival, Dad/
Café Manager, *Greek* (1988, British
première); English National Opera: Dad/
Café Manager, *Greek*; Ko-Ko, *The
Mikado*; King Gama, *Princess Ida*; Kent
Opera: Old Man, *King Priam*; Swallow,
Peter Grimes; Abbot-Astrologer, *The
Burning Fiery Furnace*; Music Theatre
Wales, William, *The Fall of the House of
Usher* (1989, British première); Opera
Factory: Choregos, *Punch and Judy*; title
role, *Eight Songs for a Mad King* and
Jimmy, *Mahagonny Songspiel*; Hummel,
The Ghost Sonata (1989, British
première); Opera London, Starveling, *A
Midsummer Night's Dream*; Opera North,
Schaunard, *La Bohème*.

RELATED PROFESSIONAL ACTIVITIES:
Numerous television appearances
including 1990, *Greek* (BBC).

RECORDINGS INCLUDE: Bernstein, *Candide*
(DG); Britten, *A Midsummer Night's Dream*
(VIRG); Purcell, *The Fairy Queen* (COLL);
Sullivan: *The Gondoliers*, *Iolanthe* (both
TER), *The Mikdao* (TELA); Turnage, *Greek*
(DECC).

VIDEOS INCLUDE: Tippett, *King Priam* (Kent
Opera).

HONOURS INCLUDE: 1990, Associate, Royal
Academy of Music.

ADDRESS: c/o Magenta Music International
Ltd, 64 Highgate High Street, London N6
5HX.

SULLIVAN GILLIAN   Soprano

PERSONAL DETAILS: b. Adelaide, Australia;
m. John Miller, two children.
PREVIOUS OCCUPATIONS: Nurse and
cartographer.
EDUCATION/TRAINING: University of
Adelaide, studied literature; privately with
Audrey Langford.
PROFESSIONAL DEBUT: 1980, Opera 80,
Countess, *The Marriage of Figaro*.
MAJOR DEBUTS INCLUDE: 1981,
Glyndebourne Touring Opera, Tytania, *A
Midsummer Night's Dream*; 1982, Opera
North, Adina, *The Elixir of Love*; 1983,
Australian Opera, Sydney, Fiordiligi, *Così
fan tutte*; 1985: Hesse State Opera,
Wiesbaden, Constanze, *Die Entführung
aus dem Serail*; Hong Kong Arts Festival,
Rosina, *Il Barbiere di Siviglia*; 1986,
Aachen Opera, Constanze, *Die
Entführung aus dem Serail*; 1987:
Cologne Opera, Musetta, *La Bohème*;
Théâtre du Châtelet, Paris, Madame Herz,
Der Schauspieldirektor; 1988, Scottish
Opera, Rosalinde, *Die Fledermaus*;
English National Opera: 1989, Governess,
The Turn of the Screw (also 1990, Soviet
Union tour: Bolshoi, Kirov and Kiev);
1991, Mimi, *La Bohème*.
OPERATIC WORLD PREMIERES INCLUDE:
1983, Opera North, The Second Mrs de
Winter, *Rebecca* by Wilfred Josephs.
CAREER INCLUDES: Since 1980: Opera 80,
Adele, *Die Fledermaus*; Opera North:
Yvonne, *Johnny Strikes Up* (1984, British
première); Gianetta, *The Gondoliers*;
Opera Northern Ireland: Fiordiligi, *Così
fan tutte*; Gilda, *Rigoletto*; Mimi, *La
Bohème*; Opera Rara at the Camden
Festival, title role, *Francesca di Foix*
(1982, British première); appearances
with Australian Opera, Sydney; Lyric
Opera of Queensland; State Opera of
South Australia, Adelaide; Victoria State
Opera, Melbourne; Western Australian
Opera, Perth; roles include: Antonia, *The
Tales of Hoffmann*; Nannetta, *Falstaff*;
Despina, *Così fan tutte*; Anne Trulove,
The Rake's Progress; Violetta, *La
Traviata*; Eurydice, *Orpheus in the
Underworld*; Donna Anna and Donna
Elvira, *Don Giovanni*; Gilda, *Rigoletto*;
Lisa, *Countess Maritza*; Hero, *Béatrice et
Bénédict*; Susanna, *Le Nozze di Figaro*;
title role, *Lucia di Lammermoor*.
RELATED PROFESSIONAL ACTIVITIES:
Numerous concert appearances in the UK
and Australia.
AWARDS INCLUDE: 1980, Leverhulme
Award, Glyndebourne.
ADDRESS: c/o Lies Askonas Ltd, 186 Drury
Lane, London WC2B 5RY.

SUMMERS JONATHAN
Baritone

PERSONAL DETAILS: b. 2 October 1946,
Melbourne, Australia; m. 1969, three
children.
PREVIOUS OCCUPATION: 1970–1974,
technical operator and recording
engineer, Australian Broadcasting
Commission Radio Division, Melbourne.
EDUCATION/TRAINING: 1964–1969, Prahran
Technical College (art school),
Melbourne; vocal studies: 1964–1974, with
Bettine McCaughan in Melbourne; 1974–
1980, with Otakar Kraus in London.
PROFESSIONAL DEBUT: 1975, Kent Opera,
title role, *Rigoletto*.
MAJOR DEBUTS INCLUDE: 1976, English
National Opera, Tonio, *Pagliacci*; 1977,
Covent Garden, Kilian, *Der Freischütz*;
1981, Australian Opera, Sydney, Germont,
La Traviata; 1982, Paris Opera, Herald,
Lohengrin; 1986: Scottish Opera, Count,
Le Nozze di Figaro; Hamburg State
Opera, Rodrigo, *Don Carlos*; 1987, Teatro
Comunale, Florence, Marcello, *La
Bohème*; 1988: Bavarian State Opera,
Munich, title role, *Le Nozze di Figaro*;
Marcello, *La Bohème*: Metropolitan
Opera, New York and La Scala, Milan in
Tokyo; 1990: Glyndebourne Festival
Opera, Ford, *Falstaff*; Lyric Opera,
Chicago, Enrico, *Lucia di Lammermoor*.
CAREER IN THE UK INCLUDES: Since 1976:
Covent Garden (1976–1986, member):
Sonora, *La Fanciulla del West*; Herald,
Lohengrin; High Priest, *Idomeneo*;

Albert, *Werther*; Hercules, *Alceste*;
Animal Tamer, *Lulu* (1981, British
première, three act version); High Priest,
Samson et Dalila; Roucher, *Andrea
Chénier*; Demetrius, *A Midsummer
Night's Dream*; Papageno, *Die
Zauberflöte*; Paolo, *Simon Boccanegra*;
Ford, *Falstaff*; Sharpless, *Madama
Butterfly*; Marcello, *La Bohème*; title role,
Le Nozze di Figaro; English National
Opera: Marcello, *La Bohème*;
Anckarström, *A Masked Ball*; Balstrode,
Peter Grimes; Rodrigo, *Don Carlos*; Don
Carlos, *The Force of Destiny*; title roles:
Simon Boccanegra, *Eugene Onegin*,
Macbeth, *Rigoletto*; Glyndebourne
Touring Opera, title role, *Falstaff*; Kent
Opera, Oreste, *Iphigenia in Tauris*;
Scottish Opera: Traveller, *Death in
Venice*; title role, *Don Giovanni*.
RELATED PROFESSIONAL ACTIVITIES:
Numerous concerts, recitals, broadcasts
and television appearances in the UK and
abroad.
RECORDINGS INCLUDE: Balfe, *The
Bohemian Girl* (ARGO); Britten, *Peter
Grimes* (PHIL); Leoncavallo, *La Bohème*
(NUOV); Orff, *Carmina Burana* (EMI); Saint-
Saëns, *Samson et Dalila* (PHIL).
VIDEOS INCLUDE: Giordano, *Andrea
Chénier*; Saint-Saëns, *Samson et Dalila*;
R. Strauss, *Der Rosenkavalier* (all Covent
Garden); Verdi, *Il Trovatore* (Australian
Opera, Sydney).
AWARDS INCLUDE: 1980, Grammy Award
(USA), *Peter Grimes*; 1988, Green Room
Theatre Award (Victoria, Australia).
ADDRESS: c/o Patricia Greenan, 19B
Belsize Park, London NW3 4DU.

SUTCLIFFE TOM
Critic and Counter-tenor

POSITION: Opera Critic, *The Guardian*.
PERSONAL DETAILS: b. 4 June 1943,
Norwich; m. 1973, Meredith Oakes (critic
and dramaturg), two children.
EDUCATION/TRAINING: 1960–1963,
Magdalen College, Oxford.

CAREER: 1963–1965, English tutor, Central
Tutorial School for Young Musicians (now
Purcell School); 1965–1971, manager,
Musica Reservata; 1966–1970, counter-
tenor, Westminster Cathedral Choir;
1968–1973, advertisement manager, then
Editor, *Music & Musicians*; 1975–1987,
music, opera and theatre critic, *Vogue*;
since 1973, *The Guardian*: Deputy Arts
Editor, sub-editor, feature writer and
opera critic; currently British
Correspondent, *Opera News*, New York.
ADDRESS: c/o *The Guardian*, 119
Farringdon Road, London EC1R 3ER.

SYRUS DAVID
Conductor, Harpsichordist,
Pianist and Accompanist,
Répétiteur and Teacher

POSITION: Senior Répétiteur, The Royal
Opera, Covent Garden.
PERSONAL DETAILS: b. 13 October 1946,
Hastings; m. 1972, Lorna Miller, three
children.
EDUCATION/TRAINING: Music Scholar, The
Queen's College, Oxford; London Opera
Centre.
CAREER: Covent Garden: 1971–1981,
member, music staff; 1981–1991, Head of
Music Staff; since 1991, Senior
Répétiteur; 1977–1984, Assistant
Conductor, Bayreuth Festival.
OPERATIC WORLD PREMIERES INCLUDE:
1980, Roundhouse, London, *The Pig
Organ* by Richard Blackford; 1989,
National Youth Music Theatre, *The Tailor
of Gloucester* by Douglas Young; Royal
Opera Garden Venture: 1989, *The
Uranium Miners' Radio Orchestra Plays
Scenes from Salome's Revenge* by
Andrew Poppy; 1991, *The Panic* by David
Sawer.
OPERA PERFORMANCES IN THE UK
INCLUDE: Since 1981: Covent Garden: *A
Christmas Carol* (1981, British première
at Sadler's Wells Theatre), *Ariadne auf
Naxos*; Jeanetta Cochrane Theatre,
London, *Pollicino* (1980, British première);

Sadler's Wells Theatre, *The Boy Who Grew Too Fast* (1986, British première).
RELATED PROFESSIONAL ACTIVITIES: Accompanist and continuo player in the UK and abroad; teacher: Royal Academy of Music, Royal College of Music.

RECORDINGS INCLUDE: Menotti: *Amahl and the Night Visitors*, *The Boy Who Grew Too Fast* (both TER).
ADDRESS: c/o Royal Opera House, Covent Garden, London WC2E 9DD.

* * * *

TATE JEFFREY   Conductor

POSITIONS: Music Director and Principal Conductor, Rotterdam Philharmonic Orchestra; Principal Conductor, English Chamber Orchestra; Principal Guest Conductor: The Royal Opera, Covent Garden; Grand Théâtre, Geneva; Orchestre National de France.
PERSONAL DETAILS: b. 28 April 1943, Salisbury.
PREVIOUS OCCUPATION: 1967–1969, doctor, St Thomas' Hospital, London.
EDUCATION/TRAINING: 1961–1967: Christ's College, Cambridge; St Thomas' Hospital; 1970–1971, London Opera Centre.
PROFESSIONAL AND OPERATIC DEBUT: 1978, Gothenburg, *Carmen*.
CAREER: 1971–1977, répétiteur, Covent Garden; 1976–1981, assistant to Pierre Boulez (Bayreuth Festival and Paris Opera); 1977–1979, assistant to John Pritchard (Cologne Opera); 1979–1985, Assistant Conductor, Metropolitan Opera, New York; Principal Conductor: 1986–1991, Covent Garden; since 1985, English Chamber Orchestra; Principal Guest Conductor: since 1983, Grand Théâtre, Geneva; since 1989, Orchestre National de France; since 1991, Covent Garden; currently Music Director and Principal Conductor, Rotterdam Philharmonic Orchestra.
MAJOR OPERATIC DEBUTS INCLUDE: 1980: Cologne Opera, *Les Contes d'Hoffmann*; Metropolitan Opera, New York, *Lulu*; 1982: Covent Garden, *La Clemenza di Tito*; Nice Opera, *Salome*; 1983, Paris Opera, *Ariadne auf Naxos*; 1984, San

Francisco Opera, *Elektra*; 1985, Salzburg Festival, *Il Ritorno d'Ulisse in Patria* (new version by Henze).
OPERATIC WORLD PREMIERES INCLUDE: 1987, Grand Théâtre, Geneva, *La Fôret* by Rolf Liebermann.
OPERA PERFORMANCES IN THE UK INCLUDE: Since 1983, Covent Garden: *Ariadne auf Naxos*, *Manon*, *Lohengrin*, *Cosi fan tutte* (also 1992, Japan tour), *Idomeneo*, *Der Rosenkavalier*, *Arabella*, *Capriccio*, *Les Contes d'Hoffmann*, *Le Nozze di Figaro* (also 1992, Japan tour), *Fidelio*.
RELATED PROFESSIONAL ACTIVITIES: Regular performances with leading orchestras in the UK and abroad.
RECORDINGS INCLUDE: Humperdinck, *Hänsel und Gretel* (EMI); Offenbach, *Les Contes d'Hoffmann* (PHIL); R. Strauss, *Arabella* (DECC).
AWARDS AND HONOURS INCLUDE: 1982, Society of West End Theatre Award, *La Clemenza di Tito* (Covent Garden); 1989, Honorary Fellow, Christ's College, Cambridge; 1990: Commander, Order of the British Empire (CBE); Chevalier de l'Ordre des Arts et des Lettres (France).
ADDRESS: c/o Royal Opera House, Covent Garden, London WC2E 9DD.

TAVENER JOHN   Composer

PERSONAL DETAILS: b. 28 January 1944, London; m. 1974, Victoria Marangopoulou; m. 1991, Maryanna Schaefer.

EDUCATION/TRAINING: 1961–1965, Royal Academy of Music, with Lennox Berkeley and David Lumsdaine.

FIRST PROFESSIONAL PERFORMANCE OF A COMPOSITION: 1962, London Bach Society, *Three Holy Sonnets* for voice and orchestra.

CAREER: Numerous compositions in all genres including three operas, four music drama works, orchestral, chamber, instrumental, vocal and choral works; since 1969, professor, Trinity College of Music.

OPERATIC WORLD PREMIERES: 1977, Bath Festival, *A Gentle Spirit*, chamber opera in one act, libretto by Gerard McLarnon after Dostoyevsky, conductor Mark Elder, director David William, designer Alan Barlow; 1979, Covent Garden, *Thérèse*, opera in one act, libretto by Gerard McLarnon, conductor Edward Downes, director David William, designer Alan Barlow; 1992, Aldeburgh Festival, *Mary of Egypt*, a moving ikon, text by Mother Thekla, conductor Lionel Friend, director Lucy Bailey, designer Jeremy Herbert.

RECORDINGS INCLUDE: *The Call* (ABCD), *Funeral Ikos*, *Ikon of Light*, *The Lamb* (all GIME), *Liturgy of St John Chrysostom*, *Orthodox Vigil Service* (both IKON), *The Protecting Veil*, *Thrinos* (both VIRG), *The Repentant Thief* (COLL), *The Sacred Music of John Tavener* (HYPE).

HONOURS INCLUDE: Honorary Fellow: Royal Academy of Music, Trinity College of Music.

ADDRESS: c/o Chester Music Ltd, 8/9 Frith Street, London W1V 5TZ.

TE KANAWA, DAME KIRI
Soprano

PERSONAL DETAILS: b. 6 March 1944, Gisborne, New Zealand; m. 1967, Desmond Park, two children.

EDUCATION/TRAINING: St Mary's College, Auckland, studied singing and piano with Sister Mary Leo; 1960–1966, privately with Sister Mary Leo; 1966–1969, London Opera Centre; privately with Vera Rozsa.

EARLY CAREER INCLUDED: 1966–1969: London Opera Centre: Second Lady, *Die Zauberflöte*; Blanche, *The Carmelites*; title role, *Anna Bolena*; Camden Festival, Elena, *La Donna del Lago*; Chelsea Opera Group, Idamante, *Idomeneo*; Northern Opera, title role, *Carmen*; 1970–1971, member, Covent Garden (debut 1971, Flower Maiden, *Parsifal*).

MAJOR DEBUTS INCLUDE: Countess, *Le Nozze di Figaro*: 1971: Covent Garden, Lyons Opera, Santa Fe Opera; 1972, San Francisco Opera; 1973, Glyndebourne Festival Opera; 1979, Salzburg Festival; Desdemona, *Otello*: 1972, Scottish Opera; 1974, Metropolitan Opera, New York; 1980, Vienna State Opera; 1982, Verona Arena; Donna Elvira, *Don Giovanni*: 1975, Paris Opera; 1978, Cologne Opera; title role, *Arabella*: 1977, Houston Grand Opera; 1985, Lyric Opera, Chicago; 1976, Australian Opera, Sydney, Mimi, *La Bohème*; 1978, La Scala, Milan, Amelia, *Simon Boccanegra*.

CAREER IN THE UK INCLUDES: Since 1971, Covent Garden: Xenia, *Boris Godunov*; Donna Elvira, *Don Giovanni*; Micaëla, *Carmen*; Desdemona, *Otello*; Amelia, *Simon Boccanegra*; Mimi, *La Bohème*; Marguérite, *Faust*; Tatyana, *Eugene Onegin*; Fiordiligi, *Così fan tutte*; Rosalinde, *Die Fledermaus*; Pamina, *Die Zauberflöte*; Violetta, *La Traviata*; Marschallin, *Der Rosenkavalier*; Countess, *Capriccio*; title roles: *Arabella*, *Manon Lescaut*.

RELATED PROFESSIONAL ACTIVITIES: Numerous concerts and recitals with leading conductors and orchestras worldwide; frequent broadcasts and television appearances including: 1981, St Paul's Cathedral, Royal Wedding; 1990, New Zealand, closing ceremony, Commonwealth Games; 1992, Last Night of the Proms.

RECORDINGS INCLUDE: Berlioz, *Nuits d'été*; Bernstein, *West Side Story* (both DG); Bizet, *Carmen*; Canteloube, *Songs of the Auvergne* (both DECC); Gounod, *Faust* (PHIL); McCartney, *Liverpool Oratorio* (EMI); Mozart: *Così fan tutte* (DG), *Don*

Giovanni (PHIL), *Le Nozze di Figaro* (DECC/
DG), *Die Zauberflöte* (PHIL), concert arias
(DECC), opera arias, sacred music (both
PHIL); Puccini: *Manon Lescaut* (DECC), *La
Rondine* (CBS), *Heroines* (CBS); Rodgers,
South Pacific (SONY); J. Strauss, *Die
Fledermaus* (PHIL); R. Strauss: Arabella
(DECC), *Der Rosenkavalier* (EMI), *Four Last
Songs* (CBS/DECC), Kiri Te Kanawa sings
Richard Strauss (CBS); Verdi: *Otello,
Simon Boccanegra* (both DECC); Wagner,
Siegfried (EMI); Puccini and Verdi, arias
(CBS); Kiri sings Gershwin, French opera
arias, Italian opera arias (all EMI); The
Essential Kiri (DECC); *Ave Maria*, Kiri
Sidetracks: The Jazz Album (both PHIL).
VIDEOS INCLUDE: Bernstein, *West Side
Story – The Making of the Recording*
(BBC); McCartney, *Liverpool Oratorio* (EMI);
Mozart: *Don Giovanni* (film by Joseph
Losey), *Le Nozze di Figaro*
(Glyndebourne Festival Opera and Vienna
State Opera); Puccini: *Manon Lescaut*
(Covent Garden), *Tosca* (Paris Opera); J.
Strauss, *Die Fledermaus*; R. Strauss, *Der
Rosenkavalier* (both Covent Garden);
Verdi: *Otello* (Verona Arena), *Simon
Boccanegra* (Covent Garden); *The
Essential Kiri, An Evening with Kiri Te
Kanawa, Kiri in Concert, Songs of the
Auvergne*, (all Polygram); *Kiri Te Kanawa
– A Profile* (LWT); *Kiri Te Kanawa sings
Mozart* (EMI); *The Maestro and the Diva*
(Sony).
PUBLICATIONS AND RELEVANT
PUBLICATIONS INCLUDE: 1982, *Kiri* by David
Fingleton (Collins); 1989, *Land of The
Long White Cloud: Maori Myths and
Legends* (Pavilion).
AWARDS AND HONOURS INCLUDE: 1965,
Sun Aria Competition (Melbourne); 1973,
Officer, Order of the British Empire (OBE);
1982, Dame Commander, Order of the
British Empire (DBE); 1983: Honorary
Doctorates of Music: Universities of
Oxford and Auckland; Honorary Fellow,
Somerville College, Oxford; 1992,
Gramophone Artist of the Year Award.
ADDRESS: c/o Fairways, Pachesham Park,
Leatherhead, Surrey KT22 ODJ.

TEAR ROBERT
Tenor and Conductor

PERSONAL DETAILS: b. 8 March 1939,
Glamorgan; m. 1961, Hilary Thomas, two
children.
EDUCATION/TRAINING: 1957–1961, Choral
Scholar, King's College, Cambridge.
PROFESSIONAL DEBUT: (1961, chorister, St
Paul's Cathedral); 1964, English Opera
Group at the Aldeburgh Festival, Quint,
The Turn of the Screw.
EARLY CAREER INCLUDED: 1964–1970,
English Opera Group: Male Chorus, *The
Rape of Lucretia*; Acis, *Acis and Galatea*;
Lysander, *A Midsummer Night's Dream*;
Arbace, *Idomeneo*; Oswald, *King Arthur.*
MAJOR DEBUTS INCLUDE: 1969, Welsh
National Opera, Jacquino, *Fidelio*; 1974,
Scottish Opera, Alfredo, *La Traviata*;
1976, Paris Opera, Loge, *Das Rheingold*;
1985, Salzburg Festival, Eumete, *Il
Ritorno d'Ulisse in Patria* (new version by
Henze); 1987, Bavarian State Opera,
Munich, Loge, *Der Ring des Nibelungen*;
1989, English National Opera, Prologue/
Peter Quint, *The Turn of the Screw*;
Aschenbach, *Death in Venice*: 1989,
Glyndebourne Touring Opera; 1992,
Glyndebourne Festival Opera.
OPERATIC WORLD PREMIERES INCLUDE:
English Opera Group at the Aldeburgh
Festival: 1966, Misael, *The Burning Fiery
Furnace*; 1968, Tempter/Younger Son,
The Prodigal Son (both by Benjamin
Britten); 1969, title role, *The Grace of
Todd* by Gordon Crosse; Covent Garden:
1970, Dov, *The Knot Garden* by Michael
Tippett; 1976, Deserter, *We Come to the
River* by Hans Werner Henze; 1979,
Rimbaud, *Thérèse* by John Tavener; 1979,
Paris Opera, Painter/Negro, three act
version of *Lulu* by Alban Berg.
CAREER IN THE UK INCLUDES: Since 1970,
Covent Garden: Lensky, *Eugene Onegin*;
Paris, *King Priam*; Prince Orlofsky, *Die
Fledermaus*; Froh and Loge, *Das
Rheingold*; Prince Shuisky, *Boris
Godunov*; Tom Rakewell, *The Rake's
Progress*; Admète, *Alceste*; David, *Die*

Meistersinger von Nürnberg; Captain
Vere, Billy Budd; Jupiter, Semele; Herod,
Salome; Director, Un Re in Ascolto (1989,
British première); Aegisth, Elektra;
Mosquito/Schoolmaster, The Cunning
Little Vixen; Méphistophélès, The Fiery
Angel; title roles: Peter Grimes, Samson.
RELATED PROFESSIONAL ACTIVITIES:
Numerous concerts, recitals and
broadcasts both as singer and conductor
in the UK and abroad; debut as
conductor: 1981, Queen Elizabeth Hall,
Thames Chamber Orchestra; 1985–1992,
first International Chair of Vocal Studies,
Royal Academy of Music; since 1992,
Artistic Adviser, London Royal Schools'
Vocal Faculty.
RECORDINGS INCLUDE: Berg, Lulu (DG);
Berlioz, Béatrice et Bénédict (PHIL);
Britten: The Burning Fiery Furnace, The
Prodigal Son (both DECC), War Requiem,
folk song Arrangements (both EMI); Elgar,
The Dream of Gerontius (CRD); Haydn, Die
Schöpfung (CFP); Janáček, The Cunning
Little Vixen (EMI); Mozart: Die Entführung
aus dem Serail (PHIL), Requiem (DECC);
Shostakovich, Lady Macbeth of Mtsensk
(EMI); Tippett, The Mask of Time (EMI);
Vaughan Williams: Hodie-Christmas
cantata, On Wenlock Edge (both EMI).
VIDEOS INCLUDE: Britten, Death in Venice
(Glyndebourne Touring Opera); J.
Strauss, Die Fledermaus (Covent
Garden).
PUBLICATIONS INCLUDE: 1980, Victorian
Songs and Duets; 1990, autobiography,
Tear Here (André Deutsch).
HONOURS INCLUDE: 1984, Commander,
Order of the British Empire (CBE); 1989,
Honorary Fellow, King's College,
Cambridge; Honorary Member, Royal
Academy of Music; Fellow: Royal College
of Music, Royal Society of Arts.
ADDRESS: c/o Harold Holt Ltd, 31 Sinclair
Road, London W14 ONS.

TEARE CHRISTINE   Soprano

PERSONAL DETAILS: b. Isle of Man.
EDUCATION/TRAINING: 1978–1982, Royal
Academy of Music, with Marjorie Thomas;
currently with Rudolf Piernay.
PROFESSIONAL DEBUT: 1983, Welsh
National Opera, Donna Anna, Don
Giovanni.
MAJOR DEBUTS INCLUDE: 1985: English
National Opera, Flower Maiden, Parsifal;
Opera North, Donna Anna, Don Giovanni;
1989, Covent Garden, Ortlinde, Die
Walküre.
CAREER IN THE UK INCLUDES: Since 1983:
Covent Garden, Helmvige, Ortlinde and
Third Norn, Der Ring des Nibelungen;
English National Opera, Berta, The
Barber of Seville; Welsh National Opera
(1985–1989, Principal Soprano): Flower
Maiden, Parsifal; Third Norn,
Götterdämmerung; Countess, Le Nozze
di Figaro; Amelia, A Masked Ball; Berta,
The Barber of Seville; Helmvige, Die
Walküre; Empress, Die Frau ohne
Schatten.
RELATED PROFESSIONAL ACTIVITIES:
Numerous recordings for BBC Radio 2
and Royal National Theatre.
RECORDINGS INCLUDE: Janáček, Osud;
Wagner, Parsifal (both EMI).
HONOURS INCLUDE: 1990, Associate, Royal
Academy of Music.
ADDRESS: c/o Music International, 13
Ardilaun Road, London N5 2QR.

TERFEL BRYN   Bass-baritone

PERSONAL DETAILS: b. 9 November 1965,
North Wales.
EDUCATION/TRAINING: 1984–1989, Guildhall
School of Music and Drama, with Rudolf
Piernay and Arthur Reckless; currently
with Rudolf Piernay.
PROFESSIONAL DEBUT: 1990, Welsh
National Opera, Guglielmo, Cosi fan tutte.
MAJOR DEBUTS INCLUDE: 1990: Welsh
National Opera, title role, The Marriage of
Figaro; Peralada Festival, Abimelech,
Samson et Dalila; 1991: title role, The

Marriage of Figaro: English National Opera, Santa Fe Opera; La Monnaie, Brussels, Speaker, *Die Zauberflöte*; 1992: Covent Garden, Masetto, *Don Giovanni* (also Japan tour); Hamburg State Opera, title role, *Le Nozze di Figaro*; Salzburg Festival: Jokanaan, *Salome*; Spirit Messenger, *Die Frau ohne Schatten*; 1993: Lyric Opera, Chicago, Donner, *Das Rheingold*; Théâtre du Châtelet, Paris, title role, *Le Nozze di Figaro*; 1993–1994, Vienna State Opera: Count, *Le Nozze di Figaro*; Lindorf/Coppelius/Dapertutto/Dr Miracle, *Les Contes d'Hoffmann*.

RELATED PROFESSIONAL ACTIVITIES: Concerts, oratorios, broadcasts and television appearances in the UK and abroad including hosting *A Fine Song for Singing* (BBC Wales).

RECORDINGS INCLUDE: Cilea, *Adriana Lecouvreur* (DECC); Handel, *Messiah* (CHAN); Monteverdi, *Vespers* (DECC); Mozart, *Don Giovanni* (L'OI); Puccini, *Tosca* (DECC); Schubert, *Schwanengesang* (SAIN); R. Strauss, *Salome* (DG).

AWARDS INCLUDE: 1988, Kathleen Ferrier Memorial Scholarship; 1989: Gold Medal, Guildhall School of Music and Drama; Cardiff Singer of the World Lieder Prize; 1992, first recipient, Critics' Circle Music Section Award.

ADDRESS: c/o Harlequin Agency Ltd, 1 University Place, Cardiff CF2 2JU.

THOMAS GWION   Baritone

PERSONAL DETAILS: b. 17 June 1954, Swansea; m. 1987, Chloë Willson-Thomas (soprano and teacher).

PREVIOUS OCCUPATION: 1972–1980, bank clerk.

EDUCATION/TRAINING: 1980–1985, Royal Northern College of Music, with Patrick McGuigan.

PROFESSIONAL DEBUT: 1985, Kent Opera, Duphol, *La Traviata*.

MAJOR DEBUTS INCLUDE: 1986, Welsh National Opera, title role, *The Barber of Seville*.

OPERATIC WORLD PREMIERES INCLUDE: 1987, Kent Opera, Chao Lin, *A Night at the Chinese Opera* by Judith Weir; 1988, Midsummer Opera at the London Opera Festival, Man, *Nell* by Alison Bauld; 1990, Welsh National Opera, First Mate, *Tornrak* by John Metcalf; 1991: BBC Television, title role, *Scipio's Dream* by Mozart/Judith Weir; Opera Theatre Company, Dublin, solo voice, *Position Seven* by Kenneth Chalmers.

CAREER IN THE UK INCLUDES: Since 1986: Aquarius Ensemble at the Aldeburgh Festival, Punch, *Punch and Judy*; Buxton Festival, Alfonso, *Torquato Tasso*; Kent Opera: Morales and Escamillo, *Carmen*; Ananias, *The Burning Fiery Furnace*; Ned Keene, *Peter Grimes*; Mecklenburgh Opera, Old Widower, *Petrified* (1992, British première); Music Theatre Wales, Orfeo, *Euridice*; Travelling Opera, Schaunard, *La Bohème*.

RELATED PROFESSIONAL ACTIVITIES: Concerts and recitals in the UK; voice tutor, Drama Department, School of Performing Arts, Leicester Polytechnic; member, Vocem Electric Voice Theatre.

AWARDS INCLUDE: 1984, Bel Canto Competition (Belgium).

ADDRESS: c/o M & M Lyric Artists, 6 Princess Road, London NW1 7JJ.

THOMPSON ADRIAN   Tenor

PERSONAL DETAILS: b. 28 July 1954, London; m. 1977, Judy Panes, two children.

EDUCATION/TRAINING: 1973–1977, Guildhall School of Music and Drama, with Duncan Robertson.

PROFESSIONAL DEBUT: 1977, chorus member, Kent Opera.

EARLY CAREER INCLUDED: 1978–1981: Aldeburgh Festival: Lensky, *Eugene Onegin*; Flute, *A Midsummer Night's Dream*; Glyndebourne Touring Opera: First Priest, *Die Zauberflöte*; Ferrando, *Così fan tutte*; Lindoro, *La Fedeltà Premiata*; Pedrillo, *Die Entführung aus dem Serail*.

267

MAJOR DEBUTS INCLUDE: 1981,
Glyndebourne Festival Opera, Snout, *A
Midsummer Night's Dream*; Pedrillo, *Die
Entführung aus dem Serail*: 1982, Scottish
Opera; 1983, Netherlands Opera; 1988,
Opera London, Arnalta, *L'Incoronazione
di Poppea*; 1990, Netherlands Opera,
Narraboth, *Salome*; 1992, English
National Opera, Iro, *The Return of
Ulysses*.

CAREER IN THE UK INCLUDES: Since 1982:
Buxton Festival: Horatio, *La Colombe*;
Rinaldo, *Il Filosofo di Campagna*;
Pedrillo, *The Seraglio*; Glyndebourne
Festival and Touring Opera: Don Basilio,
Le Nozze di Figaro; Mr Upfold, *Albert
Herring*; Handel Opera Society, Emilio,
Partenope; Opera 80: Pedrillo, *The
Seraglio*; Dancaïro, *Carmen*; Opera
Northern Ireland: Bardolph, *Falstaff*;
Alfred, *Die Fledermaus*; Phoenix Opera at
the Camden Festival, Eurimedonte,
Eritrea (1982, British première); Scottish
Opera: Vašek, *The Bartered Bride*;
Lysander, *A Midsummer Night's Dream*.

RECORDINGS INCLUDE: Britten, *A
Midsummer Night's Dream* (VIRG); Gay,
The Beggar's Opera (HYPE); Monteverdi,
L'Incoronazione di Poppea (VIRG);
Schubert, *Die Schöne Müllerin* (PICK);
Vaughan Williams: *On Wenlock Edge*, *The
Shepherds of the Delectable Mountains*
(both HYPE).

VIDEOS INCLUDE: Britten, *A Midsummer
Night's Dream* (Glyndebourne Festival
Opera).

ADDRESS: c/o Ron Gonsalves Personal
Artists & Concert Management, 10
Dagnan Road, London SW12 9LQ.

TIERNEY VIVIAN   Soprano

PERSONAL DETAILS: b. 26 November 1957,
London; one child.

EDUCATION/TRAINING: Manchester
Grammar School for Girls; since 1977,
privately with Eduardo Asquez and
Josephine Veasey.

PROFESSIONAL DEBUT: 1978, D'Oyly Carte
Opera, title role, *Princess Ida*.

EARLY CAREER INCLUDED: 1978–1982:
D'Oyly Carte Opera: Mabel, *The Pirates of
Penzance*; Elsie, *The Yeomen of the
Guard*; Yum-Yum, *The Mikado*; Gianetta,
The Gondoliers; Josephine, *HMS
Pinafore*; New Sadler's Wells Opera:
Stasi, *The Gypsy Princess*; Julietta, *The
Count of Luxembourg*.

MAJOR DEBUTS INCLUDE: 1983, Kent Opera,
Edwige, *Robinson Crusoe*; 1984,
Montpellier Festival, Mimi, *La Bohème*;
Donna Anna, *Don Giovanni*: 1985, Opera
80; 1987, Flanders Opera, Antwerp; 1988,
Opera North, title role, *The Merry Widow*;
1989: English National Opera, Regan,
Lear (British première); Freiburg, title
role, *Lady Macbeth of Mtsensk*; 1992:
Glyndebourne Festival Opera, Ellen
Orford, *Peter Grimes*; Opera Pacific,
California, title role, *Csárdásfürstin*.

OPERATIC WORLD PREMIERES INCLUDE:
1990, English National Opera, title role,
Clarissa by Robin Holloway.

CAREER INCLUDES: 1989–1991, Principal
Soprano, Freiburg: Ellen Orford, *Peter
Grimes*; Giulietta, *Les Contes
d'Hoffmann*; Jenny, *Aufstieg und Fall der
Stadt Mahagonny*; Marschallin, *Der
Rosenkavalier*; Renata, *The Fiery Angel*;
since 1991: English National Opera: Mimi,
La Bohème; Rosalinde, *Die Fledermaus*;
Málinka/Etherea/Kunka, *The Adventures
of Mr Brouček*; Opera North, Marie,
Wozzeck.

RELATED PROFESSIONAL ACTIVITIES:
Numerous concerts, recitals and
broadcasts in the UK and abroad.

RECORDINGS INCLUDE: James, *Hester Suite*
(NOVE); Lehár, *The Count of Luxembourg*
(TER).

ADDRESS: c/o Athole Still International
Management Ltd, Greystoke House, 80–86
Westow Street, London SE19 3AF.

TIMMS CLIVE   Conductor

POSITION: Head of Opera Studies, Guildhall
School of Music and Drama.
PERSONAL DETAILS: b. 16 June 1946,
Berkshire; m. Joy Roberts (soprano), two
children.
EDUCATION/TRAINING: 1965–1968,
University of Birmingham; 1969–1970,
National Opera Centre.
PROFESSIONAL DEBUT: 1970, pianist, Opera
for All.
CAREER: 1970–1971, pianist, Opera for All;
1971–1977, member, music staff and
conductor, Sadler's Wells Opera/English
National Opera; 1978–1989, Assistant
Music Director, Opera North; since 1989,
Head of Opera Studies, Guildhall School
of Music and Drama.
MAJOR OPERATIC DEBUTS INCLUDE: 1973,
Sadler's Wells Opera, *The Merry Widow*;
1978, Opera North, *Dido and Aeneas*;
1985, Opera North at Komische Oper,
East Berlin, *Tamerlano*; 1990, Icelandic
Opera, *Pagliacci*.
OPERATIC WORLD PREMIERES INCLUDE:
1972, University of Liverpool,
Tamburlaine by Marjolijn Murdock.
OPERA PERFORMANCES IN THE UK
INCLUDE: Since 1978: Barber Institute,
Birmingham, *Les Deux Journées*;
Guildhall School of Music and Drama:
Scipio (also translation), *La Clemenza di
Tito*, *Margot la Rouge/Les Mamelles de
Tirésias*; Opera North: *Les Mamelles de
Tirésias*, *Rigoletto*, *Der Fliegende
Holländer*, *The Bartered Bride*, *Werther*,
The Mastersingers of Nuremberg, *Manon*,
Aida, *Orfeo ed Euridice*.
ADDRESS: c/o Guildhall School of Music
and Drama, Barbican, London EC2Y 8DT.

TINKLER MARK   Baritone

PERSONAL DETAILS: b. 26 April 1961,
Toronto, Canada.
EDUCATION/TRAINING: 1980–1983,
University of Manchester, studied music;
1980–1986, Royal Northern College of
Music, with Nicholas Powell.

PROFESSIONAL DEBUT: 1986, Scottish
Opera, Morales, *Carmen*.
CAREER INCLUDES: Since 1986:
Glyndebourne Touring Opera, Guglielmo,
Cosi fan tutte; Scottish Opera:
Maximilian, *Candide*; title role, *Billy
Budd*; West End, Prince, *Into the Woods*;
France, Count, *Le Nozze di Figaro* (1988,
European debut).
RELATED PROFESSIONAL ACTIVITIES:
Oratorios and concerts with leading
British orchestras.
RECORDINGS INCLUDE: Bernstein, *Candide*
(TER); Sondheim, *Into the Woods* (RCA).
ADDRESS: c/o Daly Gagan Associates, 68
Old Brompton Road, London SW7 3LQ.

TINSLEY PAULINE   Soprano

PERSONAL DETAILS: b. 27 March 1928,
Wigan; m. 1956, George Neighbour, two
children.
EDUCATION/TRAINING: Northern School of
Music, Manchester, with Margaret Dillon
and Ellis Keeler; London Opera Centre,
with Joan Cross; further studies with Roy
Henderson, Eva Turner and Eduardo
Asquez.
PROFESSIONAL DEBUT: 1961, St Pancras
Festival, Desdemona, *Otello*.
MAJOR DEBUTS INCLUDE: 1962, Welsh
National Opera, Susanna, *The Marriage
of Figaro*; 1963, Sadler's Wells Opera,
Gilda, *Rigoletto*; 1965, Covent Garden,
Overseer, *Elektra*; 1970: Santa Fe Opera,
title role, *Anna Bolena*; Vancouver Opera,
Amelia, *Un Ballo in Maschera*; 1971,
Netherlands Opera, Abigaille, *Nabucco*;
1972, New York City Opera, Queen
Elizabeth, *Maria Stuarda*; 1973, Holland
Festival, title role, *Aida*; Lady Macbeth,
Macbeth: 1973, Houston Grand Opera;
1975, New Orleans Opera; 1977, Scottish
Opera, Kostelnička, *Jenůfa*; 1978, Opera
Theatre of St Louis, Lady Billows, *Albert
Herring*; 1980: Welsh National Opera on
tour (Mannheim, Leipzig Opera and
Komische Oper, East Berlin), title role,
Elektra; National Theatre, Prague, Lady
Macbeth, *Macbeth*; 1981, Deutsche Oper

am Rhein, Düsseldorf, title role, *Elektra*;
Ottawa Festival, Elettra, *Idomeneo*; 1982:
Opera North, Abigaille, *Nabucco*;
Frankfurt Opera: Kundry, *Parsifal*; title
role, *Elektra*; Gelsenkirchen, Isolde,
Tristan und Isolde; Lecce, title role,
Turandot; Verona Arena, Lady Macbeth,
Macbeth; 1983, Dublin Grand Opera,
Ortrud, *Lohengrin*; 1984: Baltimore Opera
Company, Brünnhilde, *Die Walküre*;
Cologne Opera, Ortrud, *Lohengrin*; 1986:
Dyer's Wife, *Die Frau ohne Schatten*:
Gran Teatre del Liceu, Barcelona and La
Scala, Milan; Wexford Festival, Witch,
Königskinder; 1987, Grand Théâtre,
Geneva, Mother/Witch, *Hänsel und
Gretel*; 1990, Glyndebourne Festival
Opera, Lady Billows, *Albert Herring*;
1991, Teatro La Fenice, Venice, Mother/
Witch, *Hänsel und Gretel*.

OPERATIC WORLD PREMIERES INCLUDE:
1979, Opera Theatre of St Louis, title role,
The Village Singer by Stephen Paulus.

CAREER IN THE UK INCLUDES: Since 1962:
Covent Garden: Santuzza, *Cavalleria
Rusticana*; Third Norn, *Götter-
dämmerung*; Mother Marie, *The
Carmelites*; Lady Billows, *Albert Herring*;
English Opera Group, Lady Billows,
Albert Herring; Handel Opera Society:
Zenobia, *Radamisto*; Romilda, *Serse*;
Opera North, Fata Morgana, *The Love for
Three Oranges*; Sadler's Wells Opera/
English National Opera: Leonora, *The
Force of Destiny*; Elvira, *Ernani*;
Fiordiligi, *Così fan tutte*; Marcellina and
Countess, *The Marriage of Figaro*;
Leonore, *Fidelio*; Donna Elvira, *Don
Giovanni*; Mother/Witch, *Hansel and
Gretel*; Kabanicha, *Katya Kabanova*; title
role, *Leonore*; Welsh National Opera:
Elsa, *Lohengrin*; Lady Macbeth, *Macbeth*;
Donna Elvira, *Don Giovanni*; Abigaille,
Nabucco; Kostelnička, *Jenůfa*; Dyer's
Wife, *Die Frau ohne Schatten*; title roles:
Aida, Turandot, Elektra, Tosca.

RELATED PROFESSIONAL ACTIVITIES:
Numerous concerts, recitals, broadcasts
and television appearances in the UK and
abroad.

RECORDINGS INCLUDE: Mozart, *Idomeneo*
(PHIL); R. Strauss, *Elektra* (DECC).

ADDRESS: c/o Music International, 13
Ardilaun Road, London N5 2QR.

TIPPETT, SIR MICHAEL
Composer

PERSONAL DETAILS: b. 2 January 1905,
London.

EDUCATION/TRAINING: Stamford Grammar
School; 1923–1928, Royal College of
Music: composition with Charles Wood
and C. H. Kitson, conducting with
Malcolm Sargent and Adrian Boult; 1930–
1932, further studies with contrapuntal
scholar R. O. Morris.

CAREER: Since 1930, numerous
compositions in all genres including five
operas, four symphonies, five string
quartets, four piano sonatas, choral
works including *The Vision of Saint
Augustine* and *The Mask of Time*, and the
oratorio *A Child of Our Time*, premièred
in 1944, first major work to achieve
prominence; 1927–1931, ran Choral and
Orchestral Society, Oxted, Surrey; 1929–
1931, French teacher, Hazelwood
Preparatory School, Oxted; 1932, adult
education work in music, London County
Council and Royal Arsenal Co-operative
Society Education Departments; 1940–
1951, Director of Music, Morley College.

OPERATIC WORLD PREMIERES: Covent
Garden: 1955, *The Midsummer Marriage*,
conductor John Pritchard, director
Christopher West, designer Barbara
Hepworth; 1962 (at the Coventry Festival),
King Priam, conductor John Pritchard,
director Sam Wanamaker, designer Sean
Kenny; 1970, *The Knot Garden*, conductor
Colin Davis, director Peter Hall, designer
Timothy O'Brien; 1977, *The Ice Break*,
conductor Colin Davis, director Sam
Wanamaker, designer Ralph Koltai; 1989,
Houston Grand Opera, *New Year*,
conductor John DeMain, director Peter
Hall, designer Alison Chitty (all operas in
three acts with librettos by the
composer).

RELATED PROFESSIONAL ACTIVITIES:
1969–1974, Artistic Director, Bath Festival;
1979–1989, President, Kent Opera; since
1983, President, London College of Music.

RECORDINGS INCLUDE: *The Ice Break*
(VIRG), *King Priam*, *The Knot Garden* (both
DECC), *The Midsummer Marriage* (LYRI/
PHIL), Symphonies Nos 1–4, String
Quartets Nos 1–4 (all DECC), Concerto for
double string orchestra (EMI/LOND/NIMB/
VIRG), Concerto for orchestra (PHIL),
Concerto for violin, viola, cello and
orchestra (PHIL), *A Child of Our Time*
(DECC/PHIL/RPO), *The Mask of Time* (EMI),
Songs for Dov for tenor and small
orchestra (VIRG).

VIDEOS INCLUDE: *King Priam* (Kent Opera).

PUBLICATIONS AND RELEVANT
PUBLICATIONS INCLUDE: 1959, *Moving into
Aquarius*, revised 1974 (Paladin); 1980,
Music of the Angels (Eulenburg); 1965,
*Michael Tippett: A Symposium on his 60th
Birthday*, editor Ian Kemp (Faber); 1981:
Michael Tippett by Meirion Bowen
(Robson); *Tippett: The Composer and his
Music* by Ian Kemp (Schott); 1985, Opera
Guide, *The Operas of Michael Tippett*
(Calder); 1991, autobiography, *Those
Twentieth Century Blues* (Hutchinson).

AWARDS AND HONOURS INCLUDE: 1948,
Cobbett Medal for Chamber Music; 1959,
Commander, Order of the British Empire
(CBE); 1966, Knighthood; 1976: Gold
Medal, Royal Philharmonic Society;
Honorary Member, American Academy of
Arts; Extraordinary Member, Akademie
der Künste (Berlin); 1979, Companion of
Honour (CH); 1983, Order of Merit (OM);
1988, Commandeur de l'Ordre des Arts et
des Lettres (France); honorary doctorates
from more than 20 British and foreign
universities.

ADDRESS: c/o Schott & Co. Ltd, 48 Great
Marlborough Street, London W1V 2BN.

TOMLINSON JOHN   Bass

PERSONAL DETAILS: b. 22 September 1946,
Lancashire; m. 1969, Moya Joel, three
children.

EDUCATION/TRAINING: 1964–1967,
University of Manchester, studied civil
engineering; 1967–1971, Royal
Manchester College of Music, with Patrick
McGuigan; privately with Rupert Bruce-
Lockhart and Otakar Kraus.

PROFESSIONAL DEBUT: 1968, chorus
member, Scottish Opera.

EARLY CAREER INCLUDED: 1970–1974,
numerous appearances with Chelsea
Opera Group, Glyndebourne Festival and
Touring Opera, Kent Opera, New Opera
Company; roles included: Silvano, *La
Calisto*; Banquo, *Macbeth*; Colline, *La
Bohème*; Second Priest, *Die Zauberflöte*;
Leporello, *Don Giovanni*; Reede, *Arden
Must Die* (1974, New Opera Company,
British première).

MAJOR DEBUTS INCLUDE: 1974, English
National Opera, Monk, *Don Carlos*; 1979,
Covent Garden, Fifth Jew, *Salome*; 1980,
Grand Théâtre, Geneva, Masetto, *Don
Giovanni*; 1982, Aix-en-Provence Festival,
Speaker, *Die Zauberflöte*; 1983: San
Diego Opera, Heinrich, *Lohengrin*; San
Francisco Opera, Pimen, *Boris Godunov*;
Vancouver Opera, Zaccaria, *Nabucco*;
1984, Paris Opera, Banquo, *Macbeth*;
1986, Opera North, Méphistophélès,
Faust; 1987: Scottish Opera, Claggart,
Billy Budd; Netherlands Opera, Baron
Ochs, *Der Rosenkavalier*; 1988: Bayreuth
Festival, Wotan, *Der Ring des
Nibelungen*; Deutsche Oper, Berlin,
Hagen, *Götterdämmerung*; 1990,
Saizburg Easter Fesival, Rocco, *Fidelio*;
1992: Deutsche Staatsoper, Berlin,
Gurnemanz, *Parsifal*; Vienna State
Opera, Hermann, *Tannhäuser*.

OPERATIC WORLD PREMIERES INCLUDE:
1977, English National Opera, Villac Umu,
The Royal Hunt of the Sun by Iain
Hamilton; 1991, Covent Garden, Green
Knight/Bertilak de Hautdesert, *Gawain* by
Harrison Birtwistle.

CAREER IN THE UK INCLUDES: Since 1975:
Covent Garden: Pietro, *Simon
Boccanegra*; Abimelech, *Samson et
Dalila*; Masetto, Leporello and
Commendatore, *Don Giovanni*; Hobson,
Peter Grimes; Nightwatchman and Hans

Sachs, *Die Meistersinger von Nürnberg*;
Ferrando, *Il Trovatore*; Publio, *La
Clemenza di Tito*; Trulove, *The Rake's
Progress*; Cadmus, *Semele*; Richard
Taverner, *Taverner*; Colline, *La Bohème*;
Lorenzo, *I Capuleti e i Montecchi*;
Harapha, *Samson*; Don Basilio, *Il
Barbiere di Siviglia*; Timur, *Turandot*;
Sparafucile, *Rigoletto*; Wotan, Hunding
and Hagen, *Der Ring des Nibelungen*;
English National Opera (1975–1981,
Principal Bass): Fasolt, *The Ring of the
Nibelung*; Colline, *La Bohème*; Sarastro,
The Magic Flute; Leporello, *Don
Giovanni*; Ramfis, *Aida*; Don Fernando,
Fidelio; Friar Laurence, *Romeo and
Juliet*; Achilla, *Julius Caesar*; Charon,
Orfeo; King Marke, *Tristan and Isolde*;
Arkel, *Pelléas and Mélisande*; Talbot,
Mary Stuart; Sparafucile, *Rigoletto*;
General, *The Gambler*; Méphistophélès,
Faust; Baron Ochs, *Der Rosenkavalier*;
Fiesco, *Simon Boccanegra*; title roles:
The Marriage of Figaro, *Duke
Bluebeard's Castle*, *Boris Godunov*,
Moses; Opera North: Claggart, *Billy
Budd*; Philip II, *Don Carlos*; title roles:
Boris Godunov, *Attila*.
RELATED PROFESSIONAL ACTIVITIES:
  Regular concerts, recitals, broadcasts
  and television appearances in the UK and
  abroad.
RECORDINGS INCLUDE: Birtwistle, *Punch
  and Judy* (ETCE); Donizetti, *Mary Stuart*;
  Handel: *Alcina*, *Giulio Cesare* (all EMI),
  Acis and Galatea, *Hercules*, *Messiah* (all
  ARCH); Martinů, *The Greek Passion* (SUPR);
  Monteverdi, *Orfeo* (ARCH); Mozart: *Così
  fan tutte*, *Don Giovanni*, *Le Nozze di
  Figaro* (all ERAT); Puccini: *Manon Lescaut*
  (DG), *Tosca*; Rossini, *Guillaume Tell* (both
  DECC); Verdi: *Rigoletto* (EMI), *La Traviata*
  (DECC); Wagner, *Parsifal* (ERAT).
VIDEOS INCLUDE: Britten, *Peter Grimes*
  (Covent Garden); Donizetti, *Mary Stuart*;
  Handel, *Julius Caesar*; Verdi, *Rigoletto*
  (all English National Opera).
AWARDS AND HONOURS INCLUDE: 1991,
  Royal Philharmonic Society Award;
  Honorary Member, Royal Northern
  College of Music.

ADDRESS: c/o Music International, 13
  Ardilaun Road, London N5 2QR.

TORTELIER YAN PASCAL
Conductor and Violinist

POSITION: Principal Conductor, BBC
  Philharmonic Orchestra.
PERSONAL DETAILS: b. 1947, Paris, France.
EDUCATION/TRAINING: Paris Conservatoire,
  studied violin; studied composition,
  counterpoint and harmony with Nadia
  Boulanger in Paris; studied conducting
  with Franco Ferrara in Siena.
OPERATIC DEBUT: 1978, Toulouse, *Così fan
  tutte*.
CAREER: 1974–1983, Leader and Associate
  Conductor, Orchestre du Capitole,
  Toulouse; 1989–1992, Principal Conductor
  and Artistic Director, Ulster Orchestra,
  Northern Ireland; since 1992, Principal
  Conductor, BBC Philharmonic Orchestra.
MAJOR OPERATIC DEBUTS INCLUDE: 1983:
  Opera North, *Il Trovatore*; Wexford
  Festival, *La Vedova Scaltra*; 1986, Teatro
  San Carlo, Naples, *Don Chichotte in
  Sierra Morena*; 1987, Scottish Opera, *The
  Seraglio*; 1988, English National Opera,
  Carmen.
OPERA PERFORMANCES IN THE UK
INCLUDE: Since 1985: English National
  Opera: *The Pearl Fishers*, *Werther*;
  Opera North, *Werther*.
RELATED PROFESSIONAL ACTIVITIES:
  Regular performances with leading
  symphony and chamber orchestras in the
  UK and abroad.
RECORDINGS INCLUDE: As conductor: Bizet:
  Arlesienne, *Carmen Suites* (both CHAN);
  Cantaloube, *Songs of the Auvergne* (VIRG);
  Debussy and Ravel, orchestral works;
  Saint-Saëns, Symphonies Nos 2 & 3 (all
  CHAN); as violinist: Fauré, orchestral
  works; Lalo, *Symphonie Espagnole* (both
  EMI).
ADDRESS: c/o Intermusica Artists'
  Management, 16 Duncan Terrace, London
  N1 8BZ.

TRACEY EDMUND
Administrator, Librettist and Translator

PERSONAL DETAILS: b. 14 November 1927, Preston.

EDUCATION/TRAINING: Lincoln College, Oxford; Guildhall School of Music and Drama.

CAREER: Sadler's Wells Opera/English National Opera: 1965–1966, Literary Manager; 1966–1973 and 1979–1985, Director of Drama and Text; 1973–1979, Production Director; 1985–1993, Artistic Adviser.

OPERATIC WORLD PREMIERES INCLUDE: 1969, Sadler's Wells Opera, librettist, *Lucky Peter's Journey* by Malcolm Williamson.

OTHER PROFESSIONAL ACTIVITIES INCLUDE: 1958–1965, music critic, *The Observer*; 1959–1964, Music Editor, *The Times Educational Supplement*; translations include: *La Belle Hélène*, *Die Fledermaus*, *The Merry Widow* (all dialogue only), *Sandrina's Secret*, *The Tales of Hoffmann*, (both new performing editions), *Aida*, *Cavalleria Rusticana*, *Faust*, *Louise*, *Manon*, *A Masked Ball*, *Pagliacci*, *Romeo and Juliet*, *The Sicilian Vespers*, *Tosca*, *La Traviata*.

PUBLICATIONS INCLUDE: Libretto, *Lucky Peter's Journey* (Weinberger); translations: *Aida*, *Manon*, *A Masked Ball*, *Tosca*, *La Traviata* (all Calder), *La Belle Hélène*, *Die Fledermaus*, *The Merry Widow* (all Weinberger).

ADDRESS: Not available.

TRANTER JOHN   Bass

PERSONAL DETAILS: b. 8 May 1946, Derbyshire; two children.

PREVIOUS OCCUPATION: 1961–1970, grocer.

EDUCATION/TRAINING: 1966–1970, privately with John Dethick; 1970–1972, London Opera Centre.

PROFESSIONAL DEBUT: 1972, Opera for All, Raimondo, *Lucia di Lammermoor*.

EARLY CAREER INCLUDED: 1972–1976: Kent Opera: Seneca, *The Coronation of Poppea*; Sarastro, *The Magic Flute*; Opera for All: Monterone and Sparafucile, *Rigoletto*; Commendatore, *Don Giovanni*; Prince Gremin, *Eugene Onegin*; Méphistophélès, *Faust*.

MAJOR DEBUTS INCLUDE: Commendatore, *Don Giovanni*: 1976, English National Opera; 1977, Glyndebourne Touring Opera; 1978, Opera North, Old Hebrew, *Samson et Dalila*; 1983, Welsh National Opera, Fasolt, *The Rhinegold*; 1987, Scottish Opera, Dansker, *Billy Budd*; 1990, Covent Garden, Leone, *Attila*; 1991: Marseilles Opera, Hobson, *Peter Grimes*; Pittsburgh Opera, Varlaam, *Boris Godunov*.

OPERATIC WORLD PREMIERES INCLUDE: 1977, English National Opera, Domingo, *The Royal Hunt of the Sun* by Iain Hamilton.

CAREER IN THE UK INCLUDES: Since 1977: Covent Garden: Fafner, *Siegfried*; Melcthal, *Guillaume Tell*; English National Opera: Colline, *La Bohème*; Betto, *Gianni Schicchi*; Calatrava, *The Force of Destiny*; Bartolo, *The Marriage of Figaro*; Badger, *The Cunning Little Vixen*; Nourabad, *The Pearl Fishers*; Don Fernando, *Fidelio*; Grand Inquisitor, *Don Carlos*; Angelotti, *Tosca*; Opera North: Colline, *La Bohème*; Zaccaria, *Nabucco*; Ferrando, *Il Trovatore*; Oroveso, *Norma*; Tirésias, *Oedipus Rex*; Trulove, *The Rake's Progress*; Monterone, *Rigoletto*; title role, *The Mikado*; Scottish Opera: Bonze, *Madama Butterfly*; King, *Aida*; Welsh National Opera, Fafner and Hagen, *The Ring of the Nibelung*.

RELATED PROFESSIONAL ACTIVITIES: Numerous concerts in the UK and abroad.

ADDRESS: Not available.

TRELEAVEN JOHN   Tenor

PERSONAL DETAILS: b. 10 June 1950, Cornwall; m. 1980, Roxane Folley (soprano), two children.

EDUCATION/TRAINING: 1970–1974, London College of Music, with Ivor Evans; 1974, Britten-Pears School for Advanced Musical Studies, with Peter Pears; 1975–1976, London Opera Centre, with Frederic Cox; 1977, with Nino Campanino in Naples.

PROFESSIONAL DEBUT: 1976, English National Opera on tour, Don José, *Carmen.*

EARLY CAREER INCLUDED: 1976–1979, Principal Tenor, Welsh National Opera: Mercury, *Orpheus in the Underworld* (debut); Mark, *The Midsummer Marriage*; Nemorino, *L'Elisir d'Amore*; Arminio, *I Masnadieri*; Nadir, *The Pearl Fishers*; Red Whiskers, *Billy Budd*; Don Basilio, *The Marriage of Figaro*; Flute, *A Midsummer Night's Dream*; Bob Boles, *Peter Grimes*; Pinkerton, *Madam Butterfly*; Tamino, *The Magic Flute*; Alfredo, *La Traviata.*

MAJOR DEBUTS INCLUDE: 1980, Covent Garden, Froh, *Das Rheingold*; 1982, Teatro Comunale, Bologna, title role, *La Damnation de Faust*; 1984: Scottish Opera, Florestan, *Fidelio*; Paris Opera, Pylade, *Iphigénie en Tauride*; 1985, Opera North, Dick Johnson, *La Fanciulla del West*; 1988, Hawaii Opera, Calaf, *Turandot*; 1990: San Francisco Opera, Prince Galitsin, *Khovanshchina*; Teatro Colón, Buenos Aires, title role, *Peter Grimes*; 1991: Mainz, Macduff, *Macbeth*; Mannheim, title role, *Peter Grimes.*

CAREER IN THE UK INCLUDES: Since 1979: Covent Garden, First Armed Man, *Die Zauberflöte*; title role, *Peter Grimes*; English National Opera: Don José, *Carmen*; Cavaradossi, *Tosca*; Erik, *The Flying Dutchman*; Des Grieux, *Manon*; Julien, *Louise*; Prince, *Rusalka*; Drum Major, *Wozzeck*; title roles: *Don Carlos*, *The Tales of Hoffmann*, *The Damnation of Faust*; Opera North: Radamès, *Aida*; Cavaradossi, *Tosca*; title role, *Peter Grimes*; Scottish Opera: Jeník, *The Bartered Bride*; Radamès, *Aida*; Erik, *Der Fliegende Holländer*; title roles: *Werther*, *Oedipus Rex.*

RELATED PROFESSIONAL ACTIVITIES: Numerous concerts, recitals, broadcasts, television and festival appearances in the UK and abroad.

RECORDINGS INCLUDE: Bernstein, *Candide* (DG); Donizetti, *L'Assedio di Calais* (OPRA); Meyerbeer, *Le Prophète*; Puccini, *Il Tabarro* (both CBS); Rachmaninov, *Vespers* (ABBE); Verdi, *Il Trovatore* (PHIL).

VIDEOS INCLUDE: Dvořák, *Rusalka* (English National Opera); Sullivan, *Ruddigore* (Walker).

ADDRESS: c/o Athole Still International Management Ltd, Greystoke House, 80–86 Westow Street, London SE19 3AF.

TURNAGE MARK-ANTHONY
Composer

PERSONAL DETAILS: b. 10 June 1960, Essex.

EDUCATION/TRAINING: Royal College of Music, with Oliver Knussen and John Lambert; 1983, Berkshire Music Center, Tanglewood, Massachusetts, with Hans Werner Henze and Gunter Schuller.

FIRST WORK TO ACHIEVE PROMINENCE: 1982, London Sinfonietta, *Night Dances* for orchestra.

CAREER: Compositions include two operas, orchestral, instrumental, ensemble, choral and vocal works; 1985–1986, Composer in Residence, National Centre for Orchestral Studies, University of London; Featured Composer: 1986, Bath Festival; 1987, Musica Nova Festival, Glasgow; 1989–1992, Composer in Association with the City of Birmingham Symphony Orchestra.

OPERATIC WORLD PREMIERES: 1988, first Munich Biennale of Music Theatre, *Greek*, opera in two acts, libretto adapted by the composer and Jonathan Moore from the play by Steven Berkoff, conductor Sian Edwards, director Jonathan Moore, designer David Blight (1988, British première, Edinburgh International Festival); 1992, BBC Television, *Killing Time*, libretto compiled by the composer from prisoners' poems,

274

director Rob Walker, designer Ana
Gebens.
RELATED PROFESSIONAL ACTIVITIES: 1988,
Release (BBC Television documentary
about the composer).
AWARDS INCLUDE: 1982, Guinness Prize;
1983, Benjamin Britten Young
Composers' Prize; 1988, BMW Prize,
Munich Biennale, *Greek*; 1990, Royal
Philharmonic Society/Charles Heidsieck
Award, BBC Television production of
Greek.
ADDRESS: c/o Schott & Co. Ltd, 48 Great
Marlborough Street, London W1V 2BN.

TURNER JANE   Mezzo-soprano

PERSONAL DETAILS: b. 6 March 1960,
County Durham; m., one child.
EDUCATION/TRAINING: Guildhall School of
Music and Drama, with Dorothy
Richardson; London Opera Studio, with
Silvia Beamish; currently with David
Harper.
PROFESSIONAL DEBUT: 1984, Bayreuth
Festival, Wellgunde and Siegrune, *Der
Ring des Nibelungen*.

MAJOR DEBUTS INCLUDE: 1985:
Glyndebourne Touring Opera, title role,
Carmen; Batignano Festival, Teodata,
Flavio; 1987: Covent Garden, Anne who
Strips, *The King Goes Forth to France*
(British première); English National
Opera, Maddalena, *Rigoletto*;
Glyndebourne Festival Opera, Flora, *La
Traviata*; Bayreuth Festival: 1987, Flower
Maiden, *Parsifal*; 1988, Flosshilde, *Der
Ring des Nibelungen*.
CAREER IN THE UK INCLUDES: Since 1988:
Covent Garden: Flower Maiden, *Parsifal*;
Flosshilde and Siegrune, *Der Ring des
Nibelungen*; English National Opera,
Lola, *Cavalleria Rusticana*.
RELATED PROFESSIONAL ACTIVITIES:
Concerts and recitals in the UK and
Europe.
AWARDS AND HONOURS INCLUDE:
Countess of Munster Award; The Friends
of Covent Garden Dame Eva Turner
Award; Associate, Guildhall School of
Music and Drama.
ADDRESS: c/o Lies Askonas Ltd, 186 Drury
Lane, London WC2B 5RY.

*   *   *   *

VAN ALLAN RICHARD   Bass

POSITIONS: Principal Bass, English National
Opera; Director, National Opera Studio.
PERSONAL DETAILS: b. 28 May 1935,
Nottinghamshire; m. 1976, Rosemary
Pickering (m. diss.), three children.
PREVIOUS OCCUPATIONS: 1956–1957,
policeman; 1959–1964, science teacher.
EDUCATION/TRAINING: 1957–1959,
Worcester College of Education; 1959–
1964, Birmingham School of Music, with
David Franklin; privately with Jani
Strasser.
PROFESSIONAL DEBUT: 1966, Glyndebourne
Festival Opera, Second Priest/Second
Armed Man, *Die Zauberflöte*.

EARLY CAREER INCLUDED: 1967–1971,
appearances with Covent Garden,
Glyndebourne Festival and Touring
Opera, Sadler's Wells Opera, Scottish
Opera, Welsh National Opera; roles
included: Mandarin, *Turandot*; Don
Alfonso, *Così fan tutte*; Bartolo, *La Nozze
di Figaro*; Banquo, *Macbeth*; Zaccaria,
Nabucco; Leporello and title role, *Don
Giovanni*.
MAJOR DEBUTS INCLUDE: 1975: Opera
Company of Boston, Don Pizarro, *Fidelio*;
Paris Opera, Masetto, *Don Giovanni*;
Baron Ochs, *Der Rosenkavalier.* 1975,
San Diego Opera, 1979, Teatro Colón,
Buenos Aires; 1980, Welsh National
Opera at Komische Oper, East Berlin, Da
Silva, *Ernani*; 1982, La Monnaie,

Brussels, Wurm, *Luisa Miller*; 1984, English National Opera USA tour (including Metropolitan Opera, New York): Sparafucile, *Rigoletto*; Raleigh, *Gloriana*; 1985, Greater Miami Opera, Mustafa, *L'Italiana in Algeri*; 1986: Glyndebourne Festival Opera at the Hong Kong Arts Festival, Leporello, *Don Giovanni*; Seattle Opera, Méphistophélès, *Faust*; 1987, Metropolitan Opera, New York, Count des Grieux, *Manon*; Teatro La Zarzuela, Madrid: 1991, Swallow, *Peter Grimes*; 1992, Don Jerome, *The Duenna* by Roberto Gerhard (world stage première).

OPERATIC WORLD PREMIERES INCLUDE: 1970, Glyndebourne Festival Opera, Jowler, *The Rising of the Moon* by Nicholas Maw; 1992, Almeida Opera, Man without a Conscience, *Terrible Mouth* by Nigel Osborne; English National Opera: 1992, Tiresias, *Bakxai* by John Buller; 1993, Abbot, *Inquest of Love* by Jonathan Harvey.

CAREER IN THE UK INCLUDES: Since 1972: Covent Garden (1972–1978, member): Leporello, *Don Giovanni*; Wurm, *Luisa Miller*; Don Pizarro, *Fidelio*; Don Ferrando, *Il Trovatore*; Don Alfonso, *Così fan tutte*; Colline, *La Bohème*; Theatre Director/Banker, *Lulu* (1981, British première, three act version); Mathieu, *Andrea Chénier*; Angelotti, *Tosca*; Montano, *Otello*; Count de St Bris, *Les Huguenots*; title role, *Le Nozze di Figaro*; English National Opera (since 1978, Principal Bass): Speaker, *The Magic Flute*; Baron Ochs, *Der Rosenkavalier*; Count des Grieux, *Manon*; Mustafa, *The Italian Girl in Algiers*; Water Sprite, *Rusalka*; Kecal, *The Bartered Bride*; Raleigh, *Gloriana*; Claggart, *Billy Budd*; Pooh-Bah, *The Mikado*; Collatinus, *The Rape of Lucretia*; Frank Maurrant, *Street Scene*; Tirésias, *Oedipus Rex*; Grand Inquisitor, *Don Carlos*; King Hildebrand, *Princess Ida*; title roles: *Boris Godunov*, *Don Giovanni*; Glyndebourne Festival Opera: Osmin, *Die Entführung aus dem Serail*; Trulove, *The Rake's Progress*; Tchelio, *L'Amour des Trois Oranges*;

Superintendent Budd, *Albert Herring*; Pistol, *Falstaff*; Welsh National Opera: Grand Inquisitor, *Don Carlos*; Massimiliano, *I Masnadieri*; Grigoris, *The Greek Passion* (1981, British première); Don Pizarro, *Fidelio*.

RELATED PROFESSIONAL ACTIVITIES: Since 1985, Director, National Opera Studio; Council member, British Youth Opera.

RECORDINGS INCLUDE: Britten, *Peter Grimes* (PHIL); Cavalli, *L'Ormindo* (ARGO); Massenet, *Thaïs* (EMI); Mozart: *Così fan tutte*, *Don Giovanni* (both PHIL/EMI); Puccini, *Tosca* (DECC); Sullivan, *The Mikado* (TELA/TER); Verdi: *Un Ballo in Maschera*, *La Traviata* (both EMI), *Luisa Miller* (DECC), *I Vespri Siciliani* (RCA); Weill, *Street Scene* (TER).

VIDEOS INCLUDE: Britten: *Albert Herring* (Glyndebourne Festival Opera), *Billy Budd*, *Gloriana*, *The Rape of Lucretia* (all English National Opera); Giordano, *Andrea Chénier* (Covent Garden); Prokofiev, *L'Amour des Trois Oranges* (Glyndebourne Festival Opera); Sullivan: *Iolanthe* (Walker), *The Mikado* (English National Opera).

AWARDS AND HONOURS INCLUDE: 1966, John Christie Award; 1987, Honorary Associate, Royal Academy of Music; Grammy Award (USA), *Così fan tutte* (PHIL).

ADDRESS: c/o John Coast, 31 Sinclair Road, London W14 0NS.

VAUGHAN ELIZABETH
Mezzo-soprano and Teacher

POSITION: Professor of Singing, Guildhall School of Music and Drama.

PERSONAL DETAILS: b. 12 March 1937, Llanfyllin, North Wales; m. 1968, Ray Brown (General Manager, D'Oyly Carte Opera), two children.

EDUCATION/TRAINING: 1955–1958, Royal Academy of Music, with Olive Groves; privately with Eva Turner.

PROFESSIONAL DEBUT: As soprano: 1960, Welsh National Opera, Abigaille, *Nabucco*.

EARLY CAREER INCLUDED: 1961–1972: member, Covent Garden: Isotta, *The Silent Woman*; Morgana, *Alcina*; Liù, *Turandot*; Musetta and Mimi, *La Bohème*; Andromache, *King Priam*; Tytania, *A Midsummer Night's Dream*; Amelia, *Simon Boccanegra*; Teresa, *Benvenuto Cellini*; Leonora, *Il Trovatore*; Donna Elvira, *Don Giovanni*; Violetta, *La Traviata*; Euridice, *Orfeo ed Euridice*; title role, *Madama Butterfly*; also, Welsh National Opera: Musetta and Mimi, *La Bohème*; Jemmy, *William Tell*; Violetta, *La Traviata*; Alice, *Falstaff*.

MAJOR DEBUTS INCLUDE: 1962, Covent Garden, Gilda, *Rigoletto*; 1963, Welsh National Opera, Constanze, *The Seraglio*; 1970, Vienna State Opera, Amelia, *Un Ballo in Maschera*; 1971: Deutsche Oper, Berlin, Amelia, *Simon Boccanegra*; Hamburg State Opera, title role, *Madama Butterfly*; 1972, Australian Opera, Sydney, Abigaille, *Nabucco*; 1973, Metropolitan Opera, New York, Donna Elvira, *Don Giovanni*; 1976, Cassel, title role, *Turandot*; 1978, Paris Opera, title role, *Madama Butterfly*; 1979: Opera North, title role, *Tosca*; Greater Miami Opera, title role, *Aida*; 1981, English National Opera, title role, *Madam Butterfly*; 1990, Welsh National Opera in Tokyo, Herodias, *Salome*.

CAREER IN THE UK INCLUDES: As soprano: 1972–1990: Covent Garden: Abigaille, *Nabucco*; Gayle, *The Ice Break*; Elettra, *Idomeneo*; Andromache, *King Priam* (also 1985, Athens Festival); Overseer, *Elektra*; English National Opera: Penelope, *Gloriana* (also 1984, USA tour); Leonore, *Fidelio*; title role, *Aida*; Glyndebourne Touring Opera, Leonore, *Fidelio*; Opera North: Violetta, *La Traviata*; Lady Macbeth, *Macbeth*; Abigaille, *Nabucco*; title role, *Madam Butterfly*; Scottish Opera: Violetta, *La Traviata*; title role, *Madama Butterfly*; Welsh National Opera: Leonora, *Il Trovatore*; Leonora, *La Forza del Destino*; Madeleine, *Andrea Chénier*; title roles: *Madam Butterfly*, *Manon Lescaut*, *Tosca*; as mezzo-soprano: since 1990: Chelsea Opera Group, Laura, *La Gioconda*; Scottish Opera: Herodias, *Salome*; Kabanicha, *Katya Kabanova*; Welsh National Opera, Herodias, *Salome*.

RELATED PROFESSIONAL ACTIVITIES: Numerous concerts and recitals in the UK and abroad; since 1988, Professor of Singing, Guildhall School of Music and Drama.

RECORDINGS INCLUDE: Handel, *Chandos Anthem No. 9*; Vivaldi, *Gloria in D* (both DECC).

VIDEOS INCLUDE: Britten, *Gloriana* (English National Opera).

AWARDS AND HONOURS INCLUDE: 1959, Kathleen Ferrier Memorial Scholarship; 1987, Honorary Doctorate of Music, University of Wales; Fellow, Royal Academy of Music.

ADDRESS: c/o Music International, 13 Ardilaun Road, London N5 2QR.

VEASEY JOSEPHINE
Teacher (formerly Mezzo-soprano)

POSITION: Vocal Consultant, English National Opera.

PERSONAL DETAILS: b. 10 July 1930, London; m. Ande Anderson (formerly General Manager, Royal Opera House, Covent Garden, m. diss.), two children.

EDUCATION/TRAINING: Vocal studies with Audrey Langford.

PROFESSIONAL DEBUT: 1949, chorus member, Covent Garden.

CAREER INCLUDES: 1949–1950, chorus member, Covent Garden; 1951–1955, several Opera for All and Arts Council tours; 1955–1982, member, Covent Garden, 780 performances in 60 roles including: Preziosilla, *La Forza del Destino*; Octavian, *Der Rosenkavalier*; Amneris, *Aida*; Maddalena, *Rigoletto*; Fricka and Waltraute, *Der Ring des Nibelungen*; Dorabella, *Così fan tutte*; Dido and Cassandra, *Les Troyens*; Herodias, *Salome*; Brangäne, *Tristan und*

Isolde; Eboli, *Don Carlos*; title roles: *Iphigénie en Tauride, Carmen*; also: 1957–1969, Glyndebourne Festival Opera: Zulma, *L'Italiana in Algeri*; Cherubino, *Le Nozze di Figaro*; Clarice, *La Pietra del Paragone*; Octavian, *Der Rosenkavalier*; Charlotte, *Werther*; appearances at international opera houses and festivals including: Aix-en-Provence, Vienna State Opera, Metropolitan Opera, New York and La Scala, Milan; numerous concerts, recitals and broadcasts with leading conductors and orchestras in the UK and abroad; last public performance: 1982, Covent Garden, Herodias, *Salome*; 1983–1984, Teacher of Voice Production, Royal Academy of Music; since 1984, Vocal Consultant, English National Opera and private voice teacher; Council member, British Youth Opera.

OPERATIC WORLD PREMIERES INCLUDE: Covent Garden: 1962 (at the Coventry Festival), Andromache, *King Priam* by Michael Tippett; 1976, Emperor, *We Come to the River* by Hans Werner Henze.

STUDENTS HAVE INCLUDED: Richard Angas, Kim Begley, Sally Burgess, Phyllis Cannan, Adrian Clarke, Michael Druiett, Anne Evans, Helen Field, Mary Hegarty, Simon Masterton-Smith, Felicity Palmer, Ethna Robinson, Peter Sidhom, Vivian Tierney, Alan Woodrow.

RECORDINGS INCLUDE: Berlioz: *La Damnation de Faust, Les Nuits d'été, Les Troyens* (all PHIL); Britten, *A Midsummer Night's Dream* (DECC); Purcell, *Dido and Aeneas* (PHIL); Verdi, *Requiem* (LODI); Wagner: *Das Rheingold* (DG), *Die Walküre* (NUOV).

HONOURS INCLUDE: 1970, Commander, Order of the British Empire (CBE); 1972, Honorary Member, Royal Academy of Music.

ADDRESS: 2 Pound Cottage, St Mary Bourne, Andover, Hampshire.

VENTRIS CHRISTOPHER
Tenor

PERSONAL DETAILS: b. London.

EDUCATION/TRAINING: 1982–1988, Royal Academy of Music, with Joy Mammen.

PROFESSIONAL DEBUT: 1987, chorus member, Glyndebourne Festival Opera.

MAJOR DEBUTS INCLUDE: 1988, Glyndebourne Touring Opera, Vanya, *Katya Kabanova*; 1989: Covent Garden, Major-Domo, *Der Rosenkavalier*; Glyndebourne Festival Opera, title role, *The Rake's Progress*; 1990, Opera North, Squire, *Jérusalem* (British stage première); 1992: English National Opera, Scaramuccio, *Ariadne auf Naxos*; Flanders Opera, Antwerp, Paris, *King Priam*; Leipzig Opera, Steersman, Der *Fliegende Holländer*.

OPERATIC WORLD PREMIERES INCLUDE: 1991, Opera North, Robert Lonle, *Caritas* by Robert Saxton.

CAREER IN THE UK INCLUDES: Since 1988: English National Opera, Tancredi, *The Duel of Tancredi and Clorinda*; Glyndebourne Festival and Touring Opera: Hotel Porter/Third Gondolier, *Death in Venice*; Jacquino, *Fidelio*; Števa, *Jenůfa*; Opera North: Uldino, *Attila*; Paris, *King Priam*; Novice, *Billy Budd*.

RELATED PROFESSIONAL ACTIVITIES: Numerous concerts and recitals in the UK and abroad.

RECORDINGS INCLUDE: Saxton, *Caritas* (COLL).

VIDEOS INCLUDE: Britten, *Death in Venice* (Glyndebourne Touring Opera).

AWARDS INCLUDE: 1986, Countess of Munster Award; 1988, Esso/Glyndebourne Touring Opera Award; 1990, John Christie Award.

ADDRESS: c/o Harrison/Parrott Ltd, 12 Penzance Place, London W11 4PA.

VERCO WENDY
Mezzo-soprano

PERSONAL DETAILS: b. Melbourne, Australia.

PREVIOUS OCCUPATION: 1965–1972, personal assistant in commercial industry.

EDUCATION/TRAINING: 1972–1975, New South Wales State Conservatorium of Music, Sydney, with Elizabeth Todd; 1981–1982, London Opera Studio; privately: 1975–1977, with Walther Gruner; 1977–1979, with Helga Mott; since 1979, with Audrey Langford.

PROFESSIONAL DEBUT: 1982, Opera 80, Prince Orlofsky, *Die Fledermaus*.

EARLY CAREER INCLUDED: 1982–1983: Glyndebourne Festival Opera, chorus and small roles; Opera 80, Dorabella, *Così fan tutte*; Batignano Festival, title role, *La Dori*.

MAJOR DEBUTS INCLUDE: 1984, Welsh National Opera, Amneris, *The Drama of Aida*; 1985, Opera North, Irene, *Tamburlaine* (Handel); 1986, Covent Garden, Rossweisse, *Die Walküre*; 1987, La Monnaie, Brussels, Emilia, *Otello*; Meg Page, *Falstaff*. 1989–1990, Welsh National Opera in Milan and Tokyo; 1991, Théâtre des Champs Elysées, Paris.

CAREER IN THE UK INCLUDES: Since 1984: Opera Factory, Clytemnestra, *Iphigenias*; Welsh National Opera: Maddalena, *Rigoletto*; Emilia, *Otello*; Meg Page, *Falstaff*.

RELATED PROFESSIONAL ACTIVITIES: Concerts and recitals with City of Birmingham Symphony Orchestra and London Mozart Players.

VIDEOS INCLUDE: Monteverdi, *L'Incoronazione di Poppea*; Mozart, *Idomeneo*; R. Strauss, *Arabella* (all Glyndebourne Festival Opera).

ADDRESS: c/o Ron Gonsalves Personal Artists & Concert Management, 10 Dagnan Road, London SW12 9LQ.

VICK GRAHAM   Director

POSITION: Artistic Director, City of Birmingham Touring Opera.

PERSONAL DETAILS: b. 30 December 1953, Merseyside.

EDUCATION/TRAINING: Royal Manchester College of Music.

CAREER: 1974–1978, staff director, Scottish Opera; 1976–1977, Associate Director, English Music Theatre; 1978–1981, founder and Director, Scottish Opera Go Round; 1984–1987, Director of Productions, Scottish Opera; since 1987, Artistic Director, City of Birmingham Touring Opera.

MAJOR OPERATIC DEBUTS INCLUDE: 1978, Scottish Opera, *The Elixir of Love*; 1979, Batignano Festival, *Orontea*; 1981, Wexford Festival, *I Gioielli della Madonna*; 1982, Opera North, *Così fan tutte*; 1983, English National Opera, *Ariadne auf Naxos*; 1985: La Monnaie, Brussels, *L'Elisir d'Amore*; Teatro La Fenice, Venice, *Zaide*; 1986, Opera Theatre of St Louis, *The Seraglio*; 1987, City of Birmingham Touring Opera, *Falstaff*; 1988, Bonn Opera, *Don Pasquale*; 1989: Covent Garden, *Un Re in Ascolto* (British première); Netherlands Opera, *Ariadne auf Naxos*; 1990, Maggio Musicale, Florence, *Aufstieg und Fall der Stadt Mahagonny*; 1991: Deutsche Oper, Berlin, *Otello*; Opéra Bastille, Paris, *Un Re in Ascolto*; Kirov Opera, *War and Peace*; 1992: Glyndebourne Festival Opera, *The Queen of Spades*; Lyric Opera, Chicago, *The Rake's Progress*; San Francisco Opera, *Salome*; 1993: Teatro Comunale, Bologna, *L'Incoronazione di Poppea*; Teatro San Carlo, Naples, *Der Rosenkavalier*.

OPERATIC WORLD PREMIERES INCLUDE: Scottish Opera Go Round: 1978, *Peace* by Carl Davis; 1979, *The Quest of the Hidden Moon* by Ian Robertson; 1984, Batignano Festival, *La Bella e la Bestia* by Stephen Oliver; 1985, Scottish Opera, *Hedda Gabler* by Edward Harper; 1991, English

National Opera, *Timon of Athens* by
Stephen Oliver.

OPERA PRODUCTIONS IN THE UK
INCLUDE: Since 1981: City of Birmingham
Touring Opera: *The Magic Flute, The Ring
Saga, Beauty and the Beast, Zaide, Les
Boréades*; Covent Garden, *Mitridate, Rè
di Ponto*; English National Opera: *The
Rape of Lucretia, Madam Butterfly,
Eugene Onegin, The Marriage of Figaro*;
Musica nel Chiostro: *Euridice, La Dori*;
Opera North: *Peace, Katya Kabanova,
Eugene Onegin, The Magic Flute, The
Seraglio*; Scottish Opera: *Sāvitri/Fanny
Robin, The Silken Ladder/The Marriage
Contract, Don Giovanni, La Vie
Parisienne, Oberon, Carmen*; Scottish
Opera Go Round: *Candide, La Traviata,*
The Telephone, Susanna's Secret (also
designer), *Cinderella*; Scottish Opera/
Welsh National Opera co-production, *Billy
Budd*.

VIDEOS INCLUDE: Britten, *The Rape of
Lucretia* (English National Opera).

AWARDS INCLUDE: 1990, Jury Prize, Maggio
Musicale (Florence), *Aufstieg und Fall der
Stadt Mahagonny*; 1992: Olivier Award,
Covent Garden production of *Mitridate,
Rè di Ponto*; Wagner Society's Sir
Reginald Goodall Award, City of
Birmingham Touring Opera production of
The Ring Saga.

ADDRESS: c/o Ingpen & Williams Ltd, 14
Kensington Court, London W8 5DN.

*   *   *   *

WALKER PENELOPE
Mezzo-soprano

POSITION: Principal Mezzo-soprano, Zurich
Opera.

PERSONAL DETAILS: b. 12 October 1956,
Manchester; m. Phillip Joll (bass-
baritone), two children.

EDUCATION/TRAINING: 1974–1978, Guildhall
School of Music and Drama; 1979–1980,
National Opera Studio; further studies
with Myra Ross in London, Brigitte
Fassbaender in Munich and Gerard
Souzay in Paris.

PROFESSIONAL DEBUT: 1983, Opera Rara at
the Camden Festival, title role, *Maria
Tudor*.

MAJOR DEBUTS INCLUDE: 1985: English
Bach Festival, Arcane, *Teseo*; Sosostris,
The Midsummer Marriage: English
National Opera, Opera North; 1986, Welsh
National Opera, Fricka, *The Ring of the
Nibelung*; 1989, Scottish Opera, Erda, *Das
Rheingold*; 1990, Opera London,
Hippolyta, *A Midsummer Night's Dream*;
1991: Monte Carlo Opera, Third Lady, *Die
Zauberflöte*; Zurich Opera, Hedwige,
Guillaume Tell.

OPERATIC WORLD PREMIERES INCLUDE:
1990, Welsh National Opera, Milak,
Tornrak by John Metcalf.

CAREER INCLUDES: Since 1984: English
Bach Festival at Monte Carlo Opera,
Farnace, *Mitridate, Rè di Ponto*; English
National Opera: Kate Pinkerton, *Madam
Butterfly*; Siegrune, *The Valkyrie*;
Scottish Opera, Sosostris, *The
Midsummer Marriage*; Welsh National
Opera: Anna, *The Trojans*; Geneviève,
Pelléas et Mélisande; Madame Larina,
Eugene Onegin; since 1991, Principal
Mezzo-soprano, Zurich Opera: Third
Lady, *Die Zauberflöte*; Arsace,
Semiramide.

RELATED PROFESSIONAL ACTIVITIES:
Numerous concerts, recitals, broadcasts
and television appearances in the UK and
abroad.

RECORDINGS INCLUDE: Britten, *A
Midsummer Night's Dream* (VIRG);
Mathias, *Lux Aeterna* (CHAN); Pacini,
Maria Tudor (OPRA).

VIDEOS INCLUDE: Debussy, *Pelléas et
Mélisande* (Welsh National Opera).

AWARDS INCLUDE: 1978 and 1979, Countess of Munster Award; 1979, Young Welsh Singers Competition; 1980: Kathleen Ferrier Memorial Scholarship, Miriam Licette Scholarship.

ADDRESS: c/o Robert Gilder & Company, Enterprise House, 59–65 Upper Ground, London SE1 9PQ.

WALKER SARAH
Mezzo-soprano

PERSONAL DETAILS: b. Cheltenham; m. 1972, Graham Allum (General Manager and Artistic Co-ordinator, Buxton Festival).

EDUCATION/TRAINING: 1961–1965, Royal College of Music: violin with Antonio Brosa, cello with Hervey Philips, vocal studies with Ruth Packer and Cuthbert Smith; since 1965, with Vera Rozsa.

PROFESSIONAL DEBUT: 1969, Kent Opera, Ottavia, *The Coronation of Poppea.*

EARLY CAREER INCLUDED: 1970–1978: Glyndebourne Festival Opera, Diana/Jove, *La Calisto*; Sadler's Wells Opera/English National Opera: Ottavia, *The Coronation of Poppea*; Dorabella, *Così fan tutte*; Herodias, *Salome*; Fricka, *The Valkyrie*; Countess, *The Queen of Spades*; title roles: Gloriana, *Mary Stuart*; Scottish Opera, Dido, *The Trojans.*

MAJOR DEBUTS INCLUDE: 1977, Lyric Opera, Chicago, Magdalena, *Die Meistersinger von Nürnberg*; 1979, Covent Garden, Charlotte, *Werther*; 1980, Vienna State Opera, Dido, *Les Troyens*; 1981, San Francisco Opera, Octavia, *L'Incoronazione di Poppea*; 1982, La Monnaie, Brussels, Clairon, *Capriccio*; 1983, Grand Théâtre, Geneva, Cornelia, *Giulio Cesare*; 1986, Metropolitan Opera, New York, Micha, *Samson.*

OPERATIC WORLD PREMIERES INCLUDE: English National Opera: 1977, Suzanne, *Toussaint* by David Blake; 1992, Agave, *Bakxai* by John Buller.

CAREER IN THE UK INCLUDES: Since 1979: Covent Garden: Baba the Turk, *The Rake's Progress*; Rose Parrowe, *Taverner*; Micha, *Samson*; Marcellina, *Le Nozze di Figaro* (also 1992, Japan tour); Mad Caroline, *The King Goes Forth to France* (1987, British première); English National Opera, Katisha, *The Mikado*; Kent Opera, Andromache, *King Priam*; Scottish Opera, Mistress Quickly, *Falstaff.*

RELATED PROFESSIONAL ACTIVITIES: Regular concerts, recitals, broadcasts and television appearances in the UK and abroad including Last Night of the Proms and Berlin Celebration Concert (opening of the Berlin Wall); since 1987, masterclasses at several summer festivals and universities.

RECORDINGS INCLUDE: Beethoven, Symphony No. 9 (EMI/DG); Delius: English, French and Scandinavian songs, *The Song of the High Hills*, *Songs of Sunset* (all UNIC); Gay, *The Beggar's Opera* (HYPE); Handel: *Hercules* (ARCH), *Julius Caesar* (EMI); Maw, *The Voice of Love*; Mozart, *Requiem Mass* (both CHAN); Schubert, lieder (CRD/HYPE); Schumann, lieder (CRD); Stravinsky, *The Rake's Progress* (DECC); Tippett: *The Ice Break* (VIRG), *The Mask of Time*; Verdi, *La Traviata*; Wagner, *The Valkyrie* (all EMI); Cabaret Songs (MERI), *Blah, Blah Blah* and other Trifles (HYPE), An Anthology of English Song (NOVE).

VIDEOS INCLUDE: Britten, *Gloriana*; Handel, *Julius Caesar* (both English National Opera); Tippett, *King Priam* (Kent Opera); Berlin Celebration Concert (DG).

PUBLICATIONS INCLUDE: 1989, *Sarah's Encores* (Novello).

HONOURS INCLUDE: 1987, Fellow, Royal College of Music; 1988, Honorary Member, Guildhall School of Music and Drama; 1991, Commander, Order of the British Empire (CBE).

ADDRESS: c/o Lies Askonas Ltd, 186 Drury Lane, London WC2B 5RY.

WALMSLEY-CLARK
PENELOPE   Soprano

PERSONAL DETAILS: b. London.

EDUCATION/TRAINING: Royal College of Music.

PROFESSIONAL DEBUT: Principal Soprano, BBC Singers.

CAREER INCLUDES: 1977–1986, leading concert performer in the UK and abroad; Covent Garden (1987, operatic debut): Queen of the Night, *Die Zauberflöte*; Soprano 1, *Un Re in Ascolto* (1989, British première); English National Opera, Queen of the Night, *The Magic Flute*; Glyndebourne Festival Opera, Mrs Frestln, *The Electrification of the Soviet Union*; Grand Théâtre, Geneva, Queen of the Night, *Die Zauberflöte*; Opéra Bastille, Paris, Soprano 1, *Un Re in Ascolto*; Opera Company of Boston, Queen of the Night, *Die Zauberflöte*.

OPERATIC WORLD PREMIERES INCLUDE: 1990, English National Opera, Cousin, *Clarissa* by Robin Holloway; 1991, Covent Garden, Guinevere, *Gawain* by Harrison Birtwistle.

RELATED PROFESSIONAL ACTIVITIES: Regular concerts, recitals and broadcasts with leading orchestras and conductors in the UK and abroad; particularly associated with contemporary composers.

RECORDINGS INCLUDE: Bergman, *Hathor Suite* (CHAN); Harvey, *Song Offerings* (NIMB); Holloway, *Sea Surface, Full of Clouds* (both CHAN); Ligeti, *Le Grand Macabre*; Xenakis, *Akanthos* (both WERG).

ADDRESS: c/o Allied Artists, 42 Montpelier Square, London SW7 1JZ.

WARNER KEITH
Director, Designer and Translator

POSITIONS: Artistic Director, Nexus Opera; Director of Productions, New Sussex Opera; Associate Artistic Director, Opera Omaha, Nebraska.

PERSONAL DETAILS: b. 6 December 1956, London; m. 1984, Emma Besly (translator and language coach).

PREVIOUS OCCUPATIONS: 1978–1981, actor and drama therapy teacher.

EDUCATION/TRAINING: 1975–1978, University of Bristol, studied English and drama.

PROFESSIONAL DEBUT: 1978, fringe theatre director.

OPERATIC DEBUT: 1982, English National Opera, *The Magic Flute* (revival director).

CAREER: Opera director in the UK, Europe and North America; English National Opera: 1981–1984, staff director (set up drama workshop programme and education unit); 1984–1989, Associate Director; 1985, Associate Director, Scottish Opera; since 1988, Director of Productions, New Sussex Opera; since 1989, Artistic Director, Nexus Opera; since 1992, Associate Artistic Director, Opera Omaha, Nebraska.

MAJOR OPERATIC DEBUTS INCLUDE: 1985: English National Opera, *Moses*; Scottish Opera, *Iolanthe*; 1988, New Sussex Opera, *The Flying Dutchman*; 1989: Bielefeld, *Norma*; Canadian Opera Company, Toronto, *Un Ballo in Maschera*; Dortmund, *Il Trovatore*; 1990, Opera Omaha, Nebraska: *Madama Butterfly, Golem*; 1991: Houston Grand Opera: *La Bohème, My Fair Lady*; Minnesota Opera, *Carmen*.

OPERATIC WORLD PREMIERES INCLUDE: 1992, Opera Omaha, Nebraska, *Gardens of Adonis* by Hugo Weisgall.

OPERA PRODUCTIONS IN THE UK INCLUDE: Since 1984: D'Oyly Carte Opera, *The Pirates of Penzance*; English National Opera: *The Stone Guest* (1987, British stage première), *Pacific Overtures, Werther*; New Sussex Opera: *Tannhäuser, Lost in the Stars*; Scottish Opera: *Tosca, The Magic Flute, Werther*; Scottish Opera Go Round, *Carmen*.

RELATED PROFESSIONAL ACTIVITIES: Designs include: *Carmen* (Scottish Opera Go Round), *Don Giovanni, Il Trovatore* (both Opera Omaha, Nebraska); translations include: *Carmen* (Scottish

Opera Go Round), *The Magic Flute*
(Opera Omaha, Nebraska and Opera
Tulsa, Oklahoma).

ADDRESS: c/o Athole Still International
Management Ltd, Greystoke House, 80–86
Westow Street, London SE19 3AF.

WATSON JANICE   Soprano

PERSONAL DETAILS: b. 8 April 1964,
London; m. 1990.

EDUCATION/TRAINING: 1982–1987, Guildhall
School of Music and Drama, with Johanna
Peters (since 1987, privately).

PROFESSIONAL DEBUT: 1988, Opera
London, Drusilla, *L'Incoronazione di
Poppea*.

MAJOR DEBUTS INCLUDE: Musetta, *La
Bohème*: 1989, Welsh National Opera;
1990, Covent Garden; 1991, English
National Opera, Rosalinde, *Die
Fledermaus*.

CAREER IN THE UK INCLUDES: Since 1989:
Chelsea Opera Group: Magda, *La
Rondine*; title role, *Manon Lescaut*;
English National Opera, First Lady, *The
Magic Flute*; Welsh National Opera:
Fiordiligi, *Così fan tutte*; Micaëla,
Carmen; Adele, *Count Ory*; Rosalinde,
Die Fledermaus; Pamina, *The Magic
Flute*; Tatyana, *Eugene Onegin*; Arminda,
La Finta Giardiniera; title role, *Lucia di
Lammermoor*.

RELATED PROFESSIONAL ACTIVITIES:
Concerts and recitals with leading
conductors and orchestras in the UK and
abroad.

RECORDINGS INCLUDE: Monteverdi,
L'Incoronazione di Poppea (VIRG);
Sullivan, *The Mikado* (TELA).

AWARDS INCLUDE: 1987: Kathleen Ferrier
Memorial Scholarship, Royal Over-Seas
League Music Competition.

ADDRESS: c/o Ron Gonsalves Personal
Artists & Concert Management, 10
Dagnan Road, London SW12 9LQ.

WATSON LILLIAN   Soprano

PERSONAL DETAILS: b. 4 December 1947,
London; m., two children.

EDUCATION/TRAINING: Guildhall School of
Music and Drama; London Opera Centre;
privately with Vera Rozsa; currently with
Jessica Cash.

PROFESSIONAL DEBUT: 1970, Wexford
Festival, Cis, *Albert Herring*.

EARLY CAREER INCLUDED: 1971–1975,
Principal Soprano, Welsh National Opera:
Papagena, *The Magic Flute* (debut);
Zerlina, *Don Giovanni*; Tebaldo, *Don
Carlos*; Adele, *Die Fledermaus*;
Giannetta and Adina, *L'Elisir d'Amore*;
Wanda, *The Grand Duchess of
Gérolstein*; Despina, *Così fan tutte*.

MAJOR DEBUTS INCLUDE: 1971, Covent
Garden, Barbarina, *Le Nozze di Figaro*;
1975, Glyndebourne Touring Opera,
Despina, *Così fan tutte*; 1976:
Glyndebourne Festival Opera, Susanna,
Le Nozze di Figaro; Netherlands Opera,
Despina, *Così fan tutte*; 1978: English
National Opera, Susanna, *The Marriage
of Figaro*; Holland Festival, Zerlina, *Don
Giovanni*; 1979, Bavarian State Opera,
Munich, Blonde, *Die Entführung aus dem
Serail*; 1980, Opera North, Adina, *L'Elisir
d'Amore*; 1982, Salzburg Festival,
Marzelline, *Fidelio*; 1983, Vienna State
Opera, Blonde, *Die Entführung aus dem
Serail*; 1984: Scottish Opera, Amor,
Orion; Paris Opera, Blonde, *Die
Entführung aus dem Serail*; 1985:
Purchase, New York State (Pepsico
Summerfare), Asteria, *Tamerlano*; Zurich
Opera, Blonde, *Die Entführung aus dem
Serail*; 1986, Hamburg State Opera,
Susanna, *Le Nozze di Figaro*; 1989,
Théâtre des Champs Elysées, Paris,
Sophie, *Der Rosenkavalier*; 1991, Aix-en-
Provence Festival, Tytania, *A Midsummer
Night's Dream*.

CAREER IN THE UK INCLUDES: Since 1975:
Covent Garden: Giannetta, *L'Elisir
d'Amore*; Papagena, *Die Zauberflöte*;
Young Girl, *Lulu* (1981, British première,
three act version); Fiakermilli, *Arabella*;
Woodbird, *Der Ring des Nibelungen*;

Sister Constance, *The Carmelites*; Despina, *Così fan tutte*; Frasquita, *Carmen*; Tytania, *A Midsummer Night's Dream*; Blonde, *Die Entführung aus dem Serail*; Adele, *Die Fledermaus*; Sophie, *Der Rosenkavalier*; Italian Soprano, *Capriccio*; Ismene, *Mitridate, Rè di Ponto*; title role, *The Cunning Little Vixen*; English National Opera: Eurydice, *Orpheus in the Underworld*; Adele, *Die Fledermaus*; Glyndebourne Festival Opera: Despina, *Così fan tutte*; Blonde, *Die Entführung aus dem Serail*; Tytania, *A Midsummer Night's Dream*; Sophie, *Der Rosenkavalier*; Fire/Nightingale, *L'Enfant et les Sortilèges*; Opera London, Tytania, *A Midsummer Night's Dream*; Scottish Opera, Dorinda, *Orlando*; Welsh National Opera, Blonde, *The Seraglio*.

RELATED PROFESSIONAL ACTIVITIES: Numerous concerts, recitals, broadcasts and television appearances in the UK and abroad.

RECORDINGS INCLUDE: Bizet, *Carmen* (HMV); Cilea, *Adriana Lecouvreur* (CBS); Donizetti, *L'Elisir d'Amore* (EMI); Handel, *Israel in Egypt* (ARGO); Hoddinott, *A Contemplation upon Flowers* (CHAN); Janáček, *The Cunning Little Vixen*; Mozart: *Così fan tutte* (both EMI), *Die Entführung aus dem Serail* (TELD), *Le Nozze di Figaro* (PHIL); Offenbach, *Orpheus in the Underworld* (TER); Puccini, *La Rondine* (CBS).

VIDEOS INCLUDE: Bizet, *Carmen* (film by Francesco Rosi); Mozart, *Die Entführung aus dem Serail* (Glyndebourne Festival Opera).

ADDRESS: c/o Harrison/Parrott Ltd, 12 Penzance Place, London W11 4PA.

WATT ALAN   Baritone

PERSONAL DETAILS: b. Aberdeen; m. 1988.
EDUCATION/TRAINING: 1965–1970, Royal Scottish Academy of Music and Drama, with Marjorie Blakeston.
PROFESSIONAL DEBUT: 1970, member, Scottish Opera.

MAJOR DEBUTS INCLUDE: 1973, Glyndebourne Touring Opera, Marcello, *La Bohème*; 1974, Glyndebourne Festival Opera, Helmesberger, *The Visit of the Old Lady*; 1975: Covent Garden, Marullo, *Rigoletto*; Kent Opera, Ruthven, *Ruddigore*; 1977, Grand Théâtre, Tours, Guglielmo, *Così fan tutte*; 1978, Wexford Festival, Ernesto, *Il Mondo della Luna*; 1979, English National Opera, title role, *The Marriage of Figaro*; 1983, Teatro La Fenice, Venice, Guglielmo, *Così fan tutte*; 1984, Opera North, Papageno, *The Magic Flute*; 1986: Basle, Balstrode, *Peter Grimes*; Theater an der Wien, Vienna, title role, *Le Nozze di Figaro*; 1987, Welsh National Opera, title role, *The Marriage of Figaro*; 1989, Opéra du Rhin, Strasbourg, Guglielmo, *Così fan tutte*; 1991, Tel Aviv, Papageno, *Die Zauberflöte*.

OPERATIC WORLD PREMIERES INCLUDE: 1976, Covent Garden, Soldier 3/Madman 6, *We Come to the River* by Hans Werner Henze.

CAREER IN THE UK INCLUDES: Since 1971: Buxton Festival, Marzci, *Háry János*; Covent Garden, Morales, *Carmen*; Glyndebourne Festival and Touring Opera: Dog, *The Cunning Little Vixen*; Commercial Councillor, *Intermezzo*; Guglielmo, *Così fan tutte*; Morbio, *Die Schweigsame Frau*; title role, *Le Nozze di Figaro*; Kent Opera: Papageno, *The Magic Flute*; Don Alfonso, *Così fan tutte*; Raimbaud, *Count Ory*; title role, *The Marriage of Figaro*; New Sussex Opera, Balstrode, *Peter Grimes*; Scottish Opera: Albert, *Werther*; Slook, *The Marriage Contract*; d'Obigny, *La Traviata*; Singers' Company: Don Andres, *La Périchole*; Bartolo, *The Barber of Seville*; Travelling Opera, title role, *Don Pasquale*.

RELATED PROFESSIONAL ACTIVITIES: Regular concerts, recitals and broadcasts in the UK and abroad.

RECORDINGS INCLUDE: Handel, *Israel in Egypt* (DECC); Henze, *The English Cat* (VIRG); Robert Burns Songs (CHAN).

ADDRESS: Not available.

WEBSTER GILLIAN   Soprano

PERSONAL DETAILS: b. 2 May 1964, Larbert, Scotland; m. 1988.
EDUCATION/TRAINING: 1982–1987, Royal Northern College of Music, with Sylvia Jacobs; 1987–1988, National Opera Studio.
PROFESSIONAL DEBUT: 1988, English National Opera, Klin, The *Making of the Representative for Planet 8*.
CAREER IN THE UK INCLUDES: Since 1988: Covent Garden (1988–1992, member): Page, *Rigoletto* (debut); Ida, *Die Fledermaus*; Kate Pinkerton, *Madama Butterfly*; Voice from Heaven, *Don Carlos*; Niece, *Peter Grimes*; First Maidservant, *Médée*; Inez, *Il Trovatore*; Servilia, *La Clemenza di Tito*; Ilia, *Idomeneo*; Polovtsian Girl, *Prince Igor*; Fifth Maid, *Elektra*; Berta, *Il Barbiere di Siviglia*; First Lady and Pamina, *Die Zauberflöte*; Xenia, *Boris Godunov*; Micaëla, *Carmen*; Euridice, *Orfeo ed Euridice*; Woglinde, *Der Ring der Nibelungen*; Arbate, *Mitridate, Rè di Ponto*; Lace Seller, *Death in Venice*; Giannetta, *L'Elisir d'Amore*; Mimi, *La Bohème*; Marzelline, *Fidelio*; English National Opera: Lady in Waiting, *Macbeth*; Pamina, *The Magic Flute*; Welsh National Opera, Micaëla, *Carmen*.
RECORDINGS INCLUDE: Britten, *Peter Grimes* (EMI).
VIDEOS INCLUDE: Gluck, *Orfeo ed Euridice* (Covent Garden).
AWARDS INCLUDE: 1986, John Noble Opera Award.
ADDRESS: c/o Lies Askonas Ltd, 186 Drury Lane, London WC2B 5RY.

WEIR JUDITH   Composer

PERSONAL DETAILS: b. 11 May 1954, Cambridge.
EDUCATION/TRAINING: 1973–1976, King's College, Cambridge, with Robin Holloway.
FIRST PROFESSIONAL PERFORMANCE OF A COMPOSITION: 1974, Philharmonia Orchestra, *Where The Shining Trumpets Blow* for orchestra.
CAREER: Since 1974, compositions include orchestral, instrumental, ensemble, vocal and choral works; 1976–1979, Composer in Residence, Southern Arts Association; 1979–1982, Fellow in Composition, University of Glasgow; 1983–1985, Creative Arts Fellowship, Trinity College, Cambridge; 1988–1991, Composer in Residence, Royal Scottish Academy of Music and Drama.
OPERATIC WORLD PREMIERES: 1987, Kent Opera, *A Night at the Chinese Opera*, opera in three acts, conductor Andrew Parrott, director Richard Jones, designer Richard Hudson; 1989, Second Stride and Vocem Electric Voice Theatre, *Heaven Ablaze in his Breast*, music theatre in 14 scenes after *The Sandman* by Hoffmann, choreographer Ian Spink, designer Antony McDonald; 1990, Scottish Opera, *The Vanishing Bridegroom*, opera in three parts, after *Popular Tales of the West Highlands* and *Carmina Gadelica*, conductor Alan Hacker, director Ian Spink, designer Richard Hudson; 1991, BBC Television, *Scipio's Dream*, freely adapted from *Il Sogno di Scipione* by Mozart, conductor Andrew Parrott, director Margaret Williams (all librettos by the composer).
RECORDINGS INCLUDE: *Three Operas* (NOVE), *Scotch Minstrelsey* (ABCD).
ADDRESS: c/o Chester Music Ltd, 8/9 Frith Street, London W1V 5TZ.

WHEATLEY PATRICK
Baritone

PERSONAL DETAILS: b. 1947, Leicestershire; m. 1987, Patricia O'Neill (soprano), one child.
EDUCATION/TRAINING: 1973, London Opera Centre, with Denis Dowling; privately with Esther Salaman.

PROFESSIONAL DEBUT: 1974, English National Opera, Flemish Deputy, *Don Carlos*.

EARLY CAREER INCLUDED: 1974–1980: Principal Baritone, English National Opera: Schaunard and Marcello, *La Bohème*; Albert, *Werther*; Amonasro, *Aida*; Donner and Gunther, *The Ring of the Nibelung*; King Vladislav, *Dalibor*; de Brétigny, *Manon*; Fabrizio, *The Thieving Magpie*; Goryanchikov, *From the House of the Dead*; John Sorel, *The Consul*; Speaker, *The Magic Flute*; Schelkalov, *Boris Godunov*; Sharpless, *Madam Butterfly*; also: New Opera Company, Beggar, *Julietta* (1978, British première); University College Opera: Ezio, *Attila*; Germont, *La Traviata*.

MAJOR DEBUTS INCLUDE: 1980: Opera North, Manz, *A Village Romeo and Juliet*; Opera Northern Ireland, Anckarström, *A Masked Ball*; 1984, New Sussex Opera, title role, *Gianni Schicchi*; 1987, City of Birmingham Touring Opera, title role, *Falstaff*; 1988, Scottish Opera, Zurga, *The Pearl Fishers*; 1989, Welsh National Opera, title role, *Rigoletto*.

CAREER IN THE UK INCLUDES: Since 1981: City of Birmingham Touring Opera: Papageno, *The Magic Flute*; Wotan, *The Ring Saga*; English National Opera: Ali, *The Italian Girl in Algiers*; Alidoro, *Cinderella*; Escamillo, *Carmen*; Hans Sachs, *The Mastersingers of Nuremberg*; Talbot and Cecil, *Mary Stuart*; Podkolyosin, *The Marriage*; New Sussex Opera, Michele, *Il Tabarro*; Opera North, Krušina, *The Bartered Bride*.

RELATED PROFESSIONAL ACTIVITIES: Numerous concerts, recitals and broadcasts in the UK and abroad.

RECORDINGS INCLUDE: Delius and Grainger, choral songs (CONI).

AWARDS INCLUDE: 1974, Peter Stuyvesant Foundation Scholarship.

ADDRESS: c/o Music International, 13 Ardilaun Road, London N5 2QR.

WHITE WILLARD Bass

PERSONAL DETAILS: b. 10 October 1946, St Catherine, Jamaica; m. 1972, Gillian Jackson, four children.

EDUCATION/TRAINING: 1968–1973, Juilliard School of Music, New York, with Beverley Johnson and Giorgio Tozzi; privately with Erik Thorendahl; masterclasses with Maria Callas.

PROFESSIONAL DEBUT: 1973, Washington Opera, Trulove, *The Rake's Progress*.

MAJOR DEBUTS INCLUDE: 1974, New York City Opera, Colline, *La Bohème*; 1975, Houston Grand Opera, Ned, *Treemonisha*; 1976: Welsh National Opera, Osmin, *The Seraglio* (British debut); English National Opera, Seneca, *The Coronation of Poppea*; 1977, Netherlands Opera, Water Sprite, *Rusalka*; 1978: Covent Garden, Don Diego, *L'Africaine*; Glyndebourne Festival Opera, Colline, *La Bohème*; 1979, Scottish Opera, Leporello, *Don Giovanni*; 1980, San Francisco Opera, Speaker, *Die Zauberflöte*; 1981, Bavarian State Opera, Munich, Water Sprite, *Rusalka*; 1982: Nantes Opera, title role, *Il Turco in Italia*; Teatro Comunale, Florence, Escamillo, *Carmen*; 1984, Opera North, Forester, *The Cunning Little Vixen*; 1985: Hollywood Bowl, Los Angeles, Colline, *La Bohème*; Teatro La Fenice, Venice, Osmin, *Zaide*; 1986: Glyndebourne Festival Opera, Porgy, *Porgy and Bess*; Théâtre du Châtelet, Paris, Mustafa, *L'Italiana in Algeri*; 1990, Teatro La Zarzuela, Madrid, title role, *Il Turco in Italia*; 1992, Edinburgh International Festival, Moses, *Moses and Aaron* (concert performance).

OPERATIC WORLD PREMIERES INCLUDE: 1977, English National Opera, Boukman/Moïse, *Toussaint* by David Blake.

CAREER IN THE UK INCLUDES: Since 1976: Covent Garden: Ferrando, *Il Trovatore*; Klingsor, *Parsifal*; First Nazarene, *Salome*; Orest, *Elektra*; Fafner, *Das Rheingold* and *Siegfried*; Grand Inquisitor, *Don Carlos*; Timur, *Turandot*; Porgy, *Porgy and Bess*; Don Pizarro,

Fidelio; English National Opera: Ferrando, *Il Trovatore*; First Nazarene, *Salome*; Hunding, *The Valkyrie*; Achilla, *Julius Caesar*; Boris, *Lady Macbeth of Mtsensk* (1987, British stage première); Golaud, *Pelléas and Mélisande*; Glyndebourne Festival Opera: Speaker, *Die Zauberflöte*; Osmin, *Die Entführung aus dem Serail*; Truffaldino, *Ariadne auf Naxos*; King, *L'Amour des Trois Oranges*; Alidoro, *La Cenerentola*; Scottish Opera: Timur, *Turandot*; Vulcan, *Orion*; Wotan, *Das Rheingold* and *Die Walküre*; Welsh National Opera: Massimiliano, *I Masnadieri*; Orest, *Elektra*.
RELATED PROFESSIONAL ACTIVITIES: Numerous concerts, recitals, broadcasts and television appearances in the UK and abroad; as actor: 1989, Royal Shakespeare Company, title role, *Othello*.
RECORDINGS INCLUDE: Copland, Old American Songs and Spirituals (CHAN); Gershwin, *Porgy and Bess* (DECC/EMI); Handel, *Acis and Galatea* (ARCH); Joplin, *Treemonisha* (DG); McCartney, *Liverpool Oratorio* (EMI); Mendelssohn, *Elijah* (CHAN); Monteverdi, *Orfeo* (DG); Mozart, *Requiem* (PHIL); R. Strauss, *Die Aegyptische Helena* (DECC).
VIDEOS INCLUDE: McCartney, *Liverpool Oratorio* (EMI); Mozart: *Die Entführung aus dem Serail*, *Die Zauberflöte*; Prokofiev, *L'Amour des Trois Oranges* (all Glyndebourne Festival Opera).
HONOURS INCLUDE: 1987, Prime Minister of Jamaica's Medal of Appreciation.
ADDRESS: c/o Harrison/Parrott Ltd, 12 Penzance Place, London W11 4PA.

WHITWORTH-JONES ANTHONY
Administrator

POSITION: General Director, Glyndebourne Festival Opera.
PERSONAL DETAILS: b. 1 September 1945, Buckinghamshire; m. 1974, Camilla Barlow.
EDUCATION/TRAINING: Institute of Chartered Accountants of Scotland.

CAREER: 1972–1981, Administrative Director, London Sinfonietta; 1981–1988: Opera Manager and Director of New Opera Development, Glyndebourne Festival Opera; Administrator, Glyndebourne Touring Opera; since 1989, General Director, Glyndebourne Festival Opera.
ADDRESS: c/o Glyndebourne Festival Opera, Lewes, East Sussex BN8 5UU.

WIGGLESWORTH MARK
Conductor

POSITIONS: Music Director: Opera Factory, Première Ensemble; Associate Conductor, BBC Symphony Orchestra.
PERSONAL DETAILS: b. 19 July 1964, Sussex.
EDUCATION/TRAINING: 1983–1986, University of Manchester; 1986–1989, Royal Academy of Music.
PROFESSIONAL DEBUT: 1989, Dutch Radio Philharmonic Orchestra.
OPERATIC DEBUT: 1990, Opera Factory, *Don Giovanni*.
CAREER: Since 1989, guest conductor with leading orchestras in the UK, Europe and USA; since 1991: Music Director: Opera Factory, Première Ensemble; Associate Conductor, BBC Symphony Orchestra.
OPERA PERFORMANCES IN THE UK INCLUDE: Since 1991: Opera Factory: *Cosí fan tutte*, *Yan Tan Tethera*; Scottish Opera, *The Marriage of Figaro*.
AWARDS INCLUDE: 1989, Kondrashin Competition (Netherlands).
ADDRESS: c/o Harold Holt Ltd, 31 Sinclair Road, London W14 0NS.

WILKENS ANNE
Mezzo-soprano

PERSONAL DETAILS: b. 1 July, 1948, Essex; m. 1968, one child.
EDUCATION/TRAINING: Guildhall School of Music and Drama; London Opera Centre; further studies with Eva Turner, Benjamin Britten and Peter Pears.

PROFESSIONAL DEBUT: 1972, Royal Festival Hall, appeared in *Ernani.*

MAJOR DEBUTS INCLUDE: 1973, New Opera Company, Madame Podtochina, *The Nose* (British stage première); 1974, Covent Garden, Grimgerde, *Die Walküre*; 1979, Welsh National Opera, Brangäne, *Tristan and Isolde*; 1981, Frankfurt Opera, Azucena, *Il Trovatore*; 1982: Opera North, Konchakovna, *Prince Igor*; Stuttgart State Opera, Brangäne, *Tristan und Isolde*; 1983: Bayreuth Festival, Schwertleite and Second Norn, *Der Ring des Nibelungen*; Karlsruhe, Princesse de Bouillon, *Adriana Lecouvreur.*

OPERATIC WORLD PREMIERES INCLUDE: English Opera Group at the Aldeburgh Festival: 1973, Beggar Woman, *Death in Venice* by Benjamin Britten; 1974, Marchesa Bianca, *The Voice of Ariadne* by Thea Musgrave; Covent Garden: 1976, Old Woman, *We Come to the River* by Hans Werner Henze; 1977, Astron, *The Ice Break* by Michael Tippett; 1986, Karlsruhe, Margarita, *Der Meister und Margarita* by Rainer Kunad.

CAREER INCLUDES: Since 1973: Covent Garden (1975–1979, member): Hostess, *Boris Godunov*; Marthe, *Faust*; Maddalena, *Rigoletto*; Mercédès, *Carmen*; Kate Pinkerton, *Madama Butterfly*; Dryad, *Ariadne auf Naxos*; Grimgerde and Waltraute, *Der Ring des Nibelungen*; Wowkle, *La Fanciulla del West*; Mayor's Wife, *Jenůfa*; Page, *Lohengrin*; Berta, *Il Barbiere di Siviglia*; Olga, *Eugene Onegin*; Flower Maiden, *Parsifal*; Lola, *Cavalleria Rusticana*; Mary, *Der Fliegende Holländer*; English Opera Group (1973–1974, member): Laura, *Iolanta*; Bianca, *The Rape of Lucretia*; Handel Opera Society: Cyrus, *Belshazzar*; Dejanira, *Hercules*; title role, *Ezio*; Karlsruhe (1983–1986, Principal Mezzo-soprano): Venus, *Tannhäuser*; Ortrud, *Lohengrin*; Brangäne, *Tristan und Isolde*; Fricka, *Das Rheingold* and *Die Walküre*; Waltraute, *Götterdämmerung*; Eboli, *Don Carlos*; Amastre, *Serse.*

RELATED PROFESSIONAL ACTIVITIES: Numerous concerts in the UK and abroad.

RECORDINGS INCLUDE: Gay, *The Beggar's Opera* (DECC); Puccini, *La Fanciulla del West*; Wagner, *Die Walküre* (both DG).

ADDRESS: c/o Music International, 13 Ardilaun Road, London N5 2QR.

WILLIAMS HOWARD
Conductor

POSITION: Principal Conductor and Artistic Director, Pécs Symphony Orchestra, Hungary.

PERSONAL DETAILS: b. 25 April 1947, Hemel Hempstead; m. 1977, Juliet Solomon (writer), two children.

EDUCATION/TRAINING: 1961–1965, King's School, Canterbury, studied piano with Ronald Smith and violin with Clarence Myerscough; 1965–1968, Music Scholar, New College, Oxford; 1968–1969, Guildhall School of Music and Drama; 1969–1970, University of Liverpool.

PROFESSIONAL DEBUT: 1970, BBC Northern Symphony Orchestra.

OPERATIC DEBUT: 1977, English National Opera, *A Night in Venice.*

CAREER: 1975–1981, member, music staff and Chorus Master, then Guest Conductor, English National Opera; Principal Conductor: 1981–1989, Ernest Read Symphony Orchestra; 1983–1986, Surrey Philharmonic and Fairfield Concert Orchestra; since 1989, Principal Conductor and Artistic Director, Pécs Symphony Orchestra, Hungary.

OPERATIC WORLD PREMIERES INCLUDE: 1981, English National Opera, *Anna Karenina* by Iain Hamilton.

OPERA PERFORMANCES IN THE UK INCLUDE: Since 1982: Chelsea Opera Group: *Oberon, Lady Macbeth of Mtsensk, The Snow Maiden, Ivan IV, Manon Lescaut, Ernani*; English National Opera: *Madam Butterfly, The Merry Widow, The Magic Flute*; Guildhall School of Music and Drama: *Julietta, The Journey to Rheims, La Jolie Fille de Perth, La Pietra del Paragone, The Voice of Ariadne*; Opera Factory: *Punch and Judy, The Knot Garden.*

RELATED PROFESSIONAL ACTIVITIES:
Performances with leading orchestras in
the UK and abroad.
RECORDINGS INCLUDE: Bizet, *Ivan IV* (ERAT);
Bridge, *The Christmas Rose* (PEAR).
ADDRESS: 2 Elms Avenue, London N10 2JP.

WILLIAMS-KING ANNE
Soprano

PERSONAL DETAILS: b. Wrexham.
EDUCATION/TRAINING: Royal Northern
College of Music; National Opera Studio.
PROFESSIONAL DEBUT: 1982, Berne, Anne
Trulove, *The Rake's Progress*.
MAJOR DEBUTS INCLUDE: 1983: Opera
North, Mimi, *La Bohème*; Welsh National
Opera, title role, *The Drama of Aida*;
1989, Scottish Opera, Freia, *Das
Rheingold*; 1991, English National Opera,
Foreign Princess, *Rusalka*.
OPERATIC WORLD PREMIERES INCLUDE:
1985, Arundel Festival, Guinevere,
Lancelot by Iain Hamilton.
CAREER IN THE UK INCLUDES: Since 1983:
Opera North: Juliet, *A Village Romeo and
Juliet*; Second Mrs de Winter, *Rebecca*;
Micaëla, *Carmen*; Scottish Opera: Mimi,
La Bohème; Vitellia, *La Clemenza di Tito*;
Gerhilde, *Die Walküre*; Violetta, *La
Traviata*; Fiordiligi, *Così fan tutte*; title
roles: *Jenůfa*, *Madama Butterfly*; Welsh
National Opera: Amelia, *Un Ballo in
Maschera*; Lenio, *The Greek Passion*;
Mimi, *La Bohème*; Gilda, *Rigoletto*;
Fiordiligi, *Così fan tutte*; Freia, *The Ring
of the Nibelung*; Marzelline, *Fidelio*;
Micaëla, *Carmen*.
RELATED PROFESSIONAL ACTIVITIES:
Numerous concerts, recitals and
broadcasts in the UK.
RECORDINGS INCLUDE: Bax, choral works
(CHAN).
ADDRESS: c/o Stafford Law Associates, 26
Mayfield Road, Weybridge, Surrey KT13
8XB.

WILLIAMSON MALCOLM
Composer, Organist and Pianist

POSITION: Master of the Queen's Music.
PERSONAL DETAILS: b. 21 November 1931,
Sydney, Australia; m. 1960, Dolores
Daniel, three children.
EDUCATION/TRAINING: 1943–1950, Sydney
Conservatorium of Music, studied
composition with Eugene Goossens and
piano with Alexander Sverjensky; further
studies with Elisabeth Lutyens and Erwin
Stein in London.
FIRST PROFESSIONAL PERFORMANCE OF A
COMPOSITION: 1958, BBC Radio, *Santiago
de Espada*, overture for orchestra.
CAREER: Compositions in all genres
including numerous orchestral, chamber,
instrumental, vocal and choral works,
television and film scores, ballets, three
grand operas, two chamber operas and
several operas for young people
including: 1965, *The Happy Prince*; 1966,
Julius Caesar Jones; 1967, *Dunstan and
the Devil*; 1972, *The Red Sea*; 1951–1955,
freelance organist and pianist with
leading orchestras in the UK and abroad;
1955–1958, Assistant Organist, Farm
Street Church, London; 1958–1960,
Organist, St Peter's Church, London;
1961–1962, Lecturer in Music, Central
School of Speech and Drama; Composer
in Residence: 1970–1971, Westminster
Choir College, Princeton, New Jersey;
1975, Florida State University; 1974–1981,
Creative Arts Fellow, Australian National
University; 1982–1983, Ramasciotti
Medical Research Fellow, University of
New South Wales; 1983–1986, Visiting
Professor in Music, University of
Strathclyde; since 1975, Master of the
Queen's Music.
OPERATIC WORLD PREMIÈRES INCLUDE:
Sadler's Wells Opera: 1963, *Our Man in
Havana*, libretto by Sidney Gilliat after
Graham Greene, conductor James
Loughran, director John Blatchley,
designer Carl Toms; 1966, *The Violins of
St Jacques*, libretto by William Chappell
after Patrick Leigh Fermor, conductor
Vilem Tausky, director William Chappell,

289

designer Peter Rice; 1969, *Lucky Peter's Journey*, libretto by Edmund Tracey after Strindberg, conductor John Barker, director John Cox, designer Dacre Punt (all operas in three acts); 1964, English Opera Group at the Aldeburgh Festival, *English Eccentrics*, libretto by Geoffrey Dunn after Edith Sitwell, conductor Meredith Davies, director William Chappell, designer Peter Rice; 1968, Dynevor Castle, Wales, *The Growing Castle*, libretto by the composer after Strindberg, conductor and director the composer, designer Kenneth Rowell (both chamber operas).

RELATED PROFESSIONAL ACTIVITIES: 1964, member, Executive Committee, Composers' Guild of Great Britain; President: 1977–1982, Royal Philharmonic Orchestra; since 1972, Beauchamp Sinfonietta; since 1975, Birmingham Chamber Music Society; since 1976, University of London Choir; since 1977: British Society for Music Therapy, Sing for Pleasure.

AWARDS AND HONOURS INCLUDE: 1963, Arnold Bax Prize; 1976, Commander, Order of the British Empire (CBE); 1987, Honorary Officer, Order of Australia (AO); Honorary Doctorates of Music: 1970, Westminster Choir College, USA (1971, Honorary Fellow); 1982, Universities of Melbourne and Sydney; 1983, Doctorate, Open University.

ADDRESS: c/o Campion Press, Sandon, Buntingford, Hertfordshire SG9 0QW.

WILLIS NUALA
Mezzo-soprano

PERSONAL DETAILS: b. 9 August 1941, London; m. John Rawnsley (baritone).

PREVIOUS OCCUPATION: Stage and costume designer in the UK, USA and Canada.

EDUCATION/TRAINING: 1972–1976, vocal studies with Gita Denise, David Harper and Peter Pears.

PROFESSIONAL DEBUT: 1977, Glyndebourne Festival Opera, Mother Goose, *The Rake's Progress*.

EARLY CAREER INCLUDED: 1977–1982, appearances with Glyndebourne Festival and Touring Opera, Musica nel Chiostro, University College Opera, Aldeburgh, Camden and Wexford Festivals; roles included: Innkeeper's Wife, *The Cunning Little Vixen*; Third Lady, *Die Zauberflöte*; Filipyevna, *Eugene Onegin*; Aristea, *Orontea*; Hippolyta, *A Midsummer Night's Dream*; Venus, *Euridice*; Carmela, *I Gioielli della Madonna*; title role, *The Duenna* (Prokofiev).

MAJOR DEBUTS INCLUDE: 1983, English National Opera, Franči Novaková/Kedruta, *The Adventures of Mr Brouček*; 1984: Marseilles Opera, Madame Larina, *Eugene Onegin*; Zurich Opera, Hostess, *Boris Godunov*; 1986, Covent Garden, Marthe, *Faust*; 1989: Canadian Opera Company, Toronto, Madame Arvidson, *Un Ballo in Maschera*; Stockholm Folkopera at the Edinburgh International Festival, Herodias, *Salome*.

OPERATIC WORLD PREMIERES INCLUDE: 1983, Opera North (debut), Mrs Van Hopper, *Rebecca* by Wilfred Josephs.

CAREER IN THE UK INCLUDES: Since 1983: Buxton Festival, Delfa, *Jason*; Covent Garden: Madame Larina, *Eugene Onegin*; Hippolyta, *A Midsummer Night's Dream*; Queen, *The King Goes Forth to France* (1987, British première); Opera North: Duchess of Plaza-Toro, *The Gondoliers*; Amelfa, *The Golden Cockerel*.

RELATED PROFESSIONAL ACTIVITIES: Concerts in the UK and abroad.

VIDEOS INCLUDE: Sullivan, *The Sorcerer* (Walker).

ADDRESS: c/o Athole Still International Management Ltd, Greystoke House, 80–86 Westow Street, London SE19 3AF.

WILSON PAUL   Tenor

PERSONAL DETAILS: b. 9 October 1952,
Gloucester; one child.

EDUCATION/TRAINING: 1971–1974, Jesus
College, Oxford; 1975–1978, Royal
College of Music, with Frederick Sharp;
1991, masterclass with Alberto Remedios.

PROFESSIONAL DEBUT: As baritone: 1978,
Opera for All, Germont, *La Traviata*; as
tenor: 1983, University of Warwick, Mark,
The Wreckers.

EARLY CAREER INCLUDED: 1978–1983,
appearances with Chelsea Opera Group,
Kent Opera, Opera for All, Opera Factory
Zurich, numerous university and fringe
societies; roles included: High Priest,
Idomeneo; Claudio, *Béatrice et Bénédict*;
d'Obigny, *La Traviata*; Tarquinius, *The
Rape of Lucretia*; Guglielmo, *Così fan
tutte*; 1983–1985, Covent Garden, chorus
member and small roles including:
Messenger, *Samson*; Officer, *Ariadne auf
Naxos*; 1987, chorus member, Bayreuth
Festival.

MAJOR DEBUTS INCLUDE: 1984, New
Sussex Opera, title role, *Andrea Chénier*;
1987, Welsh National Opera, Florestan,
Fidelio; 1988, English National Opera,
Monostatos, *The Magic Flute*; 1990: City
of Birmingham Touring Opera, Siegmund
and Siegfried, *The Ring Saga*; Opera
North, Torquemada, *L'Heure Espagnole*
and Gherardo, *Gianni Schicci*.

OPERATIC WORLD PREMIERES INCLUDE:
Almeida Festival: 1989, Stoikus, *Golem* by
John Casken; 1990, Tenor, *Europera 3* by
John Cage; 1991: English National Opera,
Varro, *Timon of Athens* by Stephen
Oliver; Opera North, Matthew, *Caritas* by
Robert Saxton.

CAREER IN THE UK INCLUDES: Since 1988:
Aldeburgh Festival, Achab, *Naboth's
Vineyard* and Narrator, *Shadowplay*;
Northern Stage, Stoikus, *Golem*.

RELATED PROFESSIONAL ACTIVITIES:
Recitals in the UK and abroad,
appearances in West End musicals.

RECORDINGS INCLUDE: Casken, *Golem*
(VIRG); Saxton, *Caritas* (COLL).

ADDRESS: 106 Salisbury Street, Bedford
MK41 7RQ.

WILSON TIMOTHY
Counter-tenor

PERSONAL DETAILS: b. 18 July 1961,
Winchester; m. 1989, Eirian Davies
(soprano), one child.

EDUCATION/TRAINING: 1979–1984, Royal
Academy of Music, with Geoffrey Mitchell.

PROFESSIONAL DEBUT: 1985, Scottish
Opera, Medoro, *Orlando*.

MAJOR DEBUTS INCLUDE: 1985, Frankfurt
Opera, Cupid, *Orpheus in the
Underworld*; 1986, Gelsenkirchen, Ottone,
L'Incoronazione di Poppea; 1987: Cassel,
Orfeo, *Orfeo ed Euridice*; Maggio
Musicale, Florence, Secrecy/Mopsa/
Summer, *The Fairy Queen*; 1989,
Kentucky Opera, Oberon, *A Midsummer
Night's Dream*; 1992, Covent Garden,
Voice of Apollo, *Death in Venice*.

OPERATIC WORLD PREMIERES INCLUDE:
1988, Darmstadt, Mam, *Resurrection* by
Peter Maxwell Davies; 1990, Teatro La
Zarzuela, Madrid, Androgyne, *El Viajero
Indiscreto* by Luis de Pablo; 1991:
Netherlands Opera, Shamsi, *Gassir the
Hero* by Theo Loevendie; Theater an der
Wien, Vienna, Frau Schmetterling,
Freudiana by Eric Woolfson.

CAREER IN THE UK INCLUDES: Since 1985:
Buxton Festival: Cardenio, *Don Quixote in
Sierra Morena*; Ottone, *Agrippina*;
Scottish Opera: Voice of Apollo, *Death in
Venice*; Nireno, *Julius Caesar*.

RELATED PROFESSIONAL ACTIVITIES:
Numerous concerts and recitals in the UK
and abroad.

RECORDINGS INCLUDE: Handel, *Israel in
Egypt* (EMI); Purcell, *Come Ye Sons of Art*
(EMI/DG).

AWARDS INCLUDE: 1985: John Scott Award
(Scottish Opera), Kathleen Ferrier Jury's
Prize.

ADDRESS: c/o Ingpen & Williams Ltd, 14
Kensington Court, London W8 5DN.

WILSON-JOHNSON DAVID
Bass-baritone

PERSONAL DETAILS: b. 16 November 1950, Northampton.

EDUCATION/TRAINING: 1970–1973, St Catharine's College, Cambridge, studied French and Italian; 1973–1976, Royal Academy of Music, with Henry Cummings and John Streets.

PROFESSIONAL DEBUT: 1976, Covent Garden, Official 2, *We Come to the River* by Hans Werner Henze (world première).

MAJOR DEBUTS INCLUDE: 1978: Welsh National Opera, Speaker, *The Magic Flute*; Paris Opera, title role, *Eight Songs for a Mad King*; 1980, Glyndebourne Touring Opera, Police Commissar, Der *Rosenkavalier*; 1981, Grand Théâtre, Geneva, Mr Gedge, *Albert Herring*; 1983, Grand Théâtre, Bordeaux, Don Alfonso, *Così fan tutte*; Orange Festival: 1985, Schelkalov, *Boris Godunov*; 1989, Speaker, *Die Zauberflöte*; 1989, Paris Opera, Kothner, *Die Meistersinger von Nürnberg*; 1991, English National Opera, Mr Redburn, *Billy Budd*.

OPERATIC WORLD PREMIÈRES INCLUDE: 1980, Edinburgh International Festival, Arthur, *The Lighthouse* by Peter Maxwell Davies.

CAREER IN THE UK INCLUDES: Since 1977: Covent Garden: Bosun, *Billy Budd*; Emperor of China, *The Nightingale* and Grandfather Clock/Tom Cat, *L'Enfant et les Sortilèges*; Speaker, *Die Zauberflöte*; Johann, *Werther*; Mandarin, *Turandot*; Yamadori, *Madama Butterfly*; Schelkalov, *Boris Godunov*; Opera North: Dark Fiddler, *A Village Romeo and Juliet*; Bartolo, *The Barber of Seville*; Royal Festival Hall, title role, *Saint François d'Assise* (1988, British première).

RELATED PROFESSIONAL ACTIVITIES: Numerous concerts, recitals, broadcasts and television appearances in the UK and abroad; duo partnerships with Hartmut Höll and David Owen Norris; since 1986, Director, Summer Singing Course, Ferrandou, France.

RECORDINGS INCLUDE: Berlioz, *L'Enfance du Christ* (EMI); Birtwistle, *Punch and Judy* (ETCE); Boughton, *The Immortal Hour* (HYPE); Donizetti, *Lucrezia Borgia* (DECC); Elgar, *The Kingdom* (CHAN); Handel, *Belshazzar*; Haydn, *Nelsonmesse* (both ARCH); Mozart, Masses from King's (DECC/SONY); Rachmaninov, *The Bells* (CHAN); Schubert, *Winterreise* (HYPE); Tippett: *The Ice Break* (VIRG), *King Priam* (DECC); Walton, *Belshazzar's Feast* (EMI).

HONOURS INCLUDE: Royal Academy of Music: 1984, Associate; 1988, Fellow.

ADDRESS: c/o Lies Askonas Ltd, 186 Drury Lane, London WC2B 5RY.

WINSLADE GLENN Tenor

PERSONAL DETAILS: b. 23 December 1955, Sydney, Australia.

EDUCATION/TRAINING: New South Wales State Conservatorium of Music, Sydney; Vienna Conservatorium; further studies with Evelyn Hall de Izal, William Blankenship and Valerie Collins Varga.

MAJOR DEBUTS INCLUDE: 1982, Glyndebourne Touring Opera, Don Ottavio, *Don Giovanni*; 1983: English National Opera, Tamino, *The Magic Flute*; Glyndebourne Festival Opera, Stroh, *Intermezzo*; 1985, Australian Opera, Sydney, Belmonte, *The Seraglio*; 1986, Opera North, Don Ottavio, *Don Giovanni*; 1987, Western Australian Opera, Perth, Alfredo, *La Traviata*; 1988, Wellington City Opera, Belmonte, *The Seraglio*; 1989: Scottish Opera, Don Ottavio, *Don Giovanni*; Victoria State Opera, Melbourne, Walther, *Tannhäuser*; 1990, Covent Garden, Vogelgesang, *Die Meistersinger von Nürnberg*. 1991: Netherlands Opera, High Priest, *Idomeneo*; Stuttgart State Opera, Don Ottavio, *Don Giovanni*.

CAREER IN THE UK INCLUDES: Since 1983: English National Opera: Amenophis, *Moses*; Ferrando, *Così fan tutte*; Don Ottavio, *Don Giovanni*; Glyndebourne Festival and Touring Opera: Elemer, *Arabella*; Prince, *L'Amour des Trois*

Oranges; Ferrando, *Così fan tutte*; New Sadler's Wells Opera, Camille, *The Merry Widow*; Park Lane Opera, Fracasso, *La Finta Semplice*; Scottish Opera: Lensky, *Eugene Onegin*; title role, *La Clemenza di Tito*.

RELATED PROFESSIONAL ACTIVITIES: Numerous concerts and recitals in the UK and abroad.

RECORDINGS INCLUDE: Handel, *Messiah* (PICK); Lehár, *The Merry Widow* (TER); Mozart, *Idomeneo* (ARCH).

AWARDS INCLUDE: 1981, Esso/ Glyndebourne Award; 1982, John Christie Award.

ADDRESS: c/o Lies Askonas Ltd, 186 Drury Lane, London WC2B 5RY.

WINTER LOUISE
Mezzo-soprano

PERSONAL DETAILS: b. 29 November 1959, Lancashire; m. 1990, Gerald Finley (baritone), one child.

EDUCATION/TRAINING: Royal Northern College of Music, with Frederic Cox.

PROFESSIONAL DEBUT: 1983, Glyndebourne Touring Opera, Tisbe, *La Cenerentola*.

MAJOR DEBUTS INCLUDE: 1985, Opera North, Tessa, *The Gondoliers*; 1986, Glyndebourne Festival Opera at the Hong Kong Arts Festival, Zerlina, *Don Giovanni*; 1988: Covent Garden, Flower Maiden, *Parsifal*; Netherlands Opera, Rosina, *Il Barbiere di Siviglia*; 1989, Canadian Opera Company, Toronto, Olga, *Eugene Onegin*; 1990, English National Opera, Suzuki, *Madam Butterfly*.

CAREER IN THE UK INCLUDES: Since 1983: English National Opera, title role, *Xerxes*; Glyndebourne Festival and Touring Opera: Dorabella, *Così fan tutte*; Mercédès, *Carmen*; Chinese Cup/ Dragonfly, *L'Enfant et les Sortilèges*; Nancy, *Albert Herring*; Varvara, *Katya Kabanova*; Pauline/Daphnis, *The Queen of Spades*; Opera North: Varvara, *Katya Kabanova*; Concepcion, *L'Heure Espagnole*.

RELATED PROFESSIONAL ACTIVITIES: Numerous concerts and recitals in the UK and abroad.

RECORDINGS INCLUDE: Mendelssohn, *A Midsummer Night's Dream* (COLL).

VIDEOS INCLUDE: Janáček, *Katya Kabanova* (Glyndebourne Festival Opera).

AWARDS INCLUDE: 1983: Esso/ Glyndebourne Touring Opera Award, John Christie Award.

ADDRESS: c/o Harrison/Parrott Ltd, 12 Penzance Place, London W11 4PA.

WOODROW ALAN   Tenor

PERSONAL DETAILS: b. 22 September 1952, Toronto, Canada; m. 1977, Elizabeth Stokes (mezzo-soprano).

PROFESSIONAL DEBUT: 1976, New Opera Company, Niccolò, *Bomarzo* (British première).

OPERATIC WORLD PREMIERES INCLUDE: 1977, English National Opera, Young Martin, *The Royal Hunt of the Sun* by Iain Hamilton.

CAREER INCLUDES: Since 1977, English National Opera: Jacquino, *Fidelio*; Borsa, *Rigoletto*; Don Ottavio, *Don Giovanni*; Pedrillo, *The Seraglio*; Iskra, *Mazeppa*; Major-Domo, *Der Rosenkavalier*; Monostatos, *The Magic Flute*; Young Sailor, *Tristan and Isolde*; Baroncelli, *Rienzi*; Master of Ceremonies, *Gloriana*; Eleazor, *Moses*; Vašek, *The Bartered Bride*; Canio, *Pagliacci*; Shabby Peasant, *Lady Macbeth of Mtsensk* (1987, British stage première); Herman, *The Queen of Spades*; Cock, *The Cunning Little Vixen*; Don José, *Carmen*; Edmund, *Lear* (1989, British première); Tichon, *Katya Kabanova*; Walther, *The Mastersingers of Nuremberg*; Prince, *The Love for Three Oranges*; Captain, *Wozzeck*; Tenor/ Bacchus, *Ariadne auf Naxos*; Herod, *Salome*; Sergei, *Lady Macbeth of Mtsensk*: La Scala, Milan and Opéra Bastille, Paris.

VIDEOS INCLUDE: Britten, *Gloriana* (English National Opera).

ADDRESS: c/o Athole Still International Management Ltd, Greystoke House, 80–86 Westow Street, London SE19 3AF.

WOOLLAM KENNETH
Tenor and Teacher

POSITION: Professor of Singing, Royal College of Music.
PERSONAL DETAILS: b. 16 January 1937, Chester; m. 1965, Phoebe Scrivenor (music teacher), four children.
EDUCATION/TRAINING: Chester Cathedral Choir School; Royal College of Music.
PROFESSIONAL DEBUT: 1962, chorus member, Glyndebourne Festival Opera.
EARLY CAREER INCLUDED: 1964–1972, member, BBC Singers.
MAJOR DEBUTS INCLUDE: 1972, Sadler's Wells Opera, Pierre, *War and Peace* (British stage première); 1981, Lille Opera, title role, *Les Contes d'Hoffmann*; 1984: English National Opera USA tour (including Metropolitan Opera, New York), Pierre, *War and Peace*; Frankfurt Opera, Florestan, *Fidelio*; 1986, Royal Opera, Copenhagen, David, *Saul og David*; 1988, Covent Garden, Aegisth, *Elektra*.
OPERATIC WORLD PREMIÈRES INCLUDE: 1977: Bath Festival, Man, *A Gentle Spirit* by John Tavener; English National Opera: Challcuchima, *The Royal Hunt of the Sun* by Iain Hamilton; Bricard/Millet, *Toussaint* by David Blake.
CAREER IN THE UK INCLUDES: Since 1972: Edinburgh International Festival, Herod, *Salome*; Opera North: Max, *Johnny Strikes Up* (1984, British première); Walther, *The Mastersingers of Nuremberg*; Sadler's Wells Opera/ English National Opera (1972–1984, Principal Tenor): Boris, *Katya Kabanova*; Tiresias, *The Bassarids* (1974, British stage première); Siegmund and Siegfried, *The Ring of the Nibelung*; Walther, *The Mastersingers of Nuremberg*; Gregor, *The Makropoulos Case*; Adolar, *Euryanthe*; Florestan, *Fidelio*; Radamès, *Aida*; Tenor/Bacchus, *Ariadne auf Naxos*; Tristan, *Tristan and Isolde*; title role, *Rienzi*; Scottish Opera: Tenor/Bacchus, *Ariadne auf Naxos*; Boris, *Katya Kabanova*.
RELATED PROFESSIONAL ACTIVITIES: Numerous concerts, recitals, broadcasts and television appearances in the UK and abroad; since 1985, Professor of Singing, Royal College of Music; voice teacher, University of Reading.
RECORDINGS INCLUDE: Delius, *Margot la Rouge* (BBC).
ADDRESS: 33 Blenheim Road, Chiswick, London W4 1ET.

*   *   *   *

YEARGAN MICHAEL
Designer

POSITIONS: Associate Professor in Stage Design, Yale University School of Drama; Resident Designer, Yale Repertory Theatre.
PERSONAL DETAILS: b. 13 February 1946, Dallas, USA.
EDUCATION/TRAINING: Fine arts studies: Stetson University, Florida; Yale University; Madrid University.
PROFESSIONAL DEBUT: 1968, Florida Summer Theater, *My Fair Lady*.
OPERATIC DEBUT: 1979, Santa Fe Opera, *Lucia di Lammermoor*.
CAREER: Since 1968, opera and theatre designer in the USA and abroad including West End, Broadway, American regional theatre and more than 40 productions for Yale Repertory Theatre; since 1974: Associate Professor in Stage Design, Yale University School of Drama;

Resident Designer, Yale Repertory
Theatre.

MAJOR OPERATIC DEBUTS INCLUDE: 1980:
Welsh National Opera, *Eugene Onegin*;
Nancy Opera, *Die Zauberflöte*; 1984,
Opera North, *Il Trovatore*; 1986, Scottish
Opera, *Carmen*; 1987, Frankfurt Opera,
Così fan tutte; 1989, Australian Opera,
Sydney, *Werther*; 1990: Covent Garden,
Attila; Dallas Civic Opera, *Hänsel und
Gretel*; Houston Grand Opera, *Carousel*;
1991, Lyric Opera, Chicago, *Antony and
Cleopatra*; 1993, Metropolitan Opera,
New York, *Ariadne auf Naxos*.

OPERA DESIGNS IN THE UK INCLUDE: Since
1980: Covent Garden: *Simon Boccanegra*,
I Puritani, *Stiffelio*; Scottish Opera: *La
Bohème*, *La Forza del Destino*; Welsh
National Opera: *Rodelinda*, *I Puritani*, *The
Drama of Aida*, *The Merry Widow*, *La
Bohème*, *Norma*.

VIDEOS INCLUDE: Verdi, *Simon Boccanegra*
(Covent Garden).

ADDRESS: c/o Helen Harvey Associates
Inc., 410 West 24th Street, New York, NY
10011, USA.

YURISICH GREGORY
Baritone

PERSONAL DETAILS: b. 13 October 1951,
Perth, Australia; two children.

EDUCATION/TRAINING: 1967–1969,
University of Western Australia, Perth,
studied piano and voice.

PROFESSIONAL DEBUT: 1974, Australian
Opera, Sydney, Paolo, *Simon
Boccanegra*.

CAREER INCLUDES: Since 1974: Australian
Opera, Sydney (1974–1987, Principal
Baritone): Sharpless, *Madama Butterfly*;
Marcello and Schaunard, *La Bohème*;
Yeletsky, *The Queen of Spades*; Bottom,
A Midsummer Night's Dream; Smirnov,
The Bear; Frank, *Die Fledermaus*;
Escamillo, *Carmen*; Germont, *La
Traviata*; Varlaam, *Boris Godunov*;
Bartolo, *Il Barbiere di Siviglia*; Don

Alfonso, *Così fan tutte*; Leporello, *Don
Giovanni*; Malatesta and title role, *Don
Pasquale*; Sulpice, *La Fille du Régiment*;
Pooh-Bah, *The Mikado*; Melitone, *La
Forza del Destino*; Victoria State Opera,
Melbourne: Alberich, *Siegfried*; Don
Pizarro, *Fidelio*; Telramund, *Lohengrin*;
Frankfurt Opera (1988–1990, Principal
Baritone): Bottom, *A Midsumer Night's
Dream*; Marcello, *La Bohème*; Don
Alfonso, *Così fan tutte*.

MAJOR DEBUTS INCLUDE: 1985, Lincoln
Center Trust, New York, Enrico, *Anna
Bolena*; 1988, English National Opera,
Escamillo, *Carmen*; 1990, Covent Garden,
title role, *Guillaume Tell*; 1991, Leporello,
Don Giovanni: Glyndebourne Festival
Opera and Deutsche Oper, Berlin; 1993:
Bregenz Festival, title role, *Nabucco*;
Grand Théâtre, Geneva, Shchekalov,
Boris Godunov; La Monnaie, Brussels,
Balstrode, *Peter Grimes*.

OPERATIC WORLD PREMIERES INCLUDE:
English National Opera: 1991, Alcibiades,
Timon of Athens by Stephen Oliver; 1992,
Cadmus, *Bakxai* by John Buller.

CAREER IN THE UK INCLUDES: Since 1988:
Covent Garden: Bartolo, *Il Barbiere di
Siviglia*; Lindorf/Coppelius/Dapertutto/Dr
Miracle, *Les Contes d'Hoffmann*; Don
Profondo, *Il Viaggio a Reims*; Don
Pizarro, *Fidelio*; Stankar, *Stiffelio*;
English National Opera, title roles: *The
Marriage of Figaro*, *Simon Boccanegra*.

RELATED PROFESSIONAL ACTIVITIES:
Regular concerts and recitals in the UK
and abroad.

RECORDINGS INCLUDE: Copland, Old
American Songs; Walton, *The Bear* (both
Australian labels).

VIDEOS INCLUDE: Donizetti, *La Fille du
Régiment*; J. Strauss, *Die Fledermaus*;
Sullivan, *The Mikado* (all Australian
Opera, Sydney).

ADDRESS: c/o Lies Askonas Ltd, 186 Drury
Lane, London WC2B 5RY.

295

APPENDIX 1
CROSS REFERENCES
=

ADMINISTRATORS
Bredin Henrietta   (Dramaturg, Editor, Writer)
Caulton Jeremy
Christie, Sir George
Coe Denis
Dickie Brian
Epstein Matthew
Findlay Paul
Harewood, The Earl of
Hellings Jane
Herbert Katharine
Issacs Jeremy
Jarman Richard
Jonas Peter
Katona Peter Mario
Kenyon Nicholas   (Broadcaster, Critic, Writer)
Lalandi Lina
Lloyd Hugh
McMaster Brian
McMurray John   (Dramaturg, Librettist, Writer)
Marks Dennis   (Director)
Padmore Elaine   (Broadcaster, Director – Artistic, Soprano)
Parry Elisabeth
Payne Nicholas
Peters Johanna   (Mezzo-soprano, Teacher)
Platt Norman   (Director, Librettist, Teacher, Translator)
Playfair Sarah
Pollock Adam   (Designer, Translator)
Ritchie Ian
Schmid Patric   (Editor, Record Producer, Teacher)
Shannon Randall
Stirling Angus
Stockdale Frederick   (Director)
Tracey Edmund   (Librettist, Translator)
Whitworth-Jones Anthony

BARITONES

Allen Thomas
Bailey Norman   (Teacher)
Black Jeffrey
Booth-Jones Christopher
Caproni Bruno
Clarke Adrian
Coleman-Wright Peter
Dolton Geoffrey
Donnelly Malcolm
Ebrahim Omar
Finley Gerald
Folwell Nicholas
Guy-Bromley Phillip
Hargreaves Glenville
Hayes Quentin
Herford Henry   (Teacher)
Holland Mark
Howard Jason
Howlett Neil   (Teacher)
Keenlyside Simon
Kitchiner John
Knapp Peter   (Director, Translator)
Latham Keith
Leiferkus Sergei
Luxon Benjamin
McGuigan Patrick   (Director, Teacher)
Maxwell Donald
Michaels-Moore Anthony
Mora Barry
Mosley George
Moyle Julian
Newman Henry
Oke Alan
Opie Alan
Page Steven
Poulton Robert
Rawnsley John
Rivers Malcolm   (Teacher)
Roberts Stephen
Sandison Gordon
Savidge Peter
Sharpe Terence

Shilling Eric   (Teacher)
Shimell William
Shore Andrew
Sidhom Peter
Smythe Russell
Suart Richard
Summers Jonathan
Thomas Gwion
Tinkler Mark
Watt Alan
Wheatley Patrick
Yurisich Gregory

BASS-BARITONES
Best Matthew   (Composer, Conductor)
Bryson Roger
Caddy Ian
Dean Stafford
Donnelly Patrick
Earle Roderick
Gadd Stephen
Garrett Eric
Hall John
Hayward Robert
Joll Phillip
Kennedy Roderick
Lawlor Thomas
McDonnell Tom
McIntyre, Sir Donald
Masterton-Smith Simon   (Teacher)
Morgan Arwel Huw
Rath John
Shirley-Quirk John
Terfel Bryn
Wilson-Johnson David

BASSES
Adams Donald
Angas Richard
Bannatyne-Scott Brian   (Translator)
Bayley Clive
Best Jonathan
Comboy Ian

Connell John
Druiett Michael
Howell Gwynne
Lloyd Robert
Mackie William
Miles Alistair
Moses Geoffrey
Rea Sean
Richardson Mark
Richardson Stephen
Rose Peter
Tomlinson John
Tranter John
Van Allan Richard
White Willard

BROADCASTERS
Blyth Alan   (Critic, Writer)
Douglas Nigel   (Director, Tenor, Translator, Writer)
Greenfield Edward   (Critic, Writer)
Kenyon Nicholas   (Administrator, Critic, Writer)
Osborne Nigel   (Composer, Writer)
Padmore Elaine   (Administrator, Director – Artistic, Soprano)

CHORUS MASTERS
Angus David   (Conductor)
Barker John   (Conductor, Répétiteur, Translator)
Bicket Harry   (Conductor, Harpsichordist, Organist)
Dean Timothy   (Conductor, Répétiteur)
Edwards Terry
Gellhorn Peter   (Conductor, Répétiteur)
Greenwood Andrew   (Conductor)
Halsey Simon   (Conductor)

CLARINETTISTS
Hacker Alan   (Conductor, Editor, Teacher)
Laurence Elizabeth   (Mezzo-soprano)

COMPOSERS
Barker Paul   (Conductor, Répétiteur)
Bennett Richard Rodney
Best Matthew   (Bass-baritone, Conductor)
Birtwistle, Sir Harrison

Blake David   (Conductor)
Buller John
Casken John   (Teacher)
Dove Jonathan   (Pianist and Accompanist, Répétiteur)
Finnissy Michael   (Librettist, Pianist, Teacher)
Goehr Alexander
Hamilton Iain
Harper Edward   (Conductor, Pianist)
Harvey Jonathan
Hoddinott Alun
Holloway Robin   (Librettist, Teacher, Writer)
Josephs Wilfred
Knussen Oliver   (Conductor)
Maw Nicholas
Maxwell Davies, Sir Peter   (Conductor)
Metcalf John
Musgrave Thea
Nyman Michael
Osborne Nigel   (Broadcaster, Writer)
Paintal Priti
Sams Jeremy   (Répétiteur, Translator)
Saxton Robert
Tavener John
Tippett, Sir Michael
Turnage Mark-Anthony
Weir Judith
Williamson Malcolm   (Organist, Pianist)

CONDUCTORS
Angus David   (Chorus Master)
Armstrong Richard
Atherton David
Balcombe Richard   (Répétiteur)
Barker John   (Chorus Master, Répétiteur, Translator)
Barker Paul   (Composer, Répétiteur)
Barlow Stephen
Bedford Steuart
Bernas Richard
Best Matthew   (Bass-baritone, Composer)
Bicket Harry   (Chorus Master, Harpsichordist, Organist)
Blake David   (Composer)
Bolton Ivor   (Harpsichordist)
Brydon Roderick   (Pianist and Accompanist)

Cleobury Nicholas
Daniel Paul
Davies Noel   (Editor, Harpsichordist, Répétiteur)
Davies Wyn   (Coach)
Davis Andrew   (Harpsichordist, Organist)
Davis, Sir Colin
Dean Robert
Dean Timothy   (Chorus Master, Répétiteur)
Downes, Sir Edward   (Editor, Translator)
Edwards Sian
Elder Mark
Farncombe Charles
Fifield Christopher   (Writer)
Friend Lionel
Gardiner John Eliot   (Editor)
Gellhorn Peter   (Chorus Master, Répétiteur)
Gibson, Sir Alexander
Glover Jane
Greenwood Andrew   (Chorus Master)
Hacker Alan   (Clarinettist, Editor, Teacher)
Haitink Bernard
Halsey Simon   (Chorus Master)
Harper Edward   (Composer, Pianist)
Herbert Paul
Hickox Richard
Holman Peter   (Editor, Harpsichordist, Writer)
Hose Anthony   (Translator)
Howarth Elgar
Hutchinson Stuart   (Pianist and Accompanist)
Isepp Martin   (Harpsichordist, Pianist and Accompanist, Teacher)
Jenkins Graeme
Knussen Oliver   (Composer)
Lloyd Michael   (Répétiteur)
Lloyd-Jones David   (Editor, Translator)
Lockhart James   (Pianist and Accompanist, Teacher)
Mackerras, Sir Charles   (Editor)
Manson Anne
Mauceri John
Maxwell Davies, Sir Peter   (Composer)
Montgomery Kenneth
Norrington Roger
Parrott Andrew
Parry Dayid   (Translator)

Pryce-Jones John
Rafferty Michael
Rattle Simon
Rizzi Carlo
Robinson Peter
Smith Julian
Solti, Sir Georg
Stapleton Robin
Syrus David   (Harpsichordist, Pianist and Accompanist, Répétiteur,
    Teacher)
Tate Jeffrey
Tear Robert   (Tenor)
Timms Clive
Tortelier Yan Pascal   (Violinist)
Wigglesworth Mark
Williams Howard

COUNTER-TENORS
Bowman James
Chance Michael
Esswood Paul   (Teacher)
Robson Christopher
Sutcliffe Tom   (Critic)
Wilson Timothy

CRITICS
Blyth Alan   (Critic, Writer)
Greenfield Edward   (Broadcaster, Writer)
Griffiths Paul   (Librettist, Writer)
Jacobs Arthur   (Librettist, Translator, Writer)
Kennedy Michael   (Writer)
Kenyon Nicholas   (Administrator, Broadcaster, Writer)
Loppert Max
Milnes Rodney   (Translator)
Porter Andrew   (Director, Editor, Librettist, Translator)
Sadie Stanley   (Writer)
Sutcliffe Tom   (Counter-tenor)

DESIGNERS
Bechtler Hildegard
Bjørnson Maria
Blane Sue
Brotherston Lez

Brown Paul
Bury John
Butlin Roger
Cairns Tom   (Director)
Chitty Alison
Craig Russell
Crowley Bob
Don Robin
Dudley William
Edwards Jack   (Director, Teacher, Writer)
Fielding David
Graham Colin   (Director, Librettist, Teacher, Translator)
Gunter John
Hernon Paul   (Director, Translator)
Hudson Richard
Koltai Ralph
Lazaridis Stefanos   (Director)
Lecca Marie-Jeanne
Lowery Nigel
McDonald Antony
O'Brien Timothy
Pollock Adam   (Administrator, Translator)
Prowse Philip   (Director)
Reed Tim
Roger David
Warner Keith   (Director, Translator)
Yeargan Michael

DIRECTORS
Abulafia John
Albery Tim
Alden David
Ashman Mike   (Translator, Writer)
Ayrton Norman   (Teacher)
Besch Anthony
Cairns Tom   (Designer)
Copley John
Cox John
Douglas Nigel   (Broadcaster, Tenor, Translator, Writer)
Edwards Jack   (Designer, Teacher, Writer)
Fraser Malcolm   (Teacher, Translator)
Freeman David   (Editor, Librettist, Translator)
Geliot Michael   (Translator)

Graham Colin   (Designer, Librettist, Teacher, Translator)
Hall, Sir Peter
Hawkes Tom   (Teacher)
Hernon Paul   (Designer, Translator)
Hytner Nicholas
Jones Richard
Judd Wilfred   (Translator)
Judge Ian
Knapp Peter   (Baritone, Translator)
Lang Aidan
Langford Sally
Lawless Stephen
Lazaridis Stefanos   (Designer)
McCarthy Michael
McGuigan Patrick   (Baritone, Teacher)
Marks Dennis   (Administrator)
Medcalf Stephen
Miller Jonathan
Moshinsky Elijah
Nunn Trevor
Padmore Elaine (Administrator, Broadcaster, Soprano)
Pimlott Steven
Platt Norman   (Administrator, Librettist, Teacher, Translator)
Porter Andrew   (Critic, Editor, Librettist, Translator)
Pountney David   (Translator)
Prowse Philip   (Designer)
Stockdale Frederick   (Administrator)
Vick Graham
Warner Keith   (Designer, Translator)

DRAMATURGS
Bredin Henrietta   (Administrator, Editor, Writer)
Carnegy Patrick
John Nicholas   (Writer)
McMurray John   (Administrator, Librettist, Writer)

EDITORS
Bredin Henrietta   (Administrator, Dramaturg, Writer)
Davies Noel   (Conductor, Harpsichordist, Répétiteur)
Downes, Sir Edward   (Conductor, Translator)
Freeman David   (Director, Librettist, Translator)
Gardiner John Eliot   (Conductor)
Hacker Alan   (Clarinettist, Conductor, Teacher)

Holden Amanda   (Pianist and Accompanist, Teacher, Translator, Writer)
Holman Peter   (Conductor, Harpsichordist, Writer)
Lloyd-Jones David   (Conductor, Translator)
Mackerras, Sir Charles   (Conductor)
Porter Andrew   (Critic, Director, Librettist, Translator)
Schmid Patric   (Adminstrator, Record Producer, Teacher)

HARPSICHORDISTS
Bicket Harry   (Chorus Master, Conductor, Organist)
Bolton Ivor   (Conductor)
Davies Noel   (Conductor, Editor, Répétiteur)
Davis Andrew   (Conductor, Organist).
Holman Peter   (Conductor, Editor, Writer)
Isepp Martin   (Conductor, Pianist and Accompanist, Teacher)
Syrus David   (Conductor, Pianist and Accompanist, Répétiteur, Teacher)

LIBRETTISTS
Finnissy Michael   (Composer, Pianist, Teacher)
Freeman David   (Director, Editor, Translator)
Graham Colin   (Designer, Director, Teacher, Translator)
Griffiths Paul   (Critic, Writer)
Holloway Robin   (Composer, Teacher, Writer)
Jacobs Arthur   (Critic, Translator, Writer)
McMurray John   (Administrator, Dramaturg, Writer)
Platt Norman   (Administrator, Director, Teacher, Translator)
Porter Andrew   (Critic, Director, Editor, Translator)
Tracey Edmund   (Administrator, Translator)

MEZZO-SOPRANOS
Bainbridge Elizabeth
Bardon Patricia
Bickley Susan
Botes Christine
Buchan Cynthia
Burgess Sally
Collins Anne
Davies Menai
Dickinson Meriel
Finnie Linda
Howard Ann
Howard Yvonne
Howells Anne
James Eirian

305

Jones Della
Kimm Fiona
King Mary
Knight Gillian
Laurence Elizabeth   (Clarinettist)
McCormack Elizabeth
Mason Anne
Mills Beverley
Minton Yvonne
Montague Diana
Morelle Maureen
Murray Ann
Ormiston Linda
Owens Anne-Marie
Palmer Felicity
Payne Patricia
Peters Johanna   (Administrator, Teacher)
Powell Claire
Rigby Jean
Robinson Ethna
Roebuck Janine
Squires Shelagh
Turner Jane
Vaughan Elizabeth   (Teacher)
Verco Wendy
Walker Penelope
Walker Sarah
Wilkens Anne
Willis Nuala
Winter Louise

ORGANISTS
Bicket Harry   (Chorus Master, Conductor, Harpsichordist)
Davis Andrew   (Conductor, Harpsichordist)
Williamson Malcolm   (Composer, Pianist)

PIANISTS/PIANISTS AND ACCOMPANISTS
Brydon Roderick   (Conductor)
Dove Jonathan   (Composer, Répétiteur)
Finnissy Michael   (Composer, Librettist, Teacher)
Harper Edward   (Composer, Conductor).
Holden Amanda   (Editor, Teacher, Translator, Writer)
Hutchinson Stuart   (Conductor)

Isepp Martin   (Conductor, Harpsichordist, Teacher)
Lockhart James   (Conductor, Teacher)
Syrus David   (Conductor, Harpsichordist, Répétiteur, Teacher)
Williamson Malcolm   (Composer, Organist)

RECORD PRODUCERS
Schmid Patric   (Adminstrator, Editor, Teacher)

REPETITEURS
Balcombe Richard   (Conductor)
Barker John   (Chorus Master, Conductor, Translator)
Barker Paul   (Composer, Conductor)
Davies Noel   (Conductor, Editor, Harpsichordist)
Dean Timothy   (Chorus Master, Conductor)
Dove Jonathan   (Composer, Pianist and Accompanist)
Gellhorn Peter   (Chorus Master, Conductor)
Lloyd Michael   (Conductor)
Sams Jeremy   (Composer, Translator)
Syrus David   (Conductor, Harpsichordist, Pianist and Accompanist,
   Teacher)

SOPRANOS
Angel Marie
Ashe Rosemary
Barclay Yvonne
Barker Cheryl
Barstow Josephine
Bolton Andrea
Bovino Maria
Bullock Susan
Bunning Christine
Byrne Elizabeth
Cahill Teresa
Cairns Janice
Cannan Phyllis
Christie Nan
Ciesinski Kristine
Connell Elizabeth
Cullis Rita
Davies Eirian
Davies Lynne
Dawson Anne
Dawson Lynne

Eaglen Jane
Eathorne Wendy   (Teacher)
Evans Anne
Ewing Maria
Feeney Angela
Field Helen
Gale Elizabeth
Garrett Lesley
Gomez Jill
Hagley Alison
Hannan Eilene
Harrhy Eiddwen
Harries Kathryn
Hegarty Mary
Hill Smith Marilyn
Howarth Judith
Hulse Eileen
Jones, Dame Gwyneth
Joshua Rosemary
Kelly Janis
Kenny Yvonne
Kerr Virginia
Kitchen Linda
Lloyd-Davies Mary
Lott Felicity
Mackay Penelope   (Teacher)
Mackenzie Jane Leslie
McLaughlin Marie
McLeod Linda
Mannion Rosa
Marshall Margaret
Masterson Valerie
Mills Bronwen
Moll Maria
Murphy Suzanne
O'Neill Patricia
Padmore Elaine   (Administrator, Broadcaster, Director – Artistic)
Plowright Rosalind
Pope Cathryn
Price, Dame Margaret
Ritchie Elizabeth
Rodgers Joan
Roocroft Amanda

Rozario Patricia
Slorach Marie
Steiger Anna
Stuart-Roberts Deborah
Sullivan Gillian
Te Kanawa, Dame Kiri
Teare Christine
Tierney Vivian
Tinsley Pauline
Walmsley-Clark Penelope
Watson Janice
Watson Lillian
Webster Gillian
Williams-King Anne

TEACHERS AND COACHES

Ayrton Norman   (Director)
Bailey Norman   (Baritone)
Bowden Pamela
Casken John   (Composer)
Davies Wyn   (Conductor)
Eathorne Wendy   (Soprano)
Edwards Jack   (Designer, Director, Writer)
Esswood Paul   (Counter-tenor)
Fieldsend David   (Tenor)
Finnissy Michael (Composer, Librettist, Pianist)
Fraser Malcolm   (Director, Translator)
Graham Colin   (Designer, Director, Librettist, Translator)
Hacker Alan   (Clarinettist, Conductor, Editor)
Hawkes Tom   (Director)
Herford Henry   (Baritone)
Holden Amanda   (Editor, Pianist and Accompanist, Translator, Writer)
Holloway Robin   (Composer, Librettist, Writer)
Howlett Neil   (Baritone)
Isepp Martin   (Conductor, Harpsichordist, Pianist and Accompanist)
Langford Audrey
Lockhart James   (Conductor, Pianist and Accompanist)
Mackay Penelope   (Soprano)
McGuigan Patrick   (Baritone, Director)
Masterton-Smith Simon   (Bass-baritone)
Mitchinson John   (Tenor)
Peters Johanna   (Administrator, Mezzo-soprano)
Platt Norman   (Director, Administrator, Librettist, Translator)

Power Patrick   (Tenor)
Rivers Malcolm   (Baritone)
Rozsa Vera
Schmid Patric   (Administrator, Editor, Record Producer)
Shilling Eric   (Baritone)
Syrus David   (Conductor, Harpsichordist, Pianist and Accompanist,
   Répétiteur)
Vaughan Elizabeth (Mezzo-soprano)
Veasey Josephine
Woollam Kenneth (Tenor)

TENORS
Ainsley John Mark
Archer Neill
Atkinson Lynton
Banks Barry
Barham Edmund
Begley Kim
Bottone Bonaventura
Bronder Peter
Burrows Stuart
Byles Edward
Caley Ian
Clark Graham
Crook Paul
Curtis Mark
Dale Laurence
Davies Arthur
Davies Maldwyn
Dobson John
Doghan Philip
Douglas Nigel   (Broadcaster, Director, Translator, Writer)
Egerton Francis
Elliott Alasdair
Fieldsend David   (Teacher)
Fryatt John
Gillett Christopher
Graham-Hall John
Harrhy Paul
Harris John
Hetherington Hugh
Hill Martyn
Hillman David

Jeffes Peter
Jenkins Neil
Jenkins Terry
Kale Stuart
Langridge Philip
Lavender Justin
Lawton Jeffrey
Leggate Robin
Lewis Keith
Martin Adrian
Matheson-Bruce Graeme
Mee Anthony
Milner Howard
Mitchinson John   (Teacher)
Nicoll Harry
Nilon Paul
O'Neill Dennis
Oliver Alexander
Pogson Geoffrey
Power Patrick   (Teacher)
Remedios Alberto
Remedios Ramon
Rendall David
Robson Nigel
Roden Anthony
Rolfe Johnson Anthony
Stephenson Donald
Tear Robert   (Conductor)
Thompson Adrian
Treleaven John
Ventris Christopher
Wilson Paul
Winslade Glenn
Woodrow Alan
Woollam Kenneth   (Teacher)

TRANSLATORS
Ashman Mike   (Director, Writer)
Bannatyne-Scott Brian   (Bass)
Barker John   (Chorus Master, Conductor, Répétiteur)
Douglas Nigel   (Broadcaster, Director, Tenor, Writer)
Downes, Sir Edward   (Conductor, Editor)
Fraser Malcolm   (Director, Teacher)

Freeman David   (Director, Editor, Librettist)
Geliot Michael   (Director)
Graham Colin   (Designer, Director, Librettist, Teacher)
Hernon Paul   (Designer, Director)
Holden Amanda   (Editor, Pianist and Accompanist, Teacher, Writer)
Hose Anthony   (Conductor)
Jacobs Arthur   (Critic, Librettist, Writer)
Judd Wilfred   (Director)
Knapp Peter   (Baritone, Director)
Lloyd-Jones David   (Conductor, Editor)
Milnes Rodney   (Critic)
Parry David   (Conductor)
Platt Norman   (Administator, Director, Librettist, Teacher)
Pollock Adam (Administrator, Designer)
Porter Andrew   (Critic, Director, Editor, Librettist)
Pountney David   (Director)
Ridler Anne
Sams Jeremy   (Composer, Répétiteur)
Tracey Edmund   (Administrator, Librettist)
Warner Keith   (Designer, Director)

VIOLINISTS
Tortelier Yan Pascal   (Conductor)

WRITERS
Ashman Mike   (Director, Translator)
Blyth Alan   (Broadcaster, Critic)
Bredin Henrietta   (Administrator, Dramaturg, Editor)
Douglas Nigel   (Broadcaster, Director, Tenor, Translator)
Edwards Jack   (Designer, Director, Teacher)
Fifield Christopher   (Conductor)
Greenfield Edward   (Broadcaster, Critic)
Griffiths Paul   (Critic, Librettist)
Holden Amanda   (Editor, Pianist and Accompanist, Teacher, Translator)
Holloway Robin   (Composer, Librettist, Teacher)
Holman Peter   (Conductor, Editor, Harpsichordist)
Jacobs Arthur   (Critic, Librettist, Translator)
John Nicholas   (Dramaturg)
Kennedy Michael   (Critic)
Kenyon Nicholas   (Administrator, Broadcaster, Critic)
McMurray John   (Administrator, Dramaturg, Librettist)
Osborne Nigel   (Broadcaster, Composer)
Sadie Stanley   (Critic)

APPENDIX 2
OPERAS AND THEIR COMPOSERS
==

Abbot of Drimock, The	Thea Musgrave
Acis and Galatea	George Frideric Handel
Actor's Revenge, An	Minoru Miki
Admeto	George Frideric Handel
Adriana Lecouvreur	Francesco Cilea
Adventures of Mr Brouček, The	Leoš Janáček
Africaine, L'	Giacomo Meyerbeer
Agrippina	George Frideric Handel
Aida	Giuseppe Verdi
Ajo nell'imbarazzo, L'	Gaetano Donizetti
Akhnaten	Philip Glass
Albergo Empedocle	Paul Barker
Albert Herring	Benjamin Britten
Alceste	Christoph Willibald Gluck
Alcina	George Frideric Handel
Alice in Wonderland	Wilfred Josephs
All the King's Men	Richard Rodney Bennett
Amahl and the Night Visitors	Gian Carlo Menotti
Amour des Trois Oranges, L'	Sergei Prokofiev
Anacréon	Luigi Cherubini
Andrea Chénier	Umberto Giordano
Ange de Feu, L'	Sergei Prokofiev
Angelica Vincitrice di Alcina	Johann Joseph Fux
Angélique	Jacques Ibert
Angelo	Alan Ridout
Angle of Repose	Andrew Imbrie
Anna Bolena	Gaetano Donizetti
Anna Karenina	Iain Hamilton
Antony and Cleopatra	Samuel Barber
Apollo e Dafne	George Frideric Handel
Apollo et Hyacinthus	Wolfgang Amadeus Mozart
Arabella	Richard Strauss
Arden Muss Sterben	Alexander Goehr

Arden Must Die   see: *Arden Muss Sterben*
Ariadne auf Naxos   Richard Strauss
Ariane and Bluebeard   see: *Ariane et Barbe-bleue*
Ariane et Barbe-bleue   Paul Dukas
Ariodante   George Frideric Handel
Arlecchino   Ferruccio Busoni
Armida   Joseph Haydn
Armide   Christoph Willibald Gluck
Artaxerxes   Thomas Augustine Arne
Ascanio in Alba   Wolfgang Amadeus Mozart
Aspects of Love   Andrew Lloyd Webber
Atalanta   George Frideric Handel
Attila   Giuseppe Verdi
Aufstieg und Fall der Stadt Mahagonny   Kurt Weill
Aventures et Nouvelles Aventures   György Ligeti

Bakxai   John Buller
Ballo delle Ingrate, Il   Claudio Monteverdi
Ballo in Maschera, Un   Giuseppe Verdi
Barber of Baghdad, The   see: *Barbier von Bagdad, Der*
Barber of Seville, The   see: *Barbiere di Siviglia, Il*
Barbier von Bagdad, Der   Peter Cornelius
Barbiere di Siviglia, Il (Paisiello)   Giovanni Paisiello
Barbiere di Siviglia, Il   Gioacchino Rossini
Bartered Bride, The   Bedřich Smetana
Bassariden, Die   Hans Werner Henze
Bassarids, The   see: *Bassariden, Die*
Ba-ta-clan   Jacques Offenbach
Bastien und Bastienne   Wolfgang Amadeus Mozart
Beach of Falesá, The   Alun Hoddinott
Bear, The   William Walton
Beatrice and Benedict   see: *Béatrice et Bénédict*
Beatrice Cenci   Berthold Goldschmidt
Beatrice di Tenda   Vincenzo Bellini
Béatrice et Bénédict   Hector Berlioz
Beauty and the Beast   see: *Bella e la Bestia, La*
Beggar's Opera, The   John Gay
Behold the Sun   see: *Wiedertäufer, Die*
Belisario   Gaetano Donizetti
Bella e la Bestia, La   Stephen Oliver
Belle Hélène, La   Jacques Offenbach
Belshazzar   George Frideric Handel
Benvenuto Cellini   Hector Berlioz

Bergtagna, Den	Ivar Hallström
Betrothal in a Monastery	Sergei Prokofiev
Bilby's Doll	Carlisle Floyd
Billy Budd	Benjamin Britten
Birthday of the Infanta, The	Alexander von Zemlinsky
Bitter Sweet	Noel Coward
Blood Wedding	Nicola LeFanu
Boccaccio	Franz von Suppé
Bohème, La	Giacomo Puccini
Bohemian Girl, The	Michael Balfe
Bomarzo	Alberto Ginastera
Boréades, Les	Jean-Philippe Rameau
Boris Godunov	Modest Mussorgsky
Boulevard Solitude	Hans Werner Henze
Bow Down	Harrison Birtwistle
Boy Who Grew Too Fast, The	Gian Carlo Menotti
Brickdust Man, The	Charles Dibdin
Bunbury	Paul Burkhard
Buona Figliuola, La	Niccolò Piccinni
Burning Fiery Furnace, The	Benjamin Britten

Caedmon	Edward Lambert
Calisto, La	Francesco Cavalli
Cambiale di Matrimonio, La	Gioacchino Rossini
Camera	Anthony Moore
Candide	Leonard Bernstein
Capriccio	Richard Strauss
Capture of Troy, The see: *Prise de Troie, La*	
Capuleti e i Montecchi, I	Vincenzo Bellini
Caritas	Robert Saxton
Cardillac	Paul Hindemith
Carmelites, The see: *Dialogues des Carmélites*	
Carmen	Georges Bizet
Carmen Jones	Bizet/Oscar Hammerstein II
Carousel	Richard Rodgers
Casino Paradise	William Bolcom
Castello di Kenilworth, Il	Gaetano Donizetti
Castor et Pollux	Jean-Philippe Rameau
Catiline Conspiracy, The	Iain Hamilton
Catulli Carmina	Carl Orff
Cavalleria Rusticana	Pietro Mascagni
Célèstine, La	Maurice Ohana

315

Cendrillon	Jules Massenet
Cenerentola, La	Gioacchino Rossini
Chakravaka Bird, The	Anthony Gilbert
Chalk Circle, The	Alexander von Zemlinsky
Chance, The	Orlando Gough
Chérubin	Jules Massenet
Chevalier Imaginaire, Le	Philippe Fénelon
Christmas Carol, A	Thea Musgrave
Christmas Eve	Nikolai Rimsky-Korsakov
Christopher Columbus	Offenbach/Patric Schmid
Chute de la Maison Usher, La	Claude Debussy
Cinderella (Maxwell Davies)	Peter Maxwell Davies
Cinderella see: *Cenerentola, La*	
Ciro in Babilonia	Gioacchino Rossini
Clarissa	Robin Holloway
Clemenza di Tito, La	Wolfgang Amadeus Mozart
Cléopâtre	Jules Massenet
Clytemnestra	Peter Wishart
Colombe, La	Charles Gounod
Columba	Kenneth Leighton
Combattimento di Tancredi e Clorinda, Il	Claudio Monteverdi
Comedy of Errors, The see: *Equivoci, Gli*	
Comedy on the Bridge	Bohuslav Martinů
Commedia	Edward Cowie
Comte Ory, Le	Gioacchino Rossini
Confessions of a Justified Sinner	Thomas Wilson
Consul, The	Gian Carlo Menotti
Contes d'Hoffmann, Les	Jacques Offenbach
Convenienze ed Inconvenienze Teatrali, Le	Gaetano Donizetti
Coq d'Or, Le	Nikolai Rimsky-Korsakov
Coronation of Poppea, The see: *Incoronazione di Poppea, L'*	
Corsaro, Il	Giuseppe Verdi
Così fan tutte	Wolfgang Amadeus Mozart
Count of Luxembourg, The see: *Graf von Luxembourg, Der*	
Count Ory see: *Comte Ory, Le*	
Countess Maritza	Emerich Kálmán
Cox and Box	Arthur Sullivan
Crispino e la Comare	Luigi and Federico Ricci
Crossing, The	John Metcalf
Crucible, The	Robert Ward
Csárdásfürstin, Die	Emerich Kálmán
Cubana, La	Hans Werner Henze
Cunning Little Vixen, The	Leoš Janáček

Cupid and Death	Christopher Gibbons and Matthew Locke
Curlew River	Benjamin Britten
Dalibor	Bedřich Smetana
Damnation de Faust, La	Hector Berlioz
Damnation of Faust, The see: *Damnation de Faust, La*	
Danaïdes, Les	Antonio Salieri
Dantons Tod	Gottfried von Einem
Daphne	Richard Strauss
Daughter of the Regiment, The see: *Fille du Régiment, La*	
David and Goliath	Paul Reade
David et Jonathas	Marc-Antoine Charpentier
Death in Venice	Benjamin Britten
Death of Dido, The	Johann Christoph Pepusch
Deceit Outwitted see: *Infedeltà Delusa, L'*	
Decision, The	Thea Musgrave
Deidamia	George Frideric Handel
Deux Journées, Les	Luigi Cherubini
Devil and Kate, The	Antonín Dvořák
Devil's Wall, The	Bedřich Smetana
Devils of Loudun	Krzysztof Penderecki
Dialogues des Carmélites	Francis Poulenc
Diary of One Who Disappeared, The	Leoš Janáček
Dido and Aeneas	Henry Purcell
Docteur Faustus	Konrad Boehmer
Doctor Faust see: *Doktor Faust*	
Doctor Faust	Ferruccio Busoni
Doctor und Apotheker	Karl Ditters von Dittersdorf
Don Carlos	Giuseppe Verdi
Don Chisciotte in Sierra Morena	Francesco Conti
Don Giovanni	Wolfgang Amadeus Mozart
Don Pasquale	Gaetano Donizetti
Don Quichotte	Jules Massenet
Don Quixote	Paisiello/Hans Werner Henze
Don Quixote in Sierra Morena see: *Don Chisciotte in Sierra Morena*	
Donna del Lago, La	Gioacchino Rossini
Donnerstag aus Licht	Karlheinz Stockhausen
Dori, La	Pietro Antonio Cesti
Down by the Greenwood Side	Harrison Birtwistle
Dragon of Wantley, The	John Frederick Lampe
Drama of Aida, The (adaptation of *Aida*)	

Dreigroschenoper, Die	Kurt Weill
Duchess of Malfi, The (Burton)	Stephen Douglas Burton
Duchess of Malfi, The	Stephen Oliver
Duel of Tancredi and Clorinda, The see: *Combattimento di Tancredi e Clorinda, Il*	
Duenna, The	Roberto Gerhard
Duenna, The (Prokofiev) see: *Betrothal in a Monastery*	
Duke Bluebeard's Castle	Belá Bartók

Echoes	John Hawkins
Edgar	Giacomo Puccini
Egisto, L'	Francesco Cavalli
Eight Songs for a Mad King	Peter Maxwell Davies
Electrification of the Soviet Union, The	Nigel Osborne
Elegy for Young Lovers	Hans Werner Henze
Elektra	Richard Strauss
Elisabetta, Regina d'Inghilterra	Gioacchino Rossini
Elisir d'Amore, L'	Gaetano Donizetti
Elixir of Love, The see: *Elisir d'Amore, L'*	
Emperor of Atlantis, The see: *Kaiser von Atlantis, Der*	
Enfant et les Sortilèges, L'	Maurice Ravel
Engel kommt nach Babylon, Ein	Rudolf Kelterborn
English Cat, The	Hans Werner Henze
English Eccentrics	Malcolm Williamson
Entführung aus dem Serail, Die	Wolfgang Amadeus Mozart
Ephesian Matron, The	Charles Dibdin
Equivoci, Gli	Stephen Storace
Equivoci nel Sembiante, Gli	Alessandro Scarlatti
Ercole Amante	Francesco Cavalli
Erismena, L'	Francesco Cavalli
Eritrea	Francesco Cavalli
Ermione	Gioacchino Rossini
Ernani	Giuseppe Verdi
Erwartung	Arnold Schoenberg
Erzsebet	Charles Chaynes
Esclarmonde	Jules Massenet
Esther	George Frideric Handel
Etain	Edward Maguire
Etoile, L'	Emmanuel Chabrier
Etoile du Nord, L'	Giacomo Meyerbeer
Eugene Onegin	Pyotr Ilyich Tchaikovsky
Euridice	Jacopo Peri

Europa und der Stier	Helge Jörns
Europera 3	John Cage
Euryanthe	Carl Maria von Weber
Expectation see: *Erwartung*	
Exposition of a Picture	Stephen Oliver
Ezio	George Frideric Handel

Fairy Queen, The	Henry Purcell
Falcon, The	Hugo Cole
Fall of the House of Usher, The	Philip Glass
Falstaff	Giuseppe Verdi
Fanatico Burlato, Il	Domenico Cimarosa
Fanciulla del West, La	Giacomo Puccini
Fanny Robin	Edward Harper
Faust	Charles Gounod
Faust (Lombardi)	Luca Lombardi
Faust (Spohr)	Louis Spohr
Favorita, La see: *Favorite, La*	
Favorite, La	Gaetano Donizetti
Fedeltà Premiata, La	Joseph Haydn
Feen, Die	Richard Wagner
Fennimore and Gerda	Frederick Delius
Ferne Klang, Der	Franz Schreker
Fetonte	Niccolò Jommelli
Fidelio	Ludwig van Beethoven
Fiery Angel, The see: *Ange de Feu, L'*	
Figaro's Wedding (alternative title to *The Marriage of Figaro* in some translations)	
Fille du Régiment, La	Gaetano Donizetti
Filosofo di Campagna, Il	Baldassare Galuppi
Finta Giardiniera, La	Wolfgang Amadeus Mozart
Finta Semplice, La	Wolfgang Amadeus Mozart
First Comes the Music see: *Prima la Musica e poi le Parole*	
Fisherman, The	Paul Max Edlin
Flavio	George Frideric Handel
Fledermaus, Die	Johann Strauss
Fliegende Holländer, Der	Richard Wagner
Florentine Tragedy, A	Alexander von Zemlinsky
Floridante	George Frideric Handel
Fly	Barry Conyngham
Flying Dutchman, The see: *Fliegende Holländer, Der*	
Follies	Stephen Sondheim

Force of Destiny, The see: *Forza del Destino, La*	
Fôret, La	Rolf Liebermann
Fortunio	André Messager
Forza del Destino, La	Giuseppe Verdi
Four Note Opera, The	Tom Johnson
Fra Diavolo	Daniel-François-Esprit Auber
Francesca di Foix	Gaetano Donizetti
Frau ohne Schatten, Die	Richard Strauss
Freischütz, Der	Carl Maria von Weber
Freudiana	Eric Woolfson
From the House of the Dead	Leoš Janáček
Full Circle	Robin Orr
Gabriella di Vergy	Gaetano Donizetti
Gambler, The	Sergei Prokofiev
Garden, The see: *Giardino, Il*	
Gardens of Adonis	Hugo Weisgall
Gassir the Hero	Theo Loevendie
Gawain	Harrison Birtwistle
Gawain and Ragnall	Richard Blackford
Gazza Ladra, La	Gioacchino Rossini
Gentle Spirit, A	John Tavener
Gezeichneten, Die	Franz Schreker
Ghanashyam	Ravi Shankar
Ghost Sonata, The	Aribert Reimann
Ghosts of Versailles, The	John Corigliano
Gianni Schicchi	Giacomo Puccini
Giardino, Il	Stephen Oliver
Giasone	Francesco Cavalli
Gioconda, La	Amilcare Ponchielli
Gioielli della Madonna, I	Ermanno Wolf-Ferrari
Giorno di Regno, Un	Giuseppe Verdi
Giovanna d'Arco	Giuseppe Verdi
Girl of the Golden West, The see: *Fanciulla del West, La*	
Giulio Cesare	George Frideric Handel
Giustino	George Frideric Handel
Glöckner von Notre-Dame, Der	Howard Goodall
Gloriana	Benjamin Britten
Glückliche Hand, Die	Arnold Schoenberg
Golden Cockerel, The see: *Coq d'Or, Le*	
Golden Vanity, The	Benjamin Britten
Golem	John Casken

Gondoliers, The	Arthur Sullivan
Götterdämmerung	Richard Wagner
(fourth opera, *Ring des Nibelungen, Der*)	
Grace of Todd, The	Gordon Crosse
Graf von Luxembourg, Der	Franz Lehár
Grand Duchess of Gérolstein, The see: *Grande-Duchesse de Gérolstein, La*	
Grand Macabre, Le	György Ligeti
Grande-Duchesse de Gérolstein, La	Jacques Offenbach
Greek	Mark-Anthony Turnage
Greek Passion, The	Bohuslav Martinů
Grenadier, The	Charles Dibdin
Griselda	Antonio Vivaldi
Grisélidis	Jules Massenet
Grotta di Trofonio, La	Antonio Salieri
Growing Castle, The	Malcolm Williamson
Guillaume Tell	Gioacchino Rossini
Gustave III	Daniel-François-Esprit Auber
Gwendoline	Emmanuel Chabrier
Gypsy Baron, The see: *Zigeunerbaron, Der*	
Gypsy Princess, The see: *Csárdásfürstin, Die*	
Hamlet (Searle)	Humphrey Searle
Hamlet	Ambroise Thomas
Hans Heiling	Heinrich August Marschner
Hansel and Gretel see: *Hänsel und Gretel*	
Hänsel und Gretel	Engelbert Humperdinck
Happy End	Kurt Weill
Harriet, The Woman Called Moses	Thea Musgrave
Háry János	Zoltán Kodály
Hastings Spring	Jonathan Dove
Heaven Ablaze in his Breast	Judith Weir
Hedda Gabler	Edward Harper
Hell's Angels	Nigel Osborne
Help! Help! The Globolinks!	Gian Carlo Menotti
Henri VIII	Camille Saint-Saëns
Henry VIII see: *Henri VIII*	
Hercules	George Frideric Handel
Hermiston	Robin Orr
Hero, The	Gian Carlo Menotti
Hérodiade	Jules Massenet
Heure Espagnole, L'	Maurice Ravel
Higglety Pigglety Pop!	Oliver Knussen

Hippolyte et Aricie	Jean-Philippe Rameau
HMS Pinafore	Arthur Sullivan
Hugh the Drover	Ralph Vaughan Williams
Huguenots, Les	Giacomo Meyerbeer
Huron, Le	André Grétry

Ice Break, The	Michael Tippett
Idomeneo	Wolfgang Amadeus Mozart
Imeneo	George Frideric Handel
Immortal Hour, The	Rutland Boughton
Impresario, The see: *Schauspieldirektor, Der*	
Incontro Improviso, L'	Joseph Haydn
Incoronazione di Poppea, L'	Claudio Monteverdi
Indes Galantes, Les	Jean-Philippe Rameau
Infedeltà Delusa L'	Joseph Haydn
Inquest of Love	Jonathan Harvey
Intelligence Park, The	Gerald Barry
Intermezzo	Richard Strauss
Into the Woods	Stephen Sondheim
Iolanta	Pyotr Ilyich Tchaikovsky
Iolanthe	Arthur Sullivan
Iphigenia in Aulis see: *Iphigénie en Aulide*	
Iphigenia in Tauris see: *Iphigénie en Tauride*	
Iphigenias (abridged version of *Iphigenia in Aulis* and *Iphigenia in Tauris*)	
Iphigénie en Aulide	Christoph Willibald Gluck
Iphigénie en Tauride	Christoph Willibald Gluck
Isola Disabitata, L'	Joseph Haydn
Italian Girl in Algiers, The see: *Italiana in Algeri, L'*	
Italiana in Algeri, L'	Gioacchino Rossini
Italiana in Londra, L'	Domenico Cimarosa
Ivan IV	Georges Bizet

Jacobin, The	Antonín Dvořák
Jakob Lenz	Wolfgang Rihm
Jasager, Der	Kurt Weill
Jason see: *Giasone*	
Jenůfa	Leoš Janáček
Jephtha	George Frideric Handel
Jérusalem see: *Lombardi, I*	
Jewel Box, The	Mozart/Paul Griffiths
Jewels of the Madonna, The see: *Gioielli della Madonna, I*	

Joan of Arc   see: *Giovanna d'Arco*
Job   Luigi Dallapiccola
Johnny Strikes Up   see: Jonny Spielt Auf
Jolie Fille de Perth, La   Georges Bizet
Jongleur de Notre-Dame, Le   Jules Massenet
Jonny Spielt Auf   Ernst Křenek
Joseph   Etienne Méhul
Journey, The   John Metcalf
Journey to Rheims, The   see: *Viaggio a Reims, Il*
Judgement of Paris, The   John Woolrich
Judith   Siegfried Matthus
Juditha Triumphans   Antonio Vivaldi
Juive, La   Jacques Halévy
Julia   Rudolf Kelterborn
Julietta   Bohuslav Martinů
Julius Caesar   see: *Giulio Cesare*

Kaiser von Atlantis, Der   Viktor Ullmann
Katerina Ismailova   see: *Lady Macbeth of Mtsensk*
Katya Kabanova   Leoš Janáček
Khovanshchina   Modest Mussorgsky
Killing Time   Mark-Anthony Turnage
King Arthur   Henry Purcell
King Goes Forth to France, The   Aulis Sallinen
King Priam   Michael Tippett
King Roger   Karol Szymanowski
Kiss, The   Bedřich Smetana
Kiss Me Kate   Cole Porter
Kluge, Die   Carl Orff
Knot Garden, The   Michael Tippett
Königskinder   Engelbert Humperdinck
Kopernikus   Claude Vivier

Lady Macbeth of Mtsensk   Dmitri Shostakovich
Lakmé   Léo Delibes
Lancelot   Iain Hamilton
Land des Lächelns, Das   Franz Lehár
Land of Smiles, The   see: *Land des Lächelns, Das*
Lear   Aribert Reimann
Ledge, The   Richard Rodney Bennett
Leonore   see: *Fidelio*

323

Let's Make an Opera	Benjamin Britten
Liebesverbot, Das	Richard Wagner
Lighthouse, The	Peter Maxwell Davies
Little Night Music, A	Stephen Sondheim
Lives of the Great Prisoners	Orlando Gough
Lodoïska	Luigi Cherubini
Lohengrin	Richard Wagner
Lombardi, I	Giuseppe Verdi
Lords' Masque, The	Niccolò Castiglioni
Loreley, Die	Max Bruch
Lost in the Stars	Kurt Weill
Lotario	George Frideric Handel
Louise	Gustave Charpentier
Love for Three Oranges, The see: *Amour des Trois Oranges, L'*	
Love Potion, The see: *Elisir d'Amore, L'*	
Lucia di Lammermoor	Gaetano Donizetti
Lucio Silla	Wolfgang Amadeus Mozart
Lucky Peter's Journey	Malcolm Williamson
Lucrezia Borgia	Gaetano Donizetti
Luisa Miller	Giuseppe Verdi
Lulu	Alban Berg
Lustige Witwe, Die	Franz Lehár

Macbeth	Giuseppe Verdi
Madam Butterfly see: *Madama Butterfly*	
Madama Butterfly	Giacomo Puccini
Madame Bovary	Heinrich Sutermeister
Maddalena	Sergei Prokofiev
Maestro di Capella, Il	Domenico Cimarosa
Magic Flute, The see: *Zauberflöte, Die*	
Magic Fountain, The	Frederick Delius
Magician, The	Alun Hoddinott
Mahagonny Songspiel see: *Aufstieg und Fall der Stadt Mahagonny*	
Maid of Orleans, The	Pyotr Ilyich Tchaikovsky
Making of the Representative for *Planet 8, The*	Philip Glass
Makropoulos Case, The	Leoš Janáček
Malheurs d'Orphée, Les	Darius Milhaud
Malinche, La	Paul Barker
Mamelles de Tirésias, Les	Francis Poulenc
Man at the Heels of the Wind, The	Keith Volans
Man of Feeling, A	Stephen Oliver

Man Who Mistook his Wife for a Hat, The	Michael Nyman
Mannekins	Zbigniew Rudzinski
Manon	Jules Massenet
Manon Lescaut	Giacomo Puccini
Margot la Rouge	Frederick Delius
Mari à la Porte, Un	Jacques Offenbach
Maria Golovin	Gian Carlo Menotti
Maria Stuarda	Gaetano Donizetti
Maria Tudor	Giovanni Pacini
Mario and the Magician see: *Mario ed il Mago*	
Mario ed il Mago	Stephen Oliver
Marriage, The	Modest Mussorgsky
Marriage Contract, The see: *Cambiale di Matrimonio, La*	
Marriage of Figaro, The see: *Nozze di Figaro, Le*	
Marriages Between Zones 3, 4 & 5, The	Paul Barker
Martha	Friedrich von Flotow
Martin's Lie	Gian Carlo Menotti
Martyrdom of St Magnus, The	Peter Maxwell Davies
Mary of Egypt	John Tavener
Mary, Queen of Scots	Thea Musgrave
Mary Stuart see: *Maria Stuarda*	
Masada 967	Josef Tal
Mask of Orpheus, The	Harrison Birtwistle
Masked Ball, A see: *Ballo in Maschera, Un*	
Masnadieri, I	Giuseppe Verdi
Masquerade	Carl Nielsen
Massnahme, Die	Hanns Eisler
Master Peter's Puppet Show see: *Retablo de Maese Pedro, El*	
Mastersingers of Nuremberg, The see: *Meistersinger von Nürnberg, Die*	
Matrimonio Segreto, Il	Domenico Cimarosa
Mazeppa	Pyotr Ilyich Tchaikovsky
Medea (Bryars)	Gavin Bryars
Medea see: *Médée*	
Medea in Corinto	Simone Mayr
Médée	Luigi Cherubini
Mefistofele	Arrigo Boito
Meister und Margarita, Der	York Höller
Meister und Margarita, Der (Kunad)	Rainer Kunad
Meistersinger von Nürnberg, Die	Richard Wagner
Mellstock Quire, The	Edward Harper
Menaced Assassin, The	Jeremy Peyton Jones
Menschen, Die	Detlev Müller-Siemens

Merrily We Roll Along	Stephen Sondheim
Merry Widow, The see: *Lustige Witwe, Die*	
Merry Wives of Windsor, The	Otto Nicolai
Messiah	George Frideric Handel
Metamorphoses	Richard Blackford
Midsummer Marriage, The	Michael Tippett
Midsummer Night's Dream, A	Benjamin Britten
Mignon	Ambroise Thomas
Mikado, The	Arthur Sullivan
Mines of Sulphur, The	Richard Rodney Bennett
Mireille	Charles Gounod
Miss Julie	William Alwyn
Mitridate, Rè di Ponto	Wolfgang Amadeus Mozart
Molinara, La	Giovanni Paisiello
Mondo della Luna, Il	Joseph Haydn
Monsieur Choufleuri's at Home	Jacques Offenbach
Moon and Sixpence, The	John Gardner
Mosè in Egitto	Gioacchino Rossini
Moses see: *Mosè in Egitto*	
Moses and Aaron see: *Moses und Aron*	
Moses und Aron	Arnold Schoenberg
Mozart and Salieri	Nikolai Rimsky-Korsakov
Mr Punch	Michael Finnissy
Murder in the Cathedral	Ildebrando Pizzetti
Musical Director, The see: *Maestro di Capella, Il*	
My Fair Lady	Frederick Loewe
Mystère de la Nativité, La	Frank Martin
Naboth's Vineyard	Alexander Goehr
(first part, *Triptych*)	
Nabucco	Giuseppe Verdi
Nacht in Venedig, Eine	Johann Strauss
Naïs	Jean-Philippe Rameau
Nell	Alison Bauld
Nerone	Arrigo Boito
Nevis	Kenneth Dempster
New Year	Michael Tippett
Night at the Chinese Opera, A	Judith Weir
Night in Venice, A see: *Nacht in Venedig, Eine*	
Nightingale, The	Igor Stravinsky
Nixon in China	John Adams
No. 11 Bus, The	Peter Maxwell Davies

Noche Triste, La	Jean Prodomidès
Norma	Vincenzo Bellini
Nose, The	Dmitri Shostakovich
Notte di un Nevrastenico, La	Nino Rota
Noye's Fludde	Benjamin Britten
Nozze di Figaro, Le	Wolfgang Amadeus Mozart
Nuit des Soupliantes, La	Nicos Cornelios
Oberon (Castiglioni)	Niccolò Castiglioni
Oberon	Carl Maria von Weber
Oberto, Conte di San Bonifacio	Giuseppe Verdi
Oca del Cairo, L'	Mozart/Stephen Oliver
Occasione fa il Ladro, L'	Gioacchino Rossini
Occurance at Owl Creek Bridge, An	Thea Musgrave
Oedipus Rex	Igor Stravinsky
On the Razzle	Robin Orr
On Your Toes	Richard Rodgers
One Man Show	Nicholas Maw
Orazi ed i Curiazi, Gli	Domenico Cimarosa
Orfeo	Claudio Monteverdi
Orfeo ed Euridice	Christoph Willibald Gluck
Orfeo ed Euridice (Haydn)	Joseph Haydn
Orion	Francesco Cavalli
Orlando	George Frideric Handel
Orlando Furioso	Antonio Vivaldi
Orlando Paladino	Joseph Haydn
Ormindo, L'	Francesco Cavalli
Orontea	Pietro Antonio Cesti
Orphée aux Enfers	Jacques Offenbach
Orphée et Eurydice see: *Orfeo ed Euridice*	
Orpheus and Eurydice see: *Orfeo ed Euridice*	
Orpheus' Daughter	Michael Nyman
Orpheus in the Underworld see: *Orphée aux Enfers*	
Osud	Leoš Janáček
Otello (Rossini)	Gioacchino Rossini
Otello	Giuseppe Verdi
Ottone	George Frideric Handel
Our Man in Havana	Malcolm Williamson
Owen Wingrave	Benjamin Britten
Pacific Overtures	Stephen Sondheim

Pagliacci	Ruggero Leoncavallo
Palestrina	Hans Pfitzner
Panic, The	David Sawer
Paradise Lost	Krzysztof Penderecki
Pardoner's Tale, The	Alan Ridout
Paride ed Elena	Christoph Willibald Gluck
Paris and Helen see: *Paride ed Elena*	
Parsifal	Richard Wagner
Partenope	George Frideric Handel
Passion and Resurrection	Jonathan Harvey
Passion de Gilles, La	Philippe Boesmans
Passion of Jonathan Wade, The	Carlisle Floyd
Pastor Fido, Il	George Frideric Handel
Pathelin	Wilfred Josephs
Patience	Arthur Sullivan
Patience of Socrates, The	Georg Philipp Telemann
Paul Bunyan	Benjamin Britten
Peace ˙	Carl Davis
Pearl Fishers, The see: *Pêcheurs de Perles, Les*	
Pêcheurs de Perles, Les	Georges Bizet
Peer Gynt	Werner Egk
Peleus and Thetis	William Boyce
Pelléas and Mélisande see: *Pelléas et Mélisande*	
Pelléas et Mélisande	Claude Debussy
Penny for a Song, A	Richard Rodney Bennett
Périchole, La	Jacques Offenbach
Peter Grimes	Benjamin Britten
Petrified	Juraj Beneš
Phantastes	Paul Barker
Phantom of the Opera, The	Andrew Lloyd Webber
Pharsalia	Iain Hamilton
Phoebe	Maurice Greene
Piccolo Marat, Il	Pietro Mascagni
Pietra del Paragone, La	Gioacchino Rossini
Pig	Jonathan Dove
Pig Organ, The	Richard Blackford
Pigmalione, Il	Gaetano Donizetti
Pillow Song, The	Paul Barker
Pimpinone	Georg Philipp Telemann
Pirata, Il	Vincenzo Bellini
Pirates of Penzance, The	Arthur Sullivan
Pittor Parigino, Il	Domenico Cimarosa
Platée	Jean-Philippe Rameau

329

Resurrection	Peter Maxwell Davies
Retablo de Maese Pedro, El	Manuel de Falla
Return of Ulysses, The see: *Ritorno d'Ulisse in Patria, Il*	
Rheingold, Das	Richard Wagner
(first opera, *Ring des Nibelungen, Der*)	
Rhinegold, The see: *Rheingold, Das*	
Riccardo Primo	George Frideric Handel
Riccardo III	Flavio Testi
Richard I see: *Riccardo Primo*	
Rienzi	Richard Wagner
Rigoletto	Giuseppe Verdi
Rinaldo	George Frideric Handel
Ring des Nibelungen, Der	Richard Wagner
(Rheingold, Das/Walküre, Die/Siegfried/Götterdämmerung)	
Ring of the Nibelung, The see: *Ring des Nibelungen, Der*	
Ring Saga, The (abridged version of *Ring of the Nibelung, The*)	
Rise and Fall of the City of Mahagonny, The see: *Aufstieg und Fall der Stadt Mahagonny*	
Rising of the Moon, The	Nicholas Maw
Risurrezione	Franco Alfano
Ritorno di Casanova, Il	Girolamo Arrigo
Ritorno d'Ulisse in Patria, Il	Claudio Monteverdi
Roberto Devereux	Gaetano Donizetti
Robin Hood	Norman Kay
Robinson Crusoe	Jacques Offenbach
Rodelinda	George Frideric Handel
Rodrigo	George Frideric Handel
Roi d'Ys, Le	Edouard Lalo
Romanziera, La	Gaetano Donizetti
Romeo and Juliet see: *Roméo et Juliette*	
Roméo et Juliette	Charles Gounod
Rondine, La	Giacomo Puccini
Rosenkavalier, Der	Richard Strauss
Rosmonda d'Inghilterra	Gaetano Donizetti
Royal Hunt of the Sun, The	Iain Hamilton
Ruddigore	Arthur Sullivan
Rusalka	Antonín Dvořák
Ruth	Lennox Berkeley
Saint of Bleecker Street, The	Gian Carlo Menotti
Saint François d'Assise	Olivier Messiaen
Salome	Richard Strauss

Samson	George Frideric Handel
Samson and Delilah see: *Samson et Dalila*	
Samson et Dalila	Camille Saint-Saëns
Sandrina's Secret see: *Finta Giardiniera, La*	
Sasha	Stephen Oliver
Satyagraha	Philip Glass
Satyricon	Bruno Maderna
Saul	George Frideric Handel
Saul and David see: *Saul og David*	
Saul og David	Carl Nielsen
S̄avitri	Gustav Holst
Scala di Seta, La	Gioacchino Rossini
Schauspieldirektor, Der	Wolfgang Amadeus Mozart
Schiava Liberata, La	Niccolò Jomelli
Schiavo di sua Moglie, Lo	Francesco Provenzale
Schloss, Das	André Laporte
School for Fathers, The	Ermanno Wolf-Ferrari
School for Wives, The	Rolf Liebermann
Schwarze Maske, Die	Krzysztof Penderecki
Schweigsame Frau, Die	Richard Strauss
Scipio see: *Scipione*	
Scipio's Dream	Mozart/Judith Weir
Scipione	George Frideric Handel
Semele	George Frideric Handel
Semiramide	Gioacchino Rossini
Seraglio, The see: *Entführung aus dem Serail, Die*	
Serse	George Frideric Handel
Serva e l'Ussero, La	Luigi Ricci
Serva Padrona, La	Giovanni Battista Pergolesi
Servants, The	William Mathias
Seven Deadly Sins, The	Kurt Weill
Shadowplay (second part, *Triptych*)	Alexander Goehr
Show Boat	Jerome Kern
Sicilian Vespers, The see: *Vêpres Siciliennes, Les*	
Siège de Corinthe, Le	Gioacchino Rossini
Siegfried	Richard Wagner
(third opera, *Ring des Nibelungen, Der*)	
Signor Bruschino, Il	Gioacchino Rossini
Silbersee, Der	Kurt Weill
Silent Night see: *Notte di un Nevrastenico, La*	
Silent Woman, The see: *Schweigsame Frau, Die*	
Silken Ladder, The see: *Scala di Seta, La*	
Silverlake, The see: *Silbersee, Der*	

331

Simon Boccanegra	Giuseppe Verdi
Sir Gawain and the Green Knight	Richard Blackford
Sir John in Love	Ralph Vaughan Williams
Sister Aimee	Odaline de la Martinez
Six Characters in Search of an Author	Hugo Weisgall
63: Dream Palace	Hans-Jürgen von Bose
Snatched by the Gods	Param Vir
Snow Maiden, The	Nikolai Rimsky-Korsakov
Soda Fountain	Michael Finnissy
Sogno di Scipione, Il	Wolfgang Amadeus Mozart
Soldaten, Die	Bernd Alois Zimmermann
Soldier's Tale, The	Igor Stravinsky
Sonata about Jerusalem	Alexander Goehr
(third part, *Triptych*)	
Song of Fortunio, The	Jacques Offenbach
Song of Majnun, The	Bright Sheng
Sonnambula, La	Vincenzo Bellini
Sorcerer, The	Arthur Sullivan
Sosarme	George Frideric Handel
Spectacle of the Soul and the Body, The	see: *Rappresentazione di Anima e di*
Corpo, La	
Speziale, Lo	Joseph Haydn
Spinalba, La	Francisco Antonio di Almeida
Spinning Room, The	Zoltán Kodály
Standard Bearer, The	Michael Christie
Stephen Climax	Hans Zender
Stiffelio	Giuseppe Verdi
Stone Guest, The	Alexander Dargomïzhsky
Story of Vasco, The	Gordon Crosse
Straniera, La	Vincenzo Bellini
Street Scene	Kurt Weill
Sturm, Der	Frank Martin
Sunday in the Park with George	Stephen Sondheim
Suor Angelica	Giacomo Puccini
Susanna	George Frideric Handel
Susanna's Secret	Ermanno Wolf-Ferrari
Tabarro, Il	Giacomo Puccini
Tailor of Gloucester, The	Douglas Young
Tale of Two Cities, A	Arthur Benjamin
Tales of Hoffmann, The see: *Contes d'Hoffmann, Les*	
Tamburlaine	Iain Hamilton

Tamburlaine (Handel) see: *Tamerlano*	
Tamburlaine (Murdock)	Marjolijn Murdock
Tamerlano	George Frideric Handel
Tamu-Tamu	Gian Carlo Menotti
Tancredi	Gioacchino Rossini
Tannhäuser	Richard Wagner
Tartuffe	Arthur Benjamin
Taverner	Peter Maxwell Davies
Tcherevichky	Pyotr Ilyich Tchaikovsky
Telephone, The	Gian Carlo Menotti
Temistocle	Johann Christian Bach
Tempest, The	John Eaton
Templer und die Jüdin, Der	Heinrich Marschner
Terrible Mouth	Nigel Osborne
Teseo	George Frideric Handel
Thaïs	Jules Massenet
Theodora	George Frideric Handel
Thérèse	John Tavener
Thérèse Raquin	Michael Finnissy
Thieving Magpie, The see: *Gazza Ladra, La*	
Thomas and Sally	Thomas Augustine Arne
Threepenny Opera, The see: *Dreigroschenoper, Die*	
Through the Looking Glass and What	
Alice Found There	Wilfred Josephs
Tigers, The	Havergal Brian
Tigrane, Il	Alessandro Scarlatti
Time Off? Not a Ghost of a Chance!	Elisabeth Lutyens
Timon of Athens	Stephen Oliver
Tito, Il	Pietro Antonio Cesti
Tolomeo	George Frideric Handel
Tom Jones	Stephen Oliver
Tornrak	John Metcalf
Torquato Tasso	Gaetano Donizetti
Tosca	Giacomo Puccini
Touchstone, The see: *Pietra del Paragone, La*	
Toussaint	David Blake
Tragédie de Carmen, La (adaptation of *Carmen*)	
Traviata, La	Giuseppe Verdi
Tree of Chastity, The	Martin E. Soler
Treemonisha	Scott Joplin
Trial by Jury	Arthur Sullivan
Trial by Tea Party see: *Procedura Penale*	

Triptych	Alexander Goehr
(Naboth's Vineyard/Shadowplay/Sonata about Jerusalem)	
Tristan and Isolde see: *Tristan und Isolde*	
Tristan und Isolde	Richard Wagner
Trittico, Il	Giacomo Puccini
(Tabarro, Il/Suor Angelica/Gianni Schicchi)	
Triumph of Honour, The	Alessandro Scarlatti
Troilus and Cressida	William Walton
Trojans, The see: *Troyens, Les*	
Trojans at Carthage, The see: *Troyens à Carthage, Les*	
Trouble in Tahiti	Leonard Bernstein
Trovatore, Il	Giuseppe Verdi
Troyens, Les	Hector Berlioz
Troyens à Carthage, Les (second part, *Troyens, Les*)	
Trumpet Major, The	Alun Hoddinott
Tsar's Bride, The	Nikolai Rimsky-Korsakov
Tsarina's Shoes, The see: *Tcherevichky*	
Tsuru-Kame	Michael Finnissy
Turandot	Giacomo Puccini
Turco in Italia, Il	Gioacchino Rossini
Turk in Italy, The see: *Turco in Italia, Il*	
Turn of the Screw, The	Benjamin Britten
Twilight of the Gods see: *Götterdämmerung*	
Two Fiddlers, The	Peter Maxwell Davies
Two Foscari, The	Giuseppe Verdi
Two Widows, The	Bedřich Smetana
Ubu	Andrew Toovey
Under Western Eyes	John Joubert
Undertaker, The	John Purser
Undivine Comedy, The	Michael Finnissy
Unexpected Meeting, The see: *Incontro Improviso, L'*	
Upstage and Downstage see: *Convenienze ed Inconvenienze Teatrali, Le*	
Uranium Miners' Radio Orchestra Plays	
Scenes from Salome's Revenge, The	Andrew Poppy
Valis	Tod Machover
Valkyrie, The see: *Walküre, Die*	
Vanishing Bridegroom, The	Judith Weir
Vedova Scaltra, La	Ermanno Wolf-Ferrari
Venus and Adonis	Johann Christoph Pepusch
Vêpres Siciliennes, Les	Giuseppe Verdi

Vespri Siciliani, I   see: *Vêpres Siciliennes, Les*
Vestale, La   Gasparo Spontini
Viaggio a Reims, Il   Gioacchino Rossini
Viajero Indiscreto, El   Luis de Pablo
Victory   Richard Rodney Bennett
Vida Breve, La   Manuel de Falla
Vie Parisienne, La   Jacques Offenbach
Vienna Blood   see: *Wiener Blut*
Village Romeo and Juliet, A   Frederick Delius
Village Singer, The   Stephen Paulus
Villi, Le   Giacomo Puccini
Vin Herbé, Le   Frank Martin
Violins of St Jacques, The   Malcolm Williamson
Virginia   Saverio Mercadante
Visit of the Old Lady, The   Gottfried von Einem
Visitors, The   John Gardner
Vital Statistics   Michael Nyman
Voice of Ariadne, The   Thea Musgrave
Voix Humaine, La   Francis Poulenc
Volo di Notte   Luigi Dallapiccola
Volpone   Francis Burt
Voyage, The   Philip Glass

Wager, The   Buxton Orr
Waiting   Stephen Oliver
Walküre, Die   Richard Wagner
    (second opera, *Ring des Nibelungen, Der*)
Wally, La   Alfredo Catalani
Wandering Scholar, The   Gustav Holst
War and Peace   Sergei Prokofiev
Washington Square   Thomas Pasatieri
Wat Tyler   Alan Bush
Water Bird Talk, A   Dominick Argento
We Come to the River   Hans Werner Henze
Weisse Rose, Die   Udo Zimmermann
Werther   Jules Massenet
West Side Story   Leonard Bernstein
What the Old Man Does is Always Right   Alun Hoddinott
Where the Wild Things Are   Oliver Knussen
Wiedertäufer, Die   Alexander Goehr
Wiener Blut   Johann Strauss
Wildschütz, Der   Albert Lortzing

William Tell   see: *Guillaume Tell*
Winter Cruise — Hans Henkemans
Wozzeck — Alban Berg
Wreckers, The — Ethel Smyth
Wuthering Heights — Bernard Herrmann

Xerxes   see: *Serse*

Yan Tan Tethera — Harrison Birtwistle
Yeomen of the Guard, The — Arthur Sullivan
Yes-Sayer, The   see: *Jasager, Der*
Yolande   see: *Iolanta*

Zaide — Wolfgang Amadeus Mozart
Zaide (Mozart/Mortimer) — Mozart/John Mortimer
Zampa — Ferdinand Hérold
Zauberflöte, Die — Wolfgang Amadeus Mozart
Zemire and Azor   see: *Zémire et Azor*
Zémire et Azor — André Grétry
Zigeunerbaron, Der — Johann Strauss
Zingara, La — Rinaldo di Capua

RECORD LABELS

==

ABBE	Abbey Recording Company
ABCD	Abacus
ACAD	Academy Collection
ADDA	Adda
AKAD	Akademia
AMON	Amon Ra
ARAB	Arabesque
ARCH	Archiv Produktion
ARGO	Argo
ASV	ASV
BBC	BBC
BEDI	Bedivere
BONG	Bongiovanni
BRID	Bridge
CALA	Cala
CBS	CBS
CFP	Classics for Pleasure
CHAN	Chandos
CHNT	Chant du Monde
CIRR	Cirrus
COLL	Collins
CONI	Conifer
CONT	Continuum
CRD	CRD
DECC	Decca
DENO	Denon
DG	Deutsche Grammophon
DHM	Deutsche Harmonia Mundi
EMI	EMI

ERAT	Erato
ETCE	Etcetera
EURO	Eurodisc
FACT	Factory Classical
GIME	Gimell
HARM	Harmonia Mundi
HMV	His Master's Voice (EMI)
HUNG	Hungaroton
HYPE	Hyperion
IKON	Ikon
IMP	Imp (Pickwick)
LDR	LDR
LEON	Leonarda
LIBR	Libra
LODI	Lodia
L'OI	L'Oiseau-Lyre
LOND	London
LYRI	Lyrita
MERI	Meridian
MERL	Merlin
MFP	Music for Pleasure
MMG	Moss Music Group Inc
MSCA	Musica Nova
NEW	New World
NIMB	Nimbus
NMC	NMC
NONE	Elektra-Nonesuch
NOVE	Novello
NUOV	Nuova Era

OPRA   Opera Rara
ORFE   Orfeo

PEAR   Pearl
PHIL   Philips
PICK   Pickwick
POLY   Polydor

RCA   RCA Victor
RICE   Ricercar
RODO   Rodolphe
RPO   RPO

SAGA   Saga
SAIN   Sain
SAYD   Saydisc
SILV   Silva Screen
SONY   Sony
SUPR   Supraphon

TELA   Telarc
TELD   Teldec
TER   Thats Entertainment Records
TRAX   TRAX

UNIC   Unicorn-Kanchana

VIRG   Virgin

WERG   Wergo